Psalms

BAKER COMMENTARY *on the* OLD TESTAMENT

WISDOM AND PSALMS

Tremper Longman III, Editor

Volumes now available

Psalms, vol. 1, *Psalms 1–41*, John Goldingay
Psalms, vol. 2, *Psalms 42–89*, John Goldingay
Psalms, vol. 3, *Psalms 90–150*, John Goldingay
Proverbs, Tremper Longman III
Song of Songs, Richard S. Hess

Psalms

Volume 3
Psalms 90–150

John Goldingay

B
Baker Academic
a division of Baker Publishing Group
Grand Rapids, Michigan

Published by Baker Academic
a division of Baker Publishing Group
P.O. Box 6287, Grand Rapids, MI 49516-6287
www.bakeracademic.com

Printed in the United States of America

Library of Congress Cataloging-in-Publication Data
Goldingay, John.
Psalms / John Goldingay.
p. cm. — (Baker commentary on the Old Testament wisdom and Psalms)
"The first of a three-volume commentary on the book of Psalms"—ECIP data view.
Includes bibliographical references and indexes.
ISBN 978-0-8010-2703-1 (cloth : v. 1)
ISBN 978-0-8010-2704-8 (cloth : v. 2)
ISBN 978-0-8010-3143-4 (cloth : v. 3)
1. Bible. O.T. Psalms—Commentaries. I. Title. II. Series.
BS1430.53.G65 2006
223′.2077—dc22 2006009724

25 26 27 28 29 30 31 10 9 8 7 6 5 4

Contents

Series Preface

At the end of the book of Ecclesiastes, a wise father warns his son concerning the multiplication of books: "Furthermore, of these, my son, be warned. There is no end to the making of many books!" (12:12). The Targum to this biblical book characteristically expands the thought and takes it in a different, even contradictory, direction: "My son, take care to make many books of wisdom without end."

When applied to commentaries, both statements are true. The past twenty years have seen a significant increase in the number of commentaries available on each book of the Bible. On the other hand, for those interested in grappling seriously with the meaning of the text, such proliferation should be seen as a blessing rather than a curse. No single commentary can do it all. In the first place, commentaries reflect different theological and methodological perspectives. We can learn from others who have a different understanding of the origin and nature of the Bible, but we also want commentaries that share our fundamental beliefs about the biblical text. Second, commentaries are written with different audiences in mind. Some are addressed primarily to laypeople, others to clergy, and still others to fellow scholars. A third consideration, related to the previous two, is the subdisciplines the commentator chooses to draw from to shed light on the biblical text. The possibilities are numerous, including philology, textual criticism, genre/form criticism, redaction criticism, ancient Near Eastern background, literary conventions, and more. Finally, commentaries differ in how extensively they interact with secondary literature, that is, with what others have said about a given passage.

The Baker Commentary on the Old Testament Wisdom and Psalms has a definite audience in mind. We believe the primary users of commentaries are scholars, ministers, seminary students, and Bible study leaders. Of these groups, we have most in mind clergy and future clergy, namely, seminary students. We have tried to make the commentary accessible to nonscholars by putting most of the technical discussion and interaction with secondary literature in the footnotes. We do not mean to suggest that such information is unimportant. We simply concede that, given the present state of the church, it is the rare layperson who will read such technical material with interest and profit. We hope we are wrong in this assessment, and if we are not, that the future will see a reverse in this trend. A healthy church is a church that nourishes itself with constant attention to God's words in Scripture, in all their glorious detail.

Since not all commentaries are alike, what are the features that characterize this series? The message of the biblical book is the primary focus of each commentary, and the commentators have labored to expose God's message for his people in the book they discuss. This series also distinguishes itself by restricting its coverage to one major portion of the Hebrew Scriptures, namely, the Psalms and Wisdom books (Proverbs, Job, Ecclesiastes, and Song of Songs). These biblical books provide a distinctive contribution to the canon. Although we can no longer claim that they are neglected, their unique content makes them harder to fit into the development of redemptive history and requires more effort to hear their distinctive message.

The book of Psalms is the literary sanctuary. Like the physical sanctuary structures of the Old Testament, it offers a textual holy place where humans share their joys and struggles with brutal honesty in God's presence. The book of Proverbs describes wisdom, which on one level is skill for living, the ability to navigate life's actual and potential pitfalls; but on another level, this wisdom presents a pervasive and deeply theological message: "The fear of the Lord is the beginning of knowledge" (Prov. 1:7). Proverbs also raises a disturbing issue: the sages often motivate wise behavior by linking it to reward, but in reality, bad things happen to good people, the wise are not always rewarded as they expect. This raises the question of the justice of God. Both Job and Ecclesiastes struggle with the apparent disconnect between God's justice and our actual life experience. Finally, the Song of Songs is a passionate, sensuous love poem that reminds us that God is interested in more than just our brains and our spirits; he wants us to enjoy our bodies. It reminds us that we are not merely a soul encased in a body but whole persons made in God's image.

Limiting the series to the Psalms and Wisdom books has allowed us to tailor our work to the distinctive nature of this portion of the canon. With some few exceptions in Job and Ecclesiastes, for instance, the material in these biblical books is poetic and highly literary, and so the commentators have highlighted the significant poetic conventions employed in each book. After an introduction discussing important issues that affect the interpretation of the book (title, authorship, date, language, style, text, ancient Near Eastern background, genre, canonicity, theological message, connection to the New Testament, and structure), each commentary proceeds section by section through the biblical text. The authors provide their own translation, with explanatory notes when necessary, followed by a substantial interpretive section (titled "Interpretation") and concluding with a section titled "Theological Implications." In the interpretation section, the emphasis is on the meaning of the text in its original historical setting. In the theological implications section, connections with other parts of the canon, both Old and New Testament, are sketched out along with the continuing relevance of each passage for us today. The latter section is motivated by the recognition that, while it is important to understand the individual contribution and emphasis of each book, these books now find their place in a larger collection of writings, the canon as a whole, and it is within this broader context that the books must ultimately be interpreted.

No two commentators in this series see things in exactly the same way, though we all share similar convictions about the Bible as God's Word and the belief that it must be appreciated not only as ancient literature but also as God's Word for today. It is our hope and prayer that these volumes will inform readers and, more importantly, stimulate reflection on and passion for these valuable books.

It has long been observed that the book of Psalms is a "microcosm" of the message of the Old Testament. Athanasius, the fourth-century theologian, called the Psalms "an epitome of the whole Scriptures." Basil, bishop of Caesarea in the same time period, regarded the Psalms as a "compendium of all theology." Martin Luther said the book is "a little Bible, and the summary of the Old Testament." The book of Psalms is theologically rich, so the readers of this commentary are privileged to be guided by John Goldingay, one of the foremost experts on biblical theology today. Our prayer is that as you read the Psalms with this commentary, you will grow in your knowledge of the God who reveals himself through the prayers of his ancient people.

Tremper Longman III
Robert H. Gundry Professor of Biblical Studies
Westmont College

Author's Preface

This last volume of commentary covers Books IV and V of the Psalter. The Psalter's division into books seems somewhat arbitrary, like the arrangement of the Psalter as a whole. The latter, Augustine admits, "which seems to me to contain the secret of a mighty mystery, hath not yet been revealed unto me." Of the Psalter's fivefold structure, he adds, "When I endeavoured to make out the principle of this division, I was not able."[1]

In the preface to volume 2, I noted that Psalms scholarship at the end of the twentieth century came to focus on seeking to solve Augustine's mystery; it has applied itself with more confidence to that task with regard to Books IV and V. And in some sequences these psalms contain commonality of theme (notably, Yhwh as King in Pss. 93–100) or of use (notably, the Songs of the Ascents, Pss. 120–34). Further, there are more concrete pointers to a postexilic date in many of the psalms in these last two books. Some pointers are linguistic: for instance, a number have distinctive features such as the use of the relative *š-* as a variant for *ʾăšer*, and the connective suffix *î*. It is a plausible view that many are handling the issues raised by the experience of the exile and of the disappointments as well as joys of the postexilic period. But Psalms study that focuses attention on the arrangement of the Psalter still seems to me to involve too much imagination in connecting too few dots. I remain of the view that the main focus of Psalms study needs to be the individual psalm.[2]

An opposite subject of study to that of the Psalter's arrangement is the redactional history of individual psalms, which looks behind the text as we have it. I also find this speculative and prefer to focus on the psalms

1. *Psalms*, 681.

2. Cf. Gerstenberger, e.g., *Psalms*, 2:441. For theories regarding the structure of Book V, see Gerald H. Wilson, *The Editing of the Hebrew Psalter* (Chico, CA: Scholars, 1985); Reinhard G. Kratz, "Die Tora Davids," *ZTK* 93 (1996): 1–34; Erich Zenger, "The Composition and Theology of the Fifth Book of Psalms," *JSOT* 80 (1998): 77–102; Patrick D. Miller, "The End of the Psalter," *JSOT* 80 (1998): 103–10.

as we have them. For these two forms of study, the canonical and the redactional, readers will have to look elsewhere.

My starting point for the commentary is the Masoretic Text as it appears in the Leningrad Codex published in NJPS and BHS. I have assumed that this is a broadly reliable guide to a textual tradition going back into the pre-Christian period. In the translation I have also included some alternative renderings based on the LXX or other versions, where these may reflect different Hebrew traditions (though I have assumed that much versional variation over matters such as suffixes cannot be assumed to indicate a different Hebrew tradition). The variants in 11QPs[a], the largest of the Qumran Psalms manuscripts, including part of Ps. 93 and much of Pss. 101–50, have an important place in this discussion, though this manuscript is a Psalter with its own redactional perspective.[3] I assume that variants in post-MT Hebrew manuscripts constitute post-MT errors or "corrections" rather than preserving pre-MT readings. I have noted some modern proposals for emending the text, though rarely followed them, and also rarely followed proposals for understanding Hebrew words in light of Arabic or Ugaritic.

In translating the Psalms, I have often let the Hebrew's gendered language stand where (for instance) using a gender-inclusive plural would obscure the poetry's dynamic, and in other respects I have aimed at a translation staying close to the dynamics of the Hebrew even if this sometimes means one not as elegant as a translation for reading in church. All Bible translations are my own except where otherwise noted. References are to the versification in English Bibles; where the printed Hebrew Bible differs, its references follow in square brackets (e.g., "Ps. 51:1 [3]"), except that I omit these in the case of cross-references to other verses within the psalm I am commentating on. References to parts of verses such as "v. 1a" and "v. 1b" generally denote the verses as subdivided by MT, but where verses comprise more than two cola (or where I differ from MT in understanding verse divisions), I have often used references that correspond to the subdivisions in my translation. Thus I have referred (for instance) to "v. 1c" and "v. 1d" rather than to "v. 1bα" and "v. 1bβ." I draw the reader's attention to the glossary, which comments on important words asterisked in the body of the book.

I am grateful to my research assistant, Micah Haney, to Wells Turner at Baker Academic, and to Tremper Longman as editor of this series, for saving me from many mistakes and saving you from some of my unclarities, in this and the previous two volumes; and to Damon Cha and Joel Hamme for their work on the indexes.

3. See, e.g., Flint, *Dead Sea Psalms Scrolls*, 172–227. I have referred to García Martínez et al., *Qumran Cave 11*, but for many readings I have relied on Flint.

Abbreviations

*	indicates that the word appears in the glossary
abs.	absolute
acc.	accusative
adj.	adjective, adjectival
ANET	James B. Pritchard, ed., *Ancient Near Eastern Texts Relating to the Old Testament*, 3rd ed. (Princeton: Princeton University Press, 1969)
AOAT	Alter Orient und Altes Testament
Aq	Aquila's translation of the Psalms, as printed in Fridericus Field, *Origenis Hexaplorum quae supersunt*, vol. 2 (Oxford: Oxford University Press, 1874; repr., Hildesheim: Olms, 1964)
ASTI	*Annual of the Swedish Theological Institute*
ATANT	*Abhandlungen zur Theologie des Alten und Neuen Testaments*
AUSS	*Andrews University Seminary Studies*
BASOR	*Bulletin of the American Schools of Oriental Research*
b.	Babylonian Talmud
BDB	Francis Brown, S. R. Driver, and Charles A. Briggs, *A Hebrew and English Lexicon of the Old Testament* (repr., London: Oxford University Press, 1962)
BHS	H. Bardtke, *Liber Psalmorum*, Biblia Hebraica Stuttgartensia 11 (Stuttgart: Würtembergische Bibelanstalt, 1969)
Bib	*Biblica*
BibInt	*Biblical Interpretation*
BN	*Biblische Notizen*
BSac	*Bibliotheca sacra*
BT	*The Bible Translator*
BZ	*Biblische Zeitschrift*
BZAW	Beihefte zur Zeitschrift für die alttestamentliche Wissenschaft

C	The Cairo MS of MT, as reported in *Biblia Hebraica Stuttgartensia*
CBQ	*Catholic Biblical Quarterly*
CBQMS	Catholic Biblical Quarterly Monograph Series
const.	construct
CJT	*Canadian Journal of Theology*
CP	James Barr, *Comparative Philology and the Text of the Old Testament* (Oxford: Oxford University Press, 1968)
CTJ	*Calvin Theological Journal*
CurTM	*Currents in Theology and Mission*
DCH	D. J. A. Clines, ed., *The Dictionary of Classical Hebrew* (Sheffield: Sheffield Academic Press, 1993–)
DG	J. C. L. Gibson, *Davidson's Introductory Hebrew Grammar: Syntax*, 4th ed. (Edinburgh: T&T Clark, 1994)
dittog.	dittography
DJD	Discoveries in the Judaean Desert
DTT	Marcus Jastrow, *A Dictionary of the Targumim, the Talmud Babli and Yerushalmi, and the Midrashic Literature* (New York: Choreb, 1926)
esp.	especially
EstBib	*Estudios bíblicos*
ETL	*Ephemerides theologicae lovanienses*
EvT	*Evangelische Theologie*
EVV	(Many) English versions
ExpT	*Expository Times*
f.	feminine
FRLANT	Forschungen zur Religion und Literatur des Alten und Neuen Testaments
GKC	*Gesenius' Hebrew Grammar*, ed. and enlarged by E. Kautzsch, English translation by A. E. Cowley, 2nd ed. (Oxford: Oxford University Press, 1910; repr. with corrections, 1966)
HALOT	Ludwig Koehler, Walter Baumgartner, et al., *The Hebrew and Aramaic Lexicon of the Old Testament*, 2 vols. (Leiden: Brill, 2001)
HAR	*Hebrew Annual Review*
HBT	*Horizons in Biblical Theology*
HTR	*Harvard Theological Review*
HUCA	*Hebrew Union College Annual*
IBHS	Bruce K. Waltke and Michael O'Connor, *An Introduction to Biblical Hebrew Syntax* (Winona Lake, IN: Eisenbrauns, 1990)
impv.	imperative
inf.	infinitive
Int	*Interpretation*
ITQ	*Irish Theological Quarterly*
JANESCU	*Journal of the Ancient Near Eastern Society of Columbia University*

JBL	*Journal of Biblical Literature*
JBT	Jahrbuch für biblische Theologie
Jerome	Jerome's Latin translation of the Psalms as printed in *Biblia sacra iuxta vulgatam versionem*, 3rd ed. (Stuttgart: Deutsche Bibelgeschellschaft, 1983)
JETS	*Journal of the Evangelical Theological Society*
JM	Paul Joüon, *A Grammar of Biblical Hebrew*, trans. and rev. T. Muraoka, 2 vols. (Rome: Pontifical Biblical Institute, 1991)
JNES	*Journal of Near Eastern Studies*
JNSL	*Journal of Northwest Semitic Languages*
JQR	*Jewish Quarterly Review*
JSOT	*Journal for the Study of the Old Testament*
JSOTSup	JSOT Supplement
JSS	*Journal of Semitic Studies*
JTS	*Journal of Theological Studies*
K	Kethib, the written (consonantal) Hebrew text; contrast Q
KJV	King James Version (Authorized Version)
L	Leningrad manuscript of MT, as printed in BHS
lit.	literally
LXX	Septuagint translation of the Psalms, as printed in Alfred Rahlfs, ed., *Psalmi cum Odis* (repr., Göttingen: Vandenhoeck & Ruprecht, 1979)
m.	masculine
mg	margin
MS(S)	manuscript(s)
MT	Masoretic Text, as printed in BHS
NEB	New English Bible
NedTT	*Nederlands theologisch tijdschrift*
NIDOTTE	Willem A. VanGemeren, ed., *New International Dictionary of Old Testament Theology and Exegesis*, 5 vols. (Grand Rapids: Zondervan, 1996; Carlisle, UK: Paternoster, 1997)
NIVI	*The Holy Bible, New International Version: Inclusive Language Edition* (London: Hodder, 1996)
NJPS	*JPS Hebrew-English Tanakh*, 2nd ed. (Philadelphia: Jewish Publication Society, 1999)
NRSV	New Revised Standard Version
n.s.	new series
NT	New Testament
NTS	*New Testament Studies*
obj.	object
OBO	Orbis biblicus et orientalis
OT	Old Testament
OtSt	*Oudtestamentische Studiën*
PBH	Postbiblical Hebrew
pl.	plural
prep.	preposition

ptc.	participle
Q	Qere, the Hebrew text as read out (i.e., with the vowels); contrast K
RB	*Revue biblique*
ResQ	*Restoration Quarterly*
RevExp	*Review and Expositor*
RevQ	*Revue de Qumran*
RHPR	*Revue d'histoire et de philosophie religieuses*
SBLDS	Society of Biblical Literature Dissertation Series
SBLMS	Society of Biblical Literature Monograph Series
SEÅ	*Svensk Exegetisk Årsbok*
sg.	singular
subj.	subject
SJOT	*Scandinavian Journal of the Old Testament*
ST	*Studia theologica*
Sym	Symmachus's translation of the Psalms, as printed in Fridericus Field, *Origenis Hexaplorum quae supersunt*, vol. 2 (Oxford: Oxford University Press, 1874; repr., Hildesheim: Olms, 1964)
Syr	Syriac translation of the Psalms, as printed in *The Old Testament in Syriac according to the Peshiṭta Version*, part 2.3 (Leiden: Brill, 1980)
TBü	Theologische Bücherei
TDOT	G. Johannes Botterweck et al., eds., *Theological Dictionary of the Old Testament* (Grand Rapids: Eerdmans, 1974–)
Tg	The Targum to the Psalms, as printed in *Miqrāʾôt Gĕdôlôt*, vol. 10 (repr., New York: Pardes, 1951)
Th	Theodotion's translation of the Psalms, as printed in Fridericus Field, *Origenis Hexaplorum quae supersunt*, vol. 2 (Oxford: Oxford University Press, 1874; repr., Hildesheim: Olms, 1964)
ThTo	*Theology Today*
TLOT	Ernst Jenni and Claus Westermann, eds., *Theological Lexicon of the Old Testament*, 3 vols. (Peabody, MA: Hendrickson, 1997)
TNIV	Today's New International Version
TTH	S. R. Driver, *A Treatise on the Use of the Tenses in Hebrew and Some Other Syntactical Questions*, 3rd ed. (London: Oxford University Press, 1892)
TZ	*Theologische Zeitschrift*
UF	*Ugarit-Forschungen*
v./vv.	verse/verses
Vg	The Vulgate Latin translation of the Psalms, as printed in *Biblia sacra iuxta vulgatam versionem*, 3rd ed. (Stuttgart: Deutsche Bibelgeschellschaft, 1983)
Vrs	The ancient versions (LXX, Aq, Sym, Th, Vg, Jerome, Syr, Tg) or most of them
VT	*Vetus Testamentum*
VTSup	Vetus Testamentum Supplement

WBC	Word Biblical Commentary
WMANT	Wissenschaftliche Monographien zum Alten und Neuen Testament
WTJ	*Westminster Theological Journal*
WW	*Word and World*
ZAW	*Zeitschrift für die alttestamentliche Wissenschaft*
ZTK	*Zeitschrift für Theologie und Kirche*

Old Testament

Gen.	Genesis
Exod.	Exodus
Lev.	Leviticus
Num.	Numbers
Deut.	Deuteronomy
Josh.	Joshua
Judg.	Judges
Ruth	Ruth
1–2 Sam.	1–2 Samuel
1–2 Kings	1–2 Kings
1–2 Chron.	1–2 Chronicles
Ezra	Ezra
Neh.	Nehemiah
Esther	Esther
Job	Job
Ps(s).	Psalms
Prov.	Proverbs
Eccles.	Ecclesiastes
Song	Song of Songs
Isa.	Isaiah
Jer.	Jeremiah
Lam.	Lamentations
Ezek.	Ezekiel
Dan.	Daniel
Hosea	Hosea
Joel	Joel
Amos	Amos
Obad.	Obadiah
Jon.	Jonah
Mic.	Micah
Nah.	Nahum
Hab.	Habakkuk
Zeph.	Zephaniah
Hag.	Haggai
Zech.	Zechariah
Mal.	Malachi

New Testament

Matt.	Matthew
Mark	Mark
Luke	Luke
John	John
Acts	Acts
Rom.	Romans
1–2 Cor.	1–2 Corinthians
Gal.	Galatians
Eph.	Ephesians
Phil.	Philippians
Col.	Colossians
1–2 Thess.	1–2 Thessalonians
1–2 Tim.	1–2 Timothy
Titus	Titus
Philem.	Philemon
Heb.	Hebrews
James	James
1–2 Pet.	1–2 Peter
1–3 John	1–3 John
Jude	Jude
Rev.	Revelation

Psalm 90

Yhwh and Time

Translation

Plea. Moses's, God's man.

¹My Lord, you were a shelter;[1]
    you were ours, generation after generation.[2]
²Before mountains were birthed[3]
    and you brought forth earth and world,
From age to age,
    you were there, God.[4]
³You would turn mortals to crushing;
    you said, "Turn, you people!"

1. *Māʿôn* usually denotes either an animal's lair or Yhwh's abode. LXX *kataphygē* might imply *māʿôz*, "refuge" (so some late Hebrew MSS), but the meaning of the two words overlaps.

2. MT implies "you yourself were a refuge for us, generation after generation," but this requires an implausible division of the line. I follow Briggs, *Psalms*, 2:271–72.

3. The word order is odd, the subject preceding the verb, which might explain the odd use of the qatal after *bĕṭerem* (cf. GKC 107c), but it also means that after that prep. the line works *abb′a′*.

4. EVV take v. 2 as a tricolon, but MT has the same disjunctive accent after "from age to age" as after "were birthed," and a tricolon here would be less likely. I thus understand v. 2 as two neat lines, 3-3 and 2-2. LXX reads the last word as *ʾal* rather than *ʾēl* and links with the next line, "Do not turn. . . ." Vg implies both *ʾal* and *ʾēl*; Jerome has neither.

4Because a thousand years
in your eyes were like a day,[5]
Yesterday when it passes,
or a watch in the night.
5You swept them away[6] in sleep,
though in the morning they could be like grass that can renew itself.[7]

6In the morning it can flourish and renew itself;
by evening it can wither and dry up.
7Because we are spent through your anger,
through your fury we have been overwhelmed.
8You put our wayward acts in front of you,
our youthful deeds in the light of your face.
9Because all our days have passed under your wrath,
we have spent our years as moaning.[8]
10The days of our years in themselves are seventy years,[9]
or, with strength, eighty years.
But their boisterousness[10] has been toil and trouble,
because it has passed quickly and we have flown.
11Who acknowledges the force of your anger
and in accordance with[11] reverence for you, your wrath?

5. MT links "in your eyes" with what precedes, which is odd, and takes "like a day [of] yesterday" as a construct expression, for which there is no parallel; separating these words makes for a more coherent understanding of the structure of the verse as a whole.

6. Th. Booij ("Psalm 90,5–6," *Bib* 68 [1987]: 393–96 [see 396]) renders "you pour sleep on them." For possible alternative understandings or emendations, see, e.g., N. H. Tur-Sinai, "Unverstandene Bibelworte i," *VT* 1 (1951): 307–9; D. Winton Thomas, "A Note on *zĕramtām šēnâ yihyû* in Psalm xc 5," *VT* 18 (1968): 267–68; Charles Whitley, "The Text of Psalm 90,5," *Bib* 63 (1982): 555–57; Hans-Peter Müller, "Sprachliche Beobachtungen zu Ps. xc 5f," *VT* 50 (2000): 394–400.

7. MT implies a 3-3 line, "you swept them away, they are in sleep, in the morning like grass that can renew itself"; but the 2-4 division in EVV makes better sense. I take the second colon as subordinate to the first. Elsewhere *ḥālap* qal means "pass away" (cf. LXX, Jerome), but the hiphil can also mean "renew itself," which fits better in this context, and with BDB I assume the qal can have the same double meaning. Tg has "pass away" here and "renew itself" in v. 6, Sym the reverse; either way, it seems implausible to give the word a different meaning in each colon.

8. On LXX's "like a spider" see, e.g., Johannes Schnocks, *Vergänglichkeit und Gottesherrschaft* (Berlin: Philo, 2002), 88–90.

9. The construction is difficult; I follow Schnocks, *Vergänglichkeit und Gottesherrschaft*, 92–93. One might take the prep. on *bāhem* as *b* of identity (*beth essentiae*).

10. For the hapax *rōhab*, Vrs imply *rōḥab*, "breadth" (but it is doubtful whether this more common word makes better sense; the years are long rather than wide), or the much more common *rōb*, "abundance" (which looks even more like a simplification).

11. Mitchell Dahood ("Interrogative *kî* in Psalm 90,11; Isaiah 36,19 and Hosea 13,19," *Bib* 60 [1979]: 573–74) takes the prep. as actually *kî* with an interrogative sense.

12In counting our days, so make us acknowledge it,[12]
in order that we may acquire[13] a wise mind.

13Turn, Yhwh, how long?—
relent over your servants.
14Fill us in the morning with your commitment,
so that we may resound and rejoice all our days.
15Make us rejoice in accordance with the days you have afflicted us,
the years we have seen evil.
16May your action be seen by your servants,
your majesty for their descendants.
17May the delights of my Lord come,
our God, for us.[14]
Establish the work of our hands for us,
yes, the work of our hands—establish it.

Interpretation

The Church of England *Book of Common Prayer* specifies the use of Ps. 90 or Ps. 39 at a funeral service; this takes up the psalm's meditation on the transitory nature of human life. Already in pre-Christian times, Jubilees 23.12–15 picks up its language in commenting on the shortening of the human life span in Genesis,[15] and the theme of mortality has been the focus of much Christian study of it.[16] But modern liturgical revision shortens the psalm so as to omit some or all the references to God's wrath and some or all of the plea in the last section,[17] and this reflects the fact that such use of the psalm, while appropriate and helpful, does

12. EVV have "so make us know how to number our days," but the word order works against that, as does the fact that *yādaʿ* is more often followed by a bare inf., whereas here *mĕnôt* is preceded by *l*.

13. Lit. "bring" (*bôʾ* hiphil), like the harvest (Kirkpatrick, *Psalms*, 552).

14. MT takes v. 17a–b as one colon and thus v. 17 as a tricolon, but the length of v. 17a–b suggests that it is itself more likely a bicolon. The issue parallels that in v. 1.

15. See J. T. A. G. M. van Ruiten, "Van tekst tot tekst," *NedTT* 47 (1993): 177–85; M. Eugene Boring, "Psalm 90," *Mid-Stream* 40.1–2 (2001): 111–28 (see 121–22).

16. See classically Luther, *Selected Psalms,* 2:73–141, on which see, e.g., Hans-Martin Barth, "Leben und sterben können," in *Ars moriendi*, ed. Harald Wagner (Freiburg: Herder, 1989), 45–66; Bernhard Lohse, "Gesetz, Tod und Sünde in Luthers Auslegung des 90. Psalms," in *Leben angesichts des Todes* (Helmut Thielicke Festschrift; Tübingen: Mohr, 1968), 138–55; Matthias Schlicht, *Luthers Vorlesung über Psalm 90* (Göttingen: Vandenhoeck & Ruprecht, 1994); also Gerhard von Rad, *God at Work in Israel* (Nashville: Abingdon, 1980), 210–23; Harald-Martin Wahl, "Psalm 90,12," *ZAW* 106 (1994): 116–23; Hans-Peter Müller, "Der 90. Psalm," *ZTK* 87 (1984): 265–85.

17. See, e.g., the Episcopalian *Book of Common Prayer 1979*, and the comments in Miller, *Interpreting the Psalms*, 125.

not correspond to the inherent meaning of the psalm as a whole.[18] Its last third comprises a lengthy plea, more substantial than is usual even in a prayer psalm; even Luther opens his comment by describing it as "the chief part of Moses's prayer,"[19] though he interprets it christologically. These last verses make explicit that the psalm is a prayer arising out of the people's misfortunes. This is also implicit in the lament or protest of the earlier part. Hardship has gone on year after year, perhaps decade after decade, century after century (though one should not be literalistic in interpreting the time references; trouble can seem to last an eternity when chronologically it lasts a relatively short time). The opening and closing "my Lord" may suggest that the community prayer is uttered by a person such as a king or governor, or by a minister. It parallels Ps. 85[20] and overlaps with the prayers in Ezra 9, Neh. 1 and 9, and Dan. 9.

It has a number of the regular features of a prayer psalm: after the opening invocation, it looks back on how things once were (vv. 1–5), contrasts that with how things are (vv. 6–12), then pleads with God to restore blessing (vv. 13–17).

Verses 1–5 belong together as a recollection of how things once were for *us* (vv. 1–2), which involved the way God dealt with *them* (vv. 3–5). The renewed reference to *us* running through vv. 6–12 marks the transition to a protest at the community's experience over a long period, which contrasts with the way things once were and instead compares with how things previously were for *them*. But the focus lies on how "you" have acted and how "we" have been experiencing these acts. Perhaps contemporary equivalents of the *them*, such as Persian overlords or other local communities, lie behind the psalm, but no enemies appear here and the trouble that the psalm presupposes may rather involve natural reversals such as failed harvests and epidemics. The language and thought of vv. 6–12 parallel those of wisdom, and they have thus encouraged the thesis that the psalm's focus lies on reflection. But the qatal verbs indicate that it is a lament at the community's historical experience in which wisdom motifs have been utilized to formulate a lament that leads into a plea. One might imagine it being used in a manner similar to Lamentations in contexts of communal prayer such as those presupposed in 1 Kings 8; Joel 2; Zech. 7–8. But its reflective nature and its lack of reference to enemies or disasters might suggest a background in personal devotion as a prayer composed for people praying "during hard times long endured."[21]

18. See Richard J. Clifford, "Psalm 90," in *The Book of Psalms*, ed. Flint and Miller, 190–205.

19. *Selected Psalms*, 2:130.

20. Broyles, *Conflict of Faith and Experience*, 174.

21. Tate, *Psalms 51–100*, 439. Cf. Thomas Krüger, "Psalm 90 und die 'Vergänglichkeit des Menschen,'" *Bib* 75 (1994): 191–219.

It closes with a lengthy plea (vv. 13–17).[22] Here, too, there is no concrete description of the restoration the psalm seeks, though the closing reference to establishing "the work of our hands" might suggest prospering the people's work as farmers and/or the restoration work undertaken by Ezra and Nehemiah. The plea's language has many similarities with that of vv. 1–12, though also distinctives. If it is of separate origin from vv. 1–12,[23] it has been composed in light of those verses.[24]

The psalm continues the stance of Ps. 89, repeating the question "How long?"[25] It thus does not make an encouraging beginning to Book IV. It compares with the psalms that open Books II and III, and parallels Ps. 73 in being a psalm that brings together deep-felt need and theological reflection.

Plea. Moses's, God's man.

Heading. See glossary. Moses appears only here in a psalm heading, though he appears elsewhere in Book IV (Pss. 90–106), which might even be called a "Moses-book."[26] The term "God's man" usually applies to prophets such as Elijah, as frightening characters who mediate supernatural power, but it occasionally applies more loosely to Moses to emphasize his status, not least in the "blessing" of Moses (Deut. 33:1), which is actually more a prayer for the clans and for the people as a whole. There Moses describes Yhwh as a "shelter" supporting the people with "age-long" power (Deut. 33:27).[27] Perhaps Deut. 33 was one passage that suggested the link with Ps. 90, which also has a number of verbal links with Deut. 32.[28] The link becomes ironic, as the psalm's burden is that for a long time the blessing of Deut. 33 has not been the people's experience, but in this context Moses is an appropriate person to be imagined

22. So it is hardly a psalm of trust (so, tentatively, Westermann, *The Praise of God in the Psalms*, 55) or a hymn of (self-)consolation (so David Robertson, "Literary Criticism and the Bible," *Semeia* 8 [1977]: 35–50).

23. E.g., Gunkel, *Psalmen*, 397; Werner H. Schmidt, "'Der Du die Menschen lässest sterben,'" in *Was ist der Mensch . . . ?* ed. Frank Crüsemann et al. (H. W. Wolff Festschrift; Munich: Kaiser, 1992), 115–30.

24. See analyses of its structure by Pierre Auffret, "Essai sur la structure littéraire du Psaume 90," *Bib* 61 (1980): 262–76, building on Stefan Schreiner, "Erwägungen zur Struktur des 90. Psalms," *Bib* 59 (1978): 80–90; also Matitiahu Tsevat, "Psalm xc 5–6," *VT* 35 (1985): 115–17; Schnocks, *Vergänglichkeit und Gottesherrschaft*, 35–41, and generally.

25. In v. 13, *ʿad-mātāy*; in 89:46 [47], *ʿad-mâ*.

26. Tate, *Psalms 51–100*, xxvi.

27. "Refuge" is *mĕʿōnâ*; in Ps. 90:1 *māʿôn*.

28. E.g., the two verbs in v. 2 come in Deut. 32:18; the form *yĕmôt* (v. 15) comes otherwise only in Deut. 32:7, where also the phrase *dôr wādôr* appears (cf. v. 1). Oddly, Augustine (*Psalms*, 441) reckons that Moses did not write the psalm because it lacks distinctive expressions of his.

as uttering a *plea for Israel; he did that at Sinai, urging Yhwh to "turn" from "your anger" and "relent over" the people, and to think about "your servants" (Exod. 32:12–13; cf. vv. 7, 13). Tg expands substantially on the heading and on vv. 1–2, linking the psalm with Moses's praying for the people during the rebellions in the wilderness.[29]

While the heading might have been generated by the content of the psalm, alternatively the psalm might have been written to indicate how Moses might pray for the people in their present circumstances, in light of the material in Exod. 32 and Deut. 32–33.[30] "It is as if Moses . . . himself takes up the plea of Psalm 89."[31] This would correspond to the way those prayers themselves were written, and also to the later development of material put on the lips of scriptural characters such as Adam, Enoch, and Moses.[32] Here the people's situation in a time later than Moses's (e.g., after the exile) is reckoned to be similar to their situation in Moses's time.

90:1–5. The psalm begins with a recollection of Yhwh's past faithfulness, which contrasts with the experience of the present (cf. 44:1–3 [2–4]). The qatal verbs in vv. 1b and 2a suggest reference to the past, though vv. 3–5 mix qatals and yiqtols and EVV refer them to the present. I take the whole section as reflection on Yhwh's past way of relating to the people. Verse 1 summarizes the way things once were and how they should be. Verses 2–3 then pair in expanding on their assertion, and vv. 4–5 repeat their point.

1My Lord, you were a shelter;
you were ours, generation after generation.

The opening invocation "my *Lord" is unique in the Psalms but very appropriate to Ps. 90. By its nature it appeals to the commitment a master should show his servants; the plea will spell that out (cf. vv. 13, 16, 17). If we are right to take the suffix as suggesting "my," the invocation is especially appropriate as pointing both to Yhwh's sovereign power and to Yhwh's relationship with the suppliant; neither are being expressed as might have been expected. EVV "you have been a haven" implies that Yhwh still is that; actually the psalm's problem is that this was so in the past but it no longer

29. See further Beth LaNeel Tanner, *The Book of Psalms through the Lens of Intertextuality* (New York: Lang, 2001), 85–107.

30. Cf. David Noel Freedman, "Who Asks (or Tells) God to Repent?" *Bible Review* 1/4 (1985): 56–59.

31. William J. Urbrock, "The Earth Song in Psalms 90–92," in *Earth Story*, ed. Habel, 65–83 (see 65–66); also Urbrock, "Psalm 90," *CurTM* 25 (1998): 26–29.

32. See, e.g., James H. Charlesworth, ed., *The Old Testament Pseudepigrapha*, vol. 1: *Apocalyptic Literature and Testaments* (Garden City, NY: Doubleday, 1983).

obtains. The psalm does not work with a dialectical tension between lament and trust,[33] except in the sense that any lament does; it protests the way trust is no longer possible. "Shelter" (*māʿôn*) is usually a term for an animal's lair, the secure abode it makes for itself. It is never used of human habitations, but it can refer to God's "lair" in the heavens, the place to which God retreats and which humanity cannot invade but from which God emerges to bless or deliver (68:5 [6]); Tg takes that to be the reference here. It can also refer to God's earthly "lair," the temple (26:8), to which Yhwh's people may come but which others cannot invade. Here the psalm moves from one metaphor ("Yhwh has a lair") to another, more profound one ("Yhwh *is* a lair"). Like an animal in danger from bigger animals, Israel could once run to this secure place and know it was safe. Particularly if carrying the nuance "dwelling," this declaration (the Midrash comments) indicates that the world is contained or placed in God, not God in the world. The world is second to God; God is not second to the world.[34] The affirmation that God has been the people's home is especially suggestive as one imagines it on Moses's lips, as in his day the people never had a secure home.[35] God is home for people who are or feel homeless. That was true "generation after generation," through centuries when Israel was often threatened but never overwhelmed (e.g., Pss. 46; 48).

[2]Before mountains were birthed
  and you brought forth earth and world,
From age to age,
  you were there, God.

Yhwh has been able so to protect the people "generation after generation" because Yhwh's being runs through every generation and goes back even before there were generations. Yhwh's deity antedates not merely all generations but the world's very existence. The complementarity of passive and active in v. 2a–b means the first colon raises the question "Who birthed the mountains?" and the second then gives the inevitable but striking answer, "Yhwh did." The vivid verb *ḥûl* refers to a woman's twisting, turning, and struggling as she gives birth. The answer is unexpected, as well as inevitable, because the OT does not usually speak of Yhwh's creation as birthing.[36] But the idea that the mountains were

33. So Norbert Greinacher, "Psalm 90," in *Die Freude an Gott—unsere Kraft*, ed. Johannes Joachim Degenhardt (O. B. Knoch Festschrift; Stuttgart: Katholisches Bibelwerk, 1991), 366–77 (see 366).

34. *Midrash on Psalms*, 2:93.

35. E.g., Spurgeon, *Treasury of David*, 4:61.

36. Thus Vrs. have "and the world and the earth brought [them] forth," which might imply polal *wattĕḥôlal* "and . . . were brought forth" for MT's polel *wattĕḥôlēl* (Syr has a double reading).

birthed from somewhere else, perhaps from the earth's own "creative potency" or "power to give birth,"[37] might seem in more radical tension with regular OT faith. Job 38:8–11 does speak of the seas gushing forth from an anonymous womb but then of Yhwh's sovereign action. If one is to distinguish between the earth and the world, the former will denote the material cosmos, the latter the inhabited world, which will be the focus in v. 3.

But the first line is incomplete; it is merely a pair of subordinate clauses. Initially the second line simply continues these with another temporal expression, further extending the tension: what is the point in all these temporal phrases? Indeed, this third expression raises that tension, going beyond merely looking back to the distant age when Yhwh birthed the world and extending the time reference, "from age to age"; the phrase parallels "generation after generation" (v. 1). The last colon then reveals the point of the two lines. EVV have "you are God," but the preceding lines suggest another past reference. This fits the general point of vv. 1–5: Yhwh has always been there as God (though Yhwh is not behaving like God now). Similarly, in other contexts "from age to age" could suggest Yhwh's omnipresence through time, but here it refers to the times that preceded the community's recent negative experience.

3You would turn mortals to crushing;
you said, "Turn, you people!"

NRSV renders "you turn us," assuming that v. 3 makes a statement about the way Yhwh treats Israel, but v. 3 marks a move from talking in the first person about "us" to talk in third-person terms, which continues through vv. 3–6. The way Yhwh has been a shelter for "us" is by treating "them," other people, in the way v. 3a describes. "They" have turned out to be *ʾĕnôš*, humanity in its frailty. EVV read the line as a generalization about human transience, such as would be at home in a wisdom context, and translate *dakkāʾ* as dust (something crushed). This facilitates a link with Gen. 3:19. But there is no parallel for this meaning of *dakkāʾ* (Gen. 3 uses other words to describe the raw material from which humanity was made).[38] "Crushing" usually refers to putting people down in some connection (e.g., 72:4; 89:10 [11]; 94:5; 143:3); this fits here (v. 5 will explicate how this manifested itself). Yhwh has demonstrated the capacity to put down the people from whom the community needed to find shelter.

37. Kraus, *Psalms 60–150*, 215. See further Keel, *Symbolism*, 203–4.

38. Cf. Wolfram von Soden, "Zum Psalm 90,3: Statt *dakkā* lies *dukkā*!" *UF* 15 (1983): 307–8.

Thus instead of letting the tense of the line be determined by the yiqtol in v. 3a, understood as present, in the context I let the tense of the line be determined by the qatal in v. 3b and take the yiqtol as equivalent to a temporal imperfect.

There is, however, some irony in v. 3a. Elsewhere "turn to" (*šûb ʿad*) nearly always has God as object.[39] The line might have implied that God was turning people to crushing in the sense of contrition, an inner and not merely an outward humbling (so Sym, Jerome), and urging them to turn to God. Actually they were beyond that point; God was doing away with them.

[4]Because a thousand years
in your eyes were like a day,
Yesterday when it passes,
or a watch in the night.

The "because" introduces an explanation or restatement of the point in vv. 2–3, first with another general statement about God. EVV have "*are* like a day," but the context suggests a statement about the principle underlying God's past activity.

"Mortals" (v. 3) such as the Egyptians, Canaanites, or Assyrians could last a century or two, which was as good as lasting forever. Every empire reckons it will do that; the Spanish, British, and American empires have all been characterized as the "empire on which the sun never sets." But even a millennium does not impress Yhwh (if people such as Adam and Methuselah lived nearly a millennium, so what?).[40] It does not hold Yhwh back from action, any more than a day does. A day may seem to last a long time, and a watch in the night may seem interminable, but they seem like nothing when the day has passed and become yesterday or the watch has passed uneventfully (the *k*, "like," applies to the third and fourth colon as well as the second, and the verb applies to the fourth

39. Cf. Walter Harrelson, "A Meditation on the Wrath of God," in *Scripture in History and Theology*, ed. Arthur L. Merrill and Thomas W. Overholt (J. C. Rylaarsdam Festschrift; Pittsburgh: Pickwick, 1977), 181–91 (see 186). Verse 3b has also been taken as a summons back to life after the turning of v. 3a (e.g., Luther, *Selected Psalms*, 2:97–99).

40. Cf. Jerome, *Homilies*, 1:148. Jubilees 4.30 takes up this line to explain how on human reckoning Adam lived for nearly a thousand years despite the warning that he would die on the day he ate of the tree, and then 2 Pet. 3:8 does so to respond to people who chafe at the delay of Christ's coming (see Wolfgang Schrage, "'Ein Tag ist beim Herrn wie tausand Jahre, und tausand Jahre sind wie ein Tag," in *Glaube und Eschatologie*, ed. Erich Grässer and Otto Merk [W. G. Kümmel Festschrift; Tübingen: Mohr, 1985], 267–75). Augustine warns against using it as a basis for trying to calculate the chronology of world history as lasting 6,000 years and to calculate the date of that coming (*Psalms*, 442), though he later provides the outline that designates the time beginning with John the Baptist as Day Six (*Psalms*, 457).

colon as well as the third). A millennium is like that to Yhwh. So Yhwh can easily crush an empire.

> [5]You swept them away in sleep,
> though in the morning they could be like grass that can renew itself.

EVV take the qatal verb as a gnomic qatal, but the more usual past reference of the qatal fits. Yhwh did sweep away (lit. flood away) Israel's overlords or foes in the past. Their sleep might be the sleep of death (e.g., Job 14:12) or the sleep of torpor that made them a pushover (e.g., Ps. 76:5 [6]), or v. 5b may indicate that it points to how Yhwh sweeps people away overnight. Whichever is right, the speedy fall contrasts with the flourishing vividly remembered. Grass has endless capacity to grow anew; it does not need to be reseeded. Similarly, an empire can seem to have endless capacity to reinvent itself, but this impression has turned out to be false.

90:6–12. For the rest of the psalm "they" disappear and "we" come into sharp focus, though the transition from the first section to the second is indistinct. The "because" in v. 7 makes it hard to see the transition happening there. Rather, the repetition in v. 6 is the clue to it (cf. Isa. 40:6–8, where v. 8 is a response to vv. 6b–7).

There has been little regular parallelism in vv. 1–5; there now follow four neatly parallel lines. The movement in the psalm parallels that between Ps. 44:1–8 [2–9] and 9–16 [10–17]. Here, too, the psalm moves from recollecting a positive involvement with Israel, which included the sweeping away of its enemies, to protesting the way Yhwh has more recently been relating to Israel, which is now itself withering.

> [6]In the morning it can flourish and renew itself;
> by evening it can wither and dry up.

Verse 6a, then, virtually repeats v. 5b, in order to take its point in a different direction. The grass image usually contrasts grass's capacity to grow quickly with its vulnerability to withering and drying up. So it was implicitly in v. 5, and explicitly here. A nation may flourish one moment but collapse the next.

> [7]Because we are spent through your anger,
> through your fury we have been overwhelmed.

The repetition in v. 6 began to declare that it is not just Israel's overlords and foes that illustrate that principle. In contrast to the declarations in vv.

1–5 and the comment about "them," "we" ourselves have been doing so. Instead of our foes withering like grass, we have done so (cf. Isa. 40:6–8). Instead of our foes running for their lives, overwhelmed by panic (Pss. 48:5 [6]; 83:15, 17 [16, 18]), we have done so. Instead of Yhwh's angry fury being turned on our foes, it is turned on us.

> 8You put our wayward acts in front of you,
> our youthful deeds in the light of your face.

In Pss. 44 and 74 a declaration such as v. 7 presupposes that Israel has not deserved its trouble. This psalm presupposes a time when it cannot make that claim. Israel has been guilty of *wayward acts. And instead of turning a blind eye to these and postponing anger (e.g., 103:8), Yhwh has made a point of keeping the record of them on display and looking at it, and therefore doing something about it.

Wayward acts[41] is given precision by *ʿălumēnû*, "our youthful deeds." The word follows neatly on 89:45 [46] but now refers to the deeds of Israel's youth or of the younger years of the present generation; cf. Tg. EVV take the word to mean "hidden deeds"; the reference is then to private prayer to other deities, in people's homes.[42] Even if such acts belong in the distant past or take place in darkness, they have not escaped recording, and to Yhwh it is as if they had been done in the present or out in the open, in the light of the sun (cf. 44:21 [22]). More precisely, it is as if Yhwh the FBI officer has investigated the people's entire past or come into the people's homes and by virtue of the divine presence shone a bright light on what was going on there.

> 9Because all our days have passed under your wrath,
> we have spent our years as moaning.

The "because" introduces five lines that take the point further, developing the comment on the long period that Yhwh's wrath has hung over the people because of their waywardness. "All our days" might denote the people's entire history (though the psalm's opening verse perhaps excludes that) or this generation's entire life (cf. v. 10); one could imagine (for instance) people who experienced the fall of Jerusalem and have been in a miserable state for decades. "Our years" then underlines the length of time. "Spent" picks up from v. 7, while "wrath" adds to the "anger" and "fury" of v. 7, further underlining its awfulness. Saying that the years

41. Readers might note a paronomasia with v. 1: *ʿāwôn* stands before the *māʿôn* (cf. S. D. Goitein, "'Maʿon'—a Reminder of Sin," *JSS* 10 [1965]: 52–53).

42. That is, EVV derive from *ʿālam* I, Tg from *ʿālam* II, which fits the context with its stress on time. LXX assumes *ʿôlām*, which came in v. 2 and also fits this context.

have been spent "as moaning"[43] achieves the same effect. Whereas Ps. 44 (for example) relates to a particular calamity that does not link with a particular act of rebellion, Ps. 90 relates to an ongoing experience of God's wrath, which it links with an awareness of waywardness in the community's history that justifies this. At the same time, its language suggests a sense of having come to a point of crisis. The community's days have passed; its years are spent (cf. v. 10).

The psalm is not implying that all humanity stands under God's wrath.[44] In the OT God's wrath is something that operates in particular contexts for particular reasons (though it can see the whole world as under God's curse). Here the problem is that it has been operating against God's people for such a long time to such debilitating effect.

> 10The days of our years in themselves are seventy years,
> or, with strength, eighty years:
> But their boisterousness has been toil and trouble,
> because it has passed quickly and we have flown.

In Western thinking, seventy years has traditionally suggested a normal life span, but the OT refers to seventy years in this connection only when speaking of the period of time a calamity may last—especially the exile (e.g., Jer. 25:11–12; Zech. 1:12). Nor does the OT refer to eighty years as a long life (Isa. 65:20 implies that a hundred years counts as a long life; cf. Sirach 18:9 [8]). (In a traditional society, few people would live to seventy years or keep going for eighty.) Here, as usual, seventy years suggests the community's long period of trouble. The psalm then sardonically goes beyond this conventional trope in going on to refer to eighty years. It might seem that the "boisterousness," the energy or pride, to continue to enjoy life into one's seventies would be a great blessing. Except (says the psalm) it would not, because all it would mean is experiencing more years of toil and trouble. The comment is worthy of Ecclesiastes, which indeed loves speaking of "toil" (e.g., Eccles. 1:3), as does Job (e.g., 5:7).[45] "Trouble" often accompanies it, to underline its point (e.g., Job 4:8; 5:6). The "because" introduces a final colon, also recalling Ecclesiastes: life is toil and trouble because it comes to an end, apparently quickly, which raises a question about the meaningfulness of all the preceding years.

43. Not "like" a moan, implying short-lived (BDB); it need not be! TNIV has "we finish our years with a moan," but "with" is a doubtful meaning for *k*.

44. Cf. Calvin, *Psalms*, 3:469; against (e.g.) S. W. Sykes, "Death and Doctrine," *Churchman* 95 (1981): 306–12; Claus Westermann, "Der 90. Psalm," in Westermann, *Forschung am Alten Testament*, TBü 24 (Munich: Kaiser, 1964), 344–50 (see 347).

45. Gerhard von Rad sees the psalm's links with Ecclesiastes as making it a "stranger" in the OT (*God's Work in Israel* [Nashville: Abingdon, 1980], 218). Bruce Vawter ("Postexilic Prayer and Hope," *CBQ* 37 [1975]: 460–70) also compares it with Wisdom 9; 15:1–3.

Here, in contrast, the suppliants speak of the nature of people's human life in the particular time in which they live.

> [11]Who acknowledges the force of your anger,
> and in accordance with reverence for you, your wrath?
> [12]In counting our days, so make us acknowledge it,
> in order that we may acquire a wise mind.

Why should Yhwh impose such ongoing trouble on the people, apparently going beyond what mere justice requires? Seeking to make sense of the experience of affliction, the psalm sees a purpose in it. Whereas outside OT and Christian faith people might be afraid of God, within the faith the problem is the opposite. Knowing God's love and being invited to live in relationship with God enables Israelites and Christians to be confident about that relationship. There is no reason to live in fear of God. So we can end up seeing God as simply our buddy or lover. Within Israelite and Christian faith, who acknowledges the strength of Yhwh's wrathful anger in such a way as to relate to God with proper *reverence, with the proper attitude and the proper submission? (The parallelism between the lines suggests that *yir'â* denotes reverence, not fear; acknowledging and revering are both proper positive stances toward Yhwh.)

It is the counting of days in their toilsome and troubled nature that could push the community to this acknowledgment and submission. Without it, people can live in denial and simply continue enjoying their lives without a care or a thought for God. The way they experience life can make them face questions. The psalm asks that it may do that, and thus encourage them to apply a wise mind to their understanding of life and God. The psalm again takes up wisdom ways of thinking in connecting acknowledgment, reverence, and wisdom—and also discipline (e.g., Prov. 1:7). The community as well as the individual need to pay heed to these points of connection.

A "Who?" question of this kind is often a wish, and v. 11a may imply "If only we would acknowledge . . ." (cf. TNIV). Whereas Qoheleth uses "Who knows?" questions with gloomy implications (the answer is "No one"), the psalm leaves "an open door" to a positive answer.[46] "Anger" and "wrath" are picked up from vv. 7 and 9, but the addition of "force" gives them extra effect.

90:13–17. Verses 6–12 ended with a plea that related to motifs in that section and would have made a fine climax and end to a meditative reflection. But they are not the psalm's end, destination, or climax. It closes with a more extensive plea for divine action that corresponds to

46. James L. Crenshaw, "The Expression *mî yôdēa'* in the Hebrew Bible," *VT* 36 (1986): 274–88.

the regular nature of a protest psalm.[47] In the nature of such an appeal, but with distinctive passion,[48] it throws caution to the wind and asks for fullness of blessing that implicitly contrasts with the extremes of wrath that the community has been experiencing.

> [13]Turn, Yhwh, how long?—
> relent over your servants.

The abrupt transition to urgent, insistent, and assertive plea makes for a contrast with the stance in vv. 11–12. One response to that experience of toil and trouble is to ask Yhwh to make it religiously and morally fruitful in people's lives, but another is to ask Yhwh simply to bring it to an end. "Turn" (*šûbâ*; cf., e.g., 6:4 [5]) does not presuppose that Yhwh is looking away and ignoring the people's plight and needs to turn toward them, but rather that Yhwh is set on one stance and one form of action (the expression of wrath) and needs to turn to another stance. There is some irony (or poignancy)[49] in the appeal, given the earlier references to Yhwh's bidding to turn (v. 3). "How long?" is an even more familiar plea. The question's incomplete nature (again cf. 6:3 [4]) underlines how it is not really a question, requesting information; it is indeed a plea.

"Turn" is thus a familiar bidding, but also a bold one. It often implies "repent," give up doing something you should not be doing. Verse 13b encourages us to hear this resonance with its use of *nāḥam* (niphal). This verb often denotes Yhwh's relenting of tough action; both verbs appear in Moses's plea in Exod. 32:12 (cf. also Joel 2:14; Jon. 3:9). The boldness continues as the suppliants describe themselves as Yhwh's servants. In effect, they have already acknowledged that they have not been behaving as obedient servants. Their boldness lies in the assumption that Yhwh must still be committed to treating them as servants. Their plea again parallels Moses's appeal for "your people" (Exod. 32:12), despite what this people has been doing. It also parallels his subsequent appeal to Yhwh to be mindful of "your servants Abraham, Isaac, and Israel"; they might also be in mind here.

> [14]Fill us in the morning with your commitment,
> so that we may resound and rejoice all our days.

47. On the distinction between the plea in v. 12 and the new beginning that follows, see Hossfeld and Zenger, *Psalms 2*, 419.

48. Cf. William J. Urbrock, "Mortal and Miserable Man," *Society of Biblical Literature 1974 Seminar Papers* (Cambridge: SBL, 1974), 1:1–33 (see 15).

49. Cf. Urbrock, "Mortal and Miserable Man," 13.

The plea takes off into distinctive territory. First, it asks Yhwh not merely to *show* us some *commitment but to *fill* us with it. That will correspond to the way we have been filled with troubles (88:3 [4]; 123:3–4). We want to experience so much of Yhwh's commitment that we are sated and overwhelmed. The appeal about the morning picks up that phrase from vv. 5–6, where the flourishing of the morning gives a false promise about what will follow. Here, the psalm asks that the morning may rather be the beginning of a day of divine commitment, so that things no longer work out that way. Human commitment is inclined to wither when Yhwh's breath blows on it, but Yhwh's word allegedly does not do so but stands forever (Isa. 40:6–8). The psalm asks that this may prove true.[50] "All our days" have passed under Yhwh's wrath; the psalm asks that this may be reversed, though it jumps past that to the implication that therefore we may *resound with joy (the two verbs form a hendiadys) all our days. Prosaically put, may God fill us with the fruits of divine commitment at the beginning of the day and through every day, so that we may respond to that with joyful resounding each morning and through every day.

> [15]Make us rejoice in accordance with the days you have afflicted us,
> the years we have seen evil.

The psalm restates the point, once again taking up "days" and "rejoice," and also "years": the years that may be like a day for Yhwh, but not for us (v. 4), the years consumed by moaning (v. 9), the years spent in toil and trouble (v. 10)—in other words, characterized by *bad experience.[51]

> [16]May your action be seen by your servants,
> your majesty for their descendants.

Commitment expresses itself in action that can be seen; once again a verb recurs, from the previous line (if it were not useful to make the recurrence clear, one might rather translate "be visible to"). This action will be an expression of Yhwh's majesty. "Your servants" also recurs, from v. 13. Are these simply the speakers, who are also concerned for their children? Or are "your servants" again Israel's ancestors, imagined

50. Thus there is no need to appeal to the possible notion that morning is the expected time for Yhwh to act to rescue us from trouble (cf. 30:5 [6]; 46:5 [6]; Joseph Ziegler, "Die Hilfe Gottes 'am Morgen,'" in *Alttestamentliche Studien*, ed. Hubert Junker and Johannes Botterweck [Friedrich Nötscher Festschrift; Bonn: Hanstein, 1950], 281–88).

51. Parallelism returns, with the verb applying to both cola so that the second colon has more space to describe the grimness of the past. Thus "years" pairs with "days" (the prep. also carrying over) and "we have seen evil" pairs with "you have afflicted us."

as seeing Yhwh's act of restoration, so that the present generation who experience it are themselves these descendants?

> [17]May the delights of my Lord come,
> our God, for us.
> Establish the work of our hands for us,
> yes, the work of our hands—establish it.

The appeal to Yhwh as "my Lord" completes a frame around the psalm (cf. v. 1) and also pairs with the appeal regarding "your servants" (v. 16; cf. also v. 13).[52] Asking for "delights" (*nōʿam*; cf. NEB) further suggests the abundance of the psalmist's request, for something that in its splendor corresponds to the depth and length of the community's affliction.[53] It wants to see bounteous restoration and flourishing. Tg nicely glosses "the delightfulness of the Garden of Eden."

Compared with v. 17a–b, the closing plea in v. 17c–d is prosaic in its language and in its rhetoric, as the last colon repeats the penultimate one with only slight variation (perhaps it is a congregational response).[54] In communication with God, as with human beings, there is a place for high-flown images and a place for down-to-earth language. Just grant that all the hard work we do in sowing and plowing, in building and planting, pays off rather than being a waste of time, the community asks.

Theological Implications

The psalm relates Yhwh and time, and the Israelite community and time.[55] It begins from Yhwh's eternity, not in the sense of being outside time, but in the sense of having been present through all time, through all the generations of Israel's history. Thus in the past Yhwh has always been its shelter, the place where it found a home. Making this link draws attention to the fact that Israel lives in limited time. Yhwh's time goes back before the time when Israel's generations began, before the time when the world itself was brought into being. Yhwh

52. Cf. Hubert Irsigler, "Psalm 90," in Irsigler, *Vom Adamssohn zum Immanuel* (St. Ottilien: Eos, 1997), 49–69 (see 56).

53. "Delights" (*nōʿam*) is sg., but in English "the delight of my Lord" would give a misleading impression. Jon D. Levenson ("A Technical Meaning for *nʿm* in the Hebrew Bible," *VT* 35 [1985]: 61–67) suggests that the word denotes an affirmative "omen," but this requires a lot of inference.

54. Cf. Weiser, *Psalms*, 595. Extraposing the object serves to help the line and the psalm to round off (*TTH* 197).

55. See Klaus Seybold, "Zu den Zeitvorstellungen in Psalm 90," *TZ* 53 (1997): 99–108; Schnocks, *Vergänglichkeit und Gottesherrschaft*, 145–70.

was God before that, "from age to age," as far back as time goes, which implies forever.

In the span of Yhwh's life, then, the significance of time differs greatly from its significance for human beings. Human experience helps us imagine how this is so. For us, time can go quickly or slowly. For a child, a summer lasts forever. For an older person, a decade passes in a flash and we ask, "Where did the time go?" For Yhwh, a millennium is a tiny period of time in the context of Yhwh's total experience of time. Yhwh thus has no problem being present throughout Israel's generations. Any time a nation needs putting down, Yhwh can be there to put it down. If it seems impressive because it has lasted a century or two, that is only hours in Yhwh's time frame, and the nation ceases to be impressive. Indeed, its lifetime resembles that of grass that can spring up at the beginning of a day but withers in the sun by its end. Indeed, a century or two can be like a mere day.

That is an encouragement when we consider the fate of peoples who oppose God or when a little people considers a great power's fate. It is worrying for most readers of this commentary, who belong to a great power. And it does not necessarily feel encouraging to the little people. A millennium may be only a day to Yhwh, but seventy or eighty years is seventy or eighty years to us. Flourishing and withering within a day characterizes the experience of the little people as well as that of the empire, and implicitly for the same reason; the little people looks back over its life's time frame and recognizes that it has been characterized by waywardness and thus by God's wrath. So it lives with two time frames, in a variant on the facing of two sets of facts that characterizes (for instance) Ps. 22. The solution for the tension involved in its stance in relation to time is not that it should attempt to live in God's time rather than its own, or ask to be enabled to do that. This would be another form of denial or docetism. It needs to count its days, not deny their number, but to do so in such a way as to face the facts about why they have been what they have been.

Beyond that, the solution needs to lie in Yhwh's coming to live by the people's time. "How long?" the psalm asks. The question is a common one, but it gains extra resonance in the context of this psalm's preoccupation with time. Are not seventy or eighty years enough? And Yhwh's eternity (that is, Yhwh's living on through age after age) surely makes Yhwh able to intervene in its time and take action in it. Yhwh's being God from age to age does not just apply to the past. It continues into the present and the future. And Yhwh's living in time means Yhwh can "turn" and "relent." Yhwh is not stuck forever in a pattern of action (or inaction) that must last forever because Yhwh cannot change. A great thing about Yhwh is that Yhwh can change. A traditional Compline prayer asks that "we who are wearied by the changes and chances of this fleeting world, may rest upon your eternal changelessness."[56] The psalm does not seek to escape from the changing to the constant.[57] It seeks to escape from the constant, the pattern that has obtained for seventy or eighty years, to some change. It regrets Yhwh's constancy since changing from being a shelter to being wrathful and asks that Yhwh may change once more.

The psalm has in mind a new pattern for the day. Instead of it meaning that grass grows in the morning and withers by evening, it wants the day to overflow (again) with divine commitment and wants this to become a pattern for days. Future days will thus have a different character from past days.

56. See, e.g., *Celebrating Common Prayer*, compiled by David Stancliffe and Brother Tristam SSF, rev. ed. (London and New York: Continuum, 2002), 241.

57. So Mays, *Psalms*, 294.

Psalm 91

Shadow of the Almighty

Translation

David's. [11Q11]/Praise song. David's. [LXX]

1One who lives in the shelter of the Most High,
who stays in the shade of the Almighty:
2"I say[1] to[2] Yhwh,
'My refuge and my stronghold,[3]
my God in whom I trust.' "

3Because[4] he is the one who will rescue you[5]
from the fowler's trap,
from the epidemic [MT]/word [LXX][6] that brings destruction.

1. For MT's *ʾōmar*, 11Q11 has *hʾwmr*; Jerome also has a ptc. LXX "he will say" suggests *yōʾmar*, which NRSV renders gender inclusively "you will say."

2. Or "of."

3. With Jerome, I take the colon as a vocative; a second-person noun clause without a copula (so LXX) is less likely (see examples in Pirmin Hugger, *Jahwe meine Zuflucht* [Münsterschwarzach: Vier-Türme, 1971], 61–64).

4. NJPS has "that," taking the *kî* as dependent on *ʾōmar* in v. 2.

5. LXX "me."

6. LXX, Syr, Sym (not Aq, Tg) imply *dĕbar*, "word," for MT *deber*.

[4]With his pinions he will cover[7] you,
under his wings you can take refuge.
His truthfulness will be a body shield, a rampart:[8]
[5]you will not fear[9] a terror[10] by night
or an arrow that flies by day,
[6]An epidemic[11] that walks in the dark,
or a scourge that destroys at noon.
[7]A thousand may fall at your side,
ten thousand at your right hand;
to you it will not reach.
[8]You will just look with your eyes,
see the recompense of the faithless,
[9]Because you are the one who has made Yhwh "my refuge,"
the Most High your shelter.
[10]No harm will be allowed to come upon you;
no hurt will come near your tent.
[11]Because he will command his aides for you,
to keep you in all your ways.
[12]On their hands they will carry you
so that your foot does not stumble on a stone.
[13]On cub[12] and adder you will tread;
you will trample on lion and serpent.

[14]Because I am the one he is attracted to, I will rescue him;
I will lift him to safety, because he has acknowledged my name.
[15]He can call me and I will answer him;
I will be with him in trouble.
I will save him and honor him;
[16]I will fill him with long days
and show him my deliverance.[13]

7. On the jussive, see GKC 109k.

8. The traditional understanding takes the hapax *sōḥērâ* as another word for a shield, as something that goes about (*sāḥar*) the person (cf. Aq, and LXX's paraphrase), but the verb does not really mean "go about" in this sense. Rather, see *HALOT*. A. A. Macintosh ("Psalm xci 4 and the Root סחר," *VT* 23 [1973]: 56–62) suggests it means protection in a less concrete sense. It does not mean a buckler (NRSV), which is a small, handheld shield.

9. The negative *lōʾ* might imply a statement or promise or strong prohibition.

10. Or perhaps "pack" (Dahood, *Psalms*, 2:331; and see *HALOT*).

11. LXX, Syr, Aq again imply *dābār*, "thing," for MT *deber*. But contextually this makes less sense here.

12. Cf. Tg. But LXX, Jerome have *aspis*, a word for snake, perhaps translating from the context (though see S. Mowinckel, "חלשׁ," in *Hebrew and Semitic Studies*, ed. D. W. Thomas and W. D. McHardy [G. R. Driver Festschrift; Oxford: Clarendon, 1963], 95–103).

13. The parallelism might suggest that *ʾarʾēhû* is a form from *rāwâ* or that *rāwâ* had a by-form *rāʾâ* and that it means "satiate" or that it needs emending to *ʾarwēhû*. But cf. 50:23, where "show" is more natural.

Interpretation

In content, Ps. 91 closely parallels Ps. 46,[14] but it relates to an individual's life (see especially v. 7) rather than the community's. Further, while paralleling Ps. 46 in quoting a word from God near the end, the bulk of it comprises declarations and promises of Yhwh's protection rather than testimony or expression of trust. In form, then, it closely parallels Ps. 20, or Ps. 121.[15] None of it addresses God (though v. 2 quotes some words addressed to God). It makes sense as addressed to the king, like Ps. 20. It is the king who especially needs Yhwh's rescue and protection in battle; some of the promises also parallel Ps. 72. This understanding incidentally adds bite to the tempter's quoting of the psalm (Matt. 4:6), inviting Jesus to claim promises addressed to the (messianic) king. Yet there is nothing actually to require reference to the king, and no doubt the promises could be applied to a governor and to individuals.

It begins (vv. 1–2) with an opening statement summing up its burden, though with some ambiguity about who speaks. In its main part (vv. 3–13) a human speaker (perhaps a priest or Levite or prophet) issues declarations and promises to the king. In the last part (vv. 14–16) Yhwh speaks in person about the king. These different parts might be spoken by different voices, but there is no compelling need to infer that. The psalm includes an unusual number of tricola (vv. 2, 3, 4c–5, 7, 15c–16), not all at significant moments.

While the opening and closing sections are dominated by the promise of protection, the central section elaborates on the perils necessitating this protection, in a series of images. Verse 3a presupposes an animal or bird vulnerable to a hunter. Verse 3c presupposes a human being assailed by disease (MT) or human scheming (LXX). Verse 4a–b implies a small bird threatened by a predator. Verses 4c–5 describe a warrior's danger, though using language that suggests demonic attack. Verse 6 continues to use that language, but speaking further about epidemic; this might continue the battle imagery, as epidemic can afflict an army. Verses 7–8 more explicitly resume battle imagery. Verse 12 implies someone walking along a dangerous path on a mountain or in a canyon. Verse 13 might relate to that (cf. Ps. 23): in a canyon one may meet a snake or lion.

It is impossible to be sure where imagery and literal description meet here (again, cf. Ps. 23; also Ps. 7). I shall proceed on the assumption that the military language reflects the king's literal position as commander in chief; reference to epidemic and to his tent may link

14. Weiser, *Psalms*, 604.
15. Hugger, *Jahwe meine Zuflucht*, 23–26.

with that. Traps and plots then indicate one way his enemies attempt to overcome him, and v. 4 suggests his vulnerability in this connection. Verses 12–13 provide a different image for this; facing his enemies he is like a man walking in a dangerous canyon. But the military language might actually be figurative and/or the demon language literal. In any case, the metaphors leave the psalm open to be taken differently by different people, one reason why it has been valued by Jews and Christians (once again, like Ps. 23).[16]

It offers no indication of a historical or liturgical setting. The description of perils does not give the impression that they are pressing at the moment, so the psalm hardly forms a response to a prayer psalm, and in this respect its traditional use at Compline fits its nature. It would fit an occasion such as a king's enthronement.

Like Ps. 90, it has a number of verbal links with Deut. 32: for instance, with vv. 4 and 12, compare Deut. 32:11.[17] The bulk of it appears as part of a Qumran document, 11Q11 (11Q Apocryphal Psalms), which as a whole offers resources to people in the face of attack by demons; the fragments close with a version of Ps. 91 adapted to the scroll's theme.[18] Its very many textual differences from the MT form may reflect a different tradition or looseness of quotation or adaptation to the context.

David's. [11Q11]/Praise song. David's. [LXX]

Heading. MT has no heading; 11Q11 adds a brief one, LXX a longer one. See glossary.

91:1–2. The relationship with Yhwh with which the minister wishes to encourage the king. Four expressions for God accompany four metaphors for God.

16. Cf. Leonard C. Knight, "I Will Show Him My Salvation," *ResQ* 43 (2001): 280–92. An instance is F. H. Welshman, "Psalm 91 in Relation to a Malawian Cultural Background," *Journal of Theology for Southern Africa* 8 (1974): 24–30.

17. On its links with Ps. 90, see, e.g., Auffret, *Voyez de vos yeux*, 297–300; Koenen, *Jahwe wird kommen*, 52–56.

18. See García Martínez et al., eds., *Qumran Cave 11*, 181–205; J. van der Ploeg, "Le Psaume xci dans une recension de Qumrân," *RB* 72 (1965): 210–17; also idem, "Un petit rouleau de psaumes apocryphes," in *Tradition und Glaube*, ed. Gert Jeremias et al. (K. G. Kuhn Festschrift; Göttingen: Vandenhoeck & Ruprecht, 1971), 128–39; Otto Eissfeldt, "Eine Qumran-Textform des 91. Psalms," in Eissfeldt, *Kleine Schriften* (Tübingen: Mohr, 1973), 5:45–49; Émile Puech, "*11QPsAp^a*: Un ritual d'exorcismes," *RevQ* 14 (1989–90): 377–408; also idem, "Les deux derniers Psaumes davidiques du ritual d'exorcisme, 11QPsAp^a IV 4–V 14," in *The Dead Sea Scrolls: Forty Years of Research*, ed. Devorah Dimant and Uriel Rappaport (Leiden: Brill, 1992), 64–89; Matthias Henze, "Psalm 91 in Premodern Interpretation and at Qumran," in *Biblical Interpretation at Qumran*, ed. Matthias Henze (Grand Rapids: Eerdmans, 2005), 168–93.

[1]One who lives in the shelter of the Most High,
who stays in the shade of the Almighty:

The neatly parallel opening line announces the psalm's theme, the place of protection God can provide. Such talk can refer to the temple as a refuge; Yhwh lives there, so it is a place to find safety with Yhwh. But Yhwh also *is* Israel's shelter and shade (and refuge and fortress; cf. v. 2), and here the words will refer not merely to a place of safety that Yhwh possesses or makes available. Yhwh's being shelter and shade means this shelter and shade is available not only in the temple but anywhere, because Yhwh can be present and active anywhere (cf. vv. 7–8; and 57:1–6 [2–7]). A "shelter" is more literally a place of concealment, somewhere to hide from dangerous people (1 Sam. 19:2; Ps. 27:5 in its context; 31:20 [21]). A "shade" suggests a place to get out of the punishing heat of the sun (Jon. 4:5–6). Behind the image of God's shade lies the image of the king's shadow as beneficent and protective to his people. It is Yhwh as King who is the protector (cf. Lam. 4:20).[19] Of the verbs, the second is more vivid, as it strictly refers to lodging or spending the night somewhere.

Syntactically it is natural to take v. 1 as a self-contained sentence, "One who lives . . . stays . . ." (cf. Vrs). But the parallelism[20] works against that, and the sentence would be tautologous.[21] Admittedly it is then unclear how v. 1 relates to v. 2. It might be a pair of self-contained noun phrases describing the psalm's theme. Or the description might stand in apposition to the subject of the verb in v. 2 as the beginning of the minister's self-description. Or it might be a vocative address to the person addressed in v. 2 (so NJPS).

"Almighty" (*šadday*) pairs well with "*Most High"; the two words have similar connotations and both have extra-Israelite associations.[22] "Most High" was Melchizedek's title for God (Gen. 14); "Almighty" is most common in Job. "Most High" is also a very common title in the Psalms, reflecting its pre-Israelite background and the way such pre-Israelite traditions entered Israel's way of speaking about God. In contrast, "Almighty" comes otherwise in the Psalms only at 68:14 [15], where the

19. See K. Luke, "Under the Shadow of the Almighty," *ITQ* 3 (1972): 187–93.

20. The first verb is a ptc., the second a yiqtol, but it is quite common for a ptc. to be followed by a finite verb that continues the participial meaning (cf. GKC 116x); Sym has a ptc.

21. So, e.g., Gunkel, *Psalmen*, 406.

22. Indeed, Otto Eissfeldt, "Jahwes Verhältnis zu 'Eljon und Schaddaj nach Psalm 91," in Eissfeldt, *Kleine Schriften* (Tübingen: Mohr, 1966), 3:441–47, takes them to refer to a different God from Yhwh; but readers would more likely understand them as appellatives of Yhwh; cf. v. 9.

context may point to an awareness that the title could suggest that Yhwh is the Destroyer (the verb *šādad*; this is more explicit in Isa. 13:6). The same possibility arises in v. 6.

> ²"I say to Yhwh,
> 'My refuge and my stronghold,
> my God in whom I trust.'"

In Tg, David makes the confession in v. 2 preparatory to exhorting Solomon in what follows. Comparably, NJPS apparently takes v. 2 as the minister's declaration of his commitment, which he intends to commend to the king. But it would not be a very compelling testimony; a minister does not live as vulnerable a life as a king or an ordinary person. Perhaps v. 2 is the king's own opening words of commitment, declaring from the start that Yhwh is indeed "my refuge"; the rest of the psalm would then be a response to that. But the transition at v. 3 is jerky. Perhaps v. 2, like v. 1, is a kind of statement of principle, the declaration a person such as the king must make. But resolving this ambiguity does not affect the opening words' significance.

The declaration of commitment adds two further images to the ones in v. 1. Behind the image of refuge is the need of protection from flood, rather than from sun (Isa. 4:6; 25:4; 28:15–17); that becomes a figure for the danger of being overwhelmed by attackers (Ps. 46:1 [2]; 62:7–8 [8–9]; in their context).[23] "Stronghold" makes that more explicit (2 Sam. 5:7–9), and also suggests a filling out of the picture implied by v. 1. Threatened by invasion, the people of an area come to live or stay in the safety of the city with its walls; this stronghold forms their refuge. Describing Yhwh as shelter, shade, refuge, and stronghold is a commonplace of the psalms, usually in psalms expressing ordinary Israelites' faith (e.g., 31:2, 3, 20 [3, 4, 21]; 36:7 [8]; 71:3, 7). But these expressions sometimes belong especially to kings or other leaders (e.g., 18:2 [3]; 61:3–4 [4–5]). For all, the expressions have two general implications. They imply an attitude to Yhwh rather than to some other deity (cf. Ps. 31:1–6 [2–7]) or to one's physical resources (cf. Isa. 30:1–3). And they imply an attitude of confidence rather than of fear (cf. Pss. 27; 46). LXX tellingly translates *bāṭaḥ*, the word for "trust" (the reliance that issues in confidence) by *elpizō*, "hope."

Likewise, any Israelite can see Yhwh as "my God." Encouraging people to think in terms of Yhwh being "my God" involves some risk; one could take this God for granted. The expression almost reverses the master-servant relationship. But Yhwh is happy for that risk to be taken (see

23. On the image of "refuge," see Hugger, *Jahwe meine Zuflucht*.

v. 15). "The supreme God . . . is precisely the One whom the individual may call 'my God,' as if he existed only for his sake. . . . It is only because God is *God* that absolute trust in him is at all possible."[24]

91:3–13. The minister explicitly commends this stance to the king.

> [3]Because he is the one who will rescue you
> from the fowler's trap,
> from the epidemic [MT]/word [LXX] that brings destruction.

The causal connection with what precedes is elliptical: "A person can say God is their refuge, and you can do so, because he will act in this way for you." In MT, the two perils from which Yhwh can rescue the king are human and "natural." As in English, "trap" is a common metaphor for the devices whereby enemies try to "catch" someone, though the full expression "fowler's trap" comes otherwise only in Hos. 9:8. Epidemic is a more common literal threat and reality (e.g., 1 Kings 8:37). Epidemics are by nature deadly; the description of them as "destructive" underlines the point.[25] Traps and epidemics are thus separate notions, though succeeding verses may suggest a link. A king has to be wary of his enemy's traps, and during a war his army and people are also vulnerable to epidemic.

LXX's reading of the last phrase recasts the emphasis of the verse as a whole. For the "word that destroys," compare 38:12 [13]; the expression suggests deception or plotting, which underlines the deceptive nature of the enemy's traps.

> [4a–b]With his pinions he will cover you,
> under his wings you can take refuge.

Now the king is a baby bird subject to attack by a predator, rather than to stumbling into a trap; and God is not one who diverts him from falling into the trap or opens it when it has closed, but one who provides protection from the predator (there is no reason to bring the cherubim's wings into the picture). There are two sides to the way that works, expounded by the two parallel cola.[26] The mother bird makes her wings available to her offspring; the offspring moves to hide there

24. Weiser, *Psalms*, 606–7.

25. Most occurrences of *hawwôt* are pl., like this one, suggesting it is an abstract noun (*IBHS* 7.4.2). Meir Lubetski ("The Utterance from the East," *Religion* 20 [1990]: 217–32) suggests that *hwt* means not destruction but a word, thought, or incantation.

26. The rarer noun and the rarer verb come first, so that the second colon clarifies the first, or at least reassures the reader about its meaning, and also gives time to draw breath.

when danger threatens. "Take refuge" picks up the related noun in v. 2, making explicit that what is true for that "I" can be true for the king, while "cover" implicitly takes up the declaration in v. 1.

> 4cHis truthfulness will be a body shield, a rampart:
> 5you will not fear a terror by night
> or an arrow that flies by day,
> 6An epidemic that walks in the dark,
> or a scourge that destroys at noon.

In v. 4c yet another metaphor, a more directly military one, re-expresses the point and continues into v. 5. I thus link v. 4c with what follows rather than with what precedes; the tricolon takes *abb′* form in the manner of vv. 2 and 3. Here, v. 4c makes a statement, and the two subsequent cola declare its implications in two internally parallel cola. Underlying vv. 1–4 are convictions about Yhwh's *truthfulness, steadfastness, or reliability; this implies protection such as a warrior relies on. In a battle out in the open country, God's truthfulness is like a big freestanding shield that hides the whole person. The second noun describes this shield as rampart-like or perhaps compares Yhwh's truthfulness to the rampart protecting a city, particularly its defenders, during a siege.

Verse 5 spells that out (rather than referring figuratively, for instance, to the rays of the sun or to the baleful influence of the moon). Warrior and defender need protecting from the arrow that flies by day. A night attack (see, for instance, Judg. 7) is scarier and harder to guard against (cf. Song 3:8). That also applies to attacks other than the military (e.g., Gen. 32:25; Exod. 4:24; Neh. 6:10). It is a terror, not merely in a subjective sense (it feels scary) but in an objective sense (it *is* scary). Yhwh's truthfulness protects against the unpredictable and the more predictable. The parallelism likely means we should interweave the two cola. Prosaically put, you need not fear terrifying attack by day or night.

In MT, "epidemic" picks up from v. 3. Epidemics are a problem for armies and for cities under siege; "scourge" reformulates the point by means of a rarer word. Night and day are re-expressed as dark and noon. The third pair of words stand in sharper contrast: epidemic or scourge not merely walks but destroys. Prosaically put, Yhwh will shield you from "the devastating epidemic that walks and destroys at any time of the day."

The meaning of vv. 5–6 "has been explained in such different ways that I have often thought that the main idea intended by the Holy Spirit in these words has been hidden from us."[27] Within Judaism they were reckoned to

27. Luther, *First Lectures*, 2:215.

refer to demonic attack, and this connotation could attach to the psalm as a whole.[28] Their terms correspond to Middle Eastern ways of describing the activity of hostile gods or demons, and the ancient versions refer explicitly to demons and spirits. But there is no explicit indication of this reference in the context, and it would be unique in the OT, which makes hardly any reference to demons. It rather applies the language of vv. 5–6 to Yhwh as one capable of sending epidemics or shooting arrows (e.g., 38:2 [3]; Exod. 11:5; 2 Sam. 24:16).[29] The psalm's language has mythic overtones, but it has been demythologized. Israel need not fear demonic forces, though if it does, Yhwh is greater than them.

> [7]A thousand may fall at your side,
> ten thousand at your right hand;
> to you it will not reach.

A further tricolon reverses the structure of the previous three, following *aa′b* order. After the doubled and intensified hyperbolic proposition in v. 7a–b, the final colon makes a bold promise, with "to you" in emphatic position. The deaths to which the line refers might result from epidemic (v. 6) or from battle (v. 5). The promise makes sense applied to the king; it links with his importance to the people and with the dangers attaching to his position (e.g., 1 Kings 22:29–36). The next line may make explicit who are the people who fall to them, though it may be odd to describe the enemy as "at your side . . . at your right hand."[30] This rather implies people on the same side; v. 7c also suggests people in the same danger. Perhaps, then, they are fellow Israelites who do not make Yhwh their refuge.[31]

> [8]You will just look with your eyes,
> see the recompense of the faithless,

We may imagine a king anxiously surveying the army surrounding his city: cf. 2 Kings 18–19. How can he defeat this vast horde? He will not need to do so, as 2 Kings 18–19 illustrates.[32] The pattern recurs

28. See discussion in J. de Fraine, "Le 'démon du midi,'" *Bib* 40 (1959): 372–83; Hugger, *Jahwe meine Zuflucht*, 182–206; Mitchell, *Message of the Psalter*, 278–81; Henze, "Psalm 91," 183–86 (noting the irony that the devil in Luke 4:10–11 thus "inverts the intention of the dictum" [185]).

29. See Keel, *Symbolism*, 84–85; Weiser, *Psalms*, 608.

30. The second expression gives precision to the first; it does not indicate that the first implies "left" (so Tg).

31. Cf. Spurgeon, *Treasury*, 4:91–92; against Hugger, *Jahwe meine Zuflucht*, 207–21. Spurgeon goes on to describe his experience of being preserved in an outbreak of cholera.

32. Cf. Theodoret, *Psalms*, 2:103–7.

in Israel's story (e.g., Exod. 14; Josh. 6). All he has to do is watch (cf. Exod. 14:13; Ps. 54:7 [9]). "Recompense" presupposes that Yhwh is not arbitrarily taking sides in this conflict but sees that justice is done in relation to people who are *faithless in their stance toward Yhwh and/or toward Israel.

> 9Because you are the one who has made Yhwh "my refuge,"
> the Most High your shelter.

EVV take the "because" as prospective (v. 9 then leads into v. 10); more plausibly, Jerome takes it as retrospective (v. 9 then explains what precedes). The emphatic "you" (the pronoun is expressed) then contrasts with "the faithless." In isolation one would render the first colon "because you, Yhwh, are my refuge," but the first-person statement is surprising and hard to fit with the second-person statement in v. 9b. But that second colon opens up another way of reading the first: the verb there applies to both cola, as "because you are the one who" applies to the second colon as well as the first. The first-person expression "my refuge" then describes the king's attitude in his own words, taken up from v. 2 and formulated from his perspective. "Your shelter" re-expresses the ideas in vv. 1–2 in a new way, though in this psalm's context in the Psalter it takes up the term from 90:1. The word order and the postponing of the verb gives some emphasis to the references to God (both come before the verb). The line therefore suggests "because *you* have made *Yhwh/the Most High* 'my refuge,' not to say your *shelter*." It is a particularly finely-wrought example of parallelism.

> 10No harm will be allowed to come upon you;
> no hurt will come near your tent.

Again the cola are neatly parallel, with "hurt" giving precision to "harm" (*bad) and the rare verb *ʾānâ* (pual) preceding the more common verb. But in the context "come near" (*qārab*) has sinister overtones: it and related nouns can refer to armies approaching one another for battle (not least Exod. 14:20). One might then understand "hurt" (*negaʿ*) to denote a wound (e.g., 2 Sam. 7:14, in relation to the king), and "tent" to suggest a military encampment. But usually "hurt" refers to an illness, and this would link with earlier reference to epidemics (vv. 3, 6), while "tent" could refer anachronistically to a regular home (e.g., 52:5 [7]).

> 11Because he will command his aides for you,
> to keep you in all your ways.

The "because" is again retrospective. The commanding of Yhwh's *aides suggests two significant links, with the story of Israel and Moses at the Red Sea and at Sinai (Exod. 14:19; 23:20–23; 32:34; 33:2; cf. Isa. 63:9) and with Hezekiah (2 Kings 19:35). Both link with the position of the king, though Ps. 34:7 [8] relates the action of the aide to people in general who revere Yhwh. In all these passages only one aide is mentioned (cf. 35:5–6). Whether or not we find demons in vv. 5–6, there is no doubt that angels appear here. If we find demons there, the psalm assures us that the angels are more powerful. If we do not, the psalm assures us that we are surrounded by beneficent supernatural support.

> 12On their hands they will carry you
> so that your foot does not stumble on a stone.

Once more, being thus carried recalls the exodus and Red Sea story (see Exod. 19:4), so that the psalm promises that the king will continue to have Israel's experience. But the second colon takes the image in a different direction. There, LXX has "so that you do not strike your foot on a stone," but this gives rather a trivial meaning; I rather follow Jerome, Tg, Aq. The verb *nāgap* suggests a serious smiting that can result in death (cf. 89:23 [24]), or a stumbling that has the same implication (Prov. 3:23, in its context). Stumbling on a stone when walking along a path on a mountain or in a canyon can mean falling to one's death (Jer. 13:16). The aides' carrying safeguards against this.

> 13On cub and adder you will tread;
> you will trample on lion and serpent.

The content, though not the words, recalls Gen. 1. Humanity's commission was to master the earth, and aggressive reptiles and animals would be obvious objects of that subduing. Adder and serpent also recall Gen. 3, when the snake becomes a participant in ongoing strife with humanity. In the context it is less likely that *tannîn* refers to the sea serpent. But here dangerous animals and reptiles may be other threats one encounters in walking through a canyon (cf. Ps. 23); the psalm then promises victory over them. They can also be figures for enemies (e.g., Ps. 58), and the line could function as a further metaphorical declaration that the king will crush his attackers.

91:14–16. The rhetoric changes in "spectacular" fashion.[33] God, not the minister, now speaks (though presumably still through the minister),

33. Gerstenberger, *Psalms*, 2:166.

the promises' first-person form heightening their force. Further, God speaks not *to you* but *about him*. The king now overhears himself being spoken about, a form of hearing that has its own power. To whom do these verses directly speak? Perhaps it is the community as a whole, which would be encouraged by the fact that Yhwh is committed to its leader.

> [14]Because I am the one he is attracted to, I will rescue him;
> I will lift him to safety, because he has acknowledged my name.

Literally, "because to me he is attracted": the word order takes up the emphasis of v. 9. The king does not turn to other deities or rely on physical resources. The verb *ḥāšaq* refers to a man fancying a woman (Gen. 34:8) and then to Yhwh's being attracted to Israel (Deut. 7:7); there is an affective aspect to it. "Acknowledging my *name" complements the affective with the attitudinal or conative. The king's relationship with Yhwh involves both feelings and will, both delight and submission. In contrast to that, the two verbs of which Yhwh is subject both denote the same action, looked at from different aspects. "Rescue" (*pālaṭ* piel) is often followed by "from"; it thus draws attention to the peril from which someone escapes. "Lift him to safety" (*śāgab* piel), on the other hand, suggests the position to which someone is rescued or the way they are rescued, by being raised into an inaccessible, safe position (cf. the noun *miśgāb*; e.g., 94:22; 144:2; also the complementary imagery in vv. 1–2).

> [15a–b]He can call me and I will answer him;
> I will be with him in trouble.

The further promise restates and elaborates on v. 14, reversing the "proper" relationship between master and servant. It is the master who calls and the servant who answers; but Yhwh is happy for that exchange to take place in the opposite order. The second colon restates the first: "be with him in trouble" does not denote merely sharing in his trouble and making him aware that he is not alone. When Yhwh is with a person, things happen. Calling and having Yhwh answer means Yhwh acts to get him out of trouble. The name "God is with us" makes the point (see Isa. 7:14; 8:8–10).

> [15c]I will save him and honor him;
> [16]I will fill him with long days
> and show him my deliverance.

I take v. 15c with what follows on the assumption that a tricolon is more likely to end the psalm.[34] "Saving" the king restates the thrust of vv. 14–15b. *Honoring him may restate that further: defeat would mean shame, not least the falsification of his trust in Yhwh, but victory vindicates that trust. But "honor" also may take matters further, pointing to the king's ongoing status among the people and among the nations. Certainly v. 16 goes beyond that particular victory to the life that will follow. The psalm thus points to the relationship between salvation and blessing. Salvation is the punctiliar act that gets the king out of his predicament; the psalm here makes a transition to the ongoing experience that will then characterize "normal" life. Verse 16a thus promises that this regular life will be a full and long one that he goes on to enjoy. Then, surprisingly, v. 16b returns to talk of deliverance and closes with that. Qimchi infers that it refers to eternal salvation, but in the Psalms *deliverance concerns the reality of God's involvement in the here and now. The reference to deliverance here might make vv. 15c–16 work in *aba′* order and thus achieve some closure as the psalm ends with a reaffirmation of its central point. It also suggests that the ongoing life to which v. 16a refers will be characterized by the alternation of deliverance and blessing. There is no final resolution of the antithesis in this life.

Theological Implications

"Men generally seek out a great variety of hiding-places," but "the only safe and impregnable fortress to which we can betake ourselves is the protection of God."[35] "He is the one who will rescue me . . . not I myself. Observe whether he teaches anything but this, that all our trust be in God, none in man."[36] Further, the psalm is not concerned merely with an inner attitude of trust and a feeling of security but with a practice of trust and the reality of security that derives from the fact of God's action.[37] In light of the Christian focus on eternal salvation, it is important to emphasize Yhwh's declaration that we do not experience such salvation only in the future and in heaven and in the inner person. Yhwh grants it now, on earth in the body. The point is confirmed by Paul in re-expressing these promises in Rom. 8:28–39.[38]

34. Admittedly MT sees v. 15 as a six-stress line, which one might see as a 4-2 bicolon.

35. Calvin, *Psalms*, 3:478.

36. Augustine, *Psalms*, 446.

37. Cf. Weiser, *Psalms*, 606, though Weiser later puts the emphasis rather on feelings.

38. Hossfeld and Zenger, *Psalms 2*, 433.

Of course, it is easier to believe in God's offering us a *feeling* of security and *eternal* salvation. In 1956 five United States missionaries in their twenties landed on a shore in Ecuador near the homes of a native American people, hoping to share the good news of Christ with them. These local people killed the five. They clearly did not find that Yhwh was their refuge and stronghold. Yet the widow of one, Elisabeth Elliot, subsequently wrote a memoir about her husband and titled it *Shadow of the Almighty*.[39] If ever there was a man whose life and death disproved the claims of Ps. 91, it was Jim Elliot. Yet there is something profoundly authentic about the audacity with which his wife applies its words to him. No doubt as a Christian she reckoned that the mere fact that he had died did not mean he left God's shadow. But even before Christ's death and resurrection, when that perspective does not apply, there is something profoundly authentic about maintaining such a conviction, even though experience can clash with it. Indeed, there may be something more profoundly authentic about it, as there is about the commitment of Daniel's three friends (Dan. 3:17); certainly there is something more audaciously authentic. Israelite history (like Christian history) provides much evidence that the promises in Ps. 91 do not work out. But Israel knew that Yhwh's relationship with Israel, begun at the exodus and the Red Sea, meant that such evidence could not invalidate the truths that the psalm declares.

Of course, one could misappropriate the psalm's promises (see Matt. 4:5–7);[40] they do not invite us to run into danger and put God to the test.

39. New York: Harper, 1958.
40. See Frederick J. Gaiser, "'It Shall Not Reach You,'" *WW* 25 (2005): 191–202.

Psalm 92

Testimony, Praise, and Teaching

Translation

Composition. Song. For the Sabbath day.

1 It is good to confess Yhwh,
to make music for your name, Most High,
2 To proclaim in the morning your commitment,
your truthfulness by night,[1]
3 With ten-string, with harp,
with recitation, on the lyre.

4 Because you have gladdened me with your action, Yhwh;
at the deeds of your hands I will resound.
5 How great your deeds became, Yhwh;
your plans were very deep.[2]
6 The brutish person—he would not acknowledge this,
the stupid—he would not understand it:

1. The pl. might mean "each night" or might refer to the different parts or watches of the night.

2. The "how" hardly carries over to the second colon ("How very deep your plans have been": so, e.g., DG 132); *mah mĕʾōd* would be even harsher in Hebrew than "how very" is in English. Rather the two cola use two different parallel forms of emphasis, a rhetorical question and a "very" statement.

[7]When[3] the faithless flourished like herbage
  and all who do harm thrived,[4]
It was to pass away for all time,
  [8]but you are on high forever, Yhwh.

[9]Because there—your enemies, Yhwh,
  because there—your enemies perish;
  all who do harm scatter.
[10]But you raised my horn on high like a buffalo;
  my exhaustion[5] with refreshing oil.
[11]My eye has seen my watchful foes;[6]
  the people who arose against me, acting wickedly—
  my ears could hear them.[7]
[12]The faithful person is like a date-palm flourishing,
  like a Lebanese cedar[8] growing great,[9]
[13]Ones planted in Yhwh's house,
  flourishing out in the courts of our God,
[14]Still fruiting in old age,
  being rich and fresh,[10]
[15]To proclaim that Yhwh is upright,
  my crag is one in whom there is no wickedness.[11]

Interpretation

The reference to confession in the psalm's introduction (vv. 1–3) suggests that this will be a testimony or thanksgiving psalm, which is borne

3. NJPS has "though"; while this is an implication, I doubt whether *b* before an inf. is ever literally concessive.

4. The *w*-consecutive continues the infinitive (GKC 111v; JM 83; *TTH* 118).

5. MT accentuates *ballōtî* as first-person qal from *bālal*, which would mean "I mixed" and thus makes poor sense (EVV paraphrase in different ways). Syr and Tg imply *ballōtanî*, "you mixed me," which still requires the verb's meaning to be stretched. More plausibly LXX, Sym, Jerome have "old age," implying that the word is piel inf. from *bālâ* (there is no need to emend to *bĕlōtî*). On the text, see Samuel E. Loewenstamm, "*Balloti bᵉšämän raʿᵃnān*," *UF* 10 (1978): 111–13; idem, "An Additional Remark upon Ps. 92:11ᵇ," *UF* 13 (1981): 302; Th. Booij, "The Hebrew Text of Psalm xcii 11," *VT* 38 (1988): 210–14.

6. *Bĕšûrāy* is perhaps a slip for the expected *bĕšōrĕrāy*.

7. I have translated v. 11b–c in the Hebrew word order, but added "them" for clarity.

8. Lit. "cedar in Lebanon"; the construct is not used because the expression is indeterminate (JM 130f). The prep. does not imply that the cedar is actually in Lebanon.

9. Not "flourishes like a date-palm . . . grows like a Lebanese cedar"; the word order implies that the two yiqtols are unmarked relative clauses (cf. *TTH* 34). Verse 13 confirms this as the trees are again the subject.

10. I take the yiqtol verbs in vv. 13b–14 as continuing the participial construction (cf. GKC 116x).

11. Q has *ʿawlātâ*, and K implies *ʿōlātâ*; both are variants for *ʿawlâ*.

out by subsequent references to Yhwh's deeds, done personally for the worshipper. Yet the actual beginning with its quasi-objective declaration that it is good to praise Yhwh is unusual and offers a first hint that the testimony has a didactic tone (cf. the wisdom motifs in vv. 6–7). Admittedly, that might equally be a nonstandard introduction to a praise psalm (cf. Ps. 147); the "because," too, belongs to that form (cf. Ps. 95). So this is hymnic confession with a didactic aspect. As can happen in both praise and testimony psalms, the reasons come twice, in vv. 4–8 and 9–15, each time beginning "because." Each time the psalm refers (mostly in the qatal) to the specific things Yhwh has done that require this testimony (vv. 4–5, probably vv. 6–7, vv. 9–11). It moves on to the ongoing truths about Yhwh's activity in the world and about Israel's experience that those acts illustrate and the opening declaration has already affirmed (vv. 12–14, also v. 8), and closes with a reference to the purpose of it all (vv. 7c–8, 15).

There are no indications of a historical or liturgical setting. The speaker might well be a king or governor; the psalm would then link neatly with Pss. 89 (by contrast) and 91 (whose convictions it has proved true).[12] The closing verses' move from singular to plural then points to the testimony's significance for the whole people.

Composition. Song. For the Sabbath day.

Heading. See glossary. This is the only mention of the Sabbath in the Psalms.[13] Whereas there was little difference in temple worship on the Sabbath compared to other days, the Sabbath being more a day of rest than a day of worship, in the synagogue it became a day of worship and teaching. But it is not surprising that the Sabbath should be the one day with a special psalm. Tg infers that it was composed by the first human being; the implication would be that the acts the psalm celebrates are the acts of creation.[14] On the other hand, *m. Tamid* 7 comments that this Sabbath psalm is "a song for the time that is to come, for the day that shall be all Sabbath and rest in the life everlasting." Sung in heaven, the act the psalm celebrates will be the final redemption whereby the evenings of exile come to an end.[15] Mishnah *Tamid* 7 also allocates to

12. On the psalm's links with Pss. 90–91 and 93–100, see Hossfeld and Zenger, *Psalms 2*, 442–43.

13. Augustine's exposition (*Psalms*, 452–56) is a Saturday sermon taking the heading into account, though in an anti-Jewish way. Contrast Tate, *Psalms 51–100*, 468–71.

14. N. M. Sarna ("The Psalm for the Sabbath Day [Ps 92]," *JBL* 81 [1962]: 155–68) suggests aspects of the psalm that could be read as creation themes and thus led to the choice of the psalm for the Sabbath. Cf. Jerome's comments on vv. 5–6 (*Homilies*, 1:166–69).

15. So Rashi, Qimchi. McCann ("Psalms," 1051) also calls the psalm "eschatological," though there are no pointers to this within it.

the other days of the week Pss. 24; 48; 82; 94; 81; and 93; LXX includes notes to this effect for most of these psalms.

92:1–3. The declaration about confession is equivalent to the statement of intent in a classic testimony such as Ps. 138. The three lines are neatly parallel.

> 1It is good to confess Yhwh,
> to make music for your name, Most High,
> 2To proclaim in the morning your commitment,
> your truthfulness by night,
> 3With ten-string, with harp,
> with recitation, on the lyre.

The opening affirmation recalls 54:6 [8], near the end of a testimony psalm, which also speaks of it being good to confess Yhwh's name. "*Confess" is, indeed, virtually a technical term in testimony psalms, though also appearing in praise psalms proclaiming Yhwh's great acts of deliverance (e.g., 105:1; 106:1; 107:1).[16] The affirmation in v. 1b likewise reappears in 147:1 at the beginning of a praise psalm. To say something is good or fine is to comment both on its rightness or appropriateness and on its attractiveness or pleasantness, though the parallelism in 147:1 suggests the latter is in focus.[17] "Make *music" is the verb from which "composition" comes (see the heading). The same two verbs, with a reference to Yhwh's *name, come together at the opening of Ps. 138.

Proclamation (*nāgad* hiphil), too, belongs in both testimony psalms and praise psalms, since it suggests recounting what Yhwh has done, both for contemporary individuals or communities and in the great deeds of the past. Either way, these deeds will be the expressions of Yhwh's *commitment and *truthfulness. "Morning" and "night" (*laylâ*, not *ʿereb*) suggests that the psalm does not refer to the times of morning and evening sacrifice; the expression is more likely a merism implying "all the time."[18] A mere one-time recounting of these events will not be enough; they deserve continuous and repeated proclamation (cf. 30:12 [13]).

Psalms 33:2 and 144:9 refer to the "harp of ten," the ten-stringed *harp; here "with ten-string, with harp" may be a hendiadys for the same instrument. But "with recitation, on the *lyre" seems likely not to be a compound phrase (so LXX). "Recitation" (*higgāyôn*) comes also in 9:16 [17]; 19:14 [15]; compare *hāgâ* in (for instance) 35:28; 71:24, where the context makes clear that it denotes something not so different from

16. Cf. Hossfeld and Zenger, *Psalms 2*, 435.

17. Cf. Harold Fisch, *Poetry with a Purpose* (repr., Bloomington: Indiana University Press, 1990), 128.

18. Cf. Watson, *Classical Hebrew Poetry*, 322.

confession or proclamation. If the rest of v. 3 develops the reference to music in v. 1b, this word sums up the references to confession and proclamation in vv. 1–2.[19] Thus three-quarters of vv. 1–2 refers to words, one quarter to music, and these proportions are reversed in v. 3. Calvin comments that of course the use of instrumental music belongs only to the old dispensation.[20]

92:4–8. The reasons for the confession, which are also its content.

> 4Because you have gladdened me with your action, Yhwh;
> at the deeds of your hands I will resound.

Confession is good because it corresponds to the good thing Yhwh has done. In a regular hymn, the action or deeds would be events such as creation or the Red Sea deliverance; in a testimony they are acts of deliverance performed for the worshipper. We know these acts expressed commitment and truthfulness (v. 2); we will discover something more specific about them in what follows. Meanwhile, the psalm leaps over that to the result, in gladdening me and making me *resound. In the formally parallel cola, the second goes beyond the first in speaking about the ongoing future (so that it is not strictly part of the *kî* clause), not merely the past action, and about the outward sound involved in rejoicing, not merely the attitude of heart (you cannot rejoice silently), while "your hands" makes Yhwh's involvement more concrete and "real."

> 5How great your deeds became, Yhwh;
> your plans were very deep.

The further neatly parallel cola expand on v. 4 without satisfying our curiosity about what these deeds were. Their expansion consists first in declaring how great the deeds became. It comprises not a noun clause saying simply that they *were* great, still less a generalization that they *are* great, but a verbal clause (and a fientive verb, not a stative) emphasizing the having-happened-ness of Yhwh's actual deed, which makes sense in the context.[21] The second colon expands on v. 4 further by going behind the deeds to the intentions they implemented. They were no spur-of-the-moment, instinctive response to a sudden tricky situation. Yhwh coolly formulated some intentions and implemented them. It is then not surprising if Yhwh's thoughtfully and carefully

19. NRSV and TNIV take *higgāyôn* to imply music, but that would be a unique meaning, and its cognates regularly imply something expressed in words.

20. *Psalms*, 3:495.

21. Contrast DG 62d (remark 1), which takes *gādal* as stative; cf. Kraus, *Psalms 60–150*, 227; and EVV, and see the discussion in *IBHS* 27.1c.

formulated plans are "deep." People's intentions and plans are deep in that they reside inside their minds, inaccessible to anyone unless they reveal them (64:6 [7]; Prov. 20:5). Then sometimes they are a great surprise. So it was with this action of Yhwh, which worked very differently from any plan we would have formulated (cf. Isa. 55:5–7).

> 6The brutish person—he would not acknowledge this,
> the stupid—he would not understand it:

The further parallel cola move from qatal verbs to yiqtols. In the context at the end of the colon "this" and "it" are prospective, not retrospective, and vv. 7–8 probably require them as antecedent. As usual *acknowledging and understanding imply not merely having facts available but recognizing them. It is characteristic of the brutish/stupid to refuse to face facts. Indeed, calling them brutish is an insult to many animals, which are wiser; the expression envisages a domestic animal that will not yield to the yoke, goad, or stick. The move to yiqtols might signify generalization following on the concrete statement in vv. 4–5 (though still we do not know what it was). But the line also recalls, for instance, Ps. 73 (see esp. v. 22), and perhaps the worshipper recognizes having behaved thus before the divine action that the psalm celebrates.

> 7When the faithless flourished like herbage
> and all who do harm thrived,
> It was to pass away for all time,
> 8but you are on high forever, Yhwh.

Here is what the brutish/stupid would not recognize (and what the worshipper was tempted not to believe) about the *faithless, the people who do *harm, and about Yhwh. EVV translate the infinitives as general statements, but more usually the construction (with the *w*-consecutive in v. 7b) would have past reference, and this makes sense here; they refer to the event that stimulated the testimony.[22] Thus the recognition that came parallels that in Ps. 73, but it came not because the worshipper saw something by faith, as was the case there, but through seeing something actually happen. The problem was not merely that the faithless sprouted and blossomed (cf. NJPS) in the sense that they began to flourish or threatened to do so. The verbs *pāraḥ* and *ṣûṣ* commonly suggest full growth (e.g., 72:7, 16; and cf. vv. 12–13). The extraordinary way herbage can flourish in a Mediterranean climate after rain again provides an image for such flourishing (cf. 72:16; Job 5:25).

22. Cf. Kirkpatrick, *Psalms*, 560–61.

But the point of that image is often to draw attention to the short-lived nature of this flourishing.[23] It can seem as if the herbage is abundant in the morning but withered and brown by evening after sitting through the day in the burning sun (102:4, 11 [5, 12]). Although the statement in v. 7a–b is thus a scandalous one (but at least one that recognizes reality), the person who reads the psalm is prepared for the possibility that the scandal will soon be resolved. And v. 7c resolves it in spectacular fashion by declaring that the annihilation of the faithless was the very object of their flourishing. They were being given plenty of rope, so that they could hang themselves. Although the psalm implies that Yhwh brings about their annihilation, and it has spoken of Yhwh's acts in vv. 4–5, here its rhetoric works by not directly attributing the act to Yhwh (contrast Tg), even in v. 8. The psalm incorporates the verb *šāmad* and could have used the hiphil with Yhwh as subject (cf. 145:20), suggesting "cause them to pass away/annihilate," but instead it uses the niphal, which makes the faithless the subject of the verb. They go through a process that has naturalness or inevitability built into it: you are faithless, you flourish, you pass away. Your destiny is in your hands, but you cannot evade the process working itself out.

I take v. 8 along with v. 7c. MT takes vv. 7–8 as a tricolon and a monocolon, which draws attention to v. 8.[24] More likely vv. 7–8 are two regular bicola. In v. 7c–8 the two temporal expressions (for all time, forever) correspond, underlining the way the first half of v. 8 stands in contrast to the first half of v. 7c: they pass away; you are "on high" (cf. 93:4).[25] Perhaps the noun clause implicitly continues the infinitival clause, "but in order for you to be on high." Once again, Yhwh is not the subject of an active verb but rather by a natural process the flourishing of the faithless results in the exaltation of Yhwh through causing the downfall of the faithless themselves. In another aspect to the rhetoric's subtlety, in this closing line of vv. 4–8 the first colon is much shorter than the second. The perishing of the faithless gets only two words; the focus lies on the exalting of Yhwh, which gets four.

92:9–15. The further "because" signals the fact that vv. 9–15 reprise and expand on the confession's basis and content, telling us more of what happened to rejoice the worshipper (v. 4). Qatal verbs thus reappear.

23. Indeed, MT's accents and verse division imply that this is already so in v. 7a, implying "When the faithless flourished, they were like herbage" (Tate [*Psalms 51–100*, 460–61] compares Job 27:14). Verse 7a is then paralleled by v. 7b–c as a whole.

24. For the view that v. 8 is the center of the psalm, see, e.g., Jonathan Magonet, "Some Concentric Structures in Psalms," *Heythrop Journal* 23 (1982): 365–76 (see 369–72); and Auffret's discussion, *Voyez de vos yeux*, 301–18.

25. Psalm 93:4 has *bammārôm*; this line has simple *mārôm*, lit. "you are height" (see BDB; DG 40; *TTH* 189.2).

[9]Because there—your enemies, Yhwh,
because there—your enemies perish;
all who do harm scatter.

But the section starts with yiqtols; a tricolon with staircase parallelism opens the section, rearousing attention.[26] In the first two four-word cola, the opening three words are the same, while the appellative and the verb that brings the two cola to a climax both apply to both cola; the third colon then restates the first two. The staircase form is common in Ugaritic poetry; indeed, we have an instance of a line that goes "Now thine enemy, O Baal, Now thine enemy wilt thou smite, Now wilt thou cut off thine adversary."[27] But in the manner of v. 7, the psalm simply describes what happens to these foes without attributing their destruction to Yhwh; compare also Judg. 5:31, "so all your enemies perish, Yhwh." It thus essentially resumes preceding lines, as the "there" hints. "Your enemies" corresponds to "the faithless," and "all who do harm" exactly reappears. "Perish" corresponds to "pass away," and "scatter" re-expresses the point in a way that may invite us not to take those earlier verbs too literally (you cannot scatter if you have died).

[10]But you raised my horn on high like a buffalo;
my exhaustion with refreshing oil.

The yiqtols in v. 9 were perhaps vivid ways of referring to the past; the *w*-consecutive opening v. 10 makes the past reference of these lines more explicit. The verb again takes up a term from vv. 7–8, though more tellingly. As the psalm comes to speak once more about the positive side to the events it confesses, Yhwh is once more the subject, as in v. 4a. And the verb is *rûm*, from which *mārôm* ("on high") comes. The one on high was the one who could lift me on high; and/or raising me on high established that Yhwh was on high, made Yhwh visibly on high. The point is also made by using a more positive side to a comparison of human and animal (contrast v. 6). The strength of the buffalo, wild ox, wild bull, or unicorn (LXX) is concentrated in the potentially death-dealing horn it flaunts when fighting; that gives it its victories or symbolizes its power. Yhwh has enabled the worshipper to assert huge strength like that, and thus be victorious.

26. Cf. Watson, *Classical Hebrew Poetry*, 150–54.

27. *ANET*, p. 131. On the possible links with Ugaritic poetry, see Herbert Donner, "Ugaritismen in der Psalmenforschung," *ZAW* 79 (1967): 322–50 (see 344–46); Oswald Loretz, "Psalm 92," *UF* 25 (1993): 275–88.

The second colon restates the point, though laconically, declaring in effect, "you raised me in my exhausted state." Before Yhwh's act, the worshipper was like a buffalo whose strength was gone. After Yhwh's act, he is like a person who has been covered in olive oil as a sign of celebration to replace the marks of gloom (Isa. 61:3; cf. Pss. 23:5; 45:7 [8]; 104:15), or someone whose wounds have been dressed with oil (Isa. 1:6), or someone anointed on Yhwh's behalf by a priest or prophet for their task (Ps. 89:20 [21]; 1 Sam. 10:1; 16:13). The adjective *ra'ănān* usually applies to trees, suggesting green and flourishing (cf. v. 14). Here it implies a metonymy or ellipse: it is as if Yhwh applied to this exhausted person the oil from a green olive tree and brought refreshment.

> [11]My eye has seen my watchful foes;
> the people who arose against me, acting wickedly—
> my ears could hear them.

The context indicates that this is a seeing and hearing of the enemies as defeated.[28] "Seeing" often implies looking with grief or apprehension, or with relief, satisfaction, or joy (e.g., 112:8; 118:7). Usually the verb is *rā'â*, but here *nābaṭ* (hiphil). In the context, the worshipper has been able to move from the first form of looking (apprehension) to the second (relief; BDB's pejorative "gloat" is unwarranted), presumably through being able to see the enemies fleeing rather than threatening. The implication of "hear" follows from that; the foes can be heard crying out in panic instead of in a battle shout. Their description as watchful foes who arose against me wickedly (*bad) suggests people who have attacked the worshipper or rebelled against his rule.

> [12]The faithful person is like a date-palm flourishing,
> like a Lebanese cedar growing great,
> [13]Ones planted in Yhwh's house,
> flourishing out in the courts of our God,
> [14]Still fruiting in old age,
> being rich and fresh,

Further parallel cola go on to assert the enduring truths about the *faithful that follow from the past statements. The simile is broadly familiar (e.g., 1:3), though palm tree and cedar do not otherwise feature in

28. The line is rather long to treat as a bicolon, but the second and third cola together parallel the first, the whole following *abb'a'* order. Thus the line is book-ended by first-person verbs followed by the organs that are their subject. One verb is sg. wayyiqtol, one pl. yiqtol (1QPs[a] has qatal *šm'h*, hardly the right text but a right piece of interpretation); one noun is sg., one pl. In between come object expressions to describe the enemies, the first a one-word expression, the second a compound.

this connection (they do appear in Song 5:15; 7:7 [8]). These particular trees combine fruitfulness and size. The date-palm, as well as being tall, is a major source of sweetness (cf. Joel 1:12), while the cedar (growing in Lebanon rather than in Israel proper) is a major source of timber but is known for its height and stature (e.g., Amos 2:9); fruit trees and cedars sum up the types of trees in 148:9. So the date-palm's "flourishing" compares with v. 7 and suggests its fruitfulness, while the cedar's "growing great" recalls v. 10.

Verse 13 moves from simile to metaphor. Trees grow in the temple courts, but not cedars or date-palms, though there was much cedar wood there and many representations of palms (1 Kings 6).[29] But it is the faithful who are, as it were, planted (this word does come in 1:3) in Yhwh's house, specifically in the courts that are part of it. In other words, they live in Yhwh's presence and under Yhwh's protection (see on 91:1), and there they "flourish out" (that verb again, though now declarative hiphil rather than qal, and more vigorous). Thus "in the courts of our God" gives specificity to "in Yhwh's house" and "flourishing" goes beyond "planted." The evidence of the statement's truth lies in the experience to which the psalm testifies.

The metaphor continues in v. 14. "Old age in men is dry and barren,"[30] but the old age of the faithful finds them still fruiting, continuing to resemble the date-palm. The second colon explains the kind of fruitfulness they continue to show, one characterized by richness (lit. "fat") and freshness. The second word is picked up from v. 10b, again suggesting that the psalm describes the ongoing reality of which the particular experience it has described gives evidence.

> **15**To proclaim that Yhwh is upright,
> my crag is one in whom there is no wickedness.

The opening infinitive picks up from v. 2 and thus completes a bracket around the psalm. The rest of the words closely parallel Deut. 32:4. The psalm's testimony proclaims Yhwh's commitment and truthfulness, but that is possible and necessary because the object of Yhwh's activity is also to manifest the related qualities that this closing line describes. Further, as vv. 4–8 closed with an infinitival clause declaring the covert purpose behind the short-term flourishing of the faithless, vv. 9–15 close with an infinitival clause declaring the covert purpose behind the long-term flourishing of the faithful. Again, this purpose overlaps with that one, because v. 8 spoke of Yhwh's exaltation, and so does v. 15. This exaltation

29. Cf. Fisch, *Poetry with a Purpose*, 132.
30. Cassiodorus, *Psalms*, 2:393.

involves not merely Yhwh's power but also Yhwh's uprightness. The terms of the line imply that Yhwh remains faithful to Israel, that Yhwh indeed keeps commitment and truthfulness. Yhwh proves to be my *crag. Does this form of uprightness have any moral connotations in a Western sense, or is it simply the implementing of favoritism toward Israel? The psalm has assumed that the worshipper's enemies are Yhwh's enemies (v. 9) before being his enemies (v. 11), rather than vice versa. They are people who are faithless and rebellious in relation to Yhwh and not merely in relation to Israel. The uprightness that means Yhwh cannot be involved in wickedness or injustice reflects not merely favoritism to a people or a person arbitrarily chosen. By being committed and truthful to the faithful and by putting down opponents and rebels, Yhwh acts with an integrity that is good news to be proclaimed for all.

Theological Implications

The psalm combines features of testimony, praise, and teaching. As testimony it faces the fact that God's servants can reach the point of exhaustion or burnout (v. 10). They can be overwhelmed by people's attacks and opposition and yield to the stupid conclusion that the flourishing of the faithless has the last word in history (vv. 6–7, 11). That might be especially troublesome given that their wrongful acts make these people Yhwh's enemies (v. 9). The testimony can face those facts because it relates how Yhwh then acted, in an astonishing and unpredictable way (v. 5), renewing exhausted resources with refreshing oil (v. 10). Therefore the worshipper has found renewed joy (v. 4), not merely because the attacks have gone but because the temptation to abandon faith (or rather, wisdom) is also gone.

As praise it makes two assumptions inherent in testimony psalms but more overt in this instance. Yhwh's act has ongoing implications regarding Yhwh's identity, and it is (thus) significant for people other than the person who experienced it. It says things about Yhwh's commitment and faithfulness (v. 2), about Yhwh's being on high forever (v. 8), and about Yhwh's uprightness and integrity (v. 15). It indicates something always true about Yhwh's enemies, about wrongdoers (v. 9), and a converse that is always true about faithful people (vv. 12–14)—even if it sometimes does not look like it.[31]

As teaching, it invites people to live on the basis of its being true. In his *Art Poetica*, Archibald MacLeish wrote that "a poem should not

31. Cf. Meir Weiss, "מזמור שיר ליום השבת," in *Tehillah le-Moshe*, ed. Mordechai Cogan et al. (Moshe Greenberg Festschrift; Winona Lake, IN: Eisenbrauns, 1997), 45*–51*, 317.

mean/but be."[32] Harold Fisch comments that the purpose of this poem is not just to be but to proclaim, "to strive, to make a statement." The infinitive "denies closure." The poem reaches out beyond itself to do something.[33]

Norman Wirzba invites us to read the psalm in light of the heading's reference to the Sabbath. It suggests that Sabbath observance is infused with thanksgiving and praise, the kind of appreciation of the goodness of things that is possible when we stop working to look back at the world and at how generous God is. "Sabbath practice is the focus and culmination of a life that is daily and practically devoted to honoring God, the source of all our delight and the provider of every good and perfect gift, and to sharing in God's own creative delight."[34]

32. http://www.cs.rice.edu/~ssiyer/minstrels/poems/188.html.

33. *Poetry with a Purpose*, 134.

34. Norman Wirzba, *Living the Sabbath* (Grand Rapids: Brazos, 2006), 21–23.

Psalm 93
Yhwh Began to Reign

Translation

For the day before the Sabbath, when the earth/land became inhabited. Praise song. David's. [LXX]

1Yhwh began to reign, wears grandeur,
Yhwh wears, girded himself with might.
Yes, the world stands firm [MT]/he has ordered the world [Vrs]:[1] it does not totter;
2your throne is standing firm from long ago,
you are from of old.[2]
3Rivers lifted up, Yhwh,
rivers lifted up their voice,
rivers would lift up their crushing.
4Above the voices of many waters,
majestic, the sea's breakers,[3]
Yhwh is majestic on high.

1. For MT *tikkôn* from *kûn*, Vrs imply *tikkēn* from *tākan* as in Isa. 40:12–13; Job 28:25. Cf. 11QPs[a] *tkn*.

2. Howard (*Structure of Psalms 93–100*, 37) posits that "your throne is standing firm from of old" also applies to the second colon; "you" then picks up the suffix. One might then translate the colon "yours, from of old." This makes for an elegant but rather subtle understanding.

3. The two expressions in the middle colon qualify and parallel "many waters" in the first. A redivision of the consonants into *ʾaddîr mimmišbĕrê-yām* produces the easier reading "more majestic than the sea's breakers."

[5]Your declarations[4] have been very reliable;
your holiness glorifies[5] your house,
Yhwh, for long days.

Interpretation

11QPs[a] opens the psalm "Hallelujah," recognizing that this is a praise psalm, though it lacks the exhortation to praise and the "because" that characteristically introduce such a psalm (e.g., Ps. 95). In effect, all we have here is the content of the "because." Further, most of the content of the praise is addressed to Yhwh (vv. 2, 3, 5), whereas the content of the "because" in a praise psalm characteristically speaks of Yhwh in the third person. One might, indeed, see this as a psalm of trust; such psalms often combine speaking *of* Yhwh and speaking *to* Yhwh (e.g., Pss. 4; 16; 23), though their nature is also to speak in the first person, whereas here the focus lies on Yhwh rather than on the worshipper(s). The psalm moves from qatal statements in v. 1a–b through a yiqtol in v. 1c to noun clauses in v. 2. It then goes through the same sequence again in v. 3a–b, 3c, and 4, with v. 5 expanding on that in a closing comment.[6]

The form of address varies by a different pattern. Verses 1 and 4 speak *of* Yhwh; vv. 2–3 and 5 speak *to* Yhwh. Presumably the speaker is the congregation or its representative. In MT, vv. 3–5 are tricola; I take vv. 1c–2 also as a tricolon, v. 1a–b then being a long bicolon, 4-4. The use of tricola and the alternation of qatal and yiqtol are both reminiscent of Ugaritic poetry;[7] they may be archaic or may be an archaism.[8]

The focus of the psalm's affirmation is that Yhwh has asserted kingly authority in the world, "one of the most joyous utterances which ever leaped from mortal lips."[9] The affirmation will recur especially in Pss. 95–99, and Pss. 93–100 have closer relationships with each other than

4. This regular meaning of *'ēdōt* fits; there is no need to hypothesize a homonym meaning "throne" (against James Donald Shenkel, "An Interpretation of Psalm 93,5," *Bib* 56 [1965]: 401–16 [see 404–9]).

5. 4QPs[b] *nwh* might imply "abode," and Rashi understands *na'ăwâ* itself thus, but it is then hard to construe the rest of the line.

6. Cf. Jeremias, *Königtum*, 16, though he draws different inferences. P. Auffret rather sees v. 3 as the psalm's center ("'Yahvé règne,'" *ZAW* 103 [1991]: 101–9); Rudolf Mosis sees v. 1 as stating the psalm's theme and vv. 3–4 as its center ("Ströme erheben, Jahwe, ihr Tosen . . . ," in Mosis, *Gesammelte Aufsätze zum Alten Testament* [Würzburg: Echter, 1999], 317–57).

7. See Dahood, *Psalms*, 2:339–44; Loretz, *Ugarit-Texte*, 274–303. But see Herbert Donner, "Ugaritismen in der Psalmenforschung," *ZAW* 79 (1967): 322–50 (see 346–50).

8. Helen G. Jefferson ("Psalm 93," *JBL* 71 [1952]: 155–60) argues that Ps. 93 is an adaptation of a Ugaritic psalm. See also Howard, *Structure of Psalms 93–100*, 184–89.

9. Spurgeon, *Treasury of David*, 4:222.

appear in other sequences of psalms.[10] The affirmation already came in Ps. 47, but that psalm links the theme to events in Israel's story and to Israel's relationship with the nations, and it speaks of no resistance to Yhwh's reign. Isaiah 52:7–10 uses the verb "reign" with more concrete reference to Yhwh's self-assertion in the 530s in putting down Babylon and thus making it possible for Judeans to return to Jerusalem. In contrast, Ps. 93 links the theme to the world's stability and not to Israel's history. It refers to resistance to that reign, which Yhwh had to overcome (but had no difficulty in doing so). It suggests that the assertion of Yhwh's kingship took place long ago; it is not taking place at the moment (as in Isa. 52), nor did it take place in Israel's history in taking possession of Canaan or Jerusalem (as in Ps. 47). It belongs to a primeval moment when Yhwh asserted authority in such a way as to establish the world's security. Rashi and Qimchi take the psalm to be speaking about the future, but there is no pointer to such a perspective until the last colon. Its emphasis from the beginning is that Yhwh's reign has been "from long ago/from of old."[11] Based on that, Yhwh's reign is present and actual; the last colon declares that it will continue into the future. The psalm does not give any indication of seeing Yhwh's reign as a liturgical event as opposed to a historical one. It gives no indication of a historical or liturgical context,[12] though its placing after Pss. 89–92 might invite application to broadly the same historical context as Isa. 52:7–10.[13]

For the day before the Sabbath, when the earth/land became inhabited. Praise song. David's. [LXX]

Heading. See glossary. MT has no heading. LXX's linking the psalm with Friday corresponds to *m. Tamid* 7.4. A reference to the earth being filled with inhabitants would link with God's acts of creation on the

10. On these psalms and the relationship between them, see, e.g., John H. Eaton, *Psalms of the Way and the Kingdom*, JSOTSup 199 (Sheffield: Sheffield Academic Press, 1995), 53–126; Howard, *Structure of Psalms 93–100*; Jeremias, *Königtum*; Lipiński, *Royauté de Yahwé*; Martin Leuenberger, *Konzeptionen des Königtums Gottes in Psalter*, ATANT 83 (Zürich: TVZ, 2004); Mitchell, *Message of the Psalter*; Lohfink and Zenger, *The God of Israel and the Nations*, 161–90; Koenen, *Jahwe wird kommen*.

11. Cf. Lipiński, *Royauté de Yahwé*, 107.

12. Contrast Sigmund Mowinckel's hypothesis that Israel celebrated a festival of Yhwh's enthronement and that the psalms about Yhwh's reign had their setting there (*Psalmenstudien Buch I–II* [repr., Amsterdam: Schippers, 1961], 1–209, in the second part; modified in *Psalms*, 1:106–92. But for a positive view, see J. J. M. Roberts, "Mowinckel's Enthronement Festival," in *The Book of Psalms*, ed. Flint and Miller, 97–115.

13. On links with Pss. 89–92, see Howard, *Structure of Psalms 93–100*. Bernard Gosse ("Les introductions des Psaumes 93–94 et Isaïe 59,15b–20," *ZAW* 106 [1994]: 303–6) also makes a link with Isa. 59:15b–20.

sixth day (Gen. 1:24–31); a connection with creation fits the theme of the psalm. Completing the work of creation meant God could take up the throne in the palace in heaven.[14] But a reference to the land being filled with inhabitants would link with God's restoring the land after the exile (cf. LXX's heading to Ps. 97).[15]

93:1–2. The psalm begins with a declaration about Yhwh's long ago asserting authority in a way that ensures the world remains stable.

> [1a–b]Yhwh began to reign, wears grandeur,
> Yhwh wears, girded himself with might.

In the opening long parallel bicolon, each of the four-beat cola comprises two verbal clauses; each colon is thus internally parallel.

The earliest translations translate *mālak* with a past verb (e.g., LXX aorist, Jerome perfect), which corresponds with the use of the verb elsewhere; it usually means "reigned." In passages such as 2 Sam. 5:4–5 it presupposes that the reign (or the period of the reign in question) is over. Elsewhere it denotes "became king/has become king [and therefore reigns]": that is, the reign has begun but is not over (e.g., 2 Sam. 15:10; 16:8; 1 Kings 1:11, 13, 18). There are two passages where the qatal might have stative significance and mean "reigns" (1 Sam. 12:14; Isa. 24:23), but the predominant usage elsewhere likely suggests that these, too, are fientive, "will have become king/begun to reign." If the OT wants to say that someone "reigns," it could use the yiqtol (Prov. 8:15), or say "Yhwh is king," using the noun *melek* (Ps. 10:16), or use a participle; *mālak* does not occur in this connection, but *māšal* does (Ps. 22:28 [29]).

EVV, however, have "Yhwh reigns" or "Yhwh is king."[16] This likely reflects a sense that it is odd to think of Yhwh ever *becoming* king or *starting* to reign.[17] What was Yhwh before? Who was reigning before? In Babylonian theology Marduk became king at creation, acquiring an authority he did not have before; in Israelite theology, this would not

14. See, e.g., Jon D. Levenson, *Creation and the Persistence of Evil* (reissued, Princeton, NJ: Princeton University Press, 1994), 108–9.

15. See Kirkpatrick, *Psalms*, 563.

16. JM 111h, DG 57d (remark 3) see the verb as stative.

17. See the argument in Kraus, *Psalms 60–150*, 232–34. Diethelm Michel ("Studien zu den sogenannten Thronbesteigungspsalmen," *VT* 6 [1956]: 40–68) argues the point on purely linguistic grounds. The question has been complicated by Mowinckel's revival of the translation "Yhwh has become king" in the context of his hypothesis that Israel had an annual celebration of Yhwh's becoming king (*Psalms*, 1:106–92). For the debate over the expression, see, e.g., Edward Lipiński, "*Yāhweh mâlāk*," *Bib* 44 (1963): 405–60; also idem, *Royauté de Yahwé*; Leo Perdue, "'Yahweh Is King over All the Earth,'" *ResQ* 17 (1974): 85–89.

be true of Yhwh. No other deity was king before Yhwh. But the Pentateuch never speaks of Yhwh as king except at Exod. 15:18, Deut. 33:5, and probably Num. 23:21, a parable of the fact that kingship is not a dominant image for understanding Yhwh. It was in Jerusalem, under Canaanite influence, that it came to be significant.

It does indeed then help Israel understand what went on at creation. Creation involved an assertion of sovereign authority over any other powers. Nevertheless the OT apparently thinks about this question with a different dynamic. The alternative of eternal sovereignty or recent accession[18] does not quite work here. The psalm concerns an active sovereignty.[19] The expression *yhwh mālāk* indicates that "Yahweh has succeeded to the kingship and reigns in the present."[20] There is a sense in which Yhwh began to reign at the Red Sea (Exod. 15:18), and there acted with grandeur (Exod. 15:1, 21, the verb *gā'â*); before this, Yhwh was no doubt reigning in some nominal sense but was not asserting authority over Egypt and on behalf of Israel. Yhwh did the same in taking possession of Canaan, asserting a kingly authority over Egypt or Canaan that had not been exercised before (Ps. 47). Yhwh once again began to reign in asserting authority over Babylon (Isa. 52:7; in the same connection, 12:5 uses the noun *gē'ût*); in the exile, too, Yhwh had not been exercising authority in the world in such a way as to take Israel toward its destiny, even though Babylon had been Yhwh's pawn in chastising Israel. The psalm relates an occasion of this kind that happened long before and is theologically the basis of those later acts. This was the occasion when "Yhwh established his throne in the heavens" (Ps. 103:19).

The word order *yhwh mālāk* puts into prominence the fact that it was Yhwh who began to reign. We should not exaggerate the significance of this. The subject can come first at the beginning of a statement.[21] When the formulation is used of the accession of a human king, it can have the order subject-verb or verb-subject, and can have the latter order even when the subject seems to be emphasized (see 1 Kings 1:11, 13, 18; 2 Kings 9:13; 15:1). The psalm's emphasis is not on Yhwh rather than some other deity being king but on Yhwh's reigning rather than no one being in control.

The psalm's opening colon goes on to spell out the implications of beginning to reign. In asserting authority, Yhwh wears grandeur like clothing. The expression is abstract for concrete; Yhwh wears regal

18. See A. Gelston, "A Note on יהוה מלך," *VT* 16 (1966): 507–13 (see 508).

19. Cf. Arvid S. Kapelrud, "Nochmals Jahwä mālāk," *VT* 13 (1963): 229–31 (see 231); also Jarl H. Ulrichsen, "*JHWH mālāḵ*," *VT* 27 (1977): 361–74 (see 374).

20. Lipiński, *Royauté de Yahwé*, 108.

21. JM 155nd; cf. Ps. 94:1.

garments, like a king (Esther 6:8). Yhwh indeed put on grandeur at creation (Ps. 104:1).[22]

In the parallel colon, however, the psalm follows the repeated "wears" by another qatal, "girded himself" (*ʾāzar* hitpael). The sequence of the verbs in the line is thus *abb′a′*: fientive, stative, stative, fientive. The repetition of "wears" without an object raises the question of whether its object is the same as before; the second half of the second colon makes clear that it is not. The new verb suggests equipping oneself, and specifically equipping oneself for battle, with armor and weaponry (cf. 18:32 [33]; Isa. 8:9), here with might (*ʿōz*); again abstract stands for concrete (Isa. 51:9 urges Yhwh's arm to "wear might," and the declaration that Yhwh has begun to reign in 52:7 responds to that). This parallel verb thus gives more precision to "wears grandeur." The psalm refers not to a mere ceremonial robing in regalia but to Yhwh's taking up impressive battle equipment (cf. the "putting on" of 1 Sam. 17:38) in connection with asserting kingly authority.

> 1cYes, the world stands firm [MT]/he has ordered the world [Vrs]: it does not totter;
> 2your throne is standing firm from long ago,
> you are from of old.

After that opening long bicolon, the first tricolon declares some ongoing consequences of Yhwh's assertion of kingly authority. With v. 1c the subject changes, syntactically and substantially. There is no concrete description of the exercise of might that v. 1b referred to, and no overt indication of when Yhwh's assertion of authority took place, only a declaration about the consequences of it. Its result is that the world stands firm, like the kingship in the hands of Solomon (1 Kings 2:12). The *tēbēl* is the world of humanity rather than the physical world, the earth (the *ʾereṣ*).[23] The world of humanity stands firm because it has Yhwh as its king and protector. Yet what is affirmed is that this world does not (and by implication will not) collapse or fall, like a hill in a mudslide. The declaration thus does imply an answer to the question of when Yhwh's assertion of authority took place. It was an aspect of Yhwh's activity in bringing the world into being.

Implicitly, the second colon provides the grounds for the first, taking up one of its verbs, though it moves from speaking *of* Yhwh to addressing

22. But 104:1 may refer to an event: that is, the verb *lābaštā* may be either fientive or stative. Here, the form *lābēš* must be stative (contrast Lev. 16:23; Esther 6:8, which use the fientive form *lābaš*; also the impv. in Isa. 51:9).

23. Cf. Paul Nadim Tarazi, "An Exegesis of Psalm 93," *St Vladimir's Seminary Quarterly* 35 (1991): 137–48 (see 141–42).

Yhwh. Perhaps the continuation of the form of speech in v. 1c influenced the way the verses came to be divided, though a switch from third person to second person within a line is quite common. This might also have influenced the ancient versions in understanding the first verb in v. 1c as qatal rather than yiqtol. But if v. 1c belongs with v. 2, it fits for it to be yiqtol, for the world to be the subject, and for the verb to be *kûn*, which recurs in v. 2a in keeping with the staircase nature of the tricola in vv. 3 and 4. Both third- and second-person expressions can be forms of praise or articulations of trust. In v. 1 presumably the congregation spoke to itself, or its leader addressed it; now it or its leader speaks to Yhwh. Yhwh's assertion of kingly power happened at a particular time, but once made, it had lasting implications. The world will continue to stand firm because Yhwh's assertion of kingly power (metonymically speaking, Yhwh's throne) stands firm. The line confirms that v. 1 refers to such an assertion back at the Beginning, since which time Yhwh has continued to exercise authority in the world.

The third colon more closely parallels the second. For *mēʿôlām*, "from of old," EVV have "from eternity," which the psalmist would doubtless acknowledge. But the reference of *ʿôlām* varies with the context (it can, for instance, denote a human lifetime). Here the context suggests a reference back to creation. Ever since then, Yhwh has been there, exercising authority in the world.

93:3–5. The psalm reverts to qatal as vv. 3–5 reprise the statement in vv. 1–2.

> 3Rivers lifted up, Yhwh,
> rivers lifted up their voice,
> rivers would lift up their crushing.

A more explicit staircase tricolon (*abc, abd, a′bd′*) begins the reprise. The first two cola raise the question of why the rivers are lifting up their voice. Tg has them doing so in praise;[24] Christian writers similarly see them as involved in proclamation.[25] But the third colon suggests that they do so aggressively, as v. 4 will confirm.

In Isa. 17:12–13 the roar of the waters is a figure for the roar of the nations. The rivers might thus be political powers such as the great empires.[26] And the references to their raising their voice might mean they are in subsequent rebellion against Yhwh's kingly power. But the psalm as a whole does not suggest such a historical reference (again,

24. Peter L. Trudinger revives this understanding ("Friend or Foe? Earth, Sea and *Chaoskampf* in the Psalms," in *Earth Story*, ed. Habel, 37–39).

25. E.g., Augustine, *Psalms*, 458.

26. So Rashi, Qimchi.

contrast Ps. 47 and Isa. 52:7–10). More likely v. 3 forms the beginning of a parallel account of Yhwh's assertion of kingly power at the Beginning and provides the background to that. The rivers are then the subterranean waters that appear in the oceans surrounding the world's land mass, pounding upon its shores, and gushing through the earth in springs and rivers (cf. 24:2). They threatened to overwhelm the land until Yhwh put them under constraint back at the Beginning (cf. Gen. 1:9–10).[27] Again, the yiqtol in the third colon may have past reference,[28] or it may indicate a recognition that the rivers continue to assert themselves in this way.

4Above the voices of many waters,
majestic, the sea's breakers,
Yhwh is majestic on high.

The psalm reverts to speaking *of* Yhwh; it will change to address again for the last line. Here the tricolon works *aa′b*. The noun clause could be reckoned to refer to the past, to that act of assertion; but the parallel with v. 2 makes it more likely that it describes the consequence or implication of Yhwh's action. But whether one thinks of a self-assertiveness at the Beginning or of a subsequent self-assertiveness in world history makes little difference. "Voices" elsewhere refer to thunder. The sea's breakers may be majestic; Yhwh "on high" is more so.

5Your declarations have been very reliable;
your holiness glorifies your house,
Yhwh, for long days.

The psalm closes with yet another tricolon in which the second and third cola together parallel the first.[29] Yhwh's *declarations (*ʿēdâ*) are commands Yhwh issues (cf. 25:10; 78:56; 99:7, and often in Ps. 119); specifically in this context, they will not be commands to Israel,[30] but commands to those resistant energies (cf. the command to "stop" in 46:10 [11]). Yhwh does not act violently to subdue the forcefulness of the waves. God simply issues a decree. "The seemingly fragile word of God is

27. Cf. *Midrash on Psalms*, 126–27.

28. Gunkel (*Psalmen*, 412) sees the change as purely stylistic; Seybold (*Psalmen*, 367–68) describes the yiqtol as iterative.

29. "Your declarations" are paralleled by "your holiness" (pl. by sg.); niphal "reliable" is paralleled by "beautifies," *naʾăwâ*, which looks rather like a niphal (see BDB 610a; *HALOT* 657b, 678b); and "very" is paralleled by "for long days." The appellative "Yhwh" also applies to the first colon.

30. This would parallel Ps. 19, but it would be very allusive (against, for instance, Mays, *Psalms*, 301–2).

opposed to the arrogant, intimidating actions of the world."[31] Fortunately for people who live in the world God created and ordered, over the millennia those declarative commands have been totally firm, reliable, and *true. Parallel to "your declarations" is "your holiness" (the suffix on the first word also applies to the second). Yhwh's *holiness is Yhwh's grandeur and majesty, the qualities that distinguish Yhwh from the human and earthly, and from other so-called holy ones. It is an appropriate adornment for Yhwh's house in the heavens, where Yhwh's throne is (v. 2) and where Yhwh sits in majesty (v. 4; and cf. 11:4); compare 96:5b–6.[32]

The closing time reference contrasts with the ones that preceded. It parallels, compares, and contrasts with the ones in v. 2. As well as going back as far as one can imagine, Yhwh's reign extends forward as far as one can imagine. It will always undergird the world's security. While the psalm is not eschatological in promising an assertion of Yhwh's reign one day in the future, it is eschatological in declaring that the reign Yhwh implemented at creation will continue into the future forever.

Theological Implications

"Where Psalm 29 ends, Psalm 93 begins, with the declaration that Yhwh is king."[33] Its emphasis on that thus differs from the emphasis elsewhere. Israel knew moments when Yhwh asserted kingly power in its history in putting down the power of Egypt (Exod. 15:1–19), Canaan (Ps. 47), or Babylon (Isa. 52:7–10), and knew that Yhwh exercised some kind of sovereignty throughout its history; even when the Babylonians or the Persians or the Greeks controlled its destiny, they did so by Yhwh's permission (Dan. 7–12). But Psalm 93 speaks of a sovereignty in the created world rather than in the realm of Israel's historical experience. Experience of that world raises the question whether its stability can be taken for granted. The sea with its dynamic power crashes on the sandy shore: why does it never overwhelm it? Indeed, from time to time it does. Storms buffet the land and wash away soil and rocks and anything else in their way: might they overwhelm the whole land?

31. Peterson, *Where Your Treasure Is*, 61.

32. Contrast Mowinckel's assumption that the line refers to the consecration of the temple in Jerusalem (e.g., *Psalms*, 1:126, 129, 175); cf., e.g., Bernd Janowski, "Das Königtum Gottes in den Psalmen," *ZTK* 86 (1989): 389–454 (see 416); Lipiński, *Royauté de Yahwé*, 143–63.

33. Spiekermann, *Heilsgegenwart*, 181. James L. Mays calls *yhwh mālāk* "an organizing centre for the theology of the psalms" ("The Centre of the Psalms," in *Language, Theology, and the Bible*, ed. Samuel E. Balentine and John Barton [James Barr Festschrift; Oxford: Clarendon, 1994], 231–46 [see 231]).

The raging of sea and storm are but the aftershocks or reminders of attempts to do this back at the Beginning. Way back then, Yhwh asserted kingly authority over the sea and declared, "You may come this far, but no farther," setting a limit for "the grandeur of its waves" (Job 38:11; cf. Gen. 1:9). Yhwh will never (again) let a flood overwhelm the earth (Gen. 9:11). Yhwh's sovereignty is such as to be able to guarantee that. The world stays in being and stays secure, not because of inherent stability, but because Yhwh imposed such stability on it.

It is a long time since Yhwh did that, and Yhwh's word of command to potentially recalcitrant dynamic forces has been proving itself over the millennia. Humanity may therefore live in confidence about the world's stability (though this might carry no implication that humanity itself could not fatally undermine this). Yhwh's majesty is thus the glory of Yhwh's home in the heavens and also a proper object of the glorifying of Yhwh's name on earth.

Psalm 94
God of Redress

Translation

Composition. David's. For the fourth day of the week. [LXX]

[1]The God of all redress, Yhwh,
the God of all redress has shone forth/shine forth![1]

[2]Lift yourself up as the one who exercises authority over the earth,
give their reward to the eminent people!
[3]Until when will the faithless, Yhwh,
until when will the faithless exult,
[4]Will they pour out, talk assertively,
speak out, all the people who do harm?
[5]They crush your people, Yhwh,
they afflict your possession.
[6]The widow and migrant they slay,
the orphan they murder.
[7]And they say,[2] "Yah does not look,
the God of Jacob does not take any notice."

1. MT (cf. 4QPs[b]) has qatal *hôpîaʿ* (cf. 50:2; Deut. 33:2); cf. LXX's aorist. Aq, Sym, Th, Jerome, Tg, Syr imply impv. *hôpîʿâ* (cf. 80:1 [2]). The *h* might have disappeared through haplography. It seems less likely that *hôpîaʿ* itself is an impv. form (so GKC 53m, 69v).

2. Here and in vv. 22–23 *wayyiqtol* continues yiqtol. In both places the *wayyiqtol* might have its usual past reference, despite having no preceding past verb; thus "and said" here, "and has become . . . and has turned" in vv. 22–23 (cf. LXX). But given the present

8Take notice, brutish among the people;
stupid ones, when will you show some insight?
9The one who plants the ear—does he not listen,
the one who shapes the eye—does he not discern?
10The one who instructs the nations—does he not rebuke,
the one who schools humanity about recognition?
11Yhwh recognizes the plans of humanity,
that these[3] are empty.
12The good fortune of the man whom you instruct, Yah,
and school from your teaching,
13Giving[4] him rest from times of trouble,
until a pit is dug for the faithless.
14Because Yhwh does not forsake his people,
does not abandon his possession.
15Because authority will turn to faithfulness[5]
and all the upright of heart will go after it. [Rise (LXX)]

16Who arises for me with the wrongdoers,
who stands up for me with the people who do harm?
17Were Yhwh not a help to me,
soon I would have dwelt in silence.
18If I said, "My foot has tripped,"
it is your commitment, Yhwh, holds me up.[6]
19When my anxieties multiply in my heart,
your great comfort[7] rejoices my being.
20Can the seat that brings destruction[8] join you,[9]
one that shapes troublemaking by statute?
21They gang together against the life of the faithful person,
condemn the innocent blood.
22But Yhwh becomes a haven for me,[10]
my God the crag where I find refuge,
23And turns their harmfulness upon them,
by their wrongdoing[11] puts an end to them;
Yhwh our God puts an end to them.

---

focus in both contexts, more likely the *wayyiqtol* continues the present reference of the preceding yiqtol. See *IBHS* 33.3.3c; *TTH* 82.

3. Presumably the "plans," though that was f. and "these" is m.

4. Circumstantial inf. (cf. GKC 114o); cf. Dahood, *Psalms*, 2:348.

5. For *ṣedeq*, Sym, Syr imply *ṣaddîq*, "the faithful person."

6. NRSV and TNIV have a past tense verb; TNIV has another in v. 19b. But the verbs are yiqtol (contrast v. 17b). Thus LXX has present (but past in v. 19b), Jerome future.

7. *Tanḥûmêkā* is pl.

8. See on 91:3.

9. The form of *yĕḥobrĕkā* is as easy to take as qal (see JM 63b) as pual (see BDB); qal gives better sense, and the suffix makes qal more likely.

10. See note on v. 7.

11. The context suggests "by" rather than "for" or "in" for *b*.

Interpretation

Initially, this community prayer psalm is dominated by plea and protest, but its prevailing note is confidence. Indeed, in MT it begins with a declaration that Yhwh has shone out (v. 1). This is the background for the only line of actual plea, supported by the protests in the form of rhetorical questions and statements, all addressed to Yhwh (vv. 2–7). The note of confidence is then developed in the address to brutish people who do not believe that Yhwh takes action against the faithless (vv. 8–15). The last section (vv. 16–23) resumes the rhetorical questions but is again dominated by declarations of confidence. In isolation, the "I" here might be the king's,[12] as he is troubled by foreign oppressors. But describing the wrongdoers as people who afflict widow, migrant, and orphan, and manipulate the legal system, suggests they are leaders within the community, the kind of people attacked by prophets in all periods (e.g., Isa. 1; 58–59). Yet Midrash Tehillim relates that the Levites were singing v. 23a–b when the First Temple was destroyed, and again when the Second Temple was destroyed; before they could say v. 23c, the enemies entered and took hold of them.[13] The link with 587 fits with the psalm's placing in Book IV, which may have been arranged with the exile in mind. So in itself the psalm could refer to oppression within Israel in any period, but its setting in the Psalter links it with Israel's oppression by the nations from the exile onward.

As a whole, the psalm is closer to a psalm of trust than a psalm of protest, but like Ps. 92 it has a didactic aspect. Like Ps. 93 it has features that might be archaic, such as staircase parallelism (vv. 1, 3) and the use of the name Yah, or might be archaisms; it gives no actual indications of its date.[14] Verses 1–15 would work on their own, and vv. 16–23 might be a subsequent addition, while vv. 8–15 have been seen as a "wisdom interpolation."[15] As vv. 1–15 focus on the community but go on to refer to the individual (vv. 12–13), vv. 16–23 focus on the individual but close with reference to "our God."

Composition. David's. For the fourth day of the week. [LXX]

Heading. See glossary. MT has no heading. Mishnah *Tamid* 7 also allocates the psalm to the fourth day.

94:1. A declaration about Yhwh.

12. So, e.g., Mowinckel, *Psalms*, 1:227.

13. *Midrash on Psalms*, 2:135.

14. On its links with other psalms in this part of the Psalter, see, e.g., Howard, *Structure of Psalms 93–100*.

15. Whybray, *Reading the Psalms as a Book*, 55.

> [1]The God of all redress, Yhwh,
> the God of all redress has shone forth/shine forth!

The psalm "bursts forth with exclamations"[16] as it begins with another instance of staircase parallelism (cf. 92:9 [10]; 93:3), catching attention by means of the incomplete statement in v. 1a that moves the listener to want to see this unfinished thought brought to completion, as then happens in the second colon.[17] Considerable emphasis thus attaches to the verb that eventually comes as the last word. MT's qatal "has shone forth" makes sense in the context as establishing the psalm's note of confidence; it corresponds to the qatal declaration opening Ps. 93. It offers the encouragement that Yhwh does acts to exact *redress, indeed *is* God of redress ("redress" is plural each time: hence "all redress"). It is part of Yhwh's nature not to leave wrongdoers in power. This is an aspect of Yhwh's love for the afflicted; Yhwh refuses to abandon them where they are. The declaration that Yhwh has shone forth corresponds to 50:2, where Yhwh "shone out" from Zion to announce judgment on the faithless, and earlier to Deut. 32–33, where Moses declared Yhwh's commitment to acting with redress and went on to proclaim the way Yhwh shone forth from Mount Paran in coming to meet with the people (Deut. 32:36–43; 33:2).

94:2–7. In light of that opening proclamation, the psalm exhorts Yhwh to take action now (v. 2) and backs that up with rhetorical questions about how long the faithless will be allowed to act as assertively as they do (vv. 3–4) in crushing Yhwh's people and declaring that Yhwh is not interested (vv. 5–7).

> [2]Lift yourself up as the one who exercises authority over the earth,
> give their reward to the eminent people!

"Lift yourself up" (*nāśāʾ* niphal) is not a common way to encourage Yhwh to arise to take action (*qûm* and *ʿûr* are more common). It suggests an act of self-assertion rather than a move from inaction to action. The end of the line will suggest why this is the exhortation, and the contents of vv. 3–7 will develop the point. The problem is the self-assertion of important or self-important people. As king, Yhwh wears grandeur (*gēʾût*; 93:1). Eminent (*gēʾîm*) human leaders compromise recognition of Yhwh's true eminence. "Eminent" appears in Isa. 2:12 alongside "lifting themselves up," again standing over against Yhwh's eminence (*gāʾôn*;

16. Terrien, *Psalms*, 663.

17. Bratcher and Reyburn, *Handbook on the Psalms*, 818; cf. Watson, *Classical Hebrew Poetry*, 154.

Isa. 2:10, 19, 21). The psalm urges Yhwh to look at the situation in the community as Isaiah looks at it and to act in accordance with the word declared there. It wants Yhwh not to settle for being put down from eminence by these human leaders.

Describing Yhwh as the one who exercises *authority fits with that, because Isa. 2:4 also declares Yhwh's intention to exercise authority among the nations (cf. the references to exercising authority in Isa. 1:17, 21, 23, 26, 27). In the present context, Yhwh's being "the one who exercises authority over the earth" implies there is no reason why Yhwh should not start being assertive over powerful people within Israel. "Reward" (*gĕmûl*) is in itself a neutral word, with a negative meaning in 28:4 and a positive implication in 103:2. It can appear in the company of "redress" (Isa. 35:4; Jer. 51:6) and thus point to the idea of appropriateness, as it does here. The psalm seeks for apposite action toward people whose eminence compromises Yhwh's.

3Until when will the faithless, Yhwh,
until when will the faithless exult,
4Will they pour out, talk assertively,
speak out, all the people who do harm?

Another instance of staircase parallelism follows; in structure, v. 3 corresponds to v. 1. As usual, "until when" (e.g., 74:10; 82:2) is not a request for information but a further, less direct exhortation, whose theme continues that of the direct one in v. 2. That continuity of theme begins to become explicit in the verb, which (as in v. 1) comes as the last word, with the emphasis. Exulting is fine when it takes place on the right basis (e.g., 28:7; 68:4 [5]; 96:12; 149:5); Yhwh can do it (108:7 [8]). But *faithless and exult do not go together. As in v. 1, then, the closing verb brings the line to a forceful close: in this case, a scandalous one.

The "until when" continues its effect through v. 4, which thus parallels v. 3 as well as being internally parallel. On the other hand, here three verbal expressions come first, while another noun expression closes the line. The faithless are glossed as people who do *harm, while the three verbs make explicit their offensiveness. All have the same implication. The harm-doers "pour out" words, gush out like a powerful spring (cf. Prov. 18:4). They talk assertively; the word (*ʿātāq*) suggests advancing boldly and freely (cf. 31:18 [19]; 75:5 [6]). They speak out: it is the ordinary verb for say, *ʾāmar*, but it is used uniquely in the hitpael (cf. English "he had a lot to say for himself").[18]

18. It seems unnecessary to hypothesize a second root *ʾāmar* (Seybold, *Psalmen*, 371; cf. *HALOT*).

[5]They crush your people, Yhwh,
they afflict your possession.
[6]The widow and migrant they slay,
the orphan they murder.

What is it they are saying? Verse 7 will eventually tell us. Meanwhile, the psalm goes on to the action their words relate to. Again, the two lines are parallel to each other and internally. "Crushing" makes for another link with Ps. 93 (see my translation of v. 3). "Affliction" then restates crushing. Similarly "your people" and "your *possession" constitute parallel descriptions of Israel. The suffixes particularly indicate that focus still lies on the stance of the wicked toward Yhwh. It is not (merely) that they wrong the weak; it is that they attack people who belong to Yhwh. Therein lies one aspect of their assertiveness over against Yhwh.

From v. 5 one would have inferred that the faithless are foreign peoples afflicting Israel. Verse 6 points in a different direction. The problem rather lies in the way people in power (the eminent people) treat the powerless within their own community. The former are part of "your people/your possession," but they are afflicting other people within that community. Indeed, the widow, migrant, and orphan *are* "your people/possession." The psalm is only a step away from suggesting that the people in power have forfeited their membership in this community.

Verse 6 focuses on the victims themselves in their need. Widow, migrant, and orphan are all people without a secure place in the society. A migrant belongs to no family and thus has no land and no security. Widows and orphans have lost the place in a family structure that they once had; they have no powerful man to look after them. They may have held on to their land or their house, but they are vulnerable to being swindled out of them or thrown out of them; or they may simply disappear. Migrants may do well in business, but migrants, too, have no protection; they are the victims of scams and violence, and they can even more easily disappear without anyone asking any questions.

[7]And they say, "Yah does not look,
the God of Jacob does not take any notice."

The action in v. 6 is the background to the words of which vv. 3–4 spoke, but the actual nature of these words is now clarified in another parallel line. The words of the important people parallel those of the stupid in 14:1; 53:1 [2]. Perhaps it is significant that God is referred to as *Yah, the God of the Red Sea who took the side of a weak people (Exod. 15:2) and in whom people exult as father of orphans and champion of widows

(Ps. 68:4–5 [5–6]). But it is also important that it is the vocation of a king or person exercising authority (v. 2) to safeguard the interests of such people. The important, powerful people do not question God's existence, but their conviction is that God sits in heaven without being involved in events on earth. And often their theology is supported by how life works out. They can do what they like and do their own exulting in it.

94:8–15. The psalm turns to address the "stupid" among the people, offering them insight that can encourage them to stand firm and confident in the context of the temptation to believe the assertion of the eminent people that there is no moral order in the world. The encouragement is offered in confrontational form in vv. 8–11, then less directly as reflection and promise in vv. 12–15.

8Take notice, brutish among the people;
stupid ones, when will you show some insight?

Neatly, the section begins by turning the words of the important people around. They say Yhwh does not take notice; but the brutish and stupid need to start taking some notice themselves. Likewise the "when" of v. 3 is reversed. The brutish and stupid are addressed as "you," suggesting they are not identified with the important people (though they were also brutish and stupid), who were spoken of as "they" and continue to be so termed throughout the psalm. Rather they are ordinary people in the community, tempted to stupid ways of thinking in light of the actions of the important people and the way they get away with things. "Brutish" and "stupid" are common ways of describing and addressing people who will not form their attitudes in light of the reality of God's ways in the world: see 92:6 [7]; Prov. 8:5. Such people need to take notice and find insight: compare Prov. 8:1, 5, 9, 14. Real insight lies in reverence for Yhwh, of which both the important people and these stupid people are showing no sign.

9The one who plants the ear—does he not listen,
the one who shapes the eye—does he not discern?
10The one who instructs the nations—does he not rebuke,
the one who schools humanity about recognition?

The psalm tries a little logic.[19] Yhwh, inventor of ears and eyes, possesses eyes and ears and surely therefore uses them. Why bother to invent them, unless deeming them worth using? The conviction expressed in v. 7 is totally implausible. "Planting" adds a unique sense of vividness to

19. The line is neatly parallel, but the opening of the cola provides variation as they use two different ways of introducing a question.

the creative process; the metaphor underlines its purposefulness, which makes even less plausible the idea that Yhwh does not do any listening. Yhwh is the planter and the shaper, the gardener and the potter. Yhwh shaped the first human person in that way (Gen. 2:7–8) and shapes the individual person in the womb (Isa. 44:2, 24; Jer. 1:5).

Initially, v. 10 continues the pattern of v. 9, but it reworks the logic. The people of God can be enthusiastic about God judging the world but less enthusiastic about God judging us. The psalm speaks of Yhwh "instructing" the nations (*yāsar*), a striking comment (Tg alters it to make Yhwh's people the object of the instruction).[20] But parallel to "instruct" is "rebuke" (*yākaḥ* hiphil); the two verbs appear in parallelism elsewhere and likely have similar meaning (e.g., 6:1 [2]; 38:1 [2]; and cf. 39:11 [12]).[21] The second verb usually refers to the use of words (though see Job 33:19), and the following colon also refers to schooling (*lāmad* piel). So it seems likely that the whole line refers to teaching. God instructs the nations about their behavior. God would then hardly be likely simply to leave Israel to do what it likes, and would surely issue rebukes there, too, when this instruction was ignored. In speaking of schooling humanity, v. 10b offers a parallel description to the idea of instructing the nations, varying the pattern that appeared in vv. 9–10a and thus bringing a little subsection to a close. Yhwh teaches humanity *daʿat*: not merely knowledge of God and of right and wrong but *acknowledgment or obedience.

11Yhwh recognizes the plans of humanity,
that these are empty.

The psalm picks up the idea of recognition or acknowledgment again, turning it a different way. Yhwh's efforts to teach people recognition tend to be frustrated. Their energy goes in a different direction from recognition of Yhwh and of Yhwh's ways and of Yhwh's expectations of us. Their plans are very different, as the psalm has presupposed (cf. Gen. 6:5). Yhwh recognizes that. Of course this does not mean Yhwh accepts it. Paradoxically, Yhwh's recognition works the opposite way. It means recognizing them for what they really are. Or perhaps we might say that Yhwh's recognition of them parallels their recognition of Yhwh. They decline to recognize Yhwh; Yhwh declines to recognize them. They treat Yhwh as having no power in the world; Yhwh treats them as having no power in the world. They reckon they can implement plans to act in the way vv. 3–6 describe, but they will not get away with it. Yhwh has other plans (cf. 92:5–6 [6–7]). Their plans are *hebel*, a mere breath, with no substance.

20. Unusually, the verb is here qal; for the more common piel, cf. v. 12.
21. Bratcher and Reyburn, *Handbook on the Psalms*, 822.

12The good fortune of the man whom you instruct, Yah,
and school from your teaching,
13Giving him rest from times of trouble,
until a pit is dug for the faithless.

The psalm takes further the ideas of instruction and schooling, but moves on from teaching for the nations to teaching for the individual, whose *good fortune is thus declared. Further, the reference to *Yah's *teaching (*tôrâ*)[22] suggests that the line does now have the Israelites in mind.[23]

The instruction and schooling of vv. 9–10 will have included reference to Yhwh's expectations of people, but "teaching" can also refer to broader revelation regarding Yhwh's activity and ways in the world, which contrast with empty human intentions (v. 11). That broader reference fits here, and retrospectively applies to vv. 9–10. The Psalms declare that obeying Yhwh's teaching makes for a peaceful and blessed life, but this psalm (like many others) starts from the fact that often this does not work out. But the Psalms also affirm that this experience will not have the last word. Yhwh's teaching makes promises about how Yhwh will put things right. There are then two possible senses in which Yhwh gives people rest in the meantime. Even if the faithless do not actually fall yet, Yhwh provides interim respite from their attacks; they do not finally overwhelm Yhwh's people. And further, because Yhwh is going to put things right in due course, one can stay calm in times of trouble, stay calm from them (be distanced from them), knowing that Yhwh will bring them to an end.

The pit into which the *faithless will fall is both the metaphorical one (a trap to catch a dangerous animal; e.g., 35:7) and the metaphysical one (e.g., 55:23 [24]). Who digs it? Here it is not explicit whether they dig their own pit, or God digs it, or what. It is explicit only that it will catch them.

14Because Yhwh does not forsake his people,
does not abandon his possession.
15Because authority will turn to faithfulness
and all the upright of heart will go after it. (Rise [LXX])

In vv. 12–13, the promises were expressed negatively and individualistically. Here is the other side of that, the positive and communal. Digging

22. On Yah, see on v. 7.

23. The parallelism works *abcdec′*: "the blessings of the man whom" applies also to the second colon, "from your teaching" also applies to the first, while the parallel verbs are both second person sg. piel with suffix.

a ditch to trap the faithless is the means of delivering Yhwh's people and thus the evidence that Yhwh does not abandon them. The line again emphasizes that the punishment of the faithless and the security of the faithful are based on the fact that the faithful are Yhwh's people, Yhwh's possession; compare the significance of the suffixes on these same words in v. 5. "Crushing" and "afflicting" in v. 5 are confronted by "not forsaking" and "not abandoning." Paul picks up the psalm's phraseology in reminding the Romans that even Israel's failure to recognize its Messiah does not mean that God abandons Israel (Rom. 11:1–2).

Verse 15 looks at the positive point from another angle. The OT believes passionately in the combination of *mišpāṭ* and *ṣĕdāqâ*/*ṣedeq*, *authority exercised in a way that expresses *faithfulness. At the moment that collocation is being ignored; authority is exercised for the benefit of the people who hold it, as happens in our own nations. When Yhwh acts to put the faithless down, this will mean proper order being restored. The people who exercise authority will do so in a way that recognizes their commitment to the community and safeguards faithfulness in the community. The second colon is elliptically expressed (there is no verb), but it apparently starts from the fact that at present people who are upright of heart necessarily distance themselves from the administration. When the administration turns to faithfulness again, the upright will be able to identify with and support it.

94:16–23. Only now does the psalm talk in "I" terms, making more explicit that vv. 1–15 were not talking mere theological theory or offering instruction on matters that might be issues for other people. This section, too, divides into two: twice it asks a rhetorical question relating to the attackers, and twice it answers that question by referring to Yhwh's action.

16 Who arises for me with the wrongdoers,
who stands up for me with the people who do harm?

The question "Who . . . ?" can have an urgent tone, but here the context indicates that it is a more even rhetorical question. Although it presupposes the answer "No one," the wrongdoers (*bad) and the people who do *harm are not a cause for anxiety; the statement is the background to the declaration of confidence that will continue in vv. 17–19. "Arising" and "standing up" may suggest taking forceful action but in the context may denote standing up in court.

17 Were Yhwh not a help to me,
soon I would have dwelt in silence.

The second colon underscores the implication of v. 16. If no one is standing up to take action on the suppliant's behalf, then one way or another the suppliant is doomed. The land of silence (cf. 115:17) is the grave, or Sheol (LXX has "Hades," Jerome *infernus*). Its silence is evident when one opens a tomb; there is no conversation, no praise, and no testimony there (6:5 [6]; 30:9 [10]). But in fact, Yhwh is the suppliant's *help: that is, someone who does stand up and take action.

> [18]If I said, "My foot has tripped,"
> it is your commitment, Yhwh, holds me up.

The line restates the point in v. 17, in reverse order. The image of the foot tripping presupposes the picture of someone walking a narrow mountain path and being pushed off to their death, with the further implication of tumbling into the grave/Sheol. In 91:11–12 it is Yhwh's aides who stop the suppliant from falling; here it is Yhwh's *commitment, often pictured as one of those aides, semi-separate from Yhwh (85:10–11 [11–12]; 89:14 [15]).

> [19]When my anxieties multiply in my heart,
> your great comfort rejoices my being.

In v. 17 the problem lay in the fact of danger; v. 18 referred to the fear of danger as well as the fact of it. In v. 19a the focus lies on the fear (not to imply that the fear is unjustified). Now the psalm speaks not just of a passing thought but of a consuming anxiety. And as Yhwh's commitment acts to deliver, Yhwh's *comfort acts to rejoice the person.

> [20]Can the seat that brings destruction join you,
> one that shapes troublemaking by statute?
> [21]They gang together against the life of the faithful person,
> condemn the innocent blood.

The final subsection begins with another rhetorical question, paralleling v. 16. The "seats for exercising authority" (122:5), the tribunal for issuing judgments, have become the "seat of destruction," one that issues judgments that destroy the life of the innocent. The second colon makes more concrete how it does that;[24] "shaping" picks up from v. 9, with some irony. The courts use the legal system in order to cause trouble for people instead of making statutes that embody faithfulness, in keeping

24. On the history of the interpretation of this line, see Arthur Allgeier, "Psalm 93 (94),20," in *Festschrift Alfred Bertholet*, ed. Walter Baumgartner et al. (Tübingen: Mohr, 1950), 15–28.

with Ms. Wisdom's teaching (Prov. 8:15).[25] The line thus expresses the background to v. 15's vision of things being put right. It adds the point (presupposed by v. 15) that such practices mean that people who work the legal system this way can have no common cause with Yhwh. They cannot be Yhwh's partners or associates. For the verb *ḥābar*, see Gen. 14:3 and the piel in 2 Chron. 20:36; also compare the adjective and noun *ḥābēr* in Isa. 1:23; Prov. 28:24. In theory the legal system is united with Yhwh in working for *mišpāṭ* and *ṣĕdāqâ/ṣedeq*, but in practice that is not what it works for, and therefore it is not one with Yhwh.

Verse 21 gives more specificity to the way it does work. I take the verb "band together" (*gādad*) as a denominative from *gĕdûd*, which means a company. The noun has that meaning in several different connections. It can mean a company within an army, but it can carry the connotation of a marauding band or a gang operating outside the law (Hos. 6:9; 7:1). All these offer suggestive nuances for the way the psalm characterizes the senior members of the community who form its elders and therefore constitute its court. The vocation of this court is to protect the *faithful and make sure that the innocent are recognized as such. But instead they act as a hostile army or a marauding band or an outlaw gang that treats the faithful as if they were the *faithless: the verb "condemn" (*rāšaʿ* hiphil) means treat as faithless and thus find guilty. The expression "condemn the innocent blood" involves ellipse and metonymy. The OT denounces people who "condemn the faithful" (e.g., Prov. 17:15) and thus "shed innocent blood," that is, the blood of an innocent person (e.g., 106:38). The psalmist conflates and compresses these two expressions into a phrase that means "condemn the innocent to death" (NRSV).

22But Yhwh becomes a haven for me,
my God the crag where I find refuge,
23And turns their harmfulness upon them,
by their wrongdoing puts an end to them;
Yhwh our God puts an end to them.

As vv. 17–18 responded to the question in v. 16, these closing two lines respond to the question in v. 20 and its gloss in v. 21. That question, too, does not have the anxious edge of other rhetorical questions in the Psalms, because of these facts established deep within the psalmist's awareness. When people's attacks come, the psalmist has a haven. The word (*miśgāb*) comes from the verb meaning "be high up" and thus

25. The preposition is *ʿal*, which could easily mean "against statute," with the implication "against your statute" (cf. Syr). That could then imply "against the statutes given by Yhwh to Israel," or "against the statutes that comprise the order laid down by Yhwh for the world." But either of these require some reading into the text.

suggests a refuge no one can get access to. It is a high *crag that provides refuge (cf. Ps. 91).

But finding shelter will do only as a temporary and partial expedient. The person under attack needs the attackers to be dealt with so that it is possible to emerge from hiding; and proper moral order also requires that they should be put down. The closing line affirms another side to the psalmist's awareness. EVV move to future tense for v. 23, and this may be appropriate, but the Hebrew tense remains the same as v. 22, implying that if Yhwh's being a shelter is a present reality, Yhwh's bringing about proper moral order is also not postponed into the future. Yhwh is active in the world now.

Typically, however, the psalm also affirms that Yhwh acts by seeing that people's acts bear their "natural" fruit or their natural reward (v. 2). These are people seeking to do *harm to others (vv. 4, 16). There is power in their harmfulness, and what Yhwh does is let the harmfulness have its effect, but divert it so that it boomerangs on them. Thus Yhwh puts an end to them by means of their own wrongdoing (*bad; the root recurs from v. 16 and thus book-ends this final section) as it rebounds on them.

A final unexpected third colon turns v. 23 into a tricolon to close the psalm and leaves us with an emphasis on Yhwh's own action to bring about this result. Its repetition makes for a formal book-ending of the whole psalm, given the repetition in v. 1 (cf. also v. 3). It includes the only first-person plural in the psalm, though this rounds off the concern with the community in vv. 2–7, 14. The *w*-consecutives in vv. 22–23 also pair with the one at the end of vv. 2–7.

Theological Implications

Hymnwriter John Bell tells of asking a Salvadorean musician to teach him a song from his country. Bell translated the song into English but then felt the words were far too political to regard as a hymn—they were "all about corrupt judges and corrupt courts. Then I discovered it was Psalm 94." It turned out that the Psalms "had a political and economic dimension" that perhaps our singing should have.[26]

Whereas Artur Weiser suggests that there is a contrast between this prayer for God's punishment (he calls it a prayer for vengeance) and the NT's teaching on prayer,[27] the NT's attitude to such prayer is similar to the psalm's (e.g., Rev. 6:9–11). The psalm's opening description of God

26. From an interview in *Christian Century* 123/15, July 25, 2006, p. 21.
27. *Psalms*, 623.

also fits with Paul's comment about God being the avenger (1 Thess. 4:6). Theodoret likewise notes the psalm's universal applicability,[28] while Spurgeon comments on the prayer's appropriateness, quoting John Milton's poem ("Sonnet 18") that begins "Avenge, O Lord."[29]

Augustine does observe that the person who prays this prayer needs to make sure of not being liable to its judgment.[30] Modern Westerners are wise to be uneasy about the prayer; we are likely to be its victims. We need to see ourselves as the eminent and the faithless in the psalm.

It could be easy for other Christians to become disillusioned about whether Yhwh is actually involved in the world. They are then subject to three temptations. One is to reckon that God is involved only in people's religious lives. Another is to think that God will act only at the End. A third is to reckon that they are responsible for bringing about faithfulness in the world and therefore to feel too much guilt and/or to reckon that everything depends on them.

God is indeed involved in our religious lives, God's final work does belong to the End, and we are responsible to work for faithfulness in the human community. But the psalm's witness is to remind us that God is involved in our ordinary lives, that we are encouraged to look for that involvement now,[31] and that we are to live in hope of God's achieving what we cannot.

28. *Psalms*, 2:122.

29. *Treasury of David*, 142, 149.

30. *Psalms*, 460.

31. On the psalm's noneschatological nature, see Nahum M. Sarna, "How Long Shall Evil Prevail?" *Bible Review* 9/4 (1993): 38–39.

Psalm 95
Praise, Prostration, Obedience

Translation

Praise song. David's. [LXX]

1Come on, let us resound to Yhwh,
let us shout to the crag that delivers us,
2Let us meet him face to face with confession,
we will shout to him with music,
3Because Yhwh is the great God,
the great king over all gods,
4The one in whose hand[1] are the far reaches[2] of the earth,
and to whom the peaks of the mountains belong,
5The one to whom the sea belongs (he made it),
and the dry land (he shaped it).

6Come in, let us bow low, let us bow down,
let us kneel before Yhwh our maker,
7Because he is our God
and we are the people he pastures,
the sheep in his hand.[3]

1. In poetry, the *ʾăšer* is unusual and perhaps implies "in that"; so also in v. 5 (Tate, *Psalms 51–100*, 497).

2. LXX *perata* might imply *merḥaqqê* for MT *meḥqĕrê*, or might just be a paraphrase or guess for a hapax.

3. Lit. "the people of his pasture, the sheep of his hand." Syr and Tg assimilate to the more natural expressions in 79:13; 100:3 (see Barthélemy, *Psaumes*, 667–69). On the

Today, if you listen to his voice,
8do not stiffen your attitude as at Contention,
as on the day at Testing, in the wilderness,
9When[4] your ancestors tested me;
they tried me, though[5] they saw my deed.
10Forty years I would loathe the generation[6]
and say,[7] "They are a people wandering in attitude;
they have not acknowledged my ways,"
11Of whom[8] I swore in my anger:
"If they come in to my place of rest. . . ."

Interpretation

In some respects Ps. 95 is a regular praise psalm; in others it is unique. Verses 1–7c manifest the two classic features of a praise psalm, the exhortation to worship and the reasons for worship or the content of it. Indeed, it parallels Ps. 100 in moving through this sequence twice:

Exhortation (vv. 1–2)
Reasons (vv. 3–5)
Exhortation (v. 6)
Reasons (v. 7a–c)

The two sequences are not repetitions. The first urges out-loud enthusiasm. The second is also concerned with the outward expression of worship, but now in awed prostration. Further, the reasons that back up the first exhortation concern Yhwh's supreme authority as the world's creator. The reasons that back up the second concern Yhwh's special relationship with Israel. The relationship between the form of worship and its content and rationale is thus the reverse of what one might have expected, giving the section an *abb′a′* shape.[9] Distinctively,

significance of MT's text, cf. Marc Kolden, "People of His Pasture," *CurTM* 18 (1991): 122–24.

4. Or "where."

5. Vrs render "and," but *gam* can introduce a concessive clause (cf. Jer. 36:25; Neh. 6:1 [GKC 160b]), and this makes good sense here.

6. Lit. "a generation"; the following lines define what this generation was.

7. I take the *w*-consecutive to continue the time reference of the preceding verb; see examples in *IBHS* 33.3.3c rather than 33.3.3b.

8. Gunkel (*Psalmen*, 420) takes *ʾăšer* to mean "so that"; it more likely continues the usage in vv. 4–5 (also v. 9).

9. Thus Charles Bruce Riding, "Psalm 95,1–7c as a Large Chiasm," *ZAW* 88 (1996): 418.

whereas other praise psalms (such as Ps. 100) issue their exhortation in the imperative, here, while the preliminary exhortations to "come on" and "come in" (vv. 1, 6) are imperative, these lead into sequences of cohortatives (four in vv. 1–2, three in v. 6). No other praise psalm begins with cohortatives, or with the first imperative "come on" (Ps. 100 parallels "come in").

The psalm's further distinctive feature is that vv. 7d–11 then unexpectedly ricochet into becoming a very different kind of exhortation, almost the reverse of the ones in vv. 1–7c. Whereas the psalm began by urging people to make a noise, v. 7d tells them to listen. Whereas vv. 1–7c were an exhortation in which the speaker identified with the addressees ("Let us . . ."), in v. 7d the speaker stands over against the addressees. Whereas vv. 1–7c are full of confidence, v. 7d begins "if." Whereas vv. 1–7c indirectly give enthusiastic and awed praise to Yhwh, in vv. 8–12 Yhwh responds directly with straight talking and a recollection of wrathful passion.

It might be that vv. 1–7c once existed in its own right as a perfectly good praise psalm. On some occasion when it was used, Yhwh might subsequently have inspired a minister with the confrontational response, which came to be attached to the psalm. But the combination of features overlaps with that in Pss. 50 and 81, so it is just as likely that the combination of the two divergent forms of address was integral to the psalm's nature from the beginning.[10] Perhaps the same minister leads the congregation into worship in vv. 1–7c, then issues the further exhortation in vv. 7d–11. The minister's identification with the congregation in the cohortatives then prepares the way for the exhortation in which he challenges the congregation as "you." Like a prophet, the minister has to identify both with congregation and people, and in the midst of this psalm has to move from one identification to the other, from "we" identifying with them to "I" identifying with God. Verse 7d marks the transition; it introduces the confrontation but still speaks of Yhwh as "he."

The psalm gives no indication of authorship, date, or liturgical setting. It would make sense used on an occasion commemorating the exodus and the covenant sealing at Sinai,[11] but we have no direct evidence of that. Although a praise psalm may reflect worship practice, we cannot reckon to infer a liturgy from it or reckon it is the libretto for a liturgy

10. On the psalm's unity, see Marc Girard, "The Literary Structure of Psalm 95," *Theology Digest* 30 (1982): 55–58; W. S. Prinsloo, "Psalm 95," in *The Bible in Human Society*, ed. M. Daniel Carroll et al., JSOTSup 200 (J. Rogerson Festschrift; Sheffield: Sheffield Academic Press, 1995), 393–410; George W. Savron, "The Contrasting Voices of Psalm 95," *RB* 110 (2003): 17–32.

11. Mowinckel connected it with the New Year Festival and the celebration of Yhwh's kingship.

(this is not so with Christian hymns).[12] Theodoret associates it with Josiah's time, which would fit the Deuteronomic connections of vv. 7d–11,[13] but the sermonic material in vv. 7d–11 compares with Second Temple sermonic prayers such as Neh. 9 and Ezra 9.[14]

Praise song. David's. [LXX]

Heading. See glossary. MT has no heading.

95:1–5. In the first invitation to worship, and the first set of reasons, it is not explicit who speaks. The congregation might be exhorting itself, as when we sing "O come all ye faithful." But the fact that an individual exhorts the congregation in vv. 7d–11 may imply that this is also so here.

¹Come on, let us resound to Yhwh,
let us shout to the crag that delivers us,
²Let us meet him face to face with confession,
we will shout to him with music,

The first invitation comes in two parallel lines that are also internally parallel; the opening "come on" (*hālak*) thus introduces all four first-person verbs. As in English, "come on" is not a liturgical term but a verbal convention from everyday speech suggesting mutual encouragement (e.g., Gen. 37:27).[15] It "does not denote going or coming, but an appeal to respond with alacrity."[16] For *resound, the ancient versions and EVV have expressions such as "rejoice," but again the verb comes from everyday life; it has no distinctive religious connotation, nor in itself does it suggest joy rather than grief, but loud and implicitly heartfelt noise. The parallel verb likewise denotes a shout with no distinctive religious connotation (cf. LXX) and nothing that in itself suggests joy rather than anger or fear. Joy will be the implication, but in itself the verb refers to noise. Parallel to the name Yhwh is the description of Yhwh as (literally) "the *crag of our *deliverance," our delivering crag or our crag that delivers.

In turn, "let us meet him face to face" (lit. "meet his face") is not a regular term for coming before Yhwh (though Mic. 6:6 has "meet him"). Its first distinctive connotation is that it points to the initiative of the

12. Cf. Tate, *Psalms 51–100*, 498; contrast G. Henton Davies ("Psalm 95," *ZAW* 85 [1973]: 183–95), who sees it as accompanying a movement from entry to prostration to listening.

13. *Psalms*, 2:123. Cf. Terrien, *Psalms*, 672.

14. Gerstenberger, *Psalms*, 2:185.

15. Cf. DG 68.

16. Qimchi; Jeremias renders "auf" (*Königtum*, 107–8).

person who instigates the meeting, making the first move. LXX uses the verb *prophthanō*; "anticipation means performing some action before a person thought to be approaching can be sighted."[17] People do not have to wait to be specially invited into God's presence; they can assume a standing invitation. The reference to Yhwh's "face" underlines the reality of meeting; it is as if we actually see Yhwh, look into Yhwh's eyes, catch sight of Yhwh's smile. The expression will have a background in the use of divine images, which was well known in Israel as well as among its contemporaries, even though never countenanced in the OT. Indeed, paradoxically the absence of a static image makes the lively presence of Yhwh more real and living. Coming to meet Yhwh, we come with *confession, the praise that expresses itself distinctively as thanksgiving and points to what Yhwh has done for us. The parallel colon adds further reference to shouting, now in the indicative rather than cohortative, a declaration of intent rather than a self-exhortation. It then adds reference to *music. Both the noise and clamor of shouting and the beauty and order of melody contribute to Yhwh's praise. The repetition of reference to shouting underlines further that it is not enough for worship of Yhwh to be a heart attitude. One reason is that worship has to glorify Yhwh publicly. Heart worship cannot do this. Out-loud resounding and shouting is not subject to that limitation. Another reason is that we are physical beings, with voices. Heart praise is not praise by the whole person. In worship as in other aspects of life, we naturally express ourselves with cries and shouts. It is difficult to imagine how there can be praise without these.

3Because Yhwh is the great God,
the great king over all gods,
4The one in whose hand are the far reaches of the earth,
and to whom the peaks of the mountains belong,
5The one to whom the sea belongs (he made it),
and the dry land (he shaped it).

Verse 1 hinted at the reasons for praise in its titles for God, but vv. 1–2 held back from expanding on this; indeed, it disappears from v. 2. Having held back there, the psalm expands on the point here, though vv. 3–5 do otherwise than we might have expected, not in terms of Yhwh's special relationship with Israel (to which the psalm will return in v. 7) but in terms of Yhwh's sovereign authority over the whole world. As in vv. 1–2, the lines parallel each other while also being internally parallel.

The descriptions in v. 3 are implicitly polemical. Other peoples had other candidates for the description "great God" (that is, the greatest

17. Cassiodorus, *Psalms*, 2:410.

God) or the king of the gods. As is often the case, the psalm uses the term *ʾĕlōhîm* (gods) to refer to a wider range of heavenly beings than God; God is here *ʾēl*, a term the Canaanites used to describe the top god in the pantheon, whom they would not identify with Yhwh, but Israel knows Yhwh *is* the great God. Likewise, other peoples had candidates for the description "the great king": the Assyrians spoke of their king in these terms (e.g., 2 Kings 18:19, 28). Outside temple worship, it would not look as if Yhwh was the great God or the great king over the earth (as 47:2, 7 [3, 8] declare), let alone over the other gods. The psalm invites people to make those assertions in worship in the conviction that they are the actual truth, even if it did not seem that way outside worship. In our context, they remind us that Yhwh is a great God, not a manageable one.[18]

The Assyrian king could also speak in terms of sovereignty over the whole world, though he would know that was hyperbole; he would be aware that there were vast regions beyond the bounds of his mighty empire. The psalm claims for Yhwh a true sovereignty over the whole world. The far reaches (*meḥqār*) come only here, but the root suggests distant places needing some searching and exploring; thus the high mountains form a natural parallel for them. Both are in Yhwh's hand; the parallel colon puts that more prosaically in declaring that they belong to Yhwh. They are not too far or too high for Yhwh to explore.

Sea and dry land form another, more obvious natural pairing. The verse adds the basis for the declaration that such things belong to Yhwh. If you make something, it belongs to you. As usual, the OT thinks not so much in terms of the creating of matter, whose existence is presupposed, but of the shaping of matter into something. The potter does not create the clay, but shaping the clay into a vessel gives the potter rights of ownership. No one has the right to do anything with the potter's artifacts.

95:6–7c. The psalm resumes exhortation and then gives further reasons; both exhortation and reasons are briefer than those in vv. 1–5, but they by no means simply repeat what came before. Indeed, commitment or exhortation to prostration, bowing, and kneeling is relatively rare in the OT compared with reference to resounding and shouting. The congregation thus soon becomes aware that this praise psalm is making its own way. It will eventually transpire that it is beginning a transition to the focus of vv. 7d–11. The brevity of vv. 6–7c compared with vv. 1–5 links with this.

> **6**Come in, let us bow low, let us bow down,
> let us kneel before Yhwh our maker,

18. Ronald P. Byars, "Psalm 95," *Int* 56 (2002): 77–79.

Initially, the psalm becomes more encouraging rather than more challenging. "Come in" is now the verb *bōʾ*, which in contrast to "come on" is an exhortation that does suggest movement, and specifically movement into a sanctuary (96:8; 100:2, 4; Joel 1:13; Amos 4:4);[19] again it leads into three cohortatives backed up with one phrase describing Yhwh. In the balance of the exhortation (though not its brevity) it thus compares with vv. 1–2. Although "come in" suggests horizontal movement, perhaps with irony the spelling out of the invitation involves vertical movement, and none of it upward. Whereas EVV have words such as "worship," all three Hebrew words denote downward bodily movement. There is thus a considerable difference between the form of worship urged by vv. 1–2 and that urged here. The three verbs are little different in meaning over against each other; after *bow low, "bowing down" (*kāraʿ*) implies bending the legs (*keraʿ*) and "kneeling" bending the knees.[20] None suggests bending in such a way as to keep the rest of one's body upright, but rather getting down onto one's hands and knees in the manner of Muslims at prayer.[21] The effect of the words comes from their accumulation. All imply self-humbling, but like the exhortations to praise in vv. 1–2, they make clear that self-humbling is not merely a matter of what one does in one's heart.[22] We are bodies and not merely spirits, and what we do with our bodies expresses our real selves. If there is no physical self-lowering, there can hardly be inner self-lowering. Further, this worship needs to be visible to the world and thus to draw it into similar worship. The description of Yhwh as "maker" takes up the use of that verb in the previous line, but now Yhwh is "our maker" and not merely the world's.

> 7a–cBecause he is our God
> and we are the people he pastures,
> the sheep in his hand.

A tricolon comprising three parallel cola marks the end of vv. 1–7c; it could have marked the end of the entire psalm, which would have closed quite satisfactorily here. The backing for the exhortation to worship parallels that in vv. 3–5, though like the exhortation it differs in content from the earlier one. Like that backing, too, it follows up a description of Yhwh in the exhortation (in this case, that Yhwh is "our maker") but does not so much develop it as add to it in its own way and with two

19. Cf. Frank-Lothar Hossfeld, "Psalm 95," in *Neue Wege*, ed. Seybold and Zenger, 29–44 (see 35).

20. LXX has "let us weep," implying *nibkeh*, rather than "let us kneel" (*nibrĕkâ*).

21. Cf. Keel, *Symbolism*, 308–10, with illustrations.

22. Cf. Calvin, *Psalms*, 4:35; Spurgeon, *Treasury of David*, 4:166.

new frameworks. The first is the relationship between Yhwh and Israel expressed in the fact that "Yhwh is our God" and "we are his people." One might call this the covenant relationship, though the phraseology usually occurs separately from specific reference to the covenant. The phraseology does suggest a relationship that is in broad terms covenantal, and specifically mutual (covenants need not be mutual). It implies a commitment to Yhwh on Israel's behalf and a commitment to Israel on Yhwh's behalf. Self-prostration is an expression of Israel's commitment and an awed recognition of Yhwh's.

This framework then has superimposed on it a separate one, that of Yhwh as shepherd and Israel as Yhwh's flock, which nuances the mutuality of commitment. On one hand, Yhwh looks after Israel like a shepherd, ensuring that the flock is well pastured. On the other, as Yhwh's flock Israel is "in his hand," under his sovereignty, like the world as a whole (v. 4; though here the expression is construct, "the sheep of his hand"). Once more, the fact of Yhwh's pasturing and the fact of Yhwh's sovereignty would be reason for prostration.

Nevertheless the logic of vv. 6–7c is surprising in the opposite direction from that of vv. 1–2. One might have thought that self-lowering had its basis in the mighty sovereignty of Yhwh, but actually it has its basis in Yhwh's relationship with Israel.[23]

95:7d–11. The further challenge occupying the rest of the psalm is both in continuity and in discontinuity from vv. 1–7c, and in particular from vv. 6–7c. It comes as a surprise because it does not belong to the regular nature of a praise psalm. The words are prophetic in the sense of confrontational, yet sermonic in the sense that they take up "scriptural" traditions and drive home their contemporary implications. Over against the exhortation to praise, there is a solemnity about this challenge. One can imagine that the exhortation in vv. 1–7c might be easy to accept, even welcome. Yet with hindsight we may reckon that vv. 1–7c have set us up. Yes, people might be able to enthuse about showing some noisy enthusiasm. They might even be happy about some quiet submission. But the enthusiasm concerns Yhwh's being king, and such liturgical submission to Yhwh as king presupposes that it is a liturgical expression of a submission in everyday life. The last section of the psalm implicitly raises questions about the reality of the praise and prostration in vv. 1–7c. Actually the psalm has been subtly leading the people toward this challenge. It has taken it from shouting to prostration; now it takes the people on further.

7d Today, if you listen to his voice,
8 do not stiffen your attitude as at Contention,

23. Cf. Samir Massouh, "Psalm 95," *Trinity Journal* 4/1 (1983): 85–88 (see 86).

as on the day at Testing, in the wilderness,
[9]When your ancestors tested me;
they tried me, though they saw my deed.

The new section begins with a further tricolon. "Today" and "listen to his voice" recall Deuteronomy, where Moses frequently reminds people that "today" he is issuing commands to them (e.g., Deut. 4:40; 5:1; 6:6; 7:11; 8:1) and that they need to "listen" (e.g., Deut. 4:1; 5:1; 6:3, 4). The language is not precisely the same; Moses usually addresses Israel in the singular, "today" has extra prominence in the psalm, and its function may not be quite the same. In Deuteronomy, the "today" urges the generation after Sinai to see itself as standing before Yhwh's word to it in the manner of the Sinai generation, and thus it indirectly urges each succeeding generation to see that it stands before Yhwh "today." The psalm may also have in mind the recurrent "today" of worship, which by its nature collapses the distinction between the past moment when God acted and spoke and the present moment when people stand before Yhwh. The congregation is challenged to see itself as addressed by God as at Sinai or in the Plains of Moab. Its listening takes place in worship as Yhwh's great acts are proclaimed and Yhwh's expectations again laid before the people.

EVV have "if only you would listen," but if the psalm were expressing a wish of that kind, it could have used *lû* (cf. 81:13 [14]). The sentence is constructed in the manner of an ordinary conditional clause (cf. LXX; contrast 81:8 [9]; 139:19, where the context makes clear this is a wish). Deuteronomy 11:13 uses the same construction in declaring, "If you really listen to my commands that I am commanding you today . . . I will give rain." So although the new section of the psalm raises questions about the reality of the submission that the people would show in response to vv. 6–7c, it does not necessarily imply doubt as to whether the people will show submission of will as well as submission of posture.[24]

Talk of stiffening the attitude (literally, the *heart) also overlaps with Deuteronomy's thinking, though not with its exact language. Deuteronomy 10:16 uses the more common image of stiffening the neck, and Deut. 1–3 recalls the rebellions in the wilderness. The idea of stiffening the attitude or neck suggests that people made up their mind (as we say) what they were going to do and were unwilling to show any flex-

24. Cf. Calvin, *Psalms*, 4:38; Seybold, *Psalmen*, 376. MT itself implies the assumption that v. 7d is an ordinary condition, though it attaches it to the previous sentence, suggesting "we are . . . the sheep in his hand, today, if you listen to my voice" (cf. R. Schmid, "Heute, wenn ihr auf seine Stimme hört [Ps 95,7]," in *Wort, Lied und Gottesspruch*, ed. J. Schreiner [J. Ziegler Festschrift; Würzburg: Echter, 1972], 2:91–96); LXX and Jerome more plausibly link v. 7d with what follows.

ibility in their thinking when confronted by Yhwh. For the stories about events at places that came to be called Contention and Testing, see Exod. 17:1–7; Num. 20:1–13 (cf. Ps. 81:7 [8]); and Exod. 17:1–7; Deut. 6:16; 9:22, respectively.

"Tested" in v. 9 picks up the verb (*nāsâ*) lying behind the place's name (*massâ*). Testing seeks consciously or unconsciously to find out what a person is really like and how far they can be pushed (e.g., Gen. 22:1; Exod. 15:25). In the parallel colon, "try" (*bāḥan*) has similar meaning, though it is occasionally used in such a way as to draw attention to its more literal reference to testing metal to find out how genuine it is (e.g., Jer. 9:7 [6]). The line's point is that there should have been no need for Israel to test or try Yhwh, because they had been given ample indication of what Yhwh was like. They had seen that Yhwh could provide for them and protect them, so why were they not willing to submit themselves to Yhwh in life and not just in liturgy? Yhwh's "deed" may be specifically the exodus or the Red Sea deliverance, or the word may be a collective for Yhwh's deeds of deliverance and protection in general.

10 Forty years I would loathe the generation
and say, "They are a people wandering in attitude;
they have not acknowledged my ways,"
11 Of whom I swore in my anger:
"If they come in to my place of rest. . . ."

Perhaps there is another, ironic implication in v. 10. The Israelites also knew how far Yhwh could or could not be pushed. They had seen evidence of this in their own life, and in the pharaoh's, when he stiffened his attitude in relation to Yhwh. But they took no notice of that. Thus they found that Yhwh could treat them in the same way as the pharaoh, or in almost the same way. Yhwh felt free simply to abandon the pharaoh and his people. Yhwh did not feel free to abandon Israel, or at least had to give in to Moses's argument that this was not an option; the only possibility was to abandon the recalcitrant generation (Num. 14:1–25). Again, to speak of "loathing" (*qûṭ*) corresponds to Deuteronomy's way of seeing the matter but expresses it in distinctive fashion. The verb parallels the more common *śānēʾ* (EVV "hate") in suggesting an emotion, but one expressed in a consequent action, which the lines will go on to describe. The use of the yiqtol rather than the participle suggests that Yhwh was continually being provoked to loathing by the people's continual acts of rebellion, rather than that Yhwh was continuously loathing.[25]

25. *TTH* 31.

The reason for the loathing is described a little paradoxically. In one sense the problem was the inflexibility of their attitude. In another sense the problem was its flexibility. They would not focus on Yhwh, on what Yhwh expected, and on what Yhwh had done. They were like sheep (cf. 119:176), or drunks (Isa. 28:7). Perhaps the implicit sheep image picks up from v. 7c. Certainly the word "people" picks up from there. The psalm has indeed set the people up. They have been invited to claim the fact that Yhwh is their God and they are Yhwh's people. But is that a reality in their attitude? Do they behave like Yhwh's people? The wilderness wandering that Yhwh imposed on them was a kind of ratification of their inclination to wander. The second colon re-expresses the idea of wandering in the more familiar terms of not *acknowledging: they had not taken seriously the ways Yhwh acted or the ways Yhwh expected of them. The unexpected third colon underlines the point and the strong feelings.

Verse 11 goes back to the loathing and its results. It is essentially an expansion on v. 10a (if v. 10b–c were not there, vv. 10a–11 would make a fine tricolon to end the psalm; we would not miss v. 10b–c). Swearing in anger expands on loathing; the content of the oath further explains the slightly enigmatic "the generation." The form of an oath in Hebrew often leaves the consequence of nonfulfillment unstated, in the manner of v. 11b; for the complete form, see, for example, 1 Sam. 25:22.[26] Of course, God could not swear in this way, by calling for divine sanction upon nonfulfillment; the literal logic of the oath is ignored when it appears on God's lips. Again, it is Deuteronomy that speaks of Yhwh's decision at Kadesh as an angry oath-swearing (Deut. 1:34; though see Num. 14:21). Ironically, the divine oath about the land that recurs elsewhere is the oath to give Israel the land (e.g., Num. 14:16, 23; Deut. 1:8, 34). There is thus a grievous poignancy about an oath not to give this generation the land. To think of the land as Yhwh's place of rest again links with Deut. 12:9, though the context there also refers to the place of worship that Yhwh chooses.[27] Psalm 132:8, 14 is in turn more explicit about a place that is *Yhwh's* place of rest, and it refers to Jerusalem. This links with the fact that the closing colon again speaks of "coming in"; Tg assumes that v. 11 refers to the sanctuary. In v. 6 the psalm invited people to come into the place where Yhwh is, the temple. Here it warns them that they may not be able to do so if their everyday submission does not match the liturgical submission of which v. 6 spoke.

26. See GKC 149.

27. See the discussion in Georg Braulik, "Gottes Ruhe—das Land oder der Tempel?" in *Freude an der Weisung des Herrn*, ed. Haag and Hossfeld, 33–44.

Theological Implications

Psalm 95 suggests that worship has three aspects. It begins with noise. The raucous and boisterous din associated with a World Cup soccer game or a presidential inauguration is as integral to the worship of Yhwh. Yet it also invites people into the actual presence of the President, and then we find ourselves strangely subdued and bowing down before the person who controls the mightiest power in the world. But the President is strangely unimpressed by either the shouting or the bowing and wants to ask questions about how we live our lives after the celebration is over. What attitude to the President is expressed then? Thus in the psalm "we began with exulting joy: but this Psalm hath ended with great fear."[28] "On this note of negation or divine frustration the psalm ends. . . . How could a sermon or a worship liturgy close on such a verdict?"[29] It is no way to end a psalm, as Jon. 4:9–11 is no way to end a story and Mark 16:8 is no way to end a Gospel. In each case the effect of ending as it does is to put us as readers on the spot. The point is symbolized by the place of v. 7d in the psalm.[30] There is no "if" of that kind in the average praise psalm.

In its way, Heb. 3–4 makes precisely this point in its sermon on Ps. 95.[31] It draws attention to an odd assumption implied by the psalm. Whether the resting place of which it speaks is the land as a whole or the temple in particular, there is no doubt that the people invited into this worship are there. They live in the land; they are taking part in the worship. Yet it requires the people who use the psalm to see themselves as the people of the wilderness generation who had not yet entered that rest, and indeed never did so. Its implication is that they can be physically in the resting place yet not really there. Hebrews seems to be about to argue that people who come to believe in Christ therefore do come to that resting place, but typically it does not actually set up that sharp an antithesis between old covenant and new. Rather, it argues that its Christian readers are in the same position as the wilderness generation and the readers of the psalm. The note of fear, negation, and frustration confronts the church as it confronts Israel.

28. Augustine, *Psalms*, 470.

29. Gerstenberger, *Psalms*, 2:184.

30. W. M. Schniedewind, "Are We His People or Not?" *Bib* 76 (1995): 540–50 (see 546–47); with the comments of W. Dennis Tucker, "Psalm 95," *Bib* 81 (2000): 533–41.

31. On the use of the psalm in Hebrews, see, e.g., Gerhard von Rad, "There Remains Still a Rest for the People of God," in von Rad, *The Problem of the Hexateuch and Other Essays* (Edinburgh: Oliver and Boyd; New York: McGraw-Hill, 1966), 94–102; Peter E. Enns, "Creation and Re-creation," *WTJ* 55 (1993): 255–80; Harold Weiss, "*Sabbatismos* in the Epistle to the Hebrews," *CBQ* 58 (1996): 674–89.

Psalm 95 has had a prominent place near the beginning of the church's daily worship since the time of Benedict.[32] It has thus had the potential to shape that worship, though one could hardly say that this potential has been realized.

32. See Christopher J. Renz, "Come, Let Us Listen to the Voice of the Lord," *Worship* 70 (1996): 140–53 (see 140).

Psalm 96
Why Yhwh Comes

Translation

When the house was built after the exile. Song. David's. [LXX]

1Sing for Yhwh[1] a new song,
  sing for Yhwh all the earth,
  2sing for Yhwh, worship his name.
Announce from day to day his deliverance,
  3proclaim among the nations his honor,
  among all the peoples his wonders.
4Because Yhwh is great and much to be praised,
  to be revered above all gods,
  5because all the gods of the peoples are nonentities.
Whereas Yhwh is the one who made the heavens;
  6honor and majesty are before him,
  might and glory are in his sanctuary.[2]

7Bestow on Yhwh, families of the peoples,
  bestow on Yhwh honor and might,
  8bestow on Yhwh the honor of his name.

1. Verses 2b–3 imply that this song is not sung *to* Yhwh (cf. P. A. H. de Boer, "Cantate Domino," *OtSt* 21 [1981]: 55–67 [see 58], who suggests "sing *of* Yhwh").
2. First Chronicles 16:27 has "strength and joy are in his place."

Carry an offering and come into his courts,[3]
9bow down to Yhwh in his holy majesty,[4]
quake[5] before him, all the earth.
10Say among the nations, "Yhwh began to reign;[6]
yes, the world stands firm, it does not totter,
he governs the peoples with uprightness."

11The heavens are to rejoice,
the earth is to be glad,
the sea and its fullness are to thunder,[7]
12The countryside and all that is in it are to exult,
then all the trees in the forest are to resound,
13before Yhwh, because he has come.
Because he has come to exercise authority over the earth:
he exercises authority over the world in faithfulness,
over the peoples in his truthfulness.

Interpretation

This praise psalm has parallels with Pss. 93 and 95 but corresponds more closely to the template than they do. Its first section (vv. 1–6) thus comprises biddings to praise (vv. 1–3) and reasons for it (vv. 4–6); the biddings are second-person (unlike those in Ps. 95). The second section goes through the sequence again (vv. 7–9 and v. 10), though without any "because" (cf. 100:1–3); it takes up the declaration "Yhwh began to reign" (cf. 93:1), and like Ps. 95 moves on from enthusiasm to submission. The third goes through the sequence yet again (vv. 11–12 and v. 13), though here the biddings are jussive rather than imperative. Like Ps. 93, the psalm has a number of tricola with staircase parallelism; indeed, I have understood it to be composed entirely of tricola, like Ps. 100. It speaks to the entire world throughout, urging it to come to worship Yhwh, whereas Ps. 93 does not make explicit who it addresses and Ps. 95 addresses Israel. Indeed, its horizon broadens throughout: in vv. 1–6

3. For "into his courts," 1 Chron. 16:29 has "before him."

4. "His" carries over from v. 8b (cf. LXX, though it also implies *ḥaṣrat*, "court," for *hadrat*). "Their" or "your" holy array would be alien to the context.

5. LXX has a jussive, which it will repeat in v. 11 (where the jussive corresponds to MT, but the verb is different). Briggs (*Psalms*, 2:312) translates "dance" (cf. 150:4); but see Kidner, *Psalms*, 2:348.

6. The colon comes after v. 11 in 1 Chron. 16:31. A Christian gloss adds "from the tree," which came to be seen as a prophecy of the crucifixion (see, e.g., Justin Martyr, *First Apology* 41; cf. Augustine, *Psalms*, 473; Johannes Brinktrine, "'Dominus regnavit a lingo,'" *BZ* 10 [1966]: 107–9).

7. LXX has *saleuthētō* ("is to quake") as in v. 9.

Yhwh's name is to be proclaimed among the nations, in vv. 7–10 they are urged to come to the sanctuary with offerings, and in vv. 11–13 the whole creation is to rejoice in Yhwh's governance of the whole world. Its parallels with Ps. 95 continue as it changes focus toward the end until "in the last stanza it finally discloses its point."[8]

It gives no indication of date or setting. In vv. 7–9 it has phrases in common with Ps. 29, which is usually reckoned to be a relatively old psalm upon which Ps. 96 would then be dependent. Its opening colon corresponds to one in Isa. 42:10 and phrases in vv. 11–12 are partially similar to Isa. 44:23; many of its themes also recur in Isa. 40–55 (for instance, the vision for the nations' recognition of Yhwh and the polemic against other deities). But these similarities suggest the prophet's utilization of phrases familiar from worship rather than the psalm's dependence on the prophet (that opening colon also recurs in Pss. 98:1; 149:1, and its closing tricolon is almost repeated in Ps. 98). Its stress on the everyday nature of the worship appropriate to Yhwh does not support the idea that the psalm was used on just one occasion in the year.

When the house was built after the exile. Song. David's. [LXX]

Heading. See glossary. MT has no heading, though 1 Chron. 16 makes Ps. 96 part of a confession David appointed the Asaphites to sing when he brought the covenant chest to Jerusalem. The text there is a variant on the Psalter's, lacking vv. 1a, 2a, 10c, 13c–d, and one of the occurrences of "he has come" in v. 13; I have noted other major variants from the Chronicles text, but there are many smaller variants.[9]

96:1–6. The first biddings and their reasons.

1Sing for Yhwh a new song,
  sing for Yhwh all the earth,
  2sing for Yhwh, worship his name.
Announce from day to day his deliverance,
  3proclaim among the nations his honor,
  among all the peoples his wonders.

The opening threefold exhortation to sing contrasts with the opening emphasis on noise in Ps. 95. The very first colon makes the psalm begin by setting up suspense, because it is not clear why a new song is needed (even the subsequent reference to deliverance and wonders does not require that Yhwh has done something new). The second colon hints at an answer as it goes beyond the first in introducing the psalm's emphasis

8. Fokkelman, *Major Poems*, 3:187.
9. See BHS.

on the whole world's joining in this celebration. It will eventually become clear that "the earth" embraces the natural world as well as the human world. The implication might then be that for the nations a new song is appropriate because they are now becoming aware of facts about Yhwh that they had not known before. Praising Yhwh will mean singing a song they have not sung previously, a new song that will reflect their "new orientation."[10] It is an exhortation the psalms repeat a number of times (and they never say "Let's sing a golden oldie").[11] The new phrase in the third colon provides a further verb, *worship, which implies bending the knee and thus suggests a more solemn side to this praise; it thereby anticipates vv. 8b–9. And it refers to Yhwh's *name; it is indeed God as revealed to Israel that the world is challenged to celebrate.

In vv. 2b–3 the parallel verbs move from sound to content, from music to words. While "proclaim" (*sāpar* piel) often appears in the Psalms to denote declaring the things Yhwh has done, this is its only occurrence in the imperative; compare Isa. 43:26 (with some irony when compared with this occurrence). "Announce" (*bāsar* piel) likewise comes in the imperative only here, but it is a key verb in Isa. 40–55 (40:9; 41:27; 52:7). By implication it suggests good news (cf. LXX *euangelizesthe*), though in itself it is of neutral significance like English "announce."

The move to content is also indicated by these verbs' three parallel objects, *deliverance, *honor, and wonders. The key way one praises God is by narrating what God has done, and it is this that the nations need to hear.[12] The second and third of the three prepositional phrases again emphasize the worldwide worship the psalm looks for; in light of that, the significance of "from day to day," or day after day, is to highlight how this worship deserves to embrace all time as well as all space and all peoples. Yhwh's deliverance is usually something benefiting Israel, though this deliverance can have positive significance for all the world; but there is no reference to Israel in this psalm, and the expression may rather suggest directly that Yhwh is the world's deliverer as well as Israel's. Implicitly that was so when Yhwh put down the Egyptians and the Canaanites (cf. Ps. 47 with its invitation to all the nations to join in worship); it was more directly so when Yhwh put down Babylon.

4Because Yhwh is great and much to be praised,
to be revered above all gods,
5because all the gods of the peoples are nonentities.

10. Cf. Brueggemann, *Message of the Psalms*, 144. See further Maria Russ, "Singt Ihm einen neuen Gesang!" in *Wort Gottes in der Zeit*, ed. Helmut Feld and Josef Nolte (Düsseldorf: Patmos, 1973), 15–21.

11. I owe this observation to Rusty Harding of All Saints Episcopal Church, Pasadena.

12. Cf. Jeremias, *Königtum*, 125.

Whereas Yhwh is the one who made the heavens;
[6]honor and majesty are before him,
might and glory are in his sanctuary.

As usual, the reasons for the worship and recognition are at the same time their content. It must be so; there cannot be reasons for acknowledging Yhwh beyond the facts about who Yhwh is. This means that the formal distinction between vv. 1–3 and 4–6 is belied by a substantial continuity. The psalm continues to speak of Yhwh's honor. Conversely, v. 4 fudges the distinction between exhortation and reasons in the other direction, by declaring that Yhwh is to be *praised and to be *revered.[13] The two gerundives combine wordless enthusiasm and an attitude of submission in the manner of Ps. 95:1–7c, with the same implication that enthusiasm is important but is not enough. In the parallelism, as "revere" goes beyond "praise," "above all gods" goes beyond "much," and v. 5a takes the point further. It also takes up v. 3b. Yhwh's greatness needs proclaiming among the peoples because of the feeble nature of the gods they have. For Yhwh's greatness, compare 95:3; the second and third cola in vv. 4–5a also correspond to that line as they spell out the significance of this greatness. The word "nonentities" (*ʾĕlîlîm*) is doubly attractive in this context (cf. 97:7): it looks so like the word for a proper God (*ʾĕlōhîm*), but in itself it apparently designates something as ineffective, worthless, and futile (Job 13:4; Zech. 11:17). Aq has "false," Sym "unreal," Tg "deceptions," and Jerome "images" (LXX's "demons" is more questionable). As is usual in the Bible, the psalm does not reckon we should be respectful of other people's religions. It is more important to honor the real God.

Despite the double "because," vv. 4–5a say little positive to support the exhortations in vv. 1–3. Positive content does now come in vv. 5b–6. Its logic corresponds to that of Pss. 93 and 95: Yhwh is the creator, specifically the creator of the heavens. The second and third cola move on from that. There in the heavens honor and majesty are before Yhwh; there in Yhwh's sanctuary in the heavens might and glory are present.[14] As elsewhere, aspects of Yhwh's being are personified (e.g., 42:8 [9]; 43:3), standing (as it were) before Yhwh in the sanctuary in the heavens, like the deities in other people's pantheons.[15]

13. On the assumption that these participles are gerundive (so LXX, Jerome; also DG 110, on the basis of word order). NJPS has "much acclaimed . . . held in awe," but it is odd to argue that people should sing to Yhwh and proclaim Yhwh *because* Yhwh is (already) praised and revered.

14. The two cola are thus closely parallel: might and strength pair, as do majesty and glory, then "before him" and "in his sanctuary" (cf. Calvin, *Psalms*, 4:52).

15. Qimchi (*Midrash on Psalms*, 137) sees them as the stars, ministering angels.

96:7–9. The psalm's second cycle of exhortation and reasoning functions (like 100:1–3) without using the "because" form, and thus again realistically fudges the distinction between content and reasoning. Like Ps. 95, it also subtly moves on from liturgical recognition (enthusiastic, then respectful) to recognition in life.

7Bestow on Yhwh, families of the peoples,
bestow on Yhwh honor and might,
8bestow on Yhwh the honor of his name.
Carry an offering and come into his courts,
9bow down to Yhwh in his holy majesty,
quake before him, all the earth.

For "bestow," compare Ps. 29:1–2, which addressed the gods; here it addresses their devotees. "Families of the peoples" might suggest the peoples as belonging to different ethnic groups, but it may be simply a way of emphasizing an appeal to the multitude of nations,[16] among whom proclamation is to be made and whose gods are nonentities. The gods have nothing, and therefore have nothing to bestow; but the peoples have honor and might they can bestow. As in Ps. 29, the verb (*yāhab*) does not mean merely ascribe or recognize, but give (cf. 60:11 [13]; 108:12 [13]). Of course Yhwh does have honor and might, which do need recognizing, as the psalm has affirmed. But the peoples themselves have some honor and might, and they are not to hold on to them. They bestow the honor of Yhwh's *name by bestowing honor on Yhwh's name, the honor due to or worthy of his name.[17]

The second tricolon confirms the substantial content of this "bestowing," expressed in bringing an offering before Yhwh into the courts of the earthly sanctuary. Yhwh is like an imperial ruler whom other peoples come to recognize as sovereign, abandoning the lords they previously recognized. They come to this emperor's courts with an "offering" (*minḥâ*), a word that usefully doubles as both a term for a gift to Yhwh (141:2) and for tribute offered to a sovereign (72:10). In the sovereign's courts, then, the subjects prostrate themselves before the emperor (again, cf. 95:6) in his majesty; in this case, it is a *holy majesty, God's majesty. The parallel with the movement in Ps. 95 continues in the third colon. To press the prepositions, literally the peoples quake "from before" Yhwh. The invitation to come in is thus accompanied by a caution about pulling back. It is not a mixed message but a proper recognition that confidence and reticence are both appropriate to a relationship with Yhwh. "Quake" (*ḥîl*) is a powerful word to describe this diffidence: it suggests

16. Cf. Jerome, *Homilies*, 1:186.
17. Cf. LXX, Jerome; JM 129g.

shuddering, or classically the agonized twisting of a woman giving birth (cf. 90:2). Yhwh is one who makes the earth shake (29:8; cf. 77:16 [17]; 97:4; 114:7); this psalm urges the earth to choose to do so.

> 10Say among the nations, "Yhwh began to reign;
> yes, the world stands firm, it does not totter,
> he governs the peoples with uprightness."

In the implicit reasons for the bestowing, giving, bowing, and quaking, the prescribed words in the first two cola repeat exactly from 93:1–2, with the variant. The third colon works out the implications of Yhwh's reigning in a different direction from Pss. 29, 47, or 93. Coming at this point, the first two declarations do not have the emphasis they have at the beginning of Ps. 93. The emphasis lies rather on the new comment in the third colon. Yhwh's reign undergirds not only Israel's position and the cosmos's security but also world history, and it does so in an upright way. One could translate the yiqtols in v. 10b–c as future, but this would leave the psalm, its author, and its singers stranded between a past and a future neither of which they experience. The psalm's enthusiasm (to be expressed even more fervently in vv. 11–12) suggests they do not merely look back on what Yhwh once did and forward to what Yhwh will one day do. They know Yhwh is involved in the world in the present in events such as the fall of Assyria and then of Babylon. "Governs" is *dîn*, a synonym of *šāpaṭ* ("exercise *authority"), which describes a king's task.

96:11–13. We cry, "Tell us more" than v. 10c succinctly said. Instead, the psalm builds suspense by once more commissioning joy and resounding (vv. 11–13a) before once more following that with the reasons, which do reaffirm v. 10 (v. 13b–d). It again fudges the distinction between the content of and reasons for recognition, this time by being more generous with "because" than one might have expected, letting such reasoning anticipate its way back into the end of the exhortation (v. 13a).

> 11The heavens are to rejoice,
> the earth is to be glad,
> the sea and its fullness are to thunder,
> 12The countryside and all that is in it are to exult,
> then all the trees in the forest are to resound,
> 13abefore Yhwh, because he has come.

The third exhortation gives voice to the world in its capacity to worship as its elements shine, wave, and crash. "The worshipping parties in Psalms 96–97 form a community united in celebration," a community that unites humanity and nature.[18] People who worship Yhwh and seek to draw other people into worship might well seek to free creation to offer this worship, rather than making this harder by our treatment of creation. It may be in part simply for rhetorical variation that vv. 11–12 uniquely use third-person rather than second-person formulations. In another sense, speaking about the world in the third person also keeps the psalm's human addressees in focus.

The second tricolon moves to the features of the land mass. Open country and forest complement each other, the "then" marking the end of this list of worshippers in vv. 11–12 and preparing the way for the transition to the account of Yhwh's coming.[19] The contents of the fields are their wheat and grass, waving in exultation like a congregation in worship, even as the trees that constitute the forest *resound like the congregation. They do so not "from before Yhwh," recoiling (v. 9),[20] but simply "before Yhwh," like Yhwh's own might and majesty (v. 6). And they come before Yhwh on the basis of Yhwh's having come to them, though not merely to be present with them: see v. 13b–d.

> **13b**Because he has come to exercise authority over the earth:
> he exercises authority over the world in faithfulness,
> over the peoples in his truthfulness.

The opening repetition is an instance of anadiplosis, or terrace pattern, whereby v. 13b–d makes a link with what precedes yet also creates tension.[21] The psalm is coming to its point, so the action is slowed up. In form the verb *bāʾ* could be a participle, suggesting "he is coming" (cf. LXX) and referring to a future event. But we have seen that the psalm more likely refers to the reality of Yhwh's rule in the present, based on having already asserted kingly authority. Yhwh has come (cf. Jerome). If we then translate the yiqtol verb in v. 13c as future (cf. LXX, Jerome), this must not imply a postponing of that rule, as if Yhwh were not exercising *authority in the present. It must follow on Yhwh's having come that Yhwh will indeed rule in the present over the *tēbēl*, the human world, as well as the earth, the *ʾereṣ*, with the characteristic qualities of *faithfulness and *truthfulness. Earth, world, and peoples ruled by Yhwh

18. Norman C. Habel and Geraldine Avent, "Rescuing Earth from a Storm God," in *Earth Story*, ed. Habel, 42–50 (see 50). See also C. Houtman, "De jubelzang van de struiken der wildernis in Psalm 96:12b," in *Loven en Geloven* (N. H. Ridderbos Festschrift; Amsterdam: Ton Bolland, 1975), 151–74; J. du Preez, "Reading Three 'Enthronement Psalms' from an Ecological Perspective," *Missionalia* 19 (1991): 122–30.

19. Cf. Jeremias, *Königtum*, 122.

20. Though 1 Chron. 16:33 has the "from."

21. Cf. Watson, *Classical Hebrew Poetry*, 208–10.

completes a bracket with earth, nations, and peoples called to sing and proclaim Yhwh's deeds (vv. 1–3).

Theological Implications

Who speaks in this psalm, who is addressed, and to what end? Of course, the opening makes clear that the psalm directly addresses earth and its peoples, inviting the whole world in its day to come to worship Yhwh. This longing and possibility does not await Christ's coming. But then there is a formal oddity about the relationship between the two opening tricola as the earth is both the singer (v.1b) and the recipient of the proclamation (v. 3). Verses 11–13 also bring out the question who actually hears the psalm, because there the heavens and the earth are spoken of, not spoken to. It is Israel in its worship that hears the psalm's declaration that the creation is to rejoice, and its bidding to the earth and its peoples in vv. 1–10. There is no immediate way in which the nations themselves hear it. So what is the point of Israel overhearing the psalm's exhortation to the nations?

First, it adds to the magnitude of the praise that the psalm offers Yhwh. The God Israel worships is the only real God, so that all the nations ought to acknowledge this God. By implication, Israel itself ought also to do so, rather than being attracted by other peoples' gods. Conversely, this both heightens and reduces Israel's own significance. It heightens the significance of Yhwh's deliverance of Israel; this is also designed to speak to the nations. It reduces Israel's significance, because Yhwh is not satisfied with Israel's acknowledgment; Yhwh has an eye on the whole world. Perhaps it implies a missionary commission to Israel. When Jews in the Dispersion came to commend Yhwh to the Gentile world, consciously or unconsciously, deliberately or incidentally, then they were living out the implications of this psalm. It helps us understand the Jewish people's enthusiasm about spreading knowledge of the true God.[22] Third, a fortiori, if Yhwh intends to rule the world with uprightness, faithfulness, and truthfulness, then Yhwh intends to see that Israel's destiny is worked out with these features. In the Assyrian or Babylonian or Persian period this was not obviously happening. The psalm declares that it must happen. Moments when Yhwh puts down an empire are moments when Yhwh comes to rule the earth with uprightness.

22. Contrast Spurgeon's comments on Jewish exclusiveness (*Treasury of David*, 4:180).

Psalm 97

Yhwh Began to Reign: Earth Is to Rejoice

Translation

Composition. David's. When his land was established. [LXX]

[1]Yhwh began to reign;
earth is to be glad,
many foreign coasts are to rejoice.

[2]Cloud and darkness are around him,
faithfulness and authority are the base of his throne.
[3]Fire goes before him;
it burnt up his foes around.[1]
[4]His lightning flashes lit up the world;
the earth saw and quaked.
[5]Mountains, like wax, melted before Yhwh,
before the Lord of all the earth.
[6]The heavens proclaimed his faithfulness,
all the peoples saw his honor.[2]

1. Perhaps "around him" (the reading of some late MSS), assuming that the prep. in the parallel colon carries over.

2. I take the *w*-qatal as coordinating or conjunctive (with the same time reference as the verb in v. 6a); cf. Max Rogland, *Alleged Non-past Uses of* Qatal *in Classical Hebrew*

7All those who serve an image come to shame,
those who exult in nonentities;
all the gods bowed down to him.[3]
8Zion listened and rejoiced,
the cities of Judah were glad,
for your authoritative decisions, Yhwh.
9Because you are Yhwh,
the Most High over all the earth,
you went right up above all gods.
10People dedicated to Yhwh, be against wrong,
the one who guards the lives of the people committed to him;
from the hand of the faithless he rescues them.

11Light was sown for the faithful,
and for the upright of heart, joy.
12Rejoice in Yhwh, faithful people,
confess his holy renown.

Interpretation

Beneath its surface Ps. 97 corresponds to patterns in other praise psalms that comprise summons to praise and reasons for praise, but it has an innovative and distinctive formal structure. Its opening and closing verses (vv. 1 and 11–12) issue the summons to rejoicing based on a declaration about Yhwh. They thus incorporate those two features of a praise psalm, though there is no "because" and the verses work in the opposite order to the regular one (the declaration about Yhwh comes first, the summons second). The opening summons comes in the jussive and the closing one in the imperative. This corresponds to the fact that the opening summons concerns the earth and far shores, which are not present as the psalm is used, whereas the closing summons concerns Yhwh's people, who are present. And the opening declaration concerns Yhwh's relationship with the whole world, while the closing declaration concerns how life works out for Yhwh's people.

Verses 2–6 then follow up that opening declaration about Yhwh having begun to reign, expanding on its implications for the world as a whole and providing further reasons for its rejoicing. Verses 7–10, on the other hand, speak of how things work out between Israel and Yhwh, with some contrast over against the rest of the world. Following on this, the

(Assen: Van Gorcum, 2003), 31. But it might be consequential (cf. *IBHS* 33.2.3c), "all the peoples see," which would lead into v. 7.

3. The opening verb can be taken as jussive, and the closing verb can be parsed as impv. (LXX, Jerome), but qatal better fits the context.

closing declaration functions to summarize the significance of that and to provide further reason for Israel's rejoicing.

With NJPS I read the opening line as a tricolon; vv. 2–6 are then bicola (though v. 5a is rather long, and one might read v. 5 as a tricolon). I then read vv. 7–10 as tricola, like Pss. 96 and 100, while there is no doubt that vv. 11–12 are bicola. In subject, then, vv. 1–6 and vv. 7–12 belong together; but in this aspect of form, v. 1 belongs with vv. 7–10 and vv. 2–6 belong with vv. 11–12. This feature of the prosody hooks the whole together.

The psalm has many phrases in common with other passages in the Psalms and in the Prophets, in particular with Pss. 96–99.[4] If the psalm is mostly the borrower, this might have made it a banal compilation of stereotyped expressions, but rather it thus sets itself in the context of Israel's living traditions. This is perhaps one of the moves that enables it to expound the nature of God's reign with distinctive depth and comprehensiveness.[5]

There is a variety of theories about when it was written, how it was used in liturgy, and what earlier forms it may have taken.[6] We do not have the information that would allow us to come to conclusions about these questions.

Composition. David's. When his land was established. [LXX]

Heading. See glossary. MT has no heading. The establishing of David's land might be its restoring to David after troubles in his lifetime,[7] or its restoration after the exile in fulfillment of Isa. 49:8.[8]

97:1. The opening declaration and invitation to the world.

1Yhwh began to reign;
earth is to be glad,
many foreign coasts are to rejoice.

The psalm opens like Ps. 93 but then strikes off in a distinctive direction in speaking of the appropriate response to its declaration. Further, v. 1a also corresponds to words in 96:10, while v. 1b corresponds to 96:11b, and "are to rejoice" in v. 1c is the verb in 96:11a. So v. 1 as a whole might be seen as a kind of summary of Ps. 96, introducing Ps. 97

4. See Zenger, *The God of Israel and the Nations*, 175. But it is doubtful whether the links imply simple dependence.

5. So Weiser, *Psalms*, 631–32.

6. See, e.g., Lipiński, *Royauté de Yahwé*, 173–275; Seybold, *Psalmen*, 383.

7. So Jerome, *Homilies*, 1:191.

8. Kirkpatrick, *Psalms*, 579.

as in continuity with it.[9] The only new feature here is the "foreign coasts" (*'iyyîm*)—not merely "islands" (LXX, Jerome). The expression recalls Isa. 40–66 (e.g., 42:10–12), though also Ps. 72:10. Literally it suggests countries on the other side of the Mediterranean, such as Greece, but here it points to places as far away as can be imagined, the ends of the earth.[10] It emphasizes the broadness of horizon in Ps. 96. The link with Isa. 40–66 might suggest that the moment when Yhwh began to reign is the fall of Babylon rather than the fall of Egypt at the Red Sea or the fall of Canaan when Yhwh arrived there (contrast Ps. 47).

The psalm's opening thus has a resumptive aspect. What more, then, is going to be said now about this reign of Yhwh, and about why the whole world should rejoice in response to it?

97:2–6. Five bicola give a partial answer, with a different focus from that of Pss. 93 or 96 or 47,[11] one more reminiscent of Ps. 18, though in the context in the Psalter it might be seen "to portray the coming of God mentioned in Ps 96:13."[12] Whereas Ps. 93 sees Yhwh's reign as established at creation, Ps. 97 follows Ps. 96 in seeing that kingship as asserted in history. Verse 2 constitutes a thematic statement; vv. 3–5 expand on v. 2a, then v. 6 expands on v. 2b.

2Cloud and darkness are around him,
faithfulness and authority are the base of his throne.

Paradoxically, the description of Yhwh as surrounded by cloud and darkness indicates that it really is the case that Yhwh appeared, because it signifies that this real presence had the protective shield around it that was necessary if it was not to devastate the people it was designed to help and encourage. The cloud (*'ānān*) is most familiar as the sign of Yhwh's presence that also constitutes this protective shield (e.g., Exod. 19:9, 16; 24:15–16). Darkness (*'ărāpel*) can be another way of speaking of it (Exod. 20:21; Deut. 4:11; 5:22 [19]). The two come together in the description of Yhwh's coming in Joel 2:2; Zeph. 1:15. There, that coming lies in the imminent future, and it is very bad news. Here, it has already happened (an eschatological perspective would have to be read into the psalm, not read out of it),[13] and it is reason for rejoicing.

9. So Koenen, *Jahwe wird kommen*, 71.

10. Cf. Keel, *Symbolism*, 22.

11. Lipiński (*Royauté de Yahwé*, 173) thus sees the "epiphanic character" of the psalm as its distinguishing feature over against the other kingship psalms; he goes on at length (173–275) to study it against its Middle Eastern as well as its OT background.

12. McCann, "Psalms," 1068.

13. See, e.g., *Midrash on Psalms*, 141.

The second colon explains how Yhwh's devastating coming could be reason for rejoicing; it corresponds to Ps. 89:14 [15]. The basis of Yhwh's reign is *authority exercised in *faithfulness. The second colon thus utilizes a strikingly different metaphor, speaking of the basis for the security of the king's reign rather than the frightening magnificence of the king's appearance. And its content is socio-ethical rather than phenomenal. The line as a whole is thus extraordinarily dense.

3Fire goes before him;
it burnt up his foes around.
4His lightning flashes lit up the world;
the earth saw and quaked.
5Mountains, like wax, melted before Yhwh,
before the Lord of all the earth.

The yiqtol verb in v. 3a is surprising; if there were other evidence the psalm was oriented to the future, one might take this verb that way.[14] But in the context of vv. 1–6, and of the psalm as a whole, more likely it refers to the general truth about Yhwh (like the noun clauses in v. 2), or it is a vivid way of speaking about the past (as in Ps. 18). In Ps. 18:8–9 [9–10] fire issued from Yhwh's mouth even as darkness stood under Yhwh's feet (cf. also 50:3). Here fire consumes Yhwh's foes rather than the king's foes, yet that is evidently good news for the earth and the foreign coasts. There is a sense in which they are in the same position as Israel and its king; the wiping out of Yhwh's foes in expression of Yhwh's faithful exercise of authority is the wiping out of oppressors and wrongdoers.

The fire is reflected in lightning. Again in the fashion of Ps. 18, Yhwh's coming has the drama and power of a storm with its thunder and lightning that seem to make the earth shake (Ps. 18:14 [15]). The words of v. 4a almost exactly correspond to 77:18b [19b], while those of v. 4b are close to 77:16b [17b], except that there it is the waters that quake.

Verse 5a recalls 68:2 [3] but also Mic. 1:4, again with the contrast that Micah speaks of a coming manifestation of Yhwh threatening to Judah, while the psalm speaks of an actual manifestation that is good news for the world. Literally, the mountains have melted "from before" Yhwh (see 96:9). The long line brings to a close this phenomenal or metaphorical description of Yhwh's appearing. It underlines the point with which the psalm started: the description in vv. 3–5 shows how the one who asserted monarchic authority is indeed sovereign, over the whole earth (that phrase recurs in, for instance, Mic. 4:13).

14. Cf. Kraus, *Psalms 60–150*, 259.

[6]The heavens proclaimed his faithfulness,
all the peoples saw his honor.

In turn, v. 6 returns to the moral aspect of Yhwh's appearing. This is highlighted by the words recalling Ps. 19:1 [2], yet also contrasting with them. There is no mention of *faithfulness in the opening of Ps. 19; it is the purely phenomenological aspect to the heavens that there impresses the psalmist. Here the psalm also recalls Ps. 50:6, which does include reference to Yhwh's faithfulness; in the present context this reference resumes the motif from v. 2b. In what sense have the heavens proclaimed Yhwh's faithfulness? Tg takes "the heavens" as a personification, "the aides in the heavens." I take this as a summary of the implications of Ps. 18. When Yhwh appears in the spectacular way described there, or in vv. 3–5 here, this is not merely fireworks. It is flashing of the actual weapons that fireworks symbolize, and these are weapons exercised for the sake of faithfulness. So it is Yhwh's faithfulness that the phenomena proclaim, and that all the peoples therefore see, in fulfillment of 96:3. And by a feedback process, it turns out that Yhwh's *honor lies not merely in fireworks but in faithfulness.

97:7–10. The psalm ricochets in a different direction, in form (the tricola), in content (now there is bad news for the nations, though even that bad news is disguised good news), and in intertextual context.

[7]All those who serve an image come to shame,
those who exult in nonentities;
all the gods bowed down to him.

The Decalogue prohibits Israel's making or serving images or bowing down to them, though it does not imply that the nations are to be faulted for doing so. Yet the prophets do declare that the nations are going to be shamed by their images (Isa. 42:17; 44:9–11; Jer. 10:14), because they and the gods they represent are empty and deceptive nonentities (cf. Ps. 96:5). They give no one anything truly to exult in (*praise). The coup de grace of this argument is the declaration that even these nonentities, "in a kind of 'self-undivinizing,'"[15] have the sense to recognize who they themselves need to bow down to (see the story in 1 Sam. 5).

[8]Zion listened and rejoiced,
the cities of Judah were glad,
for your authoritative decisions, Yhwh.

15. Hossfeld and Zenger, *Psalms 2*, 475.

That exulting contrasts with another kind that goes on in Zion when Yhwh's acts are proclaimed and Zion listens. Then "Mount Zion rejoices, the cities of Judah are glad for your authoritative decisions" (Ps. 48:11 [12]; the previous line speaks of this as praise or exulting, *tĕhillâ*). That psalm celebrates an occasion or occasions when Yhwh asserted kingly authority in defeating people such as the Canaanites or the Assyrians. This psalm likewise may have its mind on a particular manifestation of Yhwh's activity, which means Zion has already rejoiced and been glad in the way the world is invited to (v. 1). *Authoritative decisions is the plural of the word for authority in v. 2; there, authority accompanied faithfulness, as it often does; here, "authoritative decisions" follows on the reference to faithfulness in v. 6. Yhwh's faithfulness and authority have been expressed in that activity of Yhwh in Judah's experience. In light of the logic of other passages, this suggests that the psalm has in mind acts that directly benefited Judah, such as the defeat of Canaan or Assyria or Babylon, but ones that are also implicitly good news for other peoples. The acts have already happened, and Judah has heard about them and rejoiced in them. It has not seen them (contrast v. 6 and Ps. 48), perhaps because they happened a long time ago so that it hears about them in worship, or perhaps because they happened far away (for instance, in Babylon: see Isa. 52:7–8) and not before the walls of Jerusalem.[16] The psalm knows that they are also significant for the entire world that is under the superpower's domination. So the rejoicing that has happened in Judah can also happen elsewhere.

9Because you are Yhwh,
the Most High over all the earth,
you went right up above all gods.

The opening two cola adapt Ps. 83:18 [19], whose context also speaks about the destruction and shaming of Israel's attackers, as well as of their coming to acknowledge Yhwh. The slightly illogical two sides to that vision thus correspond to this. In turn the verbal expression in v. 9c corresponds to that in 47:9d [10d], a psalm that earlier declares how Yhwh has begun to reign over the nations. To speak of Yhwh going up is another way of referring to that taking a position of kingly power. But in keeping with the present context, v. 9c relates this to Yhwh's being on high in relation to all the gods, those nonentities (cf. 96:4–5). Yhwh's acts in relation to Egypt or Canaan or Philistia or Assyria or Babylon mean that Yhwh asserted authority over these peoples' gods.

16. Cf. Kirkpatrick, *Psalms*, 581.

> [10]People dedicated to Yhwh, be against wrong,
> the one who guards the lives of the people committed to him;
> from the hand of the faithless he rescues them.

But the background to much of the OT's polemic against other gods and their images is the attractiveness to Israel of other gods and their images. Whereas *dedicating oneself to Yhwh is a basic expectation of Israel (see esp. Deut. 6:5), Israel often dedicated itself to strangers (e.g., Jer. 2:25; 8:2). Conversely, although the challenge to be *against wrong, to repudiate wrong, comes in Amos 5:15 with reference to wrongdoing in society, in the present context the wrong that needs repudiating is the wrong of getting involved with these other deities (cf. Jer. 3:2, 5; 7:30). MT makes a surprising transition to imperative in connection with this repudiation (though imperative will be resumed in v. 12). Syr implies a statement,[17] "people dedicated to Yhwh are against wrong" (or vice versa), which fits the context better,[18] but its reading is a thin basis for emending the text.

Here, the grounds for dedication to Yhwh and repudiation of wrong lie in the facts. Israel is not challenged simply to make a choice between two equally impressive objects but to choose between *ʾĕlîlîm* and *ʾĕlōhîm*. The real God is one who has the capacity to guard and rescue. That is the fact that has been proved by the events the psalm celebrates. Yhwh does not leave the people *committed to him to the power of *faithless people such as the Canaanites, Philistines, Assyrians, and Babylonians. The verbs in the parallel cola in v. 10b–c book-end it so as to mirror the point the cola make; they stand guard at either end of the cola keeping Yhwh's people embraced and keeping the faithless under control.

97:11–12. The psalm closes by turning to another invitation to rejoice on the basis of what Yhwh has done, which pairs with the one that opened the psalm.

> [11]Light was sown for the faithful,
> and for the upright of heart, joy.
> [12]Rejoice in Yhwh, faithful people,
> confess his holy renown.

As night and gloom stand for disaster, light stands for life, deliverance, and blessing (e.g., 27:1; 36:9 [10]; 112:4; in their context). It is not

17. I.e., it implies *śōnĕʾê* for MT *śinʾû*. BHS follows this but also hypothesizes *ʾōhēb* for MT *ʾōhĕbê*, generating "Yhwh is dedicated to people who are against wrong."

18. Cf. Fokkelman, *Major Poems*, 2:254–55; oddly, Barthélemy (*Psaumes*, 673) suggests it is not very coherent.

directly a figure for joy, but when light is sown, joy is its harvest.[19] Thus it is a reason for joy on the part of the *faithful and upright.[20] To speak of light being sown (*zārua'*) is a unique image.[21] The context on either side makes it clear enough that Yhwh is the hidden agent behind the passive verb.

The closing verse begins by making explicit a call for joy in Yhwh, on the assumption that Yhwh is indeed the unnamed agent in v. 11. A bidding to make *confession is a standard element for the beginning of a psalm (e.g., 92:1 [2]; 95:2), but it can also be the note on which a psalm ends. EVV have "his holy name," but the word is not *šēm* but *zēker*, the *holy name as something people make mention of and thus celebrate in worship (cf. 6:5 [6]). The first colon corresponds fairly closely to 32:11a; the second corresponds exactly to 30:4b [5b].

Theological Implications

Yhwh reigns. Therefore Pharaoh or Sennacherib or Nebuchadnezzar or Cyrus or Caesar or Constantine or the Pope or George III or Hitler or the current British prime minister or the current American president do not reign. Yhwh reigns. Therefore Saul or David or Solomon or Rehoboam or Jeroboam or Hezekiah or Manasseh or Josiah do not reign. Yhwh reigns. Therefore the people of Britain or America do not reign.

The fact that Yhwh reigns is a worrying fact for people who think they reign. It means, among other things, that "prayer is a subversive activity" because "it involves a more or less open act of defiance against any claim of ultimacy by the current regime."[22] But for people whom others pretend to reign over, the fact that Yhwh reigns is good news. It is noteworthy that the themes of joy/gladness and faithfulness are "unifying features" of Ps. 97.[23]

19. Weiser, *Psalms*, 635.

20. Here the two nouns book-end the line and the two *l* expressions stand together at its center.

21. "Has dawned" (LXX, Jerome, Tg, Syr, implying *zāraḥ*; cf. 112:4) is a more predictable, easier reading.

22. Peterson, *Where Your Treasure Is*, 65.

23. McCann, "Psalms," 1068.

Psalm 98

God of Israel, God of the World

Translation

Composition.

1 Sing to Yhwh a new song,
   because he has done wonders;
His right hand has effected deliverance for him,
   yes, his holy arm.
2 Yhwh has made known his deliverance,
   before the eyes of the nations,
   he has revealed his faithfulness.
3 He has been mindful of his commitment[1] and his truthfulness
   to the household of Israel.
All earth's extremities
   have seen our God's deliverance.

4 Shout to Yhwh, all the earth,
   break out, resound, make music.
5 Make music for Yhwh with the lyre,
   with the lyre and the sound of music.[2]
6 With bugles and the sound of the horn,
   shout before the king, Yhwh.

1. LXX adds "to Jacob," improving the parallelism in v. 3a–b.
2. Or "with melodious voice."

7The sea and its fullness are to thunder,
the world and the beings that live in it.
8The rivers—they are to clap hands all together,
the mountains—they are to resound 9before Yhwh.[3]
Because he has come to exercise authority over the earth:
he exercises authority over the world in faithfulness,
over the peoples in uprightness.

Interpretation

Like Ps. 96 (whose opening and closing it substantially repeats), this psalm follows the template for a praise psalm whereby one first urges praise of Yhwh then gives the content or reasons for that praise. Further, like Ps. 100 it goes through that sequence twice. Thus v. 1a is a challenge to praise, vv. 1b–3 the reasons or content; then vv. 4–9a are a further challenge to praise, v. 9b–d the reasons or content. One aspect of the psalm's distinctiveness appears in the balance between these. Verses 1–3 comprise a brief challenge backed up by a very substantial *kî* clause. Verses 4–9 comprise a very substantial challenge backed up by a brief *kî* clause. This *abb′a′* feature of the emphasis in the psalm[4] parallels the *abb′a′* structure of Ps. 97.

Verses 1–3 refer to the nations in the third person and apparently address Israel, the "our" of the last colon. In contrast, vv. 4–9 (like Ps. 96) address the whole earth, these same nations. In keeping with that contrast, vv. 1b–3 refer to Yhwh's commitment and truthfulness that have already been exercised in bringing about deliverance for Israel, while v. 9b–d refers to Yhwh's authority and faithfulness that are being or are to be exercised on behalf of the peoples of the world. All the finite verbs in vv. 1–3 are qatal, while v. 9b–d speaks of what Yhwh has come to do but apparently has not yet done, of what Yhwh does or will do (yiqtol). In this way the psalm makes explicit in a new way an implication of other psalms, that Yhwh's acts of deliverance for Israel (vv. 1–3) are good news for other peoples (vv. 4–9) because they reveal the kind of God Yhwh is and the way Yhwh also acts for other peoples. Of course this addressing of the world happens only within the psalm. The psalm presumably belongs in the context of Israelite worship, so that in the first instance

3. MT links "together" with the second colon and "before Yhwh" with the next verse, but "together" usually links with the words that precede (esp. in Isa. 40–55) and the arrangement puts "before Yhwh" in an odd position. As laid out here, the lines are neatly parallel (noun–jussive verb–adverbial expression). LXX lacks "before Yhwh." LXX^{A} adds "because he has come"; the line then corresponds more precisely to Ps. 96.

4. Cf. Auffret, *Merveilles à nos yeux*, 75.

its rhetorical address to the world in vv. 4–6 (like its jussive declaration about the natural world in vv. 7–8) functions to glorify Yhwh there, to build up Israel's faith in Yhwh, and to widen its expectations.

The psalm has many phrases in common with other psalms and also with Isa. 40–55. While this might imply direct dependence of one on another, at least as likely it reflects common dependence on a shared tradition of praise.[5] As in Ps. 97, it is the utilization of this tradition, embodied also in other psalms and in the Prophets, that gives the psalm its power. Comparison with Ps. 96 highlights the prominence here of qatal clauses that put the focus on the deeds of deliverance Yhwh has done for Israel. There are no references here to God's acts of creation, nor are there noun clauses describing what God always is, as in 96:1–4. Comparison with Isa. 40–55 suggests the psalm may refer to the same historical events as those chapters reflect, so that Yhwh's coming (v. 9) is the act that lies behind the fall of Babylon,[6] though the psalm may refer to the broader chain of events that Israel's story celebrated: the Red Sea deliverance, the conquest of Canaan, the rescue from Assyria, and the fall of Babylon.

Composition.

Heading. See glossary. Only this psalm is entitled simply by this word. LXX adds "David's."

98:1–3. An exhortation to Israel to praise, with its reasons.

1Sing to Yhwh a new song,
because he has done wonders;
His right hand has effected deliverance for him,
yes, his holy arm.
2Yhwh has made known his deliverance,
before the eyes of the nations,
he has revealed his faithfulness.

So as Ps. 97 begins by taking up the opening of Ps. 93, this psalm begins by taking up the opening of Ps. 96. It then immediately segues into the reasons for or the content of the song it commissions, restating themes of Ps. 96, Yhwh's wonders and *deliverance (cf. 96:2–3). Again like Ps. 96, it also speaks in the language of Isa. 40–55. It is those chapters that emphasize Yhwh's right hand and Yhwh's holy arm as the means of

5. Cf. Weiser, *Psalms*, 636–37.

6. See also Bernhard Gosse, "Le Psaume 98 et la rédaction d'ensemble du livre d'Isaïe," *BN* 86 (1997): 29–30. Tremper Longman III ("Psalm 98," *JETS* 27 [1984]: 267–74) calls it a divine warrior song celebrating the victory Yhwh has just won.

deliverance (Isa. 41:10; 52:10). Reference to Yhwh's right hand (usually a person's more powerful hand) and to Yhwh's arm underline the might of what Yhwh has done. Qualifying Yhwh's arm as *holy further emphasizes that: this is no mere human arm, but a supernatural one. Yhwh's hand and arm are pictured as semi-independent of Yhwh (like the honor and majesty, might and glory of Ps. 96), so that they achieve things on Yhwh's behalf (cf. Isa. 51:9–11). It is as if Yhwh is in bondage as long as Israel is, but now at last Yhwh's hand and arm have terminated that.[7]

Yhwh has thus "made known his deliverance." The first colon in v. 2 slows down the rhetoric, summing up what preceded. Only at the beginning of the middle colon does the point of the line emerge. Wonders and deliverance, and the *faithfulness the line goes on to speak of, were all made known and revealed "before the eyes of the nations"; the phrase applies to both cola on either side. That revelation happened at the Red Sea, at the conquest of the land, in the rescue from Assyria, and in the deliverance from Babylon. These were public events that the nations could witness, as the OT periodically notes. But the phrase "before the eyes of the nations" again especially recalls Isa. 40–55 (see 52:10) and may suggest that it is the last of these events that the psalm especially refers to.

3He has been mindful of his commitment and his truthfulness
to the household of Israel.
All earth's extremities
have seen our God's deliverance.

It might just be possible to reckon that vv. 1–2 referred to acts whereby Yhwh delivered the nations themselves, but v. 3 makes explicit that this would be a misreading. The acts of deliverance issued from Yhwh's *commitment and *truthfulness to Israel, and from Yhwh's being *mindful of these. Yhwh thought about acts of commitment and truthfulness in the past (e.g., in delivering Israel from the Egyptians) and resolved to continue these (e.g., in delivering Israel from the Babylonians).

The second line also makes the point; it almost exactly corresponds to Isa. 52:10b. The acts are *our* God's acts of deliverance. Yet all earth's extremities saw them. And therefore (Isa. 45:22 adds) all earth's extremities can look to Yhwh for deliverance. This is the invitation that "we" are in a position to issue.

98:4–9. A second exhortation to praise, with its reasons. The implications of vv. 1b–3 for the whole world are surprising and breathtaking. The resumptive exhortation and its length reflect this.

7. *Midrash on Psalms*, 143.

[4]Shout to Yhwh, all the earth,
break out, resound, make music.
[5]Make music to Yhwh with the lyre,
with the lyre and the sound of music.
[6]With bugles and the sound of the horn,
shout before the king, Yhwh.

The psalm continues to parallel the language of Isa. 40–55 and of other psalms. “Shout” belongs in both (Pss. 47:1 [2]; 95:1–2; 100:1; Isa. 44:23), as does *resound (Pss. 33:1; 95:1; Isa. 44:23; 52:9). The exhortation to “break out” comes otherwise only in Isa. 40–55 (e.g., 44:23; 52:9); in contrast, “make music” is Psalms language (e.g., 47:6–7 [7–8]), and so is the precise exhortation to “all the earth” (e.g., 96:1, 9; 100:1). Whereas vv. 1–3 did not specify their addressees, though the “our” implies that they issued their exhortation to Israel, vv. 4–6 explicitly address the world.

The second line takes up the last verb of v. 4 in order to nuance it, but it does not do a huge amount of nuancing. As well as repeating that verb, in the second colon it repeats the noun *lyre instead of adding the harp (contrast 92:3 [4]; 108:2 [3]), and then adds a noun from that same verb “make music.” The line thus achieves its effect by repetition, as psalms sometimes do.

In contrast, v. 6 introduces variation in the sentence order and in the actual words.[8] In referring to bugles, the psalm ventures out in a distinctive direction. “Bugles” are straight metal instruments (EVV “trumpets” is misleading), ideally made from silver (Num. 10:2), and used both to get people’s attention or to signal something and as part of a musical ensemble. They seem to represent technological developments from the monarchic period, though most references to them relate to the Second Temple period.[9] Horns are “natural” instruments, made from the actual horn of an animal. They do appear in Pss. 47:5 [6]; 81:3 [4]; 150:3. They are more an instrument for gaining people’s attention than a strictly musical instrument. Trumpets and horns would be used to announce the arrival of a human king; thus they are also blown before King Yhwh. When the verb “shout” recurs, it perhaps refers to the actual “blast” of the instruments.

8. Verses 4–6 are parallel: each of the first two verses begins with an imperative verb, then has “to Yhwh,” then a qualifying phrase, with each second colon expanding on the first. The third then reverses the parallelism, with the qualifying phrases occupying the first colon, the single verb (the same as began v. 4) opening the second, and an alternative expression instead of “to Yhwh.” This has the effect of providing closure to vv. 4–6, which forms a subsection.

9. Cf. Keel, *Symbolism*, 342–43.

[7]The sea and its fullness are to thunder,
the world and the beings that live in it.
[8]The rivers—they are to clap hands all together,
the mountains—they are to resound [9a]before Yhwh.

"Earth" in vv. 4–6 referred to the human world; the psalm now turns to the rest of the created world. As is often the case, the world's praise embraces not just humanity but the whole creation. Verse 7a recurs from 96:11 (cf. also Isa. 42:10). Verse 7b corresponds to Ps. 24:1. Perhaps there, and in the context here, the colon refers not just to the world's human inhabitants but also to all its creatures (cf. 89:11 [12]).[10]

In 93:3 the rivers "lift up their voice" and thunder or roar or shout, while in Isa. 55:12 it is trees that "clap hands." But rivers can clap hands as they tumble over rocks, throwing up spurts of spray that intermingle with one another like hands joining. Likewise the mountains resound (cf. 89:12 [13]) as the wind roars over them and through their forests (cf. 96:12, which adds in v. 13 "before Yhwh, because he has come," as here). In the parallelism "all together" and "before Yhwh" apply to both rivers and mountains.

[9b]Because he has come to exercise authority over the earth:
he exercises authority over the world in faithfulness,
over the peoples in uprightness.

The final line recurs from the close of Ps. 96 (see comment), except that uprightness replaces faithfulness. In the context of this psalm with its qatal verbs, it is clearer that *bāʾ* is qatal rather than a participle.[11] After all the buildup of suspense through vv. 4–9, it at last makes explicit why the world has reason to sing a new song. Those acts of Yhwh on behalf of Israel have implications for the whole world. Putting down peoples such as the Egyptians, the Canaanites, the Assyrians, and especially the Babylonians is also good news for them. It means that Yhwh exercises *authority in a *faithful way in their lives too.

Theological Implications

The God of Israel is the God of the world; the God of the world is the God of Israel. On the one hand, Yhwh is not merely the God of Israel, never has been, and never will be. While Yhwh has been irrevocably

10. Cf. Briggs, *Psalms*, 2:308.
11. So Jeremias, *Königtum*, 135.

committed to Israel and to the Jewish people from the beginning of Israel's story, and they gain immeasurably from that, blessing Israel is not the extent of Yhwh's purpose. Yhwh's blessing of Israel has implications for the world. On the other hand, Yhwh never relates to the world independently of relating to Israel. The church relates to God on the basis of the fact that Yhwh had been at work in Israel; "salvation is from the Jews" (John 4:22).[12] The church can never grow out of or escape its indebtedness to the Jewish people. Yhwh's relationship with Israel remains the model for Yhwh's relationship with the church.

Beyond that, the God of the nations is the God of all creation. Israel's praise and the church's praise are not the only worship that the earth offers Yhwh. In an "ecology of praise"[13] the whole creation cannot but echo the human world's enthusiasm for what Yhwh has done. Yhwh made it so that it can visibly and audibly do that. When we see creation moving and sounding, we see and hear its praise.

12. Cf. Kraus, *Psalms 60–150*, 266.

13. Ellen F. Davis, "Rejoicing in Judgment," *Int* 46 (1992): 171–75 (see 174).

Psalm 99

Holy Name, Holy Place, Holy God

Translation

David's. Composition. [4QPs[k]; also LXX, transposed]

1Yhwh began to reign—the peoples tremble;
the one who sits on the cherubim—the earth shakes.
2Yhwh is great in Zion,
he is high[1] over all the peoples.
3They are to confess your name, great and to be revered[2]
(it is holy),
4and the might of a king dedicated to exercising authority.

You are the one who established uprightness;
authority and faithfulness in Jacob—
you are the one who put them into effect.
5Lift high Yhwh our God,
bow low to his footstool;
it is holy.[3]

6Moses and Aaron among his priests
and Samuel among those calling his name,

1. The *hû'* implies that *rām* is a ptc. rather than a qatal.
2. In prose, one would expect the article on each of these words if they are adjectives qualifying "your name," but poetry need not observe these rules (cf. GKC 126h).
3. Cf. v. 3; or "he is holy" (cf. v. 9).

They were people calling to Yhwh, and he himself would answer them;
7in the pillar of cloud he would speak to them.
They kept his declarations, the statute he gave them;
8Yhwh our God, you yourself answered them.
You were a God who carried things for them,
and one who exacted redress for their deeds.
9Lift high Yhwh our God,
bow low to his holy mountain,
because Yhwh our God is holy.

Interpretation

Psalm 99 parallels Ps. 97 in once again beginning with the declaration that "Yhwh began to reign" and also in working with the structure of a praise psalm (summons to praise and reasons for praise) in a distinctive way. As in Ps. 97, in effect the reasons for praise or the content of praise comes first (vv. 1–2, 4b–d, 6–8),[4] followed by the summons in the jussive or imperative (vv. 3–4a, 5, 9). The psalm thus goes through this sequence three times, like Ps. 96. In a separate pattern, it moves between speaking about Yhwh (vv. 1–2, 5–7, 9) and speaking to Yhwh (vv. 3–4, 8). The overlapping nature of these two patterns serves to hold the psalm together.[5] In speaking about Yhwh, it apparently addresses the Israelite community; the community may be addressing itself, or a worship leader may be addressing it. The psalm is also rather distinctive in the language and images with which it works out the praise psalm pattern. It lacks the links with Isa. 40–55 that appear in Ps. 98, but it has many points of contact with Exod. 15:1–18.[6] The unusual reference to Moses and Aaron coheres with this. As a whole, then, the psalm also deserves comparing with the way Ps. 47 talks about Yhwh's reign as implemented in Israel's history.

The psalm has been dated in the preexilic, exilic, and postexilic periods. As with many psalms, scholarly study makes no progress in coming to a consensus about the question.

David's. Composition. [4QPs^{k}; also LXX, transposed]

4. LXX and Jerome take the verbs in v. 1 as jussive rather than yiqtol, in keeping with the nature of a praise psalm; cf. 97:1; also 96:11–12; 98:7–8. This fits well. But the second verb, *tānûṭ*, is unequivocally a yiqtol (jussive would be *tānōṭ*), and this implies that the first (where the form of yiqtol and jussive are the same) is as well.

5. On the psalm's rhetorical features, see Auffret, *Merveilles à nos yeux*, 77–86; idem, "Dans la colonne de nuée il leur parlait," *BN* 114 (2002): 5–10.

6. Cf. McCann, "Psalms," 1074–75.

Heading. See glossary. MT has no title.

99:1–4a. Yhwh's greatness, and the challenge this puts before the world.

> [1]Yhwh began to reign—the peoples tremble;
> the one who sits on the cherubim—the earth shakes.

The psalm begins like 97:1, the question as usual arising, "What assertion of Yhwh's kingship does it refer to?" Here, the reference to the people's trembling in connection with Yhwh's reigning parallels Exod. 15:15, 18 and suggests reference to Yhwh's victory over Egypt and over Canaan (cf. also Deut. 2:25). This fits with subsequent references to Yhwh's dwelling on Zion and to Moses, Aaron, and Samuel, though not to creation or to later events.

Cherubim are winged beings of partly animal and partly human appearance. Yhwh sits on heavenly cherubim when transported about the cosmos to take action on earth (Ps. 80:1 [2]; cf. 18:10 [11]) and also sits enthroned above the cherubim in the sanctuary (1 Sam. 4:4; 2 Sam. 6:2). The image is modeled on a human king's throne, which might be supported by representations of such figures. This could also generate a picture of Yhwh sitting on a cherubim throne in the heavens,[7] which fits the parallelism, though it cannot be divorced from the fact that Yhwh reigns in and from Mount Zion (cf. v. 2). The parallelism also suggests that "earth" refers to its peoples, who shake with fear.[8]

The opening reference to the peoples and the earth corresponds to the close of Ps. 98. There is a superficial contrast between the response to Yhwh this psalm looks for and the more enthusiastic one in Ps. 98,[9] but in the Psalms there is no clash between rejoicing in Yhwh and being awed by Yhwh.

> [2]Yhwh is great in Zion,
> he is high over all the peoples.

Yhwh becomes great in Zion as the climax to the story toward which Exod. 15 points, taking the covenant chest into Canaan and, after various adventures, to Jerusalem. Yhwh reigning as the great king here relates not to other deities (as in Pss. 95 and 96) but to other peoples. Enthroned in Zion, Yhwh is in a position definitively to stand over the peoples of the region (cf. Pss. 2; 47).

7. See Hossfeld and Zenger, *Psalms 2*, 487; Keel, *Symbolism*, 167–71.

8. The meaning of the hapax *nûṭ* on the only occasion it occurs in *DTT*.

9. Cf. Calvin, *Psalms*, 4:74.

[3]They are to confess your name, great and to be revered,
(it is holy),
[4a]and the might of a king dedicated to exercising authority.

The pattern of a praise psalm as it appears here makes it likely that the verb is jussive rather than yiqtol (cf. 97:1). It then fits for *nôrāʾ* to have gerundive significance, as in 96:4; Exod. 15:11. The fact that Yhwh (and thus Yhwh's *name) is great and to be revered indicates that Yhwh (and Yhwh's name) is *holy in the sense of distinctive, supernatural, transcendent, heavenly. Like *ʾĕlōhîm*, "holy" is a word that applies to other heavenly beings, yet it comes to apply in a distinctive way to Yhwh because Yhwh's deity is so distinctive.

MT's verse division associates the third colon with the next line, but it is very difficult to construe there. There are no indications in the textual tradition of an alternative reading for v. 4a, nor any convincing emendations.[10] It is noteworthy that it begins with *w*, which would make for an odd beginning to a full line and all the more an odd beginning to a section. But attached to v. 3 it constitutes another object for the verb "confess."[11] It is easy to see why v. 4a became dissociated from v. 3: in light of vv. 5 and 9, "he is holy" looks like a refrain at the end of a section. But refrains, or repeated expressions (as it would be better to call them),[12] work in very varying ways in Hebrew poetry (see, e.g., Pss. 46; 49; 57; 62), and in this example vv. 3b, 5c, and 9c are not identical. They are not liturgical refrains, a choir or congregational response to what precedes. They function rhetorically rather than liturgically. As Hebrew poetry uses repetition in a way foreign to Western practice (as in 98:4–5), so it sometimes avoids exact repetition in a way foreign to Western practice. So in the context of v. 3, at its first occurrence "it is holy" refers to Yhwh's name. It recurs in v. 5c, signaling closure to vv. 4b–5, yet with a different reference. A similar phrase then occurs in a fuller formulation in v. 9c, closing off the psalm as a whole; its reference may again be different. Further, *rûm* ("be high") recurs two cola before v. 3b, and two cola before v. 5c, and two cola before v. 9c. So the rhetorical pattern is more complex than merely involving that brief phrase. And v. 4a rounds off the opening section, reformulating the psalm's opening line. It is as the one who began to reign at the Red Sea and in conquering Canaan and who sits enthroned on the cherubim that Yhwh is the king *dedicated to the

10. See, e.g., J. H. Eaton, "Proposals in Psalm xcix and cxix," *VT* 18 (1968): 555–58 (see 555–57).

11. Cf. J. Schiller, "Bemerkungen zur Analyse und Interpretation von Psalm 99," *BN* 91 (1998): 77–89 (see 80); Tate, *Psalms 51–100*, 526–27.

12. Cf. Howard's comments, *Structure of Psalms 93–100*, 88.

exercise of *authority, committed to acting as the world's sovereign. So the peoples would be wise to confess this king's might: the term recurs from 93:1; 96:6–7, as well as from Exod. 15.

99:4b–5. The second section restates what Yhwh did and reformulates the response appropriate to that.

> 4bYou are the one who established uprightness;
> authority and faithfulness in Jacob—
> you are the one who put them into effect.

The new statement of what Yhwh did moves on from the Red Sea to Yhwh's activity at Sinai and/or in Canaan. The length of v. 4c–d suggests we see the whole line as a tricolon, though v. 4c–d as a whole forms a lengthy parallel to v. 4b. It makes explicit an aspect of what Yhwh was doing in asserting monarchic authority over Egypt and Canaan. This was not merely an exercise of power but an act implementing uprightness and faithfulness; Egypt and Canaan flouted these and needed to be put down. Beyond that restoring of moral balance and social order in the world, Yhwh also exercised kingship in Jacob by establishing it as a community shaped by uprightness and (to put it another way) by the *faithful exercise of *authority, the qualities of Yhwh's own being (v. 4a). These qualities are embodied in the regimen Yhwh established within the people at Sinai and in settling the community in the land. Yhwh is not just about kingship, loftiness, holiness, and authority but also about uprightness and faithfulness. And Yhwh is not just about a presence in Zion but also about an activity establishing such uprightness and faithfulness in the community.[13] There is an irony about the line as it offers an implicit invitation to self-examination.

> 5Lift high Yhwh our God,
> bow low to his footstool;
> it is holy.

More unequivocally v. 5 indicates the response this activity of Yhwh requires as it (presumably) addresses the Israelite community. Yhwh *is* high over all peoples (*rām*, v. 2); therefore Israel is to lift Yhwh high (*rûm* polel). That very act is expressed in *bowing low, a symbolic expression of self-lowering in everyday life. Like Yhwh's cherubim throne, Yhwh's footstool takes two forms. The earth is Yhwh's footstool (Isa. 66:1); worship means recognizing the majesty of the God exalted in the whole cosmos. But Jerusalem or the sanctuary is also Yhwh's footstool (132:7; Lam. 2:1). So people are urged to come to bow down in worship at that *holy place.

13. Cf. Brueggemann, *Message of the Psalms*, 148.

99:6–9. The third section looks to the past from a different angle before again coming back to the appropriate response. The sudden reference to Moses, Aaron, and Samuel is surprising, but these leaders were key to Yhwh's establishing uprightness and the faithful exercise of authority in Jacob. Tg reckons that at v. 8b–c the section segues to speaking of the people as a whole,[14] but there is no positive indication of such a transition, and thus I have taken the whole of vv. 6–8 to refer to these leaders and taken the lines as four bicola rather than two tricola and a bicolon.[15]

> **6**Moses and Aaron among his priests
> and Samuel among those calling his name,
> They were people calling to Yhwh, and he himself would answer them;
> **7a**in the pillar of cloud he would speak to them.

In the OT story, Moses was the means of establishing uprightness by being *the* mediator of Yhwh's original teaching to Israel. Aaron did so and the priests continue to do so by virtue of the fact that teaching is their ongoing vocation. Moses was not a priest, though he fulfilled some priestly roles,[16] and it may be that "among his priests" applies only to Aaron.[17] Samuel likewise fulfilled some priestly roles while never being called a priest, but as a prophet he was involved in teaching the people in such a way as to assert Yhwh's kingly authority and to further uprightness and faithfulness (see 1 Sam. 8–12). The expression "calling his *name" is unusual and might refer to "calling on his name" (so EVV; cf. Lam. 3:55) but more likely refers to the proclaiming of Yhwh's name that priests, Levites, and prophets did when they were teaching. It is what Moses does in Deut. 32:3.

But an important role as intercessors for the people was played by Moses and the priests and by Samuel and the ongoing line of prophets (e.g., Exod. 32–33; 1 Sam. 12:23); Moses and Samuel appear together in this connection in Jer. 15:1.[18] They were thus involved in calling *to* Yhwh (the expression used of Samuel in 1 Sam. 12:17–18) and seeing Yhwh answer. The dynamics of the people's life thus involved their leaders calling out to Yhwh on the people's behalf, and Yhwh answering.

14. Kirkpatrick (*Psalms*, 586) finds this transition at v. 6c.

15. Cf. Seybold, *Psalmen*, 387; Loretz, *Ugarit-Texte*, 363.

16. See esp. C. Hauret, "Moïse, était-il prêtre?" *Bib* 40 (1959): 509–21.

17. GKC 119i takes the *b* to denote "Moses and Aaron *as* his priests," while John H. Eaton takes it to suggest "the most eminent of his priests" (see *Psalms of the Way and the Kingdom*, JSOTSup 199 [Sheffield: Sheffield Academic Press, 1995], 115).

18. Mark Leuchter ("The Literary Strata and Narrative Sources of Psalm xcix," *VT* 55 [2005]: 20–38 [see 27–29]) indeed argues that Aaron is a redactional addition to the psalm.

The speaking in v. 7a likely denotes Yhwh's speaking to give instruction of one kind or another (e.g., Num. 9:15–23; 12:9; Deut. 31:14–21). Thus the two lines as a whole refer both to teaching and to prayer.

> [7b]They kept his declarations, the statute he gave them;
> [8a]Yhwh our God, you yourself answered them.

Yhwh's *declarations, too, are strictly the instructions Yhwh issued in Moses's time (e.g., Deut. 6:17, 20), though "statute" can be used more broadly (e.g., Josh. 24:25; Judg. 11:39; 1 Sam. 30:25), and Samuel does lay down Yhwh's "decision" (*mišpāṭ*) concerning the monarchy (1 Sam. 10:25). In all these, it was the entire people that Yhwh was concerned to address, but there are no affirmations in the OT that they ever responded and countless declarations that they did not. More likely vv. 7b–8a affirm that leaders such as Moses, Aaron, and Samuel did follow Yhwh's word, and that this played a key part in Yhwh's being prepared to live in the calling-answering relationship that v. 6 described.

> [8b]You were a God who carried things for them,
> and one who exacted redress for their deeds.

Yet Moses, priests, and prophets were also people who from time to time fell short of Yhwh's expectations and needed Yhwh to "carry" things for them (cf. Yhwh's self-description in Exod. 34:6–7). EVV have "forgive," but here as commonly elsewhere (e.g., Pss. 32:5; 85:2 [3]) the word is *nāśā'*, the ordinary word for "carry." Forgiveness means bearing the burden of people's wrongdoing, bearing the cost oneself, instead of making them bear it.

But Yhwh is also one who exacts *redress for their deeds. The expression summarizes the negative side to Yhwh's words in Exod. 34:6–7 (with some subtlety, using *nāqam* where Exod. 34:7 uses *nāqâ*). One can see that Yhwh did this for people such as Moses and Aaron. The psalm no more resolves the tension between the two aspects of Yhwh's action than Yhwh does at Sinai.[19]

> [9]Lift high Yhwh our God,
> bow low to his holy mountain,
> because Yhwh our God is holy.

Typically, the summons to praise, following up vv. 6–8 in the closing line, in turn reprises v. 5 with some variation. Yhwh's footstool becomes

19. Sym offers the elegant alternative of having Yhwh "exact redress for their abuses," for the deeds done to them. See further R. N. Whybray, "'Their Wrongdoings' in Psalm 99,8," *ZAW* 81 (1969): 237–39; C. F. Whitley, "Psalm 99,8," *ZAW* 85 (1973): 227–30.

Yhwh's *holy mountain (cf. 2:6; 3:4; 15:1; 43:3; 48:1 [2]). The final colon makes its point more fully to bring closure to the psalm, in effect itself restating the first two cola. The title "Yhwh our God," which came in vv. 5 and 8, thus recurs twice more here (only seven times in the rest of the Psalter).[20]

Theological Implications

Psalm 99 suggests three aspects to the nature of holiness and three reasons for acknowledging the holiness of Yhwh's name, dwelling, and person. Verses 1–3a make clear that holiness is fundamentally about the distinctive authority and majesty of Yhwh. Yhwh has asserted kingly authority in Israel's history, and even the world is destined to acknowledge this. Yhwh's name as the expression of Yhwh's being is therefore to be acknowledged as holy. It would be unwise to slight it. Second, vv. 4b–5 add that Yhwh is not merely about authority and power but about uprightness and faithfulness. These two qualities are also embodied in Israel's history, and specifically in Yhwh's coming to dwell on Zion. Yhwh's dwelling place there is thus also to be honored as holy. Third, vv. 6–9 reflect the fact that this story is not one in which a purpose is being pursued by a holy but therefore rather remote God. It is a story in which Yhwh stays in ongoing dialogue with people such as Moses, Aaron, and Samuel. They call, Yhwh answers; Yhwh speaks, they respond; they fail, and Yhwh maybe lives with this or maybe disciplines them. In light of that, only in the final colon does the psalm unequivocally declare that "Yhwh our God is holy."

20. Gerstenberger, *Psalms*, 2:200.

Psalm 100

Summons to All the Earth

Translation

Composition. For confession.

1Shout to Yhwh, all the earth,
  2serve Yhwh with joy,
  come before him with resounding.
3Acknowledge that Yhwh—he is God;
  he himself made us and we are his,[1]
  his people, the flock he pastures.

4Come into his gates with confession,
  into his courts with praise;
  confess him, worship his name.
5Because Yhwh is good,
  his commitment is forever,
  his truthfulness is to generation after generation.

1. So Q, reading *wĕlô* (cf. Tg, Jerome, Aq); truly but less plausibly in the context, K has *wl'*, "and not [we ourselves]" (cf. LXX, Syr, Sym). It seems unlikely that the word would be understood as asseverative (so Joe O. Lewis, "An Asseverative לא in Psalm 100:3?" *JBL* 86 [1967]: 216).

Interpretation

This further praise psalm again goes through its sequence twice (cf. 95:1–7a), each time urging people to worship (vv. 1–2, 4) and then declaring the content of or reason for the worship (vv. 3, 5). Like Ps. 96, it comprises all tricola. While it does not explicitly refer to Yhwh as king, speaking of Yhwh as shepherd comes close to that, and in its contents Ps. 100 in other respects follows well on Pss. 93–100,[2] even if it may not have been composed in association with them.[3] Its invitation is addressed to the entire world; we would be prosaic to understand it as a hymn related to literal entry to the temple, and more prosaic to think of the two sections as representing two stages in such a procession.

The psalm has had a prominent place in synagogue worship and thus in daily Christian worship. McCann calls Ps. 100 "the banner hymn of the Reformed tradition," at least in the metrical version, "All People That on Earth Do Dwell"; while Gen. 1–2 could not have generated the Westminster Confession's definition of humanity's chief end as "to glorify God and enjoy him forever," Ps. 100 could have done so.[4] But Charles Lee Feinberg sees its invitation as relating only to the millennial temple.[5]

Composition. For confession.

Heading. See glossary. The term "confession" corresponds to the words in v. 4. Tg renders *tôdâ* "thank-offering." The theme of the psalm does not especially suggest that the psalm relates to the thank-offering; it is a praise psalm, not a thanksgiving psalm. Now headings often reflect later usage rather than a psalm's intrinsic nature, and the psalm's reference to *tôdâ* in the broader sense of praise for God's great past acts toward Israel might have led to its use in connection with *tôdâ* in the narrower sense of God's recent acts for the individual or the community. But a general statement like that in v. 5 could be entirely in place when someone brought a thank-offering; worshippers could take for granted that a particular experience of Yhwh's commitment illustrates the general point made by the psalm.

[1]Shout to Yhwh, all the earth,
[2]serve Yhwh with joy,
come before him with resounding.
[3]Acknowledge that Yhwh—he is God;

2. But see Beat Weber's comments, "Psalm 100," *BN* 91 (1998): 90–97.
3. But see Koenen, *Jahwe wird kommen*, 76–78.
4. "Psalms," 1079, 1080.
5. "'Old Hundredth,'" *BSac* 100 (1946): 53–66.

he himself made us and we are his,
his people, the flock he pastures.

100:1–3. The psalm begins with the same words as 98:4 (cf. also 47:1 [2]); this link supports the idea that it refers to all the *earth*, not all the *land*.[6] It parallels that with a more distinctive bidding to "serve" Yhwh (cf. 2:11; 102:22 [23]). In English, talk about church *services* is a dead metaphor, and that is partly so when the OT uses *ʿābad*. Other religions involved their adherents looking after the gods' physical needs (cf. *ʿābad* in 97:7); OT faith does not. Yet the verb does point to the fact that worshipping Yhwh involves a serious submission of the whole self. It involves the words of the mouth (v. 1a) and the feelings of the heart ("with joy"; it is a strange kind of servitude that is offered with joy).[7] But it is not confined to words and feelings. The verb implies that worship is done for God's sake and not for ours; servants serve their master, not themselves. And the fact that serving God mostly takes place outside worship also hints that there needs to be some coherence between what happens in worship and what happens outside. As much is indicated by the context of the only other psalmic exhortation to serve Yhwh, in 2:11. It is also suggested by Joshua's repeated talk of "service" in a worship context in Josh. 24.[8] Humanity was created to serve God, and we do that with all of our lives. The third colon adds further familiar expressions, "come before him" (cf. Pss. 95:6; 96:8) and *resounding (e.g., 95:1; 98:4). It continues to be striking that this invitation to come into Yhwh's presence with enthusiasm is issued not to Israel (as in Ps. 95) but to the world (as in Pss. 96; 98).

By its nature such worship involves *acknowledgment of who Yhwh is. The imperative is somewhat admonitory;[9] this fits the fact that it is addressed to all the earth, which does not at the moment acknowledge Yhwh. The combination of joy and admonition compares with the exhortation to foreign kings in 2:11. "Yhwh—he is God" is a Deuteronomic assertion (Deut. 4:35, 39) that recurs in the Elijah story (1 Kings 18:39). The psalmist will assume the existence of other gods in the sense of lesser heavenly beings (cf. Pss. 95:3; 96:4; 97:7, 9), but "Yhwh—he is God" is therefore stark and absolute. In reality there is no other being who can properly be designated by the word *ʾĕlōhîm*. "To praise is to reject alternative loyalties and false definitions of reality. Praise is relentlessly polemical."[10] The psalm's statement adds nothing to the faith that goes

6. Against Gunkel, *Psalmen*, 431.
7. Cf. Augustine, *Psalms*, 489; Cassiodorus, *Psalms*, 2:444.
8. Cf. Kraus, *Psalms 60–150*, 274.
9. Cf. Gerstenberger, *Psalms*, 2:204.
10. Walter Brueggemann, "Psalm 100," *Int* 39 (1985): 65–69 (see 66). He italicizes the first sentence.

back to the Song of Moses, but it expresses that faith's implications in utterly categorical terms.

The elements in the reasoning for or content of the praise that follow are then striking in another direction, though they take up a theme from Pss. 47 and 98. Yhwh is the one who made Israel, at the exodus, as in 95:6 (also, e.g., Deut. 32:6, 15; Isa. 44:2). Israel therefore belongs to Yhwh; it is Yhwh's people. In terms of a metaphor, it is the flock Yhwh pastures. Similar phrases came in Ps. 95:7, as motivation for Israel's own submission to Yhwh. Yet here, as in Pss. 47 and 98, they are motivation for the world's acknowledgment of Yhwh as God. Yet the psalm apparently slides from addressing the world (which is not present) to addressing Israel (which is). Yhwh's involvement with Israel makes Yhwh deserve the world's praise; *a fortiori* Yhwh deserves Israel's praise, and Israel's trust and confidence.

4Come into his gates with confession,
  into his courts with praise;
  confess him, worship his name.
5Because Yhwh is good,
  his commitment is forever,
  his truthfulness is to generation after generation.

100:4–5. The psalm repeats its logic. Again the whole world is invited to come into Yhwh's presence, right through the gates into the very courtyard of the house where the householder receives guests into the heart of the family, or into the court where Yhwh receives subjects or envoys. It is to come with a song of *praise, not surprisingly, but first with *confession, again implying acclamation that speaks of what Yhwh has done, in the manner of foreigners such as Jethro or Rahab when they made their confession. The conventional translation "give thanks to him" might give the impression that our attitude of thankfulness is of key importance here. But "with this *hōdû* we are not called to a sentence in which *I* am the subject, but to one in which *God* is the subject."[11]

The third colon adds *worship of Yhwh's *name, the bending of the knee. For the world as for Israel (95:1–7a), praise of Yhwh involves bodily submission as well as uninhibited enthusiasm.

Unlike v. 3, v. 5 explicitly puts the content of the praise in the form of reasons for praise. For the fourth time in the psalm's four lines, the name Yhwh comes. "The psalmist has done everything within the capacity of art to rivet attention beyond all else upon the name."[12] The declaration that Yhwh is "good"[13] is spelled out in the affirmations in v. 5b–c, though

11. Westermann, *The Praise of God in the Psalms*, 30.
12. James L. Mays, "Worship, World, and Power," *Int* 23 (1969): 315–30 (see 320).
13. See Klaus Koch, "'Denn seine Güte währet ewiglich,'" *EvT* 21 (1961): 531–44.

paradoxically they involve both ellipse and tautology. Yhwh's goodness means Yhwh is *committed and *truthful, and this commitment and truthfulness can be relied on (which is the nature of commitment and truthfulness). Again, it is the world that is formally assured of these qualities of Yhwh, which are good news for them, though it is in Israel that these qualities have been especially manifested (cf. 98:3), and the people who directly receive the assurance are the Israelites gathered for worship. Verse 5a–b almost exactly corresponds to the words Jer. 33:11 puts on the lips of people bringing a thank-offering, which fits with the psalm's heading.[14]

Theological Implications

"The verses are few, but big with great subjects."[15] The psalm brings to a powerful conclusion the stress on the interrelationship between Yhwh's involvement in Israel and Yhwh's lordship over the world that has run through Pss. 95–99. Theologically, its central affirmation is "Yhwh—he is God." Thus the whole earth is bidden to acknowledge Yhwh, not as mere overwhelmed and unwilling vassals but as people who "serve with joy." They come with confession of what Yhwh has done, with enthusiastic praise, and with willing submission. Yet they do that on the basis of what Yhwh has done for Israel. The joy is based on the fact that Yhwh made Israel, that Israel belongs to Yhwh, that it is the flock Yhwh pastures. The deeds they are confessing are the deeds Yhwh did for Israel. The goodness, commitment, and truthfulness are qualities manifested in Israel's story, and guaranteed to receive ongoing manifestation there. They are able to respond to all this because they know that Yhwh's activity in relation to Israel is not something exclusive but something inclusive. "The Gentiles have become fellow heirs, members of the same body" (Eph. 3:6).

14. Cf. Tate, *Psalms 51–100*, 538.
15. Augustine, *Psalms*, 487.

Psalm 101
Leadership with Integrity

Translation

David's. Composition.

1I shall sing of commitment and authority,
  to you, Yhwh, I shall make music.
2I shall expound on the way of integrity;[1]
  when will you come[2] to me?

I will go about with integrity of heart
  within my house.
3I will not set before my eyes
  anything worthless.
I hate the action of deviant people;[3]
  it will not stick to me.
4A crooked heart will go away from me;
  I will not acknowledge evil.

5The person who speaks against[4] his neighbor in secret—
  to him I will put an end.[5]

1. I take *tāmîm* as an adjective qualifying *derek* rather than a pl. from *tām*, "the way of people of integrity."

2. "When will it come" makes less sense in the context.

3. The inf. of *ʿāśâ* functioning as a gerund ("the doing of") is followed by the hapax noun *sēṭîm* from *sûṭ*, a by-form of *śûṭ* and *śāṭâ*, which mean "deviate" with the implication of unfaithfulness (cf. 40:4 [5]). BDB takes *sēṭîm* to refer to deviant acts (cf. GKC 115b), but the m. noun would more likely refer to people, and most of vv. 4–8 refers to people.

4. Q has *mĕlošnî*; K implies *mĕlôšĕnî*. The ending apparently makes more explicit that the noun is in the construct state (cf. GKC 90km; JM 93n).

5. Cognates suggest *ṣāmat* could also mean "silence," but in the context (see esp. the parallelism in v. 8) the traditional understanding is likely correct here (see *HALOT*).

The person who is majestic of eyes and wide of heart—
him I will not tolerate.
6My eyes will be on the trustworthy people in the land,
to live with me.
The person who walks in the way of integrity—
he will work for me.
7There will not live within my household
a person who practices deceit.
The person who speaks lies—
he will not stand before my eyes.
8Morning by morning I will put an end
to all the faithless in the land,
Cutting off[6] from the city of Yhwh
all who do harm.

Interpretation

Psalm 101 declares a commitment to live with integrity and maintain integrity in the community. The latter aspect implies that it is for the use of someone with power in the community, someone involved in leadership, such as a king or governor (cf. v. 8).[7] One can imagine various contexts in which a king or governor might make such a statement of commitment. It is needed of someone who wishes to come into God's presence (e.g., Pss. 15; 24); it indicates a commitment to meeting the expectations of the community's prayer for its leader (Ps. 72); it suggests an acceptance of direct challenges about commitment to Yhwh's ways (e.g., Pss. 81; 95); it forestalls any confrontation about wrongdoing that might entail trouble (e.g., Ps. 50); it warns people involved in deception and faithlessness to change their ways, or else. . . . The Church of England *Book of Common Prayer* prescribes its use at the anniversary of a king's accession, and in Israel a coronation or its anniversary would be a natural occasion for the king to make a commitment of this kind,[8] though we have no evidence of such a practice.

But elsewhere in the Psalter the function of a claim to integrity is to affirm that there is nothing in the suppliants' lives that should inhibit

6. Infinitive indicating attendant circumstances rather than purpose (GKC 114o).

7. Gerstenberger (*Psalms*, 2:206–10) argues that it refers to the commitment of an ordinary individual, but his parallels for this understanding are not convincing. Oswald Loretz (*Die Königspsalmen* [Münster: Ugarit, 1988], 141–76) sees it as a royal psalm that has been democratized in the course of redaction.

8. Cf. Mowinckel, *Psalms*, 1:65–68; Helen Ann Kenik, "Code of Conduct for a King," *JBL* 95 (1976): 391–403, who also emphasizes the links between the psalm and Proverbs; Michael L. Barré, "The Shifting Focus of Psalm 101," in *The Book of Psalms*, ed. Flint and Miller, 206–23, who sees it as originally designed for the instruction of the new king's courtiers.

Yhwh from answering a prayer for deliverance from trouble (e.g., 26:1–12; 44:17–22 [18–23]). In 18:20–24 [21–25], the king thus testifies to Yhwh's having delivered him because of his integrity. A claim to integrity might presuppose that the suppliant has been accused of unfaithfulness, so that if (for instance) the suppliant is ill, that is God's chastisement. The declaration of integrity then expresses before the community and before Yhwh a categorical and total commitment to Yhwh belying such accusations. Here, v. 2c–d implies that this is the context of the psalm's use. A prayer psalm can focus on a particular aspect of prayer, so that it becomes simply or primarily a protest or lament or declaration of trust. Psalm 101 focuses thus on an affirmation that one really is committed to living by Yhwh's ways.[9] One might even imagine Ps. 18 as the testimony that follows Yhwh's response to Ps. 101.

After the opening two lines, the psalm is dominated by lines with a short second colon, the rhythm characteristic of many prayer psalms. The lines come in pairs. There are many views on the larger structure of the psalm.[10] It is clear that vv. 1–2b are marked off from the rest. I have then distinguished vv. 2c–4 (as about attitude) from vv. 5–8 (as about action).

David's. Composition.

Heading. See glossary. This is the first psalm given a link with David since Ps. 86 and the only one in Book IV; the link is apposite given David's commitment to exercising authority with faithfulness (2 Sam. 8:15). But it gains irony in light of David's failure to regulate affairs in his "house," the location of his great sins of commission and omission, and in light of his lack of integrity and deceptiveness. Theodoret sees the psalm as written by David as a prediction of Josiah, whom the OT portrays in less equivocal terms.[11]

101:1–2b. The suppliant's statement of intent for the psalm. The three verbs are all cohortative.

1I shall sing of commitment and authority,
to you, Yhwh, I shall make music.

Tg assumes that the line refers to *commitment and exercise of *authority on the part of Yhwh,[12] but the suppliant does not go on to sing of

9. J. E. Weir ("The Perfect Way," *EvQ* 53 [1981]: 54–59) sees it as a wisdom psalm.

10. Pierre Auffret alone has two (*La sagesse*, 303–19; "Au milieu de ma maison," *SJOT* 11 [1997]: 124–37).

11. *Psalms*, 2:146.

12. So, e.g., Otto Kaiser, "Erwägungen zu Psalm 101," *ZAW* 74 (1962): 192–205 (see 202).

these.[13] The psalm focuses on the suppliant's own commitment and exercise of authority, though it does not again use these words. The only other OT reference to "commitment and authority" refers to human obligations (Hos. 12:6 [7]; cf. also the famous Mic. 6:8). It is this theme that the opening colon announces.[14] Yet in vv. 5–9, in effect the king's claim will be to act with the commitment and authority that Yhwh shows, so the ambiguity here may eventually be apposite. The commitment and authority of Yhwh and of the king are supposed to be one. Verse 1 thus makes for a brave start to the psalm, though one whose braveness is matched by the rest of it. As king or governor, the suppliant has people come to him to throw themselves on his mercy in appealing for support against people who are treating them wrongly, and such people have to claim an integrity that contrasts with their attackers. The suppliant does that in throwing himself on God's mercy in a way that corresponds to his position. His vocation is to exercise authority in a way that manifests commitment to other people and to Yhwh. He is going to claim to be a person who does so.

The fact that all this will be in song, in *music, in psalmody, might seem odd to us, though perhaps less odd if we think in terms of chanting or intoning. Luther notes that music adds feeling; it stops the psalm being merely a matter of the mind.[15]

> **2a–b** I shall expound on the way of integrity;
> when will you come to me?

About the verb *śākal* (hiphil), BDB comments, "meanings hard to classify; scholars differ greatly." Among other meanings, it mentions consider, understand, teach, be skillful, and succeed. The ancient versions have "consider" or "understand," but that is hardly what the psalm goes on to do. The parallelism with v. 1 suggests that the verb is here a denominative from *maśkîl*, which appears in many psalm headings (e.g., Ps. 142).[16] Admittedly this involves explaining one unknown by another, as we do not know what that noun means; perhaps "expound on" is as near as we can get to the verb's meaning. As this verb is parallel with "sing of/make music," "the way of *integrity" is parallel with "commitment and authority" and suggests further the style of life the suppliant will claim.

The question in the second colon is then a surprise, but it offers a clue to understanding the psalm. "When?" is the plea of a suppliant under pressure

13. Tg indeed needs a lengthy paraphrase to fill out its point; it then takes v. 2a–b as God's words to David.

14. Cf. Qimchi.

15. *First Lectures*, 2:294.

16. Johnson, *Sacral Kingship*, 105.

(42:2 [3]; 119:82, 84; compare the "until when" of, e.g., 74:10; 80:4 [5]; 94:3). Sometimes psalms ask when it will be possible to come to Yhwh (42:2 [3]), but they also speak of Yhwh's coming to exercise authority in the world (96:13; 98:9), and that is the direction of the coming that this psalm speaks of. It would be a solemn and dangerous longing for someone who cannot in truth say the things this psalm will go on to (see 50:3; 143:2).[17]

101:2c–4. The suppliant first makes claims about attitudes. The verbs are now yiqtol; one might render them as present ("I go about . . . I do not set . . ."), representing the stance the suppliant claims now as well as for the future; indeed, LXX is not so wrong in translating them with past-tense verbs.

> 2cI will go about with integrity of heart
> within my house.
> 3a–bI will not set before my eyes
> anything worthless.

The suppliant first speaks once more about *integrity, now making explicit that this is his commitment. The addition of reference to the *heart and to the house signifies awareness that it is one thing to behave like a person of integrity in public and another thing to be such in private (as David's story shows). The Psalms refer often to secret plotting and deceptiveness. The suppliant claims an integrity that extends to the secret life of the individual and the house (or household). Although the psalm will be chanted before the community, this means that the suppliant is taking the risk of making this claim before God. The community cannot check out whether it is true; God can.

Likewise what I "set before my eyes" points to my aims and intentions, which other people cannot know until they are implemented; and then, it is too late. Specifically, the suppliant abjures anything of "worthlessness." The understanding of *bĕlîyaʿal* as combining *bĕlî* and *yaʿal* and thus as suggesting "without worth" fits most OT occurrences of the word (e.g., 101:3), though the word's other resonances that link with the way Belial becomes a name for Satan indicate that the word is less bathetic than English "worthless" and/or that the term involves litotes.

> 3cI hate the action of deviant people;
> it will not stick to me.
> 4The crooked heart will go away from me;
> I will not acknowledge evil.

17. T. J. Booij ("Psalm ci 2," *VT* 38 [1988]: 458–62) sees Yhwh as coming in a vision, but this does not fit the context so well.

While *śānēʾ* often refers to the stance of being *against something or the act of repudiating it, here EVV's conventional "hate" may be appropriate as the suppliant speaks of inner attitudes that underlie (or contrast with) outer commitments. Hatred is an important spiritual and moral virtue (see 139:19–22), as Jesus affirms (Luke 14:26). Here, the notion of deviancy, departing from community norms, spells out the nature of worthlessness. Tg's "people who deviate from the commandments" is not so far out. In the complementarity of this pair of lines, reference to a "crooked" heart restates "deviancy," suggesting the attitude of a person who avoids being straight, the attitude that underlies the action. Thus crookedness of heart is also the antithesis of integrity of heart (v. 2).[18] The psalm is concerned not just with specific wrongs but with character, with "'the habits of the heart' out of which conduct emerges."[19] In the context the suppliant is not declaring a commitment to avoid *having* a crooked heart; this would in any case be an odd way to say that. Rather the suppliant insists on pushing away people who have a crooked heart (the expression involves synecdoche).

The vivid image of deviant action not "sticking" to me is another litotes to make the point. The suppliant makes sure it has no chance to do that. That is re-expressed another way in terms of not *acknowledging evil.

101:5–8. The suppliant now goes on to a claim about a leader's action, a claim to act like God.[20]

[5]The person who speaks against his neighbor in secret—
to him I will put an end.
The person who is majestic of eyes and wide of heart—
him I will not tolerate.

The commitment means not only avoiding crooked action, crooked attitudes, and crooked people, but taking action against crooked people. The suppliant speaks again about secret actions and inner attitudes, but now these are the secrets and attitudes of other people. Speaking against (etymologically, using one's tongue against) one's neighbor in secret implies not merely gossip but the lies that can imperil someone's life. Verse 5c–d might or might not refer to the same person; wide-heartedness (cf. Prov. 28:25) has a less positive connotation than in Isa. 60:5. That self-assessment and greed will lead to a negative assessment of people and a ruthlessness in the way one treats them. So integrity

18. Cf. Walter Brueggemann, "A Neglected Sapiential Word Pair," *ZAW* 89 (1977): 234–58 (see 245).

19. Mays, *Psalms*, 322.

20. Indeed, John S. Kselman ("Psalm 101," *JSOT* 33 [1985]: 45–62) sees vv. 6–7 as Yhwh's words. But there is no indication of a change of speaker.

involves putting such people down, in anticipation of the way they will treat others. It is always tempting to be "loving" and tolerant; the suppliant has to resist that temptation. "Like Yahweh himself, he declares לֹא־אוּכָל (Isa. 1:13)."[21]

> [6]My eyes will be on the trustworthy people in the land,
> to live with me.
> The person who walks in the way of integrity—
> he will work for me.

Positively put, the suppliant is committed to a positive relationship with trustworthy (*true) people, people of *integrity (that term again). Having eyes on them (that term again) suggests favoring (e.g., 33:18; 34:15 [16]). Not only is the suppliant committed to integrity. People who live with and work for him must also be so committed, because they act on his behalf. "Living with me" and "working for me" also take up the reference to my "house" (v. 2d), the place where work is done.

> [7]There will not live within my household
> a person who practices deceit.
> The person who speaks lies—
> he will not stand before my eyes.

The psalm retains the focus on people within the house(hold) and on people who work for the suppliant ("stand before my eyes") but moves back from the positive to the negative.[22] The opposite of integrity is deceit and lies.

> [8]Morning by morning I will put an end
> to all the faithless in the land,
> Cutting off from the city of Yhwh
> all who do harm.

The last lines become more radical. The suppliant will not merely clean up the palace and the administration but clean up the land and the city of the *faithless and the people who do *harm, and will have an ongoing commitment to this; it is not a task that is accomplished once and for all but one requiring constant attentiveness. "Morning by morning" also implies that it has a serious place in the suppliant's priorities; the first things one does each day are the things one regards as really important.

21. Kraus, *Psalms 60–150*, 279.

22. Watson (*Classical Hebrew Poetry*, 206) suggests that the lines' *abb′a′* order adds emphasis to their denial. The second line puts the subject before the verb.

In particular, it is in the morning that the king makes judicial decisions and thus delivers the oppressed and puts an end to the faithless who seek to harm them (Jer. 21:11–12; cf. 2 Sam. 15:2).

Theological Implications

"At the courts of princes," Luther comments, "there are few Josephs or Naamans, but many Ahithophels and Zibas."[23] The Christian nations, in the West and in Africa, are especially cursed by corruption in the highest levels of government and in the world of business (this seems less of a problem in the Muslim world). "It commonly happens that those who are invested with the government of kingdoms and empires are fools and blockheads" and that "although kings are not born fools, yet they are so blinded by their dignity, that they think themselves in no respect indebted to their subjects."[24] Democracy has made the problem worse, because now the rulers are people who wanted power rather than people who were born into it by accident of birth. The psalm invites their subjects (whom they are supposed to represent) to hold their government accountable, and invites boards to hold the management of their companies accountable rather than concerning themselves only with the bottom line. Given that many of the people who are deeply involved in corruption are in church on Sundays, it also invites pastors to do so in the way they arrange their teaching and preaching programs. The psalm expects people to be able to look God in the face and declare that they have exercised their leadership with commitment and integrity, to be trained in abjuring deception in their hearts and to have what happens inside the decision-making walls consistent with what the newspapers can report. It expects this to be a matter of both character and action. That action will include taking responsibility for their subordinates and being ruthless in sacking those who fall short of the highest standards. They will make this one of the highest priorities of their day. It is an aspect of the buck stopping here.

23. *Selected Psalms*, 2:180.
24. Calvin, *Psalms*, 4:88.

Psalm 102

My Time, Our Time, and Yhwh's Time

Translation

Plea. For a weak person when he is faint and pours out his murmuring
before Yhwh.

1Yhwh, listen to my plea;
my cry for help—may it come to you.
2Do not hide your face from me
at the time when trouble comes to me.
Bend your ear to me at the time when I call;[1]
answer me quickly.[2]
3Because my times have passed in[3] smoke,
my bones have burned as in a fireplace,[4]
4my heart has been crushed like grass and has withered.

1. MT links "at the time when I call" with v. 2d, but it links as well with v. 2c and, indeed, in substance applies to both.
2. Lit. "Be quick, answer me."
3. Vrs. have "like," translating loosely, though BDB suggests "as" in the sense of "in the form of" (*b* of identity or *beth essentiae*).
4. L has *kĕmô-qēd* for *kĕmôqēd*, with no difference in meaning (see Barthélemy, *Psaumes*, 220–21).

Because I have forgotten[5] to eat my food
5on account of the sound of my groaning;
my bone has stuck to my flesh.
6I have come to resemble a tawny owl of the wilderness,
I have become like a screech owl among the ruins.
7I have been wakeful and I have become like a bird
on its own[6] on a roof.
8All day my enemies have taunted me,
people I derided[7] have sworn oaths by me.
9Because I have eaten ashes like bread
and mixed my drink with tears.
10In the face of your rage and your wrath,
because you have lifted me up and thrown me away,
11My times are like an extended shadow,
and I—I wither like grass.

12But you—you, Yhwh, will sit forever,
your renown will endure generation after generation.
13You—you will arise, you will have compassion on Zion,
because it is time to show grace to her, because the appointed time has come.
14Because your servants have delighted in her stones
and they show grace to her dirt.
15Then the nations will revere Yhwh's name
and all earth's kings your splendor.
16Because Yhwh has built up Zion,
appeared in his splendor.
17He has turned to the plea of the naked person
and not despised their plea.
18This will be written down for the next generation,
and a people to be created will praise Yah.
19Because he has looked down from his holy height,
Yhwh has looked at the earth from the heavens
20To listen to the groan of the captive
and to free people doomed to death,
21So that Yhwh's name may be recounted in Zion
and his praise in Jerusalem,
22When peoples gather together,
and kingdoms, to serve Yhwh.

5. NJPS "[I am] too wasted" takes this as an instance of *HALOT*'s *šākaḥ* II; but see the discussion there.

6. Syr implies *nôdēd*, "fluttering," for MT *bôdēd*; Tg implies both words.

7. MT *mĕhôlālay* is a poal ptc. with a suffix. Although a suffix on a passive verb seems anomalous, see GKC 121. Vrs and EVV have an active verb, which requires repointing to poel (cf. *HALOT*).

[23]He has humbled my strength on my way,[8]
he has shortened my days.
[24]I say, my God, do not take me up
in the midst of my days.
Your years endure through the generations;[9]
[25]before, you established the earth,
and the heavens are the work of your hands.
[26]They may perish
but you would stand.
All of them could wear out like clothes;
like a garment you could make them pass on.
So they could pass on, [27]but you are the one
and your years do not come to an end.
[28]May the children of your servants dwell,
and their offspring endure, before you.

Interpretation

The psalm's beginning takes us a world away from Pss. 93–100 with their focus on Yhwh's reign, since vv. 1–11 follow the form of an individual prayer psalm (as the heading implies they will). They comprise address to Yhwh (v. 1), plea to Yhwh to listen (vv. 1–2), and description of the suppliant's trouble (vv. 3–11), focusing on the "I" of the suppliant's own experience and reactions (vv. 3–7, 9, 11) but also referring to the attitude of enemies (v. 8) and to that of Yhwh (v. 10).

Verses 12–22 constitute a statement of confidence such as often appears in a prayer psalm, declaring assurance that Yhwh is going to act and show compassion. They speak of "the naked person" and "the captive" in a way that could indicate a reference to an individual such as the suppliant of vv. 1–11. But these allusions are set in a context that speaks of Yhwh's having this compassion for Zion, so as to build her up. It is in this connection that Yhwh will turn to the plea of the naked and listen to the groan of the captive, and free people doomed to die. The verses go through a sequence twice, in vv. 12–17 and 18–22, each time declaring the way people will always give praise for what Yhwh will have done as a result of looking at Zion's needs and responding.

8. The suffix on "my strength" (Q, also 4QPs[b], Sym, Syr, Tg, Jerome) also applies to "way." K has *kḥw*, "his strength"; so also LXX, which takes the verb as *ʿānâ* ("he answered [in his strength]") rather than *ʿinnâ* ("he humbled"), while Tg implies *ʿānâ* ("[my strength] was humbled"). LXX then implies a variant pointing of vv. 23b–24a (cf. *IHBS* 1.6.3k), which Barthélemy (*Psaumes*, 689) sees as theologically motivated, while Tg implies *quṣṣĕrû* ("[my days] were shortened") for MT *qiṣṣar*.

9. The expression *bĕdôr dôrîm*, "in the generation of generations," comes only here, though cf. *bĕdôr wādôr* in 90:1 (itself unique to that passage).

The final section (vv. 23–28) brings the two earlier parts together. It sets the middle section's declarations in the broadest context, affirming how Yhwh's activity goes back to creation and how Yhwh's years will never end (vv. 25–27). On that basis, its frame summarizes the lament and makes the suppliant's plea more specific in taking those facts as the basis for appealing that the suppliant's life should not be cut short (vv. 23–24, 28).

No doubt vv. 1–11 could have existed independently of what follows, but we have no evidence that they ever did so, and the psalm as we have it forms a unity, with motifs recurring and the final section binding the whole.[10] What, then, is the relation between the person groaning in vv. 1–11 and the city for which vv. 12–22 pray?

Starting from the heading would locate the psalm's center of gravity in vv. 1–11. The appeal to the city's destiny then supports the personal appeal to Yhwh, addressed by a member of this community to the God committed to Zion. The converse possibility is that vv. 12–22 reframe vv. 1–11; the person groaning is someone living in the exile or afterward when Jerusalem has been devastated and not yet been restored, when it continues to be looked down on by its foes. This individual, then, speaks as a member of the Jerusalem community (or the Judean community located in Babylon), perhaps as a leader such as the king, though there are no distinctly kingly marks about the psalm as there are in some others. Or perhaps the whole community uses the psalm, and the "individual" voice speaks for the community in the manner of Lamentations (cf. esp. Lam. 3).

It transpires, then, that the psalm's setting is the same as that presupposed by many of the psalms about Yhwh's reign. Although it does not speak of Yhwh's reigning, except implicitly (v. 12), in substance it is appealing to Yhwh to start reigning. Further, its statement of hope focuses on the effect that Yhwh's act of restoration will have on the nations, who will now come to revere and serve Yhwh; this is a central theme of the psalms about Yhwh's reign. On either understanding, the psalm would come from some time in the exilic or Persian period (when Jerusalem continued to need building up).

Mishnah *Taʿanit* 2.3 prescribes the psalm for use by the community on one of the days of fasting and prayer for rain. In Christian use it became one the seven "Penitential Psalms,"[11] though like Ps. 6 it does not express penitence or contrition.[12]

10. On the psalm's unity, see esp. Christian Brüning, *Mitten im Leben vom Tod umfangen* (Frankfurt: Hain, 1992), esp. 293–96.

11. Cassiodorus's commentary on this psalm (*Psalms*, 3:2) seems to be the first extant reference to this description of those seven psalms.

12. Cf. Lindström, *Suffering and Sin*, 218–38; Mandolfo, *God in the Dock*, 88; against Weiser, *Psalms*, 653.

> Plea. For a weak person when he is faint and pours out his murmuring before Yhwh.

Heading. See glossary for *plea, *weak, and *murmur. The description of the person the psalm is designed for is unique in the Psalter but compares with headings to some Babylonian prayers[13] and corresponds to vv. 1–11. But many psalm headings reflect the psalm's use in a later period than that of its writing, and this heading may well represent its adaptation for use by an ordinary individual.[14] Pouring out one's lament *before* Yhwh might imply coming to the sanctuary and taking part in a community occasion of lament and prayer. "When he is faint . . ." parallels the terminology of an incantation for a situation of need, "This is how to pray when," though of course the psalm presupposes a different recourse for a situation of need.[15]

102:1–2. Opening plea for Yhwh to pay attention.

> 1Yhwh, listen to my plea;
> my cry for help—may it come to you.
> 2Do not hide your face from me
> at the time when trouble has come to me.
> Bend your ear to me at the time when I call;
> answer me quickly.

This appeal for Yhwh to pay attention is extraordinarily long; its extensive parallelism gives it great denseness. The suppliant wants Yhwh to listen and not look the other way, to bend an ear (to put it more vividly), but most of all to answer, and to do so fast. The following lines will suggest that this is not merely a matter of impatience ("I want it now"): the suppliant has been waiting for a long time and is sorely distressed. Thus the appeal is a *plea and a *cry for help (the two words come next to each other, which adds to their impact); the suppliant "calls" like a master summoning a servant. There is no description of the suppliant's need except as "trouble" or distress (vv. 3–11 will spell that out) nor any description of what the suppliant wants Yhwh to do (that will come implicitly and explicitly in vv. 12–22 and 23–28). The phrases used correspond to ones that appear in other psalms: practically every word can be accounted for by a comparison with 18:6 [7]; 27:9; 31:2 [3]; 39:12 [13]; 56:9 [10]; 59:16 [17]; 69:17 [18]. The nature of these links suggests the suppliant is not reworking particular lines from individual psalms, as if looking

13. Cf. Gerstenberger, *Psalms*, 2:211.
14. Cf. Mowinckel, *Psalms*, 2:9.
15. Cf. Robert P. Gordon, "*K/kI/ky* in Incantational Incipits," *UF* 23 (1991): 161–63.

at a psalms scroll. As usual, the traditional language reflects familiarity with the right way to pray, the tradition of psalmody, and the instinct to use the natural language of prayer that is sanctified by usage. These are phrases suppliants often use; they remind Yhwh of prayers that have been answered in the past. They also mean that "the singer was not as isolated as he felt,"[16] or even that he knew he was not as isolated as his words could suggest. "We are not alone when we pray; we have more support than most of us realize. We are part of a great tradition."[17]

102:3–11. The nature of the trouble. The verses focus on how it affects the suppliant: vv. 3–5 are about "my" and vv. 6–7 about "I." Verses 8–9 then turn to the enemies' action and vv. 10–11 to Yhwh's.

3Because my times have passed in smoke,
my bones have burned as in a fireplace,
4my heart has been crushed like grass and has withered.
Because I have forgotten to eat my food
5on account of the sound of my groaning;
my bone has stuck to my flesh.

It is hard to construe vv. 3–5 as bicola; v. 3 makes sense, but neither v. 4 nor v. 5 does so. They work as two tricola, parallel "because" clauses. The statement concerns my times, my bones, my heart, my food, my groaning, my bone, my flesh. In vv. 3–4a two "my" words come next together between the first two cola, and another at the end. In vv. 4b–5 they come at the end of every colon, with two at the end of v. 5.

"My times" (lit., "my days") picks up from v. 2b and 2c. The time of trouble and of calling out to Yhwh are times that have passed in smoke. The image involves an ellipse whose deeply sinister implication becomes clear only with the second colon. The suppliant's times have passed like those of someone who has been burned up. Talk of one's bones burning is doubly figurative. Having a fever means the body is consumed as by fire. But Job, too (for instance), speaks in these terms (Job 30:30) and need not imply a fever but rather that he is consumed by afflictions and pains. Even more sinister is the talk of bones burning in Ezek. 24:10. In light of vv. 12–22, that passage is the more significant. Jerusalem became the fireplace in which the Judeans' bones were burned up.[18] The third colon's talk of being crushed like grass (cf. Hos. 9:16) and withering (e.g., Isa. 40:7–8) suggests the same link. That will be true of

16. Kidner, *Psalms*, 2:360.

17. Johann Baptist Metz in *The Courage to Pray*, by Metz and Karl Rahner (London: Burns and Oates, 1980), 5.

18. Reidar Dittmann ("Fire, Smoke, and Ashes," *Pro ecclesia* 4 [1995]: 398–403) relates the psalm to the Holocaust.

the outer person; here the psalm refers to the *heart, the inner person, which can melt (Ps. 22:14 [15]) or be crushed (*šābar*, 34:18 [19]) or flag (61:2 [3]) or be pierced (109:22), rather than being set (57:7 [8]; 108:1 [2]; 112:7) or strong (76:5 [6]). The whole person, outer and inner, has been consumed.

The second "because" opening vv. 4b–5 does not explain what lies behind the first but stands parallel to it. Indeed, the experience that vv. 3–4a describes and the groaning it generates (v. 5a) could be what explains why someone would forget or neglect or *ignore eating. In turn, that neglect leads to becoming emaciated. Singular "bone" contrasts with the plural in v. 3. Either can be used (cf. Job 30:30; Prov. 15:30; 16:24); the psalm may prefer the singular here so as to have another word ending *-î*.[19] Like English "flesh," *bāśār* usually refers to the soft tissue and muscle between the skin and the bones, but occasionally denotes the skin itself.

6I have come to resemble a tawny owl of the wilderness,
   I have become like a screech owl among the ruins.
7I have been wakeful and I have become like a bird
   on its own on a roof.

Whereas vv. 3–5 offer a partly literal and partly metaphorical description, vv. 6–7 turn to simile, as they turn from "my" to "I." The *qāʾat* and the *kûs* are birds (e.g., Lev. 11:17, 18), but we do not know which kind; I have followed *HALOT* in taking them as different types of owl, birds that seem to live on their own and make weird screeching noises. This fits v. 7, which perhaps itself identifies both birds as ones that stayed awake at night, the kind that sat on a roof and made a noise when people were trying to sleep. The imagery is poignant and ironic, because birds are usually symbols of freedom and security (e.g., 55:6–7 [7–8]).[20] *Šāqad* denotes not merely being awake but deliberately staying awake and keeping watch (cf. 127:1; Jer. 1:12), as a night bird seems to do. The suppliant is not deliberately staying awake but is unable to sleep, but *resembles* a creature that seems to be deliberately doing so.

8All day my enemies have taunted me,
   people I derided have sworn oaths by me.
9Because I have eaten ashes like bread
   and mixed my drink with tears.

After five verses with the suppliant as subject, the psalm turns to speak of the enemies who make the situation worse. They are not the

19. So Allen, *Psalms 101–150*, 15.
20. Schaefer, *Psalms*, 251.

cause of the trouble; the problem is their reaction to it. One might think of the peoples the Judeans saw as taunting them after the fall of Jerusalem. Individual sufferers likewise felt their neighbors were taunting them for their suffering on the assumption that it was quite deserved. "My enemies" is expressed more forcefully as "people I derided" (lit. "derided of me"; both expressions are participles). They were people whose opposition the suppliant could have discounted and laughed at (cf. 1 Sam. 2:1, using the expression *rāḥab ʿal*), but now they turn the tables. Taunting is then expressed more forcefully in terms of swearing oaths. EVV have "curse," but the verb is *šābaʿ*. They are not saying to other people, "May you end up like that" (cf. Jer. 29:22) but "If I do not keep this oath, may I end up like that."[21]

The basis for this is the situation v. 9 describes, combined with the theological assumptions of Job's friends. Eating ashes is another metaphor. The suppliant does not join with other people in eating but sits alone like someone in mourning or sits covered in the ashes that were a symbol of grief, and instead of drinking with rejoicing in that joyful company, sits weeping.

> **10**In the face of your rage and your wrath,
> because you have lifted me up and thrown me away,
> **11**My times are like an extended shadow,
> And I—I wither like grass.

At last the psalm comes to the third way of speaking about suffering, not only in terms of "I" and "they" but in terms of "you." It might be the most painful way, and it is again forcefully expressed, in terms not of mere anger but of rage and wrath. Rage or indignation (*zaʿam*) suggests personal outrage, commonly because someone has failed to meet obligations or has acted in grossly objectionable fashion. Wrath (*qeṣep*) points to the overwhelming power of anger with its capacity to sweep all before it; it nearly always refers to divine rather than human anger. They are powerful terms to use, vividly conveying a sense of terrible personal devastation. It is as if God had treated the suppliant the way the wind treats the chaff (cf. Isa. 41:16; Job 27:21; 30:22), lifting it up (*nāśāʾ*) and carrying it off. Or the suppliant is like a dead body thrown into a common grave (Jer. 26:23) or like the tub lifted up to be taken off to Babylon in Zechariah's vision (Zech. 5:9); or like the people thrown off into exile (e.g., Jer. 7:15).

I have linked vv. 10 and 11, in keeping with the interlinking of previous lines; v. 11 then reverts to the language of times (lit. "days") and of

21. Cf. Calvin, *Psalms*, 4:104.

withering like grass that came in the first line in this subsection (vv. 3–4a) and thus completes a frame around it. At midday shadows are short, but as day draws on they become longer and longer; extended shadows are thus a sign that day is about to end. The suppliant's life is like that.

102:12–17. The statement of confidence about what Yhwh will do for Zion will reprise in vv. 18–22. It is also an implicit appeal to Yhwh to be the kind of God that the words describe, to justify the confidence the words express.

> [12]But you—you, Yhwh, will sit forever,
> your renown will endure generation after generation.

The *wĕʾattâ* opening v. 12a stands over against the *waʾănî* opening v. 11b. It makes for a dramatic shift in the psalm. The words that follow correspond to Lam. 5:19, except that they refer not to Yhwh's "throne" but to Yhwh's "renown" (*zēker*; see Ps. 97:12). They constitute a first pointer to a transition of context and content as well as stance, in pointing to the situation of the city of Jerusalem and the context where it has been long devastated and desolate. The suppliant now appeals to Yhwh like people praying in that situation. In light of what will follow, "forever" also trailers the links with the thinking of Isa. 40–66 running through vv. 12–22.[22]

The transition and some of the words in v. 12a also recall 22:3a [4a], though here the verb is yiqtol rather than a participle; "sitting" presumably refers to sitting in a position of power and authority, sitting enthroned. In substance the second colon also corresponds to 22:3b [4b]: as "the praise of Israel" Yhwh is the one whose renown Israel will forever make mention of (*zākar*) in its worship. The difference in the verb does correspond to a difference in the role of the statement. In Ps. 22 it declares what is always so and introduces a recollection of how Yhwh has acted in the past, which stands in tension with the way things are. Here it begins a statement of expectation concerning what Yhwh will surely do. The second colon thus buttresses the declaration and also anticipatorily buttresses the following statement about what must surely be. If Israel is indeed to make mention of Yhwh in the future, that presupposes that Yhwh continues to act in such a way as to call for this. At the same time the second colon reinforces the tension with vv. 1–11 and the contrast between the suppliant's relationship with time (esp. vv. 3, 11) and Yhwh's relationship with time (v. 12).[23] It epitomizes the contradictions from which the psalm lives.[24]

22. Cf. Brüning, *Mitten im Leben vom Tod umfangen*, 167–70.

23. Cf. Robert C. Culley, "Psalm 102," *Semeia* 62 (1993): 19–35 (see 28).

24. Cf. Franz Sedlmeier, "Zusammengesetzte Nominalsätze und ihre Leistung für Psalm cii," *VT* 45 (1995): 239–50 (see 239).

[13]You—you will arise, you will have compassion on Zion,
because it is time to show grace to her, because the appointed
time has come.

The yiqtols thus follow from the one in v. 12, the link between the verses emphasized by repeating the "unnecessary" pronoun and expressed again in the movement from "sit" to "arise." The first verb does not mean Yhwh is sitting doing nothing; that would be expressed in other ways (e.g., by asking why Yhwh is sleeping). Yhwh's sitting (enthroned) is good news. But when a king decides something needs to happen and/or determines to take action, he stands to make his declaration and/or to take the action. It is in this sense that Yhwh must arise from the throne, not stay seated. The king does that when hearing of oppression in the city and rising to fulfill his vocation to show compassion to the weak there. The heavenly King must do that in light of the needs of the city of Zion as a whole.

The line is dense, the longest so far (ten words, construed as 4-4), with two parallel verbs juxtaposed breathlessly in the first colon and two parallel "because" clauses juxtaposed breathlessly in the second.[25] It offers no basis for declaring that it is time to show *grace, that the "appointed time" (see, e.g., Gen. 21:2; Hab. 2:3) has come. It speaks like the widow challenging the judge to recognize that the situation demands action *now* (Luke 18:1–8). It expresses conviction about the demands issuing from what has been happening to Zion and who Yhwh is. It is a bold alternative to the rhetorical question "How long?" or "When?"

[14]Because your servants have delighted in her stones
and they show grace to her dirt.

The psalm becomes even bolder in the way it puts pressure on Yhwh. Yhwh allegedly loves and accepts and delights in (*rāṣâ*) this people and this land (Pss. 44:3 [4]; 85:1 [2]). But (as those psalms imply) Yhwh is not behaving thus, despite things Yhwh says elsewhere about Jerusalem's stones (Isa. 54:11–12). This stance thus contrasts with that of Yhwh's servants. In fact, the Master falls short of the servants! In effect, the psalm affirms the prayer in Ps. 51:18 [20], and suggests that this action will stem from sharing its attitude.

Characteristically, the parallel colon makes the point even more sharply. First, showing *grace or favor is even more Yhwh's special business than is loving, accepting, and delighting in, not least in the Psalms

25. Indeed, Brüning (*Mitten im Leben vom Tod umfangen*, 83) sees v. 13 as two internally parallel 2-2 lines.

(e.g., 123:2–3), though it is also the business of the faithful (e.g., 37:21, 26; 112:5). Indeed, here the declaration constitutes a bold taking up of the verb from v. 13b, as if to say "We show grace to Zion's dirt: it is time you did so." Second, the object of the people's favor is not only stones (which can be reassembled) but dirt, debris, or rubbish, the crumbled remains of buildings and walls that are no use for anything. Can the Judeans "revive the stones out of the heaps of dirt?" Sanballat mocked (Neh. 4:2 [3:34]). We look on these fallen stones and this dirt with love, says the psalm, challenging Yhwh to behave the same way.

> 15Then the nations will revere Yhwh's name
> and all earth's kings your splendor.

In offering another motivation for Yhwh to act, the psalm spells out the implications of v. 12b and also corresponds to the convictions of Pss. 96–100: Zion's restoration will mean nations and kings come to *revere Yhwh's *name and acknowledge Yhwh's splendor (*honor). But the language corresponds most closely to Isa. 59:19 in combination with 62:2. If the psalm is later than those prophecies, it reminds Yhwh of intentions and commitments still due to be realized. If the prophecy is later than the psalm, it constitutes a commitment Yhwh made in response to it.

> 16Because Yhwh has built up Zion,
> appeared in his splendor.
> 17He has turned to the plea of the naked person
> and not despised their plea.

The context indicates that the qatals here refer to the time when the events vv. 13–15 look forward to have actually happened, when Yhwh will have built up Zion and appeared, turned, and not despised. Thus LXX translates v. 16 as future. At the moment it is in a literal sense an open question whether these events will take place, but the psalm continues to operate with the absolute conviction that they will. Speaking as if they have already happened is another way of expressing that conviction, and thus of leaning on Yhwh. Verse 16b restates v. 16a; it is by building up Zion (cf. 51:18 [20]; 69:35 [36]) that Yhwh will appear in splendor and people will respond with awed astonishment to the transformation Yhwh brings about (cf. Isa. 60:1–2; also 40:5). Splendor (*honor) picks up from v. 15; so more subtly does "appeared," given the similarity of the verb *rāʾâ* to *yārēʾ* "revere." Appearing leads to revering.

"Turned" is the vivid verb *pānâ*, which suggests turning the face (*pānîm*); contrast v. 2a. The colon thus brings together a verb that suggests looking and a noun that suggests listening. Yhwh turns and listens, not only hears but sees. How could Yhwh then despise the *plea of the naked? Nakedness in the OT implies having no defenses or resources, being weak and helpless (cf. Gen. 3:7, 10; Isa. 58:7), the opposite of splendor (v. 16b). It was involved in the dishonoring of Jerusalem in its destruction (Lam. 1:8). So the psalm imagines the moment when the God with all resources and thus all honor applies them to the people who have neither. It is natural to despise people with nothing. Yhwh looks at naked people pleading, and responds rather than turning away.

102:18–22. The psalm goes through the sequence of expectation and confidence again.

> [18]This will be written down for the next generation,
> and a people to be created will praise Yah.

LXX takes the opening verb as a jussive, but the parallel between vv. 12–17 and vv. 18–22 rather implies that it is a simple statement (so KJV). Verse 12 spoke of Yhwh's renown lasting forever; "this" refers resumptively to the events then anticipated in vv. 13–17.[26] Writing down what Yhwh has done will ensure the renown does last, though v. 18 is content to look forward only one generation.[27] Ezra-Nehemiah are a fulfillment of this declaration; they put into writing the story of the city's restoration. Designating the people as "to be created" recalls the prominence of the verb "create" in Isa. 40–66 (see esp. 65:17–18). At the moment the people is naked and doomed to die (vv. 17, 20). It needs a work of sovereign new creation if its life is to begin again. Perhaps that is why the psalm needs to look forward only one generation; it is thereby actually looking forward to a new age. The newly created people will not be able to imagine what the old world was like. An account will need to be kept if *Yah is to be properly *praised. That archaic name for God picks up from 94:7, 12 but also marks a transition to the most familiar, later use of the name in the imperative expression "praise Yah," which will first occur in 104:35.

> [19]Because he has looked down from his holy height,
> Yhwh has looked at the earth from the heavens

26. Tg has "this prayer," but the broader implication (the prayer and its answer) fits better.

27. Tg has "last generation" (cf. Stec, *Targum*, 185), and Franz Sedlmeier ("Psalm 102,13–23," *BZ* 40 [1996]: 219–35) understands this section of the psalm as setting an eschatological hope before the sufferer; cf. Odil Hannes Steck, "Zu Eigenart und Herkunft von Ps 102," *ZAW* 102 (1990): 357–72. But *dôr ʾaḥărôn* means simply "next generation" elsewhere (48:13 [14]; 78:4, 6; Deut. 29:22 [21]; cf. Brüning, *Mitten im Leben vom Tod umfangen*, 215–17).

> [20]To listen to the groan of the captive
> and to free people doomed to death,

Again the psalm looks back from the perspective of the time when these prayers have been answered (cf. vv. 16–17). Again it focuses on Yhwh's attending to the city's needs, looking (v. 19) and listening (v. 20). This time it explicitly pictures Yhwh looking down from the palace in the heavens, the *holy height (cf. 14:2; and the appeal in Deut. 26:15; cf. Lam. 3:50).

The response will be an answer to the prayer in Ps. 79:11 about the "groan of the captive" and the "people doomed to death." People in Jerusalem are not captives like the exiles, but instead of being a free people, able to control their destiny, they are subject to the constraint of a superpower and/or a provincial government in Samaria. Thus they groan under their subjection, longing to be free of foreign domination (cf. Ezra 9; Neh. 9). In the parallel colon they describe themselves as (lit.) "children of death." Is the idea that it is as if death's forces have already overwhelmed them? Many people have been killed, and the survivors feel they have nothing to live for. But elsewhere similar expressions suggest "doomed to die" or "deserving to die" (1 Sam. 26:16; 2 Sam. 12:5). Is it Yhwh who has so doomed them (cf. vv. 10–11)? Certainly Yhwh has the power not merely to cancel the death sentence and leave them in prison for life, but actually to free the people who are on death row.

> [21]So that Yhwh's name may be recounted in Zion
> and his praise in Jerusalem,
> [22]When peoples gather together,
> and kingdoms, to serve Yhwh.

The praise in v. 18 belonged to Yhwh's people, the direct beneficiaries of Yhwh's action in restoring Zion. It is there that the story of Yhwh's action can be recounted by people who only have to point to what Yhwh has done. Once again, recounting (telling the story) is the form praise takes. Recounting indicates the mode of the praise; praise suggests the enthusiasm with which the story is told, to the honor of Yhwh's *name.

But the praise is heard much more widely. The psalm's central section closes by returning to the whole world's recognition of Yhwh (cf. v. 15). It would not do for the story to be heard only by Yhwh's people. The occasion of the telling is the gathering of peoples and kingdoms in Zion/Jerusalem, fulfilling the vision in Isa. 2:2–4; 45:20; 60:1–4; and the summons to serve Yhwh in Ps. 100. In Jerusalem they, too, will hear of what Yhwh has done, and they will be able to see the evidence of it. Thus the people of Zion will lead the nations in their worship.

102:23–28. With another sudden transition, the third section reprises the themes of the first and second, in vv. 23–24b and 24c–28. Hebrews 1:10–12 imagines vv. 25–27 being said to Christ.

> 23He has humbled my strength on my way,
> he has shortened my days.

The first line particularly reprises vv. 3–4a and 11, the opening and close of the lament. In light of vv. 12–22 we might again take this as a picture of Jerusalem's experience, in the manner of Lam. 3. Perhaps a typical individual speaks, or the community speaks as if it were an individual person. The city is like someone whose life has been brought to an end before its time. He was strong (the city often withstood its attackers); he has now been humbled (cf. Pss. 90:15; 94:5; Isa. 64:12 [11]). He knows that eventually he would have become less strong, that he would not live forever, but this has happened while he was still on his journey, while he could reckon he was still in the prime of life. So he is like a person struck down by a fatal illness in midlife (cf. Ps. 89:45 [46], referring to the king).

> 24a–bI say, my God, do not take me up
> in the midst of my days.

The plea follows from that; it is the most concrete plea so far, indeed the only overt plea apart from the appeal for Yhwh to listen. The psalm works with the typical paradox about the way suppliants picture themselves as in effect in Sheol yet asking to be preserved from Sheol; their life has come to an end before its time, yet they ask for that not to happen. The verb (*ʿālâ* hiphil) is an odd one; usually people are taken down to death, and being taken up would imply being delivered from death or being taken to be with God (cf. 2 Kings 2:1). But the qal verb occasionally means "go away," and this could generate the meaning here for the hiphil; the verb rephrases those in v. 10b.

> 24cYour years endure through the generations;
> 25before, you established the earth,
> and the heavens are the work of your hands.

Verse 24a–b forms a complete line parallel to v. 23, while the contents of v. 24c suggest that it belongs with what follows. With v. 25 it forms a tricolon at the beginning of a new subsection rather than the end of the old one. It goes on to take up the contrast between the suppliant's relationship with time and Yhwh's (see on v. 12). Human beings can find their lives cut in half, but Yhwh's years endure. "Through the generations" is a variant on the phrase in v. 12b (both cola are noun clauses). In the other two parallel cola, v. 25a–b, the psalm spells out the implications of the opening statement. Yhwh's being goes far back, back before the beginning of the cosmos for which Yhwh was responsible.

> **26a–d**They may perish
> but you would stand.
> All of them could wear out like clothes;
> like a garment you could make them pass on.

The point of that statement about Yhwh as the creator was not immediately obvious. This subsequent pair of parallel lines[28] indicates what it was. Yhwh made the earth and the heavens; that can seem to make them the very embodiment of stability (Pss. 104:5; 119:90). But unlike Yhwh, earth and heavens had a beginning, and they could also have an end (cf. Isa. 51:6). EVV affirm that they *will* have an end, but there is no need to read a yiqtol verb thus, and the OT does not elsewhere make such a statement. The psalm makes a hypothetical statement about the cosmos's nature. There is nothing about the heavens and the earth that means they must last forever; and if they do come to an end, Yhwh will outlast them. "Pass on" is *ḥālap*, hiphil the first time, qal the second time (below). It can denote change for the better or for the worse. It could point to Yhwh's capacity to renew the old and make of it something new, re-create the heavens and the earth. But the context points to a second implication: Yhwh could decide it is time for a change like a human being deciding to get rid of one set of clothes for another.

> **26e**So they could pass on, **27**but you are the one
> and your years do not come to an end.

The second occurrence of that verb is the resumptive beginning of the next line. The psalm's final point was implicit in what has preceded, and now becomes explicit. Whereas the heavens and the earth are inherently finite in time (they had a beginning and they could have an end), Yhwh is "the one." There is no basis for the rendering "you are the same";[29] the psalm rather makes the same point as the similar expression in 100:3, "Yhwh—he is God." There is a unique absoluteness about Yhwh's being, one aspect of which is that Yhwh's years do not come to an end (v. 27b forms a bracket with v. 24c around what comes in between).

28. For the understanding of v. 26a–b as a complete line, cf. Brüning, *Mitten im Leben vom Tod umfangen*, 87.

29. In contrast to GKC 135a, see DG 1, remark 1; JM 154j.

> [28]May the children of your servants dwell,
> and their offspring endure, before you.

The point of those important theological statements lies in the link between the Yhwh who has no end and the people of Yhwh who seem to have had a very definite end. With some logic the psalm asks that Yhwh's servants (or rather, their children, their offspring) may live before Yhwh, have a secure place there. Living before their master is what servants do, standing there to wait on their master to do his will, and they enjoy there his protection and provision. It is therefore a great privilege to be a servant of a great master and it is a position of security. The psalm thus closes by looking beyond the present troubles once more, and looking to the regular life that it longs should then follow deliverance. No more crises, please.

Theological Implications

The psalm has two distinctive features. One is its interweaving of the destiny of the individual and that of the city. Read from the perspective of the heading, it invites suffering individuals to set their affliction in the context of the community's destiny. Yhwh is committed to the city of God and the people of God; that is the individual's source of hope when distraught or abandoned. Read from the perspective of the psalm's latter part, conversely it invites the suffering community to express its distress and abandonment in the terms of the suffering individual. The pathos of its pain and loss then comes out vividly and has the potential to move God to act in relieving it.

The second distinctive feature is its working with the theme of my time and God's time, like Ps. 90.[30] For the psalm, mine is a time of trouble and of crying out to God. My times have passed in smoke. This trouble has been lasting a long time and goes on through each day and I therefore want speedy release from it. Otherwise my life seems to have come near its end; the shadows of its day lengthen. This is not because I have reached the natural end of my life span; Yhwh has shortened my days, broken me "on the way," when my journey should be only half over. Yhwh is about to take me up out of life in the midst of my days. The dynamics of my time thus contrast with the dynamics of Yhwh's time. "We think we have all the days we need" and/or "we think we are in the midst of our days, and suddenly we are at the end of them." But "with

30. See, e.g., Koenen, *Jahwe wird kommen*, 83–84.

the Lord time is a matter, not of days, but of years, and generations, and forever."[31] Yhwh sits there on a throne forever. Whereas I will be dead and forgotten, Yhwh's renown will endure forever. Yhwh is eternal, but this does not mean being insulated from time; it rather means being present to all time. Yhwh experiences life as years, but Yhwh's years extend through the generations. They go back to before the world's creation and they will go forward beyond its dissolution, if that ever happens. So for Yhwh there is a past, a present, and a future. It is possible to speak in terms of what Yhwh *will* do. The psalm's conviction is that Yhwh does get involved in time, and its challenge is that Yhwh should do so *now*. It is up to Yhwh to bridge Yhwh's time and our time. It is time to show grace; the appointed time has come. Then we and our children can live and last before Yhwh, sharing in the way Yhwh's being abides.

31. Mays, *Psalms*, 324.

Psalm 103

Restoration, Individual and Communal

Translation

David's.

1Worship Yhwh, my soul,
all that is within me [worship] his holy name.
2Worship Yhwh, my soul,
and do not ignore all his dealings.

3He is the one who pardons all your waywardness,[1]
who heals all your illnesses,
4who restores your life from the Abyss.
Who garlands you with commitment and compassion,
5who satiates you in your finery with good—
your youth[2] renews itself like an eagle.

6Yhwh performs faithful acts,
decisive acts for all the oppressed.
7He would make known his ways to Moses,
his deeds to the Israelites.

1. The f. suffix in vv. 3, 4, and 5b is the long, Aramaic-like form *-kî*; it makes for paronomasia with the end of *bārăkî* ("worship") in vv. 1–2 and thus further underlines the reasons for the worship. Dahood (*Psalms* 3:25) notes that it is also Ugaritic-like. 4QPs[b] has the regular *-k*.

2. Abstract pl. n. construed with f. sg. verb; see GKC 145k.

[8]Yhwh is compassionate and gracious,
slow to anger and big in commitment.
[9]He would not contend forever,
he would not hold on to it for all time.

[10]Not in accordance with our failures has he dealt with us,
not in accordance with our wayward acts has he benefited us.
[11]Because in accordance with the height of the heavens over the earth
his commitment has been strong over people who revere him.
[12]In accordance with the distance of east from west
he has distanced our rebellions from us.
[13]In accordance with the compassion a father shows to his children
Yhwh has shown compassion to people who revere him.
[14]Because he—he has acknowledged our shaping,
reminded that we are dirt.

[15]Human beings: their days are like grass,
like flowers in the countryside—so do they flourish.
[16]Because the wind passes over them[3] and they are gone,
and their place does not recognize them anymore.
[17]But Yhwh's commitment lasts from age to age,
upon people who revere him, and his truthfulness to their grandchildren,
[18]To people who keep his covenant,
to people who are mindful of his orders so that they perform them.

[19]Yhwh—he established his throne in the heavens
and his sovereignty rules over all.
[20]Worship Yhwh, you his aides,
mighty warriors, ones who perform his word,
listening[4] to the sound of his word.[5]
[21]Worship Yhwh, all his armies,
his ministers, ones who do his will.
[22]Worship Yhwh, all his works,
in all the places of his rule;
worship Yhwh, my soul.

Interpretation

Psalm 103 forms a cross between a testimony psalm and a praise psalm. Like a testimony psalm it focuses on the worship the speaker

3. Gnomic qatal.
4. Epexegetical *l* plus infinitive, see GKC 114o; *IBHS* 36.2.3e; JM 124o; DG 108.
5. 4QPs[b] has pl. *dbryw* ("words") for MT *dĕbārô* in both cola; LXX has pl. in v. 20b.

personally offers in light of what Yhwh has done, and eventually urges this worship on other beings not directly affected by Yhwh's deeds. But the language of "worship" belongs to a praise psalm, and it does not speak of concrete recent acts of Yhwh but of the pattern of Yhwh's acts and of the characteristic stance Yhwh has taken to Israel. The blessings described include ones that apply to the individual's deliverance (healing and rescue from death), whereas the pattern of God's acts in relation to Israel are described in different terms, though it still might be that the individual's self-bidding is the call of a worship leader seeking to involve the whole people in praise for what God has done for them, so that the "I" and the "we" are ultimately the same.[6] But it might be said that "the thanksgiving psalm becomes a hymn . . . where the personal experiences only enter as a starting-point and motivation."[7]

The psalm's framework is an exhortation to worship addressed to the self (vv. 1–2, 22c) and eventually to the supernatural and natural worlds (vv. 19–22b). Its main part first expands on the reasons, speaking of Yhwh's characteristic acts and nature in relation to the self who is addressed (vv. 3–5), then more generally with a reference to Moses (vv. 6–9), then in an account of Yhwh's deeds in Israel's past history (vv. 10–14). This leads into a comment on human transience and divine permanence (vv. 15–18). Rhetorically, the psalm moves from "you" (the self; vv. 1–5) to "they" (Israel of the past; vv. 6–9) to "we" (Israel of the past and present; vv. 10–14) to humanity (vv. 15–18) to the heavenly and earthly cosmos (vv. 19–22).[8]

Qimchi sees the psalm as expressed in the language of the exiles, Theodoret as relating to their restoration from exile.[9] Its Aramaisms and links with other Scriptures (esp. Isa. 40–66) indeed suggest it may be of postexilic date. It also reflects the Sinai story in Exod. 32–34, while its concern with sin compares with other postexilic prayers such as Ezra 9; Neh. 1; 9; Dan. 9.[10] Although its lack of specificity in referring to Yhwh's deeds for the individual and its subsequent emphasis on Yhwh's relationship with the people do not suggest it is a psalm to accompany a thank-offering, a general psalm such as this could have been used thus

6. So Gerstenberger, *Psalms*, 2:216.

7. Mowinckel, *Psalms*, 2:38.

8. For other analyses, see Allen, *Psalms 101–150*, 28–29.

9. *Psalms*, 2:155.

10. Christoph Dohmen further notes its manifold parallels with the Lord's Prayer and thus calls it a bridge between Jews and Christians ("Vom Sinai nach Galiläa," in *Das Drama der Barmherzigkeit Gottes: Studien zur biblischen Gottesrede und ihrer Wirkungsgeschichte in Judentum und Christentum* [ed. Ruth Scoralick; Stuttgarter Bibelstudien 183; Stuttgart: Katholisches Bibelwerk, 2000], 92–106). Cf. more broadly Otto Betz, "Jesu Lieblingspsalm," *Theologische Beiträge* 15 (1984): 253–69.

(see the comment on the heading to Ps. 100). We do not know any other context in which it could have been used.

David's.

Heading. See glossary.

103:1–2. An exhortation to the self, comprising two parallel lines that are also internally parallel.

1Worship Yhwh, my soul,
all that is within me [worship] his holy name.
2Worship Yhwh, my soul,
and do not ignore all his dealings.

The exhortation to worship Yhwh recurs six times in the psalm's opening and closing verses. It is a distinctive feature, though Ps. 104 will also have this exhortation to the self as a bracket around it (and cf. 134:1–2; 135:19–20). Psalms have asked the soul or self (*person) why it is cast down (42:5, 11 [6, 12]; 43:5) and exhorted it to be silent for God (62:5 [6]); they will exhort it to rest (116:7) and to praise (146:1). They thus assume our capacity to argue with ourselves and the need and obligation to stir ourselves up to worship.[11] The exhortation to the self concerns a bodily action, *worship, which implies kneeling before Yhwh. The parallelism of "all that is within me" makes explicit that an exhortation to the *nepeš* is not aimed at a trivial or minor part of the self. Worship essentially involves the body, but it involves the whole person. Further, "all that is within me" specifically indicates the inner person: the emotions, the mind, and the will. The parallelism of "Yhwh" and "his *holy *name" underlines this. We worship the transcendent, wholly other, Holy One; the whole inner and outer person must surely bow to this God. The parallelism of "worship" and "do not *ignore" also underlines it; being mindful or ignoring involve mind and will. Worship issues from a decision and accompanies decisions in other parts of life.

"Dealings" (*gĕmûl*) is then a surprise. "Benefits" gives the right impression if we recall the notion of a "benefits package"; the word characteristically suggests recompense, in a negative sense (94:2) or a positive one (116:7, the verb *gāmal*). But it can suggest beneficence with no relationship to deserve (119:17; Isa. 63:7). That connotation is more apposite here; the statement offers the first affirmation that, fortunately for us, Yhwh has not dealt with us as we deserve: see v. 10, though in the same

11. Cf. Calvin, *Psalms*, 4:125–26.

breath the psalm will affirm that it is people who revere Yhwh who experience Yhwh's commitment and compassion (vv. 11, 13).[12]

103:3–5. The psalm buttresses the argument with the self by reminding it of the reasons for worshipping Yhwh that lie in Yhwh's ongoing and characteristic acts and nature in relation to the self. LXX and Jerome take vv. 3–5 as a long enjambment, a series of relative clauses depending on the "his" in v. 2,[13] but this obscures the link between vv. 3–5 and vv. 6–9, which continue the reminder of Yhwh's ongoing and characteristic acts. More likely vv. 3–5 are self-contained noun-type clauses.[14]

> [3]He is the one who pardons all your waywardness,
> who heals all your illnesses,
> [4a]who restores your life from the Abyss.

While MT treats vv. 3–5 as three bicola, v. 4a seems to link with v. 3 and v. 4b with v. 5, suggesting that the verses comprise two tricola. There is a logic about the sequence. First, Yhwh pardons *waywardness and heals illnesses. "The rewards of the Lord cannot be before thine eyes unless thy sins are before thine eyes."[15] "Pardon" (*sālaḥ* and related words) is rare in the Psalms (25:11; 86:5; 130:4). It suggests the forgiveness of a person in a position of authority (e.g., a king); the more regular word translated "forgive," *nāśā'* (lit. "carry), has a less circumscribed reference and can apply to the forgiveness of peers. The psalm's other links with Exod. 34 suggest that this occurrence links with Exod. 34:9. "Heal" (*rāpā'*) is also surprisingly rare in the Psalms (e.g., 107:20; 147:3); perhaps it also links with the exodus story (Exod. 15:26).

Presumably the suppliant had noticed that Yhwh does not heal everyone's illnesses and does not pardon everyone's sins (as Exod. 34:7 declares). Perhaps the psalm's statement is simply hyperbolic. Perhaps it affirms that all pardon and healing that ever happens comes from Yhwh; none comes from any other source.

The parallelism further implies that often sin issues in sickness and conversely that often sickness issues from sin. This is a pernicious doctrine if made into a hard-and-fast rule (see Job's friends), and one that many psalms explicitly or implicitly dispute. Those psalms and Job

12. *Gāmal* also means "wean," suggesting "do not ignore all his weaning"; hence Tg's additional appreciation for Yhwh's making breasts for our mothers (cf. Stec, *Targum*, 186).

13. So JM 121r.

14. These would usually include *hû'* as subject, but this can be omitted when the subject has just been mentioned (e.g., 22:28 [29]; 107:40). See *TTH* 135.6 (esp. observation 1); DG 113a; *IBHS* 37.6a; GKC 116s.

15. Augustine, *Psalms*, 504.

suggest that the Bible as a whole expects us to treat it as a broad generalization rather than an invariable rule. Someone who lives the wrong kind of life should expect to end up losing out (an illustration would be the experience of the West, where the culture as a whole uses up a disproportionate amount of the world's resources but is on the whole rather unhappy). And people who are sick are wise to ask whether there is waywardness lying behind their sickness (cf. Mark 2:5; 1 Cor. 11:29–30; Jas. 5:15–16).

Verse 4a in turn restates v. 3b, or rather goes beyond it: not every illness takes one to the gates of death, but some do so. The last reference to "life" (*ḥayyîm*) in the Psalms came in connection with being on the verge of Sheol (88:3 [4]). Tellingly, Yhwh is similarly here characterized as one who *restores from the Abyss. When it seems we are going to die, Yhwh can rescue us. LXX and Jerome translate *šaḥat* with words for "corruption," as if it came from *šāḥat*, but the ordinary noun *šaḥat*, from *šûaḥ*, means "pit." People could be buried in a grave pit rather than in a rock-hewn tomb, so that fits here. *The* "pit" is then another term for Sheol, the place "behind" the literal pit where dead selves are (not Gehenna, as Tg has it). But burial does lead to dissolution of the body, and the connotations of *šāḥat* might carry over to *šaḥat* when used in connection with death.

> 4b Who garlands you with commitment and compassion,
> 5 who satiates you in your finery with good—
> your youth renews itself like an eagle.

The second tricolon goes systematically beyond the first. Using its first verb, *ʿāṭar*, 5:12 [13] speaks of Yhwh "surrounding" the faithful with favor as with a shield, and in isolation this would make good sense here. As well as restoring, Yhwh henceforth protects, with *commitment and compassion.

But the second, parallel colon points to the more specific significance of *ʿāṭar* and suggests a comparison with 65:11 [12], which also speaks of Yhwh garlanding with good things. Yhwh not merely restores and protects but satiates or fills. The verb *śābaʿ* denotes not merely satisfying, but something more like satiating, causing to overflow and run over. The colon literally reads "who satiates your finery";[16] it thus involves

16. Cf. Jerome, Aq. In LXX, "desire" for *ʿădî* looks like a contextual guess arising from unawareness of how the poetic construction works. Sym translates "your continuing," Tg "the days of your old age" (cf. NRSV "as long as you live"), perhaps implying *ʿōdēkî* from *ʿôd* (cf. 104:33) for MT *ʿedyēk* (cf. E. Nestle, "Ps. 103,5," *ZAW* 19 [1899]: 182). A. A. Macintosh ("A Third Root עדה in Biblical Hebrew?" *VT* 24 [1974]: 454–73), following Saadya, argues for "sustenance," but this seems an unnecessary complication.

ellipse and/or metonymy. In satiating the restored person, Yhwh puts them in finery, which goes along with their being garlanded. It is a fine reversal of the requirement at Sinai that they put off their finery because of their sin (Exod. 33:5–6); now it can be more than restored because of Yhwh's pardon.[17] And this person in their finery is the one whom Yhwh has filled with good things (cf. Exod. 33:19). The "good" with which Yhwh garlands is a way of characterizing the commitment and compassion spoken of in the parallel colon. These will be key notions in the psalm; each word (in its noun or verb form) comes four times.[18] Yhwh is big in commitment (v. 8); Yhwh's commitment has been strong over Israel (v. 11); Yhwh's commitment lasts (v. 17); thus Yhwh garlands with commitment. The first quality to be attributed to Yhwh is compassion (v. 8), compassion like a father's (v. 13); thus Yhwh garlands with compassion.

The end of the double tricolon, and the end of the participial description of Yhwh, is signaled by the verbal clause in v. 5b. Yhwh not only restores from imminent death but renews the youthfulness (the last colon of vv. 4b–5 parallels the last colon of vv. 3–4a).[19] The background to v. 5b is likely not myths about the eagle or phoenix but the promise in Isa. 40:31 with its background in the eagle's capacity to soar through the heavens (e.g., 2 Sam. 1:23).

103:6–9. Previous lines have already presupposed a link between the individual's experience of Yhwh's grace and Yhwh's acts at Sinai. Verses 6–9 speak more generally about Yhwh's relationship with Israel since Moses's time. They form two noun clauses each followed by a yiqtol clause. The transition to a different section is marked by a change to the more regular construction in which the subject of the noun clause is expressed and the participle itself does not have the article. The psalm no longer explicitly speaks of what Yhwh does for the individual, though it might still be implicitly addressing the self. And Yhwh's deeds again relate both to the needs of the whole person and to the need for forgiveness. But the outward needs are now ones issuing from the experience of oppression, and the psalm speaks of Yhwh's acts for "all the oppressed" and for "the Israelites." Relieving a group's suffering has replaced relieving the suffering of a sick individual.

17. Cf. Martin Metzger, "Lobpreis der Gnade," in *Meilenstein*, ed. Manfred Weippert and Stefan Timm (Herbert Donner Festschrift; Wiesbaden: Harrassowitz, 1995), 121–33 (see 128).

18. Fokkelman, *Major Poems*, 3:198; also J. P. Fokkelman, *Reading Biblical Poetry* (Louisville: Westminster John Knox, 2001), 159–73; James L. Mays, "Mercy Joined to Loving Kindness," *Austin Seminary Bulletin Faculty Edition* 105 (1990): 27–32 (see 27).

19. DG 87 takes the asyndetic v. 5b as a purpose clause (cf. *IBHS* 31.6.2b), GKC 156d, *TTH* 163 as a circumstantial clause that does nevertheless state a consequence.

[6]Yhwh performs faithful acts,
decisive acts for all the oppressed.
[7]He would make known his ways to Moses,
his deeds to the Israelites.

Alongside the change in construction, the familiar hendiadys, *decisive acts of *faithfulness, advertises the change in agenda. The exodus involved decisive acts on Yhwh's part (*šĕpāṭîm*; Exod. 6:6; 7:4; 12:12), the first of Yhwh's faithful acts (1 Sam. 12:7). The hendiadys neatly sums up what Yhwh did in those events.[20] Something similar is true of the "oppression" from which decisive acts of faithfulness rescue people. Within the community, it can denote extortion from weak people by powerful people, robbing them of their resources by means that may be legal (e.g., 62:10 [11]; cf. 72:4; 73:8; 119:121–22, 134), but in light of v. 7, we might think of oppression as a summary of the Israelites' experience in Egypt (105:14 comes near to using this term in this way).

The verb in v. 7 is yiqtol. It might seem to have fairly straightforward past meaning, referring as it does to the revelation Moses asked for in Exod. 33:13. Yhwh's "ways" are then goodness, grace, and compassion (33:19), qualities characterizing Yhwh's acts toward Israel. Yet Moses also asked Yhwh to take into account the fact that Israel was Yhwh's people (33:13), which it would be tempting not to do, after their making the gold calf; and while only Moses sees Yhwh pass by (33:19), the Israelites do see Yhwh's ways, including Yhwh's goodness, grace, and compassion. Here v. 7b does go on to broaden out the reference. Perhaps, then, the yiqtol verb indicates that such revelation of Yhwh's ways and deeds was not confined to one moment.

[8]Yhwh is compassionate and gracious,
slow to anger and big in commitment.
[9]He would not contend forever,
he would not hold on to it for all time.

The link with Exod. 32–34 continues as the psalm declares Yhwh to be compassionate and *gracious, slow to anger and big in *commitment (as in 34:6).

The form of expression in v. 9 overlaps significantly with that of Isa. 57:16, but in the context v. 9 continues to recall Israel's origins, though with some irony. The story is indeed one characterized by contention (e.g., Exod. 17:2, 7; Num. 20:3, 13, 24; cf. Pss. 81:7 [8]; 95:8; 106:32), a

20. Cf. T. M. Willis, "'So Great Is His Steadfast Love,'" *Bib* 72 (1991): 525–37 (see 530).

contention on the people's part, overtly with Moses though implicitly with Yhwh. Yhwh takes a confrontational stance toward Israel in response to this contentiousness; only here does the OT describe this as Yhwh contending, and even here the emphasis lies on Yhwh not contending forever. The second colon spells that out, using a rarer expression involving the ellipse of a word for anger (cf. Jer. 3:5, 12). Verse 9 thus spells out v. 8a and goes beyond v. 8b. As well as being slow actually to express anger, Yhwh does not nurse it afterward. Once it has been expressed, it is gone. Having expressed anger in Exod. 32–33, Yhwh is ready to move on (even if the relationship cannot be quite the same).

103:10–14. A further new section is marked by a transition to qatal verbs. The "testimony" continues to relate to the way Yhwh behaved in the pentateuchal story, but speaks in terms of "us" (vv. 10, 12, 14). The psalm also has in mind the way Yhwh has continued to act, and I have therefore translated the verbs as perfect, not aorist. While the *lōʾ . . . wĕlōʾ* ("not . . . and not") opening v. 10 make a link with the same expressions in v. 9, here the subsequent preposition *k* ("in accordance with") is of key significance (vv. 10a, 10b, 11a, 12a, 13a, each time at the beginning or virtually the beginning of the colon); the double *kî*, "because," in vv. 11 and 14 adds to the aural effect. The prepositional phrases make the point that there is a disparity between Yhwh's deeds and the people's deeds that (paradoxically) links with some parities that vv. 11–13 describe.

> **10**Not in accordance with our failures has he dealt with us,
> not in accordance with our wayward acts has he benefited us.

*Failures and *wayward acts again recall the Sinai story (e.g., Exod. 34:7).[21] Yes, Yhwh has been acting in accordance with the self-revelation proclaimed there. "Wayward acts" also picks up from v. 3a, following on the reference to "benefits" (v. 2b). Here, "benefited" (going beyond merely "dealt") thus makes more explicit the point in v. 2. Yhwh's "benefits" or rewards turn out to have a paradoxical relationship with what people have earned.

> **11**Because in accordance with the height of the heavens over the earth
> his commitment has been strong over people who revere him.
> **12**In accordance with the distance of east from west
> he has distanced our rebellions from us.

The negative comparison (positive in implication) is succeeded by two positive comparisons in parallel lines. Within the lines, parallelism

21. Though there the word is *ḥaṭṭāʾâ*, here *ḥēṭʾ*.

is confined to the recurrence of expressions for vertical and horizontal distance. In the first, this involves similar but unrelated words, *gĕbōah* (height) and *gābar* (has been strong); in the second it involves two forms of the same verb. *Commitment being strong over people who *revere Yhwh would elsewhere imply that it prevailed over them, but here it suggests their protection. It is strong for them rather than against them, almost strong over Yhwh rather than allowing Yhwh to abandon them. The image and the language in v. 11a parallel Isa. 55:8–9, but their linking with Yhwh's commitment also parallels Pss. 36:5 [6]; 57:10 [11] and results in the psalm making a rather different point (though Isa. 55:3 does also refer to Yhwh's acts of commitment). The complementary reference to distancing *rebellions compares with Mic. 7:19.

For the ancient reader, the height of sky over earth and the span of east from west suggests the greatest imaginable distance. For the modern reader, the comparison is even more striking because we know that the distance between heavens and earth and between east and west is actually infinity.

> 13In accordance with the compassion a father shows to his children
> Yhwh has shown compassion to people who revere him.
> 14Because he—he has acknowledged our shaping,
> reminded that we are dirt.

The simile reinforces the point. Although showing compassion might seem a distinctively female quality, it being related to the word for "womb," the psalm presupposes that it is equally natural to a father. Fathers by their nature are motherly in this respect. They can thus provide an image for Yhwh as a motherly father. There is nothing distinctively Israelite about the point; Ugaritic stories characterize the senior Canaanite god El as the compassionate one.[22] Even when confronted by his children's rebellions, a father shows compassion. Indeed, it is their rebellions that test the reality of his compassion. Hosea 11 expounds the same point without actually referring to "compassion."

The final qatal line in this recollection of Yhwh's relationship to "us" over the years prepares the way for vv. 15–18 by its reflection on the human nature of the Israelites. It makes sense to continue to translate the verbs as perfect. The recollection of the pentateuchal story goes behind Exodus to Gen. 2:7, where Yhwh "shaped" the first human being from the "dirt." In Gen. 2 there is no stress on the feebleness this implies, but that stress emerges, with regard to dirt (3:19) and shaping (6:5, the noun that comes here). The latter parallel could suggest

22. See, e.g., *ANET*, 129–55.

that "our shaping" involves not an objective genitive but a subjective one, a reference to the shaping that we do. In Gen. 8:21 Yhwh had to come to acknowledge the incorrigible waywardness of that shaping.[23] Yhwh has also had to keep acknowledging it through Israel's story. Yhwh keeps being reminded of it (the passive participle of *zākar*), keeps being caused to be *mindful of it.[24] In the context, the thing Yhwh has kept acknowledging is humanity's physical frailty rather than its moral frailty. We are on our way back to the soil. Therefore God does not treat us too hard.

103:15–18. This recollection of the Genesis story segues into a reflection on the ongoing nature of human frailty, analogous to the reflections in Pss. 90 and 102. Once again this is formulated as a reflection on human frailty in general but in the context relates to Israel in particular.

> 15Human beings: their days are like grass,
> like flowers in the countryside—so do they flourish.
> 16Because the wind passes over them and they are gone,
> and their place does not recognize them anymore.

The image corresponds to Ps. 90:5–6 but also more closely to Isa. 40:6–8, which has the flowers as well as the grass. Once again it recalls the way the winter rains in a Middle Eastern climate can transform the brown hills with abounding grass and wild flowers (v. 15; "like flowers" is *kĕṣîṣ*, "flourishes" is *yāṣîṣ*). But the way the line finishes raises suspense. *How* do they flourish?

They do so only for a short time before the sun and hot wind of summer wither them (v. 16). The place where they live can be imagined as looking about, puzzled, because it can no longer see any trace of these things that were so visible and colorful. That is what mortal human beings are like. The word *ʾĕnôš* can designate a human being in a neutral way (e.g., 55:13 [14]), but *ʾānaš* means "be weak/sick." Although there may be no etymological connection between the words, contexts sometimes imply that *ʾĕnôš* suggests mortal humanity, humanity in its frailty (e.g., 8:4 [5]; 90:3), and this is an example.

> 17But Yhwh's commitment lasts from age to age,
> upon people who revere him, and his truthfulness to their
> grandchildren,

23. In light of postbiblical usage, Tg interprets the word *yēṣer* of the human capacity to shape things for good or ill, the good or evil inclination.

24. Cf. DG 113 remark 4: the passive ptc. sometimes expresses a state resulting from the subject's own action, a use more characteristic of Aramaic (JM 50e). GKC 50f, 84[a]m rather sees this not as a passive ptc. but as an adjective denoting a quality, "mindful."

[18]To people who keep his covenant,
to people who are mindful of his orders so that they perform them.

Yhwh's lasting-ness stands over against humanity's transience. The prosody embodies the point: the line seems to go on forever.[25] Specifically, it is Yhwh's *commitment that lasts. Indeed, human transience (vv. 15–16) is surrounded fore and aft (vv. 11–14, 17) by divine commitment, compassion, and truthfulness.[26]

The psalm again links with Isa. 40:6–8, which notes how human commitment resembles the flowers of the countryside; there, too, the point expressed as a generalization about humanity applies specifically to Israel, whose commitment could not be relied on. Verse 17a makes its declaration about Yhwh's contrasting *commitment without qualification, but vv. 17b–18 then indicate a series of qualifications. First, that commitment applies to people who revere Yhwh; people who fail to do so cannot expect it to continue. Yet v. 17 closes with another declaration that lands on the side of grace. To draw out the implications of the parallelism, Yhwh's commitment and *truthfulness apply to people who revere him from age to age and thus not just to them and not even just to their children but to their grandchildren. At first sight the implication is that the attitude of the grandchildren themselves makes no difference.

Verse 18 guards against that inference in spelling out what revering Yhwh implies. It is not merely an emotion, whether fear or awe, but an attitude expressing itself in the actions v. 18 describes. Again the parallelism within the verse explicates matters. Keeping Yhwh's *covenant involves *mindfulness, attentiveness to what Yhwh has said. It implies studying these *orders, these charges that Yhwh has laid down, but being mindful in such a way as then to do what they say. This long pair of *l*-expressions follows on from the *l*-expression at the end of v. 17. It does not quite say that the promise at the end of v. 17 is conditional on the grandchildren's obedience, but it does imply that the whole of vv. 17–18 presupposes a relationship of mutual commitment. And if the response of vv. 17–18 is forthcoming, this recalibrates the implications of vv. 15–16. Humanity and its commitment is inherently fragile. But if we do revere Yhwh, Yhwh's commitment can overcome the implications of that.

103:19–22. The unusual word order in v. 19 gives a sign that once again we segue into something new. The declaration in v. 19 is the basis for the resumptive challenge to worship, addressed not just to my self

25. MT takes the line as 5-3; I have rather taken it as 4-4.

26. Walter Brueggemann, "Remember, You Are Dust," *Journal for Preachers* 14 (1991): 3–10 (see 6).

(though v. 22c will come back to that) but to the whole of reality over which Yhwh rules. Yhwh is named in each of these last four lines, and the references to "rule" act as a frame around the section. The repeated "worship" matches vv. 1 and 2, while the repeated "all" in vv. 19, 21, 22a, and 22b matches the repeated "all" in vv. 1, 2, 3a, 3b, and 6. The hyperbole there is matched by hyperbole here. While Yhwh's sovereignty may in theory rule over all, much that happens in the heavens and on the earth does not implement the sovereign God's will, which links with the fact that everyone does not get pardoned or healed or blessed or delivered.

19Yhwh—he established his throne in the heavens
and his sovereignty rules over all.

So v. 19 goes back behind the exodus and Sinai, and behind the shaping of humanity, to the moment of creation. In an image that does not come in Gen. 1, but is compatible with it, when God created the heavens and the earth, God set up a throne in the heavens in such a position that the divine feet could rest on the earth as footstool. That symbolizes sovereignty over everything in the cosmos.

20Worship Yhwh, you his aides,
mighty warriors, ones who perform his word,
listening to the sound of his word.
21Worship Yhwh, all his armies,
his ministers, ones who do his will.

The renewed bidding to *worship follows from the declaration that Yhwh's throne is established in the heavens. It implies that the "all" over which Yhwh rules includes the aides through whom Yhwh actually exercises sovereignty in the world as mighty warriors. Do the further qualifying phrases in v. 20b–c imply awareness that these aides and mighty warriors might not perform Yhwh's word or listen to the sound of that word?

Verse 21 restates the point, raising the same question. Yhwh's "armies" can refer to the planets and stars (cf. Isa. 40:26), and that would make sense here. The planets and stars are among the means by which Yhwh's will is implemented (cf. Gen. 1:14–18). They are thus Yhwh's ministers or servants (cf. Ps. 104:4).

22Worship Yhwh, all his works,
in all the places of his rule;
worship Yhwh, my soul.

The closing tricolon first moves to the worship of the creation over which the heavenly forces exercise their authority on Yhwh's behalf. Elsewhere the Psalms speak of creation's praise, and seem to refer to its capacity to make a noise and make music and wave. In referring to its *worship, Ps. 103 perhaps suggests a submission to Yhwh's will; the parallel colon with its reference to Yhwh's "rule" would fit with this.

The psalm closes with the same bidding from which it started, though this does not mean that the words have the same significance. After all that the psalm has said, the exhortation to the self has much more power. One aspect of the specific rhetorical significance of vv. 20–22 as a whole emerges here. If all those heavenly beings and all of creation should worship Yhwh, how much more we?[27]

Theological Implications

Psalm 103 forms a mirror image of Ps. 102. Here, too, the experience of the individual is seen in light of the experience of the community, but this happens not in prayer but in testimony and praise. The individual's experience of Yhwh's forgiveness, healing, deliverance, restoration, filling, and renewal is set in the context of the way Yhwh has delivered, forgiven, and blessed Israel and has related to it with commitment, grace, truthfulness, and compassion. The psalm implies that we do not understand the significance of our personal experiences of God's grace unless we see them in light of Yhwh's acts in relation to the community.[28] Yhwh does not relate simply to individuals, and then perhaps to the community as a collection of individuals. The significance of the individuals lies in their relationship with the community with which Yhwh has been at work over the generations. But conversely, the fact that Yhwh has been so at work with the community over the generations undergirds Yhwh's involvement with us as individuals. It is the community's memory of those acts of Yhwh (to be anachronistic, its Scriptures) that makes it possible for individuals to understand what Yhwh does with them, even as it is their own experience of Yhwh's involvement in their lives that enables them to understand their community's traditions concerning Yhwh's acts.[29] "The special distinctiveness of the psalm lies . . . in the inner connection between the poet's personal experience of God and the understanding of the faith worked out in the biblical testimonies of

27. Cf. Calvin, *Psalms*, 4:141.

28. Contrast N. H. Parker's comment that "ultimately all religion goes back to personal experience" ("Psalm 103," *CJT* 1 [1955]: 191–96 [see 195]).

29. Cf. Gene Rice, "An Exposition of Psalm 103," *Journal of Religious Thought* 39 (1982–83): 55–61 (see 57).

the Fathers, which are woven into an organic whole; and in that respect the psalm can still serve also today as a guide to the right interpretation of Holy Scripture."[30]

In setting in dialogue the individual's experience of God and the community's memory of that, the psalm finds itself walking around one of the trickiest of theological questions, the relationship between "divine commitment and human obligation."[31] It is possible only to walk around this question; it cannot be resolved. It is symbolized by the complementarity of the observations of Paul and James about trust and action. Our relationship with God is wholly dependent on divine commitment, yet unless that meets with a response in the form of revering and thus obeying God, an actual relationship cannot come into being. It would be misleading to say that the divine commitment is conditional on the human response, because that would imply that the relationship was a contract. But the commitment does require the response. Conversely it is not the case that our revering God is the initiative on our part that secures a response of commitment from God. But commitment, compassion, and faithfulness are for people who do revere God, because they are aspects of a relationship. Yet the double way the psalm speaks of benefits or rewards (vv. 2, 10) suggests how Yhwh's relationship with people is not contractual or legal but covenantal and personal. Verses 11–12 again underline the irresolvable nature of the relationship between deserve and blessing as they speak of the people both as revering Yhwh and as rebels. That commitment is strong for people who revere Yhwh, expressing itself in disposing of their rebellions! God cannot demonstrate commitment, forgiveness, and faithfulness to people who do not revere him; indeed, God demonstrates commitment, forgiveness, and faithfulness in order that people may emulate these.[32]

"The singer faces God's *holiness* with *respectful awe* and yet at the same time *gives himself up to the love of God* as revealed to him in God's saving deeds"; because in God there is no tension between majestic holiness and nearness of loving care. "This is the ultimately 'divine' in God that, where man sees only the chasm, God in his compassion bridges it." Indeed, "it is only in his love *for the sinner* that the sublime holiness of God fully manifests itself, and that love draws its surpassing strength and its redeeming power from the fact that it is the love of the *holy God*." Wonder is therefore appropriate.[33]

30. Weiser, *Psalms*, 657.

31. See David Noel Freedman, "Divine Commitment and Human Obligation," *Int* 18 (1964): 419–31.

32. D. F. O'Kennedy, "The Relationship between Justice and Forgiveness in Psalm 103," *Scriptura* 65 (1998): 109–21, as summarized in *Old Testament Abstracts* online.

33. Weiser, *Psalms*, 658–59.

Psalm 104

Yhwh in Relation to Creation Then and Now

Translation

David's. [11QPs[a], LXX, Aq]

[1]Worship Yhwh, my soul!

Yhwh my God, you became very great;
  you put on honor and majesty,
[2]Wrapping on light like a coat,
  stretching out the heavens like tent curtains,
[3]One fixing his lofts in the waters,
  making the clouds his chariot,
  going about on the wings of the wind,
[4]Making his aides of winds,
  his ministers of flaming fire.[1]

[5]He founded[2] the earth on its bases:
  it will never collapse, ever.
[6]With the deep like a garment you covered it:[3]
  the waters were standing above the mountains.

1. 11QPs[a] *lwhṭt* provides the f. form of the ptc. to match the f. noun; MT *lōhēṭ* is m. Spiekermann (*Heilsgegenwart*, 21) takes *lōhēṭ* as a noun, implying "fire [and] flame."

2. 4QPs[d] has ptc. *ywsd* (cf. Tg and some LXX MSS), assimilating to what precedes.

3. LXX takes *kissîtô* ("you covered it") as a noun ("its covering"), which makes good sense and avoids having a m. suffix referring to a f. noun, though the noun is usually *kĕsût*. Jerome, Aq, Th are as MT.

7At your blast they were fleeing,
at the sound of your thunder they were rushing away.[4]
8As they were rising up the mountains, so they were going down the valleys,
to the place that you founded for them.
9You set a limit that they should not pass,
they should not return to cover the earth.[5]

10You are the one who sends out springs in canyons;
between the mountains they go.
11They water every animal of the wild;
the donkeys break their thirst.
12By them the birds of the heavens dwell,
from among the branches the birds give voice.
13You are the one who waters the mountains from his lofts,
from the fruit of your works the earth drinks its fill.

14You are the one who grows grass for the cattle,
plants for the service of people,
To bring forth food from the earth,
15and wine that gladdens the human heart.
To make the face shine with oil,
and food that sustains the human heart.[6]
16Yhwh's trees[7] drink their fill,
Lebanese cedars, ones that[8] he planted,
17Where birds nest;
the stork—its home is the junipers.[9]

4. The verbs are the first of fifteen examples of energic final *nûn*, a fuller and more imposing form (JM 44e), in vv. 7, 9, 10, 12, 22, 26–30, mostly at the end of cola.

5. EVV "not again cover" takes this as an instance of *šûb*, meaning "to do again," but this usually involves the two verbs being asyndetic or linked by *w*, and here "return" is more likely in the context with the focus on movement (cf. Num. 35:32; Dan. 10:20).

6. I take "food" as a further object of "bring forth," even though v. 15c has meanwhile used a different construction (EVV obscure this difficulty). "Food" has already appeared as the object of that verb in v. 14c, and v. 15c parallels v. 15a as v. 15b parallels v. 14c. Sym has all infinitives in v. 15, implying the idiom whereby an infinitival construction is continued by finite verbs, "and wine to gladden . . . bread to sustain . . ." (cf. DG 107). Allen (*Psalms 101–150*, 36) understands the yiqtols thus but takes Yhwh as their subject and translates "with wine . . . with bread"; the word order is again a problem. GKC 114o takes the infinitives as gerunds ("in bringing forth . . . in making the face shine"), but these two verbs (and the yiqtols) introduce the objective of the participial clauses in v. 14a–b, not merely define the action; contrast v. 21b.

7. LXX "the trees of the open country" suggests *śādeh* and thus a misreading of *śadday* for *yhwh*. 4QPs[d] has this at v. 11 (see Gerhard-Wilhelm Nebe, "Psalm 104,11 aus Höhle 4 von Qumran," *ZAW* 93 [1981]: 284–90).

8. The *ʾăšer* (unnecessary in poetry) has demonstrative significance.

9. LXX "it leads" suggests that it reads *bĕrōʾšām* ("at their head") for MT *bĕrôšîm*.

18The high mountains for the ibex,
the cliffs are a refuge for the rock badgers.

19He made the moon for dates,
the sun which knows its time for setting.
20You bring darkness and it becomes night;[10]
in it every animal in the forest moves about.
21The lions roar for prey,
and that in seeking[11] their food from God.
22When the sun rises they gather[12]
and lie down in their lairs.
23Human beings go out to their work,
to their service until evening.

24How the things you made multiplied, Yhwh;
you made them all in wisdom.
The earth is full of your possessions;
25that is the sea, great and wide in reach.
There are moving things without number,
living creatures small and great.
26There ships go about,
Leviathan that you shaped to play in it.
27To you all of them look
to give them their food at its time.
28You give to them, they gather;
you open your hand, they eat their fill of good things.
29You hide your face, they panic;
you gather up their breath, they perish,
they return to their dirt.
30You send out your spirit, they are created;
you renew the face of the ground.

31May Yhwh's splendor be forever,
may Yhwh rejoice in his works,
32One who looks on the earth and it trembles,
who touches the mountains[13] and they smoke.
33I will sing for Yhwh as long as I live,
I will make music for my God as long as I last.
34May my murmuring give delight to him;
I myself will rejoice in Yhwh.

10. Strictly "bring darkness, and it shall become night"; that is, the verbs are impv. and jussive.

11. On the construction, see DG 109 remark 2; GKC 114p.

12. In the asyndetic construction, the first verb is subordinate to the second (see DG 123 remark 1).

13. Here the yiqtol verb does continue the participial construction (contrast v. 15).

35May sinners come to an end from the earth;
the faithless: may there be none of them anymore.

Worship Yhwh, my soul;
praise Yah.

Interpretation

The psalm is framed by the self-exhortation, "Worship Yhwh, my soul" (vv. 1a and 36a; cf. also vv. 33–34), suggesting it is a praise psalm for an individual. But it finally closes with the plural bidding to "praise Yah," suggesting it is actually a praise psalm in which the minister speaks individually but wants the congregation to join in (or in which each individual speaks to his or her own self).[14] The self-encouragement is designed to draw each individual into its worship of the world's creator and provider. But we do not know in what worship context it would have been used.

The frame corresponds to that of Ps. 103, which also combined the individual and the communal. Again as in Ps. 103, before the closing self-exhortation comes a longer extended declaration about the appropriate response to Yhwh (vv. 31–35).[15] All that intervenes (vv. 1b–30) expresses the content or reason for the worship, though without the characteristic "because" of a praise psalm. This content contrasts with Ps. 103. It does not mention Israel, the covenant, or Zion.[16] Yhwh, Israel's God, is the one who acts here (the name comes ten times; the ordinary word "God" comes on its own only once).[17] But that makes it more noteworthy that here the world's creation by Yhwh stands on its own ground, separate from the theme of Yhwh's involvement in salvation.[18] The psalm is totally concerned with Yhwh's relationship to the world as its creator, in two interwoven aspects, Yhwh's original activity in bringing the world into being, and Yhwh's ongoing activity in making the world work, which means that "the nearness of God is immediately experienced, each day,

14. Cf. Mowinckel, *Psalms*, 1:93.

15. Klaus Seybold sees this as a later addition ("Psalm 104 im Spiegel seiner Unterschrift," *TZ* 40 [1984]: 1–11; cf. idem, *Psalmen*, 311).

16. It is thus concerned with "existential questions" (Sabine Paulsen, "Schöpfungsverständnis im 'Psalm des Volkes' [Ps 104] und im 'Psalm der Theologen' [Ps 8]," *Ministerial Formation* 53 [1991]: 27–30, 41).

17. Cf. Francis Watson, *Text and Truth* (Edinburgh: Clark; Grand Rapids: Eerdmans, 1997), 263, noting that Ps. 104 thus does not expound a "natural theology."

18. Gerhard von Rad, "The Theological Problem of the Old Testament Doctrine of Creation," in *The Problem of the Hexateuch and Other Essays* (Edinburgh: Oliver and Boyd; New York: McGraw-Hill, 1966), 131–43 (see 140). Cf. Calvin, *Psalms*, 4:143.

each hour, in createdness itself. For this suppliant, all reality is a sign of the goodness and kindness of the creator."[19] The different sections move between reference to those initiating acts (vv. 1b–4 and 5–9, 19, 24a–b) and to the ongoing activity (vv. 10–12, 13–18, 20–23, 24c–30).[20] There is some logic about the movement: from preparing to undertake the original work of ordering on earth (vv. 1b–4) to exercising constraints on the waters there (vv. 5–9) to providing water for animals and land and thus making things grow for animals and human beings (vv. 10–18) to providing celestial guidance for the lives of animals and human beings (vv. 19–23); vv. 24–30 then summarize the whole story.[21]

The psalm has points of contact with Gen. 1–3; perhaps Gen. 1–3 utilized the psalm (among other things) in composing its creation narratives or the psalm utilized Gen. 1–3 (among other things) in formulating its celebration of Yhwh's work as creator.[22] But the two have their individual integrity and read more like independent works with overlapping foci. Comparing them nevertheless helps to highlight the nature of each.

The psalm's picture of creation as requiring the subduing of dynamic forces embodied in the sea, and its reference to Leviathan, also suggest an acquaintance with Canaanite and Babylonian stories reflected in other psalms. But Ps. 104 is more distinctive for its relationship with an Egyptian hymn.[23] In the fourteenth century, Pharaoh Akhenaton initiated a form of monotheistic religion in Egypt, which involved worshipping the sun alone. The hymn expresses that faith. There is enough similarity between hymn and psalm to make it plausible that the psalmist knew the hymn or knew hymns of this kind. Such knowledge might have been mediated by the same Canaanite culture that mediated the stories about the Sea and about Leviathan, Canaan often having been under Egyptian domination.[24] A comparison of psalm and hymn again helps to highlight the distinctive nature of each.

19. Jörg Jeremias, "Schöpfung in Poesie und Prosa des Alten Testaments," in *Schöpfung und Neuschöpfung*, JBT 5 (Neukirchen-Vluyn: Neukirchener Verlag, 1990), 11–36 (see 23).

20. Verses 16b and 26b also refer to past acts.

21. For different theories about the psalm's structure, see Allen, *Psalms 101–150*, 42–44, and his references.

22. For the first view, see, e.g., A. van der Voort, "Genèse i,1 à ii,4a et le Psaume civ," *RB* 58 (1951): 321–47; for the second, Paul Humbert, "Le relation de Genèse 1 et du Psaume 104 avec la liturgie du Nouvel-An israëlite," *RHPR* 15 (1935): 1–27.

23. See *ANET*, 369–71; Pierre Auffret, *Hymnes d'Égypte et d'Israël*, OBO 34 (Göttingen: Vandenhoeck & Ruprecht, 1981), 133–316; Paul E. Dion, "YHWH as Storm-God and Sun-God," *ZAW* 103 (1991): 43–71.

24. Cf., e.g., Georges Nagel, "À propos des rapports du Psaume 104 avec les textes égyptiens," in *Festschrift Alfred Bertholet*, ed. Walter Baumgartner et al. (Tübingen: Mohr, 1950), 395–403.

David's. [11QPs[a], LXX, Aq]

Heading. See glossary.

[1a]Worship Yhwh, my soul!

104:1a. Introductory self-exhortation. See on 103:1.[25]

104:1b–4. The content of praise first looks back to the initial stage of the work of creation, Yhwh's making a home in the heavens. Gunkel attractively reworks vv. 1–4 as five bicola,[26] but after the opening monocolon linking with v. 35c, v. 1b–c does cohere as two qatal clauses, vv. 2 and 4 each cohere as anarthrous participial clauses, and v. 3 coheres as three participial clauses with the article. While participles sometimes indicate that creation was not merely a past act, here they serve to make past event a present reality before our eyes.

[1b]Yhwh my God, you became very great;
you put on honor and majesty,

While 11QPs[a] has "our God," fitting the psalm's communal nature (and cf. v. 35d), MT's appellative "my God" begins from each individual Israelite's personal relationship with Yhwh. Jerome translates "you are very great . . . you are clothed," but LXX more appropriately translates the verbs as aorist. While the second verb could come from either the stative or fientive forms of its verb (*lābēš* or *lābaš*), the first, *gādal*, is not a stative but a fientive,[27] and the lines that follow make clear that the opening refers to Yhwh's activity in creation, not Yhwh's inherent or ongoing greatness or appearance. The psalm will assume Yhwh has the inherent greatness, honor, and majesty of a king,[28] but its interest lies in Yhwh's manifesting these in creating the cosmos.

[2]Wrapping on light like a coat,
stretching out the heavens like tent curtains,

25. Klaus Koch ("Redemption and Creation in Psalms 103–105," in *For the Sake of the Gospel*, ed. Gnana Robinson [Samuel Amirtham Festschrift; Madurai, India: TTS, 1980], 64–69 [see 65–66]) sees Ps. 104's frame as adapted from Ps. 103.

26. *Psalmen*, 445.

27. Cf. BDB, against JM 112a; DG 57a and remark 1. For "you are great," 86:10 has the noun expression *gādôl 'attâ* (cf. 96:4; 99:2).

28. Cf. Alfons Deissler, "Psalm 104," in *Standing before God*, ed. Asher Finkel and Lawrence Frizzell (John M. Oesterreicher Festschrift; New York: Ktav, 1981), 31–40 (see 34–35).

Verse 2 explicates how Yhwh became great and put on honor and majesty. The sky's brightness and light suggest brightness and light that Yhwh put on like an outer garment in getting involved in the cosmos, "a cloak which reveals God's majesty and conceals the divine nature."[29] Light thus first appears not as a gift for creation (as in Gen. 1) but as Yhwh's own clothing. Yet the parallel colon likely implies that Yhwh's appearing in light results in there being light in the cosmos (one might even compare the theologically significant assumption in Gen. 1 that light preexists the sun's creation). Yhwh brings light into the heavens, which cover the earth like tent curtains. The image simply describes the origin of the sky's expanse; it does not imply Yhwh is constructing a tent to live in, as in Isa. 40:22 (if anything, this is the tent where the world's inhabitants will live).

3One fixing his lofts in the waters,
making the clouds his chariot,
going about on the wings of the wind,

The transition to participles with the article suggests that v. 3a indeed begins a new line. It confirms that v. 2b did not refer to Yhwh's dwelling tent. Rather, Yhwh's dwelling lay above the dome of the heavens. It is a loft or penthouse; the word usually suggests rooms above the main house with relative privacy in relation to what goes on below. The problem with building in the sky is that the waters there (the source of rain) would always threaten a dwelling's stability, as would be the case on earth. So Yhwh has to make sure that the dwelling is firmly fixed.[30]

Another feature of the sky is the clouds that scud across it. So the psalm has Yhwh making these the limousine on which to ride around the cosmos, perhaps for general purposes, perhaps for the work of creation in the earthly world that the psalm will go on to. The wind resembles wings that propel the clouds and thus transport Yhwh.

4Making his aides of winds,
his ministers of flaming fire.

The further anarthrous pair of participial phrases (cf. v. 2) again link with what precedes but take it in another direction. Although the line reads more literally "making his *aides winds and his ministers a flaming fire" (cf.

29. Schaefer, *Psalms*, 257.

30. The verb *qārâ* (piel) is usually taken as a denominative from *qôrâ* ("rafter") and thus to mean "to roof," but the "waters" are below the lofts, not above them. Rather the verb reflects the meaning of the mother verb *qārâ* itself and means "cause to meet, join"—the connotation that generates the meaning "rafters" as things that fit into one another.

Heb. 1:7), it is not obvious what that would mean in this context. But the construction matches passages such as Gen. 2:7, Yhwh "shaped the man [of] the dirt" (cf. Exod. 25:25, 28); the second noun indicates the material from which something was made.[31] The four winds and the lightning bolts of the storm are means whereby Yhwh's purpose is implemented in the world, delivering people from their oppressors (e.g., Ps. 18:7–15 [8–16]). Thus, they are in effect Yhwh's aides or ministers.

104:5–9. While the psalm continues to speak of Yhwh's creating the cosmos, the transition to qatal verbs (vv. 5a, 6a, 8b, 9a) and yiqtol verbs that also refer to the past (vv. 6b–8a) matches a transition to speaking of the making of the world itself. But the lines take up motifs from vv. 1b–4 as they speak of the security Yhwh built into the earth, notwithstanding the threat that tumultuous waters can bring to it (cf. v. 3a).

[5]He founded the earth on its bases:
it will never collapse, ever.

The earth needed to be set on a secure foundation because it, too, stands over expanses of water, the waters that stream through the earth as springs and rivers and surround the land mass; the earth is thus a kind of floating island. To make it secure, then, Yhwh sank down pillars into the solid ground that eventually lies beneath that. Being a skilled engineer, Yhwh could make sure of doing this work really well.

[6]With the deep like a garment you covered it:
the waters were standing above the mountains.
[7]At your blast they were fleeing,
at the sound of your thunder they were rushing away.

The psalm now addresses God rather than speaking about God. It will keep moving between these ways of speaking. Genesis 1 almost starts with the deep covering the earth, without saying how that happened. The psalm indicates that God was responsible for this first stage of bringing into being the earth as we know it. First, that is, God created a world that was covered in water, even to the tops of the mountains.[32]

But then (Gen. 1 coolly puts it) God declared that the waters under the sky (that is, on the earth) should gather to make space for the land. The psalm uses more tumultuous language that understands the seas as

31. See further *TTH* 195. The word order suggests that EVV "making the winds his aides" cannot be right, though as a paraphrase it works.

32. Cf. the language used for the Genesis flood: see David G. Barker, "The Waters of the Earth," *Grace Theological Journal* 7 (1986): 57–80; James Barr, *The Garden of Eden and the Hope of Immortality* (London: SCM, 1992), 77.

full of dynamism of their own (perhaps "standing above" the mountains hints at their self-assertiveness). Yhwh therefore does not merely speak but shouts or roars, working through the phenomena of the storm (wind, lightning, thunder). That has the desired effect.

> 8As they were rising up the mountains, so they were going down the valleys,
> to the place that you founded for them.
> 9You set a limit that they should not pass,
> they should not return to cover the earth.

The asyndetic v. 8a (more literally, "they rose up, they went down") reprises vv. 6–7 on the way to the further point in vv. 8b–9.[33] Yhwh had appointed a place where the waters were now to be, as firmly "founded" as the earth itself (v. 5). They were therefore secure, but more to the point, the earth was therefore secure from their encroachment. Verse 9 thus nuances v. 8b. The sea can pound the shore, but it can never cross it so as to overwhelm the earth again.

The waters are in focus in every colon in vv. 7–9 yet are never mentioned. "This is an ellipse of iconic import: the waters are commanded to subside,"[34] and they disappear, even rhetorically.

104:10–18. The psalm continues to describe Yhwh's relationship with the waters but reverts again to participles (vv. 10a, 13, 14), followed by yiqtols dependent on these, describing the ongoing consequences of Yhwh's act. Thus the whole section makes the transition to describing Yhwh's ongoing activity, specifically as this involves water; it is reflected in the staircase aspect to the section.

Mountains and the wild animals (vv. 10–11)
  Trees and birds; Yhwh satiates (vv. 12–13)
    Yhwh makes things grow for animals and human beings (vv. 14–15)
  Trees and birds; Yhwh satiates (vv. 16–17)
Mountains and wild animals (v. 18)

In a good sense, there is no progress in Yhwh's involvement in the world. It is cyclic but therefore ongoing.

33. "The mountains were rising up, the valleys were going down," makes less sense in the context, as do Edmund P. Sutcliffe's suggestion ("A Note on Psalm civ 8," *VT* 2 [1952]: 177–79) that the verbs refer to the way springs continue to arise near the tops of the mountains in Israel, and Richard J. Clifford's suggestion ("A Note on Ps. 104:5–9," *JBL* 100 [1981]: 87–89) that the colon characterizes the waters as fleeing up mountain and down dale.

34. Fokkelman, *Major Poems*, 2:265.

[10]You are the one who sends out springs in canyons;
between the mountains they go.
[11]They water every animal of the wild;
the donkeys break their thirst.
[12]By them the birds of the heavens dwell,
from among the branches the birds give voice.

In "founding" a place for the fleeing waters, Yhwh was not simply stopping them from being dangerous but putting them safely into a reservoir, available as a resource. So from the waters under the earth Yhwh sends out springs in wadis that go between the mountains on either side (they do not overwhelm them, as in v. 6; they know their place).

They are therefore available as drinking water for animals, which fits the psalm's general nature (the human world will appear only, and briefly, in vv. 14–15).

Where there are streams there are trees, and where there are trees there are birds. The psalm still concerns itself with nature in its own right. The birds have homes and sing, not for human beings, nor even in praise to God, but just because that is what they do.

[13]You are the one who waters the mountains from his lofts,
from the fruit of your works the earth drinks its fill.

The further participle suggests another semi-new beginning. Water also makes things grow. But the continuity is especially clear in relation to v. 3a. The rain falls not merely because of the circular process described in Eccles. 1:7 but because Yhwh is acting as a celestial sprinkler operative. Metaphorically, the fruit of the gardener's work is the satiation of the earth; the verb suggests that the earth too is an animate entity, with a thirst that gets quenched. More literally, the work's fruit is described in vv. 14–15.[35]

[14]You are the one who grows grass for the cattle,
plants for the service of people,
To bring forth food from the earth,
[15]and wine that gladdens the human heart.
To make the face shine with oil,
and food that sustains the human heart.

Whereas the waters in vv. 10–12 directly served the animals, the rain does so indirectly by making grass grow. Further, the animals are now not

35. On the phrase, see T. Booij, "Psalm 104,13b," *Bib* 70 (1989): 409–12.

the creatures of the wild but cattle, which exist for human beings. Whereas v. 14a suggests grass that animals can eat and kindly turn into milk and meat for human beings, v. 14b suggests plants that people can eat. While the genitive might be objective (plants that serve people), in v. 23 service is something people do rather than receive (cf. Exod. 1:14; also Gen. 2:5, 15). So the colon likely refers to something of the world's ecological working; human beings serve the plants, the plants meet the human beings' needs. The picture is very different from that threatened in Gen. 3:17–18.[36]

The subject of the infinitive in v. 14c might be God (Vg) or the human servants (Jerome), and the noun *leḥem* may denote food in general or the bread made from one of the key crops that v. 14b would refer to. Verse 15a complements that. While animals drink water, human beings are more inclined to drink wine.

Once again, either God or the human servants might be the subjects of the infinitive in v. 15b. Alongside grapes, olives are one of the most important crops in Israel, with a wide range of important applications in cooking and lighting, but also makeup, as much for men as for women. The closing colon brings the little group of lines to a close by picking up *leḥem* from v. 14c and "the human heart" from v. 15a.

16Yhwh's trees drink their fill,
Lebanese cedars, ones that he planted,
17Where birds nest;
the stork—its home is the junipers.

The verses return to the trees and birds and to Yhwh's generous provision of rain (cf. vv. 12–13). Now it is the trees that are personalized, drinking to the full of the gardener's provision. Admittedly v. 16a actually distances Yhwh from the process of providing for the trees, only thereby to throw into relief the subsequent description of Yhwh as the one who planted them. Whereas v. 15 implied trees useful to humanity, v. 16 refers to trees that exist for the sake of other members of the world community. Cedar's key role in building projects is unmentioned. The psalm is interested in living trees and the enjoyment of their provision.

It *is* interested in their importance for other parts of the ecology of creation, as in vv. 12–13. They provide homes for the birds. The juniper is another tree that flourished in the forests of Lebanon, another tall, impressive, spreading, fragrant conifer.

18The high mountains for the ibex,
the cliffs are a refuge for the rock badgers.

36. Arthur Walker-Jones, "Psalm 104," in *Earth Story*, ed. Habel, 84–97 (see 92).

The section returns to where it started, with the mountains and the wild animals. The ordinary mountains are useful to humanity and to domestic animals because of things that grow there (vv. 13–15). But the high mountains are useful to no one but creatures such as the ibex, the wild goat that can be seen by the waters at En Gedi, or the rock badger, strictly the hyrax, a rabbitlike creature, though larger than the average rabbit and living in rocky situations.[37] Once again the interrelationship of creation is noted. The high mountains and the cliffs are a home, a secure refuge for these creatures (in the parallelism, "refuge" also applies in the first colon), as the trees are for the birds. Everyone needs a home.

104:19–23. The psalm turns to the mutual relationship of day and night (or rather of night and day, paralleling the "evening and morning" of Gen. 1), another instance of creation's ecology.

> 19He made the moon for dates,
> the sun which knows its time for setting.

The transition is marked by a further qatal verb, the first since vv. 5–9. The psalm again looks back to the moment of creation and compares with Gen. 1:14–18. There the role of sun and moon is to distinguish day and night and on a broader front make it possible to date months and years; Genesis adds almost as an afterthought that they also give light. The emphasis here is the same; even the afterthought is missing. The moon enables people to mark the passing of months and thus observe the rhythm of their lives in their relationship with God; the sun does the same for the years and for the rhythm of day and night.[38] Whereas v. 19a sees the moon as simply an object, something God made to fulfill a function, v. 19b asserts another aspect of the personal nature of the creation: the sun is an entity that "knows" and acts on the basis of its knowing.

> 20You bring darkness and it becomes night;
> in it every animal in the forest moves about.
> 21The lions roar for prey,
> and that in seeking their food from God.

Once again the psalm segues into describing God's ongoing activity. Genesis 1 has God establishing the pattern of day and night by the original act of creation, and v. 19 has implied a related perspective in

37. The Hebrew word *šāpān* is the origin of the name "Spain," as creatures there were mistakenly identified as hyrax.

38. The Hebrew has no *ʾăšer*, and EVV have "the sun knows its time for setting," but the word order and the conventions of parallelism suggest that v. 19b incorporates an unmarked relative clause.

seeing the sun as knowing what to do at the end of each day. Here God is actively involved each evening, effecting that transition from day to night. Further, in Gen. 1 darkness is at best of neutral significance; it is not God's positive achievement, like light. Here night has positive significance, again for the animal world. It is a safer time for animals; they are not so easily subject to being hunted and caught.

But a paradoxical aspect to the natural world's ecology is the animal world's being one where one animal eats another. Lions roar for their prey. Again there may be a contrast with Gen. 1, and certainly with Isa. 11:6–7, where lion is to lie down with lamb, content to eat hay. Genesis 1 may similarly imply that humanity's task in taming the earth was to get the animal world to live on that basis. Between creation and the End, the psalm is radically accepting of the way the world is. Lions eat other animals, and God is the farmer providing them with other creatures to eat, like the keeper of a wildlife park. And the lions are like the lions in a wildlife park, looking to their keeper so to provide. We might think of them doing this unconsciously (they are just crying out for what they will then make it their business to obtain), but in light of the way the rest of the psalm sees creation in personal terms, we should probably reckon that the psalm sees them as doing this consciously.

22When the sun rises they gather
and lie down in their lairs.
23Human beings go out to their work,
to their service until evening.

Another aspect of creation's ecology is the interrelationship of the world of wild animals and the world of humanity. The animals make the most of the night but then go home. The verb *ʾāsap* (niphal) can have the more negative meaning "withdraw" (of the moon, in Isa. 60:20; and cf. v. 29), but it more often has the positive meaning "gather together" (e.g., Ps. 47:9 [10]), specifically of animals coming to their quarters at the end of the day or to find refuge (Gen. 29:7; Exod. 9:19). The night's work done and the family's provision being won, lions can go home and relax.

Humanity's work pattern is the obverse. Sunrise is the sign for human beings to go out to their work in the fields and with the flocks, till evening again comes and the cycle starts once more. Here in the parallelism "work" (*pōʿal*) is paralleled by "service" (*ʿăbōdâ*), the first suggesting the activity and its productiveness, the second pointing to the way humanity serves nature in order to be served by it, yet another aspect of the world's ecology (see on v. 14).

104:24–30. Once again a qatal verb signals a new topic and new section. As this survey of creation draws near its end, the psalm stands back and looks at the world against the broadest horizon, spatially and metaphysically.

> **24**How the things you made multiplied, Yhwh;
> you made them all in wisdom.
> The earth is full of your possessions;
> **25a**that is the sea, great and wide in reach.

With its "multiplied,"[39] "them all," "is full," and "great and wide in reach," stretching in different directions,[40] this closing section of survey makes explicit the extraordinary range and variety of the things Yhwh made and provides for. It once again goes back to Yhwh's activity at the beginning, with v. 24 adding the new note that the creation was an expression of Yhwh's wisdom, the point expounded in Prov. 8:22–31. If wisdom here has a particular connotation, perhaps it is that interwoven ecology that the psalm has persistently described. The world is a magnificent quilt in which every thread contributes to a whole, woven by a supremely skilled craftworker.

Verses 24c–25a re-express the point. Earth and heaven is the more common pairing, but Job 11:9 and 12:8 bring together earth and sea. In that context they are a wisdom pairing, which perhaps suggests that vv. 24c–25a spell out and provide the evidence for the statement about wisdom in v. 24b.[41] Here, the sea is simply the sea; it is no longer the primeval deep, as in v. 6. But the line adds the significant notion that the world is full of Yhwh's "possessions." The verb behind *qinyān* is sometimes translated "create" (cf. LXX here), but *qinyān* itself elsewhere refers to possessions, often cattle (cf. 105:21), and this makes sense here (so Jerome). The psalm has spoken of all these features of the world in their own terms, but this term reframes their significance. The colon about the sea comprises five words, very long for a single colon. Rather than shorten it[42] or turn it into two cola (that is the sea/great and wide in reach), I take the rhetoric to match the statement.

> **25b–c**There are moving things without number,
> living creatures small and great.

39. Not "how many are the things . . ."; the qatal verb refers to an event, as in v. 1, and the "how" qualifies the verb.

40. Lit. "wide of [on] both hands," that is, in both directions (BDB 390b).

41. See further Adele Berlin, "The Wisdom of Creation in Psalm 104," in *Seeking Out the Wisdom of the Ancients*, ed. Ronald L. Troxel et al. (M. V. Fox Festschrift; Winona Lake, IN: Eisenbrauns, 2005), 71–83.

42. So Briggs, *Psalms*, 2:339.

[26]There ships go about,
Leviathan that you shaped to play in it.

Two lines spell out the preceding two cola. There are all the living creatures that move about on the earth, countless in number and diverse in size. And there are the entities of the sea, though their identity is more surprising. Ships also feature in the Aten hymn, though not with a very similar meaning, and the collocation may rather reflect a Phoenician background.[43] Their appearance here might also link with the interweaving of the needs of humanity and of the rest of creation. Sailors certainly have to look to God for food and for the continuance of life (vv. 27–29). The pairing with Leviathan suggests another perspective, that the line covers not just ordinary phenomena of the sea. How extraordinary that ships should be able to sail the sea with its dangers! How extraordinary is the great sea monster! In 74:14, as in Ugaritic stories, Leviathan is a primeval sea dragon, the embodiment of dynamic forces asserted against God and against order, a parallel image to the image of the sea itself. But in vv. 25–26 the sea is simply the sea, and the sea dragon has been demythologized. It is the Loch Ness Monster. It is another object of Yhwh's shaping as creator, shaped for a positive purpose: to frolic in the waters.[44] On the sea with its dangers the ships freely "go about" or go on their journeys (*hālak* piel), while the sea monster simply "plays" in it. Perhaps Yhwh even shaped it to play *with* it (NJPS), the meaning in Job 41:5 [40:29]: for three hours each day, according to *b. ʿAbodah Zarah* 3b (cf. Rashi, Qimchi, Ibn Ezra).

[27]To you all of them look
to give them their food at its time.
[28]You give to them, they gather;
you open your hand, they eat their fill of good things.

All earth's creatures (presumably human and animal), then, look in hope and expectation (*śābar*) to Yhwh for food as the lions do, at the time when it is due: grass in spring, grain in high summer, olives and grapes in the fall.

Verse 28 underlines positively how that works. When Yhwh gives, they are in a position to harvest. The second colon in its parallelism at each point puts the point more strongly. Yhwh gives with an open hand, with generosity, and the recipients receive not merely a sufficient portion but eat their fill, and of good things (cf. vv. 13, 16).

43. See Christoph Uehlinger, "Leviathan and die Schiffe in Ps 104,25–26," *Bib* 71 (1990): 499–526.

44. G. R. Driver ("The Resurrection of Marine and Terrestrial Creatures," *JSS* 7 [1962]: 12–22 [see 19–20]) argues that it is merely the whale.

[29]You hide your face, they panic;
you gather up their breath, they perish,
they return to their dirt.

For a moment the psalm faces a negative corollary, before closing the section on a positive note in v. 30. The lines continue the form of v. 28, where a second-person yiqtol singular verb addressing God leads asyndetically into a third-person plural yiqtol verb referring to creatures (so vv. 28a, 28b, 29a, 29b [with v. 29c as an appendage], 30a [with v. 30b as an appendage]). Each time in the asyndetic structure, the first clause is subordinate to the second.[45]

It is Yhwh's smiling that issues in the generosity v. 28 described. Conversely, Yhwh's turning away issues in the withholding of provision. It is thus a terrifying phenomenon. Verse 29b parallels v. 29a and takes it further. If Yhwh's face is turned away for long enough and provision is denied for long enough, this means death, for animals or for human beings. Yhwh is firmly made the author of the withholding of provision; if the harvest fails, it is because Yhwh's face has turned away. The psalm accepts the logic of double predestination. If God gets the credit for giving, God is also responsible when provision fails. Indeed, v. 29b pushes the logic further. The human and animal world has breath (*rûaḥ*; cf. Eccles. 3:21), and thus life, because Yhwh breathed into it (Gen. 2:7; *nĕšāmâ*) and continues to breathe into it (Isa. 42:5; Job 34:14; both *nĕšāmâ* and *rûaḥ*). When we die, Yhwh collects up that breath again (cf. Ps. 146:4; Eccles. 12:7). It is Yhwh who makes that happen. And where there is no breath, there is no life. Life is not at our disposal.[46] The unexpected third colon pushes the point home (cf. Gen. 3:19).

[30]You send out your spirit, they are created;
you renew the face of the ground.

Perhaps it is not surprising that v. 30 then returns to the positive, completing a staircase sequence in vv. 27–30:

God gives provision (vv. 27–28)
  God withdraws provision (v. 29a)
  God withdraws life (v. 29b–c)
God gives life (v. 30)

45. Cf. DG 123, remark 2.
46. Odil H. Steck, *World and Environment* (Nashville: Abingdon, 1980), 87.

The verse completes another statement of the cyclic nature of Yhwh's involvement in nature. Yhwh brings about the death of animals and human beings; Yhwh also brings into being the next generation. Yhwh sends out springs (v. 10); Yhwh sends out the divine breath or spirit. The psalm thus moves from talk in terms of "their breath" to talk in terms of "your spirit." It is the same breath/spirit that is being spoken of, but the change in expression reflects the fact that there is a level of dynamism involved when we speak of the divine breath/spirit. The human breath/spirit is an offshoot of that, but a pale one. That is in turn reflected in the association of "your spirit" with "creation." Spirit suggests the exercise of divine power; creation suggests the exercise of divine sovereignty. When live creatures come into being, there is something magically supernatural about the event.

Talk in terms of "renewal" restates the point; making things new is also a divine capacity (cf. the two uses of the imperative of *ḥādaš* piel, 51:10 [12]; Lam. 5:21). But the section's last colon also returns to the psalm's broader concern, with the "inanimate" aspect of creation, the ground itself. Here, it is renewed, not cursed.[47] Creation does not groan for its redemption (Rom. 8:22) but reveals God's nature (cf. Rom. 1:20) and experiences its redemption.

104:31–35. The psalm closes in a way analogous to Ps. 103 as it calls for and expresses a response to the account of God and the world that it has offered. The section is dominated by modal verbs, verbs expressing intent, wish, or exhortation, by means of jussives (v. 31 with v. 32 dependent on it, v. 34, v. 35), cohortatives (v. 33), and imperatives (v. 36).

> 31May Yhwh's splendor be forever,
> may Yhwh rejoice in his works,

How does v. 31a relate to what precedes? The parallel colon with its reference to Yhwh's "works" (*maʿăśeh*; cf. v. 24; also v. 13; and the mother verb *ʿāśâ* in vv. 4, 19, 24) suggests that the splendor is the way Yhwh's greatness and power are reflected and demonstrated in the acts the psalm has described, past and present (cf. 19:1 [2]), and the *honor that should there be given to Yhwh. The wish that Yhwh should also personally rejoice in these works is distinctive. Only here is Yhwh the subject of this verb,[48] though it does express forcefully and affectively the idea of God looking at creation and reckoning that it is good, indeed very good (Gen. 1). The wish is that Yhwh may look at the world not only with cool appreciation but also with enthusiasm, and may do so

47. Walker-Jones, "Psalm 104," 91; cf. Steck, *World and Environment*, 79–80.

48. Isaiah 9:16 [17] may be another example, though even there the verb is negatived.

not only in respect of its original creation but in connection with the ongoing involvement in it that the psalm has spoken of. Prosaically put, "May Yhwh's splendor be manifest in his works forever, and may Yhwh rejoice in these forever."

> [32]One who looks on the earth and it trembles,
> who touches the mountains and they smoke.

This further participial line is not surprising given the psalm's frequent use of such lines, nor is it surprising that such a line should come as the psalm draws to its close. Yet the line's specific content is surprising. The psalm's picture of Yhwh's involvement with the earth has been fundamentally upbeat, and the sentimental picture of creation in hymns such as "All Things Bright and Beautiful" finds this aspect of the psalm attractive. But the psalm has alluded to more fearsome aspects of that involvement. Winds and flaming fire were Yhwh's agents at the beginning; Yhwh's blast and thunder were involved in ordering the world (vv. 4, 8). This further line makes explicit that the more fearsome side is also an aspect of Yhwh's ongoing involvement in the world. Its emphasis lies on how slightly Yhwh needs to act in order to produce devastating effects. Only a look or a touch is required to produce the storm that will generate a mudslide or a covering with smoke-like mist or a forest fire.

> [33]I will sing for Yhwh as long as I live,
> I will make music for my God as long as I last.

The worshipper's personal declaration of intent to sing and make *music in response to the divine splendor manifest in the world corresponds to declarations near the end of other psalms (e.g., Pss. 7; 13; 18), and at the beginning of others (e.g., Pss. 101; 108; 138). In the latter case, the main body of the psalm goes on to provide the reasons for or the content of the praise, implicitly or explicitly providing the "because" for the declaration of intent that is characteristic of a hymn. In the former case, the rhetoric is reversed (a "therefore" would be in place instead of a "because"), almost as if the worshipper said, "So you see, that is why I will sing and make music for Yhwh, 'my God'" (cf. v. 1).

> [34]May my murmuring give delight to him;
> I myself will rejoice in Yhwh.

Although the worshipper's *murmur might be the psalm itself, the parallelism rather suggests it is the song that v. 33 has just referred to. But perhaps this is a false antithesis and the song of v. 33 is itself the psalm.

"Give delight" (*ʿārab*) is another affective word; it can refer to the effect of a lover's voice on their beloved (Song 2:14). There is then reciprocity about the two parallel and complementary cola. Yhwh will gain pleasure from the worshipper's praise and the worshipper will join in Yhwh's own rejoicing (cf. v. 31), rejoicing not only in Yhwh's acts but in Yhwh in person.

> 35a–bMay sinners come to an end from the earth;
> the faithless: may there be none of them anymore.

The further transition surprises us. It compares with that in Ps. 139, from vv. 1–18 to vv. 19–22, and likely has similar significance. Anyone can enthuse in worship about the wonders of the world Yhwh has made, but such enthusiastic worship can be a substitute for commitment to Yhwh and Yhwh's ways in life outside worship. But a person who is not so committed cannot take the risk of praying the prayer in v. 35. Thus its concern is not merely with other people from whom the psalm distances itself, but with people such as the worshippers who know that it would be possible to be that kind of person. The transition thus also compares with that in Ps. 19, which moves from Yhwh's splendor at the beginning to a declaration of commitment at the end.

> 35cWorship Yhwh, my soul;
> praise Yah.

The first bidding both brings the modal final section toward its close and completes a frame round the whole (cf. v. 1). The further bidding to *praise *Yah is plural (it is the first occurrence of the bidding *hallĕlû-yāh*) and is thus not addressed to the individual self but to a community that has been invisible through the psalm; it draws them into its worship, as happened in different ways within Ps. 103.[49]

Theological Implications

"As the most extended explication of God's work of creation outside of Genesis," Ps. 104 "deserves a central place in any attempt to think about God as creator and about the doctrine of creation."[50]

Over against the Egyptian hymn, the object of the psalm's praise is a God who is the source of life, who is other than creation rather than

49. Admittedly Syr lacks it, and LXX and Jerome attach it to Ps. 105 (*praise).

50. Patrick D. Miller, "The Poetry of Creation," in *God Who Creates*, ed. William P. Brown and S. Dean McBride (W. S. Towner Festschrift; Grand Rapids: Eerdmans, 2000), 87–103 (see 87).

one who is within the world.[51] Whereas the hymn concerns itself almost entirely with the sun's present relationship with the world, the psalm concerns itself in a more substantial way with God's original ordering of the world (and thus combines the emphases of Gen. 1 and the hymn). The psalm puts more emphasis on water and rain both as threat and as blessing; the hymn makes less mention of these, making clear that this relates to the difference in climate and the role of the Nile in Egypt. The psalm sees Yhwh as Lord of the darkness as well as of the day; the hymn naturally sees the darkness in more negative terms as that which comes when the deity withdraws.[52] The psalm gives the impression of being an expression of praise for anyone and everyone, all of whom may address Yhwh as "my God"; the hymn focuses on the king, for whom the sun especially rises.[53]

Over against Gen. 1–3, the psalm speaks not of a task of creation that could be completed over a week, after which God could simply rest, but of a job of work that continues as long as the world exists. It does not describe this work as something definable and divisible into six or eight discrete acts but pictures God more randomly moving from one task to another, giving a selective picture and letting individual concrete acts stand for the whole; in this respect it resembles Job 38–39 more than Genesis. It is not making an inventory of nature, as we might, but responding to it.[54] While Genesis expounds a concern for creation as a whole and comes to humanity only on Friday afternoon, the psalm is even less focused on humanity (though still more so than Job 38–39) and vividly portrays the way different parts of the world live and work together. Whereas Genesis gives humanity authority over creation, commissions it to fill the world, and thus emphasizes the sexual differentiation of man and woman, the psalm makes humanity one more part of creation; there is no hint of human domination of creation.[55] Whereas Genesis portrays creation as effortless, the psalm portrays it as requiring expenditure of divine energy in constraining and harnessing other dynamic forces. Whereas Genesis sees God as creating light

51. Jon D. Levenson does warn against overdrawing this contrast; in the psalm Yhwh "is more within nature" than is sometimes suggested (*Creation and the Persistence of Evil* [repr., Princeton, NJ: Princeton University Press, 1994], 64).

52. Cf. Walter Harrelson's comments, "On God's Care for the Earth," *CurTM* 2 (1975): 19–22 (see 20–21).

53. Cf. Otto Eissfeldt, "'Mein Gott' im Alten Testament," in Eissfeldt, *Kleine Schriften* (Tübingen: Mohr, 1966), 3:35–47 (see 46–47).

54. Cf. Virgil Howard, "Psalm 104," *Int* 46 (1992): 176–80 (see 176).

55. Cf. James Limburg, "Down-to-Earth Theology," *CurTM* 21 (1994): 340–46. William Henry Green also sees its theocentric nature as a significant message for a people coming to Christian faith out of paganism ("A Psalm for Igorots," *Anglican Theological Review* 40 [1958]: 189–203 [see 189]).

but not explicitly as creating darkness, and as introducing death only as a consequence of human disobedience, the psalm sees both darkness and light and death and life as parts of the intrinsic pattern of God's sovereignty in the world. Whereas Genesis incorporates recognition of human disobedience and its consequences, the psalm makes explicit the need that the world be purged of sinner and faithless. Whereas Genesis recognizes tensions between the human and animal world and sees both as living with a curse, the psalm speaks of none of this. Whereas Genesis describes God as blessing creation and giving over to nature the capacity to reproduce, the psalm sees God as continually involved with creation in bringing about that capacity. Whereas Genesis has God seeing the goodness of creation, the psalm's vision is that God should actually rejoice in the creation.[56]

The contrast with Genesis also points to the richness of the psalm's models for conceiving God's involvement in the world. First, the psalm shares with Genesis the model of God as the world's maker back at the beginning, the deist clockmaker who set the world going and could then leave it to run itself. God was a builder who constructed a house which he would then leave to its inhabitants to live in. God was a king who asserted control of his realm at the beginning of his reign and ensured that forces that might stop his realm working as he wanted could not do so. God was a forester who planted the trees that seem to last forever. We use the word "cosmos," but it can be a misleading one. Creation does not have a self-contained order because that is its intrinsic nature but because God made it that way.

But as king, God also constructed a palace to live in, a palace within the cosmos, as if wanting to be in a position to be involved with the world on an ongoing basis; and as controller of those potentially assertive forces, God did not merely set constraints on them at the beginning, but makes waters spring forth day by day. God put moon and sun in their place at the beginning but also brings about the movement from light to darkness each day. God makes thunder resound and lightning flash. God is a gardener sprinkling rain from the heavens. God is a farmer growing crops. God feeds the lions. Thus the beings in the world look to God for each meal. God is not on a Sabbath but continues to work. When God gives, these beings eat, to their full; when God does not, they are terrified, because they know there is no one else who will provide for them. While God breathed breath into the world's being at the beginning, God also breathes breath into each individual. And God is the one who takes it back. But God looks on to the future and

56. See further William P. Brown, "The Lion, the Wicked, and the Wonder of It All: Psalm 104 and the Playful God," *Journal for Preachers* 29/3 (2006): 15–19.

continues being involved with the world, renewing nature for the next year or the next generation.

We use the word "nature" as we use the word "cosmos," but it can also be a misleading word.[57] The natural world does not have energy, creativity, or fecundity of its own, but only energy, creativity, and fecundity that reflect the continuing involvement of God's energy, creativity, and fecundity. But it does have a being of its own. Its different parts (streams, mountains, trees, birds, wild animals, human beings) fit together. It drinks its fill. God did thereby establish a "natural" order whereby the animals get their water not directly from God but from the springs that God makes gush forth. The sun rises without being told. Animals know when to come out and when to go home, and so do human beings.

"In the Jewish tradition Psalm 104 is sung on the morning of Yom Kippur as a pledge that new life will emerge out of penance and sorrow. It is chanted on the evening of the new moon, thus consecrating another month to God. It is recited from the Sabbath of the feast of Sukkoth to Pesah (i.e., throughout the winter), in anticipation of new life in the spring. In the Orthodox tradition Psalm 104 is chanted at vespers at the setting of the sun, with the lighting of lamps, the beginning of the new day. Orthodox worshippers open the liturgy with this hymn which praises God's providence in all aspects of creation."[58] The Church of England *Book of Common Prayer* prescribes it for Pentecost, which suggests a link between the giving of God's spirit when people are born and when they are born anew.[59] The giving of God's spirit at creation finds its fulfillment at Pentecost; the giving of God's spirit at Pentecost is the consummation of the giving that happens when we are born.

57. Cf. Odil Hannes Steck, "Der Wein unter den Schöpfungsgaben," in Steck, *Wahrnehmungen Gottes im Alten Testament*, TBü 70 (Munich: Kaiser, 1982), 240–61 (see 242–47).

58. Schaefer, *Psalms*, 258–59.

59. Cf. Mays, *Psalms*, 337.

Psalm 105

Yhwh Is Still the Same

Translation

1Confess Yhwh, call in his name,[1]
make known his deeds among the peoples.
2Sing for him, make music for him,
murmur about all his wonders.
3Exult in his holy name;
may the heart of people who seek help from Yhwh rejoice.
4Have recourse to Yhwh and his might;[2]
seek help from his face continually.
5Be mindful of his wonders, the ones that he has done,[3]
his portents, the decisions of his mouth,
6Offspring of Abraham his servant,
descendants of Jacob, his chosen ones.[4]

7He is Yhwh our God;
his decisions are in all the earth.
8He has been mindful of his covenant forever,

1. LXX, Jerome begin "Praise Yah" (at the end of Ps. 104 in MT).

2. LXX "and be strengthened" implies *wĕʿuzzû* for MT *wĕʿuzzô*.

3. The suffix on "wonders" and the *ʾăšer* suggest that the line means more than merely "the wonders that he has done" (EVV).

4. 11QPs[a] has *ʿbdyw*, "his servants" (cf. LXX), and *bḥyrw*, "his chosen one." Verses 42–43 correspond to MT.

the word he commanded for a thousand generations,
9The one that he sealed with Abraham,
his sworn promise to Isaac.
10He established it as a statute for Jacob,
a lasting covenant for Israel,
11Saying, "To you I will give the land of Canaan
as the share you will possess."

12When they were few in number,
when they were little and aliens in it,
13Going about from nation to nation,
from one kingdom to another people,
14He did not let anyone oppress them
but rebuked kings on account of them:
15"Do not touch my anointed ones,
do not harm my prophets."

16He summoned hunger onto the land;
every staff of bread he broke.
17He sent someone in front of them,
sold as a slave, Joseph.
18They subjected his foot[5] to the fetter;
iron came on his person.[6]
19Until his word came about,
Yhwh's saying refined him.
20The king sent and liberated him,
the ruler of peoples [sent] and released him.
21He made him master of his household,
ruler over all his property,
22To constrain his officials according to his desire
and teach wisdom to his elders.[7]
23Israel came to Egypt,
Jacob stayed in the land of Ham.
24He made his people very fruitful,
made them stronger than their foes.

25He turned their heart so as to be against his people,
to scheme against his servants.
26He sent Moses his servant,
Aaron whom he chose.

5. Q has sg. *raglô*, K. pl. *rglyw*.

6. There is no prep., and LXX, Jerome, and Sym take "his person" as the subject, but this reverses the Hebrew word order; cf. J. Brinktrine, "Zur Übersetzung von Ps 105 (104):18," *ZAW* 64 (1952): 251–58. The links with Isa. 58 (see the comment on v. 20) suggest that *nepeš* does not mean "neck" (against, e.g., Gunkel, *Psalmen*, 460).

7. The yiqtol continues the infinitival construction (*TTH* 118).

[27]They brought on them[8] the words about his signs,
his portents[9] in the land of Ham.
[28]He sent darkness, made it dark,[10]
and they did not defy his word.[11]
[29]He turned their water into blood
and killed their fish.
[30]Their land teemed with frogs,
in their kings' rooms.
[31]He spoke and a swarm came,
mosquitoes in all their territory.
[32]He made their rain into hail,
flaming fire in their land.
[33]He struck their vine and their fig tree,
broke off the trees in their territory.
[34]He spoke and locusts came,
grasshoppers without number.
[35]They ate all the vegetation in their land,
ate the fruit of their soil.
[36]He struck every firstborn in their land,
the first of all their vigor.
[37]He brought them out with silver and gold,
not one of their clans collapsing.
[38]Egypt rejoiced at their going out,[12]
because dread of them had fallen on them.

[39]He spread a cloud for covering
and a fire to give light by night.
[40]They asked[13] and he brought quail,[14]
and he was filling them[15] with bread from the heavens.
[41]He opened a crag and waters flowed,
went in dry places as a stream.
[42]Because he was mindful of his holy word,
of Abraham his servant,
[43]He brought out his people with gladness,
his chosen ones with resounding.

8. On the use of *śîm*, see H. J. van Dijk, "A Neglected Connotation of Three Hebrew Verbs," *VT* 18 (1968): 16–30 (see 28). LXX, Syr, Jerome have a sg. verb, making Yhwh the subject, assimilating to the verses on either side.

9. The suffix on "his signs" also applies here.

10. LXX takes the hiphil as declarative, "and it became dark."

11. So Q. L has *dĕbārôw* (!); LXX implies *dĕbārāyw*, "his words."

12. Like the English "at," the prep. *b* could imply "when" or "because" they went out.

13. The verb is sg., but the subject must be Israel; perhaps a final *w* disappeared from the verb by dittog. LXX, Jerome, Tg have pl.

14. LXX "quail came" implies *wayyābōʾ* for MT *wayyābēʾ*.

15. The verb is yiqtol.

44He gave them the lands of the nations,
they came into possession of the toil of the peoples,
45So that they might keep his statutes
and observe his teachings.
Praise Yah!

Interpretation

This further praise psalm once again comprises a substantial exhortation to praise (vv. 1–6) and a very extensive account of why Yhwh is to be praised (vv. 7–45b), with a closing resumptive bidding to praise (v. 45c). But in contrast to Pss. 103 and 104, it has these elements in the more regular order (the exhortation then the reasons for or the content of the praise). It thus begins where Ps. 104 ends. And in contrast to the two preceding psalms, the reasons or content relates entirely to Yhwh's activity in Israel's story. In this, too, it forms a mirror image of Ps. 104. Its account covers the story from Israel's ancestors (vv. 7–15) via Joseph (vv. 16–24) to the oppression in Egypt and deliverance from there (vv. 25–38) to the provision through the wilderness and the occupation of the land (vv. 39–45b). It thus summarizes the familiar story in Genesis to Joshua.[16]

The first striking feature of the psalm version is the total absence of reference to Yhwh's revelation at Sinai (though see v. 45a–b) or to the rebellions in the wilderness; the people go straight from Egypt to Canaan (see esp. vv. 43–44). The psalmist and the community will have known about these events; omitting them focuses the agenda for praise on God's actual acts. These are the decisive factor in Israel's story, not the need for human response.

The omissions cohere with another feature. Where the language differs from that in Genesis to Joshua, it uses terms resonating with the community's reduced circumstances in the exile and afterward (e.g., terms from Isa. 40–66).[17] It thus encourages that community to believe that the God who related to and acted on Israel's behalf at the beginning is the same God for them. The praise psalm is thus expressed in such a way as to bring home the story's implications for the congregation. Its praise is not timeless but oriented to the worshippers' needs in a particular context. It is thus teaching;[18] but it is also worship: "It was the testimony in the

16. "Psalm 105 is the Cliff Notes of the Torah" (Marty E. Stevens, "Psalm 105," *Int* 57 [2003]: 187–89 [see 187]).

17. Cf. Svend Holm-Nielsen, "The Exodus Traditions in Psalm 105," *ASTI* 11 (1977–78): 22–30.

18. Cf. Sigmund Mowinckel, "Psalms and Wisdom," in *Wisdom in Israel and the Ancient Near East*, ed. M. Noth and D. W. Thomas, VTSup 3 (H. H. Rowley Festschrift;

Thanksgiving Psalms that offered an opportunity for teaching."[19] It thus compares and contrasts with other psalms that retell Israel's story. It has detailed similarities to Ps. 78 (e.g., vv. 4, 11, 24, 33, 36), but its overall cast is quite different, as is the case with Pss. 106 and 107.

First Chronicles 16:8–36 combines vv. 1–15 with Ps. 96 and part of Ps. 106 (the most significant differences are that for v. 6 it has Israel for Abraham and for v. 8 a plural imperative "remember") and associates them with the celebration of the covenant chest's arrival in Jerusalem, but the narrative does not say whether that happened at a particular festival and we do not know whether the psalm itself was used in a particular worship setting.

105:1–6. The extensive exhortation to praise occupies six lines in three pairs.

1Confess Yhwh, call in his name,
make known his deeds among the peoples.
2Sing for him, make music for him,
murmur about all his wonders.

The beginning already implies the link just noted, as v. 1 corresponds to words in Isa. 12:4, part of a song for singing "on that day" when troubles and exile are over and the community has been restored, when Yhwh has turned from anger and comforted it. The psalm invites the community to imagine itself in that position; they may do so on the basis of what Yhwh did at the beginning.

Once more the psalm uses the term "*confess," which puts the congregation in the position of people giving testimony to what Yhwh has done in their lives; yet the confession's subject will be what Yhwh did for Israel at the beginning, which Yhwh indeed did for the benefit of every subsequent generation. "Call in his *name" could suggest making the name of Yhwh the basis for one's pleas (e.g., 116:4; 2 Kings 5:11). But Sym takes it to suggest proclaiming in Yhwh's name, proclaiming who Yhwh is and what Yhwh has done (cf. Ps. 116:13, 17; Exod. 33:19; 34:6); this fits better between the other two clauses in v. 1. The second colon then reformulates the point, adding the common further note that although the deeds that will follow are often deeds done *against* other peoples, they are to be made known *among* the peoples.

Whereas v. 1 thus focuses on the content of Israel's praise, v. 2 then focuses on its manner: it involves song, *music, and *murmuring. In this

Leiden: Brill, 1955), 205–24 (see 213); Wallace T. Wolverton, "Sermons in the Psalms," *CJT* 10 (1964): 166–76.

19. Roland E. Murphy, "A Consideration of the Classification, 'Wisdom Psalms,'" in *Congress Volume: Bonn 1962*, VTSup 9 (Leiden: Brill, 1963), 156–67 (see 167).

parallel line there are again two internally parallel exhortations in the first colon and one clause in the second; the "deeds" are also "wonders."

[3]Exult in his holy name;
may the heart of people who seek help from Yhwh rejoice.
[4]Have recourse to Yhwh and his might;
seek help from his face continually.

The first clause reprises the point once more, but the rest of these two lines takes the agenda forward and gives further clues to the psalm's point. Bringing one's pleas to Yhwh is indeed now involved in *seeking help from Yhwh or having *recourse to Yhwh, the synonymous terms that come three times and constitute a telling way of describing the community that the psalm calls to worship. They are favorite expressions in Chronicles as it retells Israel's story to bring home its significance for people living in those disappointing times after the exile. Israel was constantly tempted to have recourse to other religious, political, and military resources, but Israel is defined as a people that looks to Yhwh for these needs. In the postexilic period, its vulnerability might seem to give it nowhere to look. The psalm invites the community to rejoice in Yhwh's holy *name on the assumption that recourse to Yhwh works.

The "continually" of v. 4 underlines the point, and the line further develops it: seeking help from Yhwh, while a matter of definition, involves deliberate choice. It also nuances v. 3 in such a way as to encourage the right choice. "And his might" reminds the addressees that they are not being asked to look to someone feeble (cf. Isa. 31:3). Further, this having recourse involves seeking help from "his face": Yhwh's face turns toward them in a love that will issue in action.

[5]Be mindful of his wonders, the ones that he has done,
his portents, the decisions of his mouth,
[6]Offspring of Abraham his servant,
descendants of Jacob, his chosen ones.

The closing exhortation in these two lines involves just the one verb, "be *mindful," which undergirds v. 4. The combination "wonders" and "portents" (*niplāʾôt, môpĕtîm*) comes only here. The first is a general purposes word for extraordinary acts of God in Israel's life, in individuals' experience, and in creation. "Portent" most characteristically refers to God's acts against Egypt (cf. v. 27); it gives precision to "wonders." The two words are then underlined as "the ones that he has done" and as "the decisions of his mouth," acts of *authority on Yhwh's part; when he speaks, things happen (33:9). If people are mindful of these things, then the seeking that vv. 3–4 describes will follow.

The extensive description of the subjects in v. 6, the addressees, reflects the fact that its deep structure is that it is functionally a set of further objects for the verb. They are to keep in mind not only the acts of v. 5 but also their own identity. They are Abraham's offspring; so what Yhwh did with Abraham and his family (vv. 7–22) is relevant to them. Abraham is otherwise "Yhwh's servant" only in v. 42, where Yhwh is "mindful" of a commitment to this servant (cf. also v. 8), and in Gen. 26:24, which also helps to explicate the point. Being someone's servant is a privilege as well as a responsibility, a guarantee that the master will be committed to the servant as well as the servant to the master. And a master's obligations extend to the servant's family ("offspring") as well as to the servant in person. But Abraham's offspring are also the descendants of Jacob; they are Israel (cf. vv. 23–45b). That expression is then accompanied not by a singular, applying to the ancestor, but by a plural that directly applies to the people. They themselves are Yhwh's chosen. Again that is a distinctive expression that recurs in v. 43 (also 106:5), once more in association with the reference to Abraham as Yhwh's servant. While the OT speaks often of God's choice, the entire people is not usually the verb's object. The psalm compares with Isa. 65:9–10, set in those discouraging years after the exile. Those verses have a number of verbal links with the psalm: they speak of Jacob's offspring, of servants, and of seeking help from Yhwh. The plural "his chosen ones" invites all the Israelites to see themselves as chosen. The psalm will go on to make clear why it begins thus: the people are to consider what God did for Abraham and Jacob/Israel and see the implications for them as their descendants.

105:7–11. The psalm begins to explicate who the God is that people should exult in and seek help from.

> 7He is Yhwh our God;
> his decisions are in all the earth.

The first colon sums up implications of vv. 1–6. The second does little more, but significantly more. "Our God" is not merely the local deity worshipped by a particular (insignificant) people in one (unimportant) place. Those decisions of Yhwh (v. 5) are effective throughout the earth. That is why "the peoples" must acknowledge them, and why Israel itself can rely on them.

> 8He has been mindful of his covenant forever,
> the word he commanded for a thousand generations,

So the people's mindfulness responds to Yhwh's *mindfulness. Yhwh had not yet been mindful of the covenant forever, or even for a thousand generations (and still has not); but the qatal verb declares that this mindfulness has started, which is part of the basis for knowing it will persist, and has been effective for twenty or thirty generations by the psalmist's day. The "thousand generations," spelling out "forever," recalls Exod. 34:7. "Covenant" is spelled out as "the word he commanded"; the emphasis is on the covenant as a commitment Yhwh made to the people. They did not take the initiative in making a commitment to Yhwh, nor was their commitment a precondition to the covenant taking effect. The covenant was a word Yhwh commanded. EVV have "promise," but Hebrew has no word for promise (cf. 85:8 [9], where translations commonly and rightly have Yhwh "promising," but the verb is the one that means "speak"), unless it is the word in v. 9b. The emphasis lies once again on the authoritative speaking that makes things happen. That is the people's encouragement.

> 9The one that he sealed with Abraham,
> his sworn promise to Isaac.
> 10He established it as a statute for Jacob,
> a lasting covenant for Israel,

The two parallel lines further explicate the covenant/word but raise suspense because they do not yet tell us its content. They also take up and spell out the references to Abraham and Jacob in v. 6, underlining the assured nature of the covenant/word. First, Yhwh sealed it. Literally, Yhwh "cut" it; the metaphor takes up the nature of the solemn ritual that sometimes guaranteed a covenant (cf. Gen. 15), a solemn self-curse in case of default. Swearing a solemn promise to keep the covenant would also imply a self-curse in case of default. Yhwh did not directly swear to Isaac or Jacob but only to Abraham (e.g., Gen. 22:16), but does later speak on the basis of the oath's applying to them (Gen. 26:3; Exod. 33:1).

Speaking of the covenant as a statute that Yhwh laid down further undergirds Yhwh's commitment. EVV have "confirm," but the verb (*ʿāmad* hiphil) does not suggest the ratification or reaffirmation of an existing statute. The verse restates the account of the covenant's original establishment, now described as like a law the king lays down and puts in writing. All this guarantees that this will be a lasting covenant, one holding to the end of the king's reign (and therefore forever!). Does the exile mean the covenant no longer holds? How could that be, in light of its origins?

> 11Saying, "To you I will give the land of Canaan
> as the share you will possess."

At last here is the content of the covenant, indeed corresponding to the original covenant to Abraham in Gen. 15. This covenant/word/promise/statute concerns land. "Land of Canaan" is the standard description in Genesis to Joshua, though this is the only subsequent occurrence of the term (otherwise it becomes "the land of Israel"). This land was to be (literally) "the share of your possession," the expression for Yhwh's allocation of the peoples and their land in Deut. 32:9, where Jacob is "the share he will possess." Here it applies to the people's relationship with their land (cf. Ps. 78:55). "Share" comes from the word for a cord, the line by means of which a village's land would be allocated to different families (cf. the solemn Amos 7:17). Yhwh parcels out the world as the elders parcel out the village's land, or as Joshua parceled out Canaan to the clans. *Possession then underlines the certainty of this tenure. In combination, the description invites Israel to believe that the land really is theirs when it does not seem so, as was the case to different degrees throughout OT times, but especially for that reduced Second Temple community. Once again the opening "you" is singular but the closing one is plural.[20] The promise was to Abraham, but it applies to all of you.

105:12–15. This section offers the first instance of a pattern that will recur: things were bad (vv. 12–13), but Yhwh acted to protect or deliver the people (vv. 14–15). Thus v. 12 relates to what follows rather than to what precedes, and v. 13 continues the construction; vv. 14–15 then form the main clause they depend on.[21] The language encourages people to make the link between their ancestors' experience and their own and thus to reckon that they can be protected and delivered.

[12]When they were few in number,
when they were little and aliens in it,
[13]Going about from nation to nation,
from one kingdom to another people,

"Few in number" is Jacob's description of himself in his insecurity in relation to the peoples around (Gen. 34:30) and also Moses's warning about how Israel may end up (Deut. 4:27). "Little" appears in the same connections (Deut. 7:7; 26:5; 28:62). It would be a telling collocation for the people who used the psalm. "Aliens" nuances the point and again parallels Gen. 15 (see v. 13; cf. also 23:4, though the noun *gēr* rather than the participle *gār* as here).

20. 11QPs[a] assimilates the sg. in the first colon to the pl. of the second.

21. TNIV takes v. 13 as the main clause, but one would not then expect it to begin with a *w*-consecutive, and in content it parallels v. 12. It continues the infinitival construction (cf. GKC 114r).

The nations and kingdoms they wandered among suggests peoples mentioned in Genesis such as the Canaanites, Egyptians, Philistines, Hittites, and Hivites. But they are not actually described there as nations, and being surrounded by the "nations" was again to be the experience of the exiles (Lev. 26:33; Deut. 4:27) and the Second Temple community (e.g., Neh. 5–6).

> 14He did not let anyone oppress them
> but rebuked kings on account of them:
> 15"Do not touch my anointed ones,
> do not harm my prophets."

The kings are again people such as the king of Gerar, whom Abraham "rebuked" (Gen. 21:25), while oppression is another description of Israel's experience in the exile (Deut. 28:29, 33; Jer. 50:33). So the psalm reminds people of when things worked in the right way, as perhaps they could again. . . .

Abraham is likewise the first prophet. Having warned Abimelech not to "touch" Sarah (Gen. 20:6–7), God promised the king that as a prophet Abraham could pray for him. Presumably the title of prophet is extended as a courtesy to the other ancestors; the Qur'an describes Abraham, Isaac, and Jacob as prophets.[22] On the other hand, Midrash Tehillim raises the question whether the prophets are the matriarchs, noting the Holy Spirit's speaking to Rebekah (Gen. 27:42).[23] In the same way the description "*anointed" strictly applies to priests and kings, but is extended metaphorically to the leaders of the ancestral family, who functioned both like priests (e.g., Gen. 12:7, 8) and like kings (see esp. Gen. 14). As people who were metaphorically anointed, they were people whom Yhwh had laid hold of and claimed, and they were therefore under Yhwh's protection; no one could attack them with impunity. The two descriptions thus form a marked contrast with the terms in the first line of this section, in v. 12.[24] This might again assure the community of Yhwh's protection for the actual prophets, anointed priests, and princes of the exile and afterward.

105:16–24. Moving on to Joseph, the recollection repeats the pattern of deprivation and provision, interweaving these through the nine lines.

> 16He summoned hunger onto the land;
> every staff of bread he broke.
> 17He sent someone in front of them,
> sold as a slave, Joseph.

22. Bratcher and Reyburn, *Handbook on the Psalms*, 895.
23. *Midrash on Psalms*, 2:182.
24. Cf. Fokkelman, *Major Poems*, 3:204.

Genesis records a series of famines, but there they simply happen; Yhwh does not summon them. That language suggests sending something as a chastisement (e.g., Jer. 29:17). The siege of Jerusalem indeed meant that Yhwh broke the staff of bread (Lev. 26:26; Ezek. 4:16; 5:16; 14:13), the only other connection in which the phrase "staff of bread" occurs (Isa. 3:1 makes explicit that "staff" suggests "support").

The implicit good news for people who have had that experience is that for Jacob's family Yhwh sent someone ahead to ensure they had food in the midst of the famine. The psalm presupposes Joseph's eventual declaration about God's intent when he came out the other side of his grim experience (Gen. 45:5; cf. 50:20).[25] Again, selling and slavery also describes Israel in the exile and afterward (Ezra 9:9; Neh. 9:36; Isa. 49:7; 50:1; 52:3). Perhaps Yhwh might still be involved in the destiny of slaves. . . .

18They subjected his foot to the fetter;
iron came on his person.
19Until his word came about,
Yhwh's saying refined him.

"Subjection" is again a term from the promise (!) in Gen. 15:13 (which also refers to enslaving) and from the experience of exile (e.g., Lam. 3:33, which uses the same verb). Otherwise v. 18 is a concrete and plausible portrayal of what prison would be like, such as partly recurs in Pss. 107:10; 149:8.

Joseph's imprisonment lasted until "his word" came true. We might initially take "his word" to refer to Joseph's word to the other prisoners and to Pharaoh (Gen. 40–41), or to Yhwh's word within those words (Gen. 41:25, 28). But the reference to refining implies that "Yhwh's saying" denotes a word Yhwh uttered before Joseph was in prison (there is no time for refining after Gen. 40–41).[26] This must be the word in Gen. 37:5–11, with "Yhwh's saying," too, referring to Yhwh's word within those words. There appears to be some development in Joseph's character from that moment (when he seems at best stupid) to the time he shows some magnanimity toward his brothers; some refining has taken place. Perhaps that has happened to Israel (Isa. 1:25; Jer. 9:7 [6]). . . . Perhaps Yhwh's promises about a permanent commitment to Israel that will outlast exile are still testing them, still refining them. . . .

20The king sent and liberated him,
the ruler of peoples [sent] and released him.

25. Cf. Calvin, *Psalms*, 4:185–86.

26. This also makes it difficult to see v. 19 as a whole as chronologically following on v. 18.

[21]He made him master of his household,
ruler over all his property,
[22]To constrain his officials according to his desire
and teach wisdom to his elders.

So Yhwh indeed restored, and more. The verbs in v. 20 all come in Isa. 58:6, though in reverse order. The more unusual word for freeing, *nātar* (hiphil), comes first and thus flags the link. The parallel points us to other links with Isa. 58, suggesting that this chapter lies behind vv. 16–20; it also talks about hunger and bread (Isa. 58:7; cf. v. 16) and about subjecting the person (Isa. 58:3, 5; cf. v. 18). The psalm invites people in the Second Temple period who are afflicted by famine and oppression to see how Yhwh used the heathen king to bring them release. Perhaps Yhwh could do that again. . . . "Ruler of peoples" (of the Egyptians, of other peoples in Egypt, and of the Egyptian empire) nuances the pharaoh's description as merely king but also prepares the way for the declaration in v. 21, which mostly follows the language of Gen. 45:8 except for the last word, "his property."

The subsequent talk of constraining Egypt's officials points to a reversal of what had happened to Joseph. The "officials" (*śārîm*) appear frequently in Gen. 39–41, and the verb (*ʾāsar*) is one of which Joseph is the object in 39:20; 40:3, 5. Joseph's *nepeš* ("desire") has been the victim (v. 18; cf. Gen. 42:21). Now it is in control.[27]

Within v. 22a, the reference of "his" changes from the pharaoh ("his officials") to Joseph ("his desire"), and it could be tempting to reckon that this change continues through v. 22b. The modern recognition of the Joseph story as a repository of wisdom teaching and of Joseph as an embodiment of wisdom (see esp. 50:20) would then encourage us to identify the elders to whom Joseph teaches wisdom as his brothers, who had so resented the implications of his dream. But in Gen. 41:8, 33, 39 the wisdom of the thirty-year-old Joseph lies in his capacity to do what the wise men of Egypt cannot do and to take over the wise government of the land. Either way, the psalm presupposes that history works itself out not simply through God's action, but through human activity.[28]

[23]Israel came to Egypt,
Jacob stayed in the land of Ham.
[24]He made his people very fruitful,
made them stronger than their foes.

27. LXX, Jerome take the verb as a form of *yāsar* ("instruct") rather than *ʾāsar* ("constrain"), which generates good parallelism but loses this link.

28. Dietmar Mathias, *Die Geschichtstheologie der Geschichtssummarien in den Psalmen* (Frankfurt and New York: Lang, 1993), 156.

The positive account ends with the journey of Joseph's father to Egypt. The verses reflect the language of Gen. 47:27–28, where "Israel" and "Jacob" appear in parallel and the narrative speaks of the people becoming "fruitful and very numerous." That comment recurs along with reference to their being "strong" in Exod. 1:7, and Exod. 1:9 has the Egyptians realizing that the Israelites are stronger than they. The narrative accounts do not use the verbs in the hiphil, and they thus leave open how this flourishing came to be. The psalm makes explicit that Yhwh caused it. The narrative does use the verb "make fruitful" with regard to Joseph and in a promise with regard to Jacob (Gen. 41:52; 48:4; there are no other occurrences of "make strong," *ʿāṣam* hiphil). For postexilic readers in their reduced and weakened state, it would draw attention to the fact that it is Yhwh who makes fruitfulness happen and strength grow, and hint at the possibility that Yhwh might do so again. . . .

105:25–38. This long section again repeats the pattern, though in a distinctive way. It refers only briefly to the people's oppression (v. 25) and hastens on to Yhwh's attacks on their oppressors (vv. 26–36) whereby Yhwh rescues Israel itself (vv. 37–38).

25He turned their heart so as to be against his people,
to scheme against his servants.

In Exod. 14:5 the heart of Pharaoh and his people turned (*hāpak*) and made them pursue the Israelites. There the verb is niphal; here it is qal, which is more often transitive (so LXX). The context in Exod. 14:4, 8 indicates that in effect it was Yhwh who did the turning; the qal here is in keeping with that. The broader context in Exodus likewise characteristically affirms that Yhwh is sovereign not only in defeating Pharaoh but also in encouraging him to be resistant so as to lay himself open to the defeat that he deserves as he acts *against Israel. Here, the stress on divine sovereignty corresponds to the earlier comment about famine (v. 16). "Scheme" (*nākal*) is an unusual word in this connection; it is no coincidence that the only other occurrence of the hitpael is Gen. 37:18. There is some irony about the fact that Jacob's descendants are the victims of scheming, designed to reduce them, weaken them, and demoralize them by making them work so hard.

26He sent Moses his servant,
Aaron whom he chose.
27They brought on them the words about his signs,
his portents in the land of Ham.

Exodus 3 makes explicit that Yhwh "sent" Moses, and "Yhwh's servant" is a standard way to describe Moses. The narrative does not speak of Yhwh "choosing" Aaron, but it does describe Yhwh commissioning him (4:14–16; 27–30). That means Aaron has the words to speak on Moses's behalf (4:15–16, 28), including the words about signs and portents (e.g., 4:17, 21; contrast the phrase in v. 5).

28He sent darkness, made it dark,
and they did not defy his word.
29He turned their water into blood
and killed their fish.
30Their land teemed with frogs,
in their kings' rooms.
31He spoke and a swarm came,
mosquitoes in all their territory.
32He made their rain into hail,
flaming fire in their land.
33He struck their vine and their fig tree,
broke off the trees in their territory.
34He spoke and locusts came,
grasshoppers without number.
35They ate all the vegetation in their land,
ate the fruit of their soil.
36He struck every firstborn in their land,
the first of all their vigor.

The account of the signs that came on Egypt corresponds to Exod. 7–12, except that darkness comes first instead of next to last, and cattle disease and boils are missing.[29] There are few parallels between the signs and the readers' own experience, but darkness is a spectacular exception. Very many references to darkness take it as a symbol of disaster and judgment and a key way of conceptualizing the day of Yhwh through which the community has gone (e.g., Ps. 107:10, 14; Lam. 3:2; 5:17). Yhwh's bringing darkness on Egypt suggests that darkness can also come for the community's later oppressors (e.g., Isa. 13:10; 45:7; 47:5). And the fact that the Egyptians eventually had to yield to Yhwh rather than continue to defy Yhwh's word suggests that this will also be true for the later oppressors.[30]

29. On the plagues in the psalm and in Genesis, see B. Margulis, "The Plagues Tradition in Ps. 105," *Bib* 50 (1969): 491–96; Samuel E. Loewenstamm, "The Number of Plagues in Psalm 105," *Bib* 52 (1971): 34–38; Archie C. C. Lee, "Genesis I and the Plagues Tradition in Psalm cv," *VT* 40 (1990): 257–63; W. Dennis Tucker, "Revisiting the Plagues in Psalm cv," *VT* 55 (2005): 401–11.

30. Assuming that Egypt is the subject of the sentence, some LXX MSS omit the "not," perhaps assimilating to 107:11 (Barthélemy, *Psaumes*, 705); NJPS and TNIV turn the

In v. 29a, Yhwh again exercises the capacity to "turn" things (cf. v. 25; and Exod. 7:17, 20). The parallel colon, like v. 25b, introduces an explicit emphasis on Yhwh's sovereign action. The fish do not merely die (*mût* qal; Exod. 7:18, 21); Yhwh makes them die (*mût* hiphil).

Frogs teeming, even in the palace's private rooms, in turn follows Exod. 8:3 [7:28]; "kings" presumably refers to the succession of monarchs who occupy these rooms. The swarm of mosquitoes (or gnats, maggots, or lice) then follows 8:16–31 [12–27], though there the two words come in the reverse order, and "territory" comes from 8:2 [7:27]. Hail and fire (lightning) come from 9:13–34.[31] Again, here Yhwh does the striking; in 9:25 the hail does it. That verse also talks about its effect in breaking off trees and other things that grew; the psalm makes this more specific in terms that would apply in Canaan, as vine and fig (cf. Ps. 78:47).

Like hail, locusts get two lines, and come near the climax of the sequence in vv. 34–35 (before the firstborn), perhaps because of the devastating nature of locust plagues in Canaan (cf. Joel 1). Locusts come from Exod. 10, grasshopper (?) and the expression "without number" to underline the point come from Joel 1:4, 6. Their eating all the vegetation in their land and eating its fruit correspond quite closely to Exod. 10:12, 15.

Finally, the description in v. 36a of Yhwh striking the firstborn follows the language of Exod. 12:29, while the second colon appends the description of a man's firstborn son that appears in Ps. 78:51. The threefold "all/every" in vv. 35–36 ends the section in frightening fashion.[32]

37He brought them out with silver and gold,
  not one of their clans collapsing.
38Egypt rejoiced at their going out,
  because dread of them had fallen on them.

"Bringing them out" and "going out" (*yāṣāʾ* hiphil and qal) are the standard expressions in Exodus for God's deliverance of the people from Egypt and their own leaving, and Exodus several times notes that they came out with silver and gold (e.g., 12:35, 41, 51). Exodus likewise emphasizes that "all" the Israelites came out (12:41). On the other hand, there is no reference to collapsing in that story, though Isa. 63:13 does

statement into a question. But "defy" (*mārâ*) is not a verb otherwise applied to foreign peoples, and the colon might refer to the plagues (Rashi) or to Moses and Aaron (Ibn Ezra), though in that case it contrasts with the declaration Yhwh eventually has to make about them (Num. 20:24; 27:14). The Sinaiticus text of the LXX has a sg. verb, and Th. Booij ("The Role of Darkness in Psalm cv 28," *VT* 39 [1989]: 209–14) takes this as original.

31. Exodus 9:33–34 also refers to rain as *māṭār* that did fall; Ps. 105:32 refers to rain as *gešem*.

32. Cf. Allen, *Psalms 101–150*, 59.

use it in this connection; the expression once again suggests the experience of Israel in the exile and afterward (e.g., Isa. 59:10; Lam. 1:14).

In the story, it is the Song of Moses that speaks of dread of Israel falling on people, and in the context it is the peoples of Canaan, though it has also made clear that the Egyptians were in a state of panic in relation to Israel and at least of relief when they went (Exod. 12:33). But it was dread on the part of the local peoples that postexilic Israel needed.

105:39–45. There is no further account of deprivation; vv. 39–45 continue seamlessly from what precedes. This account of the people's experience thus contrasts with that in Exodus and Numbers, virtually ignoring the pattern of events there with the repeated lack of food and water and interwoven rebellions.

39 He spread a cloud for covering
  and a fire to give light by night.
40 They asked and he brought quail,
  and he was filling them with bread from the heavens.
41 He opened a crag and waters flowed,
  went in dry places as a stream.

The cloud suggests the pillar of cloud accompanying the people (Exod. 13:21–22), but one cannot spread a pillar, and the cloud did not cover the people but went before them. It did cover Sinai, but talk of cloud and spreading and covering links more systematically with the wilderness sanctuary (37:9; 40:19, 21, 34–38). The colon might therefore invite the audience to see themselves as covered by Yhwh as the God present in the sanctuary, even if it did not feel like it. Verse 39b is a more straightforward reference to the pillar of fire.

"Ask" is more than an understated account of the Israelites' words that led to the arrival of quail (Exod. 16). Typically, they did not talk to Yhwh about their hunger, still less ask Yhwh to do something about it; they only complained at Moses and Aaron, and thus indirectly at Yhwh. Psalms 78:18; 106:15 do use that verb, in a pejorative context. But here it suggests another link with the Second Temple community, invited to "ask" and "seek help" and "have recourse" (Isa. 65:1; cf. v. 4). The second colon is another more straightforward summary of a complementary aspect to Yhwh's action in the language of Exod. 16.

Verse 41 then presumably takes up the next story in Exod. 17:1–7, though it again gives it a distinctive slant. Once more it omits Israel's complaining. Indirectly Yhwh does open the crag, but it is Moses who has to hit it so that water comes out. "Flow" (*zûb*) and "streams" come only here (though also in this connection in Ps. 78:16, 20; Isa. 48:21); but the verb often features in references to the land flowing with milk and honey (e.g., Exod. 13:5). "Dry places" and "streams," too, do not feature there; they suggest devastation and loss ("dry places" can be a lament motif) and its reversal (e.g., Ps. 63:1 [2]; Isa. 35:1; 41:18; 43:19–20).

> 42Because he was mindful of his holy word,
> of Abraham his servant,
> 43He brought out his people with gladness,
> his chosen ones with resounding.
> 44He gave them the lands of the nations,
> they came into possession of the toil of the peoples,

Verse 42 summarizes v. 8 (see also vv. 3 and 6; the expression "holy *word," which refers to the promise to Abraham, comes only here in the Bible); it introduces v. 43 rather than explaining v. 41. Then likewise "brought out," "his people," and "his chosen ones" reprise vv. 6, 24–25, 37–38, though "gladness" and "resounding" are new motifs. They are appropriate enough in a psalm, though they do not come elsewhere in the Psalms as a pair. They do come in an exilic or postexilic context in Isa. 35:10; 51:11.

But v. 44 shows that the last subsection of the psalm is leaping forward from the exodus and its aftermath to the occupation of the land, though this is in keeping with the dynamic of Moses's song in Exod. 15:1–18. And it is the point from which the psalm started (v. 11), the original point of the promise to Abraham. "Lands of the nations . . . peoples" may in turn take up the implicit plurals of v. 13 with its recognition that Canaan was divided among a number of people groups. But it also recalls references in the Second Temple period to the peoples of the lands, the contemporary people groups of the area around Judah, identified with or seen as the successors of those peoples from earlier days (e.g., Ezra 9:1, 2, 11). "Came into possession" is a regular term for Israel's taking control of Canaan (e.g., Deut. 3:18, which also refers to Yhwh's giving, as here), and the idea recurs that Israel comes into possession of the labor of the peoples in the sense of (for instance) houses that Israel did not build (Deut. 6:10; Josh. 24:13). But it is also noteworthy that the aftermath of the exile also sees Yhwh promising that the people will come into possession of the land, and of "the nations" and their cities in Isa. 54:3.

> 45So that they might keep his statutes
> and observe his teachings.
> Praise Yah!

That all sounds totally encouraging. Verse 45a–b then brings us up short. Sinai was omitted from the story the psalm narrated, but at its close it becomes all-important. The problem with Israel's occupation of the land is that keeping Yhwh's statutes and observing Yhwh's teachings is exactly what Israel did not do, and this is the basis of the promise that they will come into possession of the nations; hence their loss of the land. The context of those references to the peoples of the lands is that in the Second Temple period, instead of distinguishing themselves from them, the people have intermarried with them and thus made it impossible to implement Yhwh's statutes and teachings in their lives. They cannot (for instance) be households that implement the first of the Ten Words, or the second. (It would be different if the people they married committed themselves to Yhwh, like Rahab or Ruth; but that is not presupposed.) It would be an exaggeration to say that the psalm reaches its object in v. 45a–b. But whereas the psalm can put 95 percent of its stress on the grace of God, it has to make clear that a response to that grace is required.

After that, in a sense the final framing exhortation brings us up short again. The implications of v. 45a–b are very searching, but the psalm leaves us with praise, not demand.

At least that is so in MT. LXX omits v. 45c (which might be dittography from Ps. 106) and thus gives a more straightforward closure to the psalm.

Theological Implications

In retelling Israel's story in such a way as to show its significance for readers in a particular context, the psalm does on a small scale what the great OT narrative works do on a large scale. And whereas in this respect in the way they tell their story Pss. 78 and 106 correspond to Kings with its implicit indictment or self-indictment, Ps. 105 corresponds more to Chronicles with its implicit encouragement or self-encouragement. It indicates that there are times when the community needs to turn its back on the fact of its sinfulness and not focus on the demands Yhwh makes of it, and recall the reasons it has for encouragement. The God who made promises to it at the Beginning, and fulfilled them, is still its God. The fact that here the focus of Yhwh's promise is the land makes for some irony as the people do not in fact possess the land;[33] it also underlines the psalm's hopeful implications.

33. Cf. Richard J. Clifford, "Style and Purpose in Psalm 105," *Bib* 60 (1979): 420–27 (see 423–24); Anthony R. Ceresco, "A Poetic Analysis of Psalm 105," *Bib* 64 (1983): 20–46 (see 44–46); Mathias, *Geschichtstheologie*, 134–35.

The community in a particular period may need to see itself as more in the position presupposed by this psalm or that presupposed by (for instance) Ps. 106. In the time of Jeremiah, this psalm would indeed represent "pious nationalism," something like "the mentality of Jeremiah's enemies."[34] But in the time of the Ezra or Nehemiah, it would express the gospel.

34. Terrien, *Psalms*, 725.

Psalm 106

Recognizing Yhwh's Judgment

Translation

[1]Praise Yah.
Confess Yhwh, because he is good,
  because his commitment is forever.
[2]Who can utter the mighty acts[1] of Yhwh,
  declare all his praise?
[3]The good fortune of the people who keep judgment,
  of the person who does[2] faithfulness at all times!

[4]Be mindful of me, Yhwh, when you accept your people;
  attend to me when you deliver them,
[5]So that I may see the good things that come to your chosen ones,
  share in the rejoicing[3] of your nation,
  exult with your possession.

1. In 90:10, *gĕbûrōt* was abstract pl. or a Phoenician-style sg.; other occurrences in the Psalms can be understood either as sg. or pl. Here the actual references to Yhwh's acts in the psalm suggest the latter; pl. "mighty acts" and sg. "praise" then complement each other (though LXX, Jerome have pl. "praises").

2. Vrs imply pl. *ʿōśê* for MT's sg. *ʿōśēh*, but vv. 1–6 (like some preceding psalms) do mix sg. and pl., and here the sg. would take up the sg. of v. 2a. The complementarity of sg. and pl. also fits the way parallelism can work.

3. Lit. "rejoice in the rejoicing."

6We have come short with our ancestors,
been wayward, been faithless.
7Our ancestors in Egypt
did not understand your wonders,
Were not mindful of the abundance of your commitments;
they were defiant by the sea,[4] at the Reed Sea.
8But he delivered them for the sake of his name,
to cause his might to be acknowledged.
9He blasted the Reed Sea and withered it,
led them in the deeps as in a wilderness.
10He delivered them from the power of their adversary,
restored them from the power of their enemy.[5]
11The water covered their foes,
not one of them was left.
12They trusted in his words,
they were singing his praise.

13They quickly ignored his deeds,
they did not wait for his plan.
14They longed deeply[6] in the wilderness;
they tested God in the wasteland.
15He gave them what they asked;
he sent wasting among them.
16They were jealous of Moses in the camp,
and of Aaron, the holy one of Yhwh.
17The earth was opening,[7] and it swallowed Dathan,
covered over Abiram's group.
18Fire blazed among their group,
a flame that was burning up the faithless.
19They were making a bullock at Horeb,
they bowed down to an image.
20They exchanged their splendor
for the representation of a bull that eats grass.
21They ignored God their deliverer,
the one doing great things in Egypt,
22Wonders in the land of Ham,
awesome deeds at the Reed Sea.
23He said he would wipe them out,
except that Moses, his chosen,

4. LXX implies *ʿōlîm* ("those who were going up") for MT's *ʿal-yām*, an odd anticipation of *yam-sûp*; it is missing in Aq, Sym. NRSV "against the Most High" presupposes *ʿelyôn* for *ʿal-yām*, as in 78:17.

5. The suffixes on the verbs apply also to the nouns. Each time "power" is lit. "hand" (cf. vv. 41–42).

6. Lit. "they longed a longing."

7. *Pātaḥ* is usually transitive; LXX, Tg, Jerome imply niphal *tippātaḥ* for MT *tiptaḥ*.

Stood in the breach before him
  to turn his wrath from destroying.

24They rejected the lovely land,
  they did not trust in his word.
25They muttered in their tents,
  they did not listen to Yhwh's voice.
26He lifted his hand [to swear] to them
  to make them fall in the wilderness
27And make their offspring fall among the nations,
  scatter them among the countries.
28They joined the Master of Peor
  and ate sacrifices offered for the dead.
29They provoked by their deeds
  and an epidemic broke out among them.
30Phinehas stood and intervened,
  and the epidemic stopped.
31It counted for him as an act of faithfulness
  to all generations, forever.

32They angered at Strife Water,
  and it was displeasing to Moses[8] because of them,
33Because they rebelled against his spirit,
  and he was rash in his words.[9]
34They did not destroy the peoples,
  as Yhwh said to them,
35But mixed with the nations
  and learned to do as they did.
36They served their images,
  and they became a trap to them.
37They sacrificed their sons
  and their daughters to demons.
38They shed innocent blood,
  the blood of their sons and their daughters,
Whom they sacrificed to the images of Canaan;
  the land became profane through the bloodshed.
39They became taboo through their acts;
  they were immoral in their deeds.
40The anger of Yhwh burned on his people;
  he loathed his possession.
41He gave them into the power of the nations;
  their adversaries ruled over them.

8. Lit. "it was bad to/for Moses." Translations have "it went ill with Moses," but the more usual meaning of *rāʿaʿ* is "be displeasing" (e.g., Neh. 2:10). Cf. Fokkelman, *Major Poems*, 2:274.

9. Lit. "with his lips."

[42]Their enemies oppressed them;
they submitted to their power.
[43]Many times he would rescue them,
but they—they were defiant in their planning,
and sank through their waywardness.
[44]But he saw the trouble that came to them;
when he heard their resounding,
[45]He was mindful for them of his covenant
and was sorry, in accordance with the abundance of his
commitments.[10]
[46]He made them the objects of compassion
before all their captors.

[47]Deliver us, Yhwh our God,
gather us from the nations,
To confess your holy name,
to glory in your praise.

Interpretation

The main bulk of Ps. 106 is another recounting of Israel's story, but one representing a mirror image to Ps. 105. That psalm omitted all reference to the people's wrongdoing; Ps. 106 focuses on it. In Ps. 105 the repeated theme was, "We were in trouble, but Yhwh rescued us." Here, the repeated theme is, "We failed Yhwh, and Yhwh punished us, but then we were rescued." This is worked out in connection with events that led up to the Reed Sea deliverance (vv. 6–12), Moses's intercession at Sinai (vv. 13–23), Phinehas's intercession (vv. 24–31), and Yhwh's mercy in Canaan and during the exile (vv. 32–46). But the story's structuring is not done in tidy fashion. The balance of space between acknowledging the people's wrongdoing and describing their deliverance varies. Further, vv. 13–23 include reference to events after Sinai, and vv. 32–46 begin with events before Phinehas's time.

The point of the main part of the psalm is thus to confess the people's shortcomings over the centuries. It is what Gerhard von Rad called the books of Kings, a *Gerichtsdoxologie*, an act of praise at the justice of God's judgment.[11] In Kings, it is only implicit that this is the nature of the storytelling; it is even less explicit what response the storytellers seek from Yhwh. The psalm makes this explicit, though in complex ways, as

10. Q and the Cairo MS have pl. *ḥăsādāyw* (cf. Tg, Syr); K has sg. *ḥasdô* (cf. LXX, Jerome).

11. *Old Testament Theology*, 2 vols. (Edinburgh: Oliver and Boyd; New York: Harper, 1962–65), 1:357–58.

its frame comprises a summons to praise (vv. 1–3), an individual's plea to be part of Yhwh's deliverance of the people (vv. 4–5),[12] and a corporate plea for deliverance (v. 47). This is hardly enough to turn Ps. 106 into hymn, but it is enough to take the edge off the awfulness of its take on Israel's story, and it corresponds to the recurrent emphasis on Yhwh's mercy within the main body of the psalm.

Thus, whereas Ps. 105 presupposes a reading of Israel's history like that in Chronicles, emphasizing God's grace and a response of trust, Ps. 106 presupposes a reading like that in Kings (and in Ps. 78), emphasizing Israel's sinfulness and an acceptance of responsibility. Perhaps, then, the psalm comes from the exile, like Kings.[13] But penitential readings of Israel's history also appear in the Second Temple period (see Ezra 9; Neh. 9;[14] Dan. 9), and Ps. 106 could be contemporary with Ps. 105. This fits with its links with other OT material such as Isa. 63 and Ezek. 20. It also presupposes the story of ancestors as we have it in the Pentateuch and sometimes reflects its actual wording, though it does not always follow its order of events and sometimes expresses matters in its own way. It thus works in the manner of midrash, offering a creative retelling of the ancestors' story. We can hardly reckon to infer from it precisely what form of the pentateuchal narrative it presupposes.

Both Pss. 105 and 106 then embody possible responses to the sense in the Second Temple period that all was not well. They thus stand significantly next to one another. Briggs, indeed takes them as originally one psalm,[15] while Walther Zimmerli calls them "twin psalms."[16] But Zimmerli recognizes the sharp difference between them, and they indeed "stand in dialectical contrast."[17] Psalm 106 is "the dark counterpart of its predecessor."[18] They "contradict and yet complete each other in the dialectic of sin and grace."[19]

We have no information on how the psalm was used.

106:1–3. The psalm opens with an invitation to praise not unlike that in a regular praise psalm, complete with reasons in a "because" clause. In combining variant forms of vv. 1 and 47–48 with Pss. 105:1–15 and 96, the praise of 1 Chron. 16 reflects this.

12. Seybold (*Psalmen*, 321) takes vv. 1–5 as originally belonging to Ps. 105.

13. Cf. Walter Beyerlin, "Der nervus rerum in Psalm 106," *ZAW* 86 (1974): 50–64.

14. Cf. F. C. Fensham, "Neh. 9 and Pss. 104, 106, 135 and 136," *JNSL* 9 (1991): 35–51.

15. *Psalms*, 2:342.

16. "Zwillingspsalmen," in *Studien zur alttestamentlichen Theologie und Prophetie*, TBü 51 (Munich: Kaiser, 1974), 261–71; cf. Lohfink and Zenger, *God of Israel and the Nations*, 186.

17. Schaefer, *Psalms*, 261. Cf. Augustine, *Psalms*, 526.

18. Kidner, *Psalms*, 2:377.

19. Terrien, *Psalms*, 733.

[1]Praise Yah.
Confess Yhwh, because he is good,
because his commitment is forever.

The psalm is the first to begin, *Praise *Yah. After that summons, like Ps. 105 it invites people to *confess Yhwh, which once more suggests giving testimony to Yhwh's acts for the people. But these will again be the acts that characterize the people's experience over the centuries, acts characterized by God's goodness, God's generosity or kindness (LXX), and by God's *commitment, which in the parallelism spells out the implications of "goodness." This invitation recurs at the beginning of Pss. 107, 118, and 136, while 2 Chron. 20:21; Ezra 3:11; and Jer. 33:11 report slightly different forms of the wording, all suggesting that this is a well-known liturgical phrase, even though used with variations. It is actually a complete miniature praise hymn, whose content will be filled out in an unexpected way in the psalm. Yhwh has often brought trouble on the people, but Yhwh's goodness and commitment have been expressed in not casting them off but persisting despite the persistence of Israel's wrongdoing.

[2]Who can utter the mighty acts of Yhwh,
declare all his praise?

The implicit summons to praise continues in a novel way. In isolation we might take it as a rhetorical question, but it would be the only one of its kind in the Psalter, and it might seem a slightly odd one; after all, the Psalms are frequently uttering Yhwh's mighty acts,[20] though the question would imply that no one can do so adequately (as the parallelism with its "all" suggests). But v. 3 will imply that it is rather the kind of question that appears in Pss. 15 and 24: not (at least not in the same sense) a rhetorical question, but one the psalm asks and then answers.

The psalm will indeed speak of Yhwh's "mighty acts" (see vv. 7–13, 21–22, 43), but with some irony, as the problem it will own is that Israel did not really try to remember those mighty acts, let alone find itself unable to do so because they were too great. Its language, combined with that of v. 1, makes a first link with Isa. 63 (see vv. 7, 15).

[3]The good fortune of the people who keep judgment,
of the person who does faithfulness at all times!

20. But this is the only occurrence in the Psalter of the verb "utter" (*mālal*), perhaps an Aramaism or Phoenicianism; cf. Dahood, *Psalms*, 3:67.

Verse 3, then, is not a simply independent observation not very securely related to its context, but the reply to the question in v. 2.[21] Nevertheless the irony deepens as the psalm declares the *good fortune of people who are committed to *mišpāṭ* and *ṣĕdāqâ*, *faithfulness in the exercise of judgment (*authority), for the psalm will illustrate the converse point, that faithlessness (vv. 6, 18) leads to trouble, and "at all times" is what characterizes the people's faithlessness. On the other hand, the hendiadys *mišpāṭ* and *ṣĕdāqâ* appears here as a conventional formula. The faithlessness that the psalm will concern itself with is one affecting people's relationship to Yhwh more than their operating in the community. Significantly, perhaps, Isa. 56:1 makes *mišpāṭ* and *ṣĕdāqâ* the key to the postexilic community's life.

106:4–5. After vv. 1–3 this plea is a surprise, as is its first-person singular form (the Greek versions assimilate to the plural of the context), though the combination of singular and plural follows the precedent of Pss. 103 and 104 (also Ps. 89). Perhaps the same person speaks as in vv. 1–3, now articulating as an individual a prayer that worshippers are implicitly invited to make their own. It also makes explicit that this individual suppliant wants to make sure of sharing in Yhwh's dealings with the people as a whole.[22]

> [4]Be mindful of me, Yhwh, when you accept your people;
> attend to me when you deliver them,

The line jumps over a contrast in content with vv. 1–3, but assumes the setting of the rest of the psalm, as it presupposes that Yhwh's people are in trouble and therefore need *deliverance (of which there has been no hint) and that Yhwh will grant it (which at least fits with the theological convictions of v. 1). That will be the time of Yhwh's "acceptance" of the people. The exile meant Yhwh's rejection of them, but Israel looks forward to "a time/year of acceptance" when "in acceptance I show you compassion" (Isa. 49:8; 60:10; 61:2). Jumping over all that, the line's concern is that Yhwh should be *mindful of this worshipper in particular when acceptance and deliverance come. Asking for Yhwh's "attention" (*pāqad*) also contains a little irony, as it is precisely that attention that has manifested itself in bringing calamity on the people (Ps. 89:32 [33]).

> [5]So that I may see the good things that come to your chosen ones,
> share in the rejoicing of your nation,
> exult with your possession.

21. See *Midrash on Psalms*, 2:188–90.
22. Gerstenberger, *Psalms*, 2:238.

The tricolon brings the psalm's preliminaries to a close and prepares to get down to what will be its unexpected business. The aim of seeing these "good things" makes for an inclusion with v. 1 at that point. They are the generous, kind gifts of the good God. The fact that the people are Yhwh's "chosen ones" (cf. 105:6), Yhwh's nation, and Yhwh's *possession suggests reasons for confidence that the moment of acceptance and deliverance will come. Only here in the Psalms is Israel "your nation"; the term suggests a people with a secure self-identity in relation to other nations around, which was hardly the case through much of the Persian period. The parallelism indicates that (as often) "seeing" implies seeing and experiencing and/or seeing and rejoicing in.

106:6–12. In a confession or testimony, one expects the opening to lead into an account of the trouble that had come upon the worshippers and of what Yhwh has done for them. That happens here but in a distinctive way.

6We have come short with our ancestors,
been wayward, been faithless.

"After so many positive terms, the compact confession of guilt in v. 6 comes as quite a shock."[23] The people have *failed, been *wayward, been *faithless; piling up key images for wrongdoing has a cumulative effect of owning the nature of their lives over the years. The three verbs correspond to those in Solomon's account of how people in the exile may pray (1 Kings 8:47). Further, although the psalm will relate events from the past, and will start from the distant past, it does not reckon the community can distance itself from them. There is no theology like that of Exod. 34:7, nor a claim like that of Lam. 5:7. The people identify with the ancestors; they have behaved like them. In effect, they were with them. Reading their story, they see themselves. Indeed, none of the verbs in v. 6 is used of the ancestors in the Exodus story. They are the terms that recur in accounts of Israel's life in later centuries. The people do not even merely acknowledge that they have sinned "like" their ancestors, for "with" hardly means merely "like." "If it be so," Augustine nicely comments, "it should be supported by some examples of this mode of expression"; and he cannot think of any.[24] The "with" implies a negative equivalent to the Deuteronomic talk of Yhwh making a covenant not with the ancestors but with the later generation[25] (cf. Lev. 26:39–40; Jer. 14:20, where the three roots

23. Fokkelman, *Major Poems*, 2:271.

24. *Psalms*, 527. Cassiodorus (*Psalms*, 2:69) notes that this is a useful anti-Pelagian line.

25. McCann, "Psalms," 1110.

also come). "The sin is 'ours,' but it is a repetition and a prolongation of the ancestors' sins."[26]

> [7]Our ancestors in Egypt
> did not understand your wonders,
> Were not mindful of the abundance of your commitments;
> they were defiant by the sea, at the Reed Sea.

In this first retrospective section, the description of the people's wrongdoing occupies only two lines; later sections will be more expansive. The "wonders" are the signs Yhwh performed in Egypt (Exod. 3:20; and see v. 22 below). EVV have the ancestors not thinking about these wonders, and no doubt they did not, but *śākal* (hiphil) usually means more than that (cf. 94:8; 119:99). They did not draw the right implications from their awareness of these wonders. "They saw and yet they did not see."[27]

The psalm declares that this was true in Egypt itself. Exodus does not quite say that, though it is a logical inference from the people's subsequent attitude at the Reed Sea, when they showed themselves not *mindful of all those expressions of *commitment (cf. v. 1). And therefore they were defiant (*mārâ*; cf. 105:28), wishing they had never left Egypt. The psalm adds a fourth image for going wrong in our relationship with God, to add to the three in v. 6. Again, it is not one that comes in Exodus but one used to describe Israel's later life. At the Reed Sea the people panicked in a way that would not have happened if they had seen the significance of what Yhwh did in Egypt. (The psalm does not quite accuse the ancestors of faithlessness while they were still in Egypt, as Ezek. 20 does.) The ancient versions translate *yam-sûp* "Red Sea," but *sûp* is the Hebrew word for reeds or rushes, and modern translations thus include the possibility that the expression should be translated "Reed Sea." Elsewhere in the OT it nevertheless refers to one of the northern arms of the Red Sea, the Gulf of Aqaba or the Gulf of Suez. In connection with Israel's deliverance from the Egyptians, it might alternatively designate the marshy body of water that extends further north from there, the Bitter Lakes (see BDB).

> [8]But he delivered them for the sake of his name,
> to cause his might to be acknowledged.

Yhwh's response to the people's recalcitrance at the Reed Sea was to *deliver them; this implicitly begins to justify the expectation expressed in v. 4, while the reference to Yhwh's might picks up from v. 2. "For

26. Schaefer, *Psalms*, 262.
27. Jerome, *Homilies*, 1:237.

the sake of his *name" is another expression that does not appear in Exodus, but it features in connection with the exodus and wilderness events in Ezek. 20:9, 14, 22 (cf. 1 Sam. 12:22; Ps. 79:9; Isa. 48:9; Jer. 14:7, 21). In the context of the exile, it would hint at a basis for appeal to Yhwh now.

Taking up that reference to Yhwh's might spells out the implications. The aim of Yhwh's act of deliverance was that this might now be *acknowledged, a key motif in the exodus story and in Ezekiel (Exod. 14:4, 18; Ezek. 20:26, 38, 42, 44) and an aim of the deliverance the psalm longs for.

9He blasted the Reed Sea and withered it,
led them in the deeps as in a wilderness.

"Blasting" (*gāʿar*) the sea and withering it are not Exodus formulations; their background lies more in stories about a deity's victory over cosmic tumultuous waters, perhaps in connection with creation (cf. 104:9; Isa. 44:27; and 50:2, which also refers to a "wilderness" in this connection). But it was natural to apply this imagery to the Reed Sea event, a historical expression of such a victory (cf. Isa. 51:9–11). The deeps (*tĕhōmôt*) have that same background (cf. Ps. 104:6) and are also a way of picturing Yhwh's deliverance in Exod. 15:5, 8, while in Isa. 63:13, Yhwh is one "leading them in the deeps like a horse in the wilderness." All this makes links between creation, exodus, and the way people might conceive of deliverance during or after the exile.

10He delivered them from the power of their adversary,
restored them from the power of their enemy.
11The water covered their foes,
not one of them was left.
12They trusted in his words,
they were singing his praise.

Three lines summarize the Reed Sea event more in Exodus's terms. *Deliverance and *restoration from the power of the adversary (*against) or enemy (Exod. 6:6; 14:13, 30; 15:2, 6, 9, 13) and the water covering their enemies (15:10) denote an extraordinary act on behalf of a people who were being defiant by the sea, convinced of Yhwh's malevolence rather than goodness. "They trusted" (*wayyaʾămînû*) is the verb form in Exod. 14:31, while trusting in "his words" (not a common expression) again makes a link with Ps. 105:28 (cf. 145:13). Moses "was singing" then comes in the next line of Exodus, 15:1, and *praises come in Exod. 15:11. A transformation has come over the people who were described in v. 7. Or has it?

106:13–23. No, it has not. The cycle repeats with further accounts of faithlessness and mercy, though this time interwoven with punishment. Concrete links with the Pentateuch concentrate in Num. 11–16, though not in the narrative's order, but then switch focus to Exod. 32–34.

13They quickly ignored his deeds,
they did not wait for his plan.
14They longed deeply in the wilderness;
they tested God in the wasteland.
15He gave them what they asked;
he sent wasting among them.

Less idiomatically, they hastened to *ignore, they could not wait to ignore (the first asyndetic imperative, *mihărû*, suggests deliberate action; it implies more than "soon"). The distinctive formulations stress the Israelites' willfulness. In light of links with Numbers in the rest of this section, v. 13b looks like an allusion to Num. 14:26–45. Yhwh had a plan for the people's entry into the land, but after initially wanting to have nothing to do with going into the land, they ricocheted into prosecuting their own plan for that.

"Longed deeply" comes in Num. 11:4, suggesting reference to that story, though the immediate subject there is the mixed group who came out of Egypt with the Israelites; the psalm again underlines the ancestors' own responsibility. "Longing" is not wrong in itself, but their craving for real food led to their testing Yhwh by their dietary complaints. "Testing" is another motif from Num. 14 (see v. 22; also Exod. 17:1–7); it suggests seeing how far one can push God or trying to discover what God is really capable of. The "wasteland" describes where Israel is in Num. 21:20; 23:28.

Verse 15 returns to Num. 11 (esp. vv. 31–34),[28] though the language is distinctive. First, Yhwh demonstrates total capacity to do what the Israelites ask, then sends trouble as a reaction to being required to do so. "Wasting," *rāzôn*, makes for a neat paronomasia with *rāṣôn*, "acceptance" (v. 4).[29]

16They were jealous of Moses in the camp,
and of Aaron, the holy one of Yhwh.
17The earth was opening, and it swallowed Dathan,
covered over Abiram's group.
18Fire blazed among their group,
a flame that was burning up the faithless.

28. Cf. Aage Bentzen, "Die Schwindsucht in Ps 106,15b," *ZAW* 57 (1939): 152; Melvyn D. Gray, "Psalm 106,15b," *SJOT* 7 (1993): 125–33.

29. Calvin, *Psalms*, 4:218.

Three internally parallel lines sum up Num. 16, again in distinctive language, though the description of Aaron as *holy takes up a key motif (Num. 16:3, 5, 7). It is self-evident to the psalmist (as to the narrative) that the community must accept Moses and Aaron's leadership. The concern is not so much with them individually in connection with a long-ago event but with their significance for the ongoing community. Oftentimes would-be leaders urged different stances from those expressed in Moses's teaching, and other priestly groups would resist the position of Aaron's line. The psalm recalls how that has always been so.

The ordering of the community's life by Moses and Aaron is fundamental to its being. Questioning their position fundamentally imperils the community. Yhwh thus reacts in an extreme way. Verses 17–18 then follow Num. 16:32–35 (for "blazing," cf. 11:1–3). They do not mention Korah. There may be no particular reason for that; the account of the story is very brief.

19They were making a bullock at Horeb,
they bowed down to an image.
20They exchanged their splendor
for the representation of a bull that eats grass.
21They ignored God their deliverer,
the one doing great things in Egypt,
22Wonders in the land of Ham,
awesome deeds at the Reed Sea.

The psalm reverts to the story in Exod. 32–34 (with v. 19, compare 32:8). The Israelites likely thought in terms of a Yhwh image; religions have usually seen it natural to have images of their deity to bring home the deity's reality and give them something to focus on. A bullock would suggest Yhwh's strength and liveliness. But actually images cannot bring home the reality of Yhwh as someone who speaks and acts (Deut. 4). So bowing down to an image in effect means bowing down to a different deity. "Horeb" does come in those chapters of Exodus (see 33:6), but it is more characteristic of Deuteronomy; other parts of the psalm presuppose Deuteronomy's way of putting things (see v. 20b) and Deuteronomy's theology with its stress on obedience and the cost of failing to respond to Yhwh.

Verse 20 expresses more innovatively the scandal of making and bowing down to an image. It indeed involves abandoning Yhwh for another deity. "Their splendor" is a euphemism for "his [Yhwh's] splendor."[30]

30. So Ibn Ezra; Tg has "the splendor of their Lord." The text may have originally read "my/his splendor"; but see discussion in Carmel McCarthy, *The Tiqqune Sopherim*, OBO 36 (Göttingen: Vandenhoeck & Ruprecht, 1981), 97–105.

Yhwh is Israel's splendor; they have exchanged this *honored one for something feeble. It is not a bull's strength and vitality that impresses the psalmist (Tg nicely underlines the point by adding that the ox makes dung). "Representation" (*tabnît*) with this meaning comes only in the chapter that most systematically discusses the inadequacy of images, in Deut. 4:16–18.

But when Moses disappeared for a while, the people could not live by what they had experienced of Yhwh's delivering them in Egypt and at the Reed Sea. Yet the act of making an image involved *ignoring God their *deliverer, precisely because the image could not represent a God who delivered and did great things, wonders, or awesome deeds (cf. vv. 10, 13; and for the content of vv. 21–22, see also v. 7).

23He said he would wipe them out,
except that Moses, his chosen,
Stood in the breach before him
to turn his wrath from destroying.

The note of mercy at the end of vv. 13–23 takes a different form from that at the end of vv. 6–12. "Wipe out/destroy" parallels the account in Deut. 9:25–26. As "chosen" by Yhwh as leader (only here is Moses described thus), Moses can stand up to Yhwh, acting like a brave warrior blocking a breach in the city wall with his own body to stop the enemy coming in to destroy it (cf. Ezek. 22:30). The psalm stops an inch short of describing Yhwh as the enemy by picturing the enemy as Yhwh's wrath, which is thus slightly distanced from Yhwh. Tg correctly interprets "stood in the breach" to mean "showed himself strong in prayer."

106:24–31. The narrative again fast-forwards, to Num. 13–25. Its plot follows that of vv. 13–23, only now Phinehas, not Moses, acts to avert Yhwh's wrath.

24They rejected the lovely land,
they did not trust in his word.
25They muttered in their tents,
they did not listen to Yhwh's voice.

"Rejecting" the land is Yhwh's term in Num. 14:31. It is what Israel did in refusing to proceed there and wanting rather to return to Egypt. They thus spurned the "lovely land" or "desirable land" (cf. Jer. 3:19; Zech. 7:14). Why should they do that? The first colon raises a question that the second answers with Yhwh's verb from Num. 14:11, though it is also the verb from v. 12 above, but now in the negative. Yhwh said, "I am giving you the land; it is a good land; you can occupy it." They believed none of this.

"Muttering in their tents" is a formulation from Deut. 1:27 (the verb comes only once more in the OT), suggesting that people were gathered in their tents discussing the impossibility of taking the land and unwilling to set about dong so. "Not listening to Yhwh's voice" picks up another of Yhwh's comments in Num. 14:22.

> 26He lifted his hand [to swear] to them
> to make them fall in the wilderness
> 27And make their offspring fall among the nations,
> scatter them among the countries.

Human beings lift their hand in swearing an oath to call on God. Metaphorically, then, Yhwh similarly raises a hand in swearing. This is usually good news (indeed, cf. Num. 14:30, which refers to Yhwh's acting thus in connection with promising the land to the people). The second colon in v. 26 then implies an unpleasant irony. Yhwh's hand is raised in a different connection: they will fall in the wilderness (Num. 14:29, 32). The Exodus-Sinai generation will not enter the land they despise.

Specifically, they will fall among the peoples they now perversely thought they could defeat (Num. 14:43). The reference to "their offspring" suggests that the psalm also looks way beyond the wilderness to the exile, taking up Yhwh's declaration in Ezek. 20:23.[31]

> 28They joined the Master of Peor
> and ate sacrifices offered for the dead.
> 29They provoked by their deeds
> and an epidemic broke out among them.

The psalm goes on to the faithlessness in Moab, where people joined (the verb comes in this connection only here and in Num. 25:3, 5) the Master (*baʿal*) of Peor. Peor is a mountain there (23:28) and "Master of Peor" is the manifestation of the Master as worshipped there (compare expressions such as "Our Lady of Guadaloupe"). Numbers 25:2 has the Israelites eating "sacrifices of their gods"; here the phrase is more literally "sacrifices of the dead." Is "the dead" a way of characterizing the gods as lifeless? But there are no other passages where the gods are simply described thus. On the other hand, religious observances on behalf of dead family members is a common feature of religions, and Israelites did practice such observations (cf. prohibitions such as Deut. 14:1; 18:11; 26:14, and the critique in passages such as Isa. 57:1–8). One aspect of the Master's activity concerns the realm of the dead. So it would not be

31. NRSV assimilates the psalm's text to the words in Ezekiel, presupposing *ûlĕhāpîṣ* for MT *ûlĕhappîl*.

surprising if sacrifices that Israelites ate in connection with worshipping the Master of Peor were sacrifices for the dead. Given the Master's own involvement with the realm of death, and Canaanite stories about Death having the capacity to overwhelm him and his needing rescue from Death's clutches, perhaps we do not need to choose between the two possible meanings of "sacrifices for the dead."

An "epidemic" (Num. 25:8–9) follows; v. 29 once more describes it more independently, again making links with the "provocation" to anger that was more characteristic of Israel's life over the centuries. But the verb has no object, and what follows implies that Phinehas was provoked, as well as Yhwh.

30Phinehas stood and intervened,
and the epidemic stopped.
31It counted for him as an act of faithfulness
to all generations, forever.

The Master of Peor was also a god who could confer fertility, and in Numbers the event that provoked Phinehas, Aaron's grandson, seems to relate to this aspect of the religion (see Num. 25:6). The Israelite he killed was not merely marrying a non-Israelite but turning with her to the Master of Peor as the one who could make the family fertile. "Intervene" is *pālal*, a rare verb in the piel. But the preceding reference to "standing" makes for a parallel between Phinehas and Moses (v. 23) and suggests that the regular implication of the more common hitpael (plead, pray) applies here. Verse 30a thus sums up Num. 25:10–13, which includes reference to Phinehas making atonement for the Israelites; Tg has "pray," LXX "make atonement."[32] But what is the significance of the psalmist using the piel rather than the hitpael? Jerome thus has "executed judgment." Perhaps we can combine these two ideas. Phinehas took an action that appealed to Yhwh as the king who makes judicial decisions. Indeed, Yhwh had already made such a decision in sending the epidemic on the community; Phinehas's action appeals to Yhwh to reckon that enough is now enough. But the psalm (delicately?) makes no concrete allusion to Zimri's act or to Phinehas's killing him. It returns to the formulation in Num. 25:8 just for the expression "the epidemic stopped."

Yhwh's response in Num. 25:10–13 is then summed up in a phrase recalling Gen. 15:6. Phinehas's violent and distasteful act was an act of *faithfulness to Yhwh and to the community. If Israel countenanced actions such as that of Zimri setting up a family link with a Midianite clan without the woman abandoning her adherence to the Master and

32. Cf. Bernd Janowski, "Psalm cvi 28–31 und die Interzession des Pinchas," *VT* 33 (1983): 237–48.

coming to serve Yhwh (Num. 25:14–15), it would imperil its entire future as well as compromise Yhwh's honor. The stress on the permanence of the counting corresponds to and summarizes Num. 25:13.

106:32–46. The common thread through the psalm's last major section is the people's occupation of the land, which follows on the events at Peor (though vv. 32–33 again flash back). This process, too, is characterized by faithlessness and chastisement, but then by mercy.

32They angered at Strife Water,
and it was displeasing to Moses because of them,
33Because they rebelled against his spirit,
and he was rash in his words.

The account of the rebellion at Kadesh, at Strife Water (Num. 20:1–13), immediately precedes the beginning of the process whereby Israel occupies the land (see Num. 20:14–21). It first explains the strange fact that Moses himself does not enter the land, making a connection and contrast with the Phinehas story; Moses fails where Phinehas succeeded. "Angered" is the term in Deut. 9:7–8, 22, where God is the object. Here, as in v. 29, the lack of an object allows for Moses also being angered. In a sense the people are thus the cause of his not entering the land. Deuteronomy is more inclined than Numbers to suggest that it is his association with the people that explains Moses's inability to enter the land (e.g., Deut. 4:21–22); he pays the price for them. The description of their action as "displeasing" to Moses harks back to Num. 11:10–11, though there Moses gets away with his rash words, as he does not in Num. 20:1–13.

It is as rebels that Moses upbraids the Israelites at Kadesh (Num. 20:10). But *mārâ* is close to *mārar*, and here LXX and Jerome read the verb to indicate that the people have "embittered" his spirit.[33] Again there is an ambiguity about the object. Isaiah 63:10 has the people rebelling and grieving Yhwh's spirit, and v. 33a might have this reference. The two lines would then be parallel, the two first cola forming a pair and the two second cola likewise. But there has been no reference to Yhwh since v. 26, and v. 34 will make it explicit that Yhwh at last again appears, so more likely both lines refer simply to Moses. The people were indeed rebels against Yhwh, but Moses sees them as also rebels against him. They dismayed Yhwh, but they also dismayed Moses, provoking him to the rashness that forfeits his place in the land.

34They did not destroy the peoples,
as Yhwh said to them,

33. They may thus imply *hēmērû* for MT *himrû*.

35But mixed with the nations
and learned to do as they did.

The psalm moves on to Israel's occupation of the land. Actually Yhwh did not tell Israel to destroy the peoples. The verb *šāmad* is frequent in Deuteronomy, but there, it is Yhwh who is its subject; destroying the peoples is Yhwh's business. Israel's commission is to "devote" the peoples by killing them (*ḥāram* hiphil; e.g., Deut. 7:2). This feels the same to the peoples but has quite different significance for Israel in its relationship with Yhwh. But it is also to consume them (*'ākal*; e.g., 7:16), and that commission comes in a context like the present one. "Consume" suggests how it is for the people taking the action (it is like eating something up), "devote" suggests how it is for Yhwh (it is like an offering), and "destroy" suggests how it is for the objects of the action (they cease to exist).

Mixing with the nations (*'ārab* hitpael) in turn is a term that recurs only in Ezra 9:2, though it is Deut. 18:9 that warns against learning to do as the nations in Canaan do. Both links point to the significance of the psalm's observation for the postexilic community.

36They served their images,
and they became a trap to them.
37They sacrificed their sons
and their daughters to demons.

Again, Deuteronomy warns how intermarrying will result in "serving" the Canaanites' gods (e.g., 7:3–4). The psalm speaks of serving their "images" rather than their gods. Perhaps it shares the modern hesitation about dignifying these entities with the term for deity. And/or perhaps it plays with the double implication of the word for image, *'ēṣeb*. One root *'āṣab* means "shape" (hence "image"), another means "hurt" (hence nouns that mean pain; e.g., Pss. 16:4; 147:3). The images of the Canaanite gods will be something that ends up hurting the Israelites. Failing to "consume" the people will mean that their gods become a "trap" to them (Deut. 7:16). They will capture them and take them to their death.

In its warning about learning from the nations, Deut. 18:9–11 specifies that they must not make their sons and daughters pass through the fire (usually sons were sacrificed, but Deuteronomy often makes a point of being gender-inclusive). It also warns that they must not be involved in practices such as augury or spells or hexes. The second colon sums this up and offers a distinctive theological assessment: it implies involvement with demons. Deuteronomy 32:17 is the only other passage that speaks of sacrificing to demons (*šēdîm*). Deuteronomy 32:21 goes on to comment that these are no-gods (are the "sons and daughters" of Deut. 32:19

also the sons and daughters in this line in the psalm?). It downgrades deities such as the Master, whom Canaanites and Israelites would see as deities of much higher rank.

> 38They shed innocent blood,
> the blood of their sons and their daughters,
> Whom they sacrificed to the images of Canaan;
> the land became profane through the bloodshed.

"Shedding innocent blood" often denotes the execution of innocent people, but v. 38 takes up the critique in Jer. 19:4–5.

Jeremiah 3:1–2 also speaks of the land becoming profane (*ḥānēp*) through the people's wrongdoing. It was supposed to be a holy land, dedicated to Yhwh, but they turned it into a land like any other, dedicated to other deities (or rather, "images"; again the religion is downgraded). Jeremiah attributes this to the people's wrongdoing and immorality in their relationship with Yhwh (cf. v. 39); the psalm highlights their "bloodshed," the plural of the word for "blood." This usually denotes the violent shedding of blood in murder and slaughter (e.g., Pss. 51:14 [16]; 79:10), which indeed has a staining effect (cf. Gen. 4:10–11; Isa. 4:4). The psalm reframes the supreme sacrifice that a parent could offer, the sanctifying of a child, as an act of mindless violence, the profaning of something.

> 39They became taboo through their acts;
> they were immoral in their deeds.

Here the psalm follows the imagery of passages such as Jer. 2:23; 7:30–31. Normally taboo has nothing to do with sin. Although an event such as contact with a corpse makes it inappropriate to come immediately into Yhwh's presence (Yhwh as the living God has nothing to do with death), this does not imply the contact is sinful, and its effect is temporary. But the notion of taboo can be extended to cover the effects of immoral deeds and the worship of other deities. The fact that the deeds could include taking people's lives and that the deities could be involved in the realm of death might facilitate this extension. People's lives made it impossible for them to have any contact with Yhwh as inevitably as contact with a corpse made them unfit for contact with Yhwh; and there was no ceremonial act that could put this right.

Jeremiah 3:1–2 likewise speaks of the people's acting immorally (*zānâ*). The common translation "play the whore" gives too precise a meaning. It refers to sexual acts that contravene the community's standards. Offering their children, which seemed a great sacrifice, was actually an immoral act.

40The anger of Yhwh burned on his people;
he loathed his possession.
41He gave them into the power of the nations;
their adversaries ruled over them.
42Their enemies oppressed them;
they submitted to their power.
43Many times he would rescue them,
but they—they were defiant in their planning,
and sank through their waywardness.

Taboo and immorality issue in anger and loathing. There is an extraordinary mismatch between the verbs and their objects in v. 40. His people, his *possession, are the objects of Yhwh's loathing and angry burning.

Yhwh's consequent action resulted in their subjection to other nations and adversaries (*against). While the psalm will eventually refer to exile (v. 46), vv. 41–42 (like preceding verses) cover the subjection that characterized Israel's life more broadly. Israel had been rescued from oppression in Egypt and was destined to rule the nations on Yhwh's behalf, but things reverted to how they were before Yhwh intervened in its life; everything got turned upside down.

Judges, Kings, and Chronicles illustrate the repeated cycle of rescue, rebellion, and calamity summarized by v. 43; the tricolon brings the sad story to an interim close. "Defiant" recalls their stance at the Reed Sea (v. 7), while their insistence on doing their own planning rather than following Yhwh's recalls their stance at Kadesh (v. 13), and *waywardness was one of the general characteristics the psalm owned near the beginning (v. 6); nothing has changed.

44But he saw the trouble that came to them;
when he heard their resounding,
45He was mindful for them of his covenant
and was sorry, in accordance with the abundance of his commitments.
46He made them the objects of compassion
before all their captors.

Fortunately, neither does anything change in Yhwh, who still sees, hears, and is *mindful of his covenant (cf. Exod. 2:23–25). The *resounding Yhwh hears when they lament their suffering is very different from that in Ps. 105:43, but Yhwh still listens. Israel's not being mindful of the abundance of Yhwh's commitments (v. 7) does not mean Yhwh stops being so mindful. That covenant with Abraham, Isaac, and Jacob was predominantly one-sided, a solemn commitment on Yhwh's part. No obligation was formally required of Israel except the circumcision of their males. When they are deservedly punished for their faithlessness, the one-sided nature of this covenant is of crucial significance. The commitment emerged from Yhwh's own person rather than from the merit of its objects. This is the people's potential hope when they have no other claim on Yhwh.

Being sorry is an expression of that covenant; *nāḥam* (niphal) is a feelings word. It usually denotes a feeling that makes one relent about an intention, but here it rather suggests being sorry about having done something (e.g., Jer. 42:10). This need not imply regret about having done it, as if it were a mistake; but it does imply regret that the necessary deed caused such pain, and therefore a willingness to stop doing it.

So Yhwh's awareness of Israel's (deserved) suffering leads to action to ameliorate it, in keeping with Solomon's prayer in 1 Kings 8:50. Indeed, it goes beyond that. Solomon prayed for the people to find such compassion if they had turned back to Yhwh. Perhaps the psalm implies that their resounding signifies their turning back to Yhwh, but it need not do so; they could just be shouting out in pain. The psalm bases Yhwh's action simply in grace. *Commitment is the key to understanding the psalm's model for interpreting history.[34] The psalm follows the logic of the Judges period, when it is simply Yhwh's hearing the people's moaning under oppression that leads to "being sorry" (the same verb form as here).

[47]Deliver us, Yhwh our God,
  gather us from the nations,
To confess your holy name,
  to glory in your praise.

Second Chronicles 30:9 speaks in similar terms to v. 46 of the Ephraimites finding compassion with their captors if they return to Yhwh, but it adds that Yhwh will also make it possible for them to return to the land. That is now the psalm's plea. Cyrus's accession did not mean all Judeans returned to the land, and prophets continued to speak of a future *deliverance and large-scale ingathering (e.g., Isa. 60:4; 62:11; cf. Neh. 1:9). The psalm belongs in that context when a return of sorts has happened, but one that by no means satisfies such a vision. The psalm exhorts Yhwh to fulfill that vision.

There is some paradox about the closing line.[35] It combines with vv. 1–2 to frame the psalm, with its reference to confession and praise. Yet

34. Dietmar Mathias, *Die Geschichtstheologie der Geschichtssummarien in den Psalmen* (Frankfurt and New York: Lang, 1993), 201.

35. The final statement in both Pss. 105 and 106 "moves boldly against the grain of the preceding extended argument," suggesting that the relationship between God and Israel

those opening lines speak of confession and praise that can and are to be given now, while the closing line speaks of a different confession and praise that cannot be given now but will be given when Yhwh answers this prayer. Confessing Yhwh's *holy *name (cf. 103:1; 105:3) implies confessing Yhwh as the holy one.

Theological Implications

One cannot always trace a link between the faithfulness or faithlessness of God's people and its blessings or troubles (see, e.g., Ps. 44; the reigns of Manasseh and Josiah provide examples). But the Psalms and the OT narrative also make clear that often one can trace this link. They do so for the sake of the people who hear the narrative and use the Psalms. "The stories of the ancestors are also about contemporary Israel." They "blend into language about the time in which the psalm was written."[36] There is a pattern in Israel's story that is significant for a later generation.

The pattern has variants. Israel's faithlessness expresses itself in different ways. There is their disbelief in Yhwh's (proven) ability to deliver, their unwillingness to follow Yhwh's plan, their internal jealousy and strife, their making of an image, their lack of confidence in Yhwh's promise, their worship of other deities, their submission to the influences of the culture, and their acceptance of its abhorrent forms of worship. Yhwh's reaction also expresses itself in varying ways. At the Reed Sea, Yhwh simply delivers the people despite their faithlessness. In the wilderness and at Sinai, Yhwh sends terrible trouble to them, but stops short of destruction because of the intervention of Moses and Phinehas. In the land and in the exile, Yhwh gives them into the power of oppressors, but eventually gives them relief in exile because of the covenant commitment that goes back to the beginning of the story.

The story of Israel is also the story of the church.[37] One cannot always relate its flourishing and decline to its faithfulness or faithlessness, but one can often do so. One can trace this link in the cases of the near demise of the church in the Eastern Mediterranean (the church of Theodoret and Augustine, whose commentaries we refer to) and the near demise of the church in Europe (the church of Luther and Calvin, whose commentaries we refer to). If they had prosecuted their mis-

is "endlessly open, kept short of a final conclusion." Here, "after the long recital of sin, Psalm 106 nevertheless petitions for rescue" (Walter Brueggemann, *Abiding Astonishment* [Louisville: Westminster John Knox, 1991], 23).

36. Mays, *Psalms*, 342.

37. Cf. McCann, "Psalms," 1112.

sion differently, their fate might have been different. The flourishing churches in Africa and the declining church in the United States need to consider the implications of these earlier stories, which illustrate the pattern Ps. 106 finds in Israel's story. The psalm makes the pattern a basis for prayer.

Psalm 106:48
Coda to Book IV

Translation

[48]Praised be Yhwh the God of Israel
  from age to lasting age!
All the people are to say, Yes!—
  praise Yah![1]

Interpretation

[**106:48**]. The lines that MT treats as the closing praise of Ps. 106 also constitute part of the psalm in 1 Chron. 16:36, in a form slightly revised for that context. Yet the first line corresponds almost exactly to the closing praise at the end of Book I of the Psalter (Ps. 41:13 [14]), which encourages the view that the verse is actually (or also) a responsive footnote to Book IV.[2]

In 41:13 [14], after the first line the editor affirms, "Yes, yes" (LXX assimilates here). In this version, the editor puts a "Yes" (*ʾāmēn*) on the lips of the people and adds the bidding, *praise *Yah, which recurs in

1. LXX attaches to Ps. 107.

2. See the discussion in Dietmar Mathias, *Die Geschichtstheologie der Geschichtssummarien in den Psalmen* (Frankfurt and New York: Lang, 1993), 157–61.

Books IV and V. The other codas so far have contained no imperatives, and it may be that in this context we should take that bidding as part of the people's response: They say, "Yes, praise Yah."

Theological Implications

The book has provided many bases for praising Yhwh, and the coda invites the reader to respond to this note in the book as a whole.

Psalm 107

Yhwh Has Indeed Restored Israel

Translation

1Confess Yhwh, because he is good,
because his commitment is forever.
2The people restored by Yhwh should say it,
those he restored from the power of the foe.[1]
3Gathered from the countries, from east and west,
from the north and from the sea.

4People wandered in the wilderness, in the wasteland;
they did not find the way to a settled city.[2]
5Hungry and also thirsty,
their spirit within them would flag.
6But they cried out to Yhwh in the trouble that came to them;
he would rescue them from their pressures.
7He directed them by a straight way
to get to a settled city.

1. "Lit. "from the hand of the foe." "Foe" is *ṣar,* from *ṣārar* III. In vv. 6, 13, 19, and 28, *ṣar* from *ṣārar* I means "pressures," but the familiarity of this phrase in connection with enemies (e.g., 106:10) makes it more likely that "foe" is the meaning.

2. I follow LXX in associating "the way" with the second colon. MT and Jerome associate it with the first (cf. NJPS), but this makes v. 4a hard to construe, whereas "the way of" often denotes "the way to."

8They are to confess to Yhwh his commitment,
his wonders for human beings,
9Because he sated the scurrying person,
filled the hungry person with good things.

10People who lived in darkness and deathly gloom,
prisoners of affliction[3] and iron,
11Because they defied God's words,
despised Elyon's plans:[4]
12He subdued their heart with toil;[5]
they collapsed with no helper.
13But they cried out to Yhwh in the trouble that came to them;
he would deliver them from their pressures.
14He would bring them out from darkness and deathly gloom
and sever their bonds.
15They are to confess to Yhwh his commitment,
his wonders for human beings,
16Because he broke up bronze doors,
shattered iron bars.

17Fools,[6] because of their rebellious way,
and because of their acts of waywardness, would suffer affliction.
18Their very being would loathe all food
and they reached the gates of death.
19But they cried out to Yhwh in the trouble that came to them;
he would deliver them from their pressures.
20He would send his word to heal them,
release them[7] from their deep pit.
21They are to confess to Yhwh his commitment,
his wonders for human beings,
22To offer thanksgiving sacrifices
and recount his deeds with resounding.

23People who go down to the sea in ships,
who do work in great waters:
24These—they saw Yhwh's deeds,
his wonders in the deep.

3. D. W. Thomas ("Hebrew עני 'Captivity,'" *JTS,* n.s., 16 [1965]: 444–45) hypothesizes that this is not the usual *ʿŏnî* but a homonym meaning "captivity," inferred from Arabic; this seems unnecessary.

4. The participial clauses in vv. 10–11 are extraposed in relation to v. 12, where they are taken up in the "their"; so also in v. 23.

5. LXX "their heart was humbled" (cf. NRSV) implies niphal *wayyikkānaʿ* for MT's hiphil *wayyaknaʿ*.

6. LXX "he helped them" links the consonants *ʾwlm* with the root *ʾwl*/*ʾyl* (cf. 22:19 [20]; 88:4 [5]; see BDB 33b; Allen, *Psalms 101–150,* 83). NRSV emends to *ḥôlîm,* "sick people."

7. The suffix from the first colon also applies here.

25He spoke, raised a storm wind,[8]
and it lifted its waves.[9]
26They would go up to the heavens, they would go down to the depths;
their spirit would melt away in their trouble.[10]
27They would reel and stagger like a drunk
and all their wisdom would swallow up.
28But they cried out to Yhwh in the trouble that came to them;
he would bring them out from their pressures.
29He would make[11] the storm be still;
their[12] waves were silent.
30They rejoiced because they would be quiet,
and he led them to the haven they longed for.[13]
31They are to confess to Yhwh his commitment,
his wonders for human beings,
32To lift him up in the congregation of the people,
praise him in the session of the elders.

33He would make rivers into wilderness,
springs of water into thirsty land,
34Fruitful land into salt marsh,
because of the wickedness of the people who live in it.
35He would make wilderness into a pool of water,
dry land into springs of water.
36He settled the hungry there
and they built a settled city.
37They sowed fields and planted vineyards,
and they produced fruit, a harvest.[14]
38He blessed them and they increased greatly;
their cattle he would not let diminish.
39But they diminished and became low
through oppression, wickedness, and sorrow.
40He is one who pours out shame on leaders
and he made them wander in wastes without a path.
41And secured the needy from affliction
and made their families like flocks.

8. LXX "a storm wind arose" implies qal *wayyaʿămōd* for MT's hiphil *wayyaʿămēd*.

9. Grammatically, the antecedent of "its" will be the sea (v. 23), the last m. sg. noun apart from "Yhwh"; cf. Syr. They are also "his waves" (cf. 42:7 [8]), but this would need some reading in here.

10. The suffix on *nepeš* can apply also to *rāʿâ*.

11. *Yāqēm* is strictly the jussive form, but it must have yiqtol significance.

12. 4QPs[f] has *glly ym*, "the waves of the sea" (cf. Syr), which makes easier sense.

13. Lit. "the haven of their longing." On *mĕḥôz*, see *HALOT*; R. Borger, "Hebräisch *mḥwz* (Psalm 107,30)," *UF* 1 (1969): 1–3.

14. Lit. "fruit of harvest," an odd expression; Gunkel (*Psalmen*, 473) notes GKC 128q.

42The upright see and rejoice;
all wickedness has stopped its mouth.
43Who is the wise person who notes these things?—
they consider Yhwh's acts of commitment.

Interpretation

Like Ps. 106, this psalm combines worship (in the form of confession or testimony) and teaching.[15] Admittedly, the nature of a testimony psalm is to teach, witnessing to what Yhwh has done so as to draw people into deeper trust and commitment. But this can find expression in varying ways. Here, vv. 1–3 make explicit that the psalm relates to testimony, while vv. 42–43 make explicit that it seeks to teach people insight. In between, four sections review settings in which people find themselves in trouble, cry out to Yhwh, find themselves delivered, and are challenged to make their confession of all that. The experiences involve wandering in uninhabited country (vv. 4–9), languishing in prison (vv. 10–16), sickness caused by sin (vv. 17–22), and peril at sea (vv. 23–32). An additional long section describes two further similar successions of experiences (vv. 33–38, 39–41), without following the same literary sequence as the first four. But all these accounts of what Yhwh did for people are couched in the third person, so that the psalm is not itself a testimony but a challenge to testimony, and thus nearer to a piece of teaching rather than an expression of worship than is Ps. 106.

As usual, the four parallel earlier sections manifest differences rather than being completely identical: for instance, the first begins with a qatal verb, the second and fourth with participles, the third with a noun; the first and third begin with a regular sentence, the second and fourth with an extraposed clause; the first and second give reasons backing up the challenge to give testimony, the third and fourth expand on the way to give testimony; and the four sections are of varying length according to how detailed is the description of the trouble and the deliverance. The fact that the last main section (vv. 33–41) abandons the format of the first four while dealing with a similar form of experience further illustrates this liking for variety within a framework of similarity. A feature they all have in common is an alternating between qatal (or wayyiqtol) and yiqtol verbs, all referring to the past. In the first, second, and fourth sections, qatal verbs come first and establish the time reference; in the third section and in vv. 33–41 yiqtol verbs come first. Some of the yiqtol

15. See Walter Beyerlin, *Werden und Wesen des 107. Psalms*, BZAW 153 (Berlin: de Gruyter, 1979).

verbs may correspond to a European imperfect, referring to repeated action in the past, and sometimes their effect may be to portray an event vividly, but in other cases the difference may be purely stylistic. I have translated these yiqtol verbs by the English imperfect conjugation employing the auxiliary verb "would," but without implying that the difference is other than stylistic.

The opening challenge to confession indicates that the psalm is designed for people whom Yhwh has restored and gathered from all over the world, people who have received an answer to the prayer in 106:47 and are to offer the confession it speaks of. The psalm makes a number of links with Pss. 105 and 106. This suggests that the division between Books IV and V is rather artificial as it divides psalms that earlier compilers have set in relationship. It is another indication that the division of the Psalter into books (though also the juxtapositions of psalms) is not a major key to their interpretation; each psalm stands alone and has a "basic autonomy."[16]

The experiences the psalm describes are ones that could come upon individuals, a series of threats to life.[17] They presuppose that one does not need to be in the sanctuary to pray: "It can be done at sea, in the wilderness, in prison, or from the sickbed." Conversely, the temple's worship depends for its life upon people's experience of Yhwh's involvement in their everyday lives in response to such prayers.[18] But here these experiences are described as happening to a group of people. Verses 1–3 then suggest that they are aspects of what happened to people in the exile. Some got lost in uninhabited areas, some were in captivity (Tg identifies them as Zedekiah and the people taken to Babylon in 587), some experienced sickness or injury, and some crossed the Mediterranean to far shores. In all cases they then cried out to God and God brought them back. Verses 33–41 may go over similar ground or may rather relate to the situation after the exile, almost in the way Ezek. 38–39 offers a surprising vision relating to events to follow the restoration that Ezek. 33–37 has promised.

The experiences are not ones distinctively associated with exile and out of the context one would not make this association; Calvin proceeds with his exposition without referring to the exile.[19] Perhaps, then, the four accounts have been brought into relationship with the exile by being set in the context of vv. 1–3. And perhaps vv. 33–41 and/or 42–43 are ultimately of separate origin from other parts of the psalm.[20] MT marks

16. Gerstenberger, *Psalms*, 2:244.
17. Cf. Keel, *Symbolism*, 62.
18. Keel, *Symbolism*, 322, 335.
19. *Psalms*, 4:245–67.
20. See Jorge Mejía, "Some Observations on Psalm 107," *Biblical Theology Bulletin* 5 (1975): 56–66; Beyerlin, *Werden und Wesen*.

vv. 21–26 and v. 40 with an inverted *n* in the margin, which might relate to such questions, though it is not clear how it does so. Verses 39–41 and the final verses have some close verbal links with Job, which might suggest that they do have their background in reflection on the trials of ordinary life; yet the psalm as a whole also has a number of close verbal links with Isaiah, especially with Isa. 40–66, which might make it more likely that the sections do have a direct background in reflection on exile and restoration. This would also explain the otherwise puzzling inclusion of thanksgiving for rescue from disaster at sea, which must have been a very rare experience among the members of the congregations that used this psalm.

As usual, the variety of theories about the possible redactional history of the psalm suggests that if it had a redactional history, we cannot determine what this was. Likewise, there is a variety of theories about the psalm's liturgical setting; the psalm also does not give us clear information about this.[21] Weiser comments that "it is still possible clearly to recognize the liturgical, responsorial character of the hymn, with the priests' call for a prayer of thanksgiving . . . and the responses,"[22] while Mowinckel imaginatively reconstructs a service when the psalm could have been used.[23] It may indeed reflect the dynamics of liturgy, but there is no presupposition that it is itself such a responsive text (any more than the invitation "O come all ye faithful" is an invitation to an actual procession, or the form of call and response in other hymns is an indication of the way they are used). And if vv. 9 and 16 were such responses, one would not expect them to take "they" form. The psalm as we have it[24] relates to reflection and worship in connection with the experience of exile and restoration, but we do not know how it was so used.

107:1–3. The challenge to give testimony.

[1]Confess Yhwh, because he is good,
because his commitment is forever.
[2]The people restored by Yhwh should say it,
those he restored from the power of the foe,
[3]Gathered from the countries, from east and west,
from the north and from the sea.

21. Cf. the critique of John W. Roffey, "Beyond Reality: Poetic Discourse and Psalm 107," in *A Biblical Itinerary*, ed. Eugene E. Carpenter (G. W. Coats Festschrift; Sheffield: Sheffield Academic Press, 1997), 60–76.

22. *Psalms*, 685.

23. *Psalms*, 2:42–43.

24. See Auffret's initial comment, *Merveilles à nos yeux*, 105.

Apart from lacking "Praise Yah" (which LXX provides by attaching the occurrences from the end of 106:48 to the beginning of this psalm), v. 1 corresponds to the opening of Ps. 106.

Verses 2–3 then spell out the implications of that familiar exhortation but take it in a distinctive direction. In isolation, one might reckon that the people Yhwh *restored are those delivered at the Red Sea, or their descendants (see 106:10–11, where all these words come). But Isa. 62:12 uses the phrase "the restored of Yhwh" in envisioning a day when Yhwh will have delivered the people and brought them back to Jerusalem (cf. "the redeemed of Yhwh" in Isa. 35:10; 51:11). The description in v. 2 relates to a "second exodus," the restoration from exile. It assumes that the promises in Isaiah have been fulfilled. The people who experienced this restoration are the ones who should take up that conventional declaration in v. 1, given that they are in a position to affirm that it is not merely a conventional declaration but something they have proved to be true.

That is even clearer in v. 3. Psalm 106:47 pleaded with Yhwh to "gather us from the nations," in effect praying for the fulfillment of the promise in Isa. 60:4. Verse 3 presupposes that this has happened; that promise has also been fulfilled. The line works 2-2-2 and looks as if it is speaking quite conventionally about the four points of the compass, but then surprises us with its last word, where we expect a word for "south," like other passages that begin the four points of the compass but do not complete the reference (e.g., Zech. 6:6). Here, "from the north and from the sea" follows the wording of Isa. 49:12, another promise about Yhwh's bringing people back to the land that the psalm thus suggests has been fulfilled. In signifying directions, "the sea" usually denotes the west, but here might refer to the south (cf. Tg), perhaps the Red Sea, perhaps the southeast corner of the Mediterranean; one of the main countries from which people will need to return is Egypt, and they might make that journey by sea. Within the psalm, the sea as the fourth direction from which people are gathered will reappear in the fourth of the sections in vv. 4–32.

107:4–9. Again, given that there are to be four locations from which the psalm describes rescue, we might have expected that these would correspond to the four points of the compass,[25] but actually they are not this kind of location at all. They are more states or types of experience, the kind that could belong in any geographical area.

> 4People wandered in the wilderness, in the wasteland;
> they did not find the way to a settled city.

25. Cf. John Jarick, "The Four Corners of Psalm 107," *CBQ* 59 (1997): 270–87.

[5]Hungry and also thirsty,
their spirit within them would flag.

First is the experience of being lost in a trackless waste. This is not the "wandering" or stumbling about on the way to the land (*nûaʿ* hiphil; Num. 32:13); *tāʿâ* rather suggests wandering about because they had left the path or because there is no path. Like Hagar (Gen. 21:14), they were lost with nowhere to go. That is how some people were after fleeing from the land during and after the Babylonian invasion in 587. But pairing "in the wasteland" with "in the wilderness" makes a link with another promise, in Isa. 43:19–20. Here the people cannot find a way; there, Yhwh promises to make a way for them (cf. Isa. 49:11). Specifically, like Hagar they cannot find a city where they can settle (lit., "a city of settlement"). That might imply a settled city where they can also reside, or find provision or refuge, or a place where they can establish a settled city.

Again, Isa. 49:10 promises people will not hunger or thirst on the way back to the land, but that contrasts with current experience. That affects not just the outer person but the morale.

[6]But they cried out to Yhwh in the trouble that came to them;
he would rescue them from their pressures.
[7]He directed them by a straight way
to get to a settled city.

Crying out to Yhwh is what Israel did at the Red Sea (Exod. 14:10) and in the Judges period, while "the trouble that came to them" and "he would rescue them" recur from Ps. 106:43–44. "Pressures" (*mĕṣûqâ*) are often experiences that come from "oppressors"—they are troubles caused by other human beings. That fits the parallelism, since "trouble" (*ṣar*), too, tends to be humanly caused, and it also suggests a link with Isa. 51:13 (the mother verb *ṣûq*; cf. also Deut. 28:53, 55, 57).

In v. 7, the first colon, and the verb in the second, in turn parallel Isa. 42:16; 48:17, while the straightness of the way recalls Isa. 40:3; 45:2, 13. The settled city they could not find, Yhwh takes them to. Is this Jerusalem itself (so Tg)? It is Yhwh's *môšāb* in 132:13.[26]

[8]They are to confess to Yhwh his commitment,
his wonders for human beings,
[9]Because he sated the scurrying person,
filled the hungry person with good things.

26. Briggs, *Psalms*, 2:363; cf. Haglund, *Historical Motifs*, 31.

The appropriate response is one that fulfills the bidding of v. 1, which their particular experience has now embodied. They are to give their testimony to what Yhwh has done, the *confession of Yhwh's *commitment embodied in a thanksgiving psalm. Reference to Yhwh's "wonders" has recurred in Pss. 105 and 106 as a general term for the great things that Yhwh does, but there with special reference to the exodus and the Red Sea events, and it would make sense if here the word suggests that Yhwh has reprised those wonders, acting in grace for mere "human beings" (cf. 36:7 [8]).[27]

"Sating" is another motif from Ps. 105 (v. 40); Yhwh is again acting in accordance with the pattern of the wilderness period. "Good [things]" adds a link with 104:28; 106:5. The scurrying person replaces the thirsty (v. 5), suggesting people having to bustle about trying to find water.

107:10–16. The people in vv. 4–9 at least kept their freedom. The second group lost that. Further, vv. 4–9 offered no hint that people deserved their trouble; vv. 10–16 take a different stance.

10People who lived in darkness and deathly gloom,
prisoners of affliction and iron,
11Because they defied God's words,
despised Elyon's plans:
12He subdued their heart with toil;
they collapsed with no helper.

Again, "darkness" suggests the exile experience from which Yhwh promised deliverance (Isa. 49:9), while "deathly gloom" underlines the depth of darkness; *ṣalmāwet* may have been originally pointed *ṣalmût*, but MT's pointing gives extra solemnity in suggesting that this darkness is deathly shadow, the shadow of death (cf. LXX, Jerome). "Deathly" is then likely a form of superlative, as sometimes in English ("dead right"), yet here an apposite one because darkness did threaten death (cf. "dead tired"). The combination of words parallels Isa. 9:2 [1], which also formulates the promise of deliverance. The second colon explains why people are in this darkness; again, compare Isa. 49:9 (cf. 61:1). In turn Isa. 48:10 recalls Yhwh's testing people in the "furnace of affliction" (though compare also Exod. 3:7; 4:31; Lam. 1:3, 7, 9; and for "iron," Ps. 105:18 and the "iron furnace" of Deut. 4:20). People's captivity was a furnace of affliction and of iron; the iron may also imply iron chains.

Unlike people in the iron furnace of Egypt, but like the people Isa. 40–55 presupposes, these prisoners deserved their captivity. Their defying (*mārâ*) Yhwh's words makes a contrast with Ps. 105:28 (cf. also 106:33). The enormity of their attitude is underlined by the paronomasia *himrû*

27. Cf. Allen, *Psalms 101–150*, 89.

ʾimrê-ʾēl:[28] fancy juxtaposing "defy" and "words of God"! Their despising Yhwh's plans recalls Isa. 5:19, 24 and Ps. 106:13, 43. The two parts of the regular title "God Most High" are divided between the parallel cola.[29]

"Subduing" in turn picks up from 106:42, perhaps suggesting that subduing their heart involved subjecting them to their captors. Certainly the colon refers to more than mere inner pain. Like the Israelites in Egypt, they had to toil hard for their captors; the recurrence of "toil" from 105:44 carries some irony. The result of Yhwh's subjection was their collapse: cf. Isa. 59:10. It makes for an unfortunate contrast with Isa. 63:13, but at least Yhwh has declared the intention to *help them (Isa. 41:10, 13, 14; cf. 44:2; 49:8).

> 13But they cried out to Yhwh in the trouble that came to them;
> he would deliver them from their pressures.
> 14He would bring them out from darkness and deathly gloom
> and sever their bonds.

Verse 13 repeats v. 6 except for the substitution of *deliver for "rescue," making a link instead with 106:8, 10, while "he would bring them out" corresponds to 105:37; both suggest a repetition of the exodus. The rest of v. 14a repeats from v. 10a with its exilic connotations, and "he would sever their bonds" corresponds to the exilic promise in Jer. 30:8.

> 15They are to confess to Yhwh his commitment,
> his wonders for human beings,
> 16Because he broke up bronze doors,
> shattered iron bars.

Verse 15 reprises v. 8, then v. 16 offers an appropriate reason for the testimony in words corresponding to Isa. 45:2, turned into a neat *abb′a′* line whose effect is to "tie the two clauses more closely together than conj[unctive] sent[ences] and make the events or situations of which they speak in effect two sides of a single whole."[30] Yes, Yhwh fulfilled the promise, bringing exile to an end.

107:17–22. The third group of people are sick or wounded because of their sinfulness.

> 17Fools, because of their rebellious way,
> and because of their acts of waywardness, would suffer affliction.

28. Watson, *Classical Hebrew Poetry*, 243. Using the relatively unusual word for "word," *ʾēmer*, facilitates the paronomasia.

29. Ibid., 330.

30. DG 140. Watson (*Classical Hebrew Poetry*, 124) notes also the f.f., m.m. gender pattern in the line.

[18]Their very being would loathe all food
and they reached the gates of death.

The prophetic saying behind v. 17 is Isa. 35:8. "Suffer affliction" (*yitʿannû*) is one letter different from "wander" (*yitʿû*) in Isa. 35:8 (the hitpael comes only here with this meaning), and also makes for a paronomasia with waywardness (*ʿāwōn*). While the Psalms recognize that not all trouble comes from sin, in the exile *ʿāwōn* led to *ʿānâ*, as is appropriate. *Rebellion and *waywardness appear together in Isa. 50:1; 59:12.

Verse 18 does little to give more specific content to "suffer affliction," though it might imply illness or wounds (cf. v. 20a). People who give up eating because of sickness or injuries will find themselves at the gates of death; when he was ill Hezekiah saw himself sitting at the gates of Sheol (Isa. 38:10), and Tg interprets vv. 17–22 of him.

[19]But they cried out to Yhwh in the trouble that came to them;
he would deliver them from their pressures.
[20]He would send his word to heal them,
release them from their deep pit.

Verse 19 corresponds to v. 13. Once more the companion verse spells out its implications. Isaiah 55:11 almost hypostasizes the word going out from Yhwh's mouth that makes things happen; this understanding of Yhwh's word may apply here, though the expression is different and may only presuppose that things do happen when a powerful person speaks. Yhwh only has to say the word and a person gets healed. Then they are no longer sitting at death's gates waiting to be admitted or to find Death reaching out to drag them in. In Lam. 4:20 *šĕḥîtôtām* is "their deep pit" (intensive plural) in a down-to-earth sense, though perhaps still a metaphorical one; it refers to the place where someone was imprisoned. Here the context suggests that the deep pit is the pit into which we go when we die (cf. *šaḥat* in Ps. 103:4), another word for Sheol. "Release" plays a key role in Isa. 49:24–25, again suggesting the fulfillment of the promises of restoration from exile.

[21]They are to confess to Yhwh his commitment,
his wonders for human beings,
[22]To offer thanksgiving sacrifices
and recount his deeds with resounding.

Verse 21 again reprises v. 8, but then v. 22, instead of providing reasons for v. 21, restates its point. A thanksgiving sacrifice (*tôdâ*) is the regular accompaniment of the verbal thanksgiving (also *tôdâ*) referred to by the related verb *confess (*yādâ* hiphil). The instructions for the sacrifice come in Lev. 3; 7:11–18; the sacrifice makes the alleged gratefulness more than mere words. As well as expressing gratefulness, the words address other people, as confession or testimony, so that they may respond to Yhwh with their own praise and trust; we do that with the out-loud *resounding that indicates we mean it.

107:23–32. Promises of restoration from exile often refer to people coming from far shores; the fourth group are such people, who traveled across the sea to start a new life in a far country.

> 23People who go down to the sea in ships,
> who do work in great waters:

The "people who go down to the sea" thus reappear from Isa. 42:10 (see MT), though the context here may give the expression more solemnity. This participle most frequently refers to going down to Sheol or death or the pit or the dust (e.g., 22:29 [30]; 143:7), and the sea is a place of danger and the threat of death. Indeed, the expression hints not merely at going down *to* the sea (from the Judean mountains) but at going down *into* the sea (cf. Jon. 1:3 and then 2:6 [7]; Tg interprets vv. 23–32 of Jonah). People go down into the depths (v. 26), like the hapless Egyptians (Exod. 15:5). The psalm is not just talking about sailors whose job involves the danger of sea travel.[31] The people crossing the sea could include people working their passage to start a new life in a foreign country in a coast-hugging vessel from Jaffa to Egypt or traveling farther across the "great waters" of the Mediterranean to Cyprus, Greece, or Turkey.

> 24These—they saw Yhwh's deeds,
> his wonders in the deep.

This declaration then introduces what will follow. Yhwh's "deeds" are not marvels of creation but acts of deliverance (cf. v. 22; 106:13); "wonders" makes that more explicit (cf. vv. 8, 15, 21, and 31). Here, they will be wonders in the deep, of the kind Jonah experienced (Jon. 2:3 [4]). But "deep" can imply something metaphorical and metaphysical, not merely literal and physical (cf. Exod. 15:5), the unfathomable, yawning waters of death (Ps. 69:2, 15 [3, 16]).

> 25He spoke, raised a storm wind,
> and it lifted its waves.

31. In this connection, O. Loretz suggests Phoenician background for the section ("Baal—Jahwe als Beschützer der Kaufleute in Ps 107," *UF* 12 [1980]: 417–19).

26They would go up to the heavens, they would go down to the depths;
their spirit would melt away in their trouble.

In v. 20 Yhwh's word was good news, but its power works negatively as well as positively. Yhwh's powerful sovereignty in the world is not focused on what suits humanity (cf. Job 38–39). Yhwh does not order this storm to cause trouble to human beings. Such powerful phenomena are built into nature, part of creation's energy. If human beings choose to travel across the seas (or build in earthquake regions), they have to accept the consequences.

Verse 26b indicates that the "they" in the first colon is the "they" of vv. 23–24, not the waves. In a storm, waves lift the ship so high it is as if those aboard are reaching the sky. The troughs between the waves then plunge the ship so low it is as if the passengers are descending to the ocean's deepest depths, never to return; and indeed that can happen. The point is underlined by the staccato nature of the 2-2 colon.[32] It is not surprising, then, that their spirit (*person) melts or dissolves.

27They would reel and stagger like a drunk
and all their wisdom would swallow up.
28But they cried out to Yhwh in the trouble that came to them;
he would bring them out from their pressures.

Trying to fulfill their tasks as the ship tips this way and then that, the seafarers look like drunks. In the perfect storm, all the skill of sailors dissolves along with the collapse of their morale. There is nothing they can do to save themselves.

When desperate, then, one can always try prayer. Verse 28 constitutes another slight variant on the declaration in vv. 6, 13, and 19; the verb in the second colon is now *yāṣāʾ* (hiphil), the standard expression for Yhwh's bringing the people out of Egypt. Once again Yhwh's deliverance brings about a new exodus.

29He would make the storm be still;
their waves were silent.
30They rejoiced because they would be quiet,
and he led them to the haven they longed for.

Whereas the more concrete account of Yhwh's deliverance received one line in the first three sections, here it receives two, as the description of trouble was more elaborate. Objectively, the peril was perhaps no more dangerous, but it was more terrifying. Fortunately, the God who could

32. Watson, *Classical Hebrew Poetry*, 178.

call for a storm could also silence it. Although perhaps taking no account of human needs in summoning up a storm, God may take account of those needs when pressed to do so. Prayer makes a difference; it makes God take action that otherwise God would not have taken.

So the seafarers rejoiced because the waves quietened (cf. Jon. 1:11–12). A moment ago their spirit was melting away; now it can be joyful. And this joy is followed by the relief of reaching safe harbor. Yhwh led them or guided them there (*nāḥâ* hiphil). The language suggests another vivid picture of the nature of Yhwh's involvement in the world. Yhwh causes the storm; Yhwh stills the storm; Yhwh then acts like a pilot making sure that the ship not only escapes the storm Yhwh caused but also that it gets to a haven. But further, the verb also describes Yhwh's leading Israel toward the promised land (e.g., Exod. 13:21; also 15:13, though there qal). Yhwh relates to the people on their way out of the land as the people who were brought to it. The image recalls Ezekiel's picture of Yhwh's splendor appearing in Babylon as in Canaan. Their relief at reaching their haven now complements their rejoicing at their escape.

[31]They are to confess to Yhwh his commitment,
his wonders for human beings,
[32]To lift him up in the congregation of the people,
praise him in the session of the elders.

Again, the expected response reprises vv. 8, 15, and 21; v. 32 then expands on its nature in a way analogous to the expansion in v. 22. The storm lifted the waves; the people tossed about by those waves now lift up the one who rescued them from it. The psalm almost pictures the seafarers making their way straight from the quay to the place where the community gathers, to give *praise by telling of what Yhwh had done for them. One might expect "congregation" (*qāhāl*) to suggest people gathered for worship, but what place of worship would there be in this foreign haven? The second colon hints rather at the community assembly. "Session" is *môšāb*, the word for "settlement" in vv. 4, 7, and 36. The place where the community elders sit (*yāšab*) will be the plaza inside the city gate, and the seafarers' task will be to testify there to what Yhwh has done. They thus give their testimony out in the (pagan?) community, not merely inside in the synagogue. This might also be the implication in the first colon.

107:33–41. While this final major section does not follow the sequence of the preceding ones, I follow LXX and Tg in understanding it as continuing to refer to past events. Tg refers them to the natural disaster in the time of Joel. Each of its two parts moves from trouble, to divine action to undo the trouble, to consequent blessing. Each element in this structure receives two lines in vv. 33–38 and one line in vv. 39–41. The two subsections might be parallel, but the movement from v. 38 to v. 39 rather suggests that the second sequence follows on the first.

> 33He would make rivers into wilderness,
> springs of water into thirsty land,
> 34Fruitful land into salt marsh,
> because of the wickedness of the people who live in it.

The summary starts with the negative. The first colon is close to Isa. 50:2 and also recalls 42:15b, though in speaking of "wilderness" and "springs of water" it anticipates v. 35 and thus also recalls Isa. 41:18b. "Thirsty land," however, comes from the equivalent statement about a positive transformation in Isa. 35:7. The paronomasia (*mōṣāʾê mayim lĕṣimmāʾôn*) underlines the anomalous nature of the transformation. Both rivers and springs are water sources that can be relied on all year round. But Yhwh makes them not be so.

Verse 34a makes the same point in more distinctive, and perhaps more frightening, fashion. The land is actually fruitful; the colon is not referring merely to the potential for fruitfulness in the presence of rivers and springs. But Yhwh's action not merely produces drought (which might cease) or dryness (which might be put right by irrigation) but turns the land into something totally incapable of producing anything. It is again an aspect of nature that is clearly no use to humanity and must exist for its own sake or for the sake of some other part of nature (cf. Job 39:6). Here, Yhwh has deliberately turned land useful to humanity into this other kind of land. Verse 34b then explains this strange action (cf. the warnings in Deut. 29:22–23 [21–22]).

> 35He would make wilderness into a pool of water,
> dry land into springs of water.
> 36He settled the hungry there
> and they built a settled city.

The positive mirror image of that transformation corresponds closely to Isa. 41:18b. The second line again offers an explanation, though in terms of what Yhwh wants to do with the transformation, not of the human acts that caused it. There is no indication that these were good rather than wicked people, people who deserved what they received. Insofar as they offered a qualification, it was their hunger rather than their goodness. The reference to the hungry and to a settled city takes up vv. 4–7, though these people build their own city. Instead of taking them to an existing city from land where they will always be thirsty, Yhwh transforms the landscape where they are so that it can support a city. Yhwh settles them; they build. Yhwh's activity parallels that in v. 30b. As well as being the pilot who guides the ship to harbor, Yhwh is the king who establishes settlements in his realm. But Yhwh does not do everything for them. They have to build the city.

> 37 They sowed fields and planted vineyards,
> and they produced fruit, a harvest.
> 38 He blessed them and they increased greatly;
> their cattle he would not let diminish.

The divine transformation described in v. 35 makes this activity possible for the people, who build their city in the place Yhwh settles them. Both the inanimate and the animate worlds are divided into two; concrete examples stand for the whole. There are crops that people sow year by year, such as wheat and barley, and there are trees such as the olive and the vine that are planted and then tended over a period of years. Both will flourish. The prophets often speak of building houses and living in them and planting vineyards and enjoying the fruit (e.g., Isa. 65:21)—or not (Zeph. 1:13). The psalm presupposes what this formula alludes to.

Verse 38a presumably refers to Yhwh's blessing of the people themselves, which means they increase. The collocation of blessing and increase takes up that in Gen. 1. But there, blessing and increase also apply to other creatures (Gen. 1:22), though not explicitly to domestic animals (but see 8:17). Here, Yhwh is also involved in making sure that cattle (and by implication sheep, goats, and donkeys) keep their numbers. This might seem an anticlimax, though it would be a blessing not to be despised.

> 39 But they diminished and became low
> through oppression, wickedness, and sorrow.
> 40 He is one who pours out shame on leaders
> and he made them wander in wastes without a path.
> 41 And secured the needy from affliction
> and made their families like flocks.

But the diminishing of v. 38 leads into v. 39 (the two occurrences of the verb come together) to begin the reprise of the threefold sequence in vv. 39–41.[33] Their cattle may keep their numbers; the people do not, and rather get put down. The parallel with vv. 33–34 (where the word

33. Commentators make strangely heavy weather of vv. 39–41 (perhaps it is the aftereffect of the storm in vv. 23–32); thus Kraus (*Psalms 60–150*, 325) declares that "a transposition of vv. 39 and 40 is absolutely necessary." If vv. 39–41 reprise the sequence in 33–38, it is absolutely unnecessary.

"wickedness" explained what happened)[34] suggests that oppression, trouble, and sorrow are not the suffering that comes to the people but the affliction they impose on others, or the affliction that characterizes the life of the community. The city allows itself to become one where some people can impose oppression, trouble, and sorrow on others.

The "leaders" will then be the community's leaders rather than foreign rulers. A community's leaders bear special responsibility for its wickedness (partly because they usually profit from it). Thus Yhwh takes action against them. The line combines Job 12:21a and 24b, part of a long declaration that has rather cynical implications on Job's lips but quite positive ones here (the section in Job has a number of other verbal links with the psalm). Whether understood straightforwardly or cynically, it again presupposes a strong understanding of God's sovereignty. Perhaps it does not imply that Yhwh puts shame on every leader who deserves it, but it certainly reckons that Yhwh sometimes or often does that. To leaders, people's regard is very important; they want to be leaders because they want to be famous, to make their mark. But the bigger and the more famous they are, the harder and the more publicly they fall. They share the fate of the most helpless of people (cf. v. 4 of the psalm).

The *w* that begins v. 41 is more "and" than "but." The leadership's removal constitutes the deliverance of the people they have oppressed. Whereas the *needy have been brought low through the action of their leaders, Yhwh will now set them on high (*śāgab*; cf. 91:14), secure from such treatment. Yhwh not merely rescues them from affliction but puts them into a position where they have protection in the future. The final verb makes for an inclusion with the first colon of the section (v. 33a), while the final colon as a whole closes the subsection in a way that parallels the close of the parallel subsection, in v. 38.

107:42–43. The conclusion makes the psalm's didactic purpose explicit in terms that further reflect the discourse of wisdom.

> **42**The upright see and rejoice;
> all wickedness has stopped its mouth.

The first colon parallels Eliphaz's words in Job 22:19a. Ironically, this time the words are Eliphaz's, and the psalm means them in the same sense as Eliphaz does. The upright bet their lives on the principle that Yhwh does see that even if righteousness is its own reward it receives other rewards as well. They see Yhwh act in the way described in vv. 4–41 and they rejoice, not only for their own sake, but because there is moral order in the world. Meanwhile, the wicked (the psalm uses abstract for

34. EVV translate *rāʿâ* "trouble" in v. 39.

concrete and also pairs masculine and feminine and singular and plural) stop up their mouths. Isaiah 52:15 helps to establish in what sense that is so: Yhwh's actions make them shut up because those actions contradict all the assumptions upon which they have based their lives. The colon corresponds to Job 5:16b, again Eliphaz's words, and the psalm again means them in the same sense as Eliphaz does.[35]

> [43]Who is the wise person who notes these things?—
> they consider Yhwh's acts of commitment.

The wise person, then, sides with Eliphaz in his affirmation of Yhwh's moral order in the world, even if not in Eliphaz's way of making the point to Job (though here the wording actually compares with Hos. 14:9 [10]). Wise people look at the way Yhwh delivers the needy, at Yhwh's acts of *commitment (cf. Ps. 106:7, 45), and base their lives on that. They do that not least when their own experience does not match this pattern. The last verse makes the psalm (almost) close with a question that the reader has to answer.

Theological Implications

The psalm takes a distinctive stance to Yhwh's promises of restoration and their fulfillment. Promises such as those in Isa. 40–55 saw partial fulfillment in the events that followed the fall of Babylon in 539, but only very partial fulfillment. Isaiah 56–66 declares that they will receive complete fulfillment, even more splendidly than those earlier chapters described, but that the community needs to give itself in commitment to Yhwh in the meantime—with the implication that failure to do so forfeits the possibility of such fulfillment. Chronicles expresses another response as it emphasizes the privilege of being able to worship in the temple in accordance with the way David provided, and thus implies the magnitude of what Yhwh has done in making it possible for the Judean community to do that.

Psalm 107 is a variant on that latter response.[36] When one considers those glorious promises in Isa. 40–55, it is tempting to see them as quite unfulfilled. The psalm says, No, consider what Yhwh has done for us.

35. JM 60c takes the qatal as precative and, by implication, takes the whole line as jussive, but in Job the qatal seems to be gnomic, and in this line there is no clear pointer in the jussive direction.

36. An ironic fact, if Robert Meye is right to see "Psalm 107 as 'Horizon' for Interpreting the Miracle Stories of Mark 4:34–8:26" (in *Unity and Diversity in New Testament Theology*, ed. Robert A. Guelich [G. E. Ladd Festschrift; Grand Rapids: Eerdmans, 1978], 1–13).

There were people wandering and lost as they sought refuge from the aftermath of the Babylonian invasion; they found a home, and they found their way back to *the* city. There were people in captivity in Babylon; they were freed. There were people overwhelmed by their guilt who felt near death (indeed, that was true of the whole community); Yhwh healed them. There were people who had traveled far across the sea to try to find a new life, for whom any return was fraught with danger; but they found their haven. Yes, Yhwh proved to be someone who could make a well-watered land into a desert, but also someone who could do the reverse. Therefore, do not underestimate the significance of what Yhwh has done in restoring the community in fulfillment of those promises. Rejoice in what Yhwh has done, consider Yhwh's acts of commitment, testify to them.

The psalm invites the church to face the disparity between the NT's vision of it and the reality of the church as we know it, but then not to be overwhelmed but to rejoice in Yhwh's acts of commitment to it. This sinful community, too, is one gathered from the four corners of the earth (cf. v. 3).[37] It, too, has wandered about aimlessly, found itself in captivity, behaved with folly, come near shipwreck, known flourishing and diminishing, and known God meeting it in each of those experiences. Thus vv. 1–3 and 42–43 address it.

37. Jerome's key to the psalm as a whole (*Homilies*, 1:238–44).

Psalm 108

Claiming God's Promises

Translation

Song. Composition. David's.

1My heart is set, God, I will sing;
  I will make music, yes, my soul [is set].
2Wake up, harp and lyre;
  I will wake the dawn.[1]
3I will confess you among the peoples, Yhwh,
  I will make music for you among the nations.[2]
4Because your commitment is great, over the heavens,
  and your truthfulness [is great], up to the sky.

5Be on high over the heavens, Yhwh,
  over all the earth your honor.
6So that the ones you love may be rescued,
  deliver with your right hand and answer me.

7God spoke by his holiness:
  I will exult as I allocate Shechem,
  as I measure out Succot Valley.

1. LXX "I will wake up at dawn" requires the reader to treat the hiphil as having the same intransitive meaning as the qal in v. 2a and also to take *šāḥar* as if it were *baššāḥar* (cf. Hos. 10:15).

2. As elsewhere, L misdivides *ballĕʾummîm* as *bal-ʾummîm*.

[8]Gilead will be mine, Manasseh mine,
  Ephraim my helmet, Judah my scepter.
[9]Moab will be my wash basin,[3]
  over Edom I will throw my shoe,
  over Philistia I will shout out.
[10]Who will conduct me to the fortress city,[4]
  who might lead me[5] to Edom?

[11]Have you not rejected us, God?—
  you do not go out with our armies, God.[6]
[12]Grant us help against the foe,[7]
  given that[8] human deliverance is empty.
[13]Through God we will act forcefully;
  he is the one who will trample on our foes.

Interpretation

This prayer psalm divides into two; each part comes to its point with an appeal for Yhwh's deliverance (vv. 5–6 and 11–13). But each half gets to that point by a very different route, though these thus combine to achieve considerable effect. The first half starts by declaring the intent to confess among the nations Yhwh's commitment and truthfulness (vv. 1–4). The plea then builds on that confession, as if to say, "Given that confession of commitment and truthfulness, you, Yhwh, must live up to it." The second half starts by recollecting Yhwh's own words about sovereignty in relation to Israel and the peoples around Israel (vv. 7–10). The plea then

3. As at 60:8 [10], LXX "my hope basin" (cf. Sym) reflects the meaning of a second root *rāḥaṣ* in Aramaic.

4. Ps. 60:9 [11] has *'îr māṣôr* for *'îr mibṣār*, with little difference in meaning; *mibṣār* generates a paronomasia with the Edomite fortress city of Bozrah (*boṣrâ*) from that root (cf. Goulder, *Psalms of the Return*, 131).

5. As at 60:9 [11], Gunkel reads *mî yanḥēnî* for MT's *mî nāḥanî* (haplography; *Psalmen*, 259), while Barthélemy (*Psaumes*, 393) suggests that the *y* on *mî* does double duty, also functioning as a preformative on the verb, which is thus yiqtol. But the qatal itself can be used in doubtful questions (see *TTH* 19).

6. Cf. LXX for the understanding of v. 11b. Tg and TNIV assume that the interrogative carries on from the first colon, "And do you not go out. . . ." But the fact that rejecting is a bad thing and going out a good thing makes this difficult, and both have to paraphrase to cope with that. Jerome (*Homilies*, 2:252) also assumes that the interrogative carries over but takes v. 11b as an appeal, "Will you not go out. . . ." This is also difficult, where the type of statement changes from accusation to plea.

7. LXX, Jerome take *ṣar* to denote "trouble," but it denotes "foe" in the next line; cf. the comment on 107:2.

8. The *w* marks this as something more like a circumstantial clause than a causal one (see *TTH* 159, against GKC 158a; JM 170c).

builds on that declaration, as if to say, "Given that word of yours, Yhwh, you must live up to it." The two halves thus develop within themselves with some rhetorical subtlety. They also relate to one another with some subtlety. By the end of vv. 1–6 we know people need deliverance but not what they need deliverance from; we have to wait for the second half to discover that, indeed, until the latter part of the second half. To put it another way, the explicit lament element in the psalm, indicating the need the psalm brings to God, does not come until nearly the end.

The psalm's contents comprise variants on 57:7–11 [8–12] and 60:5–12 [7–14]. Both sections fit integrally into those other psalms, but also fit integrally in this context; it is particularly striking that the psalm's two-part structure does not correspond to the division between the two origins. Indeed, the rhetoric of Ps. 108 reverses those of Pss. 57 and 60 in moving from praise to plea rather than from plea or protest to declaration of confidence (both have their lament element near the beginning of the psalm), though it does finally end up in the same place as Ps. 60.[9]

It seems more likely that this psalm recycles parts of two other psalms than that two other psalmists independently found the two parts of this psalm bases for new coherent wholes. Psalm 108's retaining of the title "God" rather than "Yhwh," which is characteristic of Pss. 42–83, fits with that.[10] Its collocation with Pss. 105–7 then suggests that it represents an adaptation of this material to a postexilic context. In this setting it takes up the appeal for deliverance voiced in 106:47 in the context of the reduced state of the people in the Persian period, when Yhwh is not exercising the sovereignty in the area around Judah suggested by vv. 7–10, not least in relation to Edom (there is no particular reason to interpret Edom as an eschatological figure). In recognizing the incompleteness of Israel's restoration, it thus also presents the other side of the coin from Ps. 107. While as usual we cannot be sure of the exact period it belongs to,[11] the *kind* of period it implies is clear, one when people are aware that there are divine promises (specifically concerning their possession of the land and their relationship with surrounding peoples) that stand over their life yet are not fulfilled at present. The movement between "I" and "we" in the psalm suggests someone such as a governor addressing God on the people's behalf.

Song. Composition. David's.

9. Contrast Auffret's comment (*Voyez de vos yeux*, 84) on the "rapport" of Ps. 108 to Pss. 57 and 60.

10. The partial exception is "Yhwh" in v. 3 for *ʾădōnāy* in 57:9 [10].

11. Indeed, Ernst A. Knauf ("Psalm lx und Psalm cviii," *VT* 50 [2000]: 55–65) dates it in the second century, the time of John Hyrcanus.

Heading. The psalm is the first with a heading since Ps. 103. Its terms are all conventional (see glossary); it does not correspond at all with the headings of Pss. 57 or 60 except for the reference to David, which will recur in the next two psalms.

108:1–4. The psalm begins with an extensive commitment to praise (vv. 1–3) and a brief but far-reaching rationale for it (v. 4).

> 1My heart is set, God, I will sing;
> I will make music, yes, my soul [is set].

The content of the unconventional opening makes clear enough that this is a declaration of intent such as should lead into testimony. "Singing" and "making *music" are at home in praise and testimony psalms, but the prominence of the "I" points to the latter. Classically, "I will sing" opens Moses's Song at the Red Sea (Exod. 15:1); it commonly appears near the end of a prayer psalm to denote the singing the suppliant will offer when the plea has been answered. "I will make music" is at home in the same context (e.g., 71:22–23). MT divides the line after "God," producing a 3-3 line but one whose prosody is otherwise odd. More likely the opening participle "set" applies to both lines; "I will make music" parallels "I will sing," and "yes, my soul" parallels "my *heart."[12] "My soul" is *kĕbôdî*, which would usually denote "my honor" but in a context such as this implies (literally) "my liver" (usually *kābēd*), in the sense of "my inner being" (so, for example, 16:9). To say that my heart and soul are "set" (*nākôn*), set firm or established or made ready, is to liken them to God's throne, established of old (93:2), or to the stance of a runner about to begin a race ("ready, steady . . .").

> 2Wake up, harp and lyre;
> I will wake the dawn.

The suppliant cannot wait to begin this song; that is how firmly set and ready heart and soul are. The impatience extends to the musical instruments, *harp and *lyre (metonymy for the musicians?), which will not begin playing and ought to do so. It also extends to time itself, because the worship cannot begin until the set moment arrives (one is to imagine people irritated that the church service will not start, they are so keen to worship). Dawn is supposed to wake people (there are no alarm clocks); the suppliant wants to wake the dawn so that the time for the morning offering and its worship will arrive.

12. Psalm 57:8–9a works quite differently; LXX partly assimilates to it.

[3]I will confess you among the peoples, Yhwh,
I will make music for you among the nations.

So far, the psalm has spoken only about music, like (post)modern worshippers for whom the worship beat is more important than the words. Verse 3 puts the two necessary aspects of praise together, the words as well as the *music. The first-person nature of the commitment in vv. 1–3 means it is not surprising that the praise will take the form of *confession, testifying to what God has done for me/us. But usually one gives testimony to other Israelites, to strengthen their faith in Yhwh. Here it is to be offered among the nations. It is not an ordinary testimony. The suppliant is not an ordinary individual but someone such as a governor, who represents the whole people (cf. v. 6). The interplay of first-person speech and non-first-person content, and of confession and non-confessional content (cf. v. 4), parallels the interplay in the preceding psalms, Pss. 103–7.

[4]Because your commitment is great, over the heavens,
and your truthfulness [is great], up to the sky.

Acknowledging Yhwh's cosmos-wide *commitment and *truthfulness coheres with the worldwide reach of the praise. Yet the "because" gives another sign that this is not an ordinary testimony psalm, indeed not really a testimony psalm at all; it is praise for who Yhwh is rather than thanksgiving for what Yhwh has done for the worshipper(s). The parallelism involves ellipse, as in v. 1. Prosaically put, "your *commitment and *truthfulness are great in the realm above the heavens/sky[13] and in the realm that extends up to the heavens/sky." Perhaps the implication is that these operate not only in the realm above the heavens where God lives, which does not so directly concern us, but also in the realm beneath the heavens that does.

108:5–6. Praise gives way to a first plea. It transpires that the function of vv. 1–4 has been to set Yhwh up, in the manner of Pss. 44 or 89. For people who knew Ps. 57, this would be particularly effective, given the movement from plea to confidence there.

[5]Be on high over the heavens, Yhwh,
over all the earth your honor.
[6]So that the ones you love may be rescued,
deliver with your right hand and answer me.

13. In the first colon, 57:10 [11] has simply "up to the heavens," the same prep. as in the second colon.

If Yhwh's commitment and truthfulness are as v. 4 said, this should make a difference on earth; the psalm will go on to make more explicit that this does not seem to be so. There is a sense in which Yhwh simply *is* high over all (99:2). But other beings assert themselves and behave as if in a position of exaltation and power. So from time to time Yhwh has to assert authority. That is true in relation to supernatural powers, though the real point about v. 5 likely lies in the second colon.

In turn v. 5 as a whole is subordinate to v. 6, where the first half of the psalm reaches its goal. Thus whereas in Ps. 57 the bidding to "be on high" likely denotes an exaltation in people's thinking, in Ps. 108 it suggests an exaltation in exercising authority in events. People need *deliverance and rescue (*ḥālaṣ* niphal, suggesting being "pulled out" from a dangerous situation). It is not yet explicit what they need rescue and deliverance from; as the psalm pursues its policy of letting things unfold gradually and maintaining suspense, this will become clearer in the second half. What is clear here is another aspect of the basis for appeal. The people needing rescue are "the ones you love," "your beloved" (*yĕdîd*), a rare expression. One might use it of a favorite child (Deut. 33:12), best friend (Isa. 5:1), or spouse (Jer. 11:15). The psalm appeals to the close personal relationship between Yhwh and the people. If your child, friend, or spouse is in trouble, you do something. So surely should Yhwh in relation to this people. Following up this appeal, the closing plea to answer *me* confirms the impression that the suppliant is someone with a leadership position. And his "answer me" implies not merely a verbal reply (which might be "yes," "no," or "wait," and still count as an answer) but action.

108:7–10. The psalm ricochets in a new direction, though the link with vv. 1–6 will become clear in vv. 11–13. This word is not directly a response to the plea in vv. 1–6 but a reminder providing a way into prayer parallel to the praise of vv. 1–4, on the basis of the word's being unfulfilled.

7God spoke by his holiness:
I will exult as I allocate Shechem,
as I measure out Succot Valley.

NRSV and TNIV have "God has spoken," and one can imagine God speaking a word responding to a plea such as that in vv. 5–6 (see 2 Chron. 20:5–17), but this recalls an old word presupposing a political situation from centuries earlier.[14] That supports the view that God spoke "by his *holiness" not "in his sanctuary," as in 150:1 (cf. Tg, Jerome); compare 89:35 [36], where Yhwh refers to swearing "by my holiness" (cf. Amos 4:2). We swear oaths by something important to us, so as to bring trouble on

14. On this debate, see Jacobson, *"Many Are Saying,"* 114–17.

ourselves if we default. There is, of course, nothing Yhwh can swear by bigger than "by myself" (e.g., Gen. 22:16); swearing "by my/his holiness" is an expanded version of that, since Yhwh's holiness is the very essence of Yhwh's self. So Yhwh's commitment was a very serious one, and that point gives force to the challenge that will come in vv. 11–12. Swearing an oath, then, is a serious matter, implying reflection and considered judgment. Yet its first word concerns "exulting," a very human term for uninhibited enthusiasm, a typical expression of God's impassioned personal nature. God really enjoyed the idea of allocating the land to those people.

Warrior Yhwh owns this land and therefore can allocate it to people. The oath is one Yhwh swore when Israel was about to enter the land. Shechem was the first goal of that entering (e.g., Deut. 27), a key location near the center of the land west of the Jordan, implicitly the location of the land's allocation to the Israelite clans in Josh. 13–22. Alongside Shechem, Succot stands for the land east of the Jordan. Jacob settled there for a while after returning from Paddan-Aram and before moving on to Shechem (Gen. 33:17–18). To allocate Shechem and measure out Succot Valley[15] to Israel is thus to allocate the land as a whole. The OT does not give us an account of Yhwh's making an oath with this wording, but Yhwh could not fault vv. 7–10 as a summary of declarations Yhwh did make, beginning in Gen. 12 and 15.

> [8]Gilead will be mine, Manasseh mine,
> Ephraim my helmet, Judah my scepter.

Two more pairs of expressions make the same comprehensive geographical point as v. 7b–c, in reverse order. The verbal clauses in vv. 7b–c and 9b–c imply that these noun clauses have future reference. Gilead as the name of the area and Manasseh as the largest clan that (in part) settled there again stand for the land east of the Jordan. Ephraim and Judah are the two dominant clans west of the Jordan. The second colon also goes beyond the first in characterizing these two clans. As the dominant clans, they are not merely regular possessions but key parts of warrior Yhwh's equipment, and thus means of Yhwh's exercising sovereignty over the land. They are the warrior's helmet, literally "the protection of my head." It might seem odd to think of Yhwh needing such protection,[16] and the parallel with "scepter" may imply that the phrase

15. Not "divide" Shechem (NJPS, NRSV), which would be an odd thing to do unless you were the Israel Defense Forces; likewise "measuring out" Succot Valley does not mean dividing it but allocating it to Israel or to a specific clan.

16. *Māʿôz* can be derived either from *ʿāzaz* ("be strong") or from *ʿûz* ("take refuge"), and the two meanings will flow into each other. NJPS "my chief stronghold" takes *rōʾš* adjectivally.

points to a commander in chief's distinctive and impressive headgear. "Scepter" recurs from Gen. 49:10, where it also applies to Judah (see also Num. 21:18); literally *mĕḥōqēq* means a commander (cf. LXX, Jerome). Apparently it is a metonymy like the word "staff" applied to people. If helmet and scepter are marks of the commander's prestige and power, means whereby he wins victories, that is what Ephraim and Judah will be. The content of these references to Israel (especially the reference to Ephraim and Judah) confirms that the saying's background is the nation's early centuries in the land, when it could naturally be spoken of in these terms.

> 9Moab will be my wash basin,
> over Edom I will throw my shoe,
> over Philistia I will shout out.

For warrior Yhwh, there is a contrast between the status of Ephraim and Judah and that of Moab, Edom, and Philistia. Once more, the reference suggests the nation's early centuries in the land, specifically the period of the Judges and the united monarchy, when Israel's relationship with these peoples was of key importance. Ephraim and Judah have that honored place in Yhwh's armory. Moab, Edom, and Philistia are under Yhwh's sovereignty just as firmly, but their status is quite different. Moab is the basin in which the warrior washes off the grime and blood after a battle. Edom is the place the warrior throws his shoes in doing so. Philistia (if we are to take the line in chronological order) is the place over which he roars his shout of triumph and satisfaction at that moment. Moab and Edom were not peoples over which Yhwh needed to win a victory; Yhwh and Israel were not taking their land. But in David's day they would become part of his empire (cf. Num. 24:17–18), and the psalm reflects this reality. That fits with the mention of Philistia, which was Israel's rival for possession of Canaan; it was seeking to occupy Canaan from the west as Israel was seeking to occupy it from the east. So the shout of triumph might be a victory shout over Philistia, which David succeeded in defeating. This last colon makes for a nice variant from 60:8 [10], which has "shout out at me, Philistia!" (LXX assimilates to that).

> 10Who will conduct me to the fortress city,
> who might lead me to Edom?

Tg assumes that the suppliant now speaks (cf. NRSV, TNIV),[17] but there is no indication of a change of speaker. Rather, warrior Yhwh

17. Tg further takes "Edom" to refer to Rome, as usual.

continues to speak; spoiling for the fight and wanting to get on with the job, he asks where the scout is who will lead him as commander toward the battle's goal. The parallelism implies that the unidentified fortress city is in Edom, presumably its capital. Yhwh had no intention of dispossessing Edom for Israel's sake, but Edom was inclined to take a hostile stance in relation to Israel (e.g., Num. 20:14–21). One can hardly blame it for doubting assurances that it had nothing to worry about, and in David's day such doubts would be more than justified. Verse 10, then, is Yhwh's question preparatory to events such as those described in 2 Sam. 8:13–14.

108:11–13. The point about recollecting Yhwh's oath (like the point about the declaration in vv. 1–4) was not explicit. Now it becomes so.

> 11Have you not rejected us, God?—
> you do not go out with our armies, God.

The address to God now makes clear that there is a change of speaker. The Psalms charge God a number of times with having rejected the people. These charges sometimes come in the context of questions such as "Why?" or "Is it forever?" (e.g., 43:2; 44:23 [24]). Only here is it a (slightly) open question whether God really has rejected them, though it is a question that certainly implies an affirmative answer. LXX repeats the more poignant version of the question from 60:10 [12], "Is it not you, God, who rejected us?" Either way, the function of the rhetorical question is to press the matter into God's own thinking, to drive God to think about it and to dare to take responsibility for the answer. The evidence for the accusation lies in the second colon (cf. 44:9 [10]). Far from behaving like the warrior-commander vv. 7–10 has presupposed, Yhwh has behaved like David sitting at home in Jerusalem while the Israelite army went out to do its business (2 Sam. 11:1). And in the absence of its divine commander, the Israelite army loses the battle. Yhwh had been seeking to make the army get a move on. The army's response is to suggest that the problem lies with its commander. "God" stands at the center of each colon, but "God" is surrounded by accusation of abandonment and letdown.

> 12Grant us help against the foe,
> given that human deliverance is empty.

The line looks for the converse of v. 11b. It is a forceful request, given the meaning of *help and *deliverance. The significance of "deliverance" also means that the declaration in the second colon is not a controversial one. "Emptiness" often characterizes gods other than Yhwh, and their images. They look impressive but have no substance (e.g., 24:4); so are human efforts to gain deliverance from powerful foes. Emptiness characterizes prophecies and dreams that have no substance (Lam. 2:14; Zech. 10:2), which make promises they cannot fulfill; so are human promises of deliverance.

> 13Through God we will act forcefully;
> he is the one who will trample on our foes.

So this is how it will be when the one with you is characterized not by emptiness but by substance. The psalm thus does close with a statement of conviction cohering with the more general tone of Pss. 57 and 60. The two cola nicely complement each other in their account of the agency involved in Israel's victories. Yhwh's help and deliverance are crucial; Israel acts "through" God (*b*).[18] As the last colon affirms, it is God who tramples on Israel's foes. The point could hardly be made more vividly. Yet it is a metaphor. If any literal feet land on these foes, they are Israel's. "*We* will act forcefully."[19]

Theological Implications

Psalm 108, then, presents the other side of the coin from Ps. 107. The Psalms invite the people of God neither to underestimate what Yhwh has done in fulfilling promises nor to ignore their shortfall. "Is this [or that] all there is?" Peggy Lee has asked, as have Amy Grant, Los Lobos, and Nanci Griffith. The Psalms assume not, and they do not have in mind that there will be eternal life after this life. They rather assume that God has made commitments to the people of God that should make a difference for this life; and when they do not, we face God with them.

Psalm 108 also relates to Ps. 60 in this connection. Psalm 60 was likely already involved in "claiming" a promise from the past that ought to make a difference in a later context. Psalm 108 then assumes that the people of God can do that again. A decent word from God is not one that gets fulfilled only once. On the contrary; one fulfillment establishes that it really was a word from God, and provides the basis for looking for another. A word from God is not limited in its application to one context; it can be appealed to in different psalms at different times.[20]

18. NJPS has "with," which is fine if it denotes instrumental "with"; *b* does not denote "with" of accompaniment, though God was also with Israel in that sense.

19. Not "valiantly" (NRSV), which implies bravery; *ḥayil* implies strength rather than courage.

20. Cf. Mowinckel, *Psalms*, 2:59.

The psalm's relationship with Pss. 57 and 60 also signals the way our words to God can be adapted to new situations, as well as repeated as they have always been. It is likely that many Psalms reflect that, as redaction-critical study presupposes, but usually the nature of this process is a matter of guesswork. In a case such as Ps. 108 we can be reasonably sure about it. We repeat words that have been used before, in part as a reminder that "we are not alone when we pray."[21] We adapt them, so that they say what we ourselves need to say in our context.

21. See the comment on 102:2.

Psalm 109

How to Pray for Recompense

Translation

The leader's. David's. Composition.

1My God whom I praise,
do not be silent.
2Because it is a faithless mouth, yes a deceitful mouth,
that people have opened against me.[1]
They have spoken with me by a lying tongue,
3surrounded me by words of aggression.
They have fought me[2] for no reason;
4in return for my friendliness they accuse me and I am making a plea.
5They have brought against me bad in return for good,
aggression in return for my friendliness.

6Appoint by his side[3] a faithless person,
an accuser who will stand by his right side.[4]

1. *Pātaḥ* is transitive, so the mouths must be the objects of the verb. LXX and Jerome's passive verbs likely indicate loose translation (cf. EVV), rather than a variant text.
2. The niphal unusually has a direct object.
3. Lit. "by him."
4. The word order suggests this colon incorporates an unmarked relative clause.

7When his decision is taken, he will come out as faithless;
and his plea: it will lead to condemnation.
8May his days be few;
may someone else take his property.
9May his children become orphans,
his wife a widow.
10May his children wander about,
beg[5] and solicit,[6] away from their ruins.
11May the creditor strike[7] at everything that is his,
may strangers plunder his property.
12May there not be for him anyone showing commitment,
and may there not be anyone being gracious to his orphans.
13May his posterity be for cutting off;[8]
in the next generation may their name be blotted out.
14May his fathers' waywardness be kept in mind for Yhwh
and may his mother's sin not be blotted out.
15May they be before Yhwh continually,
and may he cut off their memory from the land.
16Because he was not mindful
to act with commitment
But pursued the person who was weak and needy,
and the one crushed in spirit, to kill him off.[9]
17He liked a curse and it came to him;
he did not care for blessing and it was distant from him.
18He put on a curse like a garment,
it came into his insides like water,
into his bones like oil.[10]
19May it be for him like the coat that surrounds him,[11]
or as[12] the belt that he puts around[13] all the time.

20May this be the payment of my accusers from Yhwh,
of the people who utter what is bad for me.
21So you, Yhwh my Lord,
act with me for your name's sake;

5. The *w*-consecutive continues the jussive; so also the next verb (JM 119k).

6. LXX "be cast out" might imply *yĕgōrĕšû* for MT *wĕdārĕšû*; but see Barthélemy, *Psaumes*, 727–30.

7. *HALOT* takes *nāqaš* as a by-form of *yāqaš*, "snare," but then emends as this does not really fit here. BDB takes it as a separate root meaning "strike." Neither meaning fits all contexts; *DCH* assumes there are two roots.

8. The odd expression generates a paronomasia, *ʾaḥărîtô lĕhakrît*.

9. The polel is resultative (see *IBHS* 24).

10. In v. 17, LXX, Jerome, and EVV have some jussives, and in v. 18 EVV have some more, but the verbs are qatal and wayyiqtol.

11. The suffix from the verb in the second colon also applies here.

12. Lit. "for."

13. The f. suffix apparently refers back to *mēzaḥ*, though that is elsewhere m.

because your commitment is good, rescue me.
22Because I am weak and needy,
and my spirit has agonized[14] within me.
23Like a shadow as it lengthens, I am gone;
I am shaken off like a locust.
24My knees have collapsed from hunger;
my flesh wastes away from being fat.[15]
25I—I have become an object of scorn to them;
when they see me,[16] they shake their head.
26Help me, Yhwh my God,
deliver me in accordance with your commitment.
27So that people may acknowledge that this is your hand,
that you, Yhwh, are the one who did it.
28Those people may curse, but you—may you bless;
may they have arisen and been shamed,[17] but may your servant rejoice.
29May my accusers put on shame
and wrap on their disgrace like a robe.

30I will confess Yhwh greatly with my mouth,
in the midst of the many I will praise him,
31Because he stands at the right hand of the needy person
to deliver him from the people who make decisions about him.

Interpretation

A number of prayer psalms (e.g., Pss. 7; 17; 35) refer to false accusations, though they also describe other forms of attack such as war and hunting, and it can be difficult to tell where metaphor ends and literal description begins. Psalm 109 also uses war language in v. 3, but it is the most systematically explicit psalm of protest and plea about being subject to false accusation. We may see the context when such a psalm might be used from passages such as Exod. 22:8 [7]; Num. 5:11–31; Deut. 17:8–13; 19:15–21; 1 Kings 8:31–32; 21:1–14. (Verses 22–25 may nevertheless indicate that the false accusations were not the original

14. Jerome takes the verb as from *ḥālal* I, "pierce" (cf. Tg, EVV), but it is doubtful if this is used in the qal, and it is hard to construe here. LXX may imply a form related to *ḥûl/ḥîl* (cf. 55:5; but see *CP* 252). I take this *ḥālal* as a by-form (cf. M. Z. Kaddary, "חלל = 'Bore,' 'Pierce'?" *VT* 13 [1963]: 486–89). BHS repoints to a form from *ḥûl/ḥîl*.

15. Lit. "from fatness"; *kāḥaš*, "waste away," is to be distinguished from *kāḥaš*, "deny, dissemble" (see *TDOT*).

16. Asyndetic conditional clause; see DG 123.

17. *TTH* 81 takes the qatal and wayyiqtol verbs as "prophetic perfect" or future perfect, but the context justifies taking them as precative (DG 60c).

background to the suppliant's difficulties; rather some illness gave the accusers excuse to attack the suppliant; cf. Job.)

The psalm begins with a very brief plea for God to act (v. 1) and a lament at the attacks that require this (vv. 2–5). The longest section comprises a prayer and a series of wishes for terrible trouble to come to someone (vv. 6–19); the suppliant is an individual but the attackers are plural, suggesting that this is their prayer and wish for the suppliant. But the next long section begins by envisaging the fate they wish for him as their own fate, and it continues with a lengthier lament at the suppliant's own affliction and further pleas for deliverance (vv. 20–29). The psalm closes with a declaration of intent to testify to Yhwh's answering this prayer (vv. 30–31). It nicely combines the expression of very strong feelings[18] with carefully wrought poetic forms of expression such as inclusion (vv. 1 and 30), stepped structure (vv. 2b–3a, 14, and vv. 20–29 as a whole), metaphor (vv. 18–20, 22–24), alongside devastatingly concrete literal description (vv. 6–16), the use of short and long lines (e.g., vv. 1 and 2–5), and the exploitation of the potentials of parallelism (e.g., vv. 2a, 14).[19]

We do not know the psalm's date or origin. Mowinckel takes it as a congregational psalm,[20] and Midrash Tehillim relates it specifically to Edom's attitude to Israel,[21] while Eaton sees it as a royal psalm[22] and Goulder as the plea of a leader in the restoration community;[23] but there are no direct pointers to such a background as opposed to use by an individual under pressure. It might have been used as part of some legal procedure such as those prescribed in the passages noted above, though the way it speaks may rather suggest use by the accused person in the company of family and friends on some less formal occasion in the temple, alongside that procedure. This would not exclude its being designed to be overheard by the accusers, even though they are not addressed like the enemies in other psalms (e.g., 55:12–13 [13–14]; 62:3 [4]), and by other people in the community. Its effect might then be to expose them and push them toward stopping what they are doing.[24]

The leader's. David's. Composition.

18. "Ps 109 is built around emotion" (Martin J. Ward, "Psalm 109," *AUSS* 18 [1980]: 163–68 [see 166]).

19. Cf. Dahood, *Psalms* 3:99.

20. *Psalms*, 1:219.

21. *Midrash on Psalms*, 2:202–4.

22. *Kingship and the Psalms*, 81.

23. *Psalms of the Return*, 132–41.

24. Cf. Gerald T. Sheppard, "'Enemies' and the Politics of Prayer in the Book of Psalms," in *The Bible and the Politics of Exegesis*, ed. David Jobling et al. (N. K. Gottwald Festschrift; Cleveland: Pilgrim, 1991), 61–82 (see 73–78).

Heading. See glossary.
109:1. The psalm begins with a distinctive short opening plea.

[1]My God whom I praise,
do not be silent.

I have followed MT in treating v. 1 as one line, but taken it as a brisk, urgent 2-2 bicolon (removing a maqqeph from *ʾal-teḥĕraš*) rather than a monocolon. There is some irony about v. 1a as the psalm is as bereft of praise as any. One might compare the opening colon of Ps. 88 with the rest of that psalm. But Yhwh is still "my praiseworthy God," literally, the "God of my praise." Yhwh is the object of the suppliant's praise in life as a whole whenever there is praise to be given. The suppliant is thus not silent, and longs to hear Yhwh not being silent. Yhwh's being the object of Jeremiah's praise (the same expression; cf. also Deut. 10:21) is implicitly the basis for Jeremiah's plea in Jer. 17:14. Here Yhwh's being the object of the suppliant's praise is implicitly the basis for the plea in v. 1b. The plea is an uncommon one; a psalm usually asks for Yhwh to listen and/or act (but cf. Pss. 28:1; 35:22; 39:12 [13]; 83:1 [2]; and especially 50:3).[25] Why does the suppliant want Yhwh to speak? Other references to Yhwh's silence do not suggest failing to give a verdict, and even in that connection the suppliant needs God not merely to speak but to speak in a certain direction, to declare "he is innocent." The point about the plea is that speaking leads to action. If Yhwh keeps silence, the court in heaven that Yhwh chairs does not make the decision the suppliant needs (see Ps. 82) and/or warrior Yhwh is sitting still instead of taking action (see Isa. 42:13–17).

109:2–5. Four lines of explanation follow. The suppliant needs Yhwh to speak and thus act because of people's unjustified and dishonest attacks. The reason for these acts is unstated, leaving the psalm open for use in varying situations, such as people desiring to defraud someone, or to prop up a theology if a person is ill (cf. vv. 22–24) and the accusers reckon there must be a reason; communities do scapegoat someone "to heap on him their own collective frustration,"[26] as any pastor or seminary dean knows.

The prosody of these lines is difficult to discern. I have reworked the division of lines and cola. The lines keep making the same point; in terms of content, one line would have been enough, but they heighten

25. In some contexts, *ḥāraš* must mean "be deaf" (e.g., Mic. 7:16), in others "be silent" (e.g., Ps. 50:3); the two are related. In psalms, an opening appeal to "listen" is common, supporting the former; but the "because" clauses suggest an appeal for action and imply the latter.

26. Gerstenberger, *Psalms*, 2:258.

the effect by repeating the same point in different words. That perhaps makes the suppliant feel better, though it is more directly designed to have an effect on Yhwh (cf. Luke 18:1–8).

> 2Because it is a faithless mouth, yes a deceitful mouth,
> that people have opened against me.
> They have spoken with me by a lying tongue,
> 3asurrounded me by words of aggression.

The "problem" in prayer psalms may be Yhwh's attitude to me, and/or how I feel in myself, and/or how other people are behaving toward me. Here, the last has all the focus. (In vv. 22–25 "I" will come into focus, but this "aggressively Yahwistic" psalm[27] never expresses any doubt or questioning about Yhwh's stance or activity; such steadfastness would also undermine any accusation of unfaithfulness to Yhwh.) The basis for the appeal in v. 1 is other people's treatment of the suppliant, a combination of hostility, such as contrasts with the suppliant's attitude to them, and deceit that uses the legal system and/or their capacity to curse in such a way as to cause trouble for the suppliant.

In v. 2a–b, the first word after the "because" is the word "mouth," and that opens up the point; the repetition then underlines it. In the internal parallelism of v. 2a, *faithless first makes the general point; "deceitful" then gives specificity to how this faithlessness expresses itself.[28]

Verses 2c–3a take a neat *abb′a′* form, more literally "They have spoken with me [by] a lying tongue, [by] words of aggression they have surrounded me." "With" has some irony. As in the expression "fight with," the speaking is formally "with" but is substantially "against." The parallel colon underlines the point by describing the words of aggression (*against) as surrounding the suppliant, like a hostile crowd surrounding an individual or hostile forces surrounding a city.

> 3bThey have fought me for no reason;
> 4in return for my friendliness they accuse me and I am making a plea.
> 5They have brought against me bad in return for good,
> aggression in return for my friendliness.

Initially the suppliant's language uses the language of battle, but then it speaks more literally in indicating that the attacks take the form of

27. Brueggemann, *Message of the Psalms*, 82.

28. The parallelism involves further variation in the way the construct is used and the way it combines concrete and abstract: lit. "the mouth of the faithless [person] and the mouth of deceit." On the former construction, see DG 42, remark 3.

accusations. But there is no basis for these; the suppliant has not wronged them. Indeed, positively, the suppliant has taken a friendly stance to them. "Aggression" (v. 3a) and "friendliness" (*śinʾâ, ʾahăbâ*; *dedicate oneself) are antonyms. The last clause, literally "I am a plea/prayer," is allusive, though it compares with "I am peace" in 120:7 and English expressions such as "he is trouble" or "he is good news."[29] "Plea" (*tĕpillâ*) usually denotes "prayer" and might suggest that the suppliant is someone who prayed for these people who are now attackers (cf. 35:13), or who now prays for Yhwh's protection and help. But that involves considerable inference. More likely, here and in v. 7 *tĕpillâ* denotes the plea or the suppliant's case before the court (cf. NJPS); that fits some uses of the mother verb *pālal*, though there are no other instances of the noun's use in this connection.

Verse 5 sums up the point, in general terms by means of the further antithesis between *bad and good, then by repeating the earlier antithesis.

109:6–19. Exegetes such as Calvin[30] assume that this plea continues the suppliant's own words; the psalm gives no direct indication that the speaker changes. But it does suggest this indirectly. The suppliant was an accused individual, speaking of a number of accusers; vv. 6–19 speak about an individual, who is that accused person. The verses bring people's accusations before Yhwh like Hezekiah showing Yhwh his letter from Sennacherib (2 Kings 19:14–19).[31] While psalms can alternate between singular and plural in referring to enemies, and the singular in vv. 6–19 could refer to the enemies who were plural in vv. 2–5, the move between plural and singular in vv. 2–5, 6–19, and 20–31 is particularly clean. A further telling difference is that vv. 1–5 addressed God, and so will vv. 21–29, but in vv. 6–19 God is not named except for the "conventional uses" in vv. 14–15.[32] The orientation of vv. 6–19 over against vv. 1–5 and 20–31 is thus very different. Both focus on real life, but vv. 1–5 and 20–31 bring God steadfastly into relationship to that life, whereas vv. 6–19 do so more nominally. The many references to the accusers' words in vv. 2–5 make it feasible enough to infer that it is these words that now follow;[33] there are other psalms where someone's words are quoted without a formula to make that explicit (e.g., 2:3; 22:8 [9]; 50:7). Does this understanding

29. See GKC 141d; *TTH* 189.2; JM 154e; DG 40.

30. *Psalms*, 4:274.

31. Cf. Hans Schmidt, *Das Gebet der Angeklagten im Alten Testament*, BZAW 49 (Giessen: Töpelmann, 1928), 41.

32. Walter Brueggemann, "Psalm 109," in *The Psalms and the Life of Faith* (Minneapolis: Fortress, 1995), 268–82 (see 271)—though he draws different inferences.

33. See Schmidt, *Das Gebet*, 40–45; Harold L. Creager, "A Note on Psalm 109," *JNES* 6 (1947): 121–23; recently Allen, *Psalms 101–150*, 102–4. But contrast David P. Wright, "Ritual Analogy in Psalm 109," *JBL* 113 (1994): 385–404 (see 393–95).

exist to avoid imprecations that people find uncomfortable?[34] Actually it is doubtful whether it does that (see v. 20), and the interpretation is hardly so implausible as to suggest special pleading. This account of the accusers' maledictions may seem very long; but "tormenting fear cries out in the descriptions of the exquisitely relentless, remorseless conduct of the enemy and the offender."[35] "This escalation of psychic and social terror . . . surrounds the one praying like a deadly, poisonous cloud," and the suppliant holds these words up before God to urge God to bring about deliverance from these threats.[36]

> [6]Appoint by his side a faithless person,
> an accuser who will stand by his right side.

The accusers' opening imperative is singular; although it does not use Yhwh's name, it presumably addresses Yhwh. Thus both parties are doing so, arguing their case before the heavenly court. The attackers ask for the appointment of someone to stand by the accused as an accuser or prosecutor (a *śāṭān*; cf. the heavenly accuser in Zech. 3). They ask for a *faithless person, someone like them (cf. v. 2), though they might not see it this way; the words are the suppliant's account of their (implicit) aims. They perhaps wanted justice to be done, but they have a twisted view of what this would mean. They were perhaps quite sincere, more like Job's friends than like Ahab, who consciously defrauded Naboth.

> [7]When his decision is taken, he will come out as faithless;
> and his plea: it will lead to condemnation.

The logical result of that action is that the court's decision (*authority) will mean that the accused emerges from its deliberations declared to be *faithless: that is, "guilty." The second colon restates the point; literally, "and his plea: it will become [into] shortcoming/condemnation" (*fail). The unambiguous yiqtol in the second colon disambiguates the verb in the first, which could be yiqtol or jussive.[37]

> [8]May his days be few;
> may someone else take his property.

34. E.g., Gerstenberger, *Psalms*, 2:257.

35. Keel, *Symbolism*, 97.

36. Zenger, *A God of Vengeance?* 59.

37. In v. 7b, LXX, Jerome have jussive; this would require *tĕhî* not MT's *tihyeh*. GKC 109a, JM 114g assume it is implicitly jussive, but why then did the psalm not use the jussive (cf. vv. 12–13)? The yiqtol makes sense after the imperative in v. 6; it is implicitly jussive in the sense of stating the result of the fulfillment of that imperative.

Grammatically, the accusers' words could be yiqtol or jussive, but in their concreteness vv. 8–11 belong with vv. 12–13, where there are three unambiguously jussive verbs. But like the yiqtols in v. 7, these jussives spell out the results of the answer to the prayer in v. 6, so they are indirectly part of the prayer (the dynamics correspond to those in Ps. 72). They paint the consequences of a guilty verdict in chilling terms. Though Naboth's story and the prophets' polemics show how a court's decisions can issue in someone's death, the expression in v. 8a suggests reference not to a court's sentence but to an event God brings about.

The accused's death would mean someone else taking over his *pĕquddâ*. The word would most obviously denote his "appointment," the position he holds (so LXX; cf. Acts 1:20), but what would that refer to? In Isa. 15:7 it refers to someone's property, which fits here (cf. BDB); vv. 9–11 will then expand on both these cola.

9May his children become orphans,
his wife a widow.
10May his children wander about,
beg and solicit, away from their ruins.
11May the creditor strike at everything that is his,
may strangers plunder his property.

The colors continue to be chilling, and the prophets' polemics again suggest they need not be overstated. The accused's death will mean his children become fatherless and his wife a widow. Those are economic realities. Orphans (not necessarily small children) and widows have no set place in society and no means of support. Some modern interpreters are especially offended by these verses in the psalm (on the assumption that they express the psalmist's wishes),[38] but the same consequences follow from economic policies with which OT scholars are complicit and from jail sentences as well as from capital punishment in modern societies. Whatever happens to an individual affects their family.

Verse 10 underlines the orphans' vulnerability. Another consequence of being found guilty can be that the person's home is demolished (see, for instance, Dan. 2:5); again one can compare practices in modern Palestine. Here, the ruins of the family home are the base from which the accused's children wander about (the expression involves repeating the verb for emphasis, "in wandering they wander") begging for sustenance.[39]

38. E.g., Kirkpatrick, *Psalms*, 652.

39. Thus "away from their ruins" qualifies the opening verbal phrase, the two parallel verbs intervening: cf. D. T. Tsumura, "Literary Insertion (AXB Pattern) in Biblical Hebrew," *VT* 33 (1983): 468–82 (see 475).

The fulfillment of the wish in v. 11 perhaps lies behind the fulfillment of that in v. 10, the verses working in hysteron-proteron order. But it is not clear why creditors or foreigners become part of the picture; perhaps these are conventional images. Passages such as 2 Kings 4:1 and Neh. 5:1–11 illustrate the power of the creditor.

> [12]May there not be for him anyone showing commitment,
> and may there not be anyone being gracious to his orphans.
> [13]May his posterity be for cutting off;
> in the next generation may their name be blotted out.

Suppose there were someone who tried to help the accused? The accusers express the wish that there will not be, that no one will show *commitment to him or *grace to his orphans. Perhaps, indeed, the reference to showing commitment presupposes that by then he is already dead; the commitment is that which would be expressed in kindness to his orphan children. A dying man is concerned for what will happen to his children, so all the wishes about the man's wife and children are there because of their relevance to him.

Indeed, the accusers wish that as he loses his life, so may they (his posterity) lose theirs, the sins of the father thereby being visited on the children. Again "cutting off" suggests God's action rather than human action (cf. v. 8a). Even the family's *name will thus be obliterated. It is another prospect to send a chill into the bones of the accused.

> [14]May his fathers' waywardness be kept in mind for Yhwh
> and may his mother's sin not be blotted out.
> [15]May they be before Yhwh continually,
> and may he cut off their memory from the land.

The accusers want the implications of his guilt to work backward as well as forward. Their wishes are now even more over the top; they feel really strongly. They want Yhwh to be kept *mindful of "his fathers' *waywardness"[40] and to make sure that his mother's failure stays registered in Yhwh's records. The implication will be that the sins of the parents have already been visited on the child: the accused's sin implies he had wayward and sinful parents. As Job's friends rewrite his sons' lives as well as Job's, these accusers rewrite the lives of the accused's parents as well as his own. They were sinners, who therefore also deserve further punishment. If Yhwh is mindful of these past sins, there will be even more trouble for the accused and his family. Whether the parents

40. I take *zākar* (niphal) *ʾel*, an unusual expression, as equivalent to a passive of *zākar* (hiphil [the hophal does not occur]), which itself practically means "accuse" (cf. BDB).

are still alive or already dead, the accusers want Yhwh to stay aware of their wrongdoing and thus be driven to ensure that every trace of them, their son, and his family disappears.

Verse 15 restates the point. Memory is *zēker*; the prayer adds that the mindfulness or remembering of v. 14a be complemented by a consequent non-mindfulness, non-remembering.

> 16Because he was not mindful
> to act with commitment
> But pursued the person who was weak and needy,
> and the one crushed in spirit, to kill him off.

In turn, the basis for the mindfulness and the non-mindfulness of vv. 14–15 lies in the alleged non-mindfulness of v. 16. If its statements were true, then the accusers have a case and anyone using the psalm has to be able to face the demand of these two lines. But the psalmist's claim is that they are indeed rewriting his life in declaring him not *mindful of the obligation to act with *commitment.

So acting involves reaching out to people in need. Ironically, they accuse him of doing what they themselves are doing in pursuing to death one who is *weak, *needy, and therefore crushed in spirit, who feels a heavy burden pressing down on his inner being and weighing him down.

> 17He liked a curse and it came to him;
> he did not care for blessing and it was distant from him.
> 18He put on a curse like a garment,
> it came into his insides like water,
> into his bones like oil.

The juxtaposition of vv. 16 and 17–18 suggests that the way the suppliant is accused of pursuing the weak and needy is by means of a curse. The irony continues, because one might see the wishes that the accusers have been developing as themselves a sequence of curses. Yet reference to cursing comes only when they give more detail on the basis for their own prayer and wishes. (Are they thus hiding from the implications of their own words? Cursing is not something they wish to admit to.) It completes a quartet of ways of understanding our relationship to events: we simply do things; we ask God to do things; we wish for things to happen; and we bless or curse. The presupposition of blessing and cursing is that God has delegated to humanity (or to some human beings in some circumstances) the power to bring good or bad to others. So people could declare a curse and it might come true, unless Yhwh frustrated it (Gen. 12:3; Num. 22–24). Curses can be undertaken in private, yet they may have terrible results (as Num. 22–24 presupposes). Whether the accused had outwardly behaved in the way v. 16 describes could be confirmed or otherwise by members of the community; perhaps that is why the accusation is rather brief. Only Yhwh knows whether the accusations in vv. 17–18 are true. That also means they can be made with impunity; an accused person cannot disprove them. There is no indication that either the supposed curse of the accused or the curselike wishes of the accusers involve "black magic" or appeal to foreign gods, and if this were so, one would expect that to be made part of the case. Both sides are sincere worshippers of Yhwh as is the case when Christians and churches accuse and demonize one another.

The accusers (the suppliant would say) are people who like curses and do not care for blessings. Curses come to them, and they welcome them; blessings stay away from them. It is curses that naturally come to their lips, while blessings naturally stay away from them. Their accusation is that this is what is true of the accused.

Verse 18 then puts the point in a vivid metaphor. A curse (they say) is like a garment that fits snugly on the accused, like a tailor-made suit. The second and third cola take the point further. A curse does not just fit him on the outside, like a garment that is separate from the person. It enters into him and becomes part of him, as refreshing and welcome as a drink of water to a thirsty person or as soothing and healing as oil to a sick person.[41] In moving away from the concrete literal wishes of vv. 6–16, vv. 17–19 gain power through their systematic use of simile and metaphor.[42]

> [19]May it be for him like the coat that surrounds him,
> or as the belt that he puts around all the time.

The last line of the accusers' series of wishes takes up the image from v. 17 and turns it back on the accused. Indeed, it takes the image much further, as it asks that his curse may overwhelm him in another sense. It is now explicitly no skimpy summer garment but a coat that envelops the whole person. Further, it is not a piece of clothing that one takes on and off but one that stays there all the time, and it has become something that consumes him.[43] It is not the means of his acting but the means of his being acted on. The divine promise in Gen. 12:3 is to be fulfilled.

109:20–29. The suppliant has been reporting the frightening prayer and wish of the accusers; now he resumes his own prayer (vv. 20–21, 26–29), with its grounds in his lament (vv. 22–25). The verses form a stepped structure:

41. Cf. Briggs, *Psalms*, 2:367.

42. Cf. Wright, "Ritual Analogy in Psalm 109," 400.

43. Wright ("Ritual Analogy in Psalm 109," 398) cites a comparable wish in Esarhaddon's Succession Treaty.

May the accusers have their plea turned back on them (v. 20)
You, Yhwh, rescue me, act, for the sake of your name, out of your commitment (v. 21)
Because I am weak (vv. 22–23)
Because I am an object of scorn (vv. 24–25)
Deliver me so that you, Yhwh, may be acknowledged as the one who acted, out of your commitment (vv. 26–27)
May the accusers have their curse turned into blessing (vv. 28–29)

20May this be the payment of my accusers from Yhwh,
of the people who utter what is bad for me.
21So you, Yhwh my Lord,
act with me for your name's sake;
because your commitment is good, rescue me.

If vv. 6–19 were the prayer of the accused, then v. 20 would bring it to a close. But the move back to speaking about a group of people confirms that vv. 6–19 were the words of the accusers (plural) about the accused (singular). Verse 20 is a noun clause and thus in isolation might be a statement about future or present, but the context suggests it is a wish, that the bad things they want for him (lit., "against my life/self/*person) will become their deserved payment, what they themselves experience. It might have seemed advantageous to avoid making vv. 6–19 the prayer of the accused; but he is quite willing to make that prayer and wish his own. (The same point applies if one takes v. 20 as an affirmation.)

The positive side to that wish is expressed as a prayer, an appeal to Yhwh as my *Lord and thus to Yhwh's sovereignty and to his relationship with Yhwh, his position as Yhwh's servant. The parallel colon appeals for action for the sake of Yhwh's own *name, which will be vindicated when the person falsely accused is vindicated. This acting "with" forms a contrast with the "with" of v. 2c.

The unexpected third colon puts the first two cola together and takes them further: it is as "my Lord" that Yhwh is characterized by *commitment, a commitment that is good (that is, kind [LXX]); and the action of v. 21b is specified as rescue. Verses 12 and 16 made commitment the (theoretical) basis of human relationships; theologically, the background is that commitment is the (actual) basis of relationships between God and us.[44]

22Because I am weak and needy,
and my spirit has agonized within me.

44. Cf. Mays, *Psalms*, 349. Walter Brueggemann ("Psalm 109") takes this word as the key to the flow of the psalm.

[23]Like a shadow as it lengthens, I am gone;
I am shaken off like a locust.

The suppliant's lament is the further reason for responding to his plea. As someone *weak and *needy, he is actually the kind of person the accusers have been claiming concern for (v. 16). Weakness and need are mostly outward matters; they concern our relationship with our community and the needs of our bodies. Thus the second colon complements the first by going on to the effect of the accusers' action on the spirit, again as in v. 16 (in both places, "spirit" is literally "*heart"). Being accused of gross wrong and losing one's acceptance in the community puts a person into a whirl.

That earlier line spoke of being crushed to death, and v. 23 expresses this point more vividly. In the evening by an irreversible process day comes to an end (cf. 102:11); that offers a picture of the process that is taking the suppliant off. In a more original picture, he is like an insect settling on someone's arm; one shake, and it is gone.

[24]My knees have collapsed from hunger;
my flesh wastes away from being fat.
[25]I—I have become an object of scorn to them;
when they see me, they shake their head.

Two lines put the point in more familiar terms. They may be meant literally or may be figures of speech (that is true of vv. 22–26 as a whole). I am like someone whose knees collapse through hunger (the context does not suggest "fasting"); I am as weak as a person whose body is emaciated.

Thus I become an object of scorn and people shake their head (cf. 22:7–8 [8–9]): that is what happens to someone reckoned to have put their life on a false basis such as the one the accusers describe.

[26]Help me, Yhwh my God,
deliver me in accordance with your commitment.
[27]So that people may acknowledge that this is your hand,
that you, Yhwh, are the one who did it.

The suppliant returns to plea, repeating key terms for such a plea, *help, *deliver, and *commitment, and adding the even more personal expression "my God" to the "my Lord" of v. 21.

Here the motivation for Yhwh to act is not the accused's need but an appeal parallel to that to Yhwh's name (v. 21). By implication, it will take a miracle if the accused is to escape from the desperate straits into which the accusers have cast him. But that means the miracle will give clear testimony to Yhwh's activity, and lead to that being *acknowledged.

> [28]Those people may curse, but you—may you bless;
> may they have arisen and been shamed, but may your servant rejoice.
> [29]May my accusers put on shame
> and wrap on their disgrace like a robe.

The suppliant returns to the wish from which v. 20 started. Initially the point is expressed positively. Yhwh's blessing is surely stronger than a human curse; may it be shown to be so. But the positive still needs to be accompanied by the negative. People who exalt themselves and thus arise to act in hostile fashion, as the accusers have, must be put down and shamed, while Yhwh's servant (again, cf. 21) is able to rejoice. The servant will rejoice both in his rescue and in their shaming. Both are vital.

Verse 29 then takes up their image from vv. 18–19. Shame and disgrace must envelop them as comprehensively as they wanted his curse to envelop him.

109:30–31. The psalm closes with the commitment to *confession that commonly closes a prayer psalm.

> [30]I will confess Yhwh greatly with my mouth,
> in the midst of the many I will praise him,
> [31]Because he stands at the right hand of the needy person
> to deliver him from the people who make decisions about him.

Once again the thanksgiving aspect of this response to Yhwh's act could not be satisfied by thankfulness in the suppliant's personal relationship with God. Thanksgiving or testimony is by its nature public. It involves the mouth, now used for a very different purpose from the one referred to at the psalm's opening (see v. 2). This *praise takes place in the midst of the many, in the most public possible gathering of the community. How did that work? Opportunity for testimonies at a great festival might seem unrealistic;[45] perhaps this testimony took place in the context of family and small-community gatherings in this broader context, like the gatherings of people in whose context laments were brought to God (compare the many little family gatherings in the plaza in front of the Western Wall in modern Jerusalem).

The basis for or content of the confession is typically expressed as a generalization. For "he stands" 11QPs[a] has "he stood";[46] but if Yhwh

45. Goulder, *Psalms of the Return*, 133.
46. *ʿmd* for *yaʿămōd* (haplography?; cf. LXX, Syr).

simply stood on this one occasion, it might have less relevance for the congregation as a whole. The public testimony presupposes that such action on Yhwh's part is the rule rather than the exception. It is not the invariable rule, but the exceptions must not obscure the rule. Yhwh does stand there at the right hand of the *needy in a position of support—not at such a person's right side in a hostile sense (v. 6). Yhwh does thus *deliver when people are having others make decisions (*authority) about them (about their life/self/*person: compare and contrast with v. 20), decisions that the powerful plan should go the wrong way (vv. 4, 7). When their lives are on the line (v. 8), Yhwh is there.

Theological Implications

A. F. Kirkpatrick comments that imprecatory psalms such as Pss. 69 and 109 "startle and shock the Christian reader"; they are "the very opposite of the spirit of the Gospel" (Matt. 5:43–47), belonging as they do in a dispensation when retribution was a fundamental principle.[47] Edmund Hill likewise refers to a Roman Catholic breviary that omits Ps. 109 as one of the psalms that "do not easily lend themselves to Christian usage."[48] Yet Kirkpatrick goes on to refer to Matt. 23:32–36;[49] in the NT retribution remains a fundamental principle.

Both the psalm and the NT speak of retribution administered not by human beings but by God. The suppliant is leaving retribution to God. "Vengeance is transferred from the heart of the speaker to the heart of God."[50] And in the NT, knowing about a resurrection life in which wrong can be righted may not change the attitude to such retribution, either for Jesus (as in Matt. 23:32–36 and other passages) or for his followers (see, e.g., 1 Cor. 16:22; 2 Thess. 1:6–10; 1 Tim. 1:20; Rev. 6:9–11). Ironically, one way the NT itself implicitly recognizes this point is by treating Ps. 109 as an illuminating theological resource (Acts 1:20). It applies to it a hermeneutic that attributes a new significance to the psalm, but it still presupposes rather than questions the retribution element in it (the same applies to the further quotation from Ps. 69 in Acts 1:20, suggesting more irony). "How did Jesus love Judas," to whom Peter applies v. 8?[51]

Retribution is not *the* fundamental principle, in OT or NT; in both, God's wrath is less central to God's character and activity than God's love.

47. *Psalms*, 652.

48. *Prayer, Praise and Politics*, 98. The others are Pss. 58 and 83.

49. *Psalms*, 652.

50. Walter Brueggemann, *Praying the Psalms* (Winona, MN: Saint Mary's Press, 1982), 70.

51. Hill, *Prayer, Praise and Politics*, 101.

But it is *a* fundamental principle. In its absence (OT and NT assume), then moral and social order cease to be realities. Because we know Yhwh is a God of recompense, we can bring to Yhwh our longing for recompense as we could not if Yhwh is just a forgiving God, in which case we would have nowhere to go. But there we surrender to God our desire and need for recompense. We relinquish it, which is an alternative to either repression or action,[52] or to indifference to the needs of others. "It is all right to feel vindictive, vengeful, reciprocally cruel." But here there is no sadism or torture but "the art of imprecation," "not the lady-like demur or the gentlemanly protest, but the well-placed curse."[53]

"As the Holy Spirit taught David and all the godly to offer up prayers like these, it must follow, that those who, in this respect, imitate them, will be promptly helped by God when he beholds them reproachfully and vilely persecuted."[54] A psalm like this "is treated with caution or disregard in Christian tradition much to our own disadvantage, exempting us from facing the realities of human life."[55] Of course, most OT scholars and most Christians in the West have no reason to pray this prayer. "Maybe you don't have any enemies. . . . Very well, but in that case who are you to repeat the injunction 'Love your enemies?'. . . Just get yourself some real enemies first; then go ahead and try to love them."[56] One way for men to do that is to imagine it on the lips of women trapped in a patriarchal system.[57] Another is for us to listen to Christians in contexts of oppression (maybe economic oppressions by the West), who may not find this psalm so uncongenial. Indeed, we ourselves cannot afford to have people praying this prayer, because we are the people it prays against.

52. Brueggemann, *Message of the Psalms*, 85–86. See further Larry Silva, "The Cursing Psalms as a Source of Blessing," in *Psalms and Practice*, ed. Reid, 220–30 (see 228–29).

53. David R. Blumenthal, *Facing the Abusing God* (Louisville: Westminster John Knox, 1993), 124–25, 143–44. (Blumenthal assumes that vv. 6–19 are the psalmist's own curse.)

54. Calvin, *Psalms*, 4:273. He is referring to vv. 6–19 in particular, understood as the suppliant's prayer. Cf. Luther, *First Lectures*, 2:353; John N. Day, *Crying for Justice* (Grand Rapids: Kregel, 2005), 81–82. Theodoret (*Psalms*, 2:200) and Spurgeon (*Treasury of David*, 4:436) are more equivocal.

55. Gerstenberger, *Psalms*, 2:257; though some caution is appropriate, given the psalm's anti-Jewish (and other) misuse in light of the NT's christological hermeneutic and its application of the psalm to Judas: see Jerome, *Homilies*, 1:255–69; Cassiodorus, *Psalms*, 2:102–11; and Zenger's comments, *A God of Vengeance?* 57–58.

56. Hill, *Prayer, Praise and Politics*, 102.

57. So Beth LaNeel Tanner, "Hearing the Cries Unspoken," in *Wisdom and Psalms*, ed. Brenner and Fontaine, 283–301.

Psalm 110
King and Priest

Translation

David's. Composition.

[1]Yhwh's utterance to my lord:
Sit at my right hand,
until I make your enemies a stool for your feet.
[2]Yhwh will send your strong staff from Zion;
prevail in the midst of your foes.
[3]Your people will offer themselves unsparingly[1] on your forceful day [MT];
[or] Nobility is with you on your forceful day [LXX];[2]
in holy splendor/on the holy mountains[3] from the womb[4] of dawn,[5]
the dew[6] of your youth[7] is yours.

1. *ʿAmmĕkā nĕdābōt,* lit. "your people are unsparing offerings."

2. LXX implies something like *ʿimmĕkā nĕdibut* (Barthélemy, *Psaumes*, 736–44).

3. Most MSS have *bĕhadrê-qōdeš;* Codex Cairensis has *bĕharĕrê-qōdeš* (cf. Jerome, Sym).

4. Translating *reḥem* "rain" rather than "dawn" (Gary A. Rendsburg, "Psalm cx 3b," *VT* 49 [1999]: 548–51) does not seem a significant improvement.

5. *Mišḥār* for the usual *šaḥar* comes only here. The form thus hardly results (e.g.) from dittography of the *m* at the end of the previous word. LXX, Th, Sym imply *miššaḥār*, which might mean "dawnward," i.e., "eastward" (William P. Brown, "A Royal Performance," *JBL* 117 [1998]: 93–96 [see 94]).

6. R. Kilian ("Der 'Tau' in Ps 110,3," *ZAW* 102 [1990]: 417–19) translates "scent" on the basis of an Egyptian parallel. Jean de Savignac ("Essai d'interpretation du psaume cx à l'aide de la littérature égyptienne," *OtSt* 9 [1951]: 107–35) interprets the psalm as a whole against the background of an Egyptian king's enthronement.

7. I take *yaldutêkā* as a composite form, combining *yaldutêkā*, "your youth," and *yĕlidtîkā*, "I beget you" (cf. LXX; assimilation to 2:7).

4Yhwh swore and will not relent:
You are a priest forever,
after the manner of[8] Melchizedek.
5The Lord by your right hand
has crushed kings on the day of his anger.
6He governs among the nations, filling them with bodies,[9]
crushing heads[10] over the breadth of the earth.[11]
7From the stream by the way he drinks;
therefore he raises his head.

Interpretation

The speaker is unidentified, but it seems likely to be a minister or prophet taking part in worship, a person such as Gad or Nathan or the figures who appear in Chronicles. He reports words of Yhwh to someone identified in v. 1 as "my lord" and in v. 4 as a priest. In light of the content of the utterance, I take "my lord" to be the king; the words in v. 1, expanded in vv. 2–3, are an "utterance" promising Yhwh's support, which will enable the king to win victories over his foes, and promising that he will also have the support from his people that will make that possible. The second declaration in v. 4, expanded in vv. 5–7, is an oath that puts the king into the position of someone such as Melchizedek, king of Salem, in Gen. 14, who was priest as well as king. In isolation, vv. 1 and 4 might be taken as referring to different people, but Yhwh's oath to the priest is similar to Yhwh's promise to the king, so more likely both designations apply to the same person. The psalm is the twin of Ps. 2, which speaks similarly of what Yhwh will do for and through the king. It is also very similar to Akkadian prophecies to the king.[12]

8. *Dibrat* is an alternative for *dābār*; it comes elsewhere only in Qohelet. GKC 90l sees *dibrātî* as having an old genitive case ending, but not all such endings can be explained thus (*melkî* may be another instance); see *IBHS* 8.2; DG 27, also JM 93lm. For *ʿal-dibrātî*, Tg's "on account of" is possible, but that usually refers to something negative. The obvious understanding is "according to my word," with Melchizedek then being vocative; cf. 11QMelch (see, e.g., Mitchell, *Message of the Psalter*, 259–60). But for *dābār* meaning "manner," see BDB 183b. There is no parallel for "after the order of" (LXX, Jerome; see Vinzenz Hamp, "Ps 110,4b und die Septuaginta," in *Neues Testament und Kirche*, ed. Joachim Gnilka [R. Schnackenburg Festschrift; Freiburg: Herder, 1974], 519–29).

9. "Them" is not expressed; Jerome implies *gēʾāyôt*, "valleys" (cf. Aq, Sym), for MT *gĕwîyôt*.

10. Sg., collective. RSV takes "heads" to mean "chiefs," but the parallelism suggests the literal meaning.

11. Lit. "over the broad earth."

12. See John W. Hilber, "Psalm cx in the Light of Assyrian Prophecies," *VT* 53 (2003): 353–66; cf. Hilber, *Cultic Prophecy*, 76–88.

It has been dated in many periods, such as the reign of David or Solomon or some other time in the early monarchy,[13] the time of Josiah,[14] the early Persian period, when the combination of high priestly and royal roles took on a new form,[15] and the time of the Hasmonean kings.[16] On the basis of its content, Midrash Tehillim can also see the psalm as David's reflection on the Abraham story in Gen. 14.[17] Any theory about its background is an inference from circumstantial evidence. We will never know its origin. Neither do we know how it might have been used in worship, though one can imagine it being used before a battle or in the context of a king's enthronement.[18] It would then be a reminder of Yhwh's promises and acts, to encourage the current king, for whom there might be a considerable gap between its promise and current reality. In the exile and afterward it would again offer encouragement, though the gap between promise and experience would be sharper; it would raise the question whether Yhwh has still not relented. There is no indication that it speaks of a future king,[19] nor any necessity to reckon that it would be interpreted messianically by the time the Psalter reached its present form; while some Jewish groups in the Persian and Greek period emphasized the importance of the coming of the Messiah, others did not. Mark 12:35–37 reflects how it would be understood messianically in Roman times, and on that basis some of its verses are applied to Jesus (e.g., Acts 2:34–35), though as a whole it does not fit him, and most of its application to him in the NT requires it to be understood in a way that would not correspond to its meaning in any OT context.[20]

13. See, e.g., Maurice Gilbert and Stephen Pisano, "Psalm 110 (109), 5–7," *Bib* 61 (1980): 343–56; E. R. Hardy, "The Date of Psalm 110," *JBL* 64 (1945): 385–90; Helen G. Jefferson, "Is Psalm 110 Canaanite?" *JBL* 73 (1954): 152–56; P. J. Nel, "Psalm 110 and the Melchizedek Tradition," *JNSL* 22 (1996): 1–14; E. Podechard, "Psaume 110," in *Études de critique et d'histoire religieuses* (L. Vaganay Festschrift; Lyon: Facultés Catholiques, 1948), 7–24; Harold H. Rowley, "Melchizedek and Zadok," in *Festschrift Alfred Bertholet*, ed. Walter Baumgartner et al. (Tübingen: Mohr, 1950), 461–72; Hans Joachim Stoebe, "Erwägungen zu Psalm 110 auf dem Hintergrund von 1. Sam. 21," in *Festschrift Friedrich Baumgärtel*, ed. Leonhard Rost (Erlangen: Universitätsbund Erlangen, 1959), 175–91.

14. E.g., Claus Schedl, "'Aus dem Bache am Wege,'" *ZAW* 73 (1961): 290–97.

15. E.g., Stefan Schreiner, "Psalm 110," *VT* 27 (1977): 216–22; Goulder, *Psalms of the Return*, 145–46. Saur (*Königspsalmen*, 222) calls it "a compromise document."

16. So M. Treves,"Two Acrostic Psalms," *VT* 15 (1965): 81–90; G. Gerleman, "Psalm cx," *VT* 31 (1981): 1–19.

17. *Midrash on Psalms*, 2:205–6; cf. Rashi; and Gerhard Bodendorfer, "Abraham zur Rechten Gottes," *EvT* 59 (1999): 252–66.

18. Cf. Klaus Homborg, "Psalm 110,1 im Rahmen des judäischen Krönungszeremoniells," *ZAW* 84 (1972): 243–46.

19. Against, e.g., Edward J. Kissane, "The Interpretation of Psalm 110," *ITQ* 21 (1954): 103–14.

20. On its use in the NT, see, e.g., A. del Agua Pérez, "Procedimentos derásicos del Sal 2:7b en el Nuevo Testamento," *EstBib* 42 (1984): 391–414; C. Breytenbach, "Das

It is one of the most difficult of the psalms, which is often assumed to indicate textual corruption.[21] Thus it has generated an above-average number of proposals for textual emendation, but it is doubtful whether we have grounds for reckoning that its text is more corrupt than average.

David's. Composition.

Heading. See glossary. It is difficult to see pattern or logic about links with David in the latter part of the Psalter.[22]

110:1–3. An oracle concerning the king's triumph.

1Yhwh's utterance to my lord:
Sit at my right hand,
until I make your enemies a stool for your feet.

"Yhwh's utterance [*nĕʾum yhwh*]" is a standard way to describe Yhwh's words, especially uttered through a prophet, and especially in Jeremiah (e.g., 2:3, 9, 12, 19, 22, 29) and Ezekiel (e.g., 14:11, 14, 16, 18, 20, 23). In the Psalms, it comes only here. Perhaps it is significant that Jeremiah and Ezekiel both had a priestly background; the expression may have its background in the prophetic words uttered in the temple. Whereas prophets commonly see themselves as Yhwh's messengers, and in this capacity say, "Yhwh has said this: . . . ," priests and Levites work with a different model for picturing the bringing of Yhwh's message. Either way, the one who speaks is claiming to pass on actual words Yhwh has uttered. "My lord" is a standard term of respect, the way anyone would speak of any superior; it is what follows that suggests it designates the king. It is again a term that would come more easily to the lips of a minister at the royal sanctuary than to the kind of prophet who needed to keep a measure of independence over against the administration.

The only other OT reference to sitting at someone's right hand concerns Bathsheba, who could sit at Solomon's right hand because she was the king's mother (1 Kings 2:19). That is often a position of great power in the Middle East, and to sit at someone's right hand is to sit

Markusevangelium, Psalm 110,1 und 118,22f," in *The Scriptures in the Gospels*, ed. C. Tuckett (Leuven: Leuven University Press, 1997), 197–222; T. Callan, "Psalm 110:1 and the Origin of the Expectation That Jesus Will Come Again," *CBQ* 44 (1982): 622–36; Michel Gourgues, *À la droite de Dieu* (Paris: Gabalda, 1978); David M. Hay, *Glory at the Right Hand*, SBLMS 18 (Nashville: Abingdon, 1973); Martin Hengel, "'Setze dich zu meiner Rechten!'" in *Le Trône de Dieu*, ed. Marc Philonenko (Tübingen: Mohr, 1993), 108–94; Elliott E. Johnson, "Hermeneutical Principles and the Interpretation of Psalm 110," *BSac* 149 (1992): 428–37; W. R. G. Loader, "Christ at the Right Hand," *NTS* 24 (1977–78): 199–217.

21. E.g., H. E. Del Medico, "Melchisédech," *ZAW* 69 (1953): 160–70.

22. Gerstenberger, *Psalms*, 2:264.

in a position of prestige and authority. One would expect someone sitting there to be one with the support of the earthly king, or in this case the heavenly King, as his servant (cf. Ps. 80:17 [18]).[23] It is difficult to imagine how the king could have literally sat at Yhwh's right hand, on a throne in the temple, and it is in any case unwise to infer some literal, concrete event from a poetic colon in a prophetic oracle in a liturgical text, whose main point is metaphorical.[24] Metaphorically, the king sits at Yhwh's right hand. This declaration then compares and contrasts with the idea that the king sits on "the throne of Yhwh's kingship over Israel" (1 Chron. 28:5; cf. 29:23; 2 Chron. 9:8; even in a prose text, one does not infer that this pictures the king enthroned in the inner room of the temple).

The king will sit there while Yhwh subdues his foes. Only here does the OT speak of making people into a footstool,[25] but it does use other analogous terms of people's symbolic subjection (e.g., Ps. 72:8–11). The enemies will be totally defeated and subservient.

> [2]Yhwh will send your strong staff from Zion;
> prevail in the midst of your foes.

The psalm continues to address the king, though it now refers to Yhwh in the third person. Perhaps this is the speaker's expansion on the oracle, though Yhwh is quite capable of self-referring in an oracle, so vv. 2–3 may continue the oracle itself. In substance, certainly, v. 2 restates v. 1, though in a superficial sense it implicitly contradicts it in picturing the king not sitting on a throne but going out to battle. "Your strong staff" is a metonymy; the powerful staff stands for the powerful king himself as the army commander in chief, commissioned by Yhwh (cf. "scepter" in 108:8 [9]). It is not Yhwh who wins the victory while the king watches, but the king who wins the victory while Yhwh watches. Zion is the place where Yhwh reigns, and where the king sits at Yhwh's right hand, and from which Yhwh acts (e.g., Amos 1:2). The king shares in that authority and action.

The second colon more precisely restates v. 1b. The verb (*rādâ*) does not denote rule in a general sense, or the regular rule the king would exercise over Israel. It indicates rule imposed on people even if they resist it (cf. Ps. 2); it describes Solomon's rule over his wide empire (1 Kings 4:24 [5:4]; cf. Ps. 72:8; also Lev. 26:17). The verb is the kind of imperative that makes a promise or offers assurance in a vivid way (cf. Tg).[26]

23. For an Egyptian parallel, see Keel, *Symbolism*, 263.
24. Against, e.g., Mowinckel, *Psalms*, 1:63–64.
25. But for an Egyptian illustration, see Keel, *Symbolism*, 255.
26. GKC 110c; *IBHS* 34.4c.

[3]Your people will offer themselves unsparingly on your forceful day
[MT];
[or] Nobility is with you on your forceful day [LXX];
in holy splendor/on the holy mountains from the womb of dawn,
the dew of your youth is yours.

The psalm continues to describe the process whereby the promise or commission in vv. 1–2 works itself out on "the day of your force [*ḥayil*]." That can hardly mean merely "the day of your power" in the sense of "the day [this day] when you are enthroned";[27] *ḥayil* suggests military might and resources (e.g., 18:32, 39 [33, 40]). The expression points to the day when the king exercises the might to which v. 2 refers (cf. Tg).[28] The king wields his staff as the means of directing his army, and v. 3a declares that he will have the forces needed in this connection.

Deborah's Song rejoices in the fact that "the people offer themselves unsparingly" for battle (Judg. 5:2), using the verb *nādab* (hitpael), which occurs most commonly in connection with offerings for the temple. In MT the psalm makes the same point by adapting the related noun *nĕdābâ*, which also usually refers to generous offerings that people make to Yhwh voluntarily, as opposed to offerings Yhwh expects them to give. For these campaigns by the king, people will not need to be drafted; they will form an enthusiastic volunteer force. The construction (lit. "they are freewill offerings") suggests "they are the very embodiment of willing offering."[29] LXX rather points to the king's honor as he fights his battles.

Verse 3b–c likely restates that in some way, but all the expressions are puzzling to one degree or another.[30] It seems plausible that "the dew of your youth" refers to the young warriors who comprise the army; they have a freshness about them or a refreshing affect on the king (cf. 133:3), or perhaps they will fall like dew on the king's foes (cf. 2 Sam. 17:12).

The opening phrase then declares that there is a *holy splendor about this king's army and/or about the king himself. Both expressions, "holy" and "splendor," belong especially to Yhwh (see Pss. 29:2; 96:9), but they can come to belong to Yhwh's servants. So the king possesses a splendor (see Pss. 21:5 [6]; and especially 45:3–4 [4–5], which relates to military action); on LXX's reading, that would follow up the reference to his

27. So Anderson, *Psalms*, 2:769.

28. Cf. Weiser, *Psalms*, 692.

29. GKC 141c.

30. "It would not be for edification to recount all the interpretations which have been given of this clause," Calvin comments (*Psalms*, 4:302), then adds with the confidence of a true OT scholar that he will now share "its true and natural import" (namely the stupendous growth of the church). Cf. Raymond Tournay, "Le Psaume 110," *RB* 67 (1960): 5–41 (see 10–12).

nobility. The king is not usually spoken of as "holy," but here that expression would lead neatly into v. 4. Likewise an army can possess splendor (Ezek. 27:10). "Holy war" is not an OT expression, but the OT does speak of "sanctifying war" (e.g., Jer. 6:4) and speaks of Israel itself as holy, so that "holy splendor" would be a feasible attribute of the king's forces. The alternative reading "on the holy mountains" (cf. 87:1) will refer to the mountainous "holy land" as a whole.

The most difficult expression is "from the womb of dawn." In Isa. 14:12 the Babylonian king is metaphorically the child of Dawn in the sense that he is destined to experience a rapid eclipse like that of the Venus star at dawn. Perhaps here that expression keeps a positive connotation, suggesting the king's meteoric rise, "a brilliant son of the rising dawn,"[31] or making a similar comment about the young men of the army. Or perhaps the expression simply reflects the fact that the dew is birthed by the morning.

110:4–7. An oath concerning the king's priesthood.

> 4Yhwh swore and will not relent:
> You are a priest forever,
>   after the manner of Melchizedek.

The person who brings Yhwh's word introduces a new word, this time an oath, an even more solemn word. Restating a promise as an oath is not remarkable, and elsewhere Yhwh does swear an oath about kingship (89:3, 35, 49 [4, 36, 50]). In the parallelism of vv. 1–3 and 4–6, the oath constitutes a heightening over the earlier "utterance." What is surprising is that the oath declares that the king is also a priest.[32] Israelite kings did not undertake regular priestly acts such as offering sacrifices; when the OT refers to kings offering sacrifices, usually it likely denotes their bringing sacrifices that the priests actually offered (as is so when this language is used of ordinary laypeople). They did undertake priestly acts such as leading worship and prayer and blessing the people, and offered sacrifice on special occasions not covered by the regular rules.[33] They could be seen as doing that because they were heirs to the position of the king of Jerusalem as it obtained before Jerusalem was an Israelite

31. Cf. Th. Booij, "Psalm 100," *VT* 41 (1991): 396–407 (see 401), though he thinks of the sun rather than the morning star.

32. H. H. Rowley suggests that here David speaks to Zadok (*Festschrift Alfred Bertholet*, 470; also "Melchizedek and David," *VT* 17 [1967]: 485). It seems unrealistic to expect readers to work that out.

33. See, e.g., John W. Bowker, "Psalm cx," *VT* 17 (1967): 31–42 (see 35–36); Willem van der Meer, "Psalm 110," in *The Structural Analysis of Biblical and Canaanite Poetry*, ed. van der Meer and Johannes C. de Moor, JSOTSup 74 (Sheffield: Sheffield Academic Press, 1988): 207–34 (see 228–29).

city, when its king was also its priest. That kingship is thus here named after Melchizedek, the priest-king of Salem in Gen. 14.

Yhwh affirms that the Israelite king has that position "forever" and promises not to relent about the commitment. Yhwh will not have a random change of mind about the matter; that is the significance of the declaration that Yhwh does not have changes of mind about things (Num. 23:19). Yhwh of course can have a change of mind for a reason, not randomly (see especially Jer. 18:1–10). Further, there are promises that might seem to apply forever but do not, such as the covenant with Phinehas (Num. 25:13). The covenant with David was to last forever, but Davidic kings sat on the throne in Jerusalem for only a few hundred years. That throne has been unoccupied for over 2,500 years. Yhwh did relent and the priesthood or kingship did not last forever, because of the human response to the promise. The promise of "forever" does not guarantee it will stand when there is no proper response. The king of Jerusalem can be sure Yhwh will not randomly have second thoughts about this oath, but this does not mean he need not make a faithful response to it (as 2 Sam. 7:11–16 notes).

5The Lord by your right hand
has crushed kings on the day of his anger.

Whereas "my lord" in v. 1 was *ʾădōnî*, here *Lord is *ʾădōnāy*, the form referring to Yhwh.[34] Evidently both Yhwh and the king had not stayed sitting, though by now they may be sitting again. Further, whereas on the throne the king sits *at* Yhwh's right hand, in the terms of another metaphor Yhwh stands *by* the king's right hand when there is action to be taken (the preposition is now *ʿal* rather than *lĕ*). Standing by someone's right hand is the position of support and protection (cf. 16:8; 109:31; 121:5). Whereas vv. 2–3 had turned the king into the protagonist in battle, v. 5 goes back to portraying Yhwh as the protagonist, in the manner of v. 1. The king speaks of crushing people (*māḥaṣ*) in 18:38 [39]; Yhwh speaks of doing so in Deut. 32:39; the reference to the king's forceful day (v. 3) is complemented by reference to Yhwh's angry day (cf. Isa. 13:13; Lam. 1:12; 2:1, 21, 22).[35] The word is the ordinary term for anger (*ʾap*), not a technical term for divine wrath. When the king fights fiercely, he expresses his anger; it is a source of his energy (1 Sam. 11:6). So it is for Yhwh. The verb is qatal, like that in v. 4 (cf. LXX, Jerome); it seems arbitrary to translate it as future (NRSV, TNIV) or present (NJPS). Like

34. For the view that the text earlier read *ʾădōnî*, see, e.g., H. Möller, "Der Textzusammenhang in Ps 110," *ZAW* 92 (1980): 287–89; Tournay, "Le Psaume 110," 5–41 (see 30).

35. For the movement between whether such acts are the king's or God's, compare the Egyptian parallel in Keel, *Symbolism*, 299.

the oath, this crushing lies in the past, and implicitly provides evidence for believing the oath.

> 6He governs among the nations, filling them with bodies,
> crushing heads over the breadth of the earth.

The psalm goes on from the acts of Yhwh that the king knows about to the ongoing conviction about Yhwh's acts that can be built on them.[36] Governing among the nations (the verb is *dîn*, a synonym of *šāpaṭ*; *authority) is of course Yhwh's business (96:10), though it too is a task in which Yhwh involves the king. As in Ps. 2, that is understood in negative terms. It means filling the nations with bodies. Psalm 2 pictures him breaking the nations (*rāʿaʿ*) with his staff (*šēbeṭ*, a synonym of *maṭṭēh* in v. 2) and smashing them (*nāpaṣ*), among the nations to the ends of the earth; this one pictures Yhwh crushing heads all over the earth.

> 7From the stream by the way he drinks;
> therefore he raises his head.

Here, the language might seem much more appropriate to a human king than a divine King. It might describe someone slaking his thirst from a stream as he prosecutes his battle, like Gideon.[37] But 1 Kings 1:38–40 relates how Solomon was anointed king by the Gihon spring outside Jerusalem. This closing line then alludes to the king being sacramentally resourced for his vocation; the line follows on the reference to Zion in v. 2. He drinks from that sacred spring by the road that descends the Valley of Siloam, and on that basis goes on to triumph. In origin, "raising the head" (cf. 3:3 [4]; 27:6) may be a legal expression, but the more general connotation applies here. Defeat would mean the king hanging his head in shame; victory means holding his head high.[38]

Yet there is no indication that the subject has changed, so the line likely continues to refer to the divine King, the divine warrior, pictured in light of the way the human king acted. Yhwh acts like a king sacra-

36. BDB 192, takes the king as the subject of v. 6, but there has been no indication of a change of subject.

37. R. Tournay, "Les Relectures du Psaume 110 (109)," *RB* 105 (1998): 321–31. John G. Gammie ("A New Setting for Psalm 110," *Anglican Theological Review* 51 [1969]: 4–17) takes this line as the key to understanding the psalm's context in prayer for rain. Joachim Becker ("Zur Deutung von Ps 110,7," in *Freude an der Weisung des Herrn*, ed. Haag and Hossfeld, 17–32) thinks of the victorious warrior drinking blood; cf. Calvin, *Psalms*, 4:308–9. Christian interpreters were more inclined to think of drinking a cup of suffering (e.g., Jerome, *Homilies*, 1:279).

38. Cf. van der Meer, "Psalm 110," 225.

mentally resourced and thus triumphant. The picture's boldness can then be compared with Isa. 42:13–14; 63:1–6.

Theological Implications

In light of NT use of the psalm, Christian exegesis traditionally took the psalm as a messianic prophecy that Jesus fulfills. Derek Kidner continues to argue trenchantly for this understanding.[39] One would never guess this interpretation from the psalm; it can only be read into it. When Yhwh spoke these words in OT times, people could not have been expected to understand them as the NT does. Herbert W. Bateman thus prefers to describe the psalm as "typological-prophetic."[40] With hindsight one can see that the text describes a pattern that Jesus will supremely embody. The relationship between NT and OT text is the one that regularly obtains. In light of Jesus's coming, the Holy Spirit inspires people to see significance in the OT that was never there before.

The text's theological implications then do not lie in its application to Jesus; that is to ignore its meaning. Its application to Jesus is part of NT study. The question is, what did the Holy Spirit offer OT believers in this text? In critical study it has been customary to discover the answer by looking at the psalm in light of its historical background or liturgical use. The effect is not very different from that of a christological approach. Once more we read the text in light of agenda that come from outside it. The psalm gives us no historical or liturgical information. We do not know and we will never know when it was written or how it was used.

Understanding has to start from the text itself. The psalm declares that Yhwh is on the side of the Israelite king and is involved in politics and history on that basis. Yhwh uses the king in governing the nations and acts in history with anger, energy, and violence. The king (and implicitly his people) is encouraged to live his life in light of ways Yhwh has made this commitment and involvement work out and in light of promises Yhwh has made about how they will work out. In Israel's history that usually means believing against the odds.

The particular distinctive insight of Ps. 110 is the fact that the king is also priest. There are things that are achieved by the combining of powers in one person. Politics and war are not allowed to escape from the context of the people's relationship with God, and the people's relationship with God is not allowed to escape from politics and war.

39. *Psalms* 2:391–92. Cf. Luther's monumental exposition in *Selected Psalms*, 2:225–348.

40. "Psalm 110:1 and the New Testament," *BSac* 149 (1992): 438–53 (see 453).

These theological insights are unfashionable in the context of modernity in which Christians work out what they reckon is a Christian view on such topics. That Christian view often corresponds to the secular view, which suggests that there is nothing very Christian about it. We neutralize the psalm's insights by claiming that we interpret it in light of the rest of the canon. And the idea of Yhwh being on the Israelite king's side against Israel's enemies does have to be set in the context of the presupposition that the enemies are resistant to Yhwh's purpose and that Israel is committed to it. But canonical interpretation must mean letting different parts of Scripture have their say, not silencing some by others that we prefer.

Psalm 111

Worship and Wisdom

Translation

1Praise Yah.
[ʾ] I confess Yhwh with all my soul
[*b*] in the council of the upright, the assembly.
[*g*] 2Yhwh's deeds are great,
[*d*] investigated[1] for all their delights.[2]
[*h*] 3His activity is majestic and splendid,
[*w*] and his faithfulness stands forever.
[*z*] 4He gained renown for his wonders;
[*ḥ*] Yhwh is gracious and compassionate.
[*ṭ*] 5He gave meat to people who revered him;
[*y*] he is mindful of his covenant forever.
[*k*] 6He proclaimed to his people the strength of his deeds,
[*l*] in giving them the possession of the nations.
[*m*] 7The deeds of his hands are true and decisive;
[*n*] all his orders are truthful.

1. The qal passive ptc. is close to gerundive (cf. Jerome, also JM 121i). Niphal (or pual) is more usual as gerundive, but it would not meet the colon's alphabetic requirement.

2. Tg, Syr, Aq apparently take *ḥepṣêhem* as a part of *ḥāpēṣ*, suggesting "by all who delight in them"; on the form, see Allen, *Psalms 101–150*, 121. But LXX, Jerome, Sym apparently take it as a part of *ḥēpeṣ*, which fits better in the context; for the prepositional expression, cf. v. 4.

[*s*] 8They are held firm forever and ever,
[ʿ] done in truth and uprightness.[3]
[*p*] 9He sent redemption to his people,
[*ṣ*] commanded his covenant forever.
[*q*] His name is holy and to be revered;
[*r*] 10reverence for Yhwh is the beginning of wisdom.[4]
[*ś*] There is good insight for all who do them;
[*t*] his praise stands forever.

Interpretation

Once again the psalm speaks in terms of confession and uses the first-person singular, but its testimony relates to Yhwh's characteristic activity as this applies to the people as a whole in whose company the worshipper stands. So this is the confession every worshipper gives when the congregation praises Yhwh; it is a confessional hymn. Like either confession or hymn it speaks *about* Yhwh but is addressed *to* other people in the congregation. Any confession or hymn thus has a didactic intent; that is more marked here (and it is reflected in the references to wisdom in the last two lines). The confession's content again works through the story of Israel's origins: the exodus and the Red Sea, the provision during the people's journey to the land, the giving of the land itself, and the teaching about the people's life. The focus on God's acts may mean it was used at Pesah or Sukkot, but we do not know anything specific about the context for its use, nor do we know when it was written.

An alphabetical psalm, its twenty-two cola begin with the successive letters of the alphabet. Verses 1–6 focus on Yhwh's acts in Israel's history and vv. 7–10 more on the revelation of Yhwh's will and its implications for Israel's life. Verse 1 introduces the whole; vv. 9c–10 close it off.[5] As usual, the observance of a form provides positive constraint for the psalmist. The alphabetic form makes it possible to suggest the content

3. The adjective *yāšār* is apparently used as if it were a noun such as *yōšer* (see DG 42, remark 4), enabling the colon to combine abstract and concrete (Watson, *Classical Hebrew Poetry*, 314–15).

4. Not "The beginning of wisdom is reverence for Yhwh" (so, e.g., NJPS). The question of word order in noun clauses is complex (see, e.g., JM 154), but here the requirements of the alphabetic structure would overwhelm any other considerations; and what is needed is a statement about reverence for Yhwh (see v. 9c) leading into the statement about wisdom (see v. 10b).

5. See further Pierre Auffret, "Essai sur la structure littéraire des Psaumes cxi et cxii," *VT* 30 (1980): 257–279; idem, "Grands sont les oeuvres de YHWH," *JNES* 56 (1997): 183–96; Dennis Pardee, "La structure du Psaume 111," *JNES* 56 (1997): 197–200; Ruth Scoralick, "Psalm 111," *Bib* 78 (1997): 190–205.

of Yhwh's praise from A to Z. Through requiring that something be said under each letter, it encourages the expression of insight that would not otherwise have emerged. It thus combines stereotyped expressions with originality. And it generates a form of poem that people may be helped to remember. Its statements are straightforward; no flights of inspiration were required to generate it. One might even imagine it as a student's composition to fulfill a professor's commission to write something that shows mastery of the alphabet; the move to wisdom language at the end would fit with that. Yet its commonplace statements make it a telling affirmation of the basic contents of Israelite faith; "the words of this psalm are big with meaning."[6] Further, the oddities generated by the alphabetic constraint produce striking statements among the obvious ones, and thus generate food for thought. It contains a marked number of instances of hendiadys (vv. 1b, 3a, 4b, 7a, 8a, 8b).

[1]Praise Yah.
[ʾ] I confess Yhwh with all my soul
[*b*] in the council of the upright, the assembly.

111:1. The opening declaration, "*Praise *Yah," stands outside the alphabetic framework, though it will turn out to form an inclusion with the last colon. While the bidding is plural, it immediately gives way to the singular commitment to *confession (*ʾôdeh*) with the whole soul (*heart). The psalmist "very properly begins with heart praise," which means our praise is genuine, the praise of the whole heart and not a heart half committed to Yhwh and half to Baal (cf. 86:11–12). But "at the same time, the person who, in secret, pours out his heart in grateful emotions toward God, will also set forth his praises in swelling strains, otherwise God would be deprived of one half of the honour which is due to him."[7] So the confession takes place in the congregation (thus plurals appear in v. 2b and subsequently, and later lines refer to "his people"). "In the council" (*bĕsôd*) suggests a gathering to make decisions for the community (cf. 89:7 [8]), glossed as the assembly (*ʿēdâ*). Neither word directly suggests the worshipping community, though they may imply that. Happy the community that has such a gathering of the upright.

[*g*] [2]Yhwh's deeds are great,
[*d*] investigated for all their delights.

111:2. The proper topic of confession is deeds, and the psalm immediately turns to these. The Cavendish Laboratory in Cambridge bears

6. Luther, *First Lectures*, 2:371.
7. Calvin, *Psalms*, 4:312.

this verse at its entrance, presumably on the assumption that Yhwh's great deeds are the work of creation, which science investigates,[8] but in this context they are more likely things Yhwh did in Israel's history. Describing them as great (*gādôl*) prepares us to read of the great things Yhwh did at the beginning of Israel's story (cf. 106:21).

The need for a *d* word generates the interesting use of *dāraš*, designating the deeds as something people have *recourse to and thus seek help from, or that are worthy of people doing so, the kind of investigation that will generate "midrash." These deeds are objectively "delights," or Israel is a people who subjectively delights in them. Either way, as they have recourse to them, they shape people's faith, hope, trust, and life.

[*h*] **3**His activity is majestic and splendid,
[*w*] and his faithfulness stands forever.

111:3. In substance v. 3 parallels v. 2. Yhwh's activity is (the embodiment of) majesty and splendor (*hôd-wĕhādār*), synonyms multiplying the affirmation of Yhwh's kingly grandeur evidenced in his activity.

In turn, the second colon (beginning "and," *w*) gives specificity to why people would investigate those deeds. They are an embodiment of Yhwh's *faithfulness, acts of faithfulness, *ṣĕdāqôt* (Judg. 5:11; 1 Sam. 12:7). Yhwh's majesty and splendor are not merely acts of power. They are harnessed to doing right by the people Yhwh is in relationship with. And that faithfulness stands forever; it is not just an aspect of the past. That makes these acts worth studying.

[*z*] **4**He gained renown for his wonders;
[*ḥ*] Yhwh is gracious and compassionate.

111:4. Yhwh made a *zēker* in connection with these acts. Elsewhere that might suggest establishing a festival such as Pesah, when they would be commemorated, but the context speaks more of the acts themselves, fitting the use of *zēker* in Exod. 3:15 (cf. also Ps. 135:13). By these acts Yhwh made a name and ensured that people would always be *mindful of it. The theme of vv. 2–3 continues. The great deeds were also wonders: the word has recurred in Pss. 105, 106, and 107 (cf. also Exod. 3:20). The parallelism reaffirms that they were not merely acts of power but acts that showed Yhwh to be *gracious (*ḥānnûn*) and compassionate, the first two adjectives in Yhwh's self-definition in Exod. 34:6, but in reverse order. While continuing the theme, the psalm also modifies it as it begins to speak in qatal verbs, more directly recalling the exodus.

8. Cf. Kidner, *Psalms*, 2:397. See the discussion in M. D. Koster, "Gods grote werken," *NedTT* 33 (1979): 10–26.

[*ṭ*] [5]He gave meat to people who revered him;
[*y*] he is mindful of his covenant forever.

111:5. The unusual word for meat, *ṭerep*, denotes a beast's prey. It reflects how eating meat is much less common in a traditional than in an urban society. Eating meat is behaving rather like a lion. Yhwh indeed provided *bāśār* (flesh, meat; Exod. 16; Num. 11), to people who *revered Yhwh (Exod. 14:31), if not for long.

At the exodus Yhwh was mindful of the covenant (Exod. 2:24; 6:5; Ps. 106:45), but *yizkōr* again means a move from Yhwh's deed at the beginning to its ongoing significance, as Yhwh is *mindful of his *covenant commitment—forever (cf. Lev. 26:42, 45).

[*k*] [6]He proclaimed to his people the strength of his deeds,
[*l*] in giving them the possession of the nations.

111:6. Yhwh manifested strength (*kōaḥ*) in the exodus and at the Red Sea (Exod. 9:16; 15:6; 32:11) and then in giving the people the land (the *l* word is the opening gerund), the "*possession of the nations" (cf. Ps. 2:8). That defines the strength of Yhwh's deeds.

[*m*] [7]The deeds of his hands are true and decisive;
[*n*] all his orders are truthful.

111:7. Together, vv. 6–7 make the same point as the two cola in v. 3 and in v. 4: Yhwh's deeds (*ma'ăśeh*) manifest not only power but decisiveness (*authority) and truth (*true). Literally, they *are* truth and decisiveness, the very embodiment of decisive truthfulness (cf. the use of nouns in v. 3). The combination is unusual; faithfulness and decisiveness is more usual. That may link with the way v. 7b takes us in a new direction and makes us reread v. 7a. At first, one would have reckoned that v. 7a again summarizes the acts described in vv. 2–6, but the second colon points in another direction by implying a link between Yhwh's bringing truth and decisiveness into effect and Yhwh's laying *orders (*piqqûdîm*) on Israel; the word comes elsewhere only in Pss. 19, 103, and 119.[9] These are themselves the embodiment of truthfulness. This second colon begins with another form of that root for truth/truthfulness, a niphal participle (so it provides an *n* word). Truthfulness is put into effect not only by Yhwh's deeds in bringing Israel from Egypt to Canaan, but by laying these orders before Israel. Indeed, the true and decisive deed to which v. 7a refers turns out to be the giving of these orders. The verse marks a

9. Cf. Mays, *Psalms*, 356–57.

move from speaking of Yhwh's acts, to speaking of Yhwh's commands, which will dominate what follows. In what sense are such behavioral requirements "truthful"? In Ps. 19:7–9, "orders" and other terms for Yhwh's commands are described by terms such as reliable, faithful, and truthful. The terms involve ellipse or metonymy, or are pregnant expressions. God's orders produce people and lives that are reliable, faithful, and truthful.

[*s*] 8They are held firm forever and ever,
[ʿ] done in truth and uprightness.

111:8. "Held firm" (*sāmak*) affirms the permanent validity of Yhwh's orders.[10] But if Yhwh has so firmly established these orders, surely they should be performed or done (*ʿāśâ*) in the *truth and uprightness that are supposed to characterize this people (cf. v. 1).[11]

[*p*] 9a–bHe sent redemption to his people,
[*ṣ*] commanded his covenant forever.

111:9a–b. Once again Yhwh's acts are restated, here beginning with reference to *redemption (*pĕdût*; cf. Exod. 8:23 [19]). Commanding (*ṣiwwâ*) the covenant is then different from establishing or sealing it, the more usual expressions. Yhwh sovereignly imposes the covenant requirements on the people (e.g., Josh. 7:11; 23:16). In the context of vv. 7–10, the thrust of the line lies in the second colon, taking further the point in vv. 7–8.

[*q*] 9cHis name is holy and to be revered;
[*r*] 10areverence for Yhwh is the beginning of wisdom.

111:9c–10a. The last two lines form an inclusion with v. 1. "To be *revered" explicates the point in *holy (*qādôš*). The second colon takes that point further in utilizing the expression "the beginning [*rēʾšît*] of wisdom" (for similar phrases see, e.g., Prov. 1:7). "Wisdom" suggests intellectual understanding expressing itself in sensible living. The psalm begins and ends with praise, enthusiastic, emotional, response to God. It does not see a tension between that and "reverence" ("fear" in many

10. The colon begins with the bare ptc., which EVV take as enjambment from v. 7. But otherwise in the psalm every line is self-contained. So more likely v. 8a is a noun clause, lacking the article in order to begin with the *s* (for such clauses, see the introductory comment on 103:3–5).

11. The qal passive *ʿăśûyim* is close to being gerundive, "to be done," rather than simply "done" (cf. v. 2).

translations), deferential submission to God. Both are essential to a relationship with God.

> [*ś*] [10b]There is good insight for all who do them;
> [*t*] his praise stands forever.

111:10b. The closing line parallels the previous one, with the two working in *abb′a′* order. Insight (*śēkel*) parallels "wisdom" in denoting understanding that makes a difference to life and makes it possible to succeed there (e.g., 1 Sam. 25:3; Prov. 3:4). "Do" and "them" pick up from vv. 7b–8, part of the rounding off of the second part of the psalm. "Praise" (*tĕhillâ*) then also forms an inclusion with the opening word.

Theological Implications

The psalm's decisive affirmation is that insight and praise belong together. Awareness of the wonder of Yhwh's deeds in delivering the people issues in heartfelt, enthusiastic praise for these great deeds, whose delight consists in the way they combine majesty, splendor, wonder, and strength with faithfulness, grace, and compassion; or rather, these deeds indicate that majesty, splendor, wonder, and strength essentially involve faithfulness, grace, and compassion. At the same time, the object of these great deeds is to establish truthfulness and uprightness in the people's life. The covenant is both a commitment Yhwh is mindful of and one Yhwh commands. Alongside the praise that claps and dances is the reverence that bows before Yhwh's holiness. And in that submission lies insight for life. Worship and wisdom are not different preferences for different groups of people. Both are part of true humanity and of the true life of God's people.

Psalm 112
Beatitudes

Translation

[1]Praise Yah.
[ʾ] The good fortune of the person who reveres Yhwh,
  [*b*] who delights greatly in his commands.
[*g*] [2]His offspring will become a mighty man in the land;
  [*d*] the generation of the upright will be blessed.
[*h*] [3]Wealth and riches are in his house,
  [*w*] and his faithfulness stands forever.
[*z*] [4]He arises as light in the darkness for the upright people;
  [*ḥ*] he is gracious, compassionate, and faithful.
[*ṭ*] [5]Good is the person who is gracious and lends,[1]
  [*y*] who completes his affairs with decisiveness.
[*k*] [6]Because he does not falter forever;
  [*l*] the faithful person will become renowned forever.
[*m*] [7]He will not be afraid of bad news;
  [*n*] his heart is established, reliant[2] on Yhwh.
[*s*] [8]His heart is held firm, he will not be afraid,
  [ʿ] until he looks on his foes.
[*p*] [9]He spreads abroad, he gives to the poor;
  [*ṣ*] his faithfulness stands forever.
[*q*] His horn will stand high in honor;
  [*r*] [10]the faithless person will look and be angry.

1. So Vrs; EVV have "it goes well for the person," but this would require *l*. Allen (*Psalms 101–150,* 127) thus suggests "it is good for a man to lend," more literally "it is good that a man lends," but his parallels show that this would require *kî*.

2. On the passive ptc., see on 103:14.

[*š*] He will gnash his teeth and grow weak;
  [*t*] the desire of faithless people will perish.

Interpretation

This further twenty-two-colon alphabetic psalm is a niece or nephew (rather than twin)[3] to Ps. 111. It starts like Ps. 111, with a bidding to worship, and like Ps. 111 combines worship and teaching, though with more stress on the latter. The alphabetic cola start where Ps. 111 ends, with reverence for Yhwh and its fruitfulness, and then expound what that fruitfulness looks like, using identical expressions to Ps. 111. But whereas Ps. 111 focuses on the way Yhwh has related to the community, Ps. 112 focuses on the individual; Ps. 111 focuses on theology, Ps. 112 on anthropology.[4] All this gives it stronger links with wisdom thinking and literature; apart from the "Praise Yah," it would fit fine in Proverbs.[5]

Most cola could stand alone, but the two in v. 8 cannot do so, and most others work with standard parallelism (e.g., vv. 1, 2, and 3), suggesting Ps. 112, like Ps. 111, comprises bicola. There are no other sections or strophes into which the psalm divides; the bicola are its only structural principle.[6] (Oddly, as with Ps. 111, MT treats the last six cola as two tricola, with more plausibility than is the case with Ps. 111.) The author of Ps. 112 knew and used Ps. 111, but there is no indication that it was the same author. Once again the psalm employs familiar material, often in innovative ways, to generate its comprehensive and novel picture. We do not know how it was used.

1Praise Yah.
[ʾ] The good fortune of the person who reveres Yhwh,
  [*b*] who delights greatly in his commands.

3. Against, e.g., Walther Zimmerli, "Zwillingspsalmen," in *Studien zur alttestamentlichen Theologie und Prophetie*, TBü 51 (Munich: Kaiser, 1974), 261–71. Cf. Beat Weber, "Zu Kolometrie und strophischer Struktur von Psalm 111—mit einem Seitenblick auf Psalm 112," *BN* 118 (2003): 62–67. In effect, Beth LaNeel Tanner (*The Book of Psalms through the Lens of Intertextuality* [New York: Lang, 2001], 141–57) invites us to see Prov. 31:10–31 as its twin, or at least its sister.

4. Seybold, *Psalmen*, 440. Stephen K. Sherwood argues that the man is the king ("Psalm 112," *CBQ* 51 [1989]: 50–64), but the evidence is circumstantial.

5. Cf. Mays, *Psalms*, 361; Leo G. Perdue, *Wisdom and Cult*, SBLDS 30 (Missoula, MT: Scholars, 1977), 291–94.

6. For attempts to trace a structure, see Pierre Auffret, "Essai sur la structure littéraire des Psaumes cxi et cxii," *VT* 30 (1980): 257–79; idem, "En mémoire éternelle sera le juste," *VT* 48 (1998): 2–14.

112:1. The opening plural exhortation to *praise *Yah corresponds to Ps. 111, though it has a different significance, as other repetitions give their words different significance. The reasons for praise lie in what follows; this actually is a praise psalm.[7]

In speaking of the *good fortune (*ʾašrê*) of the person who *reveres Yhwh (picking up from Ps. 111:10), the psalm also begins like Ps. 1. It will continue to parallel that psalm's declarations;[8] the last two words of each psalm are also the same. Its declarations also parallel another alphabetic psalm, Ps. 37,[9] though unlike Pss. 1 and 37, they focus more on the faithful person and their destiny than on the faithless. The specific declaration about good fortune attaching to revering Yhwh parallels 128:1 (though that refers to people [plural]), and the psalm's broader content parallels that psalm.

Revering Yhwh is spelled out as involving great delight in (*b*) Yhwh's commands. Delight picks up from 111:2, though now, tellingly, the object of delight is not Yhwh's acts but Yhwh's commands. The related verb came in 111:9 but "commands" is equivalent to "orders" in 111:7.

Both revering Yhwh and delighting in Yhwh's commands combine the affective and the volitional. Revering indicates respect and deference expressing itself in the practice of submission and obedience. Delight is an attitude of enthusiasm, which (applied to commands) again expresses itself in submission and obedience. If someone claimed to delight in Yhwh's commands but did not obey them, it would be odd. But the psalm also presupposes that obedience to commands that did not relate to reverence and delight would be odd.

[*g*] ²His offspring will become a mighty man in the land;
[*d*] the generation of the upright will be blessed.

112:2. In explicating the promise about good fortune the psalm moves immediately to its significance for the person's offspring, a consideration of key interest for parents (what will happen to our children?). Whereas "offspring" can be either singular or collective, "mighty" (*gibbôr*) suggests that here it denotes the person's own son.[10]

While the "generation" (*dôr*) might then be the whole next generation to which this offspring belongs, one would expect a word such as "next" to make that clear (cf. 109:13). More likely the colon refers to the whole present generation or company (cf. 14:5; 24:6) of the upright (the

7. Cf. Goulder, *Psalms of the Return*, 156.

8. See Marlin E. Thomas, "Psalms 1 and 112 as a Paradigm for the Comparison of Wisdom Motifs in the Psalms," *JETS* 29 (1986): 15–24.

9. See Goulder, *Psalms of the Return*, 157.

10. Cf. *Midrash on Psalms*, 2:211, though it refers the word to Isaac or Jacob.

word from 111:1). It will be blessed through this individual's revering of Yhwh.

> [*h*] ³Wealth and riches are in his house,
> [*w*] and his faithfulness stands forever.

112:3. The psalm moves back from the son and his contemporaries to the father. "Wealth (*hôn*) and riches" embody good fortune. Verse 3b repeats the *w* colon from 111:3b—except that there the statement related to God, whereas here it relates to one who reveres God. Read in light of what precedes, it may spell out what it is like to enjoy good fortune, but read in light of what follows, the *faithfulness may denote a continuing fruitfulness.

> [*z*] ⁴He arises as light in the darkness for the upright people;
> [*ḥ*] he is gracious, compassionate, and faithful.

112:4. "Arise" stretches the use of *zāraḥ*, apparently adapting words from Isa. 58:10 but giving them quite new significance.[11] Here vv. 3 and 4b suggest that the faithful person is the subject. The assumption is then that upright people (v. 2) do not escape darkness (that is, trouble), but that this will not have the last word because of the commitment of the faithful person. That person's faithfulness (v. 3b) works out in a willingness to use wealth and riches (v. 3a) to bring light (that is, deliverance) to the upright.

That is because of another set of qualities this person shares with Yhwh, *graciousness (*ḥānnûn*), compassion, and *faithfulness (see 111:3, 4).[12]

> [*ṭ*] ⁵Good is the person who is gracious and lends,
> [*y*] who completes his affairs with decisiveness.

112:5. LXX again assumes that being *good (*ṭôb*) suggests being kind (cf. 106:1); specifically, it thus implies *graciousness, which itself finds expression in a willingness to lend. We might think it would express itself in a willingness to give, and the psalm will come to that, but this colon makes another point. Lending and borrowing is a common feature of life. In Western society it mostly means people with resources increasing those resources by lending to people with none. In the OT lending is a means of the rich helping the poor, not helping themselves,

11. There the colon begins with a *w*-consecutive; here it needs to begin with the bare verb, which one may take as gnomic qatal. Cf. v. 9a.

12. Contrast LXX, which makes Yhwh the subject of the colon.

and not making them the recipients of charity but giving them means of reestablishing themselves, after which they would pay back the loan (see, e.g., Exod. 22:25–27). Its ideology was closer to that of credit unions and building societies. Here, goodness includes being willing to use one's surplus wealth for the benefit of others. When they pay it back, it becomes available to help yet others.

Parallel to that, this generous person is not one who leaves such tasks half done but completes them (*yĕkalkēl*)[13] with *decisiveness.

[*k*] 6Because he does not falter forever;
[*l*] the faithful person will become renowned forever.

112:6. The "because" (*kî*) may apply to both cola, as does "the *faithful person." The verb *mûṭ* often means "collapse," but in contexts referring to behavioral commitments it can denote wavering or weakening (e.g., 15:5); the colon then explicates v. 5b.

As a result he does not merely survive but triumphs. "Renown" (with *lĕ* prefixed) is yet another expression picked up from Ps. 111 (see v. 4) that there applied to Yhwh but here to the faithful person.

[*m*] 7He will not be afraid of bad news;
[*n*] his heart is established, reliant on Yhwh.

112:7. Perhaps he will not be afraid of (*min*) bad news because he knows bad news will not be coming his way; Yhwh makes things work out for him.

Or perhaps it is because his heart is established (*nākôn*), and that is because he is reliant on Yhwh.

[*s*] 8His heart is held firm, he will not be afraid,
[ʿ] until he looks on his foes.

112:8. The statement about his heart is restated by using *sāmak* from 111:8,[14] with the declaration from v. 7a then repeated and developed by the second colon. The person who reveres Yhwh (v. 1, the same verb) does not fear anything else ("Fear him, ye saints, and you will then have nothing else to fear")[15] until (*ʿad*) he looks on his foes having been put down, as he knew they would be (cf. *rāʾâ b* in 118:7 and *nābaṭ* [hiphil] in 92:11 [12]).

13. BDB makes this a unique use of *kûl* (pilpēl); more likely it is treated as if it came from *kālâ* (cf. the piel in Ruth 3:18).

14. Although that is the immediately significant parallel, the ptc. also comes in Isa. 26:3 in association with *bāṭûaḥ*, the word for "reliant" in v. 7.

15. Cf. Allen, *Psalms 101–150*, 131.

[*p*] 9a–bHe spreads abroad, he gives to the poor;
[*ṣ*] his faithfulness stands forever.

112:9a–b. So "giving" does accompany "lending." Giving is appropriate to people with no land and therefore no prospect of reestablishing themselves by means of a loan and no prospect of repaying one. "Spread abroad" (*pāzar* piel), strictly "scatter," gives a vivid picture of generosity in operation (cf. Prov. 11:24).

The second colon repeats v. 3b without the "and" so begins with *ṣidqātô* (his *faithfulness).

[*q*] 9cHis horn will stand high in honor;
[*r*] 10athe faithless person will look and be angry.

112:9c–10a. "Horn" (*qeren*) provides another image for asserting strength, like an animal raising its horn as a threat or an actual means of putting down opposition. Thus he gains *honor in the community.

That will be confirmed and enhanced by the attitude the *faithless (*rāšāʿ*) have to take. Their seeing is very different from his (the same verb form as v. 8b). The result will be vexation: the verb *kāʿas* often suggests being provoked to anger, but here one might also think of being provoked to other strong feelings such as frustration or grief.

[*š*] 10b–cHe will gnash his teeth and grow weak;
[*t*] the desire of faithless people will perish.

112:10b–c. The faithless thus gnashes his teeth (*šinnāyw*), but there is nothing he can do about it. While *māsas* (niphal) usually means "melt away" (e.g., 68:2 [3]), it is often used with the heart as its subject to mean "faint, grow fearful," and this fits here.

The final colon re-expresses the point, beginning with "desire" (*taʾăwâ*). As well as forming a contrast with the repeated "forever" applying to the faithful, it contrasts with the close of Ps. 111.

Theological Implications

The psalm implies an analysis of the good life, in two senses. It portrays the morally good life and the good life Yhwh wishes people to enjoy through living the morally good life. Both apply directly to people such as the heads of families (who have resources to lend and give) but would be open to extension to the family as a whole and to ordinary individuals.

The foundation of the morally good life is reverence for Yhwh, which expresses itself in submission to Yhwh, and in an associated enthusiasm for Yhwh's commands. In relation to other people, the good life involves faithfulness, doing right by the people in our community. This expresses itself in bringing light to people when they are in darkness by being gracious and compassionate, not so much an attitude of sympathetic concern as a practice: we lend them what they need or give them what they need, and we do not merely start on such a project but complete it.

The good life Yhwh wishes people to enjoy begins for them with the satisfaction of seeing their children flourish, and seeing themselves being a blessing to their contemporaries and having the high regard in the community that issues from that. It includes their enjoying wealth and riches, though the blessing of that lies in what they can do with them for other people. So the morally good life and the good life we enjoy turn out to overlap: being able to bring light to people in darkness, to be gracious and compassionate, is as much a blessing to the givers as it is to the receivers. The good life they enjoy also means they do not fear for themselves; their reliance on Yhwh means they do not fear trouble coming. When it threatens, they know Yhwh will deliver them. They know they will triumph, to the chagrin of their foes.

Both the implicit exhortations and the promises correspond to those in the NT. Declaring "the good fortune" of people who revere Yhwh is the form Jesus takes up in the Beatitudes. He, too, promises that such people will inherit the earth, or at least the land, and that people who seek God's reign and God's righteousness will find they have food, drink, and clothing (Matt. 5:5; 6:33). Paul takes up v. 9 and promises that people who accept its principle will be enriched in every way (2 Cor. 9:9–11). Such promises are risky and do not always correspond to experience, but that is not reason for denying them their place in the OT and NT.

Psalm 113

Yhwh Sits on High, Looks Down Low

Translation

1Praise Yah.
Praise, servants of Yhwh,
  praise Yhwh's name.
2May Yhwh's name be worshipped,
  now[1] and forever.
3From the rising of the sun to its setting,
  Yhwh's name is to be praised.[2]

4Yhwh is on high above all nations,
  his honor above the heavens.
5Who is like Yhwh, our God,
  the one who sits on high,
6The one who looks down low,[3]
  in the heavens and in the earth?—
7One who lifts the poor from the dirt,
  raises the needy from the rubbish heap,

1. The preposition on *mēʿattâ* should not be pressed (cf. NJPS, TNIV, against NRSV).
2. The context suggests that the pual ptc. is gerundive (cf. Jerome).
3. Lit. "who makes high to sit . . . makes low to see"; see GKC 114n.

8To set them[4] with the nobles,
with the nobles of his people.
9One who sets the woman who is childless in the household
as the mother of children, rejoicing.
Praise Yah.[5]

Interpretation

Psalm 113 combines aspects of a praise psalm and a testimony psalm in a different configuration from that in Pss. 104–7, though not unlike Ps. 103. Like a praise psalm, it comprises challenge to worship (vv. 1b–3) followed by reasons for worship, expressed in terms of what Yhwh is like and what Yhwh does (vv. 4–9b), with the whole set in the context of a double "Praise Yah" (vv. 1a, 9c).[6] But the praise relates not to God's acts as creator, and deliverer in Israel's history, but to God's everyday activity in lifting up the poor and giving children to the childless.

We do not know its date or the way it was used in OT times.[7] It later became the first of the Hallel (Praise) Psalms, in particular Pss. 113–18. These are used at major festivals[8] and specifically at Pesah in commemorating the exodus from Egypt, Pss. 113–14 before the meal, Pss. 115–18 afterward (cf. Mark 14:26); hence the "Egyptian Hallel." Tg thus reinterprets v. 7 as describing Yhwh's restoring Israel, for which the childless woman becomes a metaphor (as in Isa. 54).

113:1–3. After the opening "*Praise *Yah," three further lines of exhortation urge praise of Yhwh's *name. The first involves a double imperative active; vv. 2–3 expand on that in a double jussive passive. Thus the two cola in v. 1b–c are parallel, and the two whole lines in vv. 2–3 are parallel to each other and to v. 1b–c; they themselves work in *abb′a′* order.

1Praise Yah.
Praise, servants of Yhwh,
praise Yhwh's name.

4. Not "to set me"; the ending is a connective -*î* (and the object is understood). The infinitive is anomalously constructed by analogy with the participles in vv. 5–9 (see the comment on v. 7), adding to the rhyme effect.

5. LXX, Jerome associate this colon with Ps. 114.

6. Philip L. Graber ("The Structural Meaning of Psalm 113," *Occasional Papers in Translation* 4 [1990]: 340–52) analyzes the psalm's development as a series of waves.

7. Comparison with 1 Sam. 2 makes John T. Willis see it as a preexilic victory song ("The Song of Hannah and Psalm 113," *CBQ* 35 [1973]: 139–54) and David Noel Freedman see it as premonarchic ("Psalm 113 and the Song of Hannah," *Eretz-Israel* 14 [1978]: 56*–69*).

8. See, e.g., *m. Sukkah* 4.1; *m. Pesaḥim* 5.7.

[2]May Yhwh's name be worshipped,
now and forever.
[3]From the rising of the sun to its setting,
Yhwh's name is to be praised.

The people as a whole (or the choir?) is to offer praise in its capacity as Yhwh's servants, who have both the privilege and the responsibility of a servant's relationship with a master. Verses 2–3 add that Yhwh's name is to be *worshipped without limit in time or space (or perhaps all day). The psalm is fond of merism.[9]

113:4–9. Six further lines describe who Yhwh is, providing the implicit bases for the exhortation in vv. 1–3. Two relate to Yhwh's position above the heavens and the last three to Yhwh's activity on the earth; v. 6 bridges these two sets. The whole of vv. 5b–9b forms participial enjambments dependent on v. 5a—two participles with the article, then two without the article.

[4]Yhwh is on high above all nations,
his honor above the heavens.

First there is a statement, by implication directly buttressing the exhortation in vv. 2–3. Being on high could suggest Yhwh's authority extending over all earthly political power, but the second colon points to a different implication. Yhwh's *honor is recognized by all these powers and by all heavenly powers, or deserves to be so recognized. Yhwh *has* this honor; therefore Yhwh should be praised.

[5]Who is like Yhwh, our God,
the one who sits on high,
[6]The one who looks down low,
in the heavens and in the earth?—

Such rhetorical questions are a standard way of expressing the same point. They go through the motions of inviting people to think and decide something, yet they presuppose that people know the only possible answer and must affirm it. The question begins in Exod. 15:11 and Deut. 3:24 and reappears in (for instance) Pss. 35:10 and 71:19, which share the conviction that Yhwh's incomparability demonstrated at the Red Sea also works itself out in individuals' lives. Initially, however, the psalm makes the point that Yhwh's incomparability lies in that exaltation to which v. 4 referred.

But as well as rising on high to sit, Yhwh gets down to look. The verb often suggests being of modest position and low status. For a moment

9. Cf. Hans-Peter Müller, "Zum 113. Psalm," *BN* 100 (1999): 18–21.

we are left in suspense about the reason for this self-lowering. As vv. 5b and 6a thus belong together, so vv. 5a and 6b belong together; the lines work *abb′a′*, like vv. 2–3. The question asks who is like our God in the heavens or the earth (cf. Deut. 3:24; 1 Kings 8:23; thus Yhwh does not look down on the heavens, which would be a slightly odd expression). At the same time, "in the heavens and in the earth" also takes up the content of vv. 5b and 6a.

7One who lifts the poor from the dirt,
raises the needy from the rubbish heap,
8To set them with the nobles,
with the nobles of his people.

Verses 7–8a correspond to 1 Sam. 2:8a–c.[10] "Poor" (*dal*) is an economic term, suggesting people's lack of assets. "Needy" (*ʾebyôn*) draws attention to the consequence, people's lack of resources; the needy are people who lack food. While dirt and rubbish heap may be metaphors, modern experience of people living on rubbish heaps on the edge of great cities makes the language literally plausible. The OT normally mentions the poor and needy in order to emphasize the community's obligation toward them (e.g., Ps. 112:9), though the Psalms put alongside this Yhwh's acceptance of obligation toward them (e.g., 107:41; 109:31). Yhwh does not often lift up the poor by miraculous intervention but cajoles or inspires human agents to do so. Yet the psalm ignores such considerations, speaking as if Yhwh indeed acts supranaturally. Something happens that to the poor and needy looks miraculous.

Their lowliness involves not merely poverty and hunger but degradation and shame. Thus their deliverance involves not merely food but restoration to a proper position in the community. They now sit in pride among people who count there.

9One who sets the woman who is childless in the household
as the mother of children, rejoicing.
Praise Yah.

While 1 Sam. 2 thus speaks about the poor and needy, Hannah's own humiliation lay in her infertility. Her praise and rejoicing issue from Yhwh's reversing that, so that (hyperbolically) the childless woman bears seven. Here, too, such a woman thus gains her proper position in the community. In her household she now has the honorable place belonging to a mother instead of being marginal to it, not a complete

10. Except that the participial forms in vv. 5, 6, 7, and 9 have connective *-î* at the end (see GKC 90lmn; JM 93np).

woman. In 1 Sam. 2, Hannah's experience is subordinate to the grand story that Yhwh is plotting; we know about her experience because of who her son is. Such acts of Yhwh also belong in lives that have no such significance.

*Praise *Yah; the psalm closes as it began.

Theological Implications

Readers of the OT story can assume that its basic concern should be describing God's dealings with ordinary individuals like us in the context of their ordinary lives, and then can be puzzled by it or misread it. It is usually concerned with the big story in which our little stories need to be set. But this psalm does have that concern, and makes God's dealings with the individual the basis for praise. Here "the distinctiveness of Yahweh is not based on grand cosmic claims"[11] but on Yhwh's transformative interventions in the lives of the powerless. The definition of God is as one who lifts the literal poor from the literal rubbish heap and turns the literal infertile woman into a literal mother.[12] Perhaps if we want to see Yhwh at work we have to hang around rubbish heaps and keep the company of women weeping in the night because they cannot conceive.

That works only on the assumption that it takes God to fix things, which is as countercultural a notion as hanging around rubbish heaps. Ps. 112 emphasized that human beings need to care for the poor, but Ps. 113 warns against the temptation to reckon that everything depends on us; cultures differ as to which is their more dangerous temptation. Stanley Hauerwas and William H. Willimon tartly comment, "Most of our social activism is formed on the presumption that God is superfluous to the formation of a world of peace with justice. Fortunately, we are powerful people who, because we live in a democracy, are free to use our power. It is all up to us."[13] And of course we have devices to enable infertile couples to have children. So we do not need God and do not have reason to praise God.

11. Brueggemann, *Message of Psalms*, 162.

12. Thus Peter C. Craigie ("Psalm 113," *Int* 39 [1985]: 70–74) starts from vv. 7–9 in interpreting the psalm.

13. *Resident Aliens* (Nashville: Abingdon, 1989), 36; cf. McCann, "Psalms," 1140.

Psalm 114

Still the God of the Exodus

Translation

[1]When Israel came out of Egypt,
  Jacob's household from a people that jabbers,
[2]Judah became its sanctuary,
  Israel its realm.
[3]The sea saw and fled,
  the Jordan would turn back.[1]
[4]The mountains jumped like rams,
  the hills like lambs.
[5]What was with you, sea, that you would flee,
  Jordan, that you would turn back,
[6]You mountains, that you would jump like rams,
  you hills, like lambs?
[7]Tremble,[2] earth, before the Lord,
  before the God of Jacob,
[8]Who turned[3] the crag into a pool of water,
  basalt into a spring[4] of water.

1. The yiqtols in vv. 3 and 5–6 have simple past reference, but I translate them thus to draw attention to the rhetorical difference from the qatals.
2. LXX has a past verb, assimilating to vv. 1–6.
3. The ptc. has connective *-î* (cf. GKC 90m; JM 93n).
4. The construct has the connective *-ô* (see GKC 90o; JM 93r).

Interpretation

"The form of the psalm is unusual and enigmatic."[5] An idiosyncratic praise psalm, it leaps straight into reasons for praise in giving its distinctive account of the exodus and Israel's arrival in Canaan. Verses 1–2 summarize this, vv. 3–4 gloss it by a comment on what happened, and vv. 5–6 ask a series of rhetorical questions relating to that. This in turn leads in v. 7 to the equivalent of a bidding to praise, with v. 8 completing the sequence of two-line sections by summarizing Yhwh's activity in different terms and a different connection. Indeed, that last verse implies a different bidding to praise, not on the part of the earth but on the part of Israel itself. This suggests that once again the psalm combines teaching and praise. Its ultimate aim is to get the congregation itself to take the God of the exodus seriously.

As well as coming in pairs, all eight lines are internally parallel, with different phrases in the first colon also applying to the second.[6] The conservative form of the lines thus contrasts with innovative ways of expression.

We do not know what historical context the psalm emerged in, though the last line suggests it belongs after the exile. Nor do we know in what liturgical context it originally belonged; along with Ps. 113 it came to be associated with the major festivals and specifically with Pesah. LXX treats Pss. 114 and 115 as one psalm.[7]

[1]When Israel came out of Egypt,
Jacob's household from a people that jabbers,
[2]Judah became its sanctuary,
Israel its realm.

114:1–2. "Coming out of Egypt" is a standard way to speak of the exodus. The parallel colon expresses the point more distinctively. The people who went down into Egypt were Jacob's literal household (Gen. 46:27); in an extended sense the exodus generation are described thus (Exod. 19:3). But only here are the Egyptians a people that jabbers (indeed, the word comes only here), talking in a way other people cannot understand. It is of course a standard plaint of people in a foreign country. Comments

5. Terrien, *Psalms*, 767.

6. On the psalm's rhetorical features, see P. Auffret, "Notes conjointes sur la structure littéraire des psaumes 114 et 29," *EstBib* 37 (1978): 103–13 (see 103–8); W. S. Prinsloo, "Psalm 114," *JNSL* 18 (1992): 163–76; Uwe F. W. Bauer, "Eine literarische Analyse von Psalm cxiv," *VT* 51 (2001): 289–311.

7. See Hans Lubsczyk, "Einheit und heilsgeschichtliche Bedeutung von Ps 114/115 (113)," *BZ* 11 (1967): 161–73.

about oppressors with a strange language usually come in connection with foreign invasion (e.g., Deut. 28:49; Isa. 28:11; Jer. 5:15). Perhaps the exodus is here portrayed in light of that experience, so that the congregation makes a link between the Egyptians and its current overlords.

But the exodus is the means to an end, of possessing the land. EVV have "Judah became God's sanctuary, Israel his realm," which would fit well with Exod. 19:6. But there is no word for "God" here, nor will there be one until v. 7.[8] There is no other example of a psalm that requires the reader to work out the reference of a suffix thus. Further, there is no other passage where Judah (people or land) is described as Yhwh's sanctuary (*qōdeš*, Yhwh's *holy thing). So it would be doubly hard for readers to work out that Judah is Yhwh's sanctuary. The antecedent for "his/its" is rather "Jacob's household." The holy land of Judah/Israel comes to belong to this family; it is also its realm (cf. Isa. 39:2; Jer. 34:1), the land over which it rules. Set over against each other, sanctuary is a religious or theological notion, realm a political one; in the parallelism the expressions form a hendiadys.

Also set over against each other, Judah might denote the land in the south, Israel the land in the north. Or Judah might denote the whole land as the place where capital and temple were, and Israel might denote the whole land because it was more literally the whole land. Or Judah might denote the land in the south as effectively or theologically the whole land after the united monarchy or after the fall of Samaria, and Israel might then also refer to Judah because Judah *is* the whole land from this perspective.[9]

3The sea saw and fled,
the Jordan would turn back.
4The mountains jumped like rams,
the hills like lambs.

114:3–4. The events in vv. 1–2 are now described in terms of the reactions of two stretches of water. Literally, it was the Egyptians who fled before Israel (Exod. 14:25, 27); but first the sea itself fled. The Jordan likewise stopped abruptly when the Israelites were to cross, the reaction of the Amorites and the Canaanites again being similar to the river's reaction (Josh. 4:24). There was no need for this halting of the Jordan; the river is quite fordable. But it gives the new generation a Red Sea experience of its own (Josh. 4:22). Psalm 77:16 [17] has the waters seeing God; v. 3

8. In LXX the "Praise Yah" from the end of Ps. 113 prefaces Ps. 114, which can solve the problem for LXX.

9. F. pl. "realm" suggests its different parts (cf. the phrase in 103:22); cf. GKC 124b. It would be especially appropriate if "Israel" refers to the whole land, north and south.

does not. By implication, Israel's coming (vv. 1–2) is the event they see and react to, though they can tell there is something supernatural about this coming (again, cf. Exod. 14:25).

Whereas v. 3 builds metaphor on story, v. 4 comprises pure metaphor. Its language parallels Ps. 29. Although jumping can express joy (the verb also means "dance"), here as in Ps. 29 it expresses alarm. Israel's arrival had the same effect on mountains like Hermon as the coming of a thunderstorm; the ground shuddered and shook, jumping in alarm like a frightened deer. (Exod. 19:18 also describes Sinai as quaking; it also might be in mind.) Verses 3–4 become a distinctive example of the Psalms' instinct to describe God's victorious acts in delivering Israel in terms from stories about God's victorious acts in creation, subordinating and ordering the whole world to the divine will (cf. 77:11–20 [12–21]). This generates a vivid, dramatic, and personalized account of events at the Red Sea and the Jordan, which the narratives describe more prosaically (Exod. 15:1–18 is more vivid, though not as vivid as this psalm).[10] More literally, again, it was the Canaanites who jumped in fear.

> [5]What was with you, sea, that you would flee,
> Jordan, that you would turn back,
> [6]You mountains, that you would jump like rams,
> you hills, like lambs?

114:5–6. "What was with you" (lit. "What [was] to you") can be an open, or a sympathetic, or an aggressive question. Here it hardly implies they had no business responding as they did; so it might be quasi-sympathetic, though its subtext is then taunting. The rhetorical question as usual presupposes its answer, at least in general terms. Sea, river, mountain, and hill know that they are not just witnessing an ordinary group of migrants but something of earthshaking significance.

> [7]Tremble, earth, before the Lord,
> before the God of Jacob,
> [8]Who turned the crag into a pool of water,
> basalt into a spring of water.

114:7–8. Presupposing that answer, v. 7 leaps to the implications, at last with some reference to God. Red Sea, Jordan, and the mountains of Sinai or of Syria knew what they were doing. Does the world as whole? The entire earth should quake before Yhwh (cf. 96:9; 97:4) (in

10. Cf. Gerstenberger, *Psalms*, 2:282; also Stephen A. Geller, "The Language of Imagery in Psalm 114," in *Lingering over Words*, ed. Tzvi Abusch and others (W. L. Moran Festschrift; Atlanta: Scholars, 1990), 179–94.

the context, *ʾereṣ* hardly means "land," since the psalm presupposes that the people are already in the land, which has already done its quaking). Another trope is implied. Trembling is the proper response of the whole created world; therefore it is also the proper response of the human world. Yhwh is the Lord, the almighty sovereign; Yhwh is also the God of Jacob (the term forms an inclusion with the opening reference to the people as Jacob's household). "God" is the unusual *ʾĕlôah*, the singular of *ʾĕlōhîm*.

Although the closing line links with Yhwh's being "God of Jacob," its content is a surprise. It offers a very different characterization of Yhwh. Like earlier lines, it refers to Israel's experience with mountains and water, but this crag and water play a very different role from vv. 3–6. The crag now becomes a source of beneficent water. Deuteronomy 8:15 describes how Yhwh produced water from a "basalt crag" (cf. also 32:13; and Exod. 17:6 and Num. 20:10–11). In again dividing the hendiadys, the second colon goes beyond the first in underlining the hardness of the rock. Both cola also use hyperbole: Yhwh did not merely produce water out of the rock but turned the rock into water, and not just into water but into a pool and a spring. Further, "pool of water" and "spring" suggest the transformation involved in the restoration from exile in Babylon (Isa. 41:18). And alongside the overt (though unusual) exhortation in v. 7, the line implies a covert exhortation, a challenge to the congregation to hope in this God.

Theological Implications

The link with Isa. 41:18 just noted points us toward the significance of the strange move in the psalm's last verse, and the significance of the psalm as a whole.[11] As usual, the audience in the house that the psalm has in mind is the Israel/Judah whose story the psalm has spoken of. It lives in a day when Judah and Israel, however understood, are not the holy realm of Jacob's household. Judah is only a shadow of its former self. It is a long time since Israel came out of Egypt, and it is again under the domination of people who jabber in a strange tongue. It is a long time since sea, river, and mountains reacted in the way here described and since the people knew the kind of provision v. 8 describes.[12] But they once did so, and those events remain key determinants of who Israel is, and who Yhwh is. Their job is to believe and hope in that. Yhwh is still the God of the exodus.

11. Cf. Spiekermann, *Heilsgegenwart*, 155–57.
12. Cf. Gunkel, *Psalmen*, 493–95.

Long ago, the experience of the exodus generated a liturgy. Conversely, in the praying of such a psalm in worship, "the liturgy makes the experience available," not least when it has become remote and not part of obvious everyday experience. "The new world was made there and then in the moment of liberation, but it must be made and remade and made again."[13] The psalm contributes to that.

13. Brueggemann, *Israel's Praise*, 44–45.

Psalm 115
God and Other Objects of Trust

Translation

[1]Not to us, Yhwh,
  not to us,
But to your name give honor,
  because of your commitment and your truthfulness.
[2]Why should the nations say,
  "So where is their God?"
[3]But our God is in the heavens;
  everything that he wishes, he has done.
[4]Their images are silver and gold,
  the deed of human hands.
[5]They have a mouth but they do not speak,
  they have eyes but they do not see,
[6]They have ears but they do not hear,
  they have a nose but they do not smell,
[7]Their hands, but they do not feel,
  their feet, but they do not walk about,[1]
  they do not make a sound with their throat.
[8]Their makers become like them,
  everyone who relies on them.

1. GKC 143d sees v. 7a–b as involving extraposition, "as for their hands—they do not feel, as for their feet—they do not walk about." JM 154o rather sees the shortened construction as used for variety after the usual construction in vv. 5–6, which makes it possible to work out that it means "they have hands but . . ." (cf. GKC 147e).

9Israel, rely on Yhwh;
he is their help and their shield.
10Household of Aaron, rely on Yhwh;
he is their help and their shield.
11People who revere Yhwh, rely on Yhwh;
he is their help and their shield.

12Yhwh, who has been mindful of us—he will bless us,[2]
he will bless the household of Israel,
He will bless the household of Aaron,
13he will bless the people who revere Yhwh,
small along with great.

14May Yhwh add to you,
to you and to your descendants.
15You are blessed by Yhwh,
maker of the heavens and the earth.
16The heavens are heavens that belong to Yhwh,
but the earth he gave to human beings.

17The dead do not praise Yah,
not any who go down to silence.
18But we—we will worship Yah,
now and forever.
Praise Yah.[3]

Interpretation

The psalm begins with some ambiguity. Verse 1 might be an act of praise, or it might imply that the people need Yhwh to take action, and thus be the opening to a prayer psalm. Conversely, v. 2 suggests a prayer psalm, yet vv. 3–8 give a contrary impression. The psalm is something between a praise psalm and a prayer psalm, a psalm of trust: see vv. 9–11. Verses 12–13 and 14–16 then focus on blessing, while vv. 17–18 make a commitment to ongoing praise.[4] The psalm implies a situation of vulnerability, and a need for Yhwh to bless, but not a situation of desperate need. One can imagine it being prayed in the circumstances of the restoration community in the fifth century.[5]

2. The suffix on the first verb carries over to the second.
3. LXX attaches v. 18c to the next psalm.
4. On rhetorical patterns in the psalm, see Auffret, *Merveilles à nos yeux*, 148–61.
5. See Walter Beyerlin, *Im Licht der Traditionen*, VTSup 45 (Leiden: Brill, 1992), 51–137.

It gives more concrete indications than most psalms of being a liturgy in which several voices contribute.[6] In v. 1 "we" address Yhwh; in vv. 2–8 "we" speak about Yhwh; vv. 9–11 address Israel in general, the priests, and people who revere Yhwh; in vv. 12–13 "we" speak about these groups; vv. 14–15 (and perhaps v. 16) address "you"; in vv. 17–18b "we" speak and express determination; v. 18c is a closing exhortation. There are various ways of interpreting these data, but perhaps vv. 1–8 are congregational prayer and praise, while the remainder represents dialogue between minister and congregation. The minister speaks in vv. 9–11 with an exhortation and in vv. 14–16 with a wish; the congregation responds in vv. 12–13 and 17–18. Further, in vv. 9–11 the move to third person in each second colon may mean a minister utters each first colon and the choir joins in with the second. Other parts of the psalm might also have been sung thus antiphonally, while the parts expressing the congregation's attitude might actually be voiced by the choir.

L, 4QPs°, LXX, and Jerome join Ps. 115 with Ps. 114. In Pss. 113–18 this is the only transition from one psalm to another not marked by "Praise Yah" (closing one psalm or beginning the next); perhaps this explains why two separate psalms came to be run together.

115:1–8. The psalm begins with the community's plea, in its way an act of praise. Its background will come in v. 2, with a response in vv. 3–8.

1Not to us, Yhwh,
  not to us,
But to your name give honor,
  because of your commitment and your truthfulness.

The opening plea is quite distinctive. It does not ask for Yhwh to listen, and only indirectly for Yhwh to act on the people's behalf. Perhaps one reason is that (to judge from the psalm as a whole) the community is not in crisis. But the plea's presupposition is that the community could reasonably aspire to *honor, but lacks it (see, e.g., Hos. 4:7; 9:11, where the reason is the people's rebellion against Yhwh). Yet its plea does not concern its own honor but Yhwh's. (Of course action designed to affirm Yhwh's honor will also affirm Israel's.) The plea's content, though not its formulation, compares with passages such as Ezek. 36:22–23. The formulation, but not the content, compares with Isa. 42:8; 48:11, where Yhwh speaks of not giving honor to another god or to an image; that will make for a link with vv. 4–8.

6. See, e.g., K. Luke, "The Setting of Psalm 115," *ITQ* 34 (1967): 347–57.

If Yhwh acts with characteristic *commitment and *truthfulness, honor will follow. These characteristics express the essence of who Yhwh is, of what the *name Yhwh signifies.

> 2Why should the nations say,
> "So where is their God?"

Whereas v. 1 might imply an attitude of worshipful submission, the question "Why?" often belongs in a psalm of protest and plea (e.g., 42:9 [10]; 43:2). The congregation's words thus carry another unstated implication, that the nations do or could ask the question that follows in v. 2b. This compares with the questions in 42:3, 10 [4, 11]; Joel 2:17; Mic. 7:10; it is identical with that in Ps. 79:10 (except for the addition of the enclitic *-nāʾ*, "now"). One can imagine the restoration community in its unflourishing state asking the question, and imagine that the question attributed to the nations is actually the community's own. Yet the psalm never refers to reversals from which people need to be restored. Perhaps the line refers to a possibility that is real, but theoretical. Or it might indicate that whether the question is real or actual, it need not be taken too seriously; vv. 3–8 will imply that. In other words, the context of v. 2 is not the usual one in which such questions occur. Here, the question compares in particular with 2:1 in its context:[7] "Why should/do the nations say . . ." implies, "After all, it will get them nowhere."

> 3But our God is in the heavens;
> everything that he wishes, he has done.

The implication is similar. The nations' rhetorical question is treated as if it were a real question and given an answer; it will also be turned back on them in a moment. Yes, Yhwh can be located. Yhwh is not everywhere, and not located in human hearts, or in the temple, or in the company of believers, or in what human beings take with absolute seriousness. Yhwh may be in all those places, but the important affirmation in the context (and a fundamental one throughout the OT) is that God is in the heavens. This does not make God remote and uninvolved; it is "our" God who is there. It does mean God is not limited to (for instance) the realm of personal piety. Yhwh sits in a position of authority over the earth.

The second colon spells this out. Whatever Yhwh wishes, Yhwh has done. The formulation parallels the description of the king's power in Eccles. 8:3, though there both verbs are yiqtol (cf. Yhwh's statement

7. Cf. Beyerlin, *Im Licht der Traditionen*, 65.

in Isa. 46:10). As a declaration about Yhwh, the qatal statement parallels Ps. 135:6 (also Jon. 1:14).[8] Whether we translate the first, stative verb as present or past, it is natural to translate the qatal *ʿāśâ* as past. The colon does not make an abstract comment on Yhwh's sovereignty but a concrete statement about Yhwh's actual activity. Given the nature of Israel's experience with Yhwh, it is a bold statement. It leads Calvin,[9] following Augustine, into more bold (though perhaps unwise) statements about God willing and not merely permitting ills that happen.

> 4Their images are silver and gold,
> the deed of human hands.

Here is the contrast between that God and the gods the nations implicitly laud over against Yhwh with astonishing chutzpah; "their images" stands over against "our God" (v. 3a).[10] Further, "the deed [*maʿăśēh*] of human hands" stands over against "everything that he wishes, he has done [*ʿāśâ*]" (v. 3b). Typically, the OT takes the visible nature of divine images as a reliable guide to the gods' own nature and declares that the emperor has no clothes.[11] Philosophers distinguish between the image and what it represents, but the two easily get confused (like our statements of faith and the God they seek to describe). Further, the point about an image is to represent and mediate the god's presence; the psalm simply takes that claim seriously. Come on, it says, for all the monetary value of their raw material, images are made by human beings. How can they represent God? The polemic point is often developed, most systematically in Isa. 44:9–20; vv. 4–6 themselves also substantially reappear as Ps. 135:15–18 (cf. also the brief formulation in Deut. 4:28).[12] On "image," see on 106:36: "They are called *ʿṣbym* because they bring *ʿṣbwn* [pain] to those who rely on them, who are not delivered by them."[13]

> 5They have a mouth but they do not speak,
> they have eyes but they do not see,
> 6They have ears but they do not hear,
> they have a nose but they do not smell,
> 7Their hands, but they do not feel,

8. Avi Hurvitz ("The History of a Legal Formula," *VT* 32 [1982]: 257–67) argues that the expression has a legal background.

9. *Psalms*, 4:344–46.

10. Kraus, *Psalms 60–150*, 380.

11. Cf. Kidner, *Psalms*, 2:405.

12. LXX expands the psalm's text from Ps. 135.

13. Qimchi.

their feet, but they do not walk about,
they do not make a sound with their throat.

The difference between the nations' gods and Yhwh is not that the gods have body parts but Yhwh is spiritual. It is that Yhwh has body parts that work (eyes, lips, ears, hands, a face, even a shape: see, for instance, Ps. 17) rather than body parts that do not. "Each of the seven times that the negation *lo'* lashes out at them, one of the faculties is destroyed."[14] Yhwh can speak through prophets, see what Israel is doing and act accordingly, listen to Israel's prayers, smell its offerings, hold and support and touch, and walk about in Israel's midst or with it on its journeying.[15] Although its makers reckoned their gods could do those things, the gods' representations suggest they cannot. Given vv. 3–7, the nations have no right to ask the question in v. 2b.[16]

The last colon makes v. 7 into a tricolon and signals that this little polemic is coming to an end. Its significance is harder to discern, as it hardly refers simply to speaking (the verb's usual meaning), which would repeat v. 5a. Perhaps it refers to the sound of breathing (cf. 135:17).[17]

8Their makers become like them,
everyone who relies on them.

In a nice inference, the psalm declares that the image makers end up like the images, or will do so, or should do so (LXX and Jerome take the verb as jussive); they, too, end up unable to act, speak, and so on, and the same is true of the people who come to trust in the images they produce. Perhaps the logic is that a people requires gods to defend it and prevent it being annihilated. Such gods cannot do that. "Their makers" (*'ōśêhem*) again takes up the root *'āśâ* (cf. vv. 3b, 4b).

115:9–11. If Israel speaks in vv. 1–8, here it is addressed, presumably by a minister. "Relies" (v. 8) is picked up and becomes key to this next section. Even in a context when Yhwh is not bringing honor on his name (vv. 1–2), the facts about Yhwh (v. 3) set over against the facts about the gods represented by images (vv. 4–8) make trust in Yhwh appropriate.

9Israel, rely on Yhwh;
he is their help and their shield.
10Household of Aaron, rely on Yhwh;

14. Fokkelman, *Major Poems*, 3:225.
15. Cf. Gunkel, *Psalmen*, 497.
16. Cf. Kraus, *Psalms 60–150*, 380.
17. So Bratcher and Reyburn, *Handbook on the Psalms*, 973.

he is their help and their shield.
[11]People who revere Yhwh, rely on Yhwh;
he is their help and their shield.

Three groups are addressed, the entire people, the priests, and the people who *revere Yhwh (cf. 118:2–4; 135:19 adds "household of Levi"). The last usually describes Israel as whole (cf. 22:23 [24]), in which case it repeats v. 9, or brings together both laypeople (v. 9) and priests (v. 10).[18] In due course, "people who revere Yhwh" is a term for Gentiles who associate themselves with the worship of Yhwh without quite becoming Jews (see Acts 10:2, 22, 35).[19] The OT does assume that Gentiles can come to commit themselves to Yhwh, but it does not elsewhere describe them as "people who revere Yhwh."

All three groups are challenged to rely on Yhwh. In the modern world, our temptation would be to rely on ourselves, to reckon that we need to be responsible for our destiny. In a traditional culture, the temptation is to rely on other deities. This fact lies behind the movement in the psalm. Reliance on images is stupid (v. 8); reliance on Yhwh makes sense because Yhwh is both *help and shield, proactive in doing what needs to be done, protective in defending people from attack and pressure.

LXX and Jerome have finite verbs declaring that the three groups have trusted or do trust in Yhwh, which removes the harsh transition to third person in each second colon. But that transition may reflect the movements of antiphonal singing, or may simply reflect Hebrew poetry's ease in coping with such movement between cola.

115:12–13. The return to speech in "we" form suggests a response to the exhortation in vv. 9–11, though people do then go on to refer to themselves in the third person in vv. 12b–13a. They do so affirmatively. Verses 12c–13a, not v. 12, are more likely the tricolon in these two lines, closing them off with its extra phrase (v. 13b) as v. 7c closed off vv. 4–7.

[12]Yhwh, who has been mindful of us—he will bless us,
he will bless the household of Israel,
He will bless the household of Aaron,
[13]he will bless the people who revere Yhwh,
small along with great.

While Yhwh's past *mindfulness might be that embodied in Israel's earlier history, this would be an allusive way of making that point. Perhaps people are declaring the conviction that Yhwh has heard the plea

18. Cf. Joachim Becker, *Gottesfurcht im Alten Testament* (Rome: Pontifical Bible Institute, 1965), 155–60.

19. Cf. Rashi; Gunkel, *Psalmen*, 497–98.

with which the psalm opened, so that "Yhwh has been mindful of us" is "the turning point and the psychological crux of this psalm."[20] But the oddity of the expression in v. 12a (subject, qatal verb, asyndetic yiqtol verb)[21] suggests that the emphasis rather lies on the last verb, and its repetition in vv. 12b–13a supports this. Nevertheless v. 12 does correspond to the two aims of a plea, for Yhwh to listen (so Yhwh has been mindful) and to act (so Yhwh is sure to bless).

"Small along with great" suggests ordinary people or peasants and important people or landowners (cf. Deut. 1:17; Job 3:19; Jer. 6:13).

115:14–16. Once more speaker and addressees change. The speaker will again be the minister and the "you" the people addressed in vv. 9–11 who spoke in vv. 12–13; the verses respond to their statement of faith.

[14]May Yhwh add to you,
to you and to your descendants.
[15]You are blessed by Yhwh,
maker of the heavens and the earth.
[16]The heavens are heavens that belong to Yhwh,
the earth he gave to human beings.

Oftentimes, not least in the Persian period, Israel's problem is that it is small. It needs increase (cf. the exilic promises in Isa. 54). Blessing therefore needs to work itself out in numerical increase, a regular central significance of the idea of blessing (e.g., Gen. 1:22, 28). The minister prays that this may happen, in this generation and in the future, though he makes the point in the third person because he is actually speaking to the people for whom he is praying (cf. Eph. 1:15–23).

EVV translate v. 15 as a further wish.[22] It is implicitly that, insofar as this principle would lie behind the increase for which v. 14 explicitly prayed. But v. 15 is a statement, a declarative or performative one like "your sins are forgiven." It closely parallels Gen. 14:19, also a performative statement, where Melchizedek also goes on to describe Yhwh as possessor (?) of the heavens and the earth. Perhaps, then, this is a formula; it would be an apposite one. It is the maker of the heavens and the earth who is in a position to bless people in the world; "maker" (*ʿōśēh*) again makes a link with the earlier use of this root in the psalm (vv. 3b, 4b, 8a).

Verse 16 adds further to the rationale underlying vv. 14–15. Humanity cannot pretend to reach into Yhwh's realm, but the heavens belong to Yhwh as their maker, and that again underlines the cosmos-wide

20. Reuven Hammer, "Two Liturgical Psalms," *Judaism* 40 (1991): 482–510 (see 487).
21. Cf. Fokkelman, *Major Poems*, 3:225.
22. JM 132f declares that the expression always has optative meaning.

sovereignty that means Yhwh can act throughout that cosmos (cf. v. 3). Yhwh is "the God of the heavens" (e.g., Ezra 5:11–12; Neh. 1:4–5). It also means Yhwh can allocate sovereignty in the cosmos. Yhwh chooses to do that by giving sovereignty over the earth to humanity (cf. Gen. 1:28; Ps. 8:7–9). The allusion to this aspect of Gen. 1 meshes with the reference to blessing in the form of increase. In other words, the minister declares that the people will be able to fulfill their human vocation. Perhaps it also suggests that this increase will mean Judah growing not merely by the natural process of birth but through other people coming to acknowledge Yhwh.[23]

115:17–18. One final time "we" respond.

> [17]The dead do not praise Yah,
> not any who go down to silence.

The realm of the dead is within Yhwh's sovereignty, but the dead cannot *praise Yhwh. Yhwh does not choose to be active in their realm, so there is nothing for them to confess (Ps. 6). They also have the problem of lacking a working mouth and a body; people who cannot make a noise or move their hands and feet cannot worship. People who go down to the grave (the verb reflects the fact that when we die we are put under the earth) go down to silence (LXX paraphrases as Hades, or Sheol, Tg as "the house of the grave of the earth"). The grave is a very quiet place (cf. 94:17). There is nothing to say there, and no means of saying it.

> [18]But we—we will worship Yah,
> now and forever.
> Praise Yah.

So we should make the most of life, of the opportunity to *worship Yhwh now (worship, like praise, being a body word, one that implies bending the knee). "Worship" and "bless" (vv. 12–16) represent the same Hebrew word *bārak*, which symbolizes the mutual relationship of God and humanity.[24] In what sense can people reckon to worship forever? LXX glosses "we" with "who are alive," which suggests that it means throughout their life;[25] or perhaps they think of themselves as part of

23. So Beyerlin, *Im Licht der Traditionen*, 115–16.

24. Magdalene L. Frettlöh, "Gott segnen," *EvT* 56 (1996): 482–510; hence a disadvantage of rendering the verb differently according to whether God or human beings are the subject.

25. Norbert Lohfink argues that this and other LXX additions to the psalm reflect Deuteronomy (see "Ps 114/115 [M und G] und die deuteronomische Sprachwelt," in *Freude an der Weisung des Herrn*, ed. Haag and Hossfeld, 199–205).

the community that will continue to worship God forever, even when the present generation is dead and silent.

The closing "*Praise *Yah" means that both v. 18a–b and v. 18c in effect end the psalm by declaring the intention to give honor to Yhwh, the act that it urged on Yhwh at the beginning. It expresses the attitude that was implicit in that urging.

Theological Implications

In a traditional society, the people of God are tempted to rely on images or offerings; in a modern society, they are tempted to reckon that they are responsible for their own destiny. The psalm's "resounding negation"[26] directly undermines the first recourse and indirectly undermines the second. How foolish to rely on something humanly made! If there were no alternative, there would be no alternative, and modernity assumes that this is so. The psalm urges people to reckon that there is indeed an alternative, reliance on the one who is the God of the heavens and of the earth. He is the one who blesses.

26. James L. Crenshaw, *The Psalms* (Grand Rapids: Eerdmans, 2001), 128.

Psalm 116

How to Give Your Testimony (II)

Translation

1I dedicate myself, because Yhwh would listen[1]
to my voice, my plea,[2]
2Because he has bent his ear to me;
yes, through my days[3] I will call out.

3The ropes of death encompassed me,
the restraints of Sheol found me.
I would find constraint and sorrow
4and would call out in Yhwh's name,
"Oh now, Yhwh,
save my life!"
5Yhwh is gracious and faithful,
our God is one who shows compassion.
6Yhwh watches over simple people;
I sank low, and he would deliver me.

1. Qatal *šāmaʿ* would be an easier reading than *yišmaʿ*, though that could be dittog.
2. Jerome implies a construct, "my pleading voice"; the ending will then be another example of connective *-î* (cf. 113:5–9). In v. 1 the first two and last two words all end *-î*.
3. For MT *ûbĕyāmay*, Syr implies *ûbĕyôm*, "on the day I would call," conforming the text to the more familiar expression.

7Turn, my spirit, to your complete rest,[4]
because Yhwh—he has dealt with you.
8Because you have pulled away my life from death,
my eye from tears, my foot from being pushed down.[5]
9I shall walk about before Yhwh
in the lands of the living.

10I trusted, because[6] I would speak:
"I—I have become very weak";[7]
11I—I said in my trepidation,
"Every human being deceives."

12What shall I return to Yhwh
for all his dealings with me?[8]
13I will take up the chalice of deliverance[9]
and call out in Yhwh's name.
14I will fulfill my vows to Yhwh,
yes, right before[10] all his people.
15Valuable in Yhwh's eyes
is the death[11] of people committed to him.
16Oh now, Yhwh,
because I am your servant,
I am your servant, the son of your maid;

4. "Rest" is pl. (cf. 23:2, though there the more usual f. form). Each word in the colon ends -*î*; the lengthened suffix reappears on "with you" and looks like an Aramaism (JM 94i).

5. The line incorporates five more -*î* endings.

6. LXX's "therefore" (cf. 2 Cor. 4:13) for *kî* may reflect inner-Greek corruption (Allen, *Psalms 101–150*, 152), though Kraus (*Psalms 60–150*, 387) defends it. *HALOT* takes *kî* to mean "that" (cf. Lam. 4:12), but this is difficult in the context; rather, the verb is used absolutely (so *DCH*), like the opening verb in the psalm. It is questionable whether *kî* ever means "although" (against Dahood, *Psalms*, 3:148).

7. Tg takes the verb not as *ʿānâ* III but as *ʿānâ* IV ("sing") and thus takes the whole line as referring to praise; but the *mĕʾōd* (very, much) is then difficult.

8. The suffix -*ôhî* again looks like an Aramaism (GKC 91l; JM 94i).

9. *Yĕšûʿôt* is pl., or a Phoenician-style sg.

10. For the -*â* ending on *negdâ-nāʾ*, see GKC 90f; JM 93c. It is yet another example of an additional sufformative and thus not very troublesome in this psalm; it extends the assonance with *nĕdāray* at the beginning of the first colon. BDB describes *nāʾ* as "a particle of entreaty," but while it usually follows an entreaty, its own function is to add emotional force (cf. *HALOT*), usually to a verb, but this occurrence again compares with the compound *ʾānnâ* in vv. 4, 16, making it, too, not so troublesome. Tg associates *ngdh* with the *nāgad*, suggesting another commitment to proclamation (Stec, *Targum*, 208); Briggs (*Psalms*, 2:400–401) follows. Gary A. Rendsburg and J. P. Fokkelman ("נגדה נא לכל עמו," *VT* 53 [2003]: 328–36) associate the word with the Aramaic *nāgad*, "lead."

11. *Hammāwet* has another -*â* ending, serving simply to lengthen the word (see GKC 90f; JM 93i). See P. C. H. Wernberg-Møller, "The Old Accusative Case Ending in Biblical Hebrew," *JSS* 33 (1988): 155–64 (see 155–56).

you have loosed my bonds.[12]
17To you I will sacrifice a thank-offering
and call out in Yhwh's name.
18I will fulfill my vows to Yhwh,
yes, right before all his people,
19In the courts of Yhwh's house,
in the midst of Jerusalem.[13]
Praise Yah.[14]

Interpretation

The psalm is an individual's thanksgiving (the verbs sometimes address Yhwh) or testimony (they are often third person, addressing the congregation to proclaim Yhwh's action).[15] In due course qatal verbs (e.g., vv. 2a, 3a–b, 7b, 8) make clear that the worshipper indeed recounts a past experience of being afflicted, of praying, and of Yhwh responding and acting to deliver. Interwoven with these qatal verbs are yiqtols (e.g., vv. 1, 2b, 3c–4) referring to the same past events; I translate them by the modal expression "would" to mark the difference from the qatals, but the difference is purely rhetorical. While the speaker might be a leader such as the king rather than an ordinary person, there are no concrete pointers to that.

Verses 1–2 begin by summarizing the testimony to Yhwh's responsiveness. Verses 3–6 go behind that attentiveness to the predicament out of which the worshipper prayed, then go forward to the act of deliverance that issued from the attentiveness, affirming that it was an expression of Yhwh's habitual way of being and acting. Verses 7–9 then constitute a statement of confidence about the future. Verses 10–11 take us back to the beginning in reflecting again on what the worshipper went through. LXX and Jerome divide the psalm at this point into two psalms, solving the problem of the strange reversion to recollection (if it be a problem). Verses 1–9 would indeed work on their own, though vv. 10–19 hardly do so. But the splitting does point us toward the psalm's structure: vv. 1–9 and vv. 10–19 are broadly parallel, each beginning the same way, the first focusing more on Yhwh's action, the second more on the worshipper's

12. The prep. introducing the object looks like an Aramaism (GKC 117n).

13. GKC 91e; JM 94h see the ending on the prep. *bĕtôkēkî* as a feminine pronominal suffix, another apparent Aramaism, but the direct address to Jerusalem is odd in the context. Rather *tôkēk* is a reduplicated form of *tôk* (cf. the PBH words listed in *DTT*, 1668), and the *-î* is again the connective noted at 113:7–8 (cf. Allen, *Psalms 101–150*, 152).

14. LXX attaches v. 19c to the next psalm.

15. See Crüsemann, *Studien zur Formgeschichte*, 210–84 (esp. 243–46).

response.[16] The double form corresponds to that of the thanksgiving/testimony in Ps. 30 and some other praise and prayer psalms. After the renewed recollection, vv. 12–19b are an extended commitment (itself doubled) to public testimony to Yhwh's deliverance, with v. 19c a closing bidding to praise.[17] Verses 12–19b might imply that the psalm would accompany a thank-offering on an occasion when a crowd would be present (cf. Jer. 33:11), though we need not infer that "all his people" must imply one of the annual festivals.[18]

Some distinctive expressions are usually taken as Aramaisms,[19] and the psalm has close verbal links with other psalms (e.g., Pss. 18 and 56). These phenomena may indicate that it belongs in the postexilic period.

116:1–2. In the opening preliminary testimony to Yhwh's responding to prayer, the two verses make the same point, but the second reverses the order, so that they work *abb'a'*. Overlapping with that structure is the sequence of verbs, qatal with present reference, yiqtol with past reference, qatal with past reference, yiqtol with future reference.

[1]I dedicate myself, because Yhwh would listen
to my voice, my plea,
[2]Because he has bent his ear to me;
yes, through my days I will call out.

Yhwh is presumably the implicit object of the verb "*dedicate myself (to)," but the worshipper leaves the verb without object. It is at least suggestive that there is no point in the Bible when someone says that they dedicate themselves to or love God. The Bible's reticence in this regard is remarkable when compared with the ease with which modern Christians profess their love for God, though of course the Bible does urge us to love God in the sense of dedicating ourselves in this way (e.g., 31:23 [24]). Here, in any case, focus lies on the actions that drew the worshipper's self-giving. When we are in difficulties and we pray, our first need is for Yhwh to listen to our *plea, and Yhwh has done so. EVV have "because Yhwh listens" for the yiqtol, but the yiqtols in vv. 3c–4 have past reference, and here the qatal verb in v. 2a supports the idea that the same is true in v. 1a. The worshipper is beginning the testimony that the psalm will elaborate.

16. Cf. Michael L. Barré, "Psalm 116," *JBL* 109 (1990): 61–78; Jean Marcel Vincent, "'Qu'est-ce que la théologie,'" *RB* 107 (2000): 495–525.

17. On rhetorical patterns in the psalm, see W. S. Prinsloo, "Psalm 116," *Bib* 74 (1993): 71–82.

18. See further Mowinckel, *Psalms*, 2:31–43.

19. See notes on vv. 7, 12, and 16. Rendsburg (*Linguistic Evidence*, 83–86) suggests that the supposed Aramaisms are indications that the psalm is written in northern Hebrew.

The restatement in v. 2a gives no extra information, but by using the vivid image of Yhwh's head being inclined and Yhwh's ear bent in order to be fully attentive, it conveys more strongly the impression that Yhwh's listening made, its importance, and the way it drew love. In turn the second clause parallels the psalm's opening statement. The worshipper's dedication to Yhwh will be expressed in an ongoing proclamation; calling out here suggests confession (cf. vv. 13 and 17; contrast v. 4). "Through my days" (*bĕyāmay*) comes only here; but compare expressions such as "through my life" (*bĕḥayyāy*) in 104:33; 146:2.[20]

116:3–6. The psalm looks behind the prayer that vv. 1–2 recalled, and then forward beyond that to the act of deliverance that followed on Yhwh's listening, and embodied the truths Israel knew about Yhwh's character and characteristic action. Perhaps this is the content of the "calling out" of v. 2.

> 3a–bThe ropes of death encompassed me,
> the restraints of Sheol found me.

As usual, the psalm gives virtually no hard information on the peril from which the worshipper needed rescue. Indeed, v. 3a simply repeats 18:4a [5a], while v. 3b corresponds more generally to the cola that follow there.[21] The description begins from the fact that it was deathly danger. It was as if Death were a hunter throwing ropes over his prey in order to capture it. The second colon restates the point. *Sheol had gone looking for this prey, found it, and put it under confinement. At least, that was how it seemed. The constraining ropes were around the worshipper, and it looked impossible to evade their power.

LXX points to a different way of reading the line as a whole. Whereas Jerome takes *ḥeblê* as from *ḥebel*, meaning "rope," so that *mĕṣārê* will then suggest "restraints," LXX has the "pains" of death encompassing me, taking *ḥeblê* as from *ḥēbel* (cf. Tg); the parallel noun *mĕṣārê* will then suggest "torments" (NJPS).

> 3cI would find constraint and sorrow
> 4and would call out in Yhwh's name,
> "Oh now, Yhwh,
> save my life!"

The first colon neatly reuses roots from v. 3b, "find" and another noun from *ṣārar*. Restraint found him when it was looking for him (v. 3b); he

20. Cf. Allen, *Psalms 101–150*, 152.

21. Among other links is the nice recurrence of "bend" (*nāṭâ* hiphil) in v. 2 and 18:9 [10].

found constraint when he was not looking for it (v. 3c). And the constraint meant sorrow; perhaps it is no coincidence that *yāgôn* can denote the sorrow of death (Gen. 42:38; 44:31), though it is also a more general word for grief (e.g., Pss. 13:2 [3]; 107:39). (As "constraint" follows neatly from Jerome's reading of v. 3a–b, "sorrow" follows neatly from LXX's.) Fortunately, being in the grip of Sheol does not preclude calling out to Yhwh (even though in the strict sense Yhwh does not intervene in Sheol, or will not do so for some centuries yet). More literally, the worshipper had called out *in* Yhwh's *name. The psalm will use that expression twice more for proclaiming Yhwh's name (vv. 13, 17). Here, too, it suggests proclaiming who Yhwh is, and therefore urging Yhwh to act in light of the revelation expressed by the name: "Yhwh, in your own name, because of who you have revealed yourself to be, save me."

"Save," *mālaṭ* (piel), is an apposite verb in light of v. 3a–b, as it suggests providing a way of escape, and the reference to "life" matches that in light of the concern with death there.

> 5Yhwh is gracious and faithful,
> our God is one who shows compassion.

The move to a series of statements about Yhwh is a slight surprise, but it, too, is apposite. *Graciousness, *faithfulness, and compassion are the qualities that lay behind the possibility of praying and the fact that Yhwh responded. They are the qualities denoted by the name "Yhwh" (cf. Exod. 34:6). The description of this God as "our God" further invites the listeners to this testimony to keep recalling why it is given. This worshipper's experience is not a random one. Everyone is invited to see this God as "our God."

> 6Yhwh watches over simple people;
> I sank low, and he would deliver me.

After the qualities that are very familiar, the psalm segues to a much more distinctive description. Verse 6a could be a dangerous statement; the job of the simple is to grow out of it (Prov. 1:22). But we also speak positively of people with a simple faith. The worshipper was such a person, and found that Yhwh watches over such people (when they are not simply being irresponsible?). The second colon suggests that the verse as a whole once more restates v. 3a–b. The worshipper was once again on the way down to Sheol, all but there; but Yhwh *delivered.

116:7–9. The psalm returns to the present and comments on the new attitude to life that deliverance made possible.

> [7]Turn, my spirit, to your complete rest,
> because Yhwh—he has dealt with you.

The self-challenge is unique; it stands between exhortations such as 42:5 [6] in a prayer psalm, and 103:1 in a praise psalm. It lacks the urgency of 42:5 [6] because the crisis is over, but it is only recently over. The normal state of the spirit or *person is rest, the opposite of strife, toil, and turmoil. But after a crisis it takes a little while for the spirit to catch up with the relief that has come. But feelings can afford to catch up with the facts the second colon affirms. The temple itself can be referred to as Yhwh's place of rest (e.g., 132:8, 14), and it might be the place of rest where someone returns after being delivered from death; but the notion of rest is not used thus elsewhere.

For *gāmal ʿal* in v. 7b, EVV have "been good to," which is the implication, but the verb itself suggests taking the appropriate action in relation to someone; it is the context that decides whether the action is positive or negative.

> [8]Because you have pulled away my life from death,
> my eye from tears, my foot from being pushed down.

Verses 8–9 are similar to 56:13 [14] and follow that psalm's form in speaking directly to Yhwh. But there are detailed verbal differences, and the context is tellingly different. The earlier version closes a prayer psalm and represents the testimony the suppliant looks forward to offering. Here the worshipper can give that testimony. Following that precedent, the verb (*ḥālaṣ* piel) differs from that in v. 4, but the implication is similar and fits with the earlier portrayal of death; Yhwh did not let death finally take hold of the person. The last phrase has similar significance; death means losing one's footing in life and tumbling into the grave, into Sheol. Yhwh halted this process. In this context the middle phrase will refer to tears of grief (cf. Isa. 25:8; Lam. 1:2), though some transference of meaning would be needed if they are the tears of the person who dies rather than those of mourners.

> [9]I shall walk about before Yhwh
> in the lands of the living.

Having been rescued from death, the worshipper is in a position to enjoy life. The hitpael verb ("walk about") links well with the reference to rest in v. 7. The worshipper can now relax and enjoy life, the threat of death having been removed. But the prepositional phrase is at least as important. Death means separation from Yhwh, because Yhwh chooses not to get involved in Sheol. Life means being in Yhwh's presence. The whole of life is lived before Yhwh, literally to the *face of Yhwh, under Yhwh's caring and beneficent gaze. It is not the deathly nonlife, the mere existence, of Sheol, but the real life lived before God, which takes place "in the lands of the living." Whereas vv. 8–9 as a whole are a variant on 56:13 [14], this last expression recalls 27:13, though there "land" is singular. The plural again underlines the wonder of this contrast and of the fullness of life that Yhwh gives in this life, an entrancing range of scenarios for the living of life.

116:10–11. As the second half of the psalm begins, in a way parallel to vv. 1–2, the worshipper again looks back.

> **10**I trusted, because I would speak:
> "I—I have become very weak";
> **11**I—I said in my trepidation,
> "Every human being deceives."

Like vv. 1–2, these paired lines open with a qatal verb that one expects to have an object but is actually absolute and refers to the present as well as the past,[22] and is followed by a *kî* clause, then by a yiqtol verb with past reference. In vv. 10–11 as a whole this act of trust is set in connection and contrast with a series of pressures on it, or pressures that led to it. The speaker had to be trustful because there was nowhere else to turn. No doubt Yhwh is the object of the trust, but the emphasis lies on the confidence despite the pressures—or rather, because of them; the "because" in v. 10a thus applies to the whole of vv. 10b–11.

At first sight it would seem that v. 10b is not the content of what the worshipper "spoke"; *dibbēr* does not usually introduce a statement in that way (despite NRSV, TNIV; contrast NJPS). Usually the gerund "saying" mediates between such a verb and the person's words (cf. 105:11). Here the "I said" in v. 11a follows up the "I would speak" in v. 10a, and both the declarations in vv. 10b and 11b constitute the content of that speaking/saying. Prosaically put, "I came to trust because I spoke, saying in my trepidation, 'I have become very weak and every human being deceives.'" Verse 11a corresponds to 31:22a [23a].

The meaning of the opening verb *ʾāman* (hiphil) is hard to articulate, and the sparseness of hints from the context makes that especially difficult here. But the influence of 27:13 at the end of the preceding line puts us on the track of the word's specific nuance, since this actual verb

22. NJPS makes this simply a statement of present trust, but it is hard to justify that as a translation of the qatal of this fientive verb (contrast the stative with which the psalm opens), especially as it goes on to translate the yiqtol *ʾădabbēr* "I spoke."

form also comes there. The confidence expressed in v. 9 was the confidence the worshipper affirmed when going through the ordeal the psalm refers back to. Psalm 27 nuances it further by speaking of a confidence in seeing good from Yhwh in the land of the living, and that nuance makes sense here.[23]

*Weakness in v. 10b suggests not something internal and subjective but something external and objective, a powerlessness in relation to other people. The parallel colon, v. 11b, again spells that out. Weakness logically issues in trepidation or alarm and the instinct to get out of here as quickly as possible (*ḥāpaz*; cf. 48:5 [6]; 104:7). The two cola thus give some further indication of the affliction, the factors suggesting that death threatened.

Perhaps v. 11a implies that "every human being deceives" was an overreaction,[24] but for practical purposes, that was how it was. The statement could be a forceful expression of the sense that everyone is against the worshipper and is using all sorts of deceptive and dishonest methods of attack. That devastatingly compounds the implications of powerlessness; and it was this that delivered the worshipper into the arms of Sheol. But "every human being deceives" could imply a different assertion: even if there are people who are "for" the worshipper, that is no use. Human help always tends to disappoint, like a spring that fails (Isa. 58:11), and when the situation is as serious as this, it is especially bound to disappoint. The declaration that human beings always let one down thus stands in contrast to the fact that God does not do so (89:35 [36]; Num. 23:19). This comment then makes for a neat frame around the two lines. "I trusted," because while human beings always end up disappointing, Yhwh does not do so; and fortunately, it was Yhwh "I" was relying on.

116:12–19. The closing section asks about the appropriate response to Yhwh's act of deliverance. It divides into two. A question (v. 12) leads into a declaration of intent (vv. 13–14). Then statements of conviction (vv. 15–16) lead into a reformulated declaration of intent (vv. 17–19b, much of whose content repeats that of vv. 13–14) and a final bidding to praise (v. 19c).

12What shall I return to Yhwh
for all his dealings with me?

The question takes up the statement in v. 7b; the verb "return" also takes up the opening verb in v. 7. There is some internal turning that

23. Cf. Kirkpatrick, *Psalms*, 690.

24. Th. Booij ("Psalm 116,10–11," *Bib* 76 [1995]: 388–95) sees vv. 10–11 as a whole as recalling a crisis of confidence, of which this is part.

the worshipper needs to do. There is also some external turning, and the nature of that will be indicated in what follows.

> [13]I will take up the chalice of deliverance
> and call out in Yhwh's name.
> [14]I will fulfill my vows to Yhwh,
> yes, right before all his people.

In this first answer to the question, the *deliverance chalice might be the libation offered in connection with various worship occasions, including sacrifices made in fulfillment of a promise (Num. 15:1–10). The worshipper's task is to take up this chalice, perhaps in the way Western people raise their glass, yet not to drink from it but to pour it away as an indication that one is offering it to God (e.g., Gen. 35:14; Num. 28:7), like the sacrifices that were given wholly to Yhwh without the offerer sharing in them at all. Admittedly the word "chalice" does not come elsewhere in connection with libations, and the deliverance chalice might be like the chalices later passed around at Pesah or other festive meals, including a thanksgiving meal, chalices from which the offerer drank. They are analogous to the offerings that offerer and Yhwh shared (like those at a thanksgiving, indeed). Either way, there is some encouragement in being able to speak of a deliverance chalice.

As usual sacrament and word accompany one another. Like facts, sacraments without words are blind, while words without facts or sacraments are empty. There is a fruitful and necessary alliance between the two.[25] A verbal declaration of gratefulness without an expression of it that costs something would not be very impressive, but a concrete expression of gratefulness unaccompanied by interpretation would not give clear enough glory to Yhwh. So, as well as taking up the deliverance cup in honor of Yhwh, the worshipper calls out in Yhwh's *name. The expression referred to prayers in vv. 2 and 4; now it refers to praises or proclamation. The two accompany each other. Prayer is a public calling out that puts Yhwh on notice; thanksgiving is a public calling out that confesses what Yhwh has done. The worshipper thus fulfills the promises made in connection with the prayer, and does so (as is necessary) "right before all his people."

As one of the Hallel Psalms, Ps.116 was part of the observances that involved sharing four cups at Pesah (see *m. Pesaḥim* 10). This practice continued into Christian observance of the Lord's Supper, which involved

25. Cf. Daniel Bach, "Rite et parole dans l'Ancien Testament," *VT* 28 (1978): 10–19 (see 19). Contrast Keel (*Symbolism*, 323–35), who thinks in terms of a spiritualization of the sacrifices, which he thinks would be progress.

a blessing chalice (1 Cor. 10:16). Jerome notes that in speaking of the deliverance chalice, the psalm speaks of the cup of *yĕšûʿâ*, the cup of Jesus.[26] Not surprisingly, then, the psalm came to be used (at least in part) on the Thursday in Holy Week.[27] On the other hand, the Church of England *Book of Common Prayer* prescribes vv. 1–13, 18–19 for the service of Thanksgiving of Women after Child-Birth, arguably in nearer fulfillment of the psalm's original significance.

15Valuable in Yhwh's eyes
is the death of people committed to him.

The psalm begins to make the transition to the second statement of intent. Literally understood, v. 15 is an odd statement. The meaning of *yāqār* might have become stretched along lines parallel to those that apply to *kābēd*, so that it means heavy, grievous, or burdensome.[28] But there is no other indication of this stretching, and it is easier to infer that v. 15 involves a hypallage, an interchange in the application of words. Prosaically put, the life of the people *committed to him is valuable to Yhwh; or the people in danger of death who are committed to Yhwh are valuable to him.[29] The implication is that Yhwh would therefore not let their death come about; and that is what the worshipper has proved.

16Oh now, Yhwh,
because I am your servant,
I am your servant, the son of your maid;
you have loosed my bonds.

This restatement of v. 15 begins with the same emotional expostulation as v. 4b. The self-description in this double line establishes that the worshipper belongs to the category "people committed to Yhwh" (v. 15). That is the nature of the relationship presupposed by being a servant. A servant is committed to a master, but a master's protective stance toward a servant reflects a relationship of mutual commitment between master and servant. Being a servant implies having the attention and protection of one's master.

26. *Homilies*, 1:296 (the psalm actually has *yĕšûʿôt*).

27. See, e.g., *The Alternative Service Book* of the Church of England (Cambridge: Cambridge University Press, 1980), 552.

28. Cf. *Midrash on Psalms*, 2:225; J. A. Emerton, "How Does the Lord Regard the Death of His Saints in Psalm cxvi. 15?" *JTS*, n.s., 34 (1983): 146–56.

29. Fokkelman (*Major Poems*, 3:230) calls it an oxymoron: "their death is important" means "their life is important."

To be not merely a servant but the son of one who was already a family servant (cf. 86:16) underlines the point. While it draws attention to the servant's lowly status, it also makes a further claim. The worshipper is not merely someone who has recently fallen on hard times and had to submit to temporary servitude, but someone with an established, permanent position in the family arising from having been born there; not merely a servant but a servant's son (cf. 123:2). It was this that issued in the fact that the master acted to loose the servant's bonds. There is a paradox there. One might call the relationship of servant to master a form of bondage, but the positive side to it, especially in the context of the attempted imposition of ropes and restraints by another would-be master (v. 3), makes it more like a form of freedom. The potential for being captured against one's will by that other master makes this sort of servanthood preferable to that form of freedom. Indeed, this is a master "whose service is perfect freedom."[30]

17To you I will sacrifice a thank-offering
  and call out in Yhwh's name.
18I will fulfill my vows to Yhwh,
  yes, right before all his people,
19In the courts of Yhwh's house,
  in the midst of Jerusalem.
Praise Yah.

The resolution in vv. 13–14 (and the whole psalm) presupposed that the psalm is the background or foreground to the offering of a sacrifice expressing the worshipper's gratefulness for Yhwh's act of deliverance (cf. Lev. 7:11–18). Verse 17a makes that explicit; vv. 17b–18 then repeat vv. 13b–14.

Verse 19a–b makes the location more concrete. Offerings are made in the very house where Yhwh lives, in the very courts where (as is the case with any house) members of the family and friends gather to be together and join in celebration. It is a great privilege to be in those courts. Further, the offerings are thus made in the midst of the city of Jerusalem. This final phrase in vv. 10–19b parallels the final phrase of vv. 1–9, which referred to the lands of the living or the lands of life. That expression (especially in the plural) points to the breadth and the scope of the life the worshipper can now live before Yhwh, and to the depth and the focus of that life.

The psalm closes with a final bidding to *praise *Yah.

30. From a collect in the service of Morning Prayer in the Church of England *Book of Common Prayer*.

Theological Implications

The two parts of the psalm suggest that love and trust are the two bases for life with Yhwh.[31] Giving our testimony is a gesture of love to Yhwh—not a gesture of emotional love (or not only that) but an expression of the commitment of our whole life. It is the beginning of a confession that will keep recurring in our lives. It is based on the fact that Yhwh listened to us when we cried out because death was overwhelming us and there was no way for us to find an escape. In that context we were once again driven to trust in Yhwh because there was no one else to trust; specifically, we were powerless and human help could get us nowhere. It involves a renewed acknowledgment of Yhwh's grace, faithfulness, and compassion, which have been evidenced in this experience as Yhwh has watched over us. Once again we proved the privilege of being Yhwh's servants, of being committed people, and found that the master was also committed to us. It involves a confession that takes public, outward, sacrificial, sacramental form as well as private, inner, and verbal form. We can now return to that relaxed rest that is the natural habitat of God's people and walk before Yhwh in the breadth and the depth of the place of freedom where we are.

31. Cf. Hermann Spiekermann, "Lieben und Glauben," in *Meilenstein*, ed. Manfred Weippert and Stefan Timm (Herbert Donner Festschrift; Wiesbaden: Harrassowitz, 1995), 266–75.

Psalm 117
Much in a Small Compass

Translation

[1]Praise Yhwh, all you nations;
  glorify him all you peoples.
[2]Because his commitment has been strong over us,
  and Yhwh's truthfulness is forever.
Praise Yah.[1]

Interpretation

The psalm encapsulates the essential nature of a praise psalm: one line issues the challenge to praise, a second gives the reasons for or contents of that praise. Presumably the psalm was used in worship, and it is a plausible view that this very brief song had a recurrent liturgical function, like brief songs in Christian liturgies such as the *Kyrie Eleison*, but we do not know what that function was. Its link(s) with Aramaic usage may suggest an origin in the postexilic period.

[1]Praise Yhwh, all you nations;
  glorify him all you peoples.

1. LXX attaches v. 2c to Ps. 118.

Usually the people of God are urged to *praise Yhwh (e.g., 106:1, 47, 48), and only here are the nations envisaged as "glorifying" Yhwh (*šābaḥ*).[2] While other psalms have commissioned the proclaiming of Yhwh's glory among the nations and have urged the whole world to sing for, shout for, and serve Yhwh (e.g., Pss. 96; 100), only here are the nations themselves urged to do so. In a sense this is a distinction without a difference, as the nations are only rhetorically present; this line thus expresses a familiar point particularly sharply. Yet its form of expression does express sharply the real fact that the whole world is to come to acknowledge Yhwh. Its further distinctiveness lies in its not issuing its exhortation to an undifferentiated world (contrast 96:1; 100:1) but to the world of nations. It recognizes the nations as separate political and ethnic entities, and calls them as they are to worship Yhwh.

> 2Because his commitment has been strong over us,
> and Yhwh's truthfulness is forever.
> Praise Yah.

As elsewhere, the reason the world should worship is Yhwh's strong *commitment and lasting *truthfulness toward Israel. *Gābar* is a striking verb. In other contexts it would imply Yhwh has prevailed over us (e.g., 12:4 [5]); here Yhwh's warrior strength is good news, as in 103:11. The word that often refers to a military commander's power affirms that "God conquers the world . . . by the power of faithful love."[3] Yhwh's commitment stands over Israel protecting not domineering. As the verbal clause speaks about a past extending into the present, the parallel noun clause declaring the lasting nature of Yhwh's truthfulness speaks about a present extending into the future. Prosaically put, "Yhwh's truthful commitment has been strong over us and stands forever."

The regular "*Praise *Yah" rounds off the psalm again.

Theological Implications

"The shortest of all the psalms is theologically one of the grandest."[4] "It transcends all others in the economy of its utterance."[5] "This tiny psalm is great in faith, and its reach is enormous. . . . In singing this, we too

2. The rare noun *hāʾummîm* comes in the m. only here (the f. form comes only twice), though a m. form is common in Aramaic. Or is it a composite form, a cross between *hāʿammîm* and *lĕʾummîm*?

3. McCann, "Psalms," 1150.

4. Dahood, *Psalms*, 3:152.

5. Cassiodorus, *Psalms*, 3:160.

are challenged not to measure God's Kingship by His 'little flock', nor to accept the idea that different peoples have a right to different faiths. . . . This shortest psalm proves, in fact, to be one of the most potent and most seminal."[6] As usual, while rhetorically its exhortation addresses the nations, the people who hear the psalm are Israelites gathered for worship, and indirectly the psalm gives them reason for praise. But the psalm actually declares that Yhwh's faithfulness to Israel is indeed reason for the nations' worship, and explicitly for their enthusiastic *praise, not (for instance) mere grudging or enforced recognition. Thus Paul can quote v. 1 in referring to the manifestation of God's truth and mercy (LXX translates *ḥesed* in v. 2 "mercy") to Israel and to the Gentiles (Rom. 15:8–11). These attitudes and stances of Yhwh to Israel constitute good news for the nations and peoples themselves. The language is different from that of Gen. 12:1–3, but the idea is similar. Yhwh's committed truthfulness to Israel shows who Yhwh is and draws other people to Yhwh on the assumption that this committed truthfulness is not exclusive but inclusive. It does not reveal something about Yhwh that other people cannot know but something they can know. Therefore when the Jewish or Christian community sings this psalm, it reminds itself that the praise of God will be complete only when the whole world joins in.[7] These communities do not have responsibility to ensure that this happens; it is Yhwh's task to manifest committed truthfulness in such a way that it does happen. They do have the responsibility to start praising and glorifying Yhwh themselves, to be the kind of praising and glorifying communities that Yhwh can draw the nations to join.

6. Kidner, *Psalms*, 2:411, 412.
7. Mays, *Psalms*, 373.

Psalm 118

The Stone Spurned

Translation

1Confess Yhwh because he is good,
because his commitment lasts forever.
2Israel is indeed to say,[1]
"His commitment lasts forever."
3The household of Aaron are to say,
"His commitment lasts forever."
4The people who revere Yhwh are to say,
"His commitment lasts forever."

5Out of constraint I called Yah;
Yah answered me with roominess.
6Yhwh being for me, I will not be afraid;
what can a human being do to me?[2]
7Yhwh is for me as my helper,[3]
and I myself will look on the people who are against me.

8It is better to rely on Yhwh
than to depend on a human being.
9It is better to rely on Yhwh
than to depend on leaders.

1. "Indeed" represents *-nāʾ*. The *kî* that follows "say" in vv. 2, 3, and 4 introduces direct speech rather than meaning "because" (so Jacobson, *"Many Are Saying,"* 132) or being asseverative (as EVV imply).

2. Or ". . . be afraid of what a human being can do to me" (cf. Johnson, *Sacral Kingship*, 115).

3. The *b* indicating identity (*"beth essentiae"*; cf. *IBHS* 11.2.5e; JM 133c). For the pl. ptc., GKC 119i implies "as [belonging to the category of] my helpers" (cf. KJV); JM 136f, DG 20c more plausibly see the pl. as intensive, which is perhaps not very different from seeing it as an honorific pl., used of God, as are some other pl. words (*IBHS* 7.4.3d). The pl. makes for assonance and rhyme between *bĕʿōzĕrāy* and *bĕśōnĕʾāy* in the next colon (Dahood, *Psalms*, 3:157).

10All the nations surrounded me;
in Yhwh's name I indeed[4] withered them.[5]
11They surrounded me, yes they surrounded me;[6]
in Yhwh's name I indeed withered them.
12They surrounded me like bees;
they were extinguished[7] like a fire of thorns;
in Yhwh's name I indeed withered them.
13You pushed me hard,[8] so as to fall,
but Yhwh—he helped me.
14Yah became my strength and my protection[9]
and became deliverance for me.
15The noise of resounding and deliverance
in the tents of the faithful:
Yhwh's right hand acts forcefully,
16Yhwh's right hand lifts up high,[10]
Yhwh's right hand acts forcefully.
17I shall not die but live
and proclaim Yah's deeds.
18Yah really disciplined me[11]
but did not give me over to death.
19Open the faithful gates for me;
when I come through them, I will confess Yhwh.

20This is the gate that belongs to Yhwh;
the faithful—they may come through it.

4. A rare example of *kî* as purely asseverative, with no hint of connection.

5. EVV "cut them down" takes the verb as *mûl,* "circumcise," here with a stretched meaning. More likely this *mûl* is a by-form of *ʾāmal* and *mālal*. LXX *amynomai*, Jerome *ulciscor*, and Th *diathryptō* perhaps assume that. B. D. Eerdmans ("Essays on Masoretic Psalms," *OtSt* 1 [1942]: 105–300 [see 129]) has the psalmist circumcising crowds of eager foreigners. Dahood (*Psalms*, 3:157) has him circumcising his victims, comparing 1 Sam. 18:25–27; cf. Briggs, *Psalms*, 2:405.

6. The two verbs are suffixed third pl. qatal from *sābab,* but slightly different forms.

7. Barthélemy (*Psaumes*, 770–72) suggests that LXX and Tg imply *dāʿak* (pual) meaning "blaze," like a piel privative; but there is no problem about the traditional understanding of MT.

8. Lit. "[in] pushing, you pushed me." GKC 113p, JM 123i take this as an example of a stress on the contrast between v. 13a and v. 13b, "Yes, you pushed me"; but the context "so as to fall" emphasizes the degree of the pushing.

9. See *HALOT*. Samuel E. Loewenstamm ("The Lord Is My Strength and Glory," *VT* 19 [1969]: 464–70) argues for "my glory," keeping a link with the usual praise reference of *zmr*. Henning Schröer ("Gott ist mein Psalm," in *Ja und nein*, ed. Klaus Wengst et al. [Wolfgang Schrage Festschrift; Neukirchen: Neukirchener Verlag, 1998], 55–64) makes the traditional understanding ("my song") the basis for his study in the context of Jewish-Christian dialog. The suffix on the first noun carries over to the second.

10. BDB sees *rômēmâ* as a polel ptc. without preformative *m*; this seems implausible and gives poor meaning since the word does not have an object. More likely it is a reduplicated form of a qal ptc.

11. The same idiom as v. 13a with the same alternative possibilities.

[21]I confess you, because you answered me
and have been deliverance for me.

[22]A stone that the builders spurned
has become the head cornerstone.
[23]This has come from Yhwh;[12]
it has been wonderful in our eyes.
[24]This is the day Yhwh has acted;[13]
we will rejoice and be glad in him.[14]
[25]Oh now, Yhwh, do deliver;
oh now, Yhwh, do give success.
[26]Blessed is the one who enters in Yhwh's name;
we bless you[15] from Yhwh's house.
[27]Yhwh is God and has shone light[16] on us;
tie[17] the festal offering with cords, up to the horns of the altar.

[28]You are my God and I will confess you;
my God, I will lift you high.[18]
[29]Confess Yhwh, because he is good,
because his commitment lasts forever.

Interpretation

Like Ps. 116, this is a thanksgiving or testimony psalm.[19] But there were no indications that Ps. 116 represented the voice of anyone other than an ordinary individual. In Ps. 118 the language (see especially vv. 10–12) suggests a psalm for a king or other leader, delivered from a crisis issuing from his position in relation to the people as a whole. As a

12. See E. Jenni, "'Vom Herrn ist dies gewirkt,'" *TZ* 35 (1979): 55–62.

13. Cf. TNIV; Joachim Becker, "Zur Deutung von Ps 118,24," *BN* 94 (1998): 44–51. Hardly "this is the day Yhwh has made"; the OT does not elsewhere speak of Yhwh making a day (Eccles. 7:14 is the nearest parallel), but it does use this formulation to speak of "the day [when]" (e.g., Ps. 102:2 [3]; Exod. 6:28; also Mal. 4:3 [3:21], with *ʾăšer*). The word order makes it less likely that someone would read the colon as "this is what Yhwh has done today" (Adele Berlin, "Psalm 118:24," *JBL* 96 [1977]: 567–68).

14. In such contexts, rejoicing in Yhwh is more common than rejoicing in an object such as a day (e.g., 97:12; 104:34).

15. Pl.

16. *IBHS* 33.3.4c takes the *w*-consecutive as following on the noun clause and thus as having present significance, "and shines light."

17. For *ʾisrû*, 11QPs[a] has *ʾswrw* or *ʾswry*; the final letter is difficult to distinguish. With *ʾswrw*, the difference from MT is purely one of spelling. With *ʾswry*, one could point MT *ʾăsurê* and translate "the people bound [i.e., kept in order by ropes] for the festival" (cf. Godfrey Driver, "Psalm 118:27," *Textus* 7 [1969]: 130–31); but this is hardly a compelling alternative to MT.

18. Every word in this line begins with *ʾ*.

19. Again, see Crüsemann, *Studien zur Formgeschichte*, 210–84.

leader's testimony, the psalm also parallels Ps. 18 and manifests detailed points of similarity (e.g., "roominess," v. 5; cf. 18:19 [20]). It has other links with Exod. 15:1–11: v. 14 corresponds to Exod. 15:2a–b; vv. 15c–16 compares with Exod. 15:6; v. 28 compares with Exod. 15:2c–d.[20]

Mishnah tractate *Sukkah* 3.9 and 4.5 say it was used at Sukkot; as part of the Hallel (the last of the "Egyptian Hallel" collection, Pss. 113–18), it was also used at Pesah and on other festivals and occasions. But in itself it implies a particular experience of deliverance, and reflects an occasion such as that described in 2 Chron. 20: see especially v. 21, where the choir sings, "Confess Yhwh because his commitment lasts forever" (cf. v. 1 of the psalm). We might imagine it being first used at the temple dedication described in Ezra 6[21] or the feast of Sukkot described in Neh. 8–9.[22] Its regular use at Pesah and Sukkot is then a later adaptation that may have affected the order of the psalms in the Psalter but not their contents.

It also resembles Ps. 115 in giving indications that more than one voice speaks, though we again cannot be sure how it works at every point. Verses 1–4 constitute an opening invitation to worship and v. 29 pairs with that section to close the psalm; these might be the words of a minister or of the leader whose testimony we shall hear. Verses 5–7 are the initial testimony, vv. 8–9 a congregational response. Verses 10–19 are the more detailed testimony (though vv. 15–16 might be a response within that) and vv. 20–21 a briefer exchange between congregation and leader. In vv. 22–27 the congregation makes its final response and prayer, with v. 28 the leader's final summary confession before the closing exhortation in v. 29, pairing with the opening. The congregational parts might be voiced by the choir, and individual lines might have been sung antiphonally: one can imagine vv. 2a, 3a, and 4a as the minister or leader's invitation and vv. 2b, 3b, and 4b as a response.[23] As usual we would be unwise to try to infer a liturgy that was actually taking place as the psalm unfolded,[24] though no doubt the psalm reflects liturgical events.

20. But for communal interpretations, see Mowinckel, *Psalms*, 2:30; S. B. Frost, "Psalm 118," *CJT* 7 (1961): 155–66; and James L. Mays, "Psalm 118 in the Light of Canonical Analysis," in *Canon, Theology, and Old Testament Interpretation*, ed. Gene M. Tucker et al. (B. S. Childs Festschrift; Philadelphia: Fortress, 1988), 299–311.

21. Cf. Goulder, *Psalms of the Return*, 182–91.

22. Cf. Kirkpatrick, *Psalms*, 693. Harry S. May argues for a preexilic context ("Psalm 118," in *Religions in Antiquity*, ed. Jacob Neusner [E. R. Goodenough Memorial; Leiden: Brill, 1968]: 97–106).

23. For other possibilities, see Jutta Schröten, *Entstehung, Komposition und Wirkungsgeschichte des 118. Psalms* (Weinheim: Beltz Athenäum, 1995), 70–77. On verbal patterns in the psalm, see Auffret, *Merveilles à nos yeux*, 162–79.

24. Against Mowinckel, *Psalms*, 1:5–6, 120, 123, 171, 180–81; cf. Reuven Hammer, "Two Liturgical Psalms," *Judaism* 40 (1991): 484–97 (see 489–97).

Like Ps. 116, vv. 10–12 use yiqtol verbs to refer to past events; that may be true of some other yiqtol verbs.

118:1–4. The opening challenge to confession.

> [1]Confess Yhwh because he is good,
> because his commitment lasts forever.
> [2]Israel is indeed to say,
> "His commitment lasts forever."
> [3]The household of Aaron are to say,
> "His commitment lasts forever."
> [4]The people who revere Yhwh are to say,
> "His commitment lasts forever."

"*Confess" points to what kind of psalm this will be, though the verb has been used in a looser sense in Pss. 105, 106, and 107 (the line repeats 106:1). It comes five times in the psalm; no other chapter in the OT gives it such prominence. The rationale for confession does link with that looser use of the verb. For the people as a whole, the basis for confession is not the specific act of *goodness[25] and *commitment that the psalm will relate, but the more general fact about Yhwh that this specific act has evidenced. Thus as usual, the testimony's aim is to draw people into such confession; what God does for an individual can build up the whole congregation.

That point is explicit in the threefold challenge in vv. 2–4 (cf. 115:9–11). The leader's testimony is to become everyone's.

118:5–7. The leader summarizes his experience and draws inferences for his ongoing attitude to life, which implicitly is to be everyone's.

> [5]Out of constraint I called Yah;
> Yah answered me with roominess.

"Call" and "answer" correspond, epitomizing a key aspect of life with God in the Psalms. Israel's relationship with God is a dynamic personal one characterized by calling and response. In the Prophets, this involves a call or summons from God to which the people or an individual are to respond; in the Psalms, it more often involves a call or summons from the people or an individual to God to which God is to respond. Sometimes God is disappointed (as the Prophets show) and sometimes the people or the individual are disappointed (as the Psalms show), but this does not make either side finally lose faith in the dynamic of this relationship. It works often enough for both sides to persist; Ps. 118 relates to an occasion when it worked. The summons's urgency is suggested by

25. LXX renders this *ṭôb* by *agathos*, which is more literal but less illuminating than *chrēstos*. It repeats the declaration that he is good in vv. 2a, 3a, 4a.

the use of "call" as a transitive verb. The leader did not merely call to Yah, but called Yah. It might seem peremptory, like a master's calling of a servant, but evidently it is all right.

"Constraint" and "roominess" also correspond. Words from the root *ṣārar* are used to denote "distress" more generally, but etymologically the word points to restriction or straits, and the parallelism suggests this meaning here. The leader's trouble involved being pressed or confined; deliverance was a liberation into space and freedom.

The two occurrences of *Yah give God the last word in each colon.

> 6Yhwh being for me, I will not be afraid;
> what can a human being do to me?
> 7Yhwh is for me as my helper,
> and I myself will look on the people who are against me.

These yiqtol verbs might refer to the past, the stance the leader took in the crisis. But the statement of confidence is more unequivocal than ones that generally appear in this connection. More likely the initial testimony in v. 5 is being supplemented by a declaration regarding the ongoing attitude to which the leader commits himself.[26] The key word in the two lines is *lî*, "for me" in vv. 6a and 7a and "to me" in v. 6b. The double divine *lî* enfolds the human *lî* and renders it impotent. Further, v. 6 itself opens with "Yhwh" and closes with "a human being," sharpening the contrast between them by putting them as far as possible away from each other.[27]

"I will not be afraid" (*yārēʾ*) is nicely complemented by "I will look" (*rāʾâ*; for the use of the verb compare 112:8b).

118:8–9. The first person disappears; the two lines are likely a communal response to the testimony, exactly the response it seeks. "Better . . . than . . ." sayings are prominent in Proverbs and Ecclesiastes (e.g., Prov. 16:8, 16, 19), and these two lines may take up proverbial sayings of that kind or be modeled on them. They thus contrast with the form of a confessional psalm but cohere with the didactic aspect to its agenda, its concern that people draw the lesson from the testifier's story.

> 8It is better to rely on Yhwh
> than to depend on a human being.
> 9It is better to rely on Yhwh
> than to depend on leaders.

Who are the leaders, and who is inclined to *rely or depend on them? Perhaps they are foreign leaders (compare a situation such as that

26. Cf. Gerstenberger, *Psalms*, 2:302.
27. Dahood, *Psalms*, 3:156.

pictured in Isa. 7, Ezra 1–6, or Neh. 2–6). Or perhaps the communal response implies that people could have been tempted to rely on their own leader, the "human being" giving his testimony. They now heed his implicit challenge not to look to him but to look to Yhwh.

118:10–19. The leader now gives a longer account of his testimony and its implications.

10All the nations surrounded me;
in Yhwh's name I indeed withered them.
11They surrounded me, yes they surrounded me;
in Yhwh's name I indeed withered them.
12They surrounded me like bees;
they were extinguished like a fire of thorns;
in Yhwh's name I indeed withered them.

Before the exile, "all the nations" would suggest imperial forces such as the Assyrian army in 2 Kings 18–19. In the Persian period, it would suggest groups such as the peoples who put pressure on the building of the temple and the city walls: compare "surrounding" in Neh. 6:16. This verb suggests being hemmed in, and links with the expression in v. 5a. It might suggest a city besieged or an army encircled, or point to a less literal sense of being surrounded such as that applying to Nehemiah. Verse 12a then offers a different and frightening simile.

"In Yhwh's *name" perhaps suggests that the conflict concerned Yhwh's name (cf. 2 Kings 18–19). The victory needed to evidence that Yhwh was really God. But the expression also could be a restatement of the point in vv. 6–7. The victory involved a manifestation of the presence of Yhwh as revealed to Israel, the powerful and faithful person embodied in the name. To speak of "withering" the nations has a certain irony in Nehemiah's day, when their enemies not unreasonably described the Judeans themselves as withered or feeble (*ʾămēlāl*; Neh. 4:2 [3:34]). The nations looked strong, but they could be enfeebled. The extra colon in the middle of v. 12 adds yet another image. The foes were like a fire that could threaten to engulf Israel. But they were only like a fire of thorns, which blazes up but dies down as quickly. This is not to imply that this was the inherent nature of the nations. "In Yhwh's name" the leader was able to extinguish them as if that was all they were.

13You pushed me hard, so as to fall,
but Yhwh—he helped me.
14Yah became my strength and my protection
and became deliverance for me.

The second person verb is a surprise (LXX, Jerome make it easier with "I was pushed hard"). While this would be a feasible statement to Yhwh (cf. v. 18), the move to speaking of Yhwh in the third person in the parallel colon would be awkward. More likely, with vividness the leader now addresses the foe (singular) as if present, perhaps as if captured and paraded before Israel, like Agag in 1 Sam. 15. One way or another he had put huge pressure on the leader (again the imagery from v. 5a is not far away). He had reckoned to make him fall, and would have done so, were it not for Yhwh's *help. The fall is perhaps a fall into Sheol (cf. vv. 17–18).

Verse 14 then expands on v. 13b, explaining further how this worked out. The past statements on either side suggest that v. 14a is not merely a general statement ("Yhwh is my strength . . .") but a description of how Yhwh acted in the crisis; the verb in the second colon about Yhwh as *deliverance likely also applies in the first.

15The noise of resounding and deliverance
in the tents of the faithful:
Yhwh's right hand acts forcefully,
16Yhwh's right hand lifts up high,
Yhwh's right hand acts forcefully.

The *faithful is a term for Israelites as a whole, many of whom would live in tents in Jerusalem during a festival, but this looks more like a psalm used on an occasion of deliverance than a festival psalm. The tents might be the homes of the Israelites as a whole; "tents" is occasionally used anachronistically to mean homes (e.g., 78:51, 55). Or perhaps the leader is recalling the cries of an army in their tents and inviting the congregation (or, even more vividly, the enemy addressed in v. 13) to imagine they can hear them. More than anyone, the army would have a basis for *resounding at Yhwh's *deliverance.

A tricolon once again makes dramatic use of repetition. The verbs are all participles, which might suggest that with further vividness the leader imagines the faithful in the midst of perceiving and acknowledging Yhwh's act. Or this might be their subsequent declaration of faith in Yhwh as the one who characteristically works in such a way.

17I shall not die but live
and proclaim Yah's deeds.
18Yah really disciplined me
but did not give me over to death.
19Open the faithful gates for me;
when I come through them, I will confess Yhwh.

The testimony comes to an end with another summary of the experience, though again without hard information on what happened. The leader does put the threat more starkly as a matter of life and death. Again, v. 17a might be reckoned to have past reference and to point back to the crisis in which, against the odds, the leader did not die but survived. Yhwh's deliverance meant the threat of death was not fulfilled. This is why the leader has a testimony to give, that is, acts of *Yah to proclaim.

Two succeeding lines then elaborate on each of those cola. It was indeed a near-death experience. EVV have *Yah "punishing," giving a misleading impression (unless we think of the idiom whereby we speak of an athlete undergoing "punishing" training). Even when *yāsar* suggests a parent's or a teacher's chastisement, it does not denote retributive punishment but action designed to teach (cf. 16:7; 94:10, 12; LXX uses *paideuō*, but Jerome *arguo*). *Yah put the leader under severe pressures to drive him to learn the lessons the psalm has referred to (e.g., vv. 6–9; cf. 2 Cor. 1:9). To that end, Yah took him near death, through an experience like Israel's at the Red Sea, but did not let him be taken by death (cf. 116:3–9).

In turn v. 19 elaborates on v. 17b. The gates it refers to may be the gates leading into the temple court or may be the city gates.[28] The psalm might accompany a literal procession, with the leader standing at the temple gate, but this might as usual be too prosaic. But figuratively speaking, the leader returning from the crisis situation needs to come into the city or temple court, not merely to come home but to make the confession embodied in this psalm. So he seeks admission through the "*faithful gates." While that might be the actual name of a gate (a double gate?), it might rather suggest the gates of the faithful city (Isa. 1:26), the faithful abode (Jer. 31:23), or the gates of the city that embodies Yhwh's faithfulness in its own experience.[29] Perhaps the gates have been shut to stop the enemy from entering. Now they can be opened, and should be opened to hear this testimony to the fact that the city's crisis is over.

118:20–21. A minister responds to the leader's challenge, and the leader renews his confession.

> **20**This is the gate that belongs to Yhwh;
> the faithful—they may come through it.

28. David Hamidović ("'Les portes de justice' et 'la porte de YHWH' dans le Psaume 118,19–20," *Bib* 81 [2000]: 542–50) urges the latter.

29. Cf. B. J. Oosterhoff, "Het loven van God in Psalm 118," in *Loven en geloven*, ed. M. H. van Es et al. (N. H. Ridderbos Festschrift; Amsterdam: Ton Bolland, 1975), 175–90 (see 181–82).

[21]I confess you, because you answered me
and have been deliverance for me.

It is hardly a gate that leads to Yhwh (NJPS);[30] that would imply Yhwh is inside and not outside, whereas the leader knows that Yhwh has been present outside, acting to deliver. He is not coming in through the gate because Yhwh is there but because the people are there. But the gate does belong to Yhwh, because this is Yhwh's city and Yhwh's home. So the minister's response to the leader's words in v. 19 is that people who are God-like—that is, *faithful—may therefore enter through it, as the leader asked that he should.

Inside, then, he makes *confession on the basis of the way Yhwh has answered (cf. v. 5b) in words and in the act of *deliverance. Perhaps this confession is an indirect way of affirming a claim to be among the faithful who can enter the gates, an "asseveration by thanksgiving."[31]

118:22–27. The people now respond with their own confessions and affirmations (vv. 22–24, 27) and pleas (v. 25), and by blessing their leader (v. 26). Tg interestingly sees the whole of vv. 22–29 as an account of the choice of David.

[22]A stone that the builders spurned
has become the head cornerstone.

Their initial declaration is perhaps another proverbial saying. Israelite houses might be built of stone foundations and mud-brick superstructure, but public buildings used stone for superstructure as well as foundations. This stone might be unhewn or cut to shape. Either way, the builders would look at stones that were available to see which would fit into different stages of the building work. A stone unsuitable at one stage might be exactly what was required later. A nuance of this is the reusing of stones from demolished buildings, which had a practical rationale, but in connection with a temple would also symbolize and embody continuity between a rebuilt temple and its predecessor. A recycled stone might even end up in a key position, perhaps holding together two walls at right angles at the corner of a building, in the building's foundation or at the top of its superstructure. Jeremiah 51:26 mentions both a cornerstone and a foundation stone. These might be different stones or different descriptions of the same stone. The cornerstone seems to be part of the foundation in Job 38:6 (cf. Isa. 28:16), but in Zech. 4:7 the headstone seems to be the

30. Even after a verb such as "come," *l* is uncommon with this meaning (BDB 511b).

31. So S. B. Frost, "Asseveration by Thanksgiving," *VT* 8 (1958): 380–90.

top stone.[32] This aspect of building then provides a figure of speech. Something dismissed for one purpose might turn out to be exactly what was needed for another purpose, possibly a more exalted one than that for which it was rejected. That is what has happened here, the congregation comments. This leader of little Israel, or little Israel itself, seemed useless and was dismissed contemptuously by the nations. But he or it turns out to occupy a more exalted position than anyone would have dreamed.

> [23]This has come from Yhwh;
> it has been wonderful in our eyes.
> [24]This is the day Yhwh has acted;
> we will rejoice and be glad in him.

The second colon in v. 23 explains the first. The deliverance the leader has confessed can only be seen as something extraordinary, supernatural, wonderful, in continuity with the Red Sea deliverance celebrated in the Song of Moses, which the psalm echoes at other points (the noun "wonder" comes in Exod. 15:11). It has come from Yhwh.

Again, v. 24 parallels v. 23 and explains or expands on it. Without Yhwh's doing that wonder, neither leader nor people would be standing here today. The leader would be dead or the city taken or its walls not rebuilt or the temple not restored. So what happened was indeed a wonder deserving the response of joyful gladness.

> [25]Oh now, Yhwh, do deliver;
> oh now, Yhwh, do give success.

The plea is a surprise. Perhaps it reflects an awareness that one spectacular deliverance does not mean that everything is sorted out; perhaps the final outcome is still to be resolved. That would fit the circumstances of the temple dedication in Ezra 6 or the celebration of Sukkot in Neh. 8–9. Or perhaps the plea starts from the community's being in recurrent need of Yhwh's intervention because crises recur. Or perhaps (as happens in Christian usage) *deliverance or salvation is coming to coalesce with the notion of blessing, Yhwh's ongoing involvement in maintaining the community and enabling it to flourish.[33] This would fit with the reference to "success" in the parallel colon. The words in v. 25b correspond closely to Nehemiah's in Neh. 1:11.

32. Indeed, the term might simply denote a coping stone, with no implication that it was at a corner: see Michael Cahill, "Not a Cornerstone!" *RB* 106 (1999): 345–57.

33. Jakob P. Petuchowski ("'Hoshiʿah na' in Psalm cxviii 25," *VT* 5 [1955]: 266–71) suggests that this is a prayer for rain; but neither the words nor the context suggest this.

[26]Blessed is the one who enters in Yhwh's name;
we bless you from Yhwh's house.

The psalm returns to the specificity of the situation. "Blessed is" is again a declarative statement (cf. 115:15); by it blessing comes upon the leader as he enters to give his testimony.[34]

The declarative nature of v. 26a is confirmed by a further performative qatal statement ("we hereby bless you"),[35] addressed to the people whose destiny is tied to the leader's. It also makes clear that the capacity to bless does not reside in some power that people or priest possess; the blessing issues from Yhwh's house. This is where Yhwh is committed to dwelling. Therefore Yhwh's blessing can issue from there. Perhaps this disambiguates the reference to Yhwh's *name in the first colon. The word order might suggest that the leader enters in Yhwh's name, though it is not clear what that would mean (enters because he comes with his testimony to Yhwh?). The parallelism perhaps indicates that actually he is blessed in Yhwh's name.

Verses 25–26 reappear in part in the crowd's greeting to Jesus in Mark 11:9. "Hosanna" represents *hôšîʿâ nāʾ*, "do deliver"; the crowd then follows with v. 26a.[36]

[27]Yhwh is God and has shone light on us;
tie the festal offering with cords, up to the horns of the altar.

The community makes its own final declaration of faith. There is nothing more fundamental that can be said than "Yhwh is God." It is the OT's equivalent to a commitment to monotheism, but it is not the same as that, and it is arguably more significant. The OT is not very interested in how many deities there are (one or four or twenty . . .). It is interested in "Who is God?" The answer evidenced by an event such as the deliverance the leader has experienced is, "Yhwh is God." Monotheism follows (if Yhwh is God, there is only one God), but it is not a

34. "The coming one" later becomes a messianic title (see, e.g., Matt. 11:3).

35. Cf. Max Rogland, *Alleged Non-past Uses of* Qatal *in Classical Hebrew* (Assen: Van Gorcum, 2003), 123.

36. On the use of the psalm in the NT, see, e.g., James A. Sanders, "A New Testament Hermeneutic Fabric," in *Early Jewish and Christian Exegesis*, ed. Craig A. Evans and William F. Stinespring (W. H. Brownlee Memorial; Atlanta: Scholars, 1987), 177–90; revised ed. in *Luke and Scripture*, ed. Craig A. Evans and James A. Sanders (Minneapolis: Fortress, 1993), 140–53; Schröten, *Entstehung, Komposition und Wirkungsgeschichte*; J. Ross Wagner, "Psalm 118 in Luke-Acts," in *Early Christian Interpretation of the Scriptures of Israel*, ed. Craig A. Evans and James A. Sanders (Sheffield: Sheffield Academic Press, 1997), 154–78.

very interesting or significant consequence. "Yhwh is God" not "There is only one God" is the important truth.

Here the evidence of that truth is that Yhwh has shone light on the people, in fulfillment of Aaron's blessing (Num. 6:24–26). As there, this verb spells out what "blessing" looks like. Yhwh's day has come, and it has been light and not darkness (contrast Amos 5:18). As usual, whereas darkness and gloom are symbols for disaster and defeat, light is a symbol of triumph, victory, and blessing. The light has shone on "us." The leader's victory is the people's, not just his.

The second colon begins, more literally and enigmatically, "tie the festival with cords." LXX and Jerome take this as referring to the interweaving of tree branches, which in a later period were carried by people in procession at Sukkot and might therefore seem to "bind the festival procession" (NRSV). But there are no other passages where *ḥag* means "festival procession," and "branches" is a doubtful meaning for *ʿăbōt* (see BDB). Tg more plausibly assumes that *ḥag* here denotes a "festal offering," as it can in PBH and seems to in Exod. 23:18 (see NJPS, TNIV), so that the command refers to the tying of a sacrificial lamb preparatory to its being sacrificed. As far as we know animals were not tied *to* the altar; the form of expression rather implies an ellipse: "tie the festal offering with cords [until it comes] up to the horns of the altar."[37] While *ḥag* usually refers to one of the three pilgrim festivals, it can denote other festive occasions (see BDB).

118:28–29. The leader brings the psalm to a close.

28You are my God and I will confess you;
my God, I will lift you high.
29Confess Yhwh, because he is good,
because his commitment lasts forever.

The *confession now declares not only that Yhwh is God but that Yhwh is my God; that, again, has been evidenced by the deliverance Yhwh has granted. It is once more reason for this personal confession before the people. "I will lift you high" indicates what is happening when one "confesses" Yhwh. Yhwh's own hand has lifted high in acting with authority to direct the forces involved in the battle and/or to take action (v. 16); in response, the leader speaks to lift Yhwh high. Human confession has the power to exalt Yhwh.

The leader or minister goes on to urge that *confession (the verb recurs for the fifth time) on the whole congregation, repeating v. 1 to round off the psalm.

37. J. Meysing sees "up to the horns of the altar" as a gloss, and emends the earlier part of the line ("A Text Re-construction of Ps cxvii [cxviii] 27," *VT* 16 [1966]: 130–37).

Theological Implications

Psalm 118 is one of the psalms most often appealed to in the NT, particularly vv. 22–23 and 25–26. One can see how these lines helped the first Christians understand the significance of Jesus. As is often the case, the NT's use of the OT has little to do with the OT text's own meaning. The Holy Spirit inspires people to see whole new significance in the words of the text. One can articulate sophisticated theological and hermeneutical rationales for the result (if v. 22 refers to the king, then Jesus is the messianic king and it therefore applies to him; or if v. 22 refers to Israel, then Jesus is the embodiment of Israel and it therefore applies to him). These satisfy the instincts of modernity, which would like the NT to use approaches to interpretation that it approves, but they impose alien ways of thinking on the text.

If the NT regards the psalm as an important passage, it would be at least as appropriate to ask what the psalm has to say in its own right to the church. Martin Luther, often the great christological allegorist in his interpretation of the Psalms, does that in his monumental exposition of this favorite psalm of his, "my own beloved psalm,"[38] despite, or because of, seeing analogies between the psalm and the way life has worked out for him.

Because of their position, church leaders experience pressures that other Christians do not. God does not stop that from happening. In fact, God may even make it happen, but not so as finally to overwhelm them. The psalm suggests that they then call on God in urgent ways and find that God answers and that they demolish the attacks on them. They then come back to the waiting community to tell it about this and thereby encourage it. They prove Yhwh's commitment, and their story encourages the church to live confident of Yhwh's commitment. It is tempting for the church to trust in its leaders and/or for them to trust in the support of other powerful people, but their testimony shows the wisdom of rather taking refuge in God.[39] It is tempting to assume that the humanly impressive wins the day, but the humanly unimpressive is what often does so, because God's presence and activity add the x factor to the situation and overturn the odds. So leaders and church join in tumultuous celebration of the day when God has acted, processing, making offerings, rejoicing, lifting God high, and making this experience the basis for urging God to complete the work of which this is part.

38. *Selected Psalms*, 3:41–106 (see 45).
39. Cf. Mays, *Preaching and Teaching the Psalms*, 148.

Luther notes that it is experts like builders (or writers and readers of commentaries) who reject the stone, though even they can come to see things right in due course.[40]

40. See Robert C. Fulton, "Victory over Death," *CurTM* 14 (1987): 278–82. On Luther's exposition, see also Ronald M. Hals, "Psalm 118," *Int* 37 (1983): 277–83; Ernst Kutsch, "Deus humiliat et exaltat," *ZTK* 61 (1964): 193–220.

Psalm 119
The Dynamics of the Moral Life

Translation

[ʾ] 1The good fortune of people of integrity in their way of life,
who walk in Yhwh's teaching!
[ʾ] 2The good fortune of people who observe his declarations,
who have recourse to him with all their heart.
[ʾ] 3Yes, they have done no wickedness;
they have walked in his ways.
[ʾ] 4You yourself commanded your orders
to be well kept.
[ʾ] 5O that[1] my ways may be firm
in keeping your laws!
[ʾ] 6Then I shall not be shamed,
as I look on all your commands.
[ʾ] 7I will confess you with uprightness of heart
as I learn your faithful decisions.
[ʾ] 8I will keep your laws;
do not completely abandon me.

[*b*] 9How can a young person keep his path pure?—
by guarding it in accordance with your word.[2]

1. "If only" (*HALOT*) implies the psalmist thinks it unrealistic to hope to be obedient, but this hardly makes sense in the context of this psalm. *ʾAḥălay* comes only here; for the variant *ʾaḥălê* (2 Kings 5:3), "if only" would be appropriate, though not necessary.

2. There is no "it," though that can be understood; for "guarding one's way," see, e.g., 1 Kings 2:4; 8:25. LXX and Jerome have "guarding your words," but this ignores the prep.

[*b*] **10**With all my heart I have had recourse to you;
do not let me stray from your commands.
[*b*] **11**In my heart I have treasured your statement
so that I may not fall short in relation to you.
[*b*] **12**You are to be worshipped, Yhwh;
enable me to learn your laws.
[*b*] **13**With my lips I have proclaimed
all the decisions of your mouth.
[*b*] **14**In the way of your declarations I have rejoiced
as over all wealth.
[*b*] **15**About your orders I shall murmur;
I shall look on your paths.
[*b*] **16**In your laws I will delight;
I will not ignore your words.

[*g*] **17**Deal with your servant;
I shall live and keep your word.
[*g*] **18**Open my eyes so that I may look on
wonders[3] from your teaching.
[*g*] **19**I am a sojourner in the world;
do not hide your commands from me.
[*g*] **20**My spirit has shattered in connection with my longing
for your decisions all the time.
[*g*] **21**You have blasted the willful;[4]
cursed[5] are the people who stray from your commands.
[*g*] **22**Take away from me taunt and shame,
because I have observed your declarations.
[*g*] **23**Although leaders have sat speaking together against me,
your servant—he murmurs about your laws.
[*g*] **24**Yes, your declarations are my delight,
my policymakers.

[*d*] **25**My spirit has stuck to the dirt;
make me live, in accordance with your word.
[*d*] **26**I proclaimed my ways and you answered me;
enable me to learn your laws.
[*d*] **27**Enable me to understand the way of your orders

on *kidbārekā*. Throughout the psalm, MSS and Vrs vary over sg. or pl. for words such as *dābār*; I follow Codex Leningrad throughout.

3. LXX "your wonders" perhaps rightly reads the suffix back from *tôrâ*.

4. Qimchi assumes the qatal refers to the future, and DG 60b takes it as precative. Dahood (*Psalms*, 3:176) suggests that the imperative in v. 22 supports that, but that argument works less well in this psalm, where each line is self-contained. There are a number of lines that must refer to Yhwh's past acts (e.g., vv. 26, 50, 92, 93, 119), and more likely the qatal also has its usual meaning here. Cf. v. 118.

5. MT links "cursed" with v. 21a, but the effect is jerky. The word more usually comes at the beginning of a clause, as in LXX, Jerome here.

so that I may murmur about your wonders.
[*d*] 28My spirit has wept away from sorrow;
lift me up, in accordance with your word.
[*d*] 29Remove the way of falsehood from me;
grace me with your teaching.
[*d*] 30I have chosen the way of truthfulness;
I have set my mind on your decisions.
[*d*] 31I have stuck by your declarations;
Yhwh, do not shame me.
[*d*] 32I run in the way of your commands,
because you broaden my mind.

[*h*] 33Teach me, Yhwh, the way of your laws,
so that I may observe it to the utmost.[6]
[*h*] 34Enable me to understand, so that I may observe your teaching
and keep it with all my heart.
[*h*] 35Direct me in the pathway of your commands,
because I take pleasure in it.
[*h*] 36Incline my heart to your declarations
and not to gain.
[*h*] 37Make my eyes pass on from seeing emptiness;
in your way[7] make me live.
[*h*] 38Establish for your servant your statement,
which is for your revering.[8]
[*h*] 39Make my taunt, which I dread, pass on,
because your decisions are good.
[*h*] 40There: I long for your orders;
in your faithfulness make me live.

[*w*] 41So may your commitment come to me, Yhwh,[9]
your deliverance in accordance with your statement.
[*w*] 42So may I be able to answer the person who taunts me with a word,
because I have relied on your word.

6. Cf. NJPS, Tg for this understanding of *ʿēqeb*, which usually means "result." LXX translates "always," but there seems insufficient basis or need to hypothesize that further meaning.

7. 11QPs[a] has *bdbrk*, "by your word" (cf. Tg). Most lines do have an expression such as word, teaching, or laws, and Barthélemy (*Psaumes*, 787) reckons this the original reading, but one cannot conform all the lines to that general rule except by speculation.

8. EVV take as abstract for concrete, "for those who revere you"; but there is no parallel for such usage, and the next line's reference to the suppliant's dread supports the literal translation.

9. Pl. verb, sg. noun, perhaps implying a pointing slip, or the noun in v. 41b may be the second subject of the verb. The usually intransitive verb is treated as transitive (cf. v. 77).

[*w*] 43So do not take right[10] away from my mouth your[11] truthful word,
because I have waited for your decisions.
[*w*] 44So I shall keep your teaching always,
forever and ever.
[*w*] 45So I shall walk about in roominess
because I have had recourse to your orders.
[*w*] 46So I shall speak of your declarations before kings
and not be shamed.
[*w*] 47So I will delight in your commands,
which I am dedicated to.
[*w*] 48So I will lift my hands to your commands, which I am dedicated to,
and I shall murmur about your laws.

[*z*] 49Be mindful of the word to your servant,
by which you have made me wait.
[*z*] 50This is my comfort in my weakness,
that your statement has made me live.
[*z*] 51When the willful have greatly mocked me,
from your teaching I have not diverted.[12]
[*z*] 52I have been mindful of your decisions
from of old, Yhwh, and I have found comfort.
[*z*] 53Rage[13]—it has gripped me because of the faithless,
people who abandon your teaching.
[*z*] 54Your laws have been my songs/protection
in the house where I sojourn.
[*z*] 55I have been mindful at night of your name, Yhwh,
and I have kept your teaching.
[*z*] 56This is how it has been for me,
that I have observed your orders.

[*ḥ*] 57Yhwh is my allocation;
I have said I would keep your words.[14]
[*ḥ*] 58I have courted your favor with all my heart;
be gracious to me in accordance with your statement.

10. *ʿAd-mĕʾōd*, lit. "to much"; it is doubtful if it can have a time reference (so TNIV).

11. The suffix in the second colon also applies here.

12. While the subject precedes the verb to make the alphabetic arrangement work, and asyndeton need not imply the subordination of one clause to the other (many lines in the psalm are asyndetic), the combination of asyndeton with the word order invites us to take v. 51a as a circumstantial clause (see *TTH* 156–69; DG 135–37); cf. vv. 61, 69, 143, 147, 163.

13. The subject precedes the verb to make the alphabetic arrangement work, but this still gives it some emphasis.

14. The third-person statement in v. 57a is isolated, and one could render "Yhwh, my allocation . . ." (e.g., Will Soll, *Psalm 119*, CBQMS 23 [Washington, DC: Catholic Biblical Association, 1991], 162–63).

[ḥ] 59 I considered my ways [MT]/your ways [LXX]
and turned my feet to your declarations.
[ḥ] 60 I have hurried and not delayed
to keep your commands.
[ḥ] 61 Though the ropes of the faithless surrounded me,
I did not ignore your teaching.
[ḥ] 62 In the middle of the night I rise to confess you
for your faithful decisions.
[ḥ] 63 I am friend to all who revere you,
to the people who keep your orders.
[ḥ] 64 Your commitment, Yhwh—the earth is full of it;
enable me to learn your laws.

[ṭ] 65 You have done what is good for your servant,
Yhwh, in accordance with your word.
[ṭ] 66 Enable me to learn goodness of discernment and
acknowledgment,
because I have trusted in your commands.
[ṭ] 67 Before I became weak I was going astray,
but now I have kept your statement.
[ṭ] 68 You are good[15] and you do good;
enable me to learn your laws.
[ṭ] 69 The willful have smeared falsehood over me,
whereas I with all my heart observe your orders.
[ṭ] 70 Their mind is thick, like fat;
I myself have delighted in your teaching.
[ṭ] 71 It was good for me that I was made weak
so that I might learn your laws.
[ṭ] 72 The teaching that comes from your mouth is good to me,
more so than thousands of gold and silver pieces.[16]

[y] 73 It was your hands made me and founded me;
enable me to understand so that I may learn your commands.
[y] 74 People who revere you—they will see me and rejoice,
because I have waited for your word.
[y] 75 I have acknowledged, Yhwh, that your decisions are faithful,
and in truthfulness you have made me weak.
[y] 76 Do grant that[17] your commitment may come to comfort me
in accordance with your statement to your servant.
[y] 77 May your compassion come to me so that I may live,
because your teaching is my delight.
[y] 78 May the willful be shamed because they have put me in the
wrong by means of falsehood;

15. Here and in a number of other verses LXX adds "Lord."
16. Idiomatically, ". . . is better to me than thousands. . . ."
17. *-nāʾ*.

I myself murmur about your orders.
[*y*] 79 May the people who revere you turn to me,
the people who acknowledge your declarations. [Q]
[or] and acknowledge your declarations. [K][18]
[*y*] 80 May my heart be of integrity in your laws
so that I may not be shamed.

[*k*] 81 My spirit has come to an end for your deliverance;
for your word I have waited.
[*k*] 82 My eyes have come to an end for your statement
in saying "When will you comfort me?"
[*k*] 83 When[19] I have become like a waterskin in smoke
I have not ignored your laws.
[*k*] 84 How many are your servant's days—
when will you make a decision about the people who harass me?
[*k*] 85 The willful have dug pits for me,
people who do not act in accordance with your teaching.[20]
[*k*] 86 All your commands are truthful;
with falsehood people harass me, help me!
[*k*] 87 They have all but made an end of me in the land,
but I myself have not abandoned your orders.
[*k*] 88 In accordance with your commitment, make me live,
so that I may keep the declaration of your mouth.

[*l*] 89 Yhwh endures forever;
your word stands in the heavens. [MT]
[or] Your word endures forever, Yhwh;
it stands in the heavens. [LXX, Jerome, Tg]
[*l*] 90 Your truthfulness endures to all generations;
you established the earth and it has stood firm.
[*l*] 91 As for your decisions, they have stood firm today,[21]
because all are[22] your servants.
[*l*] 92 Were not your teaching my delight,
then I would have perished in my weakness.
[*l*] 93 Never will I ignore your orders,
because through them you have made me live.

18. Q has ptc. *wĕyōdĕʿê* (cf. LXX, Jerome); K has yiqtol *wydʿw* (cf. Tg).

19. Not "for" (NRSV), because there is no "yet"; and not "though" (TNIV, NJPS), because it is doubtful if *kî* ever means that.

20. Lit. "that [were] not in accordance with your teaching." Jerome, Tg, Sym refer the clause to the pits rather than the people, which "makes it sound as though the pits might conform if they were, say, a cubit less wide" (Soll, *Psalm 119*, 165).

21. The decisions are the subject, but the expression is extraposed to begin the line with *l* (against GKC 143e, which calls this instance of the idiom "very doubtful"). NJPS takes the heavens and the earth as the subject of the verb, but this requires considerable inference and goes against the self-contained nature of the psalm's lines.

22. Collective *hakkōl* is treated as pl. (cf. Josh. 23:14).

[*l*] **94**I am yours, deliver me,
because I have had recourse to your orders.
[*l*] **95**As for me, the faithless have waited to make me perish;
I show understanding of your declarations.
[*l*] **96**As for every end, I have seen the limit;
your command is very broad.

[*m*] **97**How I am dedicated to your teaching;
it is my murmur all day.
[*m*] **98**Your commands make me wiser than my enemies,
because they are mine forever.[23]
[*m*] **99**I have gained more insight than all my tutors,
because your declarations are my murmur.
[*m*] **100**I show more understanding than the elders,
because I have observed your orders.
[*m*] **101**I have held back my feet from every evil path
so that I may keep your words.
[*m*] **102**I have not departed from your decisions,
because you are the one who has taught me.
[*m*] **103**How smooth your statement has been to my taste,
more so than honey to my mouth.
[*m*] **104**I show understanding through your orders;
therefore I am against every path of falsehood.

[*n*] **105**Your word is a lamp for my foot,
a light for my pathway.
[*n*] **106**I swore, I confirmed
that I would keep your faithful decisions.
[*n*] **107**I have become very weakened;
Yhwh, make me live, in accordance with your word.
[*n*] **108**Do accept the free offerings of my mouth, Yhwh,
and enable me to understand your decisions.
[*n*] **109**My life is continually in my palm,
but I have not ignored your teaching.
[*n*] **110**The faithless laid a trap for me,
but I have not wandered from your orders.
[*n*] **111**I entered into possession of your declarations forever,
because they are the joy of my heart.
[*n*] **112**I inclined my heart to do your laws
forever, to the utmost.[24]

[*s*] **113**I am against divided people
and I am dedicated to your teaching.

23. Sg. *tĕḥakkĕmēnî* followed by pl. subject *miṣwôtekā*; cf. GKC 145k. The disagreement carries over into the second colon, where *hîʾ* is sg. One could correct the grammar by repointing *miṣwātĕkā* as v. 96 (cf. LXX).

24. See note on v. 33.

[*s*] 114You have been my shelter, my shield;[25]
for your word I have waited.
[*s*] 115Go away from me, you wrongdoers,
so that I may observe my God's commands.
[*s*] 116Hold me up in accordance with your statement so that I may live,
and do not shame me in respect of my expectation.
[*s*] 117Sustain me so that I may find deliverance,
and may have regard[26] for your laws continually.
[*s*] 118You have thrown out[27] all the people who stray from your laws,
because their deceitfulness is false.
[*s*] 119You have put an end to[28] all the faithless people in the land as dross;
therefore I have been dedicated to your declarations.
[*s*] 120My flesh tingles through awe for you;
I revere your decisions.

[ʿ] 121I have made faithful decisions;
do not leave me to my oppressors.
[ʿ] 122Pledge good things to your servant;[29]
may the willful not oppress me.
[ʿ] 123My eyes—they have come to an end for your deliverance,
for your faithful statement.
[ʿ] 124Act with your servant in accordance with your commitment
and enable me to learn your laws.
[ʿ] 125I am your servant; enable me to understand
so that I may acknowledge your declarations.
[ʿ] 126It is a time for Yhwh to act;
people have violated your teaching.
[ʿ] 127Therefore I am dedicated to your commands
more than to gold, yes than pure gold.
[ʿ] 128Therefore all the orders concerning everything[30] I have regarded as upright;
I have been against every path of falsehood.

[*p*] 129Your declarations are wonders;
therefore my spirit has observed them.

25. The time reference of the noun clause is suggested by the verbal clause.

26. LXX, Jerome, Tg render "delight," perhaps confusing *šʿh* and *šʿʿ* (Barthélemy, *Psaumes*, 797–99).

27. Qimchi assumes the qatal refers to the future; Dahood takes it as precative (*Psalms*, 3:186). See on v. 21.

28. For *hišbattā* 11QPs[a] has *ḥšbty*, "I reckoned" (cf. LXX); Aq, Sym, Jerome have "you reckoned," implying *ḥiššabtā*.

29. Lit. "pledge your servant for good."

30. For the difficult *kol-piqqûdê kōl* 11QPs[a] omits *kol*; LXX, Jerome suggest *lĕkol-piqqûdêkā*, "with regard to all your charges." Soll (*Psalm 119*, 169–71) suggests *kol-piqqûdêkā lî*, "all your orders to me," but notes that the idea of orders "to me" is surprising. The emphatic expression recurs in Ezek. 44:30 (Calvin, *Psalms*, 5:8).

[*p*] 130The opening up of your words—it gives light;
it gives understanding to the simple.
[*p*] 131I opened wide my mouth to pant,
because I longed for your commands.
[*p*] 132Turn your face to me and be gracious to me
in accordance with your decision for people who are dedicated to
your name.
[*p*] 133Establish my steps by your statement;
may no harmfulness get the mastery of me.
[*p*] 134Redeem me from human oppression
so that I may keep your orders.
[*p*] 135Shine your face on your servant
and enable me to learn your laws.
[*p*] 136My eyes have run down streams of water[31]
because people have not kept your teaching.

[*ṣ*] 137You are faithful, Yhwh,
upright in your decisions.[32]
[*ṣ*] 138You commanded the faithfulness of your declarations,
and their truthfulness, exceedingly.
[*ṣ*] 139My passion has destroyed me,
because my foes have ignored your words.
[*ṣ*] 140Your statement is much proven;
your servant is dedicated to it.
[*ṣ*] 141I am little and despised;
your orders I have not ignored.
[*ṣ*] 142Your faithfulness is a faithfulness that endures forever,
and your teaching is true.
[*ṣ*] 143Though trouble and distress have found me,
your commands have been my delight.
[*ṣ*] 144The faithfulness of your declarations stands forever;
enable me to understand, so that I may live.

[*q*] 145I have called with all my heart: Answer me, Yhwh;
I shall observe your laws.
[*q*] 146I have called you: deliver me,
so that I may keep your declarations.
[*q*] 147I have anticipated the twilight and cried for help
as I waited for your word [Q]/words [K].
[*q*] 148My eyes have anticipated the watches,
murmuring about your statement.
[*q*] 149Listen to my voice in accordance with your commitment;

31. Not "streams of water run down my eyes" (cf. Jerome); occurrences of this expression with sg. "eye" (e.g., Lam. 1:16; 3:48) clarify that the eye(s) is the subject (cf. LXX). See GKC 117z on the quasi-transitive use of the verb.

32. EVV have "and upright are your decisions"; but the adjective is sg., the noun pl.

Yhwh, in accordance with your decision, make me live.
[*q*] 150People who pursue schemes [MT]/people who harass me with
schemes [Vrs][33] are near,
but they are far from your teaching.[34]
[*q*] 151You are near, Yhwh,
and all your commands are true.
[*q*] 152Of old I have acknowledged, from your declarations,
that you founded them forever.

[*r*] 153See my weakness and rescue me,
because I have not ignored your teaching.
[*r*] 154Decide my cause and restore me;
in view of your statement, make me live.
[*r*] 155Deliverance is far from the faithless
because they have not had recourse to your laws.
[*r*] 156Your compassion is great, Yhwh;
in accordance with your decision, make me live.
[*r*] 157Though my harassers and foes are many,
I have not diverted from your declarations.
[*r*] 158I have seen betrayers and loathed them,
people who did not keep your statement.
[*r*] 159See that I have been dedicated to your orders;
Yhwh, in accordance with your commitment make me live.
[*r*] 160Truthfulness is the sum total of your word;
every faithful decision of yours stands forever.

[*ś*] 161Leaders—they have harassed me without reason,
but at your word [Q]/words [K] my heart has stood in awe.
[*ś*] 162I exult over your statement
like someone who finds much plunder.
[*š*] 163Whereas I am against falsehood and abhor it,[35]
I am dedicated to your teaching.
[*š*] 164Seven times a day I have praised you
for your faithful decisions.
[*š*] 165There is much well-being for people who are dedicated to your
teaching
and there is nothing that can make them fall.
[*ś*] 166I have looked for your deliverance, Yhwh,
and I have acted on your commands.
[*š*] 167I have kept your declarations with my whole being,
and I am very much dedicated to them.
[*š*] 168I have kept your orders and your declarations,
because all my ways are before you.

33. For MT *rōdĕpê*, LXX, Sym, Jerome imply *rōdĕpay*.

34. I take both verbs as stative, *qārēb* and *rāḥōq* (rather than fientive *qārab*, *rāḥaq*).

35. One would expect *w*-consecutive *wāʾătaʿēbâ*. *TTH* 60 assumes this form beginning *wa-* is the *w*-consecutive.

[*t*] 169May my resounding come near your face, Yhwh;
in accordance with your word, enable me to understand.
[*t*] 170May my prayer for grace come before your face;
in accordance with your statement, rescue me.
[*t*] 171May my lips pour forth[36] praise,
because you enable me to learn your laws.
[*t*] 172May my tongue sing of your statement,
because all your commands are faithful.
[*t*] 173May your hand become my help,
because I have chosen your orders.
[*t*] 174I long for your deliverance, Yhwh;
your teaching is my delight.
[*t*] 175May my spirit live so that it may praise you,
and may your decisions help me.
[*t*] 176I have wandered like a lost sheep;
search for your servant,
because I have not ignored your commands.

Interpretation

Psalm 119, by far the longest psalm, is an alphabetical composition with twenty-two sections of eight verses each. Each of the eight verses begins with the appropriate letter, is syntactically self-contained, and can be understood independently of its context, though sometimes there are links of thought and language between lines (e.g., vv. 42–43; 98–100). Like other alphabetical psalms, Ps. 119 has no structural principle beyond the alphabet—no argument or development. It covers a number of themes, but raises them throughout the composition rather than expounding them systematically. It has a distinctive, consistent focus on Yhwh's commands and promises and keeps returning to expressing attitudes of commitment and hope, praise and plea in relation to these. All but four of the 176 lines include reference to Yhwh's *teaching, word(s), statement, *decision(s), command(s), *orders, *declarations, or *laws.[37] The words "way," "path," and "pathway" also feature frequently.[38]

In a premodern context, this made the psalm a favorite of expositors such as Hilary of Poitiers,[39] Calvin,[40] and Spurgeon (chronologically

36. The context suggests that *tabbaʿnâ* is also jussive.

37. See David Noel Freedman, *Psalm 119* (Winona Lake, IN: Eisenbrauns, 1999); Josef Schreiner, "Leben nach der Weisung des Herrn," in *Freude an der Weisung des Herrn*, ed. Haag and Hossfeld, 395–424 (see 399–410); Soll, *Psalm 119*, 59–86; on other rhetorical features, see Auffret, *Voyez de nos yeux*, 319–414.

38. See LarsOlov Eriksson, "Vägen i Psaltaren 119," *SEÅ* 63 (1998): 31–40.

39. *Commentaire sur le Psaume 118*, 2 vols. (Paris: Cerf, 1988).

40. *Psalms*, 4:398–494 and 5:1–51.

modern but ideologically premodern),[41] who expounded it at some length. Augustine professes to have been long held back from commenting on it. In a superficial sense, he said, it does not need "an expositor, but only a reader and listener," and he did not think he could do justice to its depth.[42] In the modern period, its focus and its literary nature made critical scholars cold toward the psalm. Weiser called it artificial and wearisome, "a purely literary product" that reflects personal religious experience but "carries with it the germs of a development which was bound to end in the self-righteousness of the Pharisees and scribes"[43] (that comment would also now need reconsideration). He gives its 176 verses two pages of comment, less than he gives to Ps. 120 with its seven verses. In the postmodern context, as usual, such judgments have been reversed.

The form's stimulus and constraint generate two contrasting characteristics of the psalm. It often uses words or constructions in innovative or unusual ways to make lines begin with the right letter (e.g., "O that" in v. 5; "shattered" in v. 20; "wept away" in v. 28). But it does not avoid repeating a familiar word that begins with the right letter, even when it would have been possible to think of other words to use (e.g., *rāʾâ* "see" in vv. 153–60). Yet neither does it use such repetition systematically: for instance, vv. 169–76 include six third-person feminine yiqtol verbs, but randomly vv. 174 and 176 do not fit this pattern. Possibly the repetitions suggest the psalmist is not always starting from scratch but collating existent lines. This would be one of the ways the psalm compares with Proverbs, where individual lines can stand alone yet are often collated to put them into relationship with each other. The first two lines make the psalm begin with parallel statements; in vv. 4–7 each second colon continues the first by an infinitival expression, twice *l-*, twice *b-*; vv. 81–82 make parallel statements, as do vv. 98–100, 145–46, 147–48, 169–70, and 171–72.

Again, although the psalm is structured in eight-line sections and uses eight words to refer to Yhwh's teaching, it does not correlate these two eights or seek to use the eight words in any patterned way. Further, as well as leaving just four of the lines without one of the eight words (vv. 3, 37, 90, and 122), five of the lines have two of them (vv. 16, 48, 160, 168, and 172). This is hardly evidence of incompetence or textual corruption; it again instances OT psalmody's preference for leaving poetic patterns not quite perfectly realized rather than absolutely complete. This keeps readers on their toes; one can never predict how the poetry

41. *Treasury of David*, 5:130–479.
42. *Psalms*, 560.
43. *Psalms*, 739, 740, 741.

may turn out. This psalm is "endlessly inventive,"[44] using words with "no more order than in a kaleidoscope."[45]

There are more occasions than in other psalms where whole lines are broadly parallel. Many further lines involve parallelism between cola. Others involve enjambment, with the first colon incomplete without the second (e.g., vv. 13, 18, 20); this has the effect of making the line hurry on and of working against the usual dynamic of the bicolon. Many involve asyndesis, juxtaposing clauses without syntactically relating them (e.g., vv. 3, 12, 16, 57, 86, 126); this involves the reader in working out how to relate them. Many involve the "pivot pattern," whereby an element at the center of the line belongs to both cola (e.g., vv. 46, 48, 52, 105, 107, 108, 137, 138, 149); this has the effect of binding the cola. The psalm uses hendiadys (e.g., vv. 106, 114, 121) and litotes (e.g., vv. 8, 16, 19) and makes use of abstract nouns to denote concrete realities (e.g., vv. 38, 75, 86, 172). Many lines are arranged *abb'a'* (e.g., vv. 2, 3, 13 [where "lips" and "mouth" form the line's frame], 15, 16, 27, 149, 150 [where "near" and "far" form the frame]); this can have the effect of emphasizing both links and contrasts. While the psalm is thus sometimes unadventurous in its vocabulary, it manifests variety in its use of poetic devices. In its rhythm, according to MT much of it is 3-2 (e.g., vv. 2, 3, 4, 5, 9, 12, 14). Also common is 2-2 (vv. 6, 8, 10, 13, 15). The other lines in the first two sections are 2-3 (vv. 1, 16) and 3-3 (vv. 7, 11).[46] This balance fits its lament emphasis.

Ways of speaking to and of God characteristic of the Psalter reappear here. There are lines (or cola) of praise, testimony, protest, trust, plea, commitment, acknowledgment of wrongdoing, and promise of future obedience. But throughout, the psalm keeps a steady, determined, and distinctive focus on the way these correlate with Yhwh's teaching; this is the special subject of praise, testimony, protest, trust, plea, commitment, and acknowledgment of wrongdoing. In keeping with its structuring by the alphabetic scheme, another distinctive feature is that these different ways of speaking to and of God follow one another unsystematically rather than in the logical fashion that characterizes many psalms. Psalm 119 does begin with a declaration about how things work well for people who follow Yhwh's teaching, and end with a plea for Yhwh to search for the suppliant who is lost, and this suggests a standard move within a prayer psalm. But inside this beginning and end, it moves randomly between statements of trust, protest, confession, and plea.

Thus it is not the case (for instance) that the psalm simply looks back on a situation in which it was necessary to plead for Yhwh's intervention

44. David Noel Freedman and Andrew Welch in Freedman, *Psalm 119*, 87.

45. Briggs, *Psalms*, 2:415.

46. Of course the Masoretes may have changed the original rhythm by their linking of words; e.g., v. 1 might have been 3-3 (3-3 is common later in the psalm; 4-2 also recurs).

but can now speak of being free. Freedom, affliction, gratitude, protest, praise, commitment, and confession of sin are all spoken of as present realities. Further, as is the case with biblical narrative, its concrete and serendipitous form enables it to discuss issues in their subtlety and complexity. It is not bound to one statement about a question such as the link between obedience and blessing; it can make many statements that nuance one another, so that the whole can avoid oversimplification.

It thus looks more like a compendium of things one might say to God at different times than a prayer for someone to pray as a whole at the same time with the same immediacy.[47] The alphabetical form hints that it says all that needs to be said about prayer, from A to Z. Two later ways of using the psalm may give us insight on its inherent nature. It has been prayed systematically in the framework of the prayer offices of the church. In that context, it can function gradually to shape people's understanding and practice of their relationship with God. Its alphabetic form also may contribute to this end as it facilitates people's remembering the contents of this compendium.[48] How far people praying the psalm will "mean" each line would vary within the community and would vary for individuals at different times. That links with the second way of using it, as people take individual verses in isolation and treat them as resources for piety (e.g., v. 18). Jon D. Levenson suggests that the psalm itself invites the kind of reading that came to be called *lectio divina*,[49] while R. Norman Whybray calls it "*devotional* poetry: the outpouring of the most intense religious feeling."[50] But it would be unwise to try to portray the author's personality or experiences from it, as if it issued from personal journaling. It collects expressions of how anyone might relate to Yhwh.

We have noted that its form has links with Proverbs, and it has points of connection with Proverbs' ways of thinking and language. It emphasizes walking in the right "way." It assumes that right and wrong action have their "natural" results in blessing or trouble. It is concerned for the young person and the simple. It speaks much of teaching and

47. J. L. Mays calls it "a liturgical tapestry of devotional moves" ("The Place of Torah-Psalms in the Psalter," *JBL* 106 [1987]: 3–12 [see 6]). Soll (*Psalm 119*, 59–86) does see it as a prayer, and Mowinckel as a "(non-cultic) individual psalm of lamentation" (*Psalms*, 2:78). Siegfried Bergler ("Der längste Psalm," *VT* 29 [1979]: 257–88 [see 286]) suggests that it belongs at the festival of Rejoicing in the Law, Goulder (*Psalms of the Return*, 201) at Pentecost.

48. Hilary (*Commentaire*, 1:92–93) sees it as designed for young people under instruction, in keeping with 2 Tim. 3:14–15.

49. "The Sources of Torah," in *Ancient Israelite Religion*, ed. Patrick D. Miller et al. (F. M. Cross Festschrift; Philadelphia: Fortress, 1987), 559–74 (see 566).

50. "Psalm 119," in *Wisdom, You Are My Sister*, ed. Michael L. Barré, CBQMS 29 (R. E. Murphy Festschrift; Washington: Catholic Biblical Association, 1997), 31–43 (see 32).

learning, of understanding and knowledge/acknowledgment, and of the heart and mind. Like the Wisdom books, it makes no reference to the promise to the ancestors, Moses, the exodus, the covenant, holiness, or other motifs in Israel's story. But it does not refer to wisdom (the verb "be wise" comes only in v. 98, in a context that certainly does not affirm the value of the "wisdom" perspective). In all these connections, its key resource is Yhwh's teaching, and the psalmist's teacher is Yhwh, not a human mentor. It is a (or the) Torah psalm, not a wisdom psalm.[51] In general terms it often reflects the language of other Scriptures (especially Deuteronomy, where most of the terms for Yhwh's teaching come), and the talk of harassment recalls Jeremiah, but Ps. 119 is more allusive in its relationship with other books than many preceding psalms. It has no cola or verses that correspond as closely with cola or verses in other parts of the OT as they do. Indeed, its closest points of connection are within the Psalter, with Ps. 19. It is usually dated in the Persian period, but it has been dated before the exile and in the Greek period.

119:1–8. *ʾĀlep* (ʾ). The opening section combines a series of general statements (vv. 1–4) with a series of personal ones in which the psalmist professes identification with those general statements (vv. 5–8). The rest of the psalm will go on to speak resolutely for an individual "I"; the initial generalizations make explicit that it does not speak just for one individual or for particularly holy individuals but lays before the community a vision that applies to everyone but needs to be appropriated by each individual.[52]

> [1]The good fortune of people of integrity in their way of life,
> who walk in Yhwh's teaching!

Its beginning parallels the Psalter's own beginning (in part Ps. 119 could be seen as a vast expansion on Ps. 1), speaking of the *good fortune (*ʾašrê*) of people with *integrity, spelled out as walking in Yhwh's *teaching. The parallelism immediately underlines how a relationship with Yhwh is not merely a matter of what goes on inside the person but of the outward life. This is where integrity resides. Such integrity of outward life does not spoil a person's life but makes it. "The farther a man wanders from God, the happier does he imagine himself to be," yet following endless bypaths instead of the right path ends in ruin and destruction.[53] That might seem a counterintuitive affirmation, and the

51. On this question, see, e.g., A. Robert, "Le Psaume cxix et les sapientiaux," *RB* 48 (1939): 5–20; Soll, *Psalm 119*, 115–25; J. P. M. van der Ploeg, "Le Psaume 119 et la Sagesse," in *La Sagesse de l'Ancient Testament* (Leuven: Leuven University Press, 1979), 82–87.

52. Cf. Gerstenberger, *Psalms*, 2:311–12.

53. Calvin, *Psalms*, 3:403.

line does not say how it is true. It recalls Proverbs, and implicitly invites readers to reckon that life shows that it is so.

"Anyone who speaks like this assumes that the beginning has been made. . . . Life with God is not essentially a matter of ever-new beginnings" but of keeping on the way.[54]

> [2]The good fortune of people who observe his declarations,
> who have recourse to him with all their heart.

The second affirmation parallels the first, now speaking of the *good fortune (*ʾašrê*) of people who observe Yhwh's *declarations, having *recourse to him with their whole *heart. In the context, this inquiring of Yhwh indicates seeking direction over behavioral questions. Observing Yhwh's declarations is again an outward matter, but the second colon does then raise the question of the relationship of inward and outward. There needs to be a unity about the person and their relationship with life. Behavior without attitude would not be enough; attitude without behavior would not be enough. Indeed, the psalm assumes, one cannot have behavior characterized by integrity without the right attitude of heart; and one cannot have the right attitude of heart without that being expressed outwardly.

> [3]Yes, they have done no wickedness;
> they have walked in his ways.

The declaration about good fortune also applies to v. 3, whose "Yes" (*ʾap*) introduces another description of those to whom the declaration applies. The qatal verbs are perhaps gnomic, describing something that is regularly true; proverbs in Hebrew often have qatal verbs (Hebrew would find it natural to say, "Many cooks have spoiled the broth").[55] This time the parallelism contrasts a negative and a positive. Wickedness is defined not as failing to live by objective standards of right and wrong but as failing to walk in Yhwh's ways, a common expression in Deuteronomy and books that follow its mode of speaking (e.g., Deut. 8:6; 10:12; 1 Kings 2:3). Whereas talk of Yhwh commanding the people's way implies reference to the way people should walk, "Yhwh's ways" can suggest the ways Yhwh walks, which are to become the ways Israel also walks in imitation of Yhwh. Doing right involves imitation of Yhwh. "God's ways are the ways which he himself has gone and which we are

54. Dietrich Bonhoeffer, *Meditating on the Word* (Cambridge, MA: Cowley, 1986), 105.

55. See Max Rogland, *Alleged Non-past Uses of* Qatal *in Classical Hebrew* (Assen: Van Gorcum, 2003), 46.

now to go with him."[56] People's way (singular, v. 1) needs to be shaped by Yhwh's ways (plural).

> [4]You yourself commanded your orders
> to be well kept.

Verse 4 moves in a different ethical direction in emphasizing that this way is one that Yhwh personally (*ʾattâ*, "you") has given orders about. Israel's way of life does not involve making mature independent choices, like grown-ups now freed by their parents to make their own decisions. The life characterized by good fortune involves obedience to *orders Yhwh issued. Israel's job is simply to keep them. "Well" (lit. "much"), not by half-measures, the psalmist adds as the last word.

> [5]O that my ways may be firm
> in keeping your laws!

The wish (*ʾaḥălay*) recognizes that it is an open question whether one will keep Yhwh's *laws, even while recognizing its importance. Making a commitment is one thing; maintaining it is another. One needs to stand firm (*kûn* niphal), like the kingship in Solomon's hands (1 Kings 2:12, 46) or like the world itself (Pss. 93:2; 96:10). The human person is a complex entity; at one level a person can be committed to obedience, yet at another level not be so. The verse recognizes the need for an internal argument expressed in Ps. 42. But set in this context, it implies a stance about the possibility of obedience paralleling Phil. 3:6, 12–14 and the exhortations in the Sermon on the Mount rather than that of Rom. 7.

> [6]Then I shall not be shamed,
> as I look on all your commands.

NJPS runs on v. 6 from v. 5, but it would be unique for one verse in this psalm to link syntactically with another. Every verse is self-contained. One might even ask whether "then" (*ʾāz*) is simply an emphatic particle, or whether it anticipates the "as" in the second colon, rather than following on from v. 5. But the only other "O that" in the OT (2 Kings 5:3) is also followed by a "then," and logically v. 6a does follow from v. 5; in effect v. 6b is then restating v. 5. Shaming is part of the negative counterpart of good fortune (vv. 1–2), the two helping to nuance their respective significances. On one hand, good fortune is not merely a matter of blessings such as prosperity and good health, but of honor in the community, which respects a person of integrity. On the other hand, a devastating

56. Bonhoeffer, *Meditating on the Word*, 114.

consequence of refusing to walk in Yhwh's ways is losing one's honor before the community. All these interlink. Obedience generates prosperity and thus honor; disobedience generates trouble and thus shame. While the psalm recognizes that there are many exceptions to those rules, this does not mean the generalizations are without foundation. But part of the psalm's background is the way the generalizations may not work in the short term, and it will give considerable energy to pressing Yhwh to deliver and thus restore honor and remove shame.

7 I will confess you with uprightness of heart
as I learn your faithful decisions.

Confessing ('ôdĕkā*) implies giving testimony to what Yhwh has done for me; v. 7 follows from v. 6 like v. 6 from v. 5. The suppliant will prove that obeying Yhwh means prosperity and honor and will thus be able to testify to that. Verse 2 spoke of having recourse to Yhwh with the whole heart (cf. v. 10); confessing Yhwh with uprightness of *heart is an overlapping notion, suggesting the integrity of attitude lying behind integrity of life.

Another aspect of the dynamic of obedience is that as well as action and an attitude of heart, it requires attention to learning. We cannot assume we automatically know what is right, what God requires, for a variety of reasons not stated here: for instance, because our human perversity means we lose our insight into that, or because it is counterintuitive, or because God simply has rules that one could never work out by reason. No one would have worked out that we cannot worship Yhwh by means of images or ought to do no work one day each week. We have to listen and learn to discover the *authoritative decisions Yhwh has made about life that expound the nature of *faithful living in relation to God and one another.

8 I will keep your laws;
do not completely abandon me.

The desire expressed in v. 5 is now the psalmist's personal commitment. Speaking in terms of a wish took us to the inner longings; when they work right, that is potentially a powerful thing. But speaking of my wishes could be a way of avoiding obedience. Here the psalmist accepts responsibility for what was formerly the object of a wish: "I will keep your *laws [*'et-ḥuqqêkā*]."

For the first time the expected consequence of that commitment is expressed in terms of Yhwh's action; for the first time Yhwh is the subject of a verb. "Good fortune" (vv. 1–2) implies a "natural" process built into the way life works; while this is a process Yhwh devised, the phrase draws attention to the natural process. Similarly, "I shall not be shamed" (v. 6) does not make a comment on the agent of the shaming, though implicitly this will be Yhwh (cf. vv. 31, 116). Here it is explicit that Yhwh can be the agent of abandoning, which has devastating implications. It does not merely mean feeling abandoned by God. It means actually being surrendered to forces that can mean death (e.g., 22:1 [2]; 37:25, 33).

Keeping Yhwh's laws gives a basis for a plea that this should never happen, or should not happen "completely" (*ʿad mĕʾōd,* more literally "to much"), that Yhwh should not excessively or seriously abandon me. Is it possible to accept a little bit of abandonment but not abandonment on a large scale? This would be a wise and realistic stance. More likely the expression involves litotes: the psalmist means "Do not abandon me at all!" Yet issuing the plea implies an awareness of the danger, or perhaps an awareness of being rather abandoned already. The first section of the psalm thus comes to an end with the first indication of a note that will recur.

119:9–16. *Bêt* (*b*). Most lines begin with the preposition *b*, translated "how" (v. 9), "with" (vv. 10, 13), "in" (vv. 11, 14, 16), and "about" (v. 15).

> 9How can a young person keep his path pure?—
> by guarding it in accordance with your word.

In a rhetorical question, the answer to the "How?" (*bammeh*, "with what") could be assumed to be obvious. But the psalm keeps majoring on the answer stated in the second colon, suggesting this answer cannot be taken for granted. So the rhetorical continuity between the two cola stands in tension with a discontinuity. The question presupposes we want to keep our path pure, but the need to raise it with this obvious answer presupposes we do not. Like Proverbs (1:4, 22:6, 15), the psalm is concerned (among other things) for the instruction of the young (*naʿar* can cover people from babyhood to near adulthood), people who still need to learn wisdom.[57]

The few occurrences of *zākâ* ("be pure"; cf. also *zākak* and the adjective *zak*) raise complex questions. Eliphaz and Bildad ask whether anyone can be pure (Job 15:14; 25:4); before God and compared with God, all humanity stands sullied and soiled. Yet Isaiah urges people to purify themselves (Isa. 1:16). Even if we cannot make ourselves absolutely pure (Prov. 20:9), we are responsible to purify ourselves of the kind of

57. R. E. O. White ("The Student's Psalm?" *ExpT* 102 [1990–91]: 71–74) suggests that the psalmist is young and is indirectly asking "How can I as a young person keep my way pure?"

filth that Isaiah describes. The impossibility of sinless perfection does not excuse us from taking God's demands seriously. But "keep his path pure" may be overly optimistic. Given Eliphaz and Bildad's point, the question is how we can find our way into purity of life. Either way, the answer is to keep guard over our way in accordance with Yhwh's *word. The twofold content of Yhwh's word as command and promise may imply we do so both by living by Yhwh's command and by ensuring that Yhwh's promise comes to be fulfilled.

10With all my heart I have had recourse to you;
do not let me stray from your commands.

The psalmist claims to be the kind of person v. 2b prescribes, yet grants that we can never take ourselves for granted. Straying is not just a young person's problem; people stray in midlife and later life. There is some mystery about this; hence the need to appeal to Yhwh about it. So the first colon accepts responsibility for one's moral life, and the second recognizes that we need Yhwh's support to fulfill that responsibility (v. 67 will cast new light on this plea). Indeed, the second verb raises a tougher question. Elsewhere *šāgâ* (hiphil) always refers to *making* someone stray. The OT and NT recognize that God is capable of doing that as an act of chastisement (Isa. 6:9–10; Mark 4:11–12). Jerome takes it this way here. The line's logic is then that being someone who has had recourse to Yhwh with a whole *heart (*bĕkol-libbî*) means Yhwh has no reason to do that.

11In my heart I have treasured your statement
so that I may not fall short in relation to you.

Whereas "with all my heart" suggests attitude and commitment, "in my *heart" (still *b* plus *lēb*) suggests treasuring Yhwh's *statement (in the context, a word of command) in the inner person so as to shape one's thinking, decision making, and life. There this word is hidden deep so that it cannot easily be ferreted out and removed, as teachers want their insight to be buried deep in their students' hearts (cf. Prov. 2:1; 7:1; 10:14). The psalmist has stored up Yhwh's statement because that is how to make sure of not *failing or falling short of Yhwh's expectations.

12You are to be worshipped, Yhwh;
enable me to learn your laws.

The requirements of the *b* section suggest the declaration that Yhwh is to be *worshipped (qal passive participle *bārûk*). In Ps. 119 it comes only here. It does hint that we should not make too sharp a division between the worship focus and context of the psalms in general and the concerns of Ps. 119. Indeed, these two cola themselves make that point. Worshipping Yhwh and learning Yhwh's *laws go together.

This particular declaration is unique in the Psalms. Everywhere else it takes third-person form: Yhwh is to be blessed. The second-person form appears elsewhere in the OT only in 1 Chron. 29:10, though it becomes the norm in subsequent Jewish prayers.[58] The address to God makes the declaration a direct act of worship rather than a summons to other people; the two forms correspond to those of testimony and thanksgiving.

The second verb picks up from v. 7 and draws renewed attention to a related correlation. It is my responsibility to learn what Yhwh has laid down; but I need Yhwh to enable me to learn, because I have instincts that drive me in other directions. The psalm asks Yhwh to act like a wise teacher such as the person who speaks in Prov. 1–9.

13With my lips I have proclaimed
all the decisions of your mouth.

The psalmist is a teacher as well as a learner (cf. Isa. 50:4). "With my lips" (*biśpātay*) and "of your mouth" neatly book-end the line. Inside, "proclaimed" and "decisions" stand together, with similar implications: these are *authoritative decisions Yhwh made and Yhwh's mouth originally made known, but my lips make them known now. Proclaiming them is another indication of my commitment to them. While it does not guarantee that commitment (human beings can say one thing and do another), it makes it harder to evade it. When we take things on our lips they become part of us; when other people have heard us say these things, it becomes shameful to do something other than what our lips have said.

14In the way of your declarations I have rejoiced
as over all wealth.

The "way of your *declarations" (cf. v. 2) is the way of life those declarations urged (*bĕderek*). The verb introduces a new note. We know Yhwh's teaching involves the heart, the whole being, the will, the commitment (vv. 2, 7, 10, 11). In the OT, reference to the heart need not imply anything very affective. But it is important that feelings are involved; what we feel has decisive influence on our behavior. A distinctive facet of OT

58. See W. Sibley Towner, "'Blessed Be Yhwh' and 'Blessed Art Thou, Yhwh,'" *CBQ* 30 (1968): 386–99.

spirituality is joy in Yhwh's declarations concerning how we should behave. These are not a burden to us. We rejoice to affirm them because they are Yhwh's and because they prescribe what is best for us. Nevertheless, fancy getting as much kick out of doing what Yhwh says as out of having all the wealth in the world.

15About your orders I shall murmur;
 I shall look on your paths.

*Murmuring about "your *orders" (*bĕpiqqudêkā*; cf. v. 4) restates proclaiming and rejoicing; it suggests strong feelings outwardly expressed. Once more the cola correlate actions that need to belong together: "look on" suggests attentiveness expressing itself in a practical stance. Like v. 13, the line works *abb′a′*.

16In your laws I will delight;
 I will not ignore your words.

"*Laws" (*bĕḥuqqōtêkā*) comes for the fourth time in the psalm's first sixteen verses (though here for the only time feminine *ḥuqqâ*). The paradoxical nature of the psalmist's stance toward them is underlined by "*delight" (*šāʿaʿ*, here hitpalpel). The second colon may then be another litotes; the psalmist means "I will give my whole mind to them as well as rejoice in them with enthusiasm." Yet the possibility of *ignoring Yhwh's *words needs to be owned. Yhwh is often warning about that (e.g., Deut. 4:9, 23, 31), and the verb comes nine times in the psalm. Yet again, the line works *abb′a′*.

119:17–24. *Gîmel* (*g*). So far the psalm has been positive and confident; its pleas are related to being enabled to live in obedience. This third section broadens the agenda to take account of the vulnerability of the suppliant's position.

17Deal with your servant;
 I shall live and keep your word.

In itself "deal with" (*gĕmōl ʿal*) is just an appeal to Yhwh to exercise sovereignty. It is the context that indicates that it implies Yhwh doing good to us (cf. 116:7). The verb thus hints at a trust that simply asks Yhwh to exercise sovereignty and knows it will be beneficent; and it hints at a conviction that our lives are such that we can reckon Yhwh will have reason to act with beneficence, not judgment. The self-description as Yhwh's servant links with that, suggesting a claim on our master's faithfulness but presupposing that we have indeed been living as a faithful servant.

The second colon goes on to the implicit results of Yhwh's acting thus (there is no "so that," but the Psalms often leave readers to infer such links, as we do in English). The chain of verbs is striking. The result of Yhwh's "dealing" is that I shall "live," the first occurrence of a motif that will recur (the verb will reappear in vv. 77, 116, 144, 175). The suppliant prays this whole prayer presupposing pressure and harassment (e.g., vv. 23, 25, 28). I cannot assume "I shall live," stay alive. Indeed, the verb can imply "I shall revive" (e.g., v. 25); that would fit here.

The third verb in the chain states the further result of Yhwh's "dealing": "I shall . . . keep your word." The purpose of God's acting to deliver and sustain life is that we give ourselves to God as instruments of righteousness (Rom. 6:13). Yet implicitly such obedience is the presupposition of the whole line; we can take the risk of asking Yhwh to "deal with us" only on the assumption that we are living in obedience. Keeping Yhwh's word is both the line's original presupposition and its final goal. It is the entire frame of life with God.

[18]Open my eyes so that I may look on
wonders from your teaching.

"Wonders" usually refers to Yhwh's marvelous acts in delivering Israel. This would link with the preceding prayer. The suppliant's faith and hope need building up; awareness of the wonders Yhwh has done can have this effect. *The* "Teaching," or Torah, is not only a collection of instructions on what Israel must do, but a record of what Yhwh has done, which motivates what Israel must do. Under pressure, we can be overwhelmed by what Yhwh is not doing now and miss the significance of Yhwh's past deeds. So we need our eyes opened (*gal*). There is nothing mysterious about the stories. They give a clear enough account of what Yhwh has done. But we cannot see it.

But v. 129 will declare that Yhwh's declarations are "wonders." There it is the collective noun *pele'* rather than the plural participle *niplā'ôt*, but it suggests another possibility for this line. The wonders are the very commands, orders, and laws in Yhwh's teaching. This understanding fits with a characteristic of the psalm. It makes no overt reference to Yhwh's acts in Israel's history. The great wonder is the gift of Yhwh's teaching.

Why should it be seen thus? Perhaps the exodus is a long time ago. Chronicles, too, ignores the story of the ancestors, the exodus, and the giving of the land, but focuses on David and the temple as realities that relate directly to the Jerusalem community. Psalm 119 moves in a different direction in relating Yhwh's involvement with people to the individual's everyday life. Its focus on Yhwh's teaching compares more with Ezra-Nehemiah than with Chronicles, though it does not refer to it as Moses's teaching as Ezra-Nehemiah does.

Or perhaps it is marvelous not only that we should not be left in the dark about Yhwh's expectations, but that what Yhwh reveals is the key (for instance) to good fortune (vv. 1–2), honor (v. 6) and life (v. 17). Again we may not see it, perhaps because we do not want to. We may not find it natural to see commands, orders, and laws as keys to opening up our lives rather than narrowing them down. So again we need Yhwh to open our eyes.

19 I am a sojourner in the world;
do not hide your commands from me.

If we understand v. 18 in that fashion, this further plea is the negative and objective equivalent to that positive and subjective point. As well as smearing over my eyes instead of opening them (cf. Isa. 6:10), Yhwh might in Kafkaesque fashion be secretive about the commands, laws, and orders that are incumbent on me. It may seem unnecessary, but I plead with Yhwh not to do so. But the plea is perhaps another litotes. "Do not hide" means "make absolutely clear."

To speak of oneself as a sojourner (*gēr*) is a weird and sad thing. Sojourners are aliens, immigrants, people without rights. Israelites were not sojourners in Canaan; it was their country. (In a sense it is Yhwh's country, and in that sense they are indeed only sojourners; cf. Lev. 25:23.) They were secure there. The psalmist feels no more secure in the world than a landless foreigner feels in Israel, dependent on the mercy of the people who have rights there (cf. Ps. 39:12–13 [13–14]; and see 1 Chron. 29:15). That coheres with the awareness of personal insecurity from attackers that runs through the psalm and with the whole community's insecurity in the Second Temple period, surrounded by peoples such as the Samarians and the Edomites (see vv. 21, 23). Verses 21 and 23 will speak of such "willful" people, the kind of "leaders" who cause trouble to Nehemiah.

The prayer in v. 19b is then not the plea one might have expected to follow. The suppliant again presupposes that even in this situation, obedience is the key to security or life (v. 17). Obedience safeguards a relationship with Yhwh and provides a basis for trusting Yhwh to protect. "But now I must ask myself whether I am so guided by my own principles that I might not even notice if God withdrew his living commandment from me one day."[59]

59. Bonhoeffer, *Meditating on the Word*, 140.

[20]My spirit has shattered in connection with my longing
for your decisions all the time.

The psalmist reformulates the point again, as a statement rather than a plea. EVV give a positive meaning to the psalmist's spirit (*person) being shattered (*gāras*) and consumed with longing for Yhwh's *decisions. The line is then an extreme statement of a longing to know God's expectations of our lives. One might imagine someone engrossed with a demanding academic project and shattered through giving it late night and early morning hours. That would be the nature of the psalmist's ongoing study of Yhwh's expectations in light of a longing to grasp and be grasped by them.

But shattering sounds more negative than this implies. More likely such shattering of spirit is an aspect of the trouble that has come to the psalmist as a result of that enthusiastic longing for and commitment to Yhwh's decisions. Verse 25 will make that point in slightly different words.

[21]You have blasted the willful;
cursed are the people who stray from your commands.

This declaration counterbalances v. 20 and functions as a reminder for the psalmist. In principle the psalmist knows that Yhwh blesses people who heed Yhwh's decisions. The converse is not something neutral. It is not an ordinary life that lacks that blessing. Ignoring those decisions means being blasted (*gāʿar*) as Yhwh blasted the tumultuous waters that would otherwise overwhelm the earth (cf. 104:7). It means being "cursed." This is the only occurrence of *ʾārar* in the Psalms. Usually "cursed is" or "cursed are" is a performative statement (cf. v. 12), but here it is a simple affirmation, comparable to "the good fortune of" in vv. 1–2 but with the opposite implication. The active verb "blasted" is thus complemented by this passive participle whose implicit subject is Yhwh but whose form puts the stress on the experience of being under a curse rather than on the curse's agent. It also points to the "naturalness" whereby straying leads to disaster, through processes written into the universe rather than through Yhwh's intervention. Yet further, it may function as a reminder for Yhwh as well as for the psalmist.

The object of this blasting is people who are *willful.[60] Their willfulness expresses itself in their treatment of the suppliant (vv. 51, 69, 78, 85, 122), but on this first appearance the focus lies on its prior implication,

60. See Félix Asensio, "Los zēdîn del Salmo 119 en el área 'dolo-mentira,'" *EstBib* 41 (1983): 185–204.

their attitude to Yhwh's commands, which leads them to treat other people as they like. This willfulness means that "straying" (cf. v. 10) does not happen by accident, as if they are trying to walk the right path but accidentally leave it. Even if they do not realize the implications of what they are doing, they are making choices that involve abandoning the right path for the wrong one (e.g., 1 Sam. 26:21). Verse 67 will later acknowledge that the willful are not the only ones who stray, or that we can all join the company of the willful who do so, and thus give extra significance to the curse on people who stray: it will turn it into a self-curse, if we do stray.

> **22**Take away from me taunt and shame,
> because I have observed your declarations.

Perhaps the line indicates the way willfulness expresses itself in relation to the suppliant. Observing Yhwh's *declarations stands in contrast to willfulness and earns taunts and shame, either because such commitment is simply reckoned to be stupid, or because the trouble the suppliant experiences shows it is stupid. Righteousness does not pay, the willful say. Banish these taunts, the suppliant urges. The verb (*gal*) is the same as in v. 18; *gālâ* can mean remove or exile as well as uncover. But the form might also be linked with *gālal* "roll away" (cf. Josh. 5:9; and 11QPs[a] *gwl*); the suppliant might not distinguish these as forms from different verbs as we do.

The desire that taunt and shame be taken away might imply that they relate to trouble that has come on the suppliant despite being committed to righteousness or because of being so committed, so that "take away the taunt" implies "take away the trouble that causes the taunt." Or perhaps the plea reflects the importance of having good standing in the community. Being the object of taunt and shame is trouble in itself. In turn, the "because" may back up the "take away" or may explain the taunts.

> **23**Although leaders have sat speaking together against me,
> your servant—he murmurs about your laws.

The psalm becomes more explicit about this trouble. One can imagine various circumstances in which leaders (*śārîm*, a general word) might so plot (cf. v. 161). The line would fit on the lips of Naboth or Jeremiah in relation to leaders within the community, or on the lips of Nehemiah in relation to leaders of other communities. The picture of them sitting to make their plans against the suppliant recalls 1:1. Although (*gam*) they are doing that, the suppliant *murmurs about Yhwh's *laws and does so as Yhwh's servant (as the word order emphasizes); as in v. 17, that is both a declaration of the servant's commitment to the master (expressed in the rest of the colon) and an implicit appeal to the master's commitment to the servant.

> 24Yes, your declarations are my delight,
> my policymakers.

The "yes" statement (*gam* again, with a different meaning) again restates v. 23b while picking up "delight" from the last line of the previous section, v. 16, and applying it to Yhwh's *declarations. The second colon hints at a neat link with v. 23. Those leaders are formulating plans; they are policymakers (*'ēṣâ*, the word for policy, plan, or counsel, makes another link with 1:1). But the suppliant's policymaking comes from another source. The leaders' policies come from their willfulness (v. 21); the suppliant's policies for life come from Yhwh's declarations. These are the suppliant's "best friends" (Jerome's translation). *Delight and policy again suggest the strong combination of the affective and the conative. The suppliant is involved in tough decision making but is emboldened and strengthened by a love for the declarations that shape policies for life. Conversely, the suppliant is emotionally enthusiastic about Yhwh's declarations but does not stop at enthusiasm; enthusiasm makes a difference to moral commitment.

119:25–32. *Dālet* (*d*). The ethos of the *gîmel* section continues; *derek* (way) is the opening word in vv. 26, 27, 29, 30, 32.

> 25My spirit has stuck to the dirt;
> make me live, in accordance with your word.

Verse 20 declared that the psalmist's spirit was shattered. To put it another way, it has fallen to the ground and stuck (*dābaq*) there. Effectively, this spirit (*person) is glued to the dirt and cannot raise itself.

But the dirt is the place where we go when we die; our bodies are buried there, and as they decompose we become one with the dirt. So dirt can signify death (22:15, 29 [16, 30]; 30:9 [10]; 104:29). Verse 25b suggests this connotation for v. 25a. Thus the psalmist is saying, "I am as good as dead and have no way of raising myself from the realm of death; but you, Yhwh, can restore me to life." The basis for appealing for that is Yhwh's *word of promise that undertakes to protect and deliver people who live by Yhwh's commands.

> 26I proclaimed my ways and you answered me;
> enable me to learn your laws.

Elsewhere, worshippers proclaim God's commands (v. 13) or deeds (26:7), but proclaiming is an odd verb in connection with "my ways" (*dĕrākay*). It implies a bold, direct, explicit declaration of the way the psalmist has been living—by implication, living in obedience. Such declarations are part of prayer as we affirm that there are no factors in our lives that make us deserve chastisement (cf. v. 22; also passages such as 44:17–22 [18–23]). The suppliant's testimony is that this worked and Yhwh answered; evidently this line does not refer to present troubles. The plea to be enabled to learn Yhwh's *laws (cf. v. 12; also vv. 5, 7, 8, 16, 23) is then both logical and surprising. It is logical, because an experience of Yhwh's deliverance is designed to generate commitment (cf. v. 17). It is surprising, because the presupposition of v. 26a is that the suppliant had already learned them. But such learning is never finished.

> [27]Enable me to understand the way of your orders
> so that I may murmur about your wonders.

Verse 27 takes the argument on yet again, further illustrating its spiral nature, or the spiral nature of life with Yhwh. First it restates v. 26b, whose concern now becomes not an end but a new beginning. Yhwh's answering a plea does need to lead to more learning of Yhwh's laws, but the aim of understanding the way (*derek*) of Yhwh's *orders is that we may *murmur about Yhwh's wonders. As in v. 18, "wonders" could be wonders of deliverance, which will come about as commitment to Yhwh's orders issues in more experience of deliverance, or the wonders contained in those orders themselves; coming to understand them makes it possible and necessary to speak of them.

> [28]My spirit has wept away from sorrow;
> lift me up, in accordance with your word.

The line restates v. 25, with *dālĕpâ* replacing *dābĕqâ* at the beginning. The verb is another rare one (cf. Job 16:20), perhaps suggesting that the suppliant's spirit has melted in tears, because of the sorrow that trouble has caused. As in v. 25 the psalm urges Yhwh to act "in accordance with your *word." In light of v. 25 we might infer that the second verb (*qûm* piel) urges Yhwh to lift the suppliant up from the dirt (cf. *qûm* hiphil in 113:7), or it might suggest restoring to honor and power someone who has been shamed and put down (cf. *qûm* hiphil in 41:10 [11]). But the interrelationship of the cola rather suggests lifting up someone put down by sorrow (*akēdia* in LXX, which became a term for spiritual weariness or sloth, *accidie*, one of the seven deadly sins).[61]

> [29]Remove the way of falsehood from me;
> grace me with your teaching.

The psalm likely presupposes the experience of being falsely accused by people such as the leaders mentioned in v. 23, and in isolation v. 29a might denote removing people whose way (*derek*) is false, but the parallelism again points in a different direction. For all the commitment the psalm expresses, it recognizes that we can never assume we will not fall into ways of *falsehood in relationships with Yhwh and/or with other people. If we think we have arrived morally or religiously, we risk proving ourselves false. Once more, the psalm raises the question of the relationship between divine and human responsibility. Elsewhere it is our responsibility to remove the way of falsehood (e.g., Prov. 4:24, 27). Yet the wise person recognizes the depth of the problem with our human hearts and knows we need Yhwh to work in us to this end. Yet this does not take away from the fact that we ourselves have to do the removing. . . .

Significantly, the parallel colon introduces the verb *grace, which is what v. 29a had been appealing to. The psalm feels no tension between the emphasis on human obligation and the prayer for grace. Like "wonders," grace has a different reference from the one we might have expected. In vv. 58 and 132 it suggests action that delivers the psalmist from trouble; here the expression of grace lies in the very gift of Yhwh's *teaching that makes obedience possible. There is certainly no tension between grace and law.

> [30]I have chosen the way of truthfulness;
> I have set my mind on your decisions.

Paradox reappears again. In v. 29 the psalmist prayed for Yhwh to act to make righteousness possible. Verse 30 presupposes that the psalmist has already personally acted in making a choice to affirm a commitment to the right way (*derek*), the way of *truthfulness rather than the way of *falsehood. In the OT, choosing is usually Yhwh's business (e.g., 33:12; 132:13; 135:4), but in Ps. 119 it is the suppliant's (cf. v. 173; cf. Josh. 24:15; Prov. 1:29). The second colon restates that. *Šāwâ* is another

61. Cf. Theodoret, *Psalms*, 2:251, with the comments of the translator, Robert C. Hill; and Cassiodorus, *Psalms*, 3:188, with his specific reference to John Cassian, who formulated the classic definition of the seven deadly sins (see Cassian, *The Institutes* [Mahwah, NJ: Newman, 2000], 217–38).

rare verb, but it resembles the more common *śîm* in suggesting "set [the mind on]" your *decisions.[62] The choosing happens in our mind, but the choice is buttressed by our then having ways of making sure we pay attention to Yhwh's decisions, in the manner of the covenant requirements in Josh. 8:30–35.

> 31 I have stuck by your declarations;
> Yhwh, do not shame me.

The line recycles *dābaq* (v. 25) but gives it a very different, positive connotation. The psalmist has stuck to Yhwh's *declarations like a man sticking to a woman (Gen. 2:24) or Israel sticking to Yhwh (Deut. 11:22) or a man's underclothing sticking to him (Jer. 13:11). Therefore the psalmist looks to Yhwh for honor rather than shaming. Again, then, the implication is that deliverance and blessing will witness to Yhwh's being involved with us, and that will witness to our faithfulness.

> 32 I run in the way of your commands,
> because you broaden my mind.

Usually we simply walk in the way (*derek* again) of Yhwh's commands (vv. 1, 4); running in the way of them is another way of suggesting not mere compliance with Yhwh's expectations but living by them enthusiastically and energetically. The idea contrasts with that of running to do wrong (Prov. 1:16; 6:18; Isa. 59:7); the psalm assumes that running in Yhwh's way deserves at least as much enthusiasm. Suggestively, such running issues from having one's mind or *heart broadened. That has a positive connotation, as in Isa. 60:5 (contrast Ps. 101:5). There as elsewhere "broadening" is an image for deliverance; we are taken out of constraint into roominess (cf. 118:5). In this case mind and heart are perhaps being liberated from anxiety and fear. The logic is once again that Yhwh's act of deliverance liberates us into a life of obedience.

But here, the reference to broadening the mind or understanding (cf. 1 Kings 4:29 [5:9]) suggests a nuancing of the image. Living in light of Yhwh's commands is not something constraining, involving narrow-mindedness. Reading the Scriptures opens up the possibility of liberation from the limitations of our current perspective, of the attitudes that seem self-evident in our Christian culture. A broadening of horizons takes place. And that makes for running in Yhwh's ways.

62. So G. R. Driver, "Textual and Linguistic Problems," 191. Or perhaps we should understand "set [before me]" (cf. 16:8).

119:33–40. *Hē'* (*h*). Every line but the last begins with a hiphil imperative, so that the section stresses Yhwh's activity as teacher, director, and deliverer.

> 33Teach me, Yhwh, the way of your laws,
> so that I may observe it to the utmost.

"The way of your *laws" will be the way of life your laws require, while "teach" (*yārâ* hiphil) is the mother verb of the key noun *teaching. In a sense the psalmist has no need of teaching; in some version of the teaching of Moses, the prophets, and the wise, teaching is available to anyone. But the existence of that teaching and its reaching inside us are different matters. We need Yhwh to teach us in the sense of enabling that teaching to affect us. Yet Yhwh's teaching us still does not in itself generate obedience; we have to do the obeying. The two cola again recognize the two factors involved in generating a righteous life, Yhwh's teaching and our consequential observing, which needs to be done without half measures (cf. James 2:10).

> 34Enable me to understand, so that I may observe your teaching
> and keep it with all my heart.

The restatement of the point begins with the similar verb *bîn* (hiphil), then repeats "observe" and adds that famous noun *teaching. The second colon re-expresses "observing" by "keeping" and re-expresses "to the utmost" with the recognition that this keeping needs to issue from an undivided *heart, with no partial inclination to pray to other deities or occasional compromise over a matter such as pursuing wealth (v. 36).

> 35Direct me in the pathway of your commands,
> because I take pleasure in it.

The plea looks at the dynamics of the moral life from a different angle in asking that we should be "directed" (*dārak* hiphil), the mother verb of the word for "way" (v. 33). That coheres with and strengthens the reference to the "pathway" of your commands, the pathway the commands point toward and set the bounds of. The different angle is that the plea's basis is that we are already reveling in this pathway. The previous lines might have implied that something needs to be done to make our hearts incline to obedience. This line presupposes we are so inclined (cf. 112:1); inclination just needs to be given direction. We want to walk in the pathway Yhwh approves; we just need to be pointed to it.

[36]Incline my heart to your declarations
and not to gain.

The psalm reverts to that other angle, that our *heart may not delight in Yhwh's *declarations and needs to be made to incline (*nāṭâ* hiphil) to them. Perhaps the contrast suggests the awareness that we are divided people; one aspect of our being is tempted to avoid Yhwh's way, while another really wants to walk in it.

Then for the first time the psalm makes explicit the possible direction of that negative inclination, though this plea fits the comment about wealth in v. 14. As the Decalogue ends by proscribing covetousness, the psalm sees covetousness as the alternative inclination of the heart: the habit of going shopping, the desire to acquire "stuff" (e.g., Exod. 18:21; Jer. 6:13). It strikes at the heart of Western economies, dependent on covetousness for their functioning, and at the attitude that the West has propagated elsewhere in encouraging globalization.

[37]Make my eyes pass on from seeing emptiness;
in your way make me live.

The verb (*ʿābar* hiphil) implies that one inevitably sees emptiness (*šāwʾ*). The question is whether our eyes get stuck there. The parallelism with the previous line might suggest that gain, stuff, wealth is what is empty. But elsewhere, the embodiment of emptiness is a divine image (e.g., 24:4; Jer. 18:15). This would make a coherent partner for that concern with stuff. Covetousness is the typical sin in the everyday world; going after emptiness is the typical religious sin.

Whereas recourse to emptiness looks like the way to life, walking in Yhwh's way is actually the way to life. But again the psalm recognizes that "we have no power in ourselves to help ourselves."[63] Yhwh has to draw our gaze to "your way" so that we find life there.

[38]Establish for your servant your statement,
which is for your revering.

The psalm moves from focusing on Yhwh's word of command to an appeal concerning Yhwh's *statement of promise. Applied to a promise, *qûm* (hiphil) suggests fulfillment, but more than that, it suggests confirming the word, vindicating it. The action establishes that this word came from God and that God is God. "For your *revering" reformulates

63. From the collect for the Second Sunday in Lent in the Church of England *Book of Common Prayer*.

the point about the servant's commitment and builds on it in a manner that has become familiar. As Yhwh's servant, the suppliant is committed to revering Yhwh, and therefore expectant of the master's support and faithfulness. But the result of the master's acting in support of the servant will be to deepen the revering that the servant shows. The psalm may also imply that it will broaden the revering, making other people revere Yhwh. In either connection, compare 130:4.

> 39Make my taunt, which I dread, pass on,
> because your decisions are good.

The line restates v. 22, using the verb from v. 37 (*ʿābar* hiphil) in a different connection, and also making a link with "revering" (v. 38). The psalmist aspires to revere Yhwh, but is presently troubled by another preoccupation, a feeling of dread. The stative verb "dread" (*yāgōr*) is likely more than merely a synonym of *yārēʾ* ("revere/fear"); it implies a more overwhelming feeling. Either of the possibilities raised in connection with v. 22 might explain it. The psalmist may dread this taunt because of its effect on a relationship with the community, or because of what it harbingers if the taunters move from words to action.

What is the link with Yhwh's *decisions being *good? Perhaps the comment again connects with v. 38 and refers to the good things that issue from living by Yhwh's decisions; obedience to these commands means the basis for the taunts will disappear. Or perhaps v. 22 clarifies the elliptical relationship between the two cola: the suppliant has acknowledged the goodness of Yhwh's decisions and therefore lives by them, so there is no reason for Yhwh not to answer the plea. The taunts are wrong.

> 40There: I long for your orders;
> in your faithfulness make me live.

In turn, v. 40 restates v. 39. After "there" (*hinnēh*), the only *h* word that is not a hiphil verb, the verb (*tāʾabtî*) parallels the related noun "longing" in v. 20.[64] Here the object of longing is Yhwh's *orders.

The renewed plea, "make me live" (cf. vv. 25, 37), implies that the opposite is a real possibility. The related appeal to Yhwh's *faithfulness recurs in the Psalms (e.g., 5:8 [9]; 143:1), but oddly not elsewhere in Ps. 119. In substance, its implications are not very different from the claim to be Yhwh's servant (v. 38). Masters have an obligation of faithfulness to servants who have the right attitude to their orders.

64. I take the verb as stative, *tāʾēb*.

119:41–48. *Wāw* (*w*). Each line begins with a verb prefaced by a simple *w* (LXX treats some as *w*-consecutive).

> [41]So may your commitment come to me, Yhwh,
> your deliverance in accordance with your statement.

The line is the first of three developing the sense of being under pressure and needing to experience Yhwh's *commitment, which will be expressed in an act of *deliverance in fulfillment of Yhwh's *statement, Yhwh's promise.

> [42]So may I be able to answer the person who taunts me with a word,
> because I have relied on your word.

Again the pressure takes the form of taunting, which will imply (for instance) that the suppliant's trouble is an indication of Yhwh's abandonment, itself a sign of the suppliant's sin. "With a word" might refer to the answer or the taunting; either way it might seem redundant, but the parallel colon suggests its point. Relying on Yhwh's *word is what enables us to keep going when people taunt with their word, and/or to answer them with a word (perhaps, indeed, the suffix also applies to the first colon, which then denotes "answer with your word"). When does the suppliant give this answer? Perhaps that happens in the midst of the trouble, but the answer will be really effective only when the trouble is over, when Yhwh has acted (v. 41), so perhaps that is when it will be possible to give this answer. Verse 42b will then imply not only that the suppliant has relied on Yhwh, but also that this reliance has been vindicated.

> [43]So do not take right away from my mouth your truthful word,
> because I have waited for your decisions.

The *truthful *word is then that reliable word of promise; and it belongs in "my mouth" because when Yhwh acts, I can and must testify to its fulfillment (cf. v. 7). Indirectly, then, this is another plea for Yhwh to act in deliverance. Asking for Yhwh not to take that word "right away" might be litotes, implying "do not take it away at all." Or perhaps at the moment Yhwh has taken it away, so that the suppliant cannot at the moment testify to its faithfulness. Either way, part of the basis for the plea is the nature of that faithful word, Yhwh's *authoritative decisions, because they promise that people who observe them find they are followed by blessing, not trouble (cf. v. 39). So it is possible to *wait for their fulfillment.

44So I shall keep your teaching always,
forever and ever.

If one may press the significance of the *w*, the awareness that Yhwh's decisions or *teaching carries those promises is a further motivation for keeping it; and the threefold time references balance the "right away" in v. 43.

45So I shall walk about in roominess
because I have had recourse to your orders.

The line returns to the expectation of knowing Yhwh's deliverance, here expressed in terms of being delivered from constraint to roominess (cf. 118:5),[65] though the psalmist leaps over the actual act of deliverance to the consequential freedom to "walk about." Again the psalm assumes the link between thus knowing Yhwh's faithfulness and paying attention to Yhwh's *orders. Here attentiveness is expressed as having *recourse to them; that implies study and the assumption that they are a resource. If I want to know what to do, that is where I go.

46So I shall speak of your declarations before kings
and not be shamed.

The implicit link between Yhwh's commands and Yhwh's actions continues. One can imagine a person such as Ezra or Nehemiah speaking of Yhwh's teaching and its promises before Persian emperors, knowing Yhwh will honor their commitment to the *declarations and their reliance on the promises.

47So I will delight in your commands,
which I am dedicated to.

Again, if one may press the *w*, the psalmist's *delight and *dedication issues not merely from a selfless affirming of whatever Yhwh approves, but from an awareness that such affirming is in our interests.

48So I will lift my hands to your commands, which I am dedicated to,
and I shall murmur about your laws.

The final *w* makes the point again, that confidence in Yhwh's faithfulness to the promises attached to Yhwh's commands makes for an

65. Hilary (*Commentaire*, 1:236–37) compares 2 Cor. 4:8.

openness to these commands. Lifting hands is an attitude of recognition and worship (63:4 [5]) and also of request (141:2). Elsewhere hands are lifted to Yhwh (Lam. 2:19; 3:41) or to the sanctuary (Pss. 28:2; 134:2). Here they are lifted to Yhwh's commands. This implies recognizing and honoring them, and thus being *dedicated to them (the point is underlined from v. 47) and *murmuring about these *laws (cf. v. 23). Given the other common significance of lifting up hands, it also implies appeal to those commands for their guidance and promise.

119:49–56. *Zayin* (*z*). *Zākar* (be mindful) begins three of the lines.

> 49Be mindful of the word to your servant,
> by which you have made me wait.

*Mindfulness begins as a stance urged on Yhwh. Once again the suppliant's position of servant makes a claim on Yhwh as master. The *word is the promise attached to Yhwh's teaching. The second colon thus underlines its significance. Whereas one usually waits *for* Yhwh's word (*l*), the moment when that word will be fulfilled, here the psalm speaks of being made to wait *by* Yhwh's word (*'al*). This formulation looks back to the giving of that word. That put the psalmist into a *waiting attitude, a positive hopefulness. But the interrelationship of the cola points to the sense of tension when we live in light of the promises Yhwh has given but do not see them fulfilled.

> 50This is my comfort in my weakness,
> that your statement has made me live.

The need of hope continues to be in focus, and the reference to Yhwh's word or *statement is taken further. The second colon makes it evident that relying on that word does not involve simply whistling in the dark. Yhwh has kept this promise in the past, given life when death threatened, so it is possible to find *comfort during a subsequent experience of *weakness—for instance, when I am under attack and powerless.

> 51When the willful have greatly mocked me,
> from your teaching I have not diverted.

Such attackers are again characterized as the *willful. They are people who decide for themselves how to live, and then mock people stupid enough to let Yhwh's *teaching decide for them. Being reduced to powerlessness could tempt the one who is mocked to change that stance; the suppliant has resisted the temptation.

> 52I have been mindful of your decisions
> from of old, Yhwh, and I have found comfort.

*Mindfulness is not just Yhwh's business but ours. Yhwh's mindfulness toward the word with its demands and promises inspires us to be mindful toward those same *authoritative decisions with their demands and promises. The suppliant has been mindful and can find *comfort (cf. v. 50) on the basis of having fulfilled their expectations and therefore of having confidence that their promises will be fulfilled.

Once again (cf. v. 50) the psalm indicates that this is no new stance. The suppliant can look back over a long commitment to the expectations and a long proving of the promises. Or perhaps the word order suggests that the decisions themselves are "from of old"; it is their antiquity that increases their capacity to be a comfort.

> 53Rage—it has gripped me because of the faithless,
> people who abandon your teaching.

The psalmist's attitude toward the *faithless sounds a new note with extraordinary force in speaking of rage or fury (*zalʿāpâ*); the word refers more concretely to a raging fire or a raging wind. Inner tumult grips and overwhelms the person like a forest fire consuming acres of land.

What causes this is not personal threats from the faithless but their abandoning Yhwh's *teaching. Raging at their attitude to Yhwh and to life indirectly indicates the psalmist's own commitment to Yhwh's teaching, like the commitment against evil people in Ps. 139.

> 54Your laws have been my songs/protection
> in the house where I sojourn.

Far from abandoning Yhwh's laws, the psalmist has let them be something to sing about. In 118:14 *zimrāt* means protection rather than song, and NJPS understands *zĕmirôt* thus here. Although the general idea of Yhwh's commands as a reason for rejoicing is a familiar one (e.g., v. 14), these commands as a topic for songs does not recur. Yet MT's vocalization may be designed to preserve the difference between "protection" and "songs" (though it may then be that at an earlier stage it was "protection" that the line referred to). Either understanding links well with the parallel colon, which takes up a note from v. 19. Wherever I dwell, I do so with the vulnerability of a sojourner, someone without security or rights. But I can still sing or be safe because of those laws.

[55]I have been mindful at night of your name, Yhwh,
and I have kept your teaching.

The third occurrence of *zākar* follows on from the second (v. 52). *Mindfulness characterizes not only the long haul of the psalmist's life but also the day-to-day life and night-to-night life. The long hours of the night when one cannot do much manual work can be a time for study and prayer, though also a time of danger and anxiety. For either reason they become a time to be mindful of Yhwh's *name. Keeping Yhwh's *teaching issues from the study and/or is a means of laying oneself under Yhwh's protection.

[56]This is how it has been for me,
that I have observed your orders.

Jerome translates "because" rather than "that," but it then requires some inference to work out what "this" refers to. More likely, "this" refers forward: it is defined as observing Yhwh's *orders; the line repeats the explicit and implicit claims in vv. 51–55.

119:57–64. *Ḥêt* (*ḥ*). The combination of allocation (*ḥēleq*) and commitment (*ḥesed*) nicely frames the section.

[57]Yhwh is my allocation;
I have said I would keep your words.

A family's allocation (*ḥēleq*) is the land allotted to it in the area belonging to its village, part of the broader allocation to their clan. Israel is Yhwh's allocation or special possession among the peoples of the world (Deut. 32:9); and Yhwh is the allocation or special possession of the priests (they have no land, but share in the produce that comes to Yhwh from the people's land). But like the idea of "wonders" and "grace" (vv. 18, 27, 29), "allocation" has a different reference from usual: Yhwh is the allocation or special possession of the ordinary Israelite. The declaration is especially at home on the lips of people who are aware of their vulnerability (like those landless priests; cf. 73:26; 142:6; Lam. 3:24) and choose to accept it.[66] That will fit this psalmist. But keeping Yhwh's *words is a necessity for cashing this commitment of Yhwh's.

[58]I have courted your favor with all my heart;
be gracious to me in accordance with your statement.

66. Cf. Hilary, *Commentaire*, 1:258–59.

"Courted [*ḥālâ* piel] your favor" is literally "sweetened your face," implying that this face is at best neutral, at worst hostile, and needs to be won to showing favor.[67] While it can thus presuppose that the person (human or divine) has reason for hostility and needs to be won over, it need not imply this (e.g., 45:12 [13]; Zech. 8:21–22), and the psalmist gives no other evidence of seeing God that way. So TNIV's "seek your face" gives a fair impression of its implication. With a whole *heart the psalmist seeks for Yhwh to show *grace, once again appealing to the *statement or promise attached to Yhwh's commands.

> **59**I considered my ways [MT]/your ways [LXX]
> and turned my feet to your declarations.

The psalm may refer to a time of consideration (*ḥāšab* piel) or self-examination that led to recognizing the need to turn the feet from one way to another (it makes little difference whether we read with MT or with LXX). In the qal, "turning" (*šûb*; here hiphil) can mean "turn back" or repent, and this would fit the testimony in v. 67. But the words need not imply a need to change course; they may simply describe the stance the psalmist once took and then has continually taken, one of reflection and commitment to walking by Yhwh's *declarations. The first understanding would fit a more negative reading of v. 58 (if the suppliant knew that Yhwh had reason to be hostile); the second would fit v. 60.

> **60**I have hurried and not delayed
> to keep your commands.

So the psalmist hastened (*ḥûš*) and (to underline the point) did not delay turning the feet so as to keep those declarations or commands. There are feet (cf. v. 59) that hurry to deceit (Job 31:5); with the same eagerness, the psalmist hastens to keep those commands.[68]

> **61**Though the ropes of the faithless surrounded me,
> I did not ignore your teaching.

We know about the ropes (*ḥebel*) of Death encompassing a suppliant (116:3), like the ropes of a hunter capturing an animal. The *faithless have been known to act like such hunters (cf. 140:4–5 [5–6]). Their ropes, too, have surrounded this psalmist. There seemed no escape from being captured and confined or killed. EVV translate the qatal

67. On the expression's court background, see Klaus Seybold, "Reverenz und Gebet," *ZAW* 88 (1972): 2–16.
68. Cf. Anderson, *Psalms*, 2:825.

verbs as present, but this could hardly be happening as the psalmist is acting as described in vv. 62–63, so perhaps v. 61 looks back on such an attack. It did not lead to *ignoring, or putting out of mind, Yhwh's *teaching.

> 62In the middle of the night I rise to confess you
> for your faithful decisions.

There is a long tradition of getting up in the middle of the night (*ḥăṣôt-laylâ*) for prayer, as well as for praying in the morning, in the middle of the day, and in the evening, but it is a tradition that marks the lives of people especially committed to prayer. The psalmist claims to be that kind of person, one who rises thus to *confess Yhwh for the *faithful *decisions that have been proved true in life in the past and/or will be proved true in the future.

> 63I am friend to all who revere you,
> to the people who keep your orders.

The converse of being enraged at the faithless (v. 53) and by implication of having nothing to do with them is to be an associate (*ḥābēr*) of people who *revere Yhwh and keep Yhwh's *orders. These are the people whose company we seek out and want to identify with.

> 64Your commitment, Yhwh—the earth is full of it;
> enable me to learn your laws.

The first colon corresponds to 33:5, except that here the words are addressed to Yhwh. The context there points us to the confession's significance. In Ps. 33 Yhwh's *commitment stands alongside Yhwh's uprightness, truthfulness, and faithfulness in authoritative decision making, the characteristics of Yhwh's acts in the world (not just in Israel). These thus need to be characteristics of the way we live in the world, and we are to ask for that to come about as we are enabled to learn Yhwh's *laws. Superficially, this again looks like an unnecessary prayer. Yhwh's laws are publicly available; anyone can learn them. But not everyone does so, which highlights our human need of something beyond the simple deposit of the truth before us. It is as well that the divine teacher has ways of reaching into minds and hearts.

119:65–72. *Ṭêt* (*ṭ*). "Good" (*ṭôb*/*ṭûb*) opens five of the lines.

> 65You have done what is good for your servant,
> Yhwh, in accordance with your word.

Yhwh's "decisions are *good [ṭôb]" (v. 39). One aspect of this is their having promises attached to them. Heeding them means Yhwh's *word finds fulfillment as Yhwh does good for us.

66Enable me to learn goodness of discernment and acknowledgment,
because I have trusted in your commands.

*Goodness (ṭûb) of discernment is the capacity to make insightful decisions, which will also be ones that have good outcomes. They will be morally good, and therefore experientially good. De facto, "goodness" will also apply to *acknowledgment. We ask Yhwh to teach us to acknowledge things that are good to acknowledge, such as Yhwh's decisions and declarations (vv. 75, 79, 125); these, too, will be good for us. We do so on the basis of being people who have trusted that Yhwh's commands can be Yhwh's means of bringing all this about.

67Before I became weak I was going astray,
but now I have kept your statement.

The psalmist usually claims a life characterized by integrity, but here almost acknowledges what the willful said. There were reasons why Yhwh could have been acting in chastisement; at least, this has been so in the past. The psalm does not indicate wherein the *weakness consisted; v. 50 implied a sense of powerlessness in relation to other people. This might be the trouble that the willful then make their excuse for harassing the psalmist, or it might be the harassment itself.

But before (*ṭerem*) becoming powerless, the psalmist acknowledges having gone astray. Straying has been the subject of a plea (v. 10) and a curse (v. 21), though there the verb was *šāgâ*, whereas here it is *šāgag*. While the meaning of these two verbs overlaps, like their form, they are apparently not simply synonyms. *Šāgag* suggests accidental straying; *šāgâ* implies straying for which one accepts responsibility.[69] So the psalmist is not quite admitting guilt in the terms implied by vv. 10 and 21. Nevertheless the straying led to a wrong moral or religious path. The psalmist claims now to have come back onto the path and to be keeping Yhwh's *statement.

68You are good and you do good;
enable me to learn your laws.

Behind Yhwh's doing *good is the fact that Yhwh is *good. Goodness is not merely a pleasantness about some things we experience but an

69. See, e.g., *TLOT* on *šāgag*.

objective feature of our experience that emanates from and reflects God. No wonder we want to learn the *laws that will put us in the way of that goodness (cf. vv. 12b, 26b, 64b).

> 69The willful have smeared falsehood over me,
> whereas I with all my heart observe your orders.

The *willful appear again. Their relentless headstrongness expresses itself in boundless false accusation, here vividly expressed as smearing (*ṭāpal*) *falsehood over the psalmist like plaster (cf. Job 13:4). The person of integrity thus becomes invisible and looks like someone who consistently ignores Yhwh's orders. That makes for a grievous contrast with the real nature of the psalmist's life as one whose whole *heart or energy is given to observing those orders.

> 70Their mind is thick, like fat;
> I myself have delighted in your teaching.

The line parallels and looks behind the assertion in v. 69a and contrasts the psalmist's *heart or mind (v. 69b) and that of the *willful. It begins with another vivid *ṭ* word: this heart or mind is thick (*ṭāpaš*) with fat, as if encased with suet like the stomach, preventing the truth getting through to heart or mind, stopping it from understanding anything outside itself. The second colon restates the contrast, in collocating *delight and Yhwh's *teaching.

> 71It was good for me that I was made weak
> so that I might learn your laws.

The line takes further the point in v. 67. The verb is pual, not qal. Somebody or something made the psalmist *weak, though the agent (God or the willful?) is unidentified. But it was "*good for me." That statement further nuances the notion of goodness. The good is again a matter of the psalmist's experience (cf. v. 68), but it is a moral experience as well as a sensible one. Somehow, instead of driving the psalmist into sin, being reduced to powerlessness engenders an openness to learning Yhwh's *laws. Elsewhere, learning Yhwh's laws brings good. Here, learning these laws *is* itself the good thing.

> 72The teaching that comes from your mouth is good to me,
> more so than thousands of gold and silver pieces.

The last *good line restates the point. Perhaps observing Yhwh's *teaching brings material reward; so Jesus and Paul indicate (Matt. 6:33; 2 Cor.

9:6–11). The psalm recognizes that nevertheless the teaching itself does good to the psalmist that far outweighs the value of vast riches. Since the teaching comes from Yhwh's mouth, that is not surprising. Yhwh is thus vividly painted as wisdom teacher. Being taught by Yhwh is like sitting and listening to the words coming out of the teacher's mouth. That is how real is their origin in Yhwh. They are certainly not mere human teaching.

119:73–80. *Yôd* (*y*). Lines 5 to 8 begin with a third-person jussive verb.

> [73]It was your hands made me and founded me;
> enable me to understand so that I may learn your commands.

The vivid picture of Yhwh's hands-on (*yādayim*) making of humanity fits with the image in Gen. 2 of Yhwh initially shaping humanity like a potter. "Found" (*kûn* polel) is a more surprising verb. It may suggest "establishing" us so that we are secure, or "preparing" us so that we fulfill our role. But Exod. 15:17 also speaks of Yhwh's hands being involved in the founding or establishing of a sanctuary. That would suggest creating us was like constructing a building.

The link between the cola is elliptical. Perhaps Yhwh's involvement in creating us implies the capacity to make us understand things. Perhaps this involvement is why Yhwh goes on to make us understand things, not leaving the creative task half finished. Translating *kûn* as "prepare" would suggest we are made to live by Yhwh's commands, so we pray to be enabled to understand and learn them. The psalm touchingly assumes that if we understand and learn them, we will live by them. That makes for a comparison with Jesus's observation that people open to doing the will of God will know whether or not his teaching comes from God (John 7:17): what you are willing to do decides what you are willing and able to see. The psalm makes the same assumption concerning our unity or interwovenness as human beings but approaches it from the other end. If we really understand what Yhwh expects, of course we will do it. (If we are not prepared to do it, we will never let ourselves understand it.)

> [74]People who revere you—they will see me and rejoice,
> because I have waited for your word.

Oddly, the psalm does not begin the line with the first verb (*yirʾûnî*), which would be the regular word and would make it the first instance of the pattern in vv. 76–80. The order instead puts the stress on "people who revere you" (*yĕrēʾêkā*). Either order repeats the recurrent juxtaposition of "revere/fear" (*yārēʾ*) and "see" (*rāʾâ*), suggesting a link between them.

The link's nature becomes clearer in light of the declaration that in turn revering and seeing leads to rejoicing, another characteristic conviction of the Psalms that sounds counterintuitive to modern ears.

Here the ellipse between the cola is easier to bridge. The psalmist has *waited for Yhwh's *word, knowing it will find fulfillment and looking for that, because it is Yhwh's word and because of having lived in obedience to its expectations. That will give encouragement to other people who also revere Yhwh and see that fulfillment in the psalmist's life.

> [75]I have acknowledged, Yhwh, that your decisions are faithful,
> and in truthfulness you have made me weak.

This *acknowledgment (*yāda'*) is the psalmist's own recognition of the truth presupposed by v. 74. Yhwh's *decisions are *faithful in the sense that they promise blessing to people who obey them.

The second colon makes a more surprising and courageous statement of faith. In other contexts it might be an acknowledgment of the justice of God's judgment,[70] but here the context offers no acknowledgment of disobedience, which would have justified Yhwh in making the suppliant *weak and powerless in relation to people involved in attacks and harassment (cf. v. 50; contrast v. 67). The suppliant confesses Yhwh's *truthfulness on the basis of faith. Sometimes we cannot see why our life works out as it does, but we nevertheless affirm (on the basis of other evidence) that Yhwh is truthful and faithful. Perhaps that truthfulness lies in what I learn through such an experience (cf. v. 71).

> [76]Do grant that your commitment may come to comfort me
> in accordance with your statement to your servant.

The prayer links with the comment about weakness. Recognizing that Yhwh caused that weakness does not mean having simply to lie down under it until Yhwh decides to do something. In other contexts, Yhwh's *commitment becoming (*yĕhî*) one's *comfort could indeed mean that one accepts that the powerlessness and harassment will continue but that an awareness of Yhwh's commitment makes it possible to live with that. More often the Psalms assume that a relationship with Yhwh means that acceptance can be combined with plea for change, and one can press Yhwh to change the situation, not just to change the person. The following verses suggest that this is the psalm's burden here (and cf. "comfort" in v. 82). Once again the servant-master relationship provides a double basis for the appeal. The psalmist has been behaving like an obedient servant, and

70. So, e.g., Kraus, *Psalms 60–150*, 417.

the master is supposed to be committed to the servant. Both support the appeal that Yhwh's *statement should be fulfilled.

> [77]May your compassion come to me so that I may live,
> because your teaching is my delight.

The line restates the point, with Yhwh's compassion taking the place of Yhwh's commitment, and *delight in Yhwh's *teaching paralleling v. 76b. When that compassion "comes to me" (*yĕbōʾûnî*; cf. v. 41), the anticipated result is that "I may live," supporting the idea that Yhwh's commitment or compassion changes more than merely the psalmist's inner attitude: compare vv. 37 and 40. It means a renewed whole life, not merely a renewed inner life.

> [78]May the willful be shamed because they have put me in the wrong by means of falsehood;
> I myself murmur about your orders.

It is even more explicit that the psalm looks for action in the outer world, not just the inner world. For the truth to be proclaimed, the *willful must be exposed and shamed (*yēbōšû*). The line expresses their willfulness in more explicitly legal language. "Put me in the wrong" (*ʿāwat* piel) implies "subvert my case," "subvert justice for me" (cf. Job 8:3; 34:12; Lam. 3:36). Their accusations are lies; the psalmist's *murmuring about Yhwh's *orders provides evidence. They cannot get the psalmist convicted without utilizing *falsehood. That murmuring is also the basis for appealing to Yhwh for vindication.

> [79]May the people who revere you turn to me,
> the people who acknowledge your declarations. [Q]
> [or] and acknowledge your declarations. [K]

The people who *revere Yhwh reappear from v. 74. Especially when read in light of v. 78, the plea that they may "turn to me" (*yāšûbû*) suggests they have understandably turned away, having bought into the propaganda of the *willful. The psalm asks that they may turn back, again recognize the psalmist's integrity, and offer honor and support.

Revering Yhwh is re-expressed, familiarly enough, in terms of *acknowledging Yhwh's *declarations (Q), or is reckoned to lead to such acknowledging (K).

> [80]May my heart be of integrity in your laws
> so that I may not be shamed.

Again the two cola look at realities that lie behind the actual obeying of Yhwh's *laws, and that follow on it. On one side is the necessity that this not merely involve one's outward life but be an expression of what one is at *heart; there must be *integrity there. The profound reason for that is contained within the statement itself. Integrity means moral wholeness; there cannot be a moral wholeness of the person unless this affects the mind and spirit as well as the hands and feet. But here the psalm focuses more overtly on the pragmatic reason for this necessity. If there is no integrity in the inner person, there will hardly be integrity in the outer person's behavior in the long run or when the pressures are on. There is no shame in lacking integrity in the inner person; no one can see it in order to shame it. But eventually this inner problem will issue outwardly and thus will issue in shame.

119:81–88. *Kap* (*k*). The section is dominated by the psalmist's sense of being under pressure.

> 81My spirit has come to an end for your deliverance;
> for your word I have waited.

In the restatement of v. 20a, "come to an end" (*kālâ*) is less vivid, but at least as final. The psalmist's spirit (*person) has been consumed with longing for Yhwh to *deliver, in light of that *word that has been the object of *waiting, but deliverance does not come, and that spirit has no energy left.

> 82My eyes have come to an end for your statement
> in saying "When will you comfort me?"

The point is repeated, using the same verb (*kālâ*), but it is now the eyes that fail through the concentrated strain of continuing to look for Yhwh to fulfill that *statement. "Statement" is *ʾimrâ*, so the familiar prosaic "in saying" (*lēʾmōr*) picks up the root.

The question confronts that promising statement, or rather confronts Yhwh over its not issuing in *comfort, in action bringing restoration. The question "When?" or "Until when?" is typical of a prayer psalm (e.g., 42:3; 74:10; 94:3). It makes clear that prayer is not bound to submit to God's timing, any more than to God's inaction (cf. v. 76).

> 83When I have become like a waterskin in smoke
> I have not ignored your laws.

The simile was perhaps familiar, but it is now unclear. Commentators usually hypothesize that a waterskin would shrivel and blacken in the smoky atmosphere of an Israelite courtyard, though this seems to be pure guesswork.[71] But the image offers another description of the experience depicted in vv. 81a and 82a. Even when (*kî*) this is how things are and hope has all but died, the psalmist has not *ignored Yhwh's *laws, but rather been mindful of them.

84How many are your servant's days—
when will you make a decision about the people who harass me?

In isolation, the question "How many?" (*kammâ*) might be an indirect comment on how few are the suppliant's days; life is short. But here, the second colon clarifies the question. The suppliant's harassment will come to an end only when Yhwh makes a *decision about the tormentors and puts them down. So when will that be? The questions in vv. 82b and 84b are two sides of the same coin. The psalm again assumes that we can press God about timing; and once again the suppliant's position as God's servant is the basis for appeal.

85The willful have dug pits for me,
people who do not act in accordance with your teaching.

The action of the *willful is now described in terms of a familiar metaphor. They resemble people hunting a wild animal: for digging (*kārâ*), compare 7:15 [16]; 57:6 [7] (the latter passage also has the word for "pit"), and also v. 61 with its reference to ropes.

As willful people, these hunters do not live by Yhwh's *teaching. Further, there is no basis for their attacks, so this specific action has no basis in Yhwh's teaching. Their hostility and harassment are expressions of their rejecting it.

86All your commands are truthful;
with falsehood people harass me, help me!

Again the argument is that Yhwh's commands, all (*kol*) of them, are *truthful in their promise that life will work out for people who heed them. The psalm can therefore point to people's harassment and argue that this cannot be allowed to continue. The two cola set over against each other Yhwh's truthfulness and the tormentors' *falsehood (the words come next to each other at the center of the line) and almost allow this to speak for itself; but only almost. The last asyndetic word appeals for *help.

71. Cf. Dahood, *Psalms*, 3:183. LXX, Jerome have "frost" for "smoke," suggesting the image was already unclear.

> [87]They have all but made an end of me in the land,
> but I myself have not abandoned your orders.

"Come to an end" (vv. 81, 82) recurs once more, now piel to describe the tormentors' action. They have all but (*kimʿaṭ*) finished off the suppliant. In the Psalms, *ʾereṣ* usually denotes the earth, but here the context suggests it denotes the attackers' imperiling of the suppliant's place in the land or worthwhile life in the land. One might again think of the way the Persian authorities and the surrounding communities made life difficult for the little postexilic community (see, e.g., Neh. 9:36–37).

Once again there is more than one way to read the relationship between the two cola. Is it that despite the pressure, the suppliant has not abandoned Yhwh's *orders? This suggests an implicit appeal to Yhwh to act before it is finally too late. But the "I myself" suggests seeing a contrast in the cola between the attackers' troublemaking and the suppliant's faithfulness. That too implicitly makes an appeal.

> [88]In accordance with your commitment, make me live,
> so that I may keep the declaration of your mouth.

This closing plea reverses some of that argument, still aiming to get Yhwh to act. Once more the psalm appeals to Yhwh's *commitment as a basis for restoring the suppliant to life. That will contrast with the tormentors' attempts to bring life to an end. But here the motivation for Yhwh to act is not only that this will be consistent with that commitment but also that it will enable the suppliant to continue to keep Yhwh's *declaration (the singular comes only here in the psalm). "Of your mouth" (cf. vv. 13, 72) adds to the sense of wonder and responsibility at having this declaration. A prayer psalm often adds as motivation that the result of Yhwh's acting will be that the suppliant will be in a position to praise Yhwh for this act; the motivation here compares and contrasts with that in noting how the suppliant who has been delivered will then be in a position to live a life of obedience to Yhwh. Both are summed up by phrases such as "for your glory," which Christians sometimes add to their prayers as motivation for God to answer.

119:89–96. *Lāmed* (*l*). The opening and closing lines suggest the theme that Yhwh's teaching endures and thus contrasts with all else.

> [89]Yhwh endures forever;
> your word stands in the heavens. [MT]
> [or] Your word endures forever, Yhwh;
> it stands in the heavens. [LXX, Jerome, Tg]

MT's punctuation generates an assertion that is indeed a fundamental conviction of the psalm. *Forever (*lĕʿôlām*) means we never run out of a situation where Yhwh is present and active, faithful to the promises the psalm keeps referring to. The alternative punctuation generates a different suggestive assertion, which the parallel statements in vv. 90 and 91 support.

Either way, the second colon gives precision to the statement in the first, even while the statement in the first undergirds that in the second. Yhwh's *word is personified as something that has taken its stand for a purpose, in the heavens. It is therefore in a position to exercise authority on earth.[72]

> **90**Your truthfulness endures to all generations;
> you established the earth and it has stood firm.

Verse 90 starts again from Yhwh's permanence (*lĕdōr wādōr*): the permanence of Yhwh's *truthfulness undergirds that conviction that Yhwh's word will indeed exercise authority and thus find fulfillment.

The abiding nature of Yhwh's truthfulness and the authority of Yhwh's word in the heavens are evidenced in the world we can see, as we cannot see those other realities. Truthfulness implies having the moral capacity and the sovereign power to fulfill one's promises; Yhwh's truthfulness is evidenced by the nature of the world we experience, as a place Yhwh established. "The world stands firm, does it not? That reflects Yhwh's truthfulness."

> **91**As for your decisions, they have stood firm today,
> because all are your servants.

In another take on the link between the stability of creation and of Yhwh's word, Yhwh's *decisions (*lĕmišpāṭêkā*) not surprisingly share in the stability of Yhwh's world. Both have stood firm even to today.

The secret of the earth's stability and of Yhwh's decisions is that everything in existence exists to serve Yhwh. (Servants can disobey, of course, but the master does not let things get out of hand.)

> **92**Were not your teaching my delight,
> then I would have perished in my weakness.

"Were not [*lûlê*] your *teaching my *delight" reaffirms the point in v. 77b. Verse 77a affirmed that this delight means Yhwh shows compassion, which issues in renewed life. Conversely, lack of this delight means

72. Cf. Th. Booij, "Psalm 119,89–91," *Bib* 79 (1998): 539–41 (see 539).

that when we are in a position of *weakness and powerlessness, we have forfeited any basis for appealing to Yhwh for compassion and would properly expect to perish. (Yhwh may still act in grace and mercy, not being bound to such rules; but we cannot claim or expect that.)

> 93Never will I ignore your orders,
> because through them you have made me live.

The first colon re-expresses the point negatively, while the second re-expresses the companion point positively rather than negatively. Delighting in Yhwh's teaching or *orders will issue in being mindful of them and doing what they say, not ever (*lĕʿôlām*) simply *ignoring them and failing to live by them.

The second colon also makes even more definite than v. 92b that this is not mere theological theory but testimony based on experience. Any appeal for life in the present (e.g., v. 88) bases part of its confidence on Yhwh's having given life in the past in a way that demonstrates the link between obedience and life (cf. v. 50). Whereas v. 92b presupposed the "natural" link between obedience and life (cf. Lev. 18:5), v. 93b draws attention to the divine involvement in effecting this link (Deut. 30:15–20 interweaves these two models for understanding how life works).

> 94I am yours, deliver me,
> because I have had recourse to your orders.

"I am yours" (*lĕkā-ʾănî*) indicates that the psalmist accepted a servant's responsibility and Yhwh accepted a master's responsibility. Verse 94 appeals for that to continue to be true. One who belongs to Yhwh can appeal to Yhwh to *deliver. The line again emphasizes Yhwh's direct involvement in our lives. Yhwh is not just the deist clockmaker. But part of the basis for expecting Yhwh to behave as if we belong to Yhwh is that we have so behaved. The second colon claims to have fulfilled that condition by having had *recourse to Yhwh's *orders, making it our business to treat Yhwh's commands as our resource for knowing how to live.

> 95As for me, the faithless have waited to make me perish;
> I show understanding of your declarations.

Formally, the line opens in a way that balances v. 94a (*lî* over against *lĕkā*), and the rest of the first colon provides the background to its appeal for deliverance. The psalmist has been looking forward expectantly (vv. 43, 49, 74, 81, 114, 147), but unfortunately so have the *faithless (the psalm uses *yāḥal* for that good waiting and *qāwâ* for this bad waiting, but the two verbs have similar meaning and elsewhere the latter usually has the good significance). In v. 92b the psalmist spoke of having been near perishing; v. 95a makes explicit that this perishing would have had agents. The power of the faithless stands over against the psalmist's weakness.

Like v. 92a, the second colon then once more claims that the psalmist is the kind of person who delights in Yhwh's teaching, here expressed as involving understanding Yhwh's *declarations. The verb (*bîn*) has occurred three times in the hiphil in pleas to "enable me to understand"; it now occurs three times in the hitpolel to indicate a claim to "show understanding/attentiveness" (cf. vv. 100, 104). The psalm again thus affirms both the involvement of God and that of the human agent in the process of understanding and the practical responsiveness this issues in. It is suggestive that the pleas to Yhwh come first and are then followed by the human statements.

> **96**As for every end, I have seen the limit;
> your command is very broad.

Yhwh's command is broad; it is not surprising, then, that it can broaden the mind (v. 32). Yhwh's purview is wide ranging; Yhwh's commands cover many eventualities. All the guidance we need is there.

The first colon makes for a contrast with that. Its general point is clear, the details less so. The noun in the expression "as for every end" (*lĕkol tiklâ*) is a hapax. There are two aspects to the meaning of its mother verb (*kālâ*); either is elliptical in this context. The verb often means "come to completion," so the noun could mean completion or completeness in a positive sense (cf. Jerome; but NRSV and TNIV "perfection" gives a misleading impression). Over against the second colon, v. 96a might then grant the broadness of human insight but imply that it is not so broad; it has its limit. "Limit" then qualifies "completeness."

But vv. 81 and 82 have used the verb with its other, more negative connotation, "come to an end." (LXX has *synteleia*, nicely keeping the ambiguity.) So the more likely understanding is that v. 96a begins by pointing out more directly that all things come to an end. That is the nature of the limitations built into human life. "Limit" then restates "coming to an end."

On either understanding, the much broader perspective of Yhwh's commands makes for a contrast.[73]

73. An easier understanding would be "for everything I have seen the end, the limit"; this would require repointing *lĕkol* as *lakkōl*.

119:97–104. *Mêm* (*m*). The preposition *min* dominates, with the three lines where it means "than" (vv. 98, 99, 100) making a powerful claim. The section makes no pleas; it is all statement.

97How I am dedicated to your teaching;
it is my murmur all day.

For the claim to be *dedicated to Yhwh's commands, compare vv. 47–48, and for *murmuring, vv. 15, 23, 27, 48, 78. Yhwh's *teaching has also been mentioned often enough, though not in these connections, which leads Cassiodorus to comment that for the psalmist the law is the object of love, not fear.[74] The new expressions in the line are "how" (*mâ*) and "all day," which are related. The all-day nature of this murmuring indicates how dedicated the suppliant is. The expression involves some hyperbole; the suppliant is "always" reflecting on Yhwh's teaching and talking about it.

98Your commands make me wiser than my enemies,
because they are mine forever.

The contrast with "my enemies" (*mēʾōyĕbay*) involves the psalm's only reference to "wisdom." Even its references to understanding (*bîn*) have expressed an aspiration, not a claim (e.g., v. 27; but contrast vv. 99–100). So v. 98a stands out, though its point could be reckoned implicit throughout the psalm. Wisdom opens up the possibility of living life in accordance with how things really are, and thus in a way that works. Obviously, people attacking the psalmist without reason and/or with deceit ignore both the content of Yhwh's commands and the promises attached to them. They are stupid. They are ultimately bound to fail.

This may not seem to work in the short term, but it works in the long term and for the long haul.

99I have gained more insight than all my tutors,
because your declarations are my murmur.

The parallel contrast with all the people who have enabled me to learn (*mikkol-mĕlammĕday*) is more surprising. Perhaps the psalm refers to people who do not base their instruction on *the* Teaching, the Torah; this would fit the word order in the second colon and the polemic against human wisdom in the Prophets. But perhaps the psalm presupposes that anyone who has been taught from the Torah, takes it seriously,

74. *Psalms*, 3:217.

and applies it to their life (when they make Yhwh's *declarations their *murmur) becomes (at least potentially) the wisest person in the world. Mere knowledge does not make for insight, but this commitment does. Even the enemies would know Yhwh's commands, if they were Israelites, but their actions indicate they did not obey them. They never had knowledge converted into wisdom.

> 100 I show more understanding than the elders,
> because I have observed your orders.

This third parallel line raises the same question. The elders are the community's senior members who make decisions for it, settle disputes, witness transactions, and offer advice (e.g., Deut. 21; Ruth 4; 1 Kings 12). Perhaps the psalmist has more understanding than the elders (*mizzĕqēnîm*) because they, too, base their insight on human wisdom gained through their life experience, so that attentiveness to Yhwh's teaching gives even a junior member of the community more understanding than they possess. Or perhaps it is again the actual observing of Yhwh's *orders (not merely knowledge of them) that makes the difference.

> 101 I have held back my feet from every evil path
> so that I may keep your words.

The way or path is sometimes a dead metaphor, but here the psalm presses its literal meaning. Ahead of us in life are a number of good paths we may choose to put our feet on, and a number of evil ones from (*min*) which we hold back. A good path is one that makes it possible to keep Yhwh's *words.

> 102 I have not departed from your decisions,
> because you are the one who has taught me.

"From your *decisions" (*mimmišpāṭêkā*) pairs with and contrasts with "from every evil path." The path image continues in the talk of not departing; contrast Israel at Sinai departing from the way Yhwh commanded (Exod. 32:8).

A particular effectiveness obtains when Yhwh does the *teaching. In isolation one might reckon that the decisions are the means whereby Yhwh teaches the suppliant, but the many pleas elsewhere for Yhwh to "enable me to understand" (e.g., v. 27) suggest that the suppliant has known Yhwh teaching what the decisions mean and demand, not merely their content. To have insight, one needs both the objectively existent teaching treasured in the community and the subjective work of Yhwh using it, interpreting it, and bringing it home. This reference to Yhwh's teaching also undergirds the claims in vv. 98–100. It is Yhwh's teaching that means one understands more than enemies, tutors, or elders.

> 103How smooth your statement has been to my taste,
> more so than honey to my mouth.

"How" (*mah*) recurs, now to comment on Yhwh's *statement rather than on the person who reads. Yet it is a comment on the effect of that word on the reader. Reading the statement is like eating something that slides down the throat in most agreeable fashion, like honey. As well as bee honey, that can denote the more common sweet syrup made from dates, the most common source of sweetness in the Middle East (cf. 19:10 [11]). What can be true of the effect of another person's words to us (Prov. 16:24) and of Yhwh's revelations to a prophet (Ezek. 3:3) is also true of the effect of the word that declares Yhwh's expectations but also attaches Yhwh's promises to them.

> 104I show understanding through your orders;
> therefore I am against every path of falsehood.

In closing the section the line again reformulates the claim about wisdom/insight/understanding in vv. 98–100, though here in absolute terms without any comparison with other people. Rather it goes on from the understanding that comes through Yhwh's *orders (*mippiqqûdêkā*) to its results, also taking up the image of the path. The enemies are fond of falsehood (vv. 69, 78, 86), but people who are theoretically committed to truth can also yield to the temptation to let their feet tread the way of *falsehood. Once again the prayer to be kept from that (v. 29) combines with an expression of commitment to keep from it, a commitment important enough to be repeated in vv. 128 and 163. The colon gives a good example of *śānē'*, conventionally translated "hate," denoting not merely emotional feelings but personal moral commitment; what we hate is what we are *against.

119:105–12. *Nûn* (*n*). Declarations concerning the effectiveness of Yhwh's word and the suppliant's consequent resolution to follow it bracket the pleas in vv. 107–8.

> 105Your word is a lamp for my foot,
> a light for my pathway.

The familiar image of the path now has a slightly different significance. The psalm speaks not of the various paths before us, which might be good or evil, but of the one pathway each one personally treads. In literal darkness we can lose our way or lose our footing and stumble, perhaps with fatal results. In metaphorical darkness the same is true; one might not realize (or might not face the fact) that certain sorts of offerings or certain forms of sexual activity are wrong, and might end up losing one's religious or moral footing, with fatal results (as Prov. 1–9 points out with regard to the latter). Yhwh's *word is thus our lamp (*nēr*), our source of light or our actual light.

106I swore, I confirmed
that I would keep your faithful decisions.

The *decisions are *faithful because they do give light that keeps us on the path of life and blessing, as long as we keep them. Thus swearing (*nišbaʿtî*) such an oath and confirming it (a hendiadys) logically follows from the awareness expressed in v. 105. Why would the psalmist now need to make this commitment the subject of an oath? Perhaps v. 107 suggests the answer: in weakness (and danger and pressure, vv. 109–10), one might abandon Yhwh's decisions because they do not look faithful.

107I have become very weakened;
Yhwh, make me live, in accordance with your word.

"Be *weak" (*naʿănêtî*) has come in qal (v. 67), pual (v. 71), and piel (v. 75); here it is niphal, qualifying it for first place in the line. Piel refers to Yhwh's activity in weakening, pual to the experience of being weakened by some agency, and qal to the experience of being weak. The rare niphal stands somewhere between the qal and the pual. The second colon suggests how far this weakening has gone; near death, the suppliant again appeals for life on the basis of how Yhwh's *word is supposed to work.

108Do accept the freewill offerings of my mouth, Yhwh,
and enable me to understand your decisions.

A literal freewill offering (*nĕdābâ*) is a sacrifice made as an act of free devotion to Yhwh, as opposed to one prescribed, or required because (for instance) of a particular answer to prayer. A verbal freewill offering is an analogous act of praise.[75] The suppliant often expresses praise for Yhwh's words; it is such praise that this line asks Yhwh to accept (*rāṣâ*) as Yhwh accepts a sacrifice (e.g., Lev. 1:4).

75. Christian writers such as Hilary (*Commentaire*, 2:142–43) think of a voluntary verbal undertaking such as a commitment to celibacy or vegetarianism.

The line's logic is that accepting this praise will also incline Yhwh to enable the suppliant to understand Yhwh's *decisions. The praise turns out to be also a kind of prayer. Further, the line implies another aspect of the spiral nature of a relationship with God. Understanding Yhwh's decisions leads to praise; praise leads to understanding Yhwh's decisions.

> 109My life is continually in my palm,
> but I have not ignored your teaching.

To take your life (*nepeš*; *person) into your hand is an image for risking your life (1 Sam. 19:5; 28:21). "Palm," *kap*, rather than the general word *yād*, helps to explain the idea: having your life on your open hand makes it easy for your enemies to take it. Tg "on the back of my hand" would have the same implication.

Continuing to follow Yhwh's *teaching rather than *ignoring it acts as a continual provocation to some people. The suppliant nevertheless continues to behave this way.

> 110The faithless laid a trap for me,
> but I have not wandered from your orders.

The line re-expresses the point. The suppliant's life is endangered through a trap the *faithless have laid (*nātan*); the word refers to a trap with nets such as those used by someone trying to catch birds. The trap thus complements the ropes of v. 61 and the pits of v. 85. Despite the danger, the suppliant has still not strayed out of the way laid out by Yhwh's *orders.

> 111I entered into possession of your declarations forever,
> because they are the joy of my heart.

Like v. 103, the line puts the point in a more affective way. Entering into possession (*nāḥal*) parallels receiving an allocation (v. 57). Both apply to a family possessing an allocation of land in the village, and on the larger scale to the clan and the whole people doing so. The suppliant sees Yhwh's *declarations to be as important, precious, or valuable as a family sees the land on which life depends. Entering into possession of these declarations was like Israel entering the land or like the clan and the family receiving its allocation when the process of occupation was (notionally) over. Like that tract of land, it is the suppliant's possession forever.

There is a thrill about that, which the second colon spells out in terms of the joy of the *heart.

> 112I inclined my heart to do your laws
> forever, to the utmost.

Once again the enthusiasm is not merely an emotion but a fervor expressing itself in action, in doing Yhwh's *laws. But between the joy and the action is the inclining (*nāṭâ*) of the *heart. The heart, the locus of joy in v. 111b, is now the locus of decision making, the will. The line suggests another instance of the interweaving of divine and human action in connection with our obedience. Yhwh has to incline our heart (v. 36); we have to incline our heart. The second colon doubly underlines that.

119:113–20. *Sāmek* (*s*). The section contrasts an attitude of dedication to Yhwh's teaching and commands (vv. 113, 119) with the stance of the divided and faithless.

> 113I am against divided people
> and I am dedicated to your teaching.

Divided people (*sēʿăpîm*) stand in contrast to someone *dedicated to Yhwh's *teaching. They are people like those Elijah upbraids for being unwilling to decide whether to follow Yhwh or Baal (1 Kings 17:21; cf. Josh. 24:15; Matt. 6:24). They cannot make up their mind whether or not to live by Yhwh's commands and promises. They will not make a stand.

The verbs make for a further contrast. Being *against and being *dedicated to (*śānēʾ* and *ʾāhēb*) are antonyms, usually translated "hate" and "love." They underline the choice the psalm urges, which the psalmist claims to have made.

> 114You have been my shelter, my shield;
> for your word I have waited.

The psalmist looks back, though (as is common in the psalm) what the qatal verb describes continues to be a present reality. There might be a tension between the cola, one the life of faith often has to handle. Yhwh has been the psalmist's shelter (*sēter*) and shield, a shield to shelter behind (the expression acts as a hendiadys). But the psalmist has had to *wait for Yhwh. The psalm implies there have been times when the psalmist waited and experienced Yhwh acting. But some lines picture waiting as the present reality; such waiting implies not yet experiencing the fulfillment of Yhwh's *word, not being protected or shielded from attack (vv. 43, 49, and esp. 81). In the ultimate sense there is protection; the psalmist did not die. But in the midst of aggression and assault, the psalmist has to continue believing Yhwh is shelter and shield even when it does not look like it, until the moment of deliverance proves its truth again.

> [115]Go away from me, you wrongdoers,
> so that I may observe my God's commands.

The vast bulk of Ps. 119 addresses Yhwh. A few verses (e.g., vv. 1–3) speak of Yhwh in the third person, addressing people who need to learn to obey and trust Yhwh, who are perhaps the audience that is intended to overhear the psalm as a whole. Although it speaks much of the psalmist's opponents or attackers, it addresses them only here. The sense of being under attack running through much of the psalm makes it natural to have this longing for them to "go away!" (*sûr*). Yet this exclamation is likely an expression of confidence and conviction, not anguish. That might be suggested by the rest of the psalm, but also by the setting and significance of such a cry elsewhere. In Ps. 6:8 [9] it emerges from the conviction that Yhwh has indeed determined to deliver the suppliant. In 139:19–22 it indicates the psalmist's dissociation from wrongdoers and signifies evidence that one really is against their lifestyle (cf. v. 113).

Here the psalmist wants them out of the way to make it possible or easier to observe Yhwh's commands; they will no longer be a pressure tempting toward compromise for the sake of a quiet life, or toward sharing their lifestyle because of its short-term benefits. Calling Yhwh "my God" is the converse to speaking as "Yhwh's servant," with the implication that observing God's commands is what is to be expected of someone in such a relationship with God.

> [116]Hold me up in accordance with your statement so that I may live,
> and do not shame me in respect of my expectation.

That pressure or temptation could make us fall over, or the attacks themselves could knock us over. The suppliant thus pleads with Yhwh to hold us up (*sāmak*), to stop us falling or to catch us as we fall and stand us up again (see 37:17, 24; 71:6; 145:14) so that we may live.

Failing to do that would bring shame on us, make us look stupid, but it would also bring discredit on Yhwh, because it is Yhwh's *statement that we made the basis of that "expectation" that we would be held up (the rare word *śēber*, more common in Aramaic; cf. v. 166).

> [117]Sustain me so that I may find deliverance,
> and may have regard for your laws continually.

"Sustain me" (*sāʿad*) is a similar plea to "hold me," and the reference to *deliverance parallels that to "life." The niphal verb ("find deliverance") again stands somewhere between a qal and a passive (though there is no other passive of *yāšaʿ*).[76]

The second colon goes in a different direction, though a familiar one. Having regard for (*šāʿâ*) Yhwh's *laws suggests a steady gaze implying trust, devotion, or acceptance; it is the word for Yhwh's accepting Abel and his offering, and not Cain and his (Gen. 4:4–5). So "continually" underlines part of the verb's own significance.

> **118**You have thrown out all the people who stray from your laws,
> because their deceitfulness is false.

The opposite of regard for Yhwh's *laws is straying from them, which as usual implies a deliberate rather than an accidental turning away. In that connection, working with the constraints and stimulus of the letter samek (one of the less common initial letters for words) generates another rare verb for throw out or spurn (*sālâ*). Presumably this spurning is something the psalmist knows has happened in the past, though elsewhere the psalm indicates it does not seem to be a present reality. Not all such qatal verbs can be precative,[77] but some instances, such as this, though of past meaning, may rhetorically function to remind Yhwh of this pattern of action that needs to be repeated.

The reason for Yhwh's spurning is expressed in what is formally a tautology (lit. "because their deceitfulness is *falsehood"),[78] but in substance it makes its point powerfully; one might paraphrase "because of their deceitfulness, their falsehood."

> **119**You have put an end to all the faithless people in the land as dross;
> therefore I have been dedicated to your declarations.

This further line first restates v. 118a, then v. 117b or 113b. "Dross" (*sigîm*) implies a process of testing that reveals what is true metal and what is not, but OT references usually presuppose that the difference has already become obvious (e.g., Isa. 1:22–26; Ezek. 22:17–19) and concern themselves with the action that follows, and so it is here. The *faithless

76. The niphal also makes for alliteration between *wĕʾiwwāšēʿâ* and the following *wĕʾešʿâ*.

77. See the note on v. 21.

78. LXX, Jerome have "their thought is falsehood," which might mean that for *tarmîtām* they read a word from *rāʿâ* III, such as the Aramaic *tarʿîtām*, or it might mean that they understood *tarmîtām* to have that meaning (cf. G. R. Driver, "Textual and Linguistic Problems," 191).

in the land[79] have already been exposed as dross by their faithlessness, and Yhwh has put an end to them. Once more, the psalmist speaks of Yhwh's past habitual activity that is thus also ongoing practice, and that Yhwh needs to take up again. The rest of the psalm suggests that this activity of Yhwh is not the only basis for being *dedicated to Yhwh's *declarations, but it is one basis, or an encouragement to maintain that dedication. To see the link another way, eliminating faithless people is the other side of the coin to being a shelter and shield (v. 114) or being enabled to live or find deliverance (vv. 116, 117). It provides evidence that the promises in Yhwh's declarations can be relied on.

[120]My flesh tingles through awe for you;
I revere your decisions.

The last samek word, "tingle" (*sāmar*), is another rarity. It otherwise occurs only in Job 4:15, which makes clear that it hardly suggests that the psalmist's flesh creeps (BDB) but that it shivers or trembles. "Awe" (*paḥad*) is a strong synonym for *reverence; the two words can signify terror and fear, but the psalm's usual way of speaking suggests that here again it denotes a positive awe for Yhwh in person (v. 120a) and for Yhwh's *decisions (v. 120b).

Likewise *reverence usually emphasizes the practical outworking of submission and obedience; here the image emphasizes that the affective and conative go together. There is no tension between love and dedication (v. 119) and awe and reverence (cf. Deut. 10:12), partly because both express themselves in obedience.

119:121–28. *'Ayin* (ʿ). Prominent at the center of this section is the declaration, "I am your servant" (v. 125; cf. vv. 122, 124).

[121]I have made faithful decisions;
do not leave me to my oppressors.

The precise expression for "*faithful *decisions" (*mišpāṭ wāṣedeq*) comes otherwise only in Eccles. 5:8 [7]: people ignore this priority in favor of encouraging oppression (*ʿōšeq*) (cf. Ps. 146:7). That is exactly the psalmist's experience. Ecclesiastes witnesses it; the psalmist endures it. With the Hebrew words in the opposite order, faithful decision making is the foundation of Yhwh's throne (89:14 [15]; 97:2), though also (or rather, and therefore) a key human aspiration (cf. Prov. 2:9). The psalmist claims to have given it priority: "I have made . . ." (*ʿāśâ*). There would therefore be justice about Yhwh demonstrating that this is indeed the

79. Cf. Gunkel, *Psalmen*, 530. EVV have "the earth."

foundation of Yhwh's throne, the priority basic to Yhwh's rule, by not abandoning the psalmist to oppressors.

> [122]Pledge good things to your servant;
> may the willful not oppress me.

Asking Yhwh to "make a pledge [*ʿārab*] to your servant for *good" is a bold metaphor, though related to the idea of Yhwh being restorer (*gōʾēl*). The metaphor recurs from Isa. 38:14, where Hezekiah, as one who is "oppressed" (cf. vv. 121b, 122b here), asks Yhwh to do this. A needy person will beseech someone with resources to pledge some of these to get a creditor off the debtor's back. "Oppression" often denotes extortion, so here the financial image is not far away. The suppliant is indeed like someone in financial straits at the hands of the *willful and needs Yhwh to spend resources on this needy person's behalf. It is again as Yhwh's servant that the suppliant makes that request; because of this relationship, an obligation hangs on the master.

> [123]My eyes—they have come to an end for your deliverance,
> for your faithful statement.

Words from vv. 81–82 recur (adding the familiar *faithful), in a slightly varied configuration, partly in order to open the line with "my eyes" (*ʿênay*).

> [124]Act with your servant in accordance with your commitment
> and enable me to learn your laws.

Again the suppliant appeals to the position of servant (*ʿebed*) to whom the master owes *commitment, and asks to be enabled to learn Yhwh's *laws, a servant's appropriate correlative desire. But this makes the cast of the request different from usual. The master's commitment is expressed not in an act of deliverance but in the educative task of opening the servant's mind.

> [125]I am your servant; enable me to understand
> so that I may acknowledge your declarations.

The repetition again appeals to the position of servant and charges Yhwh to take action if the servant is to *acknowledge (that is, obey) the master's *declarations.

> [126]It is a time for Yhwh to act;
> people have violated your teaching.

The theme of vv. 118 and 119 returns. The word order is "it is time [*ʿēt*] to act for Yhwh" (cf. LXX), though that would give a misleading impression of the meaning of the second *l* ("for"). Jerome thus has "it is time that you should act, Yhwh," implying *yhwh* for *lyhwh*. Further, while the notion of acting for God suits modern Western readers, it would be a strange note in this psalm. The psalm is more concerned to prevail on Yhwh to act, and that is the aim here, as the second colon also implies.

The appeal's basis is people's violating (*pārar* hiphil) Yhwh's *teaching. The verb often has the covenant as its object, and EVV refer to "breaking the covenant," an ambiguous expression that could suggest (usually misleadingly) that people have terminated the covenant. Usually it denotes contravening it, violating it, making it *de facto* ineffectual. Such is the idea here.

127Therefore I am dedicated to your commands
more than to gold, yes than pure gold.

"Therefore" (*ʿal-kēn*) provides a convenient way to open an *ʿayin* line, though the logic is elliptical. Violating Yhwh's teaching is scandalous, v. 126 has implied; so the psalmist is *dedicated to the commands expressed in that teaching, more than to things of greatest earthly value (cf. v. 72). Reference to oppression or exaction and pledging gives heightened significance to the comparison. Is gold the ultimate value? Not for this suppliant.

128Therefore all the orders concerning everything I have regarded as upright;
I have been against every path of falsehood.

The first colon again begins "therefore" (*ʿal-kēn*) and restates v. 127 as a whole. One dedicates oneself to commands and *orders because of regarding them as upright, and vice versa. The expression emphatically suggests all orders, no matter what they are or what they apply to.

Being *against paths of *falsehood, paths that involve walking deceitfully in the way of the *willful, is again the antonym of dedicating oneself to such paths (cf. v. 113).

119:129–36. *Pê* (*p*). Even Soll, who argues that the psalm as a whole develops in coherent fashion, cannot point to movement of thought in the *ʿayin*, *pê*, and *ṣādê* sections, which simply take further themes that have already been elaborated; he summarizes this section as "petitions and protestations of loyalty."[80]

80. *Psalm 119*, 105, 109.

> [129]Your declarations are wonders;
> therefore my spirit has observed them.

For Yhwh's *declarations as "wonders" (here the collective *pele'* to provide a *p* word), see vv. 18 and 27. The amazing nature of these revelations about Yhwh's will, which make it possible to put one's life on the right track and see the fruitfulness of that, makes it natural to observe them with enthusiasm of spirit (*person).

> [130]The opening up of your words—it gives light;
> it gives understanding to the simple.

In 49:4 [5], "opening up" (*pētaḥ*) refers to a mystery needing explanation; so it is the expounding of Yhwh's *words that brings illumination. Or the expression may picture Yhwh's words as contained on a scroll, rolled up until one unrolls it; the words' mere presence on the scroll brings no light until someone opens the scroll. Sym takes it to picture Yhwh's words as a gateway opening out into the light, though one would expect *petaḥ* for "gateway." *Pētaḥ* comes only here and may rather link with *pātaḥ* II, "engrave" (cf. Tg). It then traces the light-giving back to Yhwh's bringing these words into being, and describes this in terms of writing them (as if on stone) rather than uttering them (contrast vv. 13, 72, 88).[81]

On any understanding, God's words consequently enlighten our path, specifically the path of simple people. That might suggest people who have not yet gained experience in recognizing dangers and deviations that are to be avoided and signs that a path leads somewhere safe and positive (e.g., Prov. 1:32; 9:6; 14:15; 22:3). But in Ps. 116:6 it suggested, more positively, someone such as the psalmist, someone of simple faith in a good sense.

Light is regularly a symbol not merely of guidance but of blessing (e.g., 97:11; 112:4; and this verb in 118:27). Reading this line after v. 129 suggests that common broader connotation; conversely, v. 130 explains something of how Yhwh's declarations are wonders and why one's spirit would observe them.

> [131]I opened wide my mouth to pant,
> because I longed for your commands.

Again the psalm makes explicit (as Proverbs also emphasizes) that Yhwh's words or commands are not just for the simple. Opening wide

81. 11QPs[a] *ptḥ* implies impv. (Allen, *Psalms 101–150*, 179).

my mouth (*pî*) suggests desire and craving (cf. Job 29:23; Isa. 5:14). "Panting" underlines the image (cf. Job 5:5; 7:2; 36:20), and "longing" (*yāʾab*, a hapax Aramaism) underlines it yet again. Longing for Yhwh's commands is like a hungry person's longing for food, or a laborer's longing for the end of the day, or the ground's desire for rain, or Sheol's desire for people to die.

132Turn your face to me and be gracious to me
in accordance with your decision for people who are dedicated to your name.

Turning the face (*pānâ*) has its natural result in showing *grace. When someone's face lights up with a smile (cf. v. 130), that both signifies affection and promises blessing.

This is not a random affair, as if a suppliant cannot know whether the king will look with favor today. There is a principle underlying Yhwh's attitude. Yhwh long ago made known a policy *decision that people *dedicated to Yhwh's *name would be treated thus. (This may compromise the meaning of "grace," because strictly grace ought not to be something that can be earned or calculated. Perhaps we should say that the experience will be gracelike in its positiveness, even if it is actually something more like the working out of mutual commitment.)

133Establish my steps by your statement;
may no harmfulness get the mastery of me.

The psalm again assumes that both God and we are involved in what happens to us. We have responsibility for our feet (vv. 59, 101), but we also ask God to establish our steps (*pĕʿāmay*). Mediating between these two is God's *statement being a lamp for our foot (v. 105). We may fall because we fail to direct our feet aright, or because someone or something trips us. There are lots of people doing harm to others out there: "doers of harm" is a recurrent phrase (e.g., 92:7, 9 [8, 10]; 94:4, 16). So may they not get power over us. Given that possibility, however, while we need to accept our responsibility for directing our steps, we also need God to keep our steps firm. We ask for that to happen in accordance with God's word, because that word promises that things will work out if we fulfill our responsibility by obeying it.

134Redeem me from human oppression
so that I may keep your orders.

Strictly, "*redeem" (*pādâ*) implies spending money (cf. 49:7 [8]), but usually it has a more general sense of procuring someone's freedom or release from oppression (e.g., 25:22; 26:11; 78:42). Again, the object of liberation is not to be able to do as one wishes but to keep God's *orders. "*Redemption," recalling the redemption of a slave, helps underline that point. Yhwh's procuring Israel's freedom from oppression in Egypt gave Yhwh some rights over Israel (e.g., Deut. 9:6–11). They are obliged to keep Yhwh's orders.

> **135**Shine your face on your servant
> and enable me to learn your laws.

The notions of the face (*pānêkā*; cf. v. 132) and of shining like light (v. 130) now come together. As a servant, the psalmist appeals for the master's smile and thus for the good that this brings.

Here that good lies not in prosperity or long life or a sense of God's goodness, but in the capacity to learn God's *laws. Priority in the psalmist's desires (cf. v. 131) lies there.

> **136**My eyes have run down streams of water
> because people have not kept your teaching.

The converse to personal joy in Yhwh's *teaching, and commitment to keeping it, is grief that many people do not share that commitment. Hyperbolically, the grief makes rivers (*peleg*) of tears run down the psalmist's face. While significance attaches to the affective meaning of that statement, it is another marker of personal commitment. Someone who cries like that in witnessing disobedience to Yhwh's teaching surely cannot blatantly ignore that teaching.

119:137–44. *Ṣādê* (*ṣ*). The section opens and closes by celebrating the faithfulness of Yhwh and Yhwh's declarations (vv. 137, 144; cf. also vv. 138, 142).

> **137**You are faithful, Yhwh,
> upright in your decisions.

"*Faithful" (*ṣaddîq*) makes a natural opening for the *ṣ* section; here it is explicated as uprightness (cf. Deut. 32:4). In adding reference to *decisions, the line incorporates variants on the expression "faithful decisions" (*mišpāṭ wāṣedeq*; v. 121). The two roots bring out how faithfulness must find expression in action, while decisions must reflect relational priorities.

> **138**You commanded the faithfulness of your declarations,
> and their truthfulness, exceedingly.

To restate the point, Yhwh issued *declarations embodying *faithfulness and *truthfulness. Out of the context, that might suggest declarations demanding faithfulness and truthfulness; here it suggests declarations with these qualities as their fruit for people who observe them. The adverb "exceedingly" (*mĕʾōd*) should qualify a verb, suggesting that "command" (*ṣāwâ* piel) and this adverb constitute a bracket round the three nouns in the line; the adverb emphasizes the firmness of Yhwh's command.[82]

> **139**My passion has destroyed me,
> because my foes have ignored your words.

"Passion" (*qinʾâ*) often implies jealousy or anger, but it directly refers to depth and intensity of emotions, often felt by human beings for God's honor (69:9 [10]; cf. John 2:17). Here the word might have suggested a deep personal anger in relation to the psalmist's attackers, but the second colon nuances that. The foes are not mentioned until the very end of the line, which gives prominence to their *ignoring Yhwh's *words. That is why passion has destroyed (*ṣāmat* piel) the psalmist. Passion consumes like fire (Song 8:6). The psalmist might have wished not to feel so strongly about people's ignoring Yhwh's word, but passion does not give options. No doubt declaring this passion again signals that the psalmist is definitely not someone who fails to be mindful of Yhwh's words.

> **140**Your statement is much proven;
> your servant is dedicated to it.

In what sense is Yhwh's *statement proven (*ṣārap*)? The image suggests something that contains dross and needs refining (e.g., 105:19), but it would be odd to suggest a need to purify what Yhwh says. But in 18:30 [31] the suppliant has proved Yhwh's word, having been forced to rely on Yhwh's promises and to discover Yhwh does keep them. Verse 140a could refer to that personal proving. It provides a basis for a servant's being *dedicated to the master's word.

> **141**I am little and despised;
> your orders I have not ignored.

82. It is often difficult to tell how translations construe the elliptical line (though it makes little difference to the meaning). Following NRSV generates "in faithfulness you commanded your declarations." But MT's conjunctive accent on "faithfulness" suggests that *ṣedeq ʿēdōtêkā* is a construct phrase (cf. Jerome), which requires less inference. I have then reckoned that *ʿēdōtêkā* also applies in the second colon.

Being the little (*ṣāʿîr*) son, the youngest, or being small of stature, means being insignificant and not counting (e.g., 1 Sam. 9:21). That is the suppliant's status in the community; it likely reflects the troubles the psalm has referred to. Trouble leads to being discounted and disregarded.

But being despised has not made the suppliant abandon commitment to Yhwh, that is, start *ignoring Yhwh's *laws. Or is it that people's disregard has come despite the suppliant's not having ignored those laws? Or is it that not ignoring those laws is a basis for appeal to Yhwh to do something about the way the suppliant is being marginalized?

> [142]Your faithfulness is a faithfulness that endures forever,
> and your teaching is true.

Verse 141 could have looked as if it indicated the opposite, but the suppliant affirms that Yhwh's *faithfulness actually is forever and that Yhwh's *teaching is *true; it can be relied on. Alternatively, that declaration could back up the implicit plea in v. 141.

> [143]Though trouble and distress have found me,
> your commands have been my delight.

Again to restate v. 141: it is as if trouble and distress are active agents going about seeking to cause trouble and finding their victims, like Sheol (cf. 116:3); hence the psalmist's insignificance and shame. But the psalmist was *delighting in Yhwh's commands (cf. vv. 16, 24, 47, 70, 77, 92) before things went wrong, and/or has continued to do so after things went wrong, and now looks to be treated accordingly by Yhwh.

> [144]The faithfulness of your declarations stands forever;
> enable me to understand, so that I may live.

The closing line opens as the section began, referring to Yhwh's *faithfulness (*ṣedeq*), specifically the faithfulness of Yhwh's *declarations (cf. v. 138) and the lasting nature of this faithfulness (cf. v. 142).[83]

The familiar plea to be enabled to understand explains that this leads to life. If I am to receive the benefits of Yhwh's faithful declarations, namely life, I need Yhwh also to enable me to understand (and do) them.

119:145–52. *Qôp* (*q*). In an interesting pattern, the first two lines pair, both beginning with *qārāʾ*; the next two also pair, both beginning with

83. MT's accent implies it does not see *ṣedeq ʿēdwōtêkā* as a construct phrase, as in v. 138; thus Jerome suggests "Your declarations are faithful forever" (cf. NRSV). More likely the phrase works in the same way as in v. 138 (cf. NJPS).

qādam piel; vv. 150–51 pair, both beginning with a form of *qrb*; and the closing line begins with *qedem*, from which *qādam* derives.

145I have called with all my heart: Answer me, Yhwh;
I shall observe your laws.

The *qôp* section leads the psalm for the first time to speak of calling to Yhwh (*qārāʾ*), though it has often been doing that or referring to having done it, and with a whole *heart. And v. 26 did speak of Yhwh's having answered such an appeal. Here it might be looking back on such an experience. But as there is no reference to an answer, more likely "answer me" is the plea the psalmist is still uttering. The motivation for Yhwh's answering is, "I shall observe your *laws."

146I have called you: deliver me,
so that I may keep your declarations.

"Call" (*qārāʾ*) now has the suffix that makes it more urgent and direct, even peremptory, while the content of the appeal moves on from "answer me" to urge with more specificity, "deliver me." The second colon makes more specific that it is a purpose clause but then simply restates words from v. 145 by speaking of keeping Yhwh's *declarations.

147I have anticipated the twilight and cried for help
as I waited for your word [Q]/words[K].

The theme continues as the psalmist recalls pleading that has been going on and still persists. "Twilight" (*nešep*) is usually taken to denote the transition from dark to light. Anticipating (*qādam* piel) the twilight then implies rising before the sun; that is how urgent the need feels and how importunate the psalmist is driven to be (so Sym). But twilight usually refers to the transition from light to dark (it is not certain that it ever refers to morning); this leads well into v. 148. The idea then is of anticipating the time for evening prayer and the offering of the evening sacrifice. *Crying for help re-expresses the "call" of vv. 145–46, with more emphasis on its urgency.

The second colon again brings the line to a close by referring to Yhwh's teaching, here as Yhwh's *word; but it is the promise aspect of that word that is noted.

148My eyes have anticipated the watches,
murmuring about your statement.

In the parallelism of the two lines, "my eyes" gives precision to the subject of the verb, while the object of anticipation is now the night watches, the night's divisions as these govern the changes between look-outs (e.g., Judg. 7:19). The psalmist is even keener than a sentry is supposed to be about going on watch, and resembles a sentry arriving for duty early. Allen suggests an allusion to the last of the three watches of the night (2 a.m. to 6 a.m.),[84] the watch leading to the dawn, the time of morning prayer when the morning sacrifice was due. The psalmist is then speaking of rising to pray well before the set time for prayer. The line then complements the previous line if that spoke of praying before the evening time for sacrifice and prayer (it restates it, if that already referred to the dawning).

This prayer is accompanied by murmuring about Yhwh's *statement, which might embrace declaring both the importance of its demands and trust in its promise; each adds to the reason for Yhwh to respond.

> **149**Listen to my voice in accordance with your commitment;
> Yhwh, in accordance with your decision, make me live.

Yhwh's statement implies a *commitment to people who live by it, so either understanding of v. 148b is a basis for urging Yhwh to listen. The second colon explicitly appeals to the promise aspect of Yhwh's decision, which promises life.

> **150**People who pursue schemes [MT]/people who harass me with schemes [Vrs] are near,
> but they are far from your teaching.

The line sets up a nice contrast between being near (*qārēb*) and being far (*rāḥōq*). The people who pursue or harass the psalmist (*rādap*, vv. 84, 86) are people who in connection with that pursuit also pursue "schemes." Like the English word, *zimmâ* need not suggest something wrong, and Yhwh can be the subject of related words, but they usually denote planning to do something by way of judgment, and commonly suggest scheming to do wrong. So it is worrying that these people are physically near. The negative connotation of their scheming is confirmed by their being morally far away—from Yhwh's *teaching. The word order helps bring out the contrast and the scandal as it separates "near" and "far away," and juxtaposes "schemes" and "from your teaching": "Near are people who pursue schemes but from your teaching they are far."

84. *Psalms 101–150*, 191.

> [151]You are near, Yhwh,
> and all your commands are true.

The reference to Yhwh's being near (*qārôb*) makes for a nice and relieving contrast with v. 150 (cf. 34:18 [19]; 145:18). Subjectively, one can cope with schemers being near if Yhwh is near; and objectively, their being near will not mean their schemes succeed if Yhwh is near. Likewise, the fact that they are far from Yhwh's teaching counts for less (subjectively and objectively) in light of Yhwh's commands being *true and trustworthy, reliable guides to conduct that matches the way the world really is and to conduct Yhwh will honor.

> [152]Of old I have acknowledged, from your declarations,
> that you founded them forever.

Verse 152 confirms and expands on v. 151. "Of old" (*qedem*) picks up the root of the denominative verb that opened vv. 147 and 148. Those verses spoke of what the psalmist did before the twilight and before the night watches; this verse looks back to a much earlier "before," which indeed came before those "befores" and constitutes their foundation. If it were not for this "before," those "befores" never would have happened. The psalmist's life from way back has been based on studying Yhwh's *declarations, becoming convinced by their wisdom and their promises, and thus *acknowledging from them that they indeed came from Yhwh and that therefore they will stand forever (cf. vv. 142, 144); they will share in Yhwh's eternity (cf. v. 89). "Of old" and "forever" thus embrace the entire time of the psalmist's human life.

119:153–60. *Rêš* (*r*). A bidding to "see" frames the section (vv. 153, 159; cf. v. 158); the section also three times urges, "make me live" (vv. 154, 156, 159).

> [153]See my weakness and rescue me,
> because I have not ignored your teaching.

Often the aim of a psalm is to get Yhwh to pay attention; action then must follow. So here the idea is to get Yhwh to look at (*rāʾâ*) the suppliant's *weakness and vulnerability and therefore to rescue. Again the appeal's basis is the fact of not having *ignored or neglected Yhwh's *teaching.

> [154]Decide my cause and restore me;
> in view of your statement, make me live.

"Decide my cause" (*rîbâ rîbî*) uses *r* words for the more familiar words from *špṭ*. In effect the suppliant is on trial; indeed, the accusers have already turned in a "guilty" verdict and are behaving accordingly. But Yhwh is in a position to determine the decision of the metaphorical court. The suppliant urges Yhwh to do so, ruling in the suppliant's favor. This will issue in *restoration and release, to new life. The second colon re-expresses the point in familiar terms, except for the preposition referring to Yhwh's *statement.

155Deliverance is far from the faithless
because they have not had recourse to your laws.

The statement that *deliverance is far (*rāḥôq*) from the *faithless because they have not had *recourse to Yhwh's *laws is the converse of that implied by v. 154. It carries the usual assumption that there is a link between the demands of the laws and the promises attached to them.

156Your compassion is great, Yhwh;
in accordance with your decision, make me live.

Yet again the line reformulates v. 154 with its appeal to Yhwh's compassion (*raḥămîm*) and its appeal for life based on the nature of Yhwh's *decision.

157Though my harassers and foes are many,
I have not diverted from your declarations.

And once more the psalm repeats the contention (most recently formulated in v. 153) not to have forfeited a claim on Yhwh. For all the pressure by these many (*rabbîm*), the suppliant has not swerved from the path laid out by Yhwh's *declarations (cf. v. 51). Thus Yhwh has already been answering the prayer in v. 36 (using this verb, *nāṭâ*). The double usage again illustrates the complementarity of divine and human action. I need Yhwh to incline my heart; I too have to incline my heart to Yhwh's declarations, not away from them. Yhwh's inclining requires and makes possible my inclining; my inclining requires and makes actual Yhwh's inclining.

158I have seen betrayers and loathed them,
people who did not keep your statement.

The line puts flesh on v. 157b. Seeing (*rāʾâ*) things can be a means of temptation; we see the attractiveness of what people do and get drawn into imitating them. Here, seeing has had the opposite effect, leading to loathing. The language (*qûṭ*) and the logic will recur in 139:21, with the same implication that being disgusted by people's behavior indicates we would not dream of going that way ourselves (see on vv. 53, 115). The language also implies being imitators of Yhwh (95:10).

The description of the loathsome betrayers as people who did not keep Yhwh's *statement may seem tame; yet the language's strength then indicates how serious a business it is when we fail to keep Yhwh's word. It also indicates that while the psalm sometimes pictures trouble coming from outside the community, sometimes it comes from within.

159 See that I have been dedicated to your orders;
Yhwh, in accordance with your commitment make me live.

The further bidding to see (*rāʾâ*) pairs with and contrasts with that in v. 153. The psalmist has pointed to weakness but can also point to *dedication to Yhwh's *orders, and therefore again reckon that being enabled to live will fit with Yhwh's *commitment.

160 Truthfulness is the sum total of your word;
every faithful decision of yours stands forever.

This double conviction is one that essentially underlines the psalmist's spirituality. We can keep being dedicated to Yhwh's orders because we know that Yhwh's *word or *decision is not merely a matter of laying down the law but is an expression of *truthfulness and *faithfulness. There is some inevitability about that. A person's word and decision reflect who they are. Yhwh is truthful and faithful; so then are Yhwh's word and decision.

That is so "forever," because these are Yhwh's characteristics forever. This qualifier at the beginning of the second colon pairs with the qualifier with which the whole line opens, the *r* word that is its distinctive new expression, *rōʾš*. It usually means "head," but occasionally means something like sum total (cf. 139:17). The essence of Yhwh is truthfulness.

119:161–68. *Śîn/Šîn* (*ś/š*). One of the psalm's understandably favorite words, *šāmar* ("keep") opens the last two lines and sums up the section's tone.

161 Leaders—they have harassed me without reason,
but at your word [Q]/words [K] my heart has stood in awe.

The leaders (*śārîm*) appeared in v. 23 (see comment). Here they have moved on to implement their plots; the psalmist claims to be innocent of any action that should have provoked them.

The pressure has not changed the psalmist's attitude to Yhwh's *teaching. Perhaps it has deepened it: for the *heart to be in awe (*pāḥad*; cf. the noun in v. 120) involves a less familiar word than "revere" (the parallel word in v. 120), and may suggest something more intense. But the expression still implies an attitude that issues in heeding this word, not a paralyzing dread.

> 162I exult over your statement
> like someone who finds much plunder.

Emotion again does come into attitudes to Yhwh's *statement, namely exultation or joy (*śûś*): for such celebration at finding plunder, see 1 Sam. 14:31–32; 30:16, and for the simile, Isa. 9:3 [2]. Finding plunder results from winning a great victory; it is quite something that the psalm can speak of such exulting when threatened with devastating defeat (v. 161).

> 163Whereas I am against falsehood and abhor it,
> I am dedicated to your teaching.

There is a contrast between *falsehood and Yhwh's *teaching (the line works *aba′b′*). Then there is a contrast between being *against or opposing or hating (*śānē'*) and its antonym, being *dedicated to or loving (*'āhēb*) (cf. v. 113). The former is supplemented by the further verb "abhor," which underlines the emotional aspect to *śānē'*. The line thus continues the emotional tone of vv. 161–62.

> 164Seven times a day I have praised you
> for your faithful decisions.

A person of faith gives *praise to Yhwh morning and evening, the times of the offerings. A person of great faith might pray a third time, presumably in the middle of the day, like Daniel (Dan. 6; cf. Ps. 55:17 [18]?), or even in the middle of the night (cf. v. 62). Hyperbolically, the psalmist claims to have given praise seven times (*šeba'*) a day for Yhwh's *faithful *decisions, which again both give direction for life and promise that blessing will issue from following them.

> 165There is much well-being for people who are dedicated to your teaching
> and there is nothing that can make them fall.

This further declaration follows from that. Only here does the psalm speak of *well-being (*šālôm*), which will indeed issue from being *dedicated to Yhwh's *teaching; cf. v. 163b. Again the parallel colon makes an antithetical statement. NRSV and TNIV have "stumble," but *kāšal* (here the noun *mikšôl*) does not suggest losing one's footing in a way that might be momentary, but falling so as not to be able to recover. The psalm again presupposes the image of the way that we walk. For all the hazards of the path, we will be able to walk it.

> 166I have looked for your deliverance, Yhwh,
> and I have acted on your commands.

"Looked" (*śābar* piel) in the sense of "hoped" suggests a sure expectation of Yhwh's *deliverance; it is the mother verb of "expectation" in v. 116. Yet again the two cola make the link between expecting to see Yhwh's promises fulfilled and obeying Yhwh's commands.

> 167I have kept your declarations with my whole being,
> and I am very much dedicated to them.

The line expands on the attitude expressed in v. 166a, again implying the link between action, attitude, and emotion (cf. vv. 161–63). Keeping (*šāmar*) Yhwh's *declarations involves action. But the involvement of the whole being (*person) implies this is not only an obedience of the outward person but a response of the spirit, will, and heart. Both carry over into the reference to being totally *dedicated to those declarations.

> 168I have kept your orders and your declarations,
> because all my ways are before you.

The last line in the section re-expresses the point about keeping (*šāmar*) those *orders and *declarations, but focuses on the action this implies rather than the inner attitude. In an ideal world, or rather if we were ideal people, the idea that God sees everything we do might be an unworthy motivation for obedience, but in the actual world seminary students need to be proctored when they are taking tests (cf. Heb. 4:13).

The notion that our ways are before Yhwh carries a further connotation. In 38:9 [10] its implication is not that Yhwh knows what we do but that Yhwh knows what happens to us (cf. "before you" in 88:1 [2]; "before me" in 89:36 [37]). A similar implication makes sense here. Yet again the line links Yhwh's commands and God's promises. Our living obedient lives means God keeps an eye on us.

119:169–76. *Tāw* (*t*). Six lines begin with a third-person feminine yiqtol or jussive, giving the final section a sustained tone of plea.

169May my resounding come near your face, Yhwh;
in accordance with your word, enable me to understand.

*Resounding can suggest both prayer (e.g., 106:44) and praise (e.g., 118:15). While either might be possible here (see vv. 170–72), the plea that this cry may come near (*tiqrab*) Yhwh's face and the immediate parallel between vv. 169 and 170 suggest that the sound is an urgent cry rather than enthusiastic praise. In the hiphil the verb "is practically a technical term for the presenting of an offering to God,"[85] suggesting that on either understanding of the resounding, the aim is that it should reach and be acceptable to God like an offering (cf. v. 108).

The cry's content, then, is that the psalmist may be able to understand. Presumably the object of understanding is the regular one, Yhwh's teaching. Yhwh's *word implicitly promises Yhwh will grant this understanding, so the suppliant asks for it.

170May my prayer for grace come before your face;
in accordance with your statement, rescue me.

In this parallel line, "prayer for *grace" (the content) complements "resounding" (the sound). "*Statement" complements "word." Simple "come" (*tābôʾ*) complements "come near," both aiming that the prayer may reach Yhwh's face and thus get Yhwh's attention. "Rescue me" complements "enable me to understand," the two exemplifying the basic recurrent prayers.

171May my lips pour forth praise,
because you enable me to learn your laws.

Two wishes (implicitly promises) about praise complement the two prayers. *Praise by its nature suggests something gushing and abounding; like resounding, it refers to the sound of the suppliant's words rather than the content. The point is underlined by picturing it as pouring forth (*tabbaʿnâ*) like waters gushing after heavy rain or flowing from a spring. One's lips will gush with such wordless praise because one is enabled to learn Yhwh's *laws (cf. v. 169b).

172May my tongue sing of your statement,
because all your commands are faithful.

85. Anderson, *Psalms*, 2:846.

The second promise-full wish restates the first, as happened between vv. 169 and 170. "My tongue" complements "my lips." "Sing [*taʿan*] of your *statement" complements "pour forth praise."[86] "Sing" suggests something more controlled and tuneful than "pour forth" and links with "your statement," pointing to the utterance's verbal content, whereas "praise" suggested its sound. The objective comment that Yhwh's commands are *faithful then complements the relational statement in v. 171b about God's activity toward the psalmist.

> [173]May your hand become my help,
> because I have chosen your orders.

Two further lines go together. Yhwh's hand is the means whereby Yhwh acts, striking out or directing forces; the psalm asks that it may become so (*tĕhî*) where the suppliant needs *help. Once more the plea appeals to the suppliant's stance toward Yhwh's *orders, here described as choosing (cf. v. 30).

> [174]I long for your deliverance, Yhwh;
> your teaching is my delight.

The parallel line expresses longing (*tāʾabtî*; cf. v. 40), instead of referring to longing in a jussive, and speaks of *deliverance instead of help. *Delighting in Yhwh's *teaching likewise parallels v. 173b in content and function as it offers an argument for Yhwh's acting.

> [175]May my spirit live so that it may praise you,
> and may your decisions help me.

The next-to-last line begins by once more restating vv. 173a and 174a in its prayer for the psalmist's spirit (*person) to live (*tĕḥî*), but then strikes off in a different though familiar direction in buttressing the prayer by noting that this will enable that spirit to *praise Yhwh.

The second colon in turn parallels the first and thus those earlier first cola rather than relating to the previous second cola. It restates the plea, picking up its verb from v. 173a: may Yhwh's *decisions *help the suppliant. In other contexts Yhwh's decisions being the suppliant's means of deliverance could mean that Yhwh acts decisively to deliver; here, decisions more likely continue to denote declarations about how Israel should live. These once more relate to help and deliverance because of the promises attached to obeying them.

86. The parallelism suggests that the verb is *ʿānâ* IV, though Tg assumes it is *ʿānâ* I ("respond"), and LXX, Jerome imply the same understanding.

> 176 I have wandered like a lost sheep;
> search for your servant,
> because I have not ignored your commands.

We know before we read it that this is the eighth and therefore last line in the section dedicated to the final letter of the alphabet; nevertheless, v. 176 marks closure for the psalm with a tricolon, the only definite example in Ps. 119. In content, however, there is nothing to suggest closure. Indeed, the line leaves things open more than most. Initially it also surprises us by its reversion to speaking of wandering (*tāʿâ*), especially when it then goes on to claim not to have *ignored Yhwh's commands. It seems too subtle to reckon that the first colon refers to an isolated or accidental act and the last colon to a more consistent or deliberate pattern of life. More likely the comparison with a lost sheep (more literally, a dying sheep) indicates that wandering refers here not to abandoning Yhwh's commands (as was explicit in the talk of wandering in v. 110 and of straying in vv. 10, 21, and 118, and was implicit in v. 67) but to getting lost through no fault of our own, as in 107:4 and like the sheep in Ezek. 34. So the psalm asks for Yhwh to search for this servant (to mix the metaphors, though both metaphors imply a concern on the part of the stronger party for the weaker party). And the basis for the appeal is that the psalmist has indeed still been behaving as a servant.

The psalm's close thus makes for a strong contrast with its opening. The tension is the one that often appears in laments (e.g., Pss. 44; 89) and appears in the relationship between Proverbs on one hand and Job and Ecclesiastes on the other.

Theological Implications

The psalm comprises a manual of moral and religious spirituality. Life is a walk along a way, path, or track. What counts is not (for instance) the development of our thinking, our self-understanding, our prayer life, or our profession, but our walk. But the whole person is involved in this walk, heart or spirit and mouth or lips, as well as feet. That is so because heart, mouth, and feet are parts of the one person, and it is the whole person who is so to walk. It is not enough if the heart enthuses for Yhwh but the mouth does not laud Yhwh's ways or the feet do not walk in them; it is not enough if the feet walk Yhwh's way and the mouth professes allegiance to it but in secret the person worships other deities. The heart needs to treasure and delight in Yhwh's word for that word to influence the way the feet walk and for the mouth to honor that word.

Reverence, dedication, and joy are expressed in the walk, the feelings, and the words on our lips. There is no tension between love and dedication, and awe and reverence.

The walk is guided by Yhwh's teaching. What counts is not my unique individual walk in which I find out who I am and what role I play in Yhwh's purpose. What counts is the generic question whether my walk is guided by Yhwh's teaching. That is my resource for shaping my life. It is a gift of God's grace. That teaching is both one coherent whole (teaching, word) and something made concrete in many specific injunctions and promises (statements, declarations, orders, decisions, laws, commands). I am concerned both for my way and for my ways, both to walk in Yhwh's way and to walk in Yhwh's ways. Both the unity and coherence of that teaching and the detailed injunctions and promises are designed to shape my life. I thus need to apply myself to learning the content of it, to concentrate on it and remain mindful of it rather than ignoring or neglecting it.

The teaching comprises both command and promise. It is appropriate that most of the terms used to describe it (teaching, word, statements, declarations, orders, decisions) are capable of referring to both. That itself points to some theological insights. One is that there is an intrinsic link between the two. The link is not extrinsic (driving too fast risks getting arrested) but intrinsic (driving fast risks having an accident). It does not imply that the relationship between God and us is contractual. Both command and promise are expressions of Yhwh's truthfulness and faithfulness. Psalm 19 puts creation in its place by first suggesting the ambiguity and limitation of what creation reveals and then rejoicing unequivocally over Yhwh's teaching. Psalm 119 puts creation in its place by ignoring it (the isolation of a colon such as v. 90b underlines the point) and focusing wholly on Yhwh's teaching. It also puts the exodus and the covenant in their place. All that matters is the word of command and promise.

In this psalm, Yhwh's word is the object of attitudes that elsewhere apply to Yhwh. It is the object of reliance, dedication, appeal, hope, and trust; it is my precious possession. But at the same time I have a very personal relationship with Yhwh. Yhwh is my personal teacher. Yhwh is my master, and I am Yhwh's servant; we are mutually committed. Yhwh is my allocation. So there are many verbs of which Yhwh is the object. I have recourse to Yhwh, fall short of Yhwh, worship Yhwh, am dedicated to Yhwh.

Yhwh does not always provide a rationale for the commands, and we sometimes obey them simply because they are commands (Midrash Tehillim instances the prohibition on cooking a kid goat in its mother's milk).[87] Yet they are not random; they issue from the way God is, the way

87. *Midrash on Psalms*, 2:251.

humanity is, and the way the world is. Yhwh's way and Yhwh's ways lie behind Yhwh's word and Yhwh's words. The revelation of Yhwh's way and Yhwh's ways is given so that our way and ways may be directed so as to correspond to them. To follow Yhwh's commands is to align oneself with the nature of the world as Yhwh made it; to resist them is to pretend that the world is other than it is. Following them therefore makes me wiser than all the people who might think they are the embodiment of insight. Yhwh's teaching reveals wonders.

That being so, following these commands and aligning oneself with the actual world will mean we fit in that world harmoniously, honorably, and joyfully, and it relates to us harmoniously, honorably, and joyfully. Yhwh's teaching is a means to understanding and to obedience and thus to life, life in all its fullness. The walk that follows Yhwh's ways is one that experiences good fortune. There are many exceptions to this rule, but this should not make us lose sight of the rule. It also means we align ourselves with the way Yhwh is. Thus we find ourselves living within the sphere of Yhwh's faithfulness. Yhwh is personally involved with us as we walk this walk. We rejoice in being Yhwh's servant and having Yhwh as master.

Our relationship with Yhwh is founded on Yhwh's grace, commitment, and compassion, and in appealing to Yhwh we appeal to who Yhwh is. Yet our relationship also depends on our obedience, and in appealing to Yhwh we appeal to that obedience. I am myself responsible for walking in Yhwh's way, yet I depend on Yhwh's help in doing so. My wholehearted commitment is a necessary but not a sufficient prerequisite to my living by Yhwh's teaching. I need to be committed to walking the right way, but I need Yhwh's help in not straying from it. I need to direct my feet, but I need Yhwh to establish them. I need Yhwh to incline my heart to Yhwh's declarations, but I need to incline my heart to Yhwh's declarations. Yet the fact that God's grace is decisive means I can face the fact that I have been known to stray.

Indeed, I need Yhwh in order to understand these declarations. One might have thought that Yhwh had done all that was needed in giving us this corpus of teaching, but this is not so. We also need Yhwh to work in us to open our eyes to its wonders, to make us enthuse over it and therefore commit ourselves to it. We need Yhwh to broaden our minds. I cannot assume Yhwh will teach me; Yhwh's teaching might remain hidden from me. There is a paradoxical form of insecure security about this relationship with Yhwh, such as often obtains in relationships. I can be confident about it, but I cannot take it for granted.

The need to guard my way indicates that there are pressures not to walk this way. It is easy to stray. One pressure is the strange fact that not everyone enthuses over the wonders embodied in this teaching. Many people resist it. They like making up their own minds about how to live their lives. (They do not want to confine their worship to Yhwh alone, or to abjure worship by means of images, or to keep the Sabbath. . . .) That in its own right causes me to be overcome by strong feelings, both sadness and rage. And people attack and scorn and misrepresent those who press the importance of Yhwh's teaching. Thus whereas the psalm begins by declaring the good fortune of people of integrity, it goes on to complain about the oppression and sufferings of the righteous.[88]

We know that Yhwh has put down oppressors in the past, but it may not be easy to live by that fact in the present. So my enthusiasm about Yhwh's teaching is combined with a sense of vulnerability and weakness that come from my adherence to it. That leaves me living with a tension between the two aspects of Yhwh's teaching. I should walk in a certain way and life will work out as I do so, but I live anxiously in the space between these two declarations, my spirit stuck to the dirt.

So I live waiting and expecting and hoping. I am not whistling in the dark; I have seen Yhwh act in the past and thus find comfort under pressure. My hope is not an eschatological one. I expect to see Yhwh act again soon. Further, I can live with the experience of weakness because I know it is somehow part of Yhwh's purpose and that I learn from it. But all this does heighten the need for Yhwh to keep helping me walk the way by continuing to give me insight into this teaching and the will to live by it.

88. Cf. Bonhoeffer, *Meditating on the Word,* 111.

Psalm 120
War and Peace

Translation

Song of the Ascents.

1To Yhwh, in the distress that came to me,
   I called and he answered me.
2Yhwh, save my life from false lips,
   from a tongue of deceit.[1]
3What will you be given, what more will you be given,
   tongue of deceit?
4A warrior's arrows, sharpened,
   with coals of broom shrubs.
5Oh, oh, for me, that I have sojourned with Meshek,[2]
   stayed with the tents of Kedar.
6So long[3] have I been staying[4]
   with someone who is against peace.
7I am for peace,
   but when I speak, they are for war.

1. Lit. "from a tongue, deceit"; the nouns stand in apposition rather than as a construct phrase. Cf. v. 3.

2. The prep. *ʿim* in v. 5b also applies in v. 5a. It is natural there; ironically it is odder where it actually appears in v. 5b, as the translation reflects. EVV "among" obscures the point. "Near" would be acceptable, but this would obscure the significance of the repetition in v. 6.

3. The f. sg. adjective is used adverbially.

4. Lit. "long has my soul [been] staying for itself."

Interpretation

The opening would give the impression that this is a thanksgiving or testimony psalm. Such psalms often recall the prayer that the suppliant prayed and that Yhwh answered (e.g., 30:8–10 [9–11]); vv. 2–7 would then be the recollection of such a prayer.[5] But this psalm does not introduce vv. 2–7 by telling us, "This is how I prayed," nor follow them up by describing how Yhwh acted. Indeed, vv. 2–7 so dominate the psalm that it is hard to see them as purely recollection.

Perhaps, then, v. 2 alone is the recollection of the prayer; Yhwh has heeded this, though the suppliant has not yet seen the answer implemented.[6] Verses 3–7 are then comments that reflect that present situation, a little like 6:8–10 [9–11]. Again, the difficulty arises that the psalm does not say that v. 2 is a recollection of a past prayer. Further, there is no clear parallel for a psalm talking as if Yhwh has answered a prayer when this means only that Yhwh has heard the prayer but not yet acted.

TNIV and NRSV translate v. 1 as present; the verses that follow are then presumably this present prayer. But the verbs are qatal, which would be an odd way to make this point (contrast the yiqtol in 3:4 [5]).[7] The same applies to the suggestion that the verbs constitute a statement of confidence concerning what Yhwh will do.[8]

More likely the psalm follows a recurrent pattern in the psalms whereby a suppliant recalls a past answer to prayer (v. 1)[9] and then builds on that with a new prayer (v. 2), a confrontation of the foes to whom the prayer refers (vv. 3–4), and a lament at the situation, supporting the prayer and designed for Yhwh's hearing (vv. 5–7). The psalm thus compares in function to Ps. 119.[10] Psalms 9–10 and 40 are large-scale examples of psalms that build prayer on recollection in this way (there has also been some debate about the right understanding of these other psalms, and on the relationship of thanksgiving and prayer within them). Several key expressions recur in the psalm in "terrace" fashion, both moving

5. So Seybold, *Psalmen*, 476–77.

6. Cf. Allen, *Psalms 101–150*, 199.

7. Weiser (*Psalms*, 742) calls this translation "hardly legitimate." Crow (*Songs of Ascents*, 32) sees *qārā'tî* as performative, which is in itself plausible, but then has to translate *wayyaʿănēnî* "that [God] should answer me," which is hardly legitimate; one would need to repoint to *wĕyaʿănēnî* (so, e.g., Gunkel, *Psalmen*, 538).

8. Gerstenberger, *Psalms*, 2:318; he compares 7:1 [2]; 31:1–2 [2–3], but the only qatals there refer to taking refuge, which is a literal past act.

9. Cf. Kirkpatrick, *Psalms*, 733.

10. Kirsten Nielsen ("Why Not Plough with an Ox and an Ass Together?" *SJOT* 14 [2000]: 56–66) in fact suggests reading Pss. 119 and 120–34 together as expounding the nature of the way of Torah and the way of pilgrimage.

the argument on and binding it together: "tongue of deceit" in vv. 2 and 3, "stay with" in vv. 5 and 6, "peace" in vv. 6 and 7.

The geographical references in v. 5 would give the impression of a psalm used by someone living in dispersion. Presumably it became part of the Psalter through also being used in Jerusalem, perhaps because it was a psalm pilgrims used. But the geographical references allude to widely separated places; the suppliant could not have lived in both. This suggests they are metaphors for a location where people are hostile. The suppliant could then be literally living in Jerusalem and the psalm can have the same background in prayer in the temple as others have. It might be used there by a king or governor or by an ordinary person. One can see the Judeans in Daniel or Esther, or in Ezra-Nehemiah, as people who might pray this way.

Song of the Ascents.

Heading. See glossary. The reference to Meshek and Kedar, understood as standing for places where Judeans lived, might have encouraged its being used as a pilgrimage psalm.

[1]To Yhwh, in the distress that came to me,
I called and he answered me.

120:1. The recollection. The psalm begins in a unique way, "To Yhwh," which gives the impression of introducing a testimony psalm. Given that it turns out to be a prayer psalm, however, perhaps we are to imagine the suppliant praying it in the company of other people. Initially it recalls an occasion that had the threefold sequence that recurs in testimony psalms (e.g., 34:4, 6 [5, 7]; 118:5), distress, then calling, then answering (cf. 138:3). In this context "answering" covers both hearing and acting; answering means delivering (cf. 86:1, 7; 102:2 [3]; 108:6 [7]).

[2]Yhwh, save my life from false lips,
from a tongue of deceit.

120:2. The plea builds on the recollection. In speaking of what Yhwh once did, the psalm addressed other people. In turning to pray, it addresses Yhwh; the move between third and second persons is common in the Psalms. The problem it speaks of is the same as that in Ps. 119. Indeed, every word in this plea has already come there, except that the form of the word for deceit there is *tarmît* (v. 118), whereas here it is *rĕmîyâ*. Once again the problem the suppliant needs Yhwh to handle is people's falsehood.

120:3–4. The declaration of defiance.

> [3]What will you be given, what more will you be given,
> tongue of deceit?

As quickly as the psalm turned to plea, it turns in another direction. Indeed, perhaps vv. 3–4 indicate that v. 1 already addressed the attackers. Certainly vv. 3–4 now do so, utilizing synecdoche as the deceitful tongue stands for the person acting deceitfully by using the tongue. The attackers might be present literally in the wider gathering of people in the temple and its courts, or they might simply be present rhetorically, like the nations when they are urged to join in worship.

Literally, v. 3a asks "What will it/he give to you and what will it/he increase [i.e., give more] to you?" The expression is a variant on "so may God do to me and so may he increase [do more] to me" (e.g., 2 Sam. 3:9, 35), a formula of cursing that calls down trouble on the speaker in case of default on an undertaking. Evidently the deceptive person has used words of this kind to swear solemnly to bring trouble on the suppliant, who is in turn now declaring that the self-curse involved will indeed come true. If the expression follows that formula, "he" (Yhwh) is the implicit agent referred to by the passive verbs. The suppliant's question then implies, "What is Yhwh going to do with you for your deceit, in fulfillment of your curse?"

Alternatively, the difference in the expression over against the recurrent version, and the naturalness of looking for continuity with v. 2, could mean that "it," the act of deceit, is the agent. The question then implies, "What do you think you are going to gain from your deceit?"

> [4]A warrior's arrows, sharpened,
> with coals of broom shrubs.

Either way, the question was a rhetorical one, though different from some rhetorical questions. Here is the actual answer. On the first understanding, the irony is that the answer is the one the attacker presupposed, though the suppliant implies that it will come in spades. The attacker's action will turn out to be self-destructive. On the second, it is the kind of question the addressee could have answered by saying (for instance), "It will give us land," whereas the speaker reckons that the true answer is quite different.

The OT can describe sharpened tongues and words as arrows (e.g., Ps. 64:3–4 [4–5]) and can associate the idea of burning arrows with that; they are a means of doing damage by deceit (Prov. 26:18–19). So the idea might be that Yhwh will shoot some words back to respond to the words in vv. 2–3. But that is not explicit, and it is not clear what it would refer to. More likely the psalmist refers to literal burning arrows shot by warrior Yhwh—though the whole statement will be a metaphor. The parallelism means the verse need not be promising two separate unpleasant experiences, arrows and fire. What Yhwh will give, or what the deceit will give, is a hail of burning arrows. They might be simply the arrows a good human warrior shoots, though the statement would have more point if Yhwh is the warrior (cf. 24:8). That is their first threatening characteristic. The second is that they have been well sharpened, as would be the case with a warrior's arrows. The third is that they are equipped with burning coals. In ancient warfare, the purpose of arrows was not merely to kill individual members of the opposition; it was to set fire to a city. Arrows were missiles, not merely bullets. And these coals were made from the wood of the broom tree, which presumably made them especially effective. Apparently this wood produced especially fierce fire and retained its heat for a long time, and it was used for making charcoal. With some hyperbole, Midrash Tehillim tells of two men who returned after a year to a place where they had made a fire from this wood, and found the ashes still burning.[11]

120:5–7. The lament or protest.

> 5Oh, oh, for me, that I have sojourned with Meshek,
> stayed with the tents of Kedar.

A combination of features suggests that the beginning of v. 5 echoes the Psalm's beginning. "Oh, oh" (*ʾôyâ*) is a unique long form of the regular "impassioned expression of grief and despair" (*ʾôy*).[12] It thus parallels the unique long form of the word for distress (*ṣārātâ*). Then "for me" (*lî*) echoes v. 1 (translated "to me").[13] The pattern of people causing distress to me is being repeated; but as v. 1 recalled Yhwh's answering prayer, this line hints that this might happen again.

The psalmist's vulnerability is described as if issuing from life in a foreign country. But the line again has a figurative aspect, because Meshek and Kedar are very different places, in opposite directions from Canaan.[14] Meshek is in Turkey, to the northwest (cf. Ezek. 27:13; 38:2). Kedar is a nomadic shepherding tribe (hence the reference to tents) in the Arabian desert, to the east and south of Canaan (cf. Isa. 21:13–17;

11. *Midrash on Psalms*, 291–92. See Harold N. Moldenke and Alma L. Moldenke, *Plants of the Bible* (repr., New York: Dover, 1986), 201.

12. BDB 17.

13. Cf. Allen, *Psalms 101–150*, 200.

14. But Goulder (*Psalms of the Return*, 37–39) ingeniously and intriguingly links them with Sanballat and Geshem in Nehemiah.

42:11; 60:7). These two peoples were not thought of as more warlike or hostile to Judeans than many others. They are simply alien, mysterious, far-off peoples. They might then simply stand for typical places where Judeans might live as a scattered people as a result of "the" exile. The line would imply both an acceptance and a nonacceptance of that. People living in dispersion (as opposed to exile) are in some sense free to go "back" to Jerusalem, though that freedom may exist more in theory than in practice. They choose to live where they do, yet they do so with its frustrations and troubles, such as the Jewish people have experienced throughout their history. Both verbs help to make this point. "Sojourn" is *gûr*, the verb that generates the noun *gēr*, which describes a foreigner resident in a country on a semipermanent basis but without the rights of a citizen. "Stay" is the less technical *šākan*, which can denote permanent settlement but still says less than *yāšab*, "live."

6So long have I been staying
  with someone who is against peace.
7I am for peace,
  but when I speak, they are for war.

The "Oh, oh," however, indicates not merely that this is not home, but that the suppliant has been staying for a long time in the company of hostile foreigners. The next line suggests the "someone" is collective, denoting the people of Meshek or Kedar as people *against peace. Thus LXX, Jerome have a plural, though Tg identifies the "someone" as Edom (that is, Rome). The singular matches the singular in v. 3. "The trail of word repetitions in vv 5–7 expresses a demoralizing series of woes."[15]

Verse 7a is literally "I am peace" (see the comment on 109:4). But the parallelism suggests that the preposition on "war" also applies to "peace" (cf. the prepositions in v. 5). In another context, vv. 6–7 might refer to the peoples' attitude toward their own enemies, but in the context of this psalm, they presumably refer to the hostile stance they take toward the suppliant. The reference to speaking fits with this motif's significance in vv. 2–3. The psalmist's words are words of peace; the other peoples speak only to make trouble by falsehood. But the closing line, and specifically the closing word, speak not merely of words but of war, and thus bring the psalm to a solemn ending, the sharpest expression of "a uniform tone of despair" in the psalm[16] and an implicit call for Yhwh to answer in the way recalled in v. 1.

15. Allen, *Psalms 101–150*, 201.

16. Grossberg, *Centripetal and Centrifugal Structures*, 26; he analyzes the psalm's verbal patterns.

The psalmist's words hardly suggest a person who is for peace. But typically of the Psalms, hostility is channeled into prayer rather than expressed or acted out toward the people one feels hostile toward. Thus the suppliant's closing words are doubly a statement of self-defense, a claim that those people have no reason to be hostile and that Yhwh has no reason to ignore this prayer.

Theological Implications

The psalm thus deconstructs, though not fatally. On one hand, the psalmist "is for peace" or "is peace" or "is peaceful," in contrast to people who are "for war." Yet the psalm relishes the idea that these people should find themselves set on fire by a warrior's arrows, sharpened and fired by high-grade charcoal. These are not the words of someone who is for peace. The tension is implicitly explored by Jerome, who expounds at great length the psalm's implicit challenge to be peaceful people, because of the challenge it brings to Christian communities.[17] We can do our best to be forgiving yet not be able to get rid of the poison of resentment in our hearts. We need to be delivered not only from the tongues of other people but from our own.

How does that deliverance come about? The Psalms suggest an invitation not to deny that poison's existence but to own it and bring it to God. It is at least possible that bringing our warring instincts to God will make it possible to leave them there.

17. *Homilies*, 1:314.

Psalm 121
Yhwh as Helper, Maker, Guard

Translation

Song for the Ascents.

1 I raise my eyes to the mountains:
from where does my help come?[1]
2 My help comes from Yhwh,
the maker of the heavens and the earth.

3 May he not give your foot to faltering;[2]
may he not doze, your guard.
4 Indeed, he will not doze and he will not sleep,
Israel's guard.
5 Yhwh is your guard, Yhwh is your shade,
at your right hand.
6 By day the sun will not hit you,
nor will the moon by night.
7 Yhwh: he will guard you from all harm;
he will guard your life.
8 Yhwh: he will guard your going and your coming
from now and forever.

1. Not "mountains from where . . ." (Jerome); *mēʾayin* is used only as an interrogative, not as a relative.

2. The article on *lammôṭ* marks *môṭ* as a noun, not an infinitive, as it is in this expression in 55:22 [23]; 66:9.

Interpretation

Psalm 121 bears comparison with Ps. 91[3] in that the bulk of it comprises promises of Yhwh's protection. Like Ps. 91, none of it addresses God; all of it brings good news about God to a human listener. Like Ps. 91, it speaks of feet not being allowed to stumble, of Yhwh as shade, of the subject's right hand, of being guarded from the dangers of night and day, and of being kept from harm. Like Ps. 91, it does not make explicit who speaks to whom, especially at the beginning; here there is some mystery about the movement between the "I" of vv. 1–2 and the "you" of vv. 3–8. Like Ps. 91, one can imagine it being applied to an ordinary person, but much of it comes into clearer focus if it relates specifically to a king or governor.[4] In Ps. 91, the opening "I" represents the voice of a minister who first speaks of his own trust in Yhwh and then goes on to commend that trust to the king,[5] but here the change from "I" to "you" in v. 3 makes it more natural to see the king himself speaking in vv. 1–2, with vv. 3–8 constituting a minister's response. Given that an internal dialogue happens between vv. 1 and 2, that movement from "I" to "you" hardly represents an internal argument like that in Pss. 42–43.

In origin Ps. 121 will relate to the leadership role of the king as one who goes out to face challenges, dangers, and battles and is promised a safe return. When it became associated with pilgrimage, it would make sense addressed to people going home. It was perhaps originally written before the exile but set in the context of the other "Songs of the Ascents" after the exile.[6]

Like Ps. 120, it uses key expressions in "terrace" fashion: "help" (vv. 1–2); "doze" (vv. 3–4); the participle "guard" (vv. 3, 4, 5); the yiqtol "guard" (vv. 7–8). The lines are structured in other subtle ways. Both vv. 3 and 4 hold back the subject's identification until the end of the line. While hardly setting up suspense, this does put some emphasis on the fact that the subject of the verses is indeed the guard. Verse 5 follows *aba′* order. Both vv. 6 and 7 follow the "pivot pattern" whereby a phrase at the center ("will not hit you" and "from all harm") applies to both cola

3. Cf. Otto Eissfeldt, "Psalm 121," in Eissfeldt, *Kleine Schriften* (Tübingen: Mohr, 1966), 3:494–500 (see 498–99).

4. On the range of understandings of it, see John T. Willis, "Psalm 121 as a Wisdom Poem," *HAR* 11 (1987): 435–51; Armin Schmitt, "Zum literarischen und theologischen Profil von Ps 121," *BN* 97 (1999): 55–84.

5. So here Goulder, *Psalms of the Return*, 41.

6. James Limburg interprets it as a pilgim's song ("Psalm 121," *WW* 5 [1985]: 180–87).

and thus binds the line together. In both vv. 7 and 8 the subject comes first and is thus given emphasis.[7]

> Song for the Ascents.

Heading. See glossary, though the formulation here with the preposition is unique. Its form avoids the ungrammatical nature of the usual construct form of the expression, which should strictly mean "the song of ascents."

121:1–2. A question and a confession.

> [1]I raise my eyes to the mountains:
> from where does my help come?

Why and where would someone lift their eyes to the mountains? When these expressions appear elsewhere, "raise my eyes" does not suggest looking apprehensively, and "mountains" do not generally suggest something dangerous.[8] Raising the eyes can suggest looking expectantly or looking to a resource (cf. 123:1), and the mountains could be an illegitimate resource to look to, perhaps as the location of sanctuaries dedicated to other gods (cf. Ezek. 18:6, 15, with the references to the mountains in the context).[9] But mountains are often a positive image. Indeed, the mountains surrounding Jerusalem suggest an image for Yhwh's surrounding Israel (Ps. 125:2). It would be natural to assume that this psalm was written for use in Jerusalem and that the person using it indeed looks at the mountains and attributes that significance to them: they suggest Yhwh's protective strength.

The question that follows is then "a rhetorical foil for the following declaration,"[10] though this does not make its point less real. The psalm does assume that life is surrounded by danger, even if the mountains do not symbolize that; this is so for an ordinary person, but much more for a king. From where does *help then come? Again the question links with one of the songs of ascent that is soon to follow (see 124:8).

> [2]My help comes from Yhwh,
> the maker of the heavens and the earth.

7. See further Bernd Willmes, *Jahwe—ein schlummernder Beschützer* (Neukirchen: Neukirchener Verlag, 1998), 22–23.

8. Against Julius Morgenstern, "Psalm 121," *JBL* 58 (1939): 311–23; P. Hewison Pollock, "Psalm 121," *JBL* 59 (1940): 411–12.

9. So, e.g., John T. Willis, "An Attempt to Decipher Psalm 121:1b," *CBQ* 52 (1990): 241–51.

10. Mays, *Psalms*, 389.

Verse 1a had implied the answer to the question in v. 1b; v. 2 makes it explicit. The mountains' symbolic significance means that the suppliant and the people who listen to this testimony know without thinking that *help comes from Yhwh. Yet suppose someone asked, "But how do you know?" In the parallelism, the first colon implicitly raises a question that the second answers. The worship of the Jerusalem sanctuary had long emphasized the importance of the maker of heaven and earth,[11] and this fact answers that implicit question. The mountains no doubt supported this answer. They are not only a symbol of Yhwh's might but an indication of it; Yhwh created them in their impressiveness, along with the whole earth, and the heavens, so how impressive is Yhwh?

121:3–8. The king's promise. The genitive is intentionally ambiguous; the promise could be made by the king, who thus continues to speak through the psalm. But more likely the change from "I" to "you" indicates that the promise is made to the king; a minister now speaks and confirms the king's testimony.

3May he not give your foot to faltering;
  may he not doze, your guard.
4Indeed, he will not doze and he will not sleep,
  Israel's guard.

The minister's words begin with a third-person jussive declaration. In v. 3, that is, the double "not" is not the regular negative *lōʾ*, which would suggest the translation "he will not" or "he does not," but the less common negative *ʾal*, "denying . . . not objectively as a fact (like *lōʾ*, [Greek] *ou*) but subjectively as a wish (like [Greek] *mē*), expressing thereby a *deprecation* or *prohibition*."[12] The regular negative will appear in v. 4; the distinction, observed by LXX and Jerome, is ignored by EVV, but it seems unlikely that the psalm would use *ʾal* and mean nothing or hardly anything by the distinction.[13] Minister or people thus respond to the statement of faith by declaring the longing that Yhwh may indeed make it work out in this way.[14]

The line uses two parallel images. The familiar image of losing one's footing has a literal significance; on the average path it would be easy to do so. That would have particular significance if we emphasize the

11. See Norman C. Habel, "'Yahweh, Maker of Heaven and Earth,'" *JBL* 91 (1972): 321–37.

12. BDB 39a.

13. As GKC implies, more convincingly at 109e than at 107p.

14. So, e.g., DG 67; *IBHS* 34.3b; Jerome F. D. Creach, "Psalm 121," *Int* 50 (1996): 47–51 (see 49).

journey motif in the psalm; the image here would link with v. 8.[15] But we also tumble into Sheol, and the idea of the foot faltering further suggests that possibility. The second image goes behind this. A guard's key duty is to stay awake, though that is not always easy (cf. 127:1; 130:6). If he drops off, the city may fall, the palace be invaded, or the king be assassinated. Indeed, v. 3b might refer to the king's human guard.[16] The king's guards were supposed to look after his safety during all his comings and goings (cf. v. 8; see 2 Kings 11:7–8). But given the parallelism, more likely the guard is Yhwh. Yhwh's keeping our footing firm depends on Yhwh's staying alert, and the verse affirms that Yhwh must do so.

In case v. 3 should seem to treat Yhwh's wakefulness as an open question, in v. 4 the psalm hastens to make an appropriate affirmation of faith, using the regular negative. Yhwh will not drop off and will not fall into proper sleep. If v. 3b actually referred to a human guard, v. 4 makes a contrast with such a person. A human guard may indeed drop off, as some gods might;[17] Yhwh does not.

5Yhwh is your guard, Yhwh is your shade,
at your right hand.
6By day the sun will not hit you,
nor will the moon by night.

The psalm maintains continuity by the repetition of "guard," but then it changes the metaphor to "shade" (cf. 91:1). The ensuing reference to Yhwh's being at the king's right hand further interlinks the imagery, because it is as guard that Yhwh will stand at the right hand (cf. 16:8; 109:31), whereas it is as shade that Yhwh will protect from the sun and moon (v. 6).

The sun is a danger in the Middle East. It can literally make someone collapse, and one so stricken is unlikely to rise again. So it is an image for peril. The subsequent reference to the moon is usually taken to presuppose that the full moon can send a person crazy, and this idea may lie behind the verse, though again it is a metaphor. Indeed, Qimchi assumes that the verse rather refers to the freezing cold of night in the mountains.[18] In any case, the moon may be present simply as makeweight, to make the parallelism work and to complete a merism affirming how Yhwh's protection covers any danger at any time, day or night.[19]

15. Cf. Auffret, *La sagesse*, 450–53; but see also Auffret, *Merveilles à nos yeux*, 182–90.

16. Cf. Augustine's comment, *Psalms*, 591; also Cassiodorus, *Psalms*, 3:267.

17. On the question whether v. 4 makes a polemical point over against other religions, see Willmes, *Jahwe—ein schlummernder Beschützer*, 58–62.

18. Cf. Calvin, *Psalms*, 5:67.

19. Cf. Kidner, *Psalms*, 2:432. It seems less likely that v. 6 refers to demonic forces (Keel, *Symbolism*, 97–98).

[7]Yhwh: he will guard you from all harm;
he will guard your life.
[8]Yhwh: he will guard your going and your coming
from now and forever.

In closing, the psalm moves to more literal generalizations rather than images. Both fulfill significant functions. An image appeals to the imagination and has affective results. A generalization offers something whose cash value can be spelled out; of course the trouble with a literal statement of this kind is that one can measure whether it turns out to be true. The finite verb "guard" takes up from the participle and becomes the means of making the generalization; three occurrences of the finite verb balance three occurrences of the participle, underlining and affirming it. Yhwh will "guard you from all harm" (*bad) and thus "guard your life" (*person). The verb, and even the specific verb form, recalls the priestly blessing in Num. 6:24 and applies it to this individual king or pilgrim.

The significance of that is then spelled out further in the declaration that it covers the individual's going out and coming in. Yhwh will be with the king as he sets out from the city on a campaign and as he returns (cf. 1 Sam. 29:6).[20] It covers an ordinary person's going out to the fields in the morning and returning in the evening, and the other everyday activities of life (Deut. 28:6, 19; 31:2). It would cover Israel's exile and return.[21] It covers a pilgrim's going home and returning next festival[22] (LXX reverses the verbs' significance so that they refer to coming and going, which might refer to pilgrims arriving for the festival and leaving at its end). And that will be true now and all through your life.

Theological Implications

The psalm starts with Yhwh as *help. Help is a synonym of deliverance; it suggests Yhwh's involvement in the crises of Israel's history or the crises of the pilgrim's life.

But when the suppliant asks the rhetorical question in v. 1b, the answer in v. 2 is an interesting one, and not necessarily the obvious one. Yhwh is the maker of the heavens and the earth. Although help is a reality associated not with creation but with Yhwh's involvement in Israel's

20. Cf. Anthony C. Ceresko, "Psalm 121: Prayer of a Warrior?" *Bib* 70 (1989): 496–510.

21. So Qimchi.

22. See David G. Barker, "'The Lord Watches over You,'" *BSac* 152 (1995): 163–81 (see 180).

history, here it is not on this involvement that the suppliant bases the conviction about Yhwh's being a source of help ("Yhwh has been a help before, so will be again"). The conviction has its basis in a much more fundamental fact about Yhwh; Yhwh's particular acts of deliverance are made possible by the fact that Yhwh is the maker of the heavens and the earth. "The Creator-God is not dormant, but continues to act; he is forever the *living* God."[23] So the God of creation is indeed the God of history.

The image of "guard," which then appears and goes on to dominate the psalm, constitutes a further subtle move over against the initial motif of "help."[24] An aspect of the "distinctive character of the Old Testament concept of creation comes out clearly here. It ministers not to a theoretical explanation of the universe but to the mastering of a concrete situation in life in a practical way. It represents not a piece of knowledge but a decision to submit oneself to God's creative will and power."[25] "He's got the whole world in his hand"; and therefore "he's got you and me, sister/brother, in his hands."[26] Ten times in the rest of the psalm the pronominal suffix "you/your" brings this point home.[27]

23. Weiser, *Psalms*, 748.
24. Cf. Fokkelman, *Major Poems*, 3:272.
25. Weiser, *Psalms*, 747. I would say "It represents not merely. . . ."
26. McCann, "Psalms," 1181.
27. Schaefer, *Psalms*, 299.

Psalm 122

For Jerusalem

Translation

Song of the Ascents. David's.[1]

[1]I rejoiced in the people who said[2] to me,
"We are going[3] to Yhwh's house."
[2]Our feet have been standing
within your gates, Jerusalem,
[3]Jerusalem which is built[4]
as a city that is joined together to itself,
[4]To which the clans went up,[5]
Yah's clans,

1. Tg omits "David's," as do some LXX MSS, but it is present in 1Q11Ps[a].

2. To generate the conventional translation "I rejoiced when they said to me," one would expect *bĕʾomrām*; thus Crow (*Songs of Ascents*, 43) has "I rejoiced among those who had said to me." But further, *śāmaḥ b* regularly means "rejoice in" (e.g., 32:11; 97:12; Judg. 9:19); cf. LXX.

3. Lit. "we will go" (cf. LXX); not "let us go" (NRSV, TNIV), which would require *nēlĕkâ* (as in 1 Sam. 11:14).

4. Not "Jerusalem is built" (making v. 3 begin a new sentence), for which one would not expect the article on *habbĕnûyâ*.

5. TNIV and NRSV have present tense, NJPS imperfect tense, but the qatal is odd for either of these.

(A declaration[6] for Israel),
to confess Yhwh's name,
[5]Because thrones sat there to make decisions,
thrones belonging to David's household.

[6]Ask for well-being for Jerusalem:
"May people be at ease who are dedicated to you.
[7]May there be well-being within your rampart,
ease in your citadels."
[8]For the sake of my brothers and friends
I shall indeed[7] speak of well-being for you.
[9]For the sake of the house of Yhwh our God
I shall seek good for you.

Interpretation

Along with Pss. 46, 48, 76, 84, and sometimes others, Ps. 122 has been called a Zion song, but those other Zion songs focus at least as much on Yhwh as on Zion. Ps. 122 is unique for its focus on Zion itself—or rather on Jerusalem (vv. 2–3, 6) since "Zion" does not occur. Yhwh features in vv. 1, 4, and 9 but is never addressed (as happens in those other psalms). Only Jerusalem is addressed. That coheres with the actual use of the name Jerusalem rather than Zion. While Jerusalem and Zion can have similar reference, the names have different connotations. Jerusalem points more to an earthly city, the capital of Israel, a city of stone and brick, inhabited by people. Zion points more to a religious entity, the place where the temple is, the abode of Yhwh—even though Jerusalem of course is the place where the temple actually is (see v. 1). Psalm 122 celebrates Jerusalem (vv. 1–5) and prays for its well-being (vv. 6–9). The person who speaks in the psalm is not a resident there but someone who comes for a festival, marvels at being able to do that, and then goes on to seek blessing for the city.

After the opening recollection, the psalm comprises two parts, vv. 2–5 and 6–9. The first is characterized by a massive enjambment as the four lines comprising vv. 3–5 hang suspended on the declaration in v. 2. Such enjambment is unusual; each line in a psalm is usually self-contained. The construction builds up suspense line by line: When will the breathless enthusiasm of this huge sentence, announced by v. 1, come to an

6. 11QPs[a]'s *ʿdt* (assembly; cf. Sym) for *ʿēdût* makes for smoother sense (cf. Rick R. Marrs, "Psalm 122,3.4," *Bib* 68 [1987]: 106–9 [see 108–9]), but the subsequent *lĕ* (which 11QPs[a] omits) is then difficult. Th. Booij ("Psalm cxxii 4," *VT* 51 [2001]: 262–66) seeks to account for it, but the end result seems no improvement on MT.

7. *-nāʾ*; see also the emphatic ending on the verbs in vv. 8 and 9.

end? In contrast, vv. 6–9 comprise a neat example of a more traditional piece of Hebrew prosody. Each line closes with a reference to "you." The first two lines are parallel in content, as are the second two, with each pair of first cola and each pair of second cola manifesting some parallelism ("well-being" then "ease" in vv. 6–7, "for the sake of" then a first-person singular cohortative verb in vv. 8–9). These thus comprise a much tighter poetic composition than vv. 2–5. The whole psalm expounds the significance of *yĕrûšālaim*, the city (*ʿîr*) of peace/well-being (*šālôm*).[8] Both parts use words in "terrace" fashion, which holds the argument together but simultaneously presses it forward: Jerusalem (vv. 2–3), clans (v. 4), thrones (v. 5), well-being/ease (vv. 6–7; cf. also well-being/good in vv. 8–9), for the sake of (vv. 8–9). "The house of Yhwh" in vv. 1 and 9 then holds together the psalm as a whole. There are no indications of its date, though the relative prefix *š-* in vv. 3 and 4 and the full spelling of *dāwîd* in v. 5 may suggest a postexilic date.

Song of the Ascents. David's.

Heading. See glossary. This is the most explicitly pilgrim psalm, the one psalm out of Pss. 120–34 that most looks as if it might have been actually composed in connection with pilgrimage. So v. 1 recalls the expectation of making pilgrimage, while v. 2 suggests that it specifically looks back on coming to the city and thus belongs to the moment of leaving to go back home; "there" in v. 5 supports the idea that the pilgrim is on the way from the city rather than speaking as a recent arrival. The psalm thus pairs with Ps. 121, which has come to be used in the same connection. Calvin links the reference to David with the plan to move the covenant chest to Jerusalem (cf. Ps. 132).[9]

122:1–5. A celebration of Jerusalem. The pilgrim rejoices in Jerusalem because of its physical impressiveness (v. 3), its being where the whole community gathers to confess what Yhwh did for it (v. 4), and its being where decisions for the community are taken (v. 5).

[1]I rejoiced in the people who said to me,
"We are going to Yhwh's house."

The psalm looks back to the moment when the family or village community proposed to go to Jerusalem for a festival. The Torah urges all

8. Cf. Luis Alonso Schökel and Andrzej Strus, "Salmo 122," *Bib* 61 (1980): 234–50; also Schaefer, *Psalms*, 301. But it is not clear that there is an etymological link between *šālôm* and *yĕrûšālaim*, nor is there any indication that the OT saw Jerusalem as the "city of peace."

9. *Psalms*, 5:70.

Israelites to make the pilgrimage for the three major festivals, but if that involved going to the central sanctuary people who lived any distance away would doubtless find this impractical. It would require a huge amount of effort and organization, not least to cover the needs at home (who will look after the animals?). Even Elkanah and his family made the pilgrimage to the sanctuary at Shiloh (not so distant from where they lived) only once a year (1 Sam. 1). But there would be occasions when the community made the effort, and the psalm belongs to such an occasion. It would likely be Sukkot in September/October, the climax of the year when the harvest had been gathered in and it was feasible to pause before beginning the next year's work. The opening verb speaks of the rejoicing this moment caused the psalmist.

The basis for that rejoicing is indeed that it means not merely a visit to the big city but a visit to the house where Yhwh lives. The word order underlines the point: "to Yhwh's house we are going."

"Our joy, in like manner, should be doubled, when God by his Holy Spirit not only frames each of us to the obedience of his word, but also produces the same effect upon others, so that we may be united together in the same faith."[10] We rejoice "when we find companions in this pilgrimage."[11]

2Our feet have been standing
   within your gates, Jerusalem,
3Jerusalem which is built
   as a city that is joined together to itself,
4To which the clans went up,
   Yah's clans,
(A declaration for Israel),
   to confess Yhwh's name,
5Because thrones sat there to make decisions,
   thrones belonging to David's household.

The verbal expression in v. 2 could signify "our feet have become standing" and therefore are standing now (so NRSV, TNIV) rather than "our feet have been standing," but a noun clause would be the more natural way to say "our feet are standing.[12] Further, the rest of the psalm reads naturally

10. Calvin, *Psalms*, 5:70.

11. Augustine, *Psalms*, 593.

12. Thus LXX has a past tense verb. See further JM 113, remark 2, and JM 121f, which comments that in general the point of adding a form of *hāyâ* to a participle is "in order clearly to express time past." In late biblical Hebrew, the combination of *hāyâ* and a participle functions as a periphrastic verb form, in imitation of Aramaic. The verb might then simply have qatal meaning, "our feet stood." But in regular biblical Hebrew, this combination would suggest "our feet were standing [on an ongoing basis]" or "there

as a pilgrim's reflection and prayer on coming to the end of a time in Jerusalem, though no doubt in practice someone could use it on arrival or during the week's stay there. The verse underlines the solid physical nature of the pilgrimage. The person is someone with feet, and the city is a place with gates, with an inside and an outside. Neither are ethereal realities.

The repetition of the city's name at the beginning of v. 3 underlines the pilgrim's sense of joy and wonder announced and reflected in vv. 1–2 ("our feet have been standing in *Jerusalem*!"). Tg understands v. 3 to refer to the heavenly Jerusalem, while Midrash Tehillim[13] links that with the assumption that it refers to the community fellowship of the city (cf. LXX). This draws our attention to the fact that the Hebrew itself goes on further to emphasize the earthly city's solid physical reality (cf. 48:12–13 [13–14]). This is a city that is built up. There is no particular reason to take this to mean "rebuilt" after destruction, though a person living after the restoration who had known the city in its desolation would have extra reason to marvel at its rebuilt state. But even before the exile, one can imagine a pilgrim being struck by the city's bounded compactness, with the houses all built closely together, partly as imposed by the physical constraints within which the older parts of the city were constructed (and reconstructed in Nehemiah's day)[14] because it was almost surrounded by canyons. The redundancy in the expressions in v. 3b underlines the impression of togetherness and compactness made on the pilgrim.

Verse 4a–b moves on from the city's striking physical form to its significance for the community, as the pilgrim looks back on the clans' going up there. This made it indeed a place of community and fellowship, rather overwhelmingly (it must have seemed) when the clans so gathered for this festival. They are usually "the clans of Israel" (e.g., 78:55); "clans of Yhwh" never appears, and "clans of Yah" appears only here.

But the expression leads well into v. 4c–d. These clans came because of a *declaration for Israel, something Yhwh laid down as a requirement on the people (in passages such as Exod. 23:14–17). And they came to *confess Yhwh's *name, because the point of the festival was to celebrate what Yhwh had done. These festivals did that in two ways. They were nature or harvest festivals, marking stages in the farming year and celebrating what Yhwh was doing in making the crops grow. They also had links with Israel's own story, marking stages in its gaining its freedom from Egypt and its journey to its own land and celebrating what Yhwh had done for Israel in particular.

---

were our feet, standing" (cf. JM 121g). *IBHS* 37.7.1, however, notes that here the participle precedes *hāyû* and takes this as an indication that "standing" functions as an adjective (cf. Josh. 5:5), "our feet were [in a state of] standing."

13. *Midrash on Psalms*, 2:300.

14. Goulder (*Psalms of the Return*, 44–47) imagines the psalm used by Nehemiah.

What, then, is the link between v. 5 and what precedes? The question arises even if (with TNIV) one were to reckon that the opening *kî* (because) is really just an asseverative, meaning "indeed" (here and often elsewhere, TNIV does not translate the word). "Thrones" is metonymy for the people who sat on thrones (unless we translate "people sat [on] thrones").[15] The thrones belonging to David's household might relate to the country's political processes; these are the places where *decisions are made about whom to ally with or whom to submit to or whom to resist. The link with the city's significance for a pilgrim would then be the excitement of visiting the place where these decisions are made. The thrones would also be where community disputes were resolved, which might be more directly relevant to pilgrims who brought here disputes they could not settle through the local community's processes. The king would thus ensure that decisions were taken in a faithful way for Israel (e.g., 2 Sam. 8:15; 15:2–6). The plurality of thrones reflects the king's associating his son(s) and potential successor(s) ("David's household") with him in such aspects of government; further, the demands of dispute resolution could be overwhelming and would not be undertaken by the king alone but by a judiciary appointed by him (again, cf. 2 Sam. 15:2–6; also Exod. 18:13–26). The reference to David's household also *prima facie* implies that the psalm belongs before the exile, though it does not require this; when the psalm was used after the exile, it would suggest the great days when David's household did rule[16] and/or would indicate that Davidic leaders such as Zerubbabel were involved in these processes.

122:6–9. The latter part of the psalm turns quite sharply to speak of the psalmist's concern for the city.

> 6Ask for well-being for Jerusalem:
> "May people be at ease who are dedicated to you.
> 7May there be well-being within your rampart,
> ease in your citadels."

We need hardly ask who are encouraged to do this asking; the imperative is a rhetorical one the pilgrim goes on to obey. The psalm uses an ordinary word for "ask" (*šāʾal*) rather than a word for asking God for something (e.g., *pālal* hitpael). Indeed, in isolation one might translate v. 6a "ask about the well-being of Jerusalem."[17] But vv. 6b–7

15. So, e.g., Seybold, *Psalmen*, 479.

16. Cf. Herbert Donner, "Psalm 122," in *Text and Context*, ed. W. Claassen, JSOTSup 48 (F. C. Fensham Festschrift; Sheffield: Sheffield Academic Press, 1988), 81–92 (see 88).

17. Cf. Jer. 15:5 (though there the construction is significantly different) and Sym here, also Cassiodorus, *Psalms*, 3:275.

make clear that the lines refer to prayer. Both *šālôm* (well-being) and *šālâ* (be at ease) are capable of a narrower and a wider meaning, and the psalm contains indications that both apply here.[18] In the narrower sense *šālôm* refers to peace, while *šālâ* and its related words can suggest being quiet, secure, relaxed, and at ease (e.g., Prov. 17:1; Jer. 49:31). Jerusalem often needed that, and this meaning would fit with the reference to rampart and citadels in v. 7. The rampart is the city wall and the citadels the impressive fortified dwellings in the city. These are signs of the city's possessing secure defenses, but that means they are signs of being susceptible to attack. The words recur from Ps. 48:13 [14], though the reference here has a different slant. There the psalm marveled at these symbols of Yhwh's protection; here the psalm in effect prays that they may continue to be that. The gender matching in the two cola, two masculine nouns followed by two feminines, itself expresses the harmony the psalm prays for.[19]

On the other hand, eventually the psalm will close with reference to "good," and that links with the common broader meaning of *šālôm* as *well-being and the common broader meaning of *šālâ* as suggesting flourishing in different ways (e.g., Ps. 30:6 [7]; Jer. 22:21). It might always be a matter of selfish and unselfish concern for people from the country as a whole that their capital and its residents should prosper. Both pilgrims and residents are in different senses *dedicated to the city.

So it is natural to reckon that the psalm might be asking both for Jerusalem to enjoy peace and security and for it to blossom and thrive, in keeping with the kind of promises that appear in the prophets (e.g., Isa. 54; 60). Once more, such a desire would be natural in the preexilic period, but would have special significance in the sixth and fifth centuries, the time to which those prophecies belong.

8For the sake of my brothers and friends
I shall indeed speak of well-being for you.
9For the sake of the house of Yhwh our God
I shall seek good for you.

Speaking of *well-being will be another way of referring to asking for well-being. The brothers and friends are the people who are dedicated to the city, not least because they live there. The pilgrim does not live there but is invited by the psalm (actually written by a Jerusalemite?!) to identify with people who do, to see them as brothers (they are indeed fellow members of the family of Israel) and friends and neighbors (members of the same community).

18. *Ša'ălû šĕlôm yĕrûšālāim* makes for a nice alliteration.
19. So Watson, *Classical Hebrew Poetry*, 126.

Seeking *good for the city is yet another way of characterizing the prayer the pilgrim prays. (Tg takes it to denote seeking to *do* good for the city, as the expression means with irony in Neh. 2:10, but in this context a reference to prayer fits.) But this verse identifies the psalmist's concern as with the house that belongs to the God whom pilgrims and residents have in common ("our God"). The closing line thus makes an inclusion with the opening line. The pilgrim opens with a recollection of the joy involved in going to Yhwh's house and closes with the commitment to continuing prayer for the city where it stands, because it is this house that ultimately makes the city important. Thus the psalm's failure to make much reference to Yhwh as opposed to the city is qualified by the fact that really the thing that matters about the city is the fact that Yhwh lives there.

Theological Implications

Jerusalem is of decisive theological importance for OT faith and for NT faith. It is important during the preparatory and opening scenes of Jesus's life (even though he did not live there) and during his ministry. "The joy of this psalm and its concern for the peace of Jerusalem stand in tragic contrast with the arrival of the pilgrim who, when he 'saw the city, wept over it' (Luke 19:42–44). . . . Tears and lament disclose how deeply Jesus cared and shared the psalm's concern for the peace of Jerusalem;"[20] Jesus's actual phraseology about "the things that relate to peace" follows that of v. 8 (LXX). He goes on to speak subsequently of the distressing day when Jerusalem will once again be trampled on by the Gentiles (Luke 21:24). He himself then died there and rose there, the Holy Spirit was poured out there on the community that named his name, and the telling of his story throughout the world went out from there. Jerusalem, not Rome or Constantinople or Geneva or Canterbury or Los Angeles, is the city of God. Its associations make it a city that Jews and Christians rejoice to visit; and Muslims do so too, because it also became important for Mohammed. All that has made it more a place of conflict than it ever was in OT times. In recent decades it has become a place of prosperity and flourishing for some people, but not for others, and not a place of peace. This pilgrim (the writer of this commentary) no longer rejoices at the invitation to go up to Jerusalem because it has come to symbolize conflict. The city is vastly built up, but no thrones sit there for the making of decisions that will implement God's faithfulness. For the sake of my brothers and sisters and friends, Jewish and Christian and Muslim, and for the sake of Yhwh's house, then, the psalm issues a challenge to pray for peace.

20. Mays, *Psalms*, 394.

Psalm 123
The Servant Looks to the Master

Translation

Song of the Ascents.

1Toward you I have raised my eyes,
you who sit[1] in the heavens.
2Now: like the eyes of servants
toward their masters' hand,
Like the eyes of a maid
toward her mistress's hand,
So are our eyes
toward Yhwh our God,
until he is gracious to us.

3Be gracious, Yhwh, be gracious,
because we have become so full of shame.
4Our whole being[2] has become so full for itself
of scorn in relation to[3] the secure,
of shame in relation to the majestic.[4]

1. On the connective *î* ending, see the note on the translation of 113:8.
2. If *nepeš* can mean "throat," this could apply here; but *nepeš* is often used in connection with *śāba'* without that implication (e.g., 88:3 [4]).
3. The *l* in the second colon also applies to the first (cf. LXX). Alternatively, the juxtaposed absolute nouns might denote "of scorn, [the scorn of] the secure" (cf. GKC 127g).
4. Q has *lig'ê yônîm*, "in relation to the majestic of the oppressors," i.e., "the most majestic oppressors." I follow K, which takes the phrase as one word, presumably *lĕga'ăyônîm*.

Interpretation

Over against Ps. 122, this psalm has no inherent connection with pilgrimage, but the situation of the people as described in vv. 3–4 would match the circumstances of the postexilic community that collected the psalms of ascent. This could have attracted it to them, whenever it was written.

Psalm 123 is a prayer psalm, concerned (notwithstanding the opening "I") with the community's needs rather than an individual's. As a prayer psalm, it manifests a distinctive balance between its elements. Verses 1–2 comprise an extended appeal for Yhwh to pay attention, expressed as a recollection of the suppliant's seeking for Yhwh to pay attention. This no doubt continues into the present, but the qatal suggests it has been going on for a while. Verses 3–4 then begin with a plea for Yhwh to act, though this occupies only one colon (v. 3a), and back that up with a lament at the trouble that makes the plea necessary (vv. 3b–4). Both vv. 1–2 and vv. 3–4 come to an end with a tricolon, the closing one being longer (v. 2e–g is merely 2-2-2). In that sense the prayer comes to an end; but it incorporates no response or assurance that Yhwh has responded. Thus, whereas the opening lines could give one the impression that this will be a psalm of trust, its movement reverses the usual one for such a psalm. It begins by recalling an attitude of trust but ends up stressing awareness of need.[5]

The combination of "I" and "we" may indicate that the psalm was designed for a king or community leader such as Nehemiah, or a worship leader such as a Levite. There is no particular reason to infer that its speakers or singers changed; a leader can speak both as "I" and as "you." It compares with community prayers such as Ps. 44 and Lamentations, and it might be used on occasions of fasting and prayer such as those referred to by Zech. 7–8. It would fit the community's gloomy state in Hezekiah's time or during the exile or that of the postexilic community overshadowed by the imperial power and looked down on by other local communities.

The psalm again uses "terrace" parallelism to bind the whole: "my eyes" and "our eyes" in v. 1 and v. 2e; "like the eyes" in v. 2a and 2c; "hand" in v. 2b and 2d; the pairing of "servants" and "maid" and of "toward their masters' hand" and "toward her mistress's hand" in v. 2; the inclusion of "Toward you . . . you who sit in the heavens" and "toward Yhwh our God" in vv. 1 and 2f; "gracious" in vv. 2g and 3a; "become so full" in vv. 3b and 4a;[6] and "shame" in vv. 3b and 4c.

5. Cf. Auffret, *La sagesse*, 453.

6. The first time the word is m. *rab* used adverbially, the second time f. *rabbat* used adverbially (as in 120:6), matching the move from "we" to f. "our *nepeš*."

Song of the Ascents.

Heading. See glossary.

123:1–2. A reminder of the way the suppliant has been seeking Yhwh's attention.

[1]Toward you I have raised my eyes,
  you who sit in the heavens.

The opening phrase takes up from 121:1, except that here the qatal verb suggests an action in the past (though continuing in the present), whereas the yiqtol in 121:1 suggested a habitual or durative act. Here, further, it is explicit that Yhwh is the one to whom the suppliant looks, and it is thus clear that this is an expectant look rather than (for instance) a fearful look to something threatening. Names such as Elioenai, "My eyes to Yhwh," recur in passages such as Ezra 10:22, 27.[7]

Sitting in the heavens does not suggest remoteness or noninvolvement in this world but rather that Yhwh is enthroned, and from there as sovereign Yhwh can and does come to intervene in the world down below the palace.

[2]Now: like the eyes of servants
  toward their masters' hand,
Like the eyes of a maid
  toward her mistress's hand,
So are our eyes
  toward Yhwh our God,
  until he is gracious to us.

Three lines make this explicit in working out the implications of the looking. The sentence's length compares and contrasts with that of 122:2–5 following on the one-line opening to that psalm. This sentence does not involve enjambment, but it raises suspense as we wait for the main clause in v. 2e–g. The poetry reflects the contents: the effect of the sentence is "to express the feeling of waiting and suspense it portrays."[8]

Most manuscripts of Tg have "haughty" servants and a "haughty" maid looking to their masters and mistress, and later have the suppliants thus looking anxiously to their God. All this carries with it some irony as their haughtiness makes them just like the people they complain about

7. Keel, *Symbolism*, 317; he provides a figure picturing Assyrian captives thus looking to their overseer (*Symbolism*, 320, 322).

8. Watson, *Classical Hebrew Poetry*, 368.

in v. 4.[9] Qimchi likewise has the servants and the maid looking anxiously to the hand that strikes them, as Yhwh's hand had struck Israel. But the affirmative tone of the psalm rather suggests a positive form of looking, like that invited by 104:27–28 and described by 145:15–16.[10] Servants and maids look to their masters and mistresses to provide for them and act on their behalf.

The singular and plural, masculine/male and feminine/female complement each other in v. 2a–d (we need hardly infer that a household had many male servants and only one female, which in any case seems inherently impractical).[11] While it would be possible to translate *ʿebed* and *šipḥâ* "slave" and "slave girl," the very implications of the simile show that this would be misleading, as elsewhere in the OT. An *ʿebed* and a *šipḥâ* are not chattels. They have limited rights and freedoms and extensive obligations, but they have a relationship with their masters and mistresses that also involves the latter in responsibilities and obligations. The psalm presupposes the use of *ʿebed* to describe the Israelite as a "servant" of God, implying that such a mutual understanding of the relationship is the regular one. Abraham's servant with his responsible position in Gen. 24 conveys some idea of the servant-master relationship, while the willingness of some feisty women (Ruth, Hannah, Abigail) to describe themselves metaphorically as "maids" suggests this cannot have been too despicable a term.

So the reliance of male and female servants on their masters and mistresses provides an image for the stance the community has taken to Yhwh, who is "our God," as masters and mistresses are "their masters" and "her mistress." In 145:15–16 people's eyes are looking for food. Here they are looking for *grace. There is some tension involved in the use of that word (as in 119:132). The relationship of master and servant does not work on the basis of grace but of mutual commitment. But it may have started in an act of grace, if the master took on this person as servant when the person was in desperate need. And it is such a gracelike act that the suppliant needs now. LXX and Jerome translate *ḥānan* as "pity,"[12] and that gives the right idea.

As well as completing the section with a tricolon, v. 2e–g completes an *abb′a′* sequence in vv. 1–2. The first and fourth lines refer directly to the psalm's topic; the middle two lines provide a double simile for it. Verse 2e–g thus binds the four lines together and initiates a transition to what

9. But the MSS evidence for both verses in Tg is complicated (the word for "haughty" does not appear in either of the editions of *Miqrāʾôt Gĕdôlôt* that I use), and Tg evidently has gone through some reworking (see Stec, *Targum*, 221).

10. Cassiodorus (*Psalms*, 3:279) postmodernly allows for either reading.

11. Against Gunkel, *Psalmen*, 544.

12. Though LXX obscures the continuity in v. 3 by there translating "have mercy."

follows. It also marks the transition to speaking in the plural. Perhaps v. 1 constitutes the leader's affirmation of faith into which v. 2e–g draws the congregation.

123:3–4. The suppliant's plea, and the need that lies behind it.

> ³Be gracious, Yhwh, be gracious,
> because we have become so full of shame.
> ⁴Our whole being has become so full for itself
> of scorn in relation to the secure,
> of shame in relation to the majestic.

The reference to Yhwh's graciousness now becomes a plea rather than merely featuring in a report of one. The verb's recurrence also bridges that transition from recollection to plea in the two parts of the psalm. Initially, v. 3 simply underlines the plea's urgency by twice more repeating the verb; in between, for the first time it actually calls on "Yhwh." Holding back that invocation also adds force to the plea.

But why does the suppliant's community need grace or mercy? Verse 3b begins to explain. Being full is a nice experience, if you are full of the right thing, such as food or good things generally, or Yhwh's commitment, or simply full of Yhwh (90:14; 91:16; 105:40; 107:9; 132:15; 147:14). But here the community is full of shame. There were many situations when that was true of Israel: in Hezekiah's day, and in the exile, and in Nehemiah's day, the only concrete context in which this root for shame (*bûz*) occurs (Neh. 4:4 [3:36]).

Verse 4 expands on the point at some length; again, the move in the poetry from v. 3 to v. 4 is bridged by the continuity of subject and words. So first the verb "be full" recurs, with the impact of this shame underlined by noting how the whole being (*person) can become consumed by it. "Shame" itself recurs in the third colon, adding to the continuity and the underlining, but meanwhile it is reconfigured in the middle colon as "scorn"; the root recurs in connection with Hezekiah (Isa. 37:22) and the exile (Ezek. 36:4), as well as Nehemiah (Neh. 2:19; 4:1 [3:33]). Shame can involve both our own awareness and perception and that of other people; scorn focuses on that of other people. In those different contexts, it can be the attitude of people who see themselves as more powerful than we are and despise our weakness, or the attitude of bystanders who do not get as far as saying, "There but for the grace of God go I" and may rather say, "Where is your God?" (42:10 [11]; 115:2).[13]

Here, the bystanders could be the "secure" (*šaʾănān*). EVV have "complacent," and these people may well be that, but the root also (perhaps

13. Mays, *Psalms*, 395.

first) refers to an objective state of safety and security (e.g., Isa. 33:20; Zech. 1:15). It would rather be the powerful people, whom one would call the "majestic" (*gaʾăyônîm*). Once more EVV have an attitude word, "proud," and no doubt these people were proud, but again the root refers to an objective state, of exaltation and majesty.[14] It makes its first and most proper appearances applied to Yhwh (Exod. 15:1, 7, 21; cf. Ps. 93:1), though more often it is applied to human beings (for example, Pss. 94:2; 140:5 [6]). But precisely its original and proper connection with Yhwh means it is almost impossible for it to apply to human entities without that becoming blasphemy. It is almost impossible to become majestic without becoming arrogant. In this context, the scorners will be eminent and impressive people like the Assyrians, Babylonians, and Persians, but also the local opponents of people such as Nehemiah, who will often have seemed worryingly powerful on a smaller scale. All will no doubt have been confident and self-assured, too, and not without (apparent) reason. They could certainly look down on little Judah. The community longs for Yhwh to do something about that. The description of them as majestic or arrogant constitutes an implicit appeal for Yhwh to act because the problem is not merely that the community is being ridiculed but because Yhwh is being scorned. Further, the exaltation of these scorners at the end of the psalm contrasts with the exaltation of Yhwh at its beginning.[15]

Theological Implications

For the church in a situation like the present, in North America and in Europe, "what then remains to be done, but . . . that our soul, although it may be filled to satiety with all kinds of reproaches, breathe forth prayers to God for deliverance with the importunity of the famished?"[16] The priestly blessing with its promise of grace (Num. 6:25) is both the basis for this prayer and the response to it.[17]

In this connection the psalm offers a simple, clear theological insight. Our relationship to Yhwh is like that of servants to their masters and mistresses. Yhwh, then, is in a position of exaltation and power. This would make it possible to be authoritarian and demanding, but rather it makes it possible to be authoritative and protective. There is a quasi-

14. LXX and Jerome have an objective word ("prosperous") for the first word and an attitude word for the second ("proud"). The second colon will then take the first further (as Augustine implies [*Psalms*, 597–98]).

15. Cf. Grossberg, *Centripetal and Centrifugal Structures*, 35–36.

16. Calvin, *Psalms*, 5:83.

17. *Midrash on Psalms*, 2:303.

covenantal relationship between servants and their masters; the servants serve, and the masters provide and protect. There is an analogous relationship between a people and Yhwh. The human reality of servanthood may seem to generate the theological insight, but substantially and metaphysically, and even epistemologically, and certainly ethically, the movement is the other way around. It is because Yhwh is master and we are servants that we come to perceive the nature of human masterhood and servanthood. Admittedly there is a theological tension here, because the creation stories in Genesis would rather imply that God's design did not envisage such a thing as human masterhood and servanthood. But outside the Garden of Eden these came to be, and the nature of Yhwh's masterhood and of human servanthood then provides the model for masterhood and servanthood within humanity. Being a boss means being someone who protects and provides. Being a servant means having someone who protects and provides, and being able to appeal for them to show grace.

Psalm 124
Our Help Is Yhwh's Name

Translation

Song of the Ascents. David's.

1Were it not Yhwh who was for us,[1]
  Israel is indeed[2] to say,
2Were it not Yhwh who was for us
  when human beings arose against us,
3Then they would have swallowed us alive
  when their anger burned against us.
4Then the waters—they would have carried us off;
  the torrent[3]—it would have passed right over us.[4]
5Then it would have passed right over us,
  the seething waters.[5]

1. LXX, Jerome understand "Were it not that Yhwh was with us," treating the relative prefix *še* on *hāyâ* as pleonastic (cf. *TTH* 139). This puts the emphasis on the fact that Yhwh *was for us*. I rather follow Aq, Sym, Th, who translate the relative and assume that *lûlê* is here used to introduce a noun clause as in 94:17; 119:92. This puts the emphasis on the fact that *Yhwh* was for us, which fits the emphasis of the psalm.

2. *-nāʾ*.

3. *Naḥlâ* has the additional *â* ending (see the note on 116:15).

4. Lit. "passed over our being," perhaps "our neck" (*nepeš*); so also in v. 5a.

5. The sg. verb thus eventually has a pl. subject, which can happen in Hebrew, though here it is facilitated by the way v. 5a repeats v. 4b with its sg. subject.

[6]Yhwh be worshipped,
who did not give us as prey for their teeth.
[7]We ourselves are[6] like a bird
that has escaped from the fowlers' trap.
The trap—it broke,
and we—we escaped.
[8]Our help is the very name of Yhwh,[7]
maker of the heavens and the earth.

Interpretation

The psalm is a thanksgiving or testimony by the community, as is reflected in the prominence of the suffix *-nû* "us/our" (vv. 1a, 2a, 2b, 3a, 3b, 4a, 4b, 5a, 6b, 7a, 7d, 8a). Yet it does not follow the regular form of such a psalm; this may be related to the fact that most thanksgiving/testimony psalms celebrate what Yhwh has done for an individual. They commonly tell the story of an experience of distress, of praying, of Yhwh responding, and of Yhwh acting. While most of these features are implicitly present in Ps. 124, it is not structured by them in the manner of Pss. 116 and 118. This psalm perhaps recycles the imagery of an individual thanksgiving/testimony in order to speak of the community's experience.[8]

It then also makes for illuminating comparison with Pss. 103; 105; 107; 108. These in one way or another announce themselves as thanksgiving or testimony psalms and/or organize themselves as such, but in content or function they are more like praise psalms. Psalm 124 does not announce itself as a thanksgiving or testimony psalm, but that is what it constitutes.

Testimony is the more appropriate designation, since it never addresses Yhwh. It is not clear whom it does address, though implicitly it is sung both for the hearing of Israel itself and for that of the nations. It is sung for Israel's hearing, because testimony gives the testifier opportunity to articulate what has happened and thus to know what has happened and to be built up by it. The testifier is thus able to recognize future situations that resemble this one and to react in light of this experience. And the psalm is sung for the nations' hearing (cf. Pss. 105; 108) because Yhwh's deeds for Israel are also good news for the nations.

The psalm divides into two parts, of five and four lines. Verses 1–5 contemplate what might have been if Yhwh had not acted. As in Pss.

6. Lit. "our being is" (*nepeš*).

7. Not "our help is in the name of Yhwh"; the *b* is *beth* of identity, *beth essentiae* (see *IBHS* 11.2.5e). The statement thus bears comparison with the *lûlê* statement in 94:17.

8. See Crüsemann, *Studien zur Formgeschichte*, 161–68.

122 and 123, some of the effect comes from the incorporation of a long, suspenseful sentence, here occupying at least three lines and forming the opening of the psalm.[9] Once again attention and curiosity are aroused by the incomplete nature of the first line, and then of the second, and the hearer listens closely to discover the outcome.[10] Further, while the syntax thus holds together vv. 1–3, parallelism of structure holds together vv. 3–5. The whole is thus tightly bound.

Verses 6–8 then declare how Yhwh should be worshipped for what happened because Yhwh did act. This second part corresponds more closely to the form of a testimony psalm, with its declaration that Yhwh is to be worshipped, its recollection of what Yhwh did, and its closing affirmation of the ongoing implications. Reference to Yhwh appropriately frames the section; it also frames the psalm as a whole. Whereas Pss. 121 and 123 gain their power from their systematic exploring of one metaphor, Ps. 124 gains its power from its speedy movement from one metaphor to another; but the reference to Yhwh holds it together.[11] Once again, the psalm achieves some of its effect through the use of "terrace" parallelism, especially in the first section: see vv. 1–2; vv. 2–3 (the second cola are similarly structured); vv. 3–5 ("then"); vv. 4a and 5b; vv. 4b–5a; v. 7b–c.

One can once more imagine the psalm being sung in relation to the crisis in Hezekiah's day (see Isa. 36–37). The actual language of fire and flood (vv. 3–5) recurs in the context of the exile and the prospect of escape from Babylon (Isa. 43:2), though it might again have been used subsequently as the community looked back to the exile, and some of the language of vv. 1–3 also parallels that in Nehemiah. The reference to David in the heading has suggested a reference to Philistine attacks in his day. But typically, the psalm is unspecific about particular foes, facilitating its use in different contexts. It thus noticeably speaks only of "human beings" and then in metaphorical terms about fire and flood and fowlers. Thus the attempt to relate the psalm to a context works against its own nature and aim.

Once again its nature does not suggest it was by origin a pilgrimage psalm, but its testimony to Yhwh's deliverance of the people would make it open to being used to this end.

Song of the Ascents. David's.

9. Indeed, *IBHS* 39.3.4f sees vv. 1–5 as one sentence (cf. NRSV; TNIV). On the other hand, Gerstenberger (*Psalms*, 2:333) sees v. 1 as the worship leader's bidding, vv. 2–9 being the congregation's response.

10. So Watson, *Classical Hebrew Poetry*, 154.

11. Cf. Grossberg, *Centripetal and Centrifugal Structures*, 36.

Heading. See glossary.

124:1–5. How things could have been.

> [1]Were it not Yhwh who was for us,
> Israel is indeed to say,
> [2]Were it not Yhwh who was for us
> when human beings arose against us,
> [3]Then they would have swallowed us alive
> when their anger burned against us.

In the complex opening sentence, "for us" in the first colon and "against us" in the last colon act as a frame and set up the basic antinomy with which it works. The middle line underlines the point by itself antithesizing "for us" and "against us" (though in v. 2 "against us" is *ʿālênû*; in v. 3, *bānû*).

The expression in v. 1b belongs in testimony speech (cf. 118:2–4; 129:1; also 107:2). Thus "Israel is indeed to say" is another way of urging Israel to "confess" Yhwh. If we go on to look at that antinomy between "for us" and "against us" in the reverse of the psalm's order, we see vv. 2b–3 offering a threefold description of the problem that Israel had. Fairly literally, human beings "arose" against Israel; the verb often suggests a sudden and unexpected attack. And second, they could easily have swallowed up Israel, as Lam. 2:16 imagines Jerusalem's enemies reckoning they have done (cf. Isa. 49:19; Jer. 51:34–35), swallowed them like a monster so suddenly it would have been like swallowing them alive. The image is one applied to Death with its insatiable appetite and its desire to take people before their time (e.g., Prov. 1:12). Third, these people's anger "burned" against Israel. As usual, this expression need not mean that the attackers necessarily felt angry; the point is that the effect of their action on Israel was like that of someone being angry and lashing out. But the king of Babylon, for instance, was indeed angry with Judah for rebelling, and Sanballat and others were angry at Nehemiah's achievements (Neh. 4:1, 7 [3:33; 4:1]).

Such is the description of Israel's problem. But the psalm actually begins with a conjunction that "provides the hearers with basic security" because it "shifts the entire series of ten cola . . . into the counterfactual mode." Although the description of peril is given more and more space as the poem unfolds, its teeth have already been drawn by this "signal of the counterfactual mode,"[12] for what vv. 2b–3 describe is how things would have been were it not for the fact that Yhwh was "for us" or was

12. Fokkelman, *Major Poems*, 3:275–76.

"ours." The expression parallels the testimony in 116:6 and some words of Nehemiah (Neh. 4:20 [14]); it also recalls the phrase "I will be your God," more literally "I will be God for you" (Exod. 6:7; Jer. 7:23). The testimony Israel is to give itself and the nations is that having Yhwh for you draws the monster's teeth.

> 4Then the waters—they would have carried us off;
> the torrent—it would have passed right over us.
> 5Then it would have passed right over us,
> the seething waters.

The psalm continues to describe that would-have-been peril in two parallel lines that are syntactically separate from vv. 1–3 and expound a different image for the peril the people were in. But they also parallel v. 3, as the further opening "then" in v. 4 and again in v. 5 signal. For a city in the ancient world, fire (v. 3) is a great peril. In the open country, flood can be a great peril. Camping in a wadi (1 Kings 17:4–5) could be a tempting idea because things grow there and there is often a continuing water supply. But people camping in a wadi can suddenly be overwhelmed by floodwaters flowing down from the mountains as the result of a storm there (cf. Judg. 5:21). So the raging torrent that from time to time rushes down a wadi, a *naḥal,* becomes a figure for an army overwhelming a country (Isa. 8:7–8; Jer. 47:2). At the same time, talk of waters and torrent suggests forces of more than natural significance, the forces of chaos that assert themselves against order and against God and/or the forces of death (which would follow well on v. 3); compare, for example, Pss. 69:1–2, 14–15 [2–3, 15–16]; 93:3–4.

In the last word of the lines and of the section, the enemies themselves become visible again, as "seething" comes from a root that can refer to the literal boiling of food but more often refers to human assertiveness (the recurrent "willful" in Ps. 119 comes from this root). The waters become a torrent, and the torrent becomes seething waters, so that the effect heightens through vv. 4–5, though at the same time, the *abb'a'* order of the two lines brings the first section to a close.[13]

124:6–9. The psalm's confession.

> 6Yhwh be worshipped,
> who did not give us as prey for their teeth.

"Yhwh be worshipped" is a declaration that can be based simply on who Yhwh is (especially in the declarations at the end of each book in the Psalter), but it also commonly arises when people are aware of

13. Cf. Bratcher and Reyburn, *Handbook on the Psalms*, 1063.

Yhwh having done things for them personally (18:46 [47]; 28:6; 31:21 [22]; 66:20), and so it is here.[14] Thus it is yet another way of urging people to "confess" Yhwh. The confession's basis lies in the action Yhwh took "for us" (vv. 1–2), here pictured in yet another way (or perhaps it takes further the image of being eaten alive). It is as if we were a rabbit and the enemy was a lion; but Yhwh plucked us from the jaws of the lion.

[7]We ourselves are like a bird
  that has escaped from the fowlers' trap.
The trap—it broke,
  and we—we escaped.

Like the alternatives of fire and flood, the section goes on to work with the alternatives of a lion catching its prey and a fowler catching a bird, both common images for an enemy's attacks. Again the victim has a narrow escape from being eaten. "Escape" (*mālaṭ* niphal) is a verb that can be used theologically of being delivered by God and can also be used with its ordinary literal meaning; here both connotations will apply.

It was a very narrow escape. The bird actually did get caught, but the trap broke. (The Assyrian king Sennacherib describes his attack on Hezekiah as resulting in shutting up Hezekiah like a bird in a cage.)[15] The phraseology subtly leaves open whether this was a supranatural event. All three verbs (escaped, broke, escaped) are niphal; in keeping with the common meaning of the niphal I have translated them as intransitives. Yet all three could be taken as passive ("has been delivered . . . was broken . . . were delivered") with Yhwh the implicit agent of the deliverance and the breaking. The verse leaves the question open.

[8]Our help is the very name of Yhwh,
  maker of the heavens and the earth.

The closing verse resolves any ambiguity. Like the deliverance of Hezekiah, this was not a purely "natural" event. The psalm moves to language with strong supranatural implications in speaking of *help and of Yhwh's *name and sets the deliverance in the broadest of theological contexts in v. 8b (cf. 121:2). Once again Yhwh's work of deliverance is one with Yhwh's work as creator.

14. Westermann (*Living Psalms*, 52–54) emphasizes the link of this phrase with narratives of what Yhwh has done.

15. See *ANET*, 287–88.

Theological Implications

"If God is for us, who can be against us?" (Rom. 8:31). The experience of deliverance is not really very surprising when one thinks about it. How could you fret when your help is the maker of the heavens and the earth? This declaration in v. 8 came to feature at the beginning of the order for the last prayers of the day, called Compline (an abbreviation for "The Completion of the Day").[16] It is thus transferred from its context in a testimony psalm to a statement of faith that applies every day, specifically every evening when one needs to call on God's protection for the night. There is some irony about this, because theologically the statement will have its original setting in what Westermann calls descriptive praise rather than declarative praise (that is, the speech of praise psalms rather than that of thanksgiving/testimony psalms).[17] The psalm transfers this to the context of declarative praise, and Compline moves it back again. But this is fine; it reflects the dialectical relationship between praise and thanksgiving. Praise depends on testimony to keep it alive; testimony is designed to lead into praise. Psalm 124 fulfills an aspect of its vocation when Christian communities make its closing declaration at the end of each day. On the other hand, opening with a line from a thanksgiving psalm might encourage these communities, as they pray, to begin by recalling the evidence this day has given that "Our help is the name of Yhwh." That is in keeping with the statement's background in the rest of the psalm.

16. See, e.g., the Society of St. Francis service book *Celebrating Common Prayer*, rev. ed. (London and New York: Continuum, 2002), 235.

17. See *The Praise of God in the Psalms*.

Psalm 125
Well-Being on Israel

Translation

Song of the Ascents.

1People who rely on Yhwh are like Mount Zion,
which will not fall down, it will abide, forever.
2Jerusalem: mountains are around it,
and Yhwh: he is around his people,
from now and forever.

3Because the faithless staff will not rest
on the allotment of the faithful,
So that the faithful do not put
their hands to wickedness.[1]

4Do good, Yhwh, to the good,
to the upright in heart.
5But people who bend [their ways so that they become] quite
crooked—
may Yhwh make them go, the people who do harm;[2]
well-being on Israel.

1. The noun has the additional *-â* ending (see the note on 116:15).

2. I take *ʾet* as object marker rather than as the preposition meaning "with" (cf. Crow, *Songs of Ascents*, 55–56; he then sees the phrase as a gloss). On such nouns in apposition to a preceding suffix, see GKC 131m; *IBHS* 12.4. DG 39 remark 3 notes that it is an Aramaic usage.

Interpretation

Once more, the psalm's background lies in pressure on Israel from outside. But whereas Ps. 124 testified to deliverance and implied a sense of confidence in Yhwh on the basis of that, Ps. 125 focuses on and begins from a declaration of confidence, expressed first positively (vv. 1–2) and then negatively (v. 3). In due course it comes to plea (vv. 4–5), but its focus suggests it is more a psalm of trust than a prayer psalm.[3] Briggs sees the original kernel of the psalm as lying in vv. 1–3b, the rest being later additions.[4] Crow sees the original kernel as lying in vv. 3–5b,[5] giving the psalm a wisdom cast,[6] with vv. 1–2 being a later introduction.

Song of the Ascents.

Heading. See glossary. Once more this is not by nature a pilgrimage psalm; it was evidently adapted to that usage.

125:1–2. The positive declaration of confidence.

[1]People who rely on Yhwh are like Mount Zion,
which will not fall down, it will abide, forever.

The presupposition of vv. 1–2 is that mountains are both stable and protective. Historically it was the case that being located in a strange place on top of a mountain ridge made Jerusalem more secure than a capital city on the plain; other things being equal, it was not worth besieging, and (politically speaking) this was what saved it when Sennacherib reduced the rest of the cities in Judah. Geophysically, mountains look and are stable and strong. There is a particular strength about Mount Zion, constituting as it does a thumb-shaped crest with steep slopes on three sides. Even a handful of deaf and blind people could defend it, its pre-Israelite inhabitants perhaps thought (see 2 Sam. 5:6; though the meaning of the verse is notoriously uncertain); admittedly they turned out to be wrong. But the psalm will have in mind a whole other level of strength that Mount Zion came to have. It is Yhwh's holy mountain, the place where Yhwh lives, the place Yhwh is dedicated to (Pss. 2:6; 74:2; 78:68). How could it fall down, even if some other mountains did (see

3. Cf. Gunkel, *Psalmen*, 548.

4. *Psalms*, 2:454.

5. *Songs of Ascents*, 57.

6. Cf. Walter Beyerlin, *Weisheitliche Vergewisserung mit Bezug auf den Zionskult*, OBO 68 (Göttingen: Vandenhoeck & Ruprecht, 1985); Seybold, *Psalmen*, 484. But Beyerlin (27–45) sees the basic contents of the whole psalm as fixed from the beginning; only a few phrases are later additions.

Ps. 46:2–5 [3–6])? "On Mount Zion rests the promise of God" (cf. Isa. 28:16).[7] (One might also reverse that: Mount Zion rests on the promise of God.) Therefore Mount Zion will surely sit there (the verb in v. 1b is *yāšab*), forever (the word comes between "fall down" and "abide" and likely applies to both).

And people who rely on Yhwh are like that. Formally the statement is purely a simile, but there is a substantial link and not merely a figurative one between Yhwh and Zion and thus between the people and Zion, as well as between the people and Yhwh. They all stand or fall, or rather stand and do not fall, together.

[2]Jerusalem: mountains are around it,
and Yhwh: he is around his people,
from now and forever.

The second line works the simile in a different way. Zion, or Jerusalem (interestingly, the psalm now uses the more political title for the city), is secure because of its own physical characteristics, notwithstanding the fact that it is surrounded by bigger mountains. These are not a threat; enemies do not have missiles they could shoot from that far away. They look more like a protective shield. Thus they provide a figure for Yhwh's relationship with the people whose life centers on Zion. Admittedly, the image of Yhwh as "around" the people stretches the imagination. In 34:7 [8] Yhwh's aide camps around them, which perhaps suggests that the aide stands for an army; that would make sense here. Or perhaps one is to imagine a mother whose arms envelop her child and protect it from danger. As in English, being surrounded is often a negative image (e.g., 3:6 [7]; 27:6; 31:13 [14]). This is a more positive surrounding.

The last colon makes the line into a tricolon and advertises that the first short section is coming to an end. It takes up the theme of the last clause in v. 1. We could also read v. 1 as a tricolon, 2-2-2; this further tricolon is then systematically longer. In keeping with that formal point, the statement about Yhwh being around the people "now and forever" goes beyond the statement that Zion merely "abides forever."

125:3. The negative declaration of confidence.

[3]Because the faithless staff will not rest
on the allotment of the faithful,
So that the faithful do not put
their hands to wickedness.

7. Weiser, *Psalms*, 757.

The "because" follows on from vv. 1–2: the people are secure because they will not fall or remain under oppressors. It is easy to imagine the staff of the *faithless one resting on the allotment of the *faithful. Isaiah spoke in those terms of Assyria and Babylon (Isa. 9:4 [3]; 14:4–5, 29; 30:31). Sennacherib thought his staff was going to rest on Jerusalem, and so did Sanballat. The staff (*šēbeṭ*) is a club or rod, a substantial or formal sign of authority (cf. Pss. 2:9; 45:6 [7]). Its resting might suggest heavy imposition or might suggest descending and staying there. There is no necessary implication that it must already be present, so that the promise is that it will not continue there (one might then expect another word such as "forever"); the verb "rest" (*nûaḥ*) often denotes the arrival of something, which comes to rest (e.g., Num. 10:36; 11:25, 26). But the psalm could be used with either implication.

The impossibility of the faithless staff being allowed to come to dominate Israel is suggested by v. 3b. Like English "allotment," *gôrāl* can refer either to the process of allotting something or to the result, specifically in terms of land (e.g., Josh. 14:2; 15:1; 16:1). So the allocation of the faithful is the land that has been allocated to them, allocated by the drawing of lots and thus by Yhwh (cf. Prov. 16:33). So surely, having superintended this allocation, Yhwh will not allow it to be frustrated. The allocation belongs to the faithful, the people in committed relationship with Yhwh, which makes that even more inconceivable.

There is also a pragmatic (though still theological) reason why that surely could not be allowed. The effect of foreign sovereignty is often to impose the overlord's religion; that would lead the faithful to "put their hands" to the wickedness of apostasy. But "wickedness" usually denotes wrongful behavior in relation to other people, the opposite of faithfulness to them. The psalmist reckons that falling under the authority of the faithless will lead to such wickedness in the community. Why that is so, the psalm does not explain, though one can guess at some reasons. The new regime will operate on an immoral basis, and anyone who wants to succeed will be tempted to do the same. The new regime will show that wickedness pays and thus tempt the faithful to live thus. Alternatively, the success of the faithless may make the faithful lose faith and give in to "moral nihilism."[8] Nehemiah 5 shows how (people may claim) the demands of an occupying power (on which cf. also Neh. 9:36–37) indeed lead people to abandon their faithfulness to one another.[9] The faithless staff has indeed come to rest on the faithful. The only question is whether it will continue to do so.

8. Carol Bechtel Reynolds, "Psalm 125," *Int* 48 (1994): 272–75 (see 274).

9. Cf. Goulder, *Psalms of the Return*, 56–59.

125:4–5. The plea.

> [4]Do good, Yhwh, to the good,
> to the upright in heart.

Paradoxically, perhaps, the statements of conviction in vv. 1–3 do not make prayer unnecessary; perhaps they are what makes it possible. Just now, "faithful" was a courtesy title for the community. That is their status. It parallels the NT's calling Christians "saints." Verse 4 speaks of the same people but applies to them more unequivocally moral terms, "*good" and "upright in *heart"; the last phrase indicates that their goodness and uprightness must not be skin-deep but must reach down into the inner person and thus affect what they do in private as well as what they do in public. It is on the basis of their being good that the psalm can bid Yhwh to do *good, to bless them and prosper them. The hearers or singers of the psalm then have to reflect on the possible tension between having the position "the faithful" and having the vocation of being the "good" and "upright." Being the faithful implies a vocation to be the good and upright, as being saints implies a vocation to be holy.

> [5]But people who bend [their ways so that they become] quite
> crooked—
> may Yhwh make them go, the people who do harm;
> well-being on Israel.

In the context, following on v. 4, I take this closing line (another tricolon) as a continuation of the plea rather than simply a statement about what Yhwh will do. The word for crooked is a strong one, doubly or triply so; it is very rare, it is reduplicated (the root is *ʿāqal*; this adjective is *ʿăqalqāl*), and the plural may be intensive. The expression in which it comes seems to involve an ellipse and to presuppose a word for "ways," a common image in the psalms.[10] The faithless are people who do not walk a straight way but deliberately walk a way that is morally and socially warped and twisted. The image of walking a path may also underlie the middle colon. The OT assumes that crooked paths lead to destruction, and the psalm may be asking that Yhwh simply make the faithless walk that way, as the people who *harm others that they are. Or it may be asking that Yhwh just make them go away.

10. Vrs take the verb intransitively, suggesting "bend [to] crookednesses," but this involves a doubly unusual usage: there are no other instances of *nāṭâ* (hiphil) used thus, and we have to provide "to" before "crookednesses."

The final colon stands syntactically isolated, its relationship with what precedes being left for inference. It is widely regarded as a gloss,[11] but Kraus calls it "the real theme of the psalm."[12] The context suggests it is another wish, expressing the converse of the preceding two cola. *Šālôm* might have its narrow meaning; Israel's attackers have gone, and thus may "peace" prevail. But I have assumed its broader meaning, *well-being, which contrasts with the fate of the crooked troublemakers as well as with the trouble they bring. It is a motif that recurs in the Songs of the Ascents (120:6–7; 122:6–8; 128:6).

Theological Implications

In today's religion/culture wars, the faithless are winning[13] and have led the faithful to put their hands to wickedness in the sense that church culture like secular culture is dominated by money, possessions, size, individualism, family breakdown, narcissism, overwork, and an acceptance of the gulf between rich and poor. Thus it is hard to make the affirmations in vv. 1–2. But perhaps it was hard in the psalmist's day; certainly this was so in the time of Hezekiah, Ezekiel, Haggai, and Nehemiah. The difficulty of the affirmations means it is the more important to make them, along with the psalm's pleas.

11. E.g., Gunkel, *Psalmen*, 549.
12. *Psalms 60–150*, 446.
13. Cf. Reynolds, "Psalm 125," 274–75.

Psalm 126

Weeping and Laughter

Translation

Song of the Ascents.

1When Yhwh brought about the restoration of Zion,
  we became like people dreaming/healing.
2Then our mouth filled with laughter,
  our tongue with resounding.
Then they said among the nations,
  "Yhwh has done something great[1] with these people."
3Yhwh has done something great with us;
  we became people rejoicing.

4Yhwh, bring about our restoration,
  like channels in the Negeb.
5People who sow with weeping
  will reap with resounding.
6He does go crying,
  the one who carries the bag of seed.[2]
He will indeed come with resounding,
  the one who carries his sheaves.

1. Lit. "has shown greatness in acting"; *higdîl* is an "internal" or "inwardly transitive" hiphil (*IBHS* 27.2f; GKC 53d–f).

2. The phrase in v. 6b (and 6d) is the subject of the preceding verb (cf. Crow, *Songs of Ascents*, 61). The meaning of *mešek* is a matter of guesswork, but it is usually taken to mean a leather bag (cf. *HALOT*). Tg apparently takes it to mean "ox" and makes it the subject. LXX simply omits the word. Jerome paraphrases "seed for sowing," and NRSV, TNIV follow.

Interpretation

Yet again this community prayer psalm does not read like a psalm composed for pilgrimage, but one can see how it could come to be used in that connection. Its background is the people's need for some restoring of their fortunes, and the second of the two neat four-line sections (vv. 4–6) implies that the trouble it presupposes is that crops have not been growing, apparently because of drought (or perhaps that the trouble can be spoken of metaphorically in those terms). The psalm anticipates that being reversed, with the result described in faith and hope in vv. 5–6.

NJPS translates the first section (vv. 1–3) as also a statement of faith and hope ("When the LORD restores the fortunes of Zion . . . our mouths shall be filled with laughter. . . . The LORD will do great things for us . . ."), which gives the yiqtol verbs in v. 2 their common future meaning.[3] But they follow *ʾāz* ("then") and thus can just as easily refer to the past; and the verbs in vv. 1b, 3a, and 3b are qatals. While these could be qatals of certainty, there is no obstacle to giving them their regular meaning and assuming that the whole of the first section refers to the past. Indeed, "it is unnatural and forced to suppose, with some expositors, that this is a prediction of what was to come."[4] Rather it provides background for the prayer in the second section, in a fashion that recurs in prayer psalms. It particularly corresponds to Ps. 85, which also begins from Yhwh's restoration in the past and urges Yhwh to do something like that again (cf. also Ps. 44). So here, Yhwh's past act (vv. 1–3) contrasts with the situation now but encourages the community in its prayer in the present (vv. 4–6) and encourages God to answer it.

The past reversal of fortunes in vv. 1–3 looks like the restoration after the exile. The trouble presupposed by vv. 4–6 then belongs somewhat later. The crop failure presupposed by Haggai may be too soon to be the background, but it instances the kind of experience the psalm refers to, as does the locust blight in Joel and the earlier drought referred to in Jer. 14 (see also the problems reflected in Isa. 56–66 and Nehemiah). Walter Beyerlin notes a series of links with Joel (notably Joel 2:21, 26, 28 [3:1]; 3:1 [4:1]), inferring that the psalmist knew the prophecy, utilized its phrases, and shared some of its perspectives.[5] The most remarkable

3. LXX has past in vv. 1–2a and 3 (and 6a) but future in v. 2c (and 5, 6c). Jerome has future in v. 2.

4. Calvin, *Psalms*, 5:96. Contrast Luther, *First Lectures*, 2:550!

5. See *We Are Like Dreamers* (Edinburgh: Clark, 1982), 43–50. His arguments for the two works' respective dating and for the psalm's semi-polemical relationship to Joel (50–54) are less convincing than his view that the psalm has utilized phrases and thinking from Joel. See also Rudolf Mosis's discussion, "'Mit Jauchzen werden sie ernten," in *Gesammelte Aufsätze zum Alten Testament* (Würzburg: Echter, 1999), 359–81.

difference between them is the psalm's not referring to the need for repentance as the key to restoration.

The first section works *abb'a'*: "We became . . . then . . . then . . . we became."[6] The second section does not have a comparable neat structure. It first goes back to the beginning (that is, vv. 4–5 pick up from vv. 1–2b), with a reference to bringing about restoration, a simile for this, and a reference to weeping and resounding that pairs with the earlier reference to laughter and resounding; this itself works *abb'a'*. The second section then concludes in v. 6 with two more lines expanding on v. 5. This arrangement is worked out partly through further uses of variants on "terrace" structure: compare vv. 1a and 4a; vv. 1b and 3b; v. 2a–b and 2c–d; vv. 2d and 3a; v. 5a and 5b; v. 6a–b and 6c–d.

Presumably the psalm was used in community worship, and Sukkot/New Year would be a plausible occasion, especially if it was an occasion when people prayed for the restoration of Israel.[7]

Song of the Ascents.

Heading. See glossary.
126:1–3. The recollection.

[1]When Yhwh brought about the restoration of Zion,
we became like people dreaming/healing.

LXX, Jerome, and Tg assume that the opening colon refers to bringing back the exiles to Zion, though the expression *šûb šîbâ* more literally means simply "turn a turning." It suggests that whereas a situation had once been one of blessing and fulfillment that then went wrong, eventually Yhwh took it back to what it had been. While this precise phrase comes only here, the more common expression *šûb šĕbût/šĕbît* (see v. 4)[8] usually does refer to the community's restoration after the exile, and the Vrs' inference is plausible. So the psalm begins by looking back to that event. The time reference of the infinitival phrase (more lit. "at the time of Yhwh's bringing about") is determined by the qatal verb in the second colon.

LXX and Tg take the participle in v. 1b to come from *ḥālam* I, "be healthy" ("like people comforted," LXX paraphrases).[9] That fits well with the motif of restoration. The transformation was like that of someone

6. Cf. Fokkelman, *Major Poems*, 3:280.
7. So Mowinckel, *Psalms*, 1:223.
8. 4QPs[e] assimilates v. 1 to v. 4 K.
9. 11QPs[a] *ḥlwmym* also points toward a form of *ḥālam* I; cf. Seybold, *Psalmen*, 485–86; Tobias Nicklas, "Der Text und die Texte," *Bib* 81 (2000): 252–61 (see 256).

regaining health after an illness. They had looked as if they might die, but now they are full of life again.[10] Jerome, however, takes it as *ḥālam* II, "dream." The simile might then refer to the experience of a wonderful dream; we were like people waking after what we took to be a great dream and finding that the dream is reality (contrast Isa. 29:7–8; also Ps. 73:20; Job 20:8).[11] We pinched ourselves to check that we were awake, and found we were. But OT reference to dreaming commonly alludes not merely to that regular human experience but to dreams as a means of revelation (e.g., Dan. 7; Joel 2:28 [3:1]). So the psalm may also refer to Yhwh's having given Israel visionary dreams of restoration from exile. They had turned out not to be empty dreams such as Jeremiah dismissed (Jer. 23:25–28; 29:8). They had come true.

2Then our mouth filled with laughter,
our tongue with resounding.
Then they said among the nations,
"Yhwh has done something great with these people."

But Jeremiah dreamed of restoration, too (cf. 31:26), and spoke of Yhwh's bringing a restoration of Israel that would mean laughter or merrymaking (Jer. 30:18–19; 31:4) and *resounding or shouting (31:7, 12). His promises came true when the community began to rebuild the temple and people sang and shouted and testified and praised Yhwh and wept with joy and shouted for joy in such a way that the noise could be heard from miles away (Ezra 3:10–13). It was indeed as if they were people waking from a dream and finding it was reality, or perceiving that the dreams God had given their prophets had come true, or recovering from illness and finding themselves full of life.

That reference to the noise being heard miles away, and then to the reaction of Judah's adversaries (Ezra 4:1–5), is as near as the Ezra narrative gets to the nations acknowledging that Yhwh has done great things for Judah and Benjamin. The motif is familiar from the story of Israel's beginnings (e.g., Josh. 2:8–11), from psalms summoning the nations to acknowledge Yhwh (e.g., Ps. 96:3, 10), and from declarations of a prophet such as Jeremiah (e.g., 31:10; 33:9). It forms a marked contrast to the scornful question, "Where is your God?" (Pss. 42:3 [4]; 79:10; 115:2; also Joel 2:17).[12] In this psalm, every line is a bicolon with a short (two-stress) second colon, except for v. 2c–d, which is 3-4. The length of v. 2d thus underlines the wonder of what people say among the nations.

10. Cf. John Strugnell, "A Note on Ps. cxxvi.1," *JTS* 7 (1956): 239–43.

11. Or perhaps "we became veritable dreamers/healed people" (cf. NJPS); see the comments on *k* in *HALOT*; GKC 118x; JM 133g.

12. Cf. Kraus, *Psalms 60–150*, 450; Beyerlin, *We Are Like Dreamers*, 43.

But no doubt the declaration in v. 2c–d is as much a statement about what would be an appropriate reaction on the nations' part as a factual statement about their actual reaction. It thus parallels Exod. 15:14–15, an imaginative account of the reaction that would be appropriate on the part of the nations.

> [3]Yhwh has done something great with us;
> we became people rejoicing.

Dramatically, the worshippers conclude this recollection by confirming what the nations said, as if they had not quite realized the significance of Yhwh's action until they heard it on the nations' lips. That is sometimes how things work; when someone else formulates what has happened to us, we see it more clearly ourselves. Simply imagining the nations having that appropriate reaction could have that result. (This would be especially so if these people are enemies rather than friends, as in Ezra-Nehemiah, though that is not explicit.) Indeed, the nations' recognition increases the greatness of what Yhwh has done, so the statement is now more true than it would have been before the nations spoke.

126:4–6. The prayer built on the recollection.

> [4]Yhwh, bring about our restoration,
> like channels in the Negeb.

The psalm goes back to the beginning and reformulates the recollection of what Yhwh once did, in a plea for Yhwh to do it again, or perhaps to do it somewhere else (as v. 4 does not mention Zion). In K, the expression is now the more usual *šûb šĕbût*, which is more easily open to being understood to mean "turn the captivity," on the natural assumption that *šĕbût* comes from the verb *šābâ* "take captive" (cf. BDB). But this does not fit all occurrences of that phrase (esp. Ezek. 16:53; Job 42:10), and more likely *šĕbût* is simply a variant on *šîbâ* in v. 1 (or rather, vice versa) and also comes from *šûb* itself, so that this phrase also means "turn a turning" (cf. *HALOT*). It, too, can thus have broader meaning and need not refer to the exile.[13] To complicate matters further, Q has *šûb šĕbît*. This noun looks more like one that comes from *šābâ*, so that the phrase would mean "turn the captivity." The variants suggest some confusion between the two possibilities in MT (see *HALOT*). Paradoxically, however, in v. 4 the expression does have the more general meaning, and the use of a slightly different word here from v. 1 draws attention to the difference in what the psalm now asks for.

13. See John M. Bracke, "*Šûb šᵉbût*," *ZAW* 97 (1985): 233–44.

The second colon refers to the extraordinary transformation that rain can bring to the Negeb. It need not imply that the Negeb actually does get transformed like that; its miraculous transformation may happen only in the psalmist's imagination. Its actual untransformed state thus provides an image for the untransformed state of the people.[14] But perhaps the psalm has in mind the way winter rains can transform the Negeb landscape, turning the desert briefly but miraculously into flourishing greenery and flowers (as Tg makes explicit)[15] and replenishing such sources of water as will last through the summer. Psalm 124:4–5 referred to such storms in a negative connection; here is the positive side. Núñez sees this image as the key to the psalm: "a pregnant and eloquent simile illuminates the different aspects of this restoration."[16]

> [5]People who sow with weeping
>   will reap with resounding.

The subsequent lines extend the simile, though it is more than a simile. The gift of rain is what people need if v. 4 is to come true, and here "it is almost as if the desert is first watered with tears and rains follow."[17] In Ezra 3:10–13, weeping seems to be a sign of joy just as shouting was, but here weeping and *resounding are set over against each other. There may be a link between this weeping and rejoicing and the same motif that appears in ancient Middle Eastern stories and rituals associated with the agricultural year,[18] but the fact that harvests sometimes fail is enough indication that farmers would sow their seed with fear and anxiety. Will the next harvest be poor again? The reversal in the *abb′a′* structure of the line ("People who sow with weeping, with resounding will reap") puts weeping and resounding next to one another and thus mirrors and emphasizes the reversal the line refers to. NRSV has "may they reap," and that is at least implicit in the line. The declaration in v. 5b describes what will happen if and when Yhwh answers the prayer in v. 4 and repeats the rejoicing to which v. 2 refers. This time, there will be a real harvest, and thus people will utter the shouts of relief that should characterize harvest time. Verses 5–6 might be a promise from a prophet in response to the plea in v. 4, but they are also plausible as

14. So Weiser, *Psalms*, 761–62.

15. Cf. Nelson Glueck, *Rivers in the Desert* (New York: Farrar, 1959), 92–94.

16. Angel Gonzáles Núñez, "Cual torrentes del Neguev," *EstBib* 24 (1965): 349–60 (see 355).

17. Schaefer, *Psalms*, 306.

18. See, e.g., the references to weeping for Baal in the Baal and Anat poems (e.g., *ANET*, 138–41), and see Flemming F. Hvidberg, *Weeping and Laughter in the Old Testament* (Leiden: Brill, 1962), esp. 133–34. But the evidence is circumstantial and the hypothesis hardly necessary, or very illuminating.

the community's declaration of confidence about what will follow from Yhwh's answering its prayer.

> 6He does go crying,
> the one who carries the bag of seed.
> He will indeed come with resounding,
> the one who carries his sheaves.

The final two lines restate v. 5, this time working *aba'b'*.[19] They do not involve a relative clause ("one who goes . . . will come"; cf. NRSV, TNIV) or a concessive clause ("though he goes . . . he will come"; so NJPS); the two lines are quite parallel. Each first colon begins with an infinitive absolute followed by the third-person singular yiqtol of the same verb, the verbs being close to antonyms (go and come) and the infinitival expression conveying emphasis and underlining the contrast.[20] Each second colon begins with the participle "carrying." Here the contrast of winter and summer is expressed first as crying (in the sense of weeping) over against *resounding with joy and relief, and of carrying a bag of seed for sowing over against carrying sheaves of ripened wheat or barley.

Theological Implications

Like life, the psalm is full of weeping and laughter. "One historical reversal of fates, like the return of some captives from exile, does not yet end, once and for all, the fateful course of human suffering and joy."[21] In many parts of the world, people might recall times of blessing but have to contrast them with a current fear that there might not be enough food for next year; the psalm encourages them to remember and to pray.

At the same time, the fact that vv. 4b–6 started off as a simile raises the question whether these lines as a whole are an extended simile. They do not refer to the need of a good harvest; that is a simile for restoration

19. Briggs (*Psalms*, 2:455–57) continues the jussive understanding through v. 6.

20. The line involves an inf. absolute of *hālak*, the finite form of *hālak*, and an inf. absolute of *bākâ*. The inf. absolute of *hālak* can suggest continuity or regularity, but it would usually come after the finite verb and before the second inf., and, anyway, continuity or regularity seems irrelevant here. Putting the inf. first can suggest a concessive meaning ("he will go, albeit weeping"), but that also seems irrelevant. The words are similar to 2 Sam. 3:16, where they suggest simultaneity ("he went, and as he went he wept"), and that is more likely the point here. Admittedly, there the inf. comes second, as one would expect; putting the inf. first makes for emphasis, specifically in the context of the contrast that will follow in v. 6c, where the construction will recur. See JM 123; *IBHS* 35.3.1f (rather than 35.3.2c).

21. Gerstenberger, *Psalms*, 2:341.

that might take other forms. This possibility at least makes the psalm open to being prayed in contexts where the restoration that people need takes forms other than those to which the success of the harvest is key (as has happened in the history of the psalm's interpretation). In the United States, the psalm is one of those set for use on Thanksgiving Day,[22] and people who do not need to wonder whether there will be food in the supermarket might use it to express their thanksgiving for what God has been to the church over the centuries but then contrast that with the state of the church in the parts of the world where the harvest seems less secure.

Rabbi Johanan inferred from v. 2 that our mouths should not be filled with laughter until they made this declaration among the nations, and Rabbi Simeon ben Lachish therefore never laughed again all his life.[23] The psalm's logic seems to be the opposite: it is because we have reason to laugh that the nations come to make their declaration.

22. See, e.g., the *Revised Common Lectionary* (http://divinity.library.vanderbilt.edu/lectionary).

23. *Midrash on Psalms*, 2:308.

Psalm 127

Yhwh Gives, Yhwh Fills

Translation

Song of the Ascents. Solomon's.

1If Yhwh himself does not build a house,
in vain will the builders have labored on it.[1]
If Yhwh himself does not guard a city,
in vain will the guard have been wakeful.
2In vain are you,
people who are early to rise, late to sit down,
People who eat the bread of great toil;
yes,[2] he gives sleep[3] to his beloved one.[4]

3Now: sons are a possession from Yhwh;
the fruit of the womb is a reward.
4Like arrows in the hand of the warrior,
thus are the sons of youth.[5]

1. I take the qatal verbs in vv. 1a and 1c as future perfect, with JM 112i.

2. I take this as an instance of *HALOT*'s *kēn* I (cf. BDB 467), not the more common *kēn* II (BDB 485–87), "thus," which makes poor sense in the context (hence LXX's paraphrase "because").

3. The spelling *šēnā'* for *šēnâ* is Aramaic. For other possible meanings, see J. A. Emerton, "The Meaning of *šēnā'* in Psalm cxxvii 2," *VT* 24 (1954): 15–31; and further Allen, *Psalms 101–150*, 235. None seems an improvement on the traditional understanding.

4. LXX, Jerome have pl., perhaps assimilating to the context.

5. LXX "sons of outcasts" takes *nĕʿûrîm* as from *nāʿar* II. Vg thus renders *excussorum*, which Cassiodorus (*Psalms*, 3:299–300) can then understand to mean "researchers": "as arrows in the hand of the mighty, so also the children of the researchers."

[5]The good fortune of the man
  whose quiver he has filled;
Of them people will not be ashamed[6]
  when they speak with enemies in the gate.[7]

Interpretation

Most of the Songs of the Ascents can be linked to regular Psalms genres, even if they are idiosyncratic instances of them. It is harder so to link Ps. 127. It has a human audience in mind and comprises two four-line teaching poems that might seem quite unrelated. Both could have appeared in Proverbs; there, too, apparently unrelated material can be juxtaposed (e.g., Prov. 30).[8] But if the two sections are of separate origin, they have been juxtaposed as one unit.[9] Attempts have been made to argue for the psalm's original unity on the basis of rhetorical features. For instance, the first section concerns *bônāyw* (its builders), the second concerns sons (*bānîm*); the psalm begins with the city and ends with the city, in the sense that it refers to the city gate. Both sections begin with reference to Yhwh's involvement with us, which is expressed in general terms; both end with a comment on how this affects an individual. This individual is the kind of person who has a position of responsibility in home and community, who has to make sure his household has something to eat and is well protected. It would be a fair inference that the psalm is concerned to bring its message home to such individuals. To do that, its two sections start from those generalizations that might seem uncontroversial and might be widely accepted, and then point out their implications. No one will dispute vv. 1 and 3. Verses 2a–c and 4 sharpen the point, the first by speaking of "you" (but plural, so that the individual is not yet confronted) and the second by beginning to make specific what is good about having sons. Verses 2d and 5 then drive the implications home to this individual, both speaking of what Yhwh has done for him. Both sections move from the family to the city.[10] A Sumerian song in which these two themes also appear (though not as closely as in the

6. I follow MT in linking *mēhem* with "be ashamed" rather than with "filled," which fits the more common usage of *min* and generates a more plausible understanding of the prosody.

7. NRSV emends the verbs to sg.

8. See Leo G. Perdue, *Wisdom and Cult*, SBLDS 30 (Missoula, MT: Scholars, 1977), 297–99.

9. Patrick D. Miller argues strongly for the psalm's unity in *Interpreting the Psalms*, 131–37.

10. This parallelism makes it less likely that vv. 3–5 solve the "problem" set up by vv. 1–2 (so Daniel J. Estes, "Like Arrows in the Hand of a Warrior," *VT* 41 [1991]: 304–11).

psalm) describes the goddess Nisaba as one whose activity undergirds human house building and city building, and later as one who makes possible the conception and birth of children.[11]

The first section includes examples of "terrace" structuring: v. 1a–b and 1c–d both begin "if Yhwh does not" and follow that with a statement beginning "in vain," while "in vain" then also opens the third line. The psalm's similarity to material in Proverbs raises the question why it is in the Psalter rather than there. Presumably this implies it was used in worship, though we do not know how.

Song of the Ascents. Solomon's.

Heading. See glossary. Yet again, nothing in the psalm suggests pilgrimage; indeed, the psalm's horizon is the settled state of city dwellers. The reference to Solomon is apposite given that he was responsible for putting great effort into building a particular house, for Yhwh (v. 1), and into other tasks, according to Ecclesiastes (v. 2), and also for teaching about the implications of these matters, according to Proverbs and Ecclesiastes. He was Yhwh's "beloved" (v. 2); see 2 Sam. 12:25.

127:1–2. The first half of the poem is a four-line reflection on the "vanity" of our activities if Yhwh is not involved or if we forget that Yhwh is involved. The section resembles groups of sayings in Proverbs in which the point lies in the last (e.g., Prov. 30:29–31 and 33). The opening sayings serve to arouse interest and/or establish a common framework for thinking, one nobody would dispute. They thus prepare the way for the more contentious or more important saying with which the series ends.

1 If Yhwh himself does not build a house,
   in vain will the builders have labored on it.
If Yhwh himself does not guard a city,
   in vain will the guard have been wakeful.

There are many senses in which Yhwh builds a house. Yhwh built a house in the heavens (Amos 9:6) and built "his sanctuary" in Jerusalem (Ps. 78:69). The OT often speaks of Yhwh's building a household (e.g., 1 Sam. 2:35; 2 Sam. 7:27; 1 Kings 11:38) and also of Yhwh's (re)building David's fallen shelter (Amos 9:11). The notion of building a household might be stretched further. Yhwh builds Zion (Ps. 102:16 [17]), the cities of Judah (69:35 [36]), and Jerusalem (147:2, there referring to the building up of the community). Yhwh needs to build Jerusalem's walls (51:18 [20]), Yhwh builds David's throne (89:4 [5]), and Yhwh will build

11. See Kraus, *Psalms 60–150*, 455, quoting from A. Falkenstein and W. von Soden, eds., *Sumerische und akkadische Hymnen und Gebete* (Zürich: Artemis, 1953), 66, 67.

Judah and Israel after the exile rather than demolishing them (e.g., Jer. 24:6; 33:7; 45:4). Any of those connections in which one might speak of house building have their equivalents when the second colon moves on to speaking of human house builders. Reference to building a city, building Zion, or building Jerusalem would lead well into v. 1c–d; reference to building a house or household (cf. Ruth 4:11; Prov. 14:1) or building the community after the exile would lead well into vv. 3–5. But there is no need to tie down the saying's meaning to one of these. It is the nature of a proverb to be open.

Laboring (*ʿāmal*) suggests hard work and effort that take a lot of energy and may or may not tire a person in a way that seems negative rather than positive. Its being vain (*šāwʾ*), like human deliverance (108:12 [13]; cf. Jer. 46:11), recalls Ecclesiastes, which declares it to be *hebel* (see especially 2:9–26). Yet the two notions are different. Ecclesiastes means we may succeed in what we seek to do, but it may then be pointless. The psalm means we may not succeed in what we seek to do. Ecclesiastes simply assumes that God is not involved in what we do. The psalm assumes that God might or might not be so involved, and whether that is the case is crucial to whether our efforts succeed. But the psalm's point is in fact like one that recurs in Ecclesiastes and in Proverbs. We can plan something carefully, work hard at it, and be responsible and creative in implementing our plans, and everything can go wrong in a way we could never have foreseen.

The notion of guarding a city is more clearly defined than that of building a house.[12] The Psalms often refer to Yhwh guarding people (e.g., 97:10; 116:6; 121:2, 3, 5, 7; 145:20). The assumption will doubtless be that people also seek to look after themselves, as v. 1d implies; Yhwh's guarding does not mean people can be careless. The psalm does not assume that Yhwh's guarding the city means it need not put guards on duty through the night watches. Its security depends on both human and divine action. Thus the lookout has battled sleep through his watch and made himself stay awake on the assumption that it makes a difference. But the psalm's polemic is not attacking human carelessness that evades taking responsibility but again noting that the best human carefulness cannot guarantee results.

Deuteronomy 28 warns that disobedience to Yhwh might mean that a man would build a house but not be able to live in it and that all the towns in the land might fall. Three rabbis visited a city where there was no teacher of Scripture or instructor in the oral law. They sent for the

12. "House" and "city" are a recurrent word pair (see Daniel E. Fleming, "'House'/'City,'" *JBL* 105 [1986]: 689–93; idem, "Psalm 127," *ZAW* 107 [1995]: 435–44). But this does not settle exegetical questions in the psalm.

city's chief watchmen and declared them actually to be the destroyers of the city because "the watchmen of the city are the teachers of Scripture and instructors of Oral Law."[13] But sometimes there is no such explanation for a man's not being able to live in the house he has built and for the failure of the committed watchfulness of the guards. Yhwh does not make it possible. This is "just one of those things."

The declarations in v. 1 are uncontroversial, to judge from the way they parallel statements in Proverbs and Ecclesiastes (though they are often evaded both by Christians and non-Christians in Western culture, where we like to feel we are in control of our destinies). But the point about articulating them lies in what will now follow.

> **2**In vain are you,
> people who are early to rise, late to sit down,
> People who eat the bread of great toil;
> yes, he gives sleep to his beloved one.

In the opening two words (v. 2a) the psalm signals that we are coming to the significance for the listeners of the sayings in v. 1. Literally it says "Vanity to you." Fokkelman calls this a "swearword" and "near-curse."[14] With emphasis the verse first takes up the word translated "in vain" and makes it the opening word in the sentence. It then follows with an expression that involves the listeners rather than leaving them objectively distanced.

The two lines work *abb'a'*, with the middle cola comprising parallel participial clauses.[15] They generalize the lifestyle referred to by v. 1b and 1d as that of people who get up early to work and work all day without a break until evening. The point of v. 2c might then be that they thus eat only at the end of a very long day of great toil or that they thus never sit down during the day but eat their lunch on the run. Either way, they "eat the bread of great toil" (intensive plural): their eating is mixed up with the toilsomeness of their work. Whereas labor (v. 1b) is an ambiguous word, which can be negative but also can denote the positive if tiring expenditure of energy, toil is unambiguous. It is work that is simply tiring. That is how work is if one never takes a break. One expects toilsomeness to characterize work since human life went wrong (Gen. 3:16–17). As with other consequences of that disobedience, such as the tension in relationships between human beings and between humanity and the animal world, it is possible to work against this feature of human life. But if we do not do so, it overwhelms. Thus it is with the toilsomeness

13. *Midrash on Psalms*, 2:310.

14. *Major Poems*, 3:284.

15. MT thus links v. 2b and 2c, placing the mid-verse division after v. 2c.

of work. By working through a long day without intermission, we give in to sin. Sym assumes the word refers to toilers rather than toil, and this would make good sense. It might suggest that the householder is behaving like a mere laborer.

The opening and closing cola thus form a frame around these two descriptions of the listeners. The separation of the two elements in the frame underlines the contrast between them. On one hand there is vanity. What is true about building and guarding is true about all work. It is vain if it is not accompanied by Yhwh's involvement; it may unaccountably achieve nothing. On the other hand, if we recognize that Yhwh not only needs to be involved with our life but actually is involved with our life, then we do not fall into the trap that the middle two cola describe. Therefore (the final colon says), we take advantage of the fact that he gives sleep to his beloved one. The line as a whole thus completes a reversal of the order of statements over against that in v. 1a–b and 1c–d. There we had references to Yhwh's involvement, then to our activity. Here we have had three cola about our activity, but reference to Yhwh's activity rounds off the section and brings it to a close. It underscores the line's point if we translate v. 2d "he gives in sleep to his beloved one."[16] The statement then makes a related point to those in v. 1. Our activity is not the only factor in making things happen; Yhwh's activity also contributes. We can afford to relax and sleep, because Yhwh continues to be active when we do so. "Yhwh's blessing makes rich; toil does not add to it" (Prov. 10:22). But the more straightforward translation "he gives sleep" also fits well. As well as getting up early and depriving themselves of sleep, the excessively hard workers not only decline to take a lunch break but decline to take the siesta that should follow, or they not only work late but decline to go to bed when they should, despite the fact that sleep is Yhwh's gift.

The verse thus clarifies the point about v. 1. The builder and the guard are both figures or metaphors for the man who needs to make sure that everything gets done, and also illustrations of what is involved in his leadership in family and community. The head of a household is responsible for building the household and for sharing in the guarding of the city. He is not to get overwhelmed by that. Yhwh gives sleep. The last colon also individualizes the point in order to bring it home to individuals, but in doing so it speaks of this man as Yhwh's "beloved." Yhwh loves him! That is why Yhwh gives him sleep. The surprising comment also closes off vv. 1–2 in another way. The observations about human effort

16. So GKC 118i; DG 117b; Th. Booij, "Psalm 127,2b," *Bib* 81 (2000): 262–68. But see the discussion in Vinzenz Hamp, "'Der Herr gibt es den Seinen im Schlaf,'" in *Wort, Lied und Gottesspruch*, ed. J. Schreiner (J. Ziegler Festschrift; Würzburg: Echter, 1972), 2:71–79.

and divine involvement in vv. 1–2 are reason for some anxiety; hence the human instinct is to avoid their implications. We can never know whether the efforts we expend in what we are trying to do will lead anywhere. Yhwh may cause or allow them to be frustrated by events we could never have predicted and made allowance for. But that aspect of Yhwh's involvement in our lives is counterbalanced by the fact that Yhwh loves us. Even the disappointments, frustrations, and reversals can be embraced by that.

127:3–5. The second half of the poem reflects on the blessings of having a large family.

> 3Now: sons are a possession from Yhwh;
> the fruit of the womb is a reward.

"Possession" (*naḥălâ*) is most familiar as a term for the land or people as Yhwh's possession (e.g., 106:5, 40). Here it has a less technical meaning, as in Job 20:29; 27:13; 31:2. There it stands in parallelism with "allocation" (*ḥēleq*), here with "reward" or wages (*śākār*). There it carries some irony, denoting something unpleasant that Yhwh gives in return for people's wrongdoing. Here the meaning is more straightforward, though we cannot press the idea that what Yhwh gives is a payment (any more than in Gen. 15:1).[17] The emphasis lies rather on the value of what the man receives and the certainty that it really belongs to him (which is also the point of *naḥălâ*). These sons, then, here have no significance for themselves or for the owner of the womb that bears them; the only interest within the psalm's purview is their father's.[18] But vv. 4–5 will eventually make clear that this usefulness of the sons positively affects the whole family, including mother and daughters, and Gerstenberger suggests it might have been written by a woman.[19] The psalmist would have granted that daughters were also a possession from Yhwh and were among the fruit of the womb that were Yhwh's reward; there is no direct suggestion in the OT that (for instance) the birth of a daughter would be unwelcome, and there are many indications of an awareness of the importance and responsibility of daughters and mothers in their own right and not merely in their potential or actual capacity to bear children (sons!) (for instance, Deut. 5:14; 12:12, 18). But in connection

17. Contrast Tg's gloss "for good deeds," part of a thoroughgoing moral reading of the psalm: the people in v. 2 get up early to commit robbery, stay up late to commit fornication, and eat the food of the poor, and here in v. 3 it is upright sons that are a gift from God.

18. Cf. Madipoane Masenya, "An Eco*bosadi* Reading of Psalm 127.3–5," in *Earth Story*, ed. Habel, 109–22 (see 116–21).

19. *Psalms*, 2:347.

with the matter vv. 4–5 go on to discuss, in the social context it is sons that are significant. Thus NRSV is right not to gender-inclusivize v. 3 (contrast TNIV).

> [4]Like arrows in the hand of the warrior,
> thus are the sons of youth.

So why are sons valuable? The psalm offers only one reason. They are like weapons that can be used for offense or defense. This is particularly so if they are born when the father is young. They will then be grown up by the time their father is middle-aged and is a person of responsibility and position in the community, and therefore sometimes has the need v. 5 presupposes (the point here is not that they will be able to offer their parents support in their old age). But the line offers only a simile; such sons are *like* arrows in a warrior's hand.

> [5]The good fortune of the man
> whose quiver he has filled;
> Of them people will not be ashamed
> when they speak with enemies in the gate.

The first two cola declare the good *fortune of the man in the position v. 4 described, though going beyond it in making explicit that he has *many* sons. His quiver is full of these arrows. The context (see v. 3) suggests it is Yhwh who has filled his quiver rather than the man himself.[20]

Only in the second line does the psalm come closer to clarifying how the sons are useful, though it has more than one possible meaning. The final verb is *dābar* (piel). If this is the rare verb *dābar*, meaning "destroy, drive away" (e.g., 18:47 [48]),[21] then the sons are people capable of playing a key part in the defense of the city. That fits with the earlier references to guarding it and to weapons. Yet guarding is different from fighting, and the stress there was on the insufficiency of the human action. Further, the reference to guarding the city related to the point then made in v. 2, while the weaponry language in v. 4 was a simile.

More likely, then, the verb is the very familiar *dābar*, meaning "speak," as the Vrs take it. "Speaking with" here refers to legal or quasi-legal confrontation (as, for instance, Josh. 17:14; 20:4).[22] Anyone can be the victim of scams, false accusations, or theft, as the Psalms often make

20. Cf. Allen, *Psalms 101–150*, 235.

21. See *HALOT*.

22. Cf. Estes, "Like Arrows in the Hand of a Warrior," 308.

clear. A man with a houseful of hefty young men will be no pushover in these circumstances. They will stand up to such adversaries. Perhaps the psalm refers to the semiformal gathering of the community court in the plaza inside the city gate (cf. Tg). But it may simply refer to that same public location as the place where they would confront such adversaries in public, without this being a legal or semiformal legal situation. They will do so with confidence, and people will be impressed by them; or the man himself will have reason to be proud of them (so some LXX MSS, which have a singular verb in v. 5c; this would make good sense).

Theological Implications

"When philosophers argue concerning the political affairs of a state, . . . they discourse with consummate skill upon everything that is necessary to be known on this subject, except that they omit the principle point," the need that "God stretches forth his hand to them, or rather makes use of them as his instruments."[23] The same will be true of sociologists of the family. If we leave God out of consideration, we will not understand the city or the family, or be able to work for their upbuilding.

But we have noted that the concern with the house and the city introduces a more general point. The two sections of the psalm combine to urge a simple message on the man who bears the burden of responsibility for his household: relax. In the United States, people are getting less and less sleep in order to be able to do their work, and they are incurring more and more of a sleep deficit that generates illness and accident. Apparently this is not merely a North American problem.[24] Commentators on the psalm hasten to assure their readers that it does not imply a countenancing of laziness.[25] When commentators or preachers reassure people that a text should not be taken too radically, it is a sign it has something important to say. Commentators, of course, are people who rise early and stay up late at their work, as if it were crucial to the kingdom of God as well as to their careers. The text confronts us in our pretensions about our work being indispensable and bids us relax. We

23. Calvin, *Psalms*, 5:105–6.

24. Benjamin A. Ntreh ("Towards an African Biblical Hermeneutical," *Africa Theological Journal* 19 [1990]: 247–54 [see 251–52]) notes the challenge of v. 2 in his African context.

25. Cf. Midrash Tehillim, which neatly reverses v. 2d by taking *yĕdîdô* as from *nādad* rather than *yādad* and renders "he will surely give to those who banish sleep" (*Midrash on Psalms*, 2:310, 518); cf. Rashi.

are to be vigilant against *irreligiosa solicitudo pro Deo,* "a blasphemous anxiety to do God's work for him."[26]

In the context of Western society, it is extraordinary to think of the family being able to function in the way presupposed here. It would be nice to think that the church could model an alternative way of being human and being family, such as the psalm points to.

26. Eugene H. Peterson, *A Long Obedience in the Same Direction* (repr., Downers Grove: InterVarsity, 2000), 109. He attributes the Latin to Hilary of Tours, perhaps meaning Hilary of Poitiers, but I have not been able to locate the quotation anywhere. It's a nice quote, though.

Psalm 128
Work, Home, Family

Translation

Song of the Ascents.

1The good fortune of everyone who reveres Yhwh,
who walks in his ways.
2The fruit of your hands you will surely eat:
your good fortune, good things for you!
3Your wife like a fruiting vine,
in the inner rooms of your house,
Your sons like the slips of olive trees,
around your table.

4Now: surely thus will the man be blessed,
who reveres Yhwh.
5May Yhwh bless you from Zion;
look upon the good things of Jerusalem
All the days of your life;
6look at your grandchildren.

Well-being on Israel.

Interpretation

The psalm begins like the aleph colon in Ps. 112, and like that psalm it is for the most part a poem that could have appeared in Proverbs.

It thus also resembles Ps. 127, and it begins as Ps. 127 closed, with a declaration of "good fortune." But as Ps. 112 actually begins "Praise Yah," before it ends Ps. 128 is praying for Yhwh's blessing in a way that a poem in Proverbs would not, and praying for Yhwh's well-being for Israel. So this declaration about the good fortune of people who revere Yhwh does compare with other psalms that begin with that expression (Pss. 1; 32; 41; 119). Like Ps. 112 it focuses on the individual, and as in Ps. 127, that individual is the male head of a household.

The psalm comprises two sections that work out the implications of being someone who reveres Yhwh. The first (vv. 1–3) does so by exclamations on the "good fortune" that issues from revering Yhwh. The second (vv. 4–6) moves on to talk in terms of the "blessing" that comes from that stance and speaks in terms of a prayer or pronouncement of blessing. After their initial declarations, both sections give most space to the concrete fruits that embody the nature of good fortune or blessing. Each section begins by speaking in the third person (vv. 1, 4) and then moves to direct address of the individual who can enjoy the fruit. Each spells out its key word (good fortune/bless) with reference to "good." The psalm closes with an exclamatory prayer for Israel, repeating the prayer that closes Ps. 125.

One can imagine the psalm being declaimed at a festival. Its focus on men might fit the fact that there was more specific obligation on men than on women to attend the festivals. For better and for worse, their position put extra responsibility and pressure on them, and like Ps. 127 the psalm promises them Yhwh's support. It would be natural to infer that the blessing in vv. 5–6b was declared by a priest, and then that this might be true of the whole psalm.

Song of the Ascents.

Heading. See glossary. Of all the Songs of the Ascents, Ps. 128 might most plausibly be seen as belonging inherently to a pilgrimage context.

128:1–3. The declaration.

1The good fortune of everyone who reveres Yhwh,
who walks in his ways.

Having declared the *good fortune of the person who *reveres Yhwh, the opening line answers the question "What does revering Yhwh look like?" by defining it as walking in Yhwh's ways (see 119:3). But why does the psalm make this declaration of good fortune? It might have the effect of inspiring people to revere Yhwh, or it might encourage people who do revere Yhwh by assuring them that the fruits of this stance will follow.

[2]The fruit of your hands you will surely eat:
your good fortune, good things for you!

The transition to direct address is unexpected (contrast Ps. 1); it has the effect of bringing the objective point home to the individual in a way that demands appropriation. Psalm 127 implicitly warned about the possibility of working too hard to make sure that the family had enough to eat. That is unwise because it presupposes that everything depends on us; it is acting as if God did not exist. Psalm 128 has started from reverence for Yhwh, which is a very different starting point from that confronted by Ps. 127. It now begins to spell out the implications of the declaration in v. 1 by making the converse point to the one Ps. 127 made. We can have confidence about eating the fruit of our labors (lit. eating "the labor of your hands") if we revere Yhwh rather than assuming everything depends on us. This attitude means Yhwh gets involved with us.

In a moment, the psalm will continue to spell things out in a way that corresponds to the agenda of Ps. 127, but first in v. 2b it underlines the promise in general terms, in a further pair of exclamations that expand on the first word of the psalm. It is *your* *good fortune. The objective exclamation makes the important general point; the second-person suffix makes sure that the listener hears it as personally applied. That dynamic continues in the further exclamation that this good fortune means something *good for you.

[3]Your wife like a fruiting vine,
in the inner rooms of your house,
Your sons like the slips of olive trees,
around your table.

In Ps. 127, only the womb of the man's wife appeared. Here she herself is mentioned, but once again the psalm is really concerned only with her womb; it is her capacity to have children that is in focus. Women of course can be valued from other angles in the OT; there are women prophets, women worship leaders, and women enjoying a sexual relationship whose focus does not lie on having children. But the topic of concern in Ps.128 is different. In a traditional society, having children can no more be taken for granted than the availability of food. These could be taken for granted even less in a context such as Judah in the Persian period. The promise of good fortune in the form of food or fertility therefore means a lot.

Likewise, other parts of the OT emphasize the role the woman of the house plays outside the house itself (see especially Prov. 31:10–31);

because of the psalm's topic of concern, this line emphasizes her role inside the house, in the private life of the family in its inner rooms.[1] The psalm rather corresponds to Gen. 3:16–19, noted in connection with Ps. 127, where the specified role of the woman is to bear children and that of the man is to work the ground.

The sons also reappear from Ps. 127. They are likely grown-up sons, whose wives will also be present as the household sits around the dining table in those inner parts of the house, though they remain unmentioned for the same reasons that emerge from the focus of the psalm. "Slips" are the transplanted shoots of a plant; the man who is addressed is the actual olive tree. Once again, the flourishing of family and society that is concretized not only in the birth of sons but in their coming to adulthood cannot be taken for granted in a traditional society; in the twenty-first century we can think in terms of the AIDS pandemic.

The two lines are parallel, mother ("wife") and sons, and inner rooms and table. Neither the OT nor archeological discoveries tell us what the inner rooms are, but there is no particular reason to reckon that they are the women's quarters, and the parallelism in the psalm would suggest that they are where the family meets and eats. And both lines involve not mere prosaic literal references to a wife and children, but inviting similes. The vine and the olive are key trees without which life would be impossible, and they thus generate key metaphors; Israel itself is both a vine and an olive. That would add further resonance to these declarations.[2]

128:4–6. The prayers.

> [4]Now: surely thus will the man be blessed,
> who reveres Yhwh.

One might have thought that this line with its further reference to *revering Yhwh nicely rounded off vv. 1–4, but the new declaration begins by speaking of "blessing" rather than "good fortune" (TNIV uses "blessed" for both words), and this language will be taken further in v. 5. This suggests that v. 4 parallels v. 1 as the beginning of a section rather than forming an inclusion; or perhaps it constitutes an interlocking hook between the two sections, the first colon looking forward and the

1. If the psalm had used the form from *yārēk*, which means thighs or loins as well as occasionally sides (e.g., of the altar), one might have reckoned that there was a sexual reference in this word (cf. Grossberg, *Centripetal and Centrifugal Structures*, 43–44); but its use of the form from *yarkâ*, which is not used for parts of the body, means that any such allusion is very indirect.

2. Cf. Weiser, *Psalms*, 768–69. See further David R. Blumenthal, *Facing the Abusing God* (Louisville: Westminster John Knox, 1993), 75.

second backward. The transition also raises the question of the difference between good fortune and blessing.[3] Both can look to the future and be designed to arouse anticipation and motivate toward commitment to Yhwh. But "good fortune" describes a state or an experience and does not comment on the agency that brings it about, while "bless" refers to the personal action that generates that state or experience. Thus the pual verb in v. 4 indeed describes an action or process; it is not a description of a state.

> **5**May Yhwh bless you from Zion;
> look upon the good things of Jerusalem
> All the days of your life;
> **6a**look at your grandchildren.

While v. 4 could have been a continuation of the speech of Proverbs, vv. 5–6 make us retrospectively reframe it as marking a transition to a different way of thinking. Yhwh would be assumed to be behind good fortune, but the term itself works within the framework of a recognition that a natural process leads from obedience to good fortune. Yhwh does not need to take direct action to make that happen. In contrast, Yhwh is the implicit agent behind the passive verb in v. 4, and now becomes the explicit agent of this blessing. And because blessing does involve Yhwh's action, it is naturally the subject of prayer, which puts into the form of a plea or wish the matter that was apparently a simple declaration in v. 4. Far from inhibiting prayer, then, a statement such as that in v. 4 encourages prayer.

As well as moving from declaration to prayer, in v. 5 the geographical focus moves from that of a home, perhaps in a village rather than in the city, to that of Jerusalem. There is no precise parallel for the idea of blessing coming from Zion, with the implications for ordinary life that are worked out here (134:3, where the actual words recur, is nearest, if this refers to ordinary people). But it would be natural to speak in such terms. People gathered in Zion/Jerusalem as an expression of their reverence for Yhwh and their commitment to walking in Yhwh's ways, and there they sought blessing on their family life from the God who had agreed to make a permanent home in Zion/Jerusalem. Their blessing thus issues from there.

The cola in vv. 5–6a interweave in a variety of ways. Structurally, the lines work *aba'b'*; the two second cola express parallel biddings, suggesting that in turn "all the days of your life" continues "May Yhwh

3. Cf. Carl Keller, "Les 'béatitudes' de l'Ancien Testament," in *Hommage à Wilhelm Vischer* (Montpellier: Causse, Graille, Castelnau, 1960), 88–100, who is inclined to assimilate them.

bless you from Zion." The two parallel biddings instance the Hebrew idiom whereby a promise can be expressed by means of imperatives that follow on a jussive.[4]

In content, however, the two parts of each line complement each other. Thus experiencing Yhwh's blessing from Zion is re-expressed as looking upon the good things of Jerusalem; that is, Zion/Jerusalem is the source of blessings/good things. The parallelism in v. 5a–b then makes it likely that v. 5b refers to good things coming *from* Jerusalem to people who live elsewhere, rather than to good things coming *to* Jerusalem. It will make sense if the context in which the psalm is used is the worship of the temple there, and it will also make sense if many of the people who hear this blessing are pilgrims who would want the blessing that comes from Yhwh's presence there to extend to their homes in Judah and elsewhere.

In turn, "all the days of your life" is re-expressed as the opportunity to "look at your grandchildren." The expression in v. 6b is thus slightly different from that in v. 5b. There it is *rā'â b*, which often has the implication of looking at something with feeling, almost enjoying (cf. 27:13; 106:5 and the parallelism). Here it is *rā'â* alone, which simply means "see." When your children have had children and you have seen them, you have seen the evidence that you have fulfilled your purpose as a man and an Israelite. You have not only brought the next generation into the world but witnessed the arrival of the generation after that.

6bWell-being on Israel.

The horizon has broadened through the psalm, from the individual who reveres Yhwh, to his marriage, to his household, to his relationship with Zion/Jerusalem. It eventually widens to become a prayer for the *well-being of the whole people that meets there.

Theological Implications

The maxim in v. 1 "is so much at variance with the common opinion of men, that very few will give it their assent. . . . So much the more requisite then is it to dwell upon the consideration of this truth."[5] The psalm is therefore a challenge to live in faith and hope. Admittedly, the assumption that one cannot take for granted one's supply of food,

4. See GKC 110i; *TTH* 65; DG 86b; JM 116f. The use of this idiom also makes it likely that the preceding verb means "may Yhwh bless" (cf. 29:11), not "Yhwh will bless" (cf. 115:12–13).

5. Calvin, *Psalms*, 5:113, 114.

the fertility of a woman's womb, and the expectation that one's children will grow to adulthood, is also alien to much Western experience. Yet there are many women who want to have children and find that they cannot conceive; and there are parts of Los Angeles where it cannot be assumed that sons will grow up to adulthood. The psalm invites us not to take such things for granted. "Psalm 128 articulates a theology of blessing as it celebrates the daily realms of work and family as gifts of God." It thus resists "our persistent tendency to view the world purely in secular terms."[6]

The stress on wives and children is a stumbling block to ancient commentators for whom celibacy was a key value.[7] Amusingly, it can also be a stumbling block to modern commentators for whom a wife is more than a womb and daughters count as much as sons.[8] Once more, when Scripture is saying something that we do not like, we do well to pay attention. Having rightly deplored the sexist attitudes that people could derive from the psalm, we would be wise to reflect on the significance (for men and for women) of having children, particularly if we are people who are inclined to downplay it. The psalm also speaks to modern Western attitudes by inviting men and women to value what happens inside the house and not to think that value attaches only to what happens outside, in the community, business, society, and politics.

6. McCann, "Psalms," 1201.

7. E.g., Augustine, *Psalms*, 609; Cassiodorus, *Psalms*, 3:303; cf. Jerome, *Homilies*, 1:317.

8. See esp. Marc Zvi Brettler, "Women and Psalms," in *Gender and Law in the Hebrew Bible and the Ancient Near East*, ed. Victor H. Matthews and others, JSOTSup 262 (Sheffield: Sheffield Academic Press, 1998), 25–56 (see 27–37); he overpresses the point in suggesting, e.g., that the OT in general and this psalm in particular views a wife as her husband's sexual chattel.

Psalm 129

The Promise of Empty Harvest

Translation

Song of the Ascents.

1So much[1] did people attack me from my youth,
Israel is indeed[2] to say,
2So much did people attack me from my youth,
though they did not prevail over me.
3Over my back plowers [MT] faithless people [LXX, 11QPs[a]] plowed,
they made their long furrow(s).[3]
4Yhwh—he is faithful;
he cut the rope of the faithless.[4]

5May they/They shall be shamed and turn away back,
all who are against Zion.
6May they/They shall become like the grass on roofs,
which before it has been plucked,[5] has withered,
7With which a reaper has not filled his hand,
a gatherer his arm,

1. For the use of *rabbat,* see 120:6; 123:4. LXX has "often," but contrast the expression in Neh. 9:28.

2. *-nāʾ.*

3. Q has sg. *lĕmaʿănîtām,* a hapax; K has pl. *lmʿnwtm,* which comes only one other time (but see *DTT*, 818).

4. LXX, Jerome understand "Faithful Yhwh—he cut . . . ," but MT's disjunctive accent on *yhwh* along with its locating the midpoint division of the verse after the first two words suggests that the words are a noun clause, as is usually the case with phrases such as *yhwh ṣaddîq*.

5. Lit. "before [someone] has plucked [it]." Aq, Jerome, Tg suggest "before it has shot up" (cf. BDB), but this requires considerable stretching of the meaning of *šālap*. Rather, cf. LXX, Th, Sym.

[8]And passersby have not said,
"Yhwh's blessing to you;[6]
we bless you[7] in Yhwh's name."

Interpretation

Like Pss. 124–28, the psalm begins by speaking *of* Yhwh rather than *to* Yhwh; indeed, it does so throughout. As was the case with Ps. 126, the first section (vv. 1–4) recalls troubles from the past and Yhwh's act of deliverance, and the second section (vv. 5–8) builds on that background in envisaging a further act of deliverance in a present crisis.[8] A difference is that Ps. 129 explicitly recalls attacks from other people, and vv. 5–8 also have that focus (whereas Ps. 126:4–6 related to hopes for the harvest). Thus here the recollection in vv. 1–4 concerns "them"; so do vv. 5–8, which are thus jussive rather than second-person. Further, the recollection in Ps. 126 concerned Yhwh's restoration of "Zion." The recollection in Ps. 129 concerns "Israel," the subject of the OT's story going back to its beginning; it is the present problems that affect "Zion," the little postexilic community focused on Jerusalem.

But there are two ways in which a congregation might understand the verbs in vv. 5–8 and thus might use the whole psalm. One is to take it as another instance of the pattern of Ps. 126, where the second section is a plea for deliverance to happen again. The verbs are then jussive, the section is a further such plea, and the psalm as a whole is a community prayer psalm. The other is to take the verbs in vv. 5–8 as yiqtol, the second section thus being a declaration of confidence in what Yhwh will do, repeating the pattern of vv. 1–4. The psalm as a whole is then a psalm of confidence, in significance more like Ps. 124 (which starts in a similar way, with a colon and a summons to Israel and the first colon repeated) or Ps. 125 than Ps. 126.

Once again vv. 1–2 begin with an example of "terrace" parallelism, while the second section incorporates a further three-line enjambment, taking the picture of the attackers' downfall to ever-increasing gravity (but encouragement for the congregation).

Song of the Ascents.

Heading. See glossary.

6. *ʾĂlêkem*, not usual *ʿălêkem* (for which cf. 11QPs[a]).

7. Performative qatal.

8. For other approaches to the structure, see A. J. O. van der Wal, "The Structure of Psalm cxxix," *VT* 28 (1988): 364–67.

129:1–4. The recollection.

[1]So much did people attack me from my youth,
Israel is indeed to say,
[2]So much did people attack me from my youth,
though they did not prevail over me.

The congregation begins to tell Israel's story as if it is the story of an individual human being; the psalm recycles the language of an individual prayer to put it on the community's lips.[9] It looks right back to its "youth" (cf. Jer. 2–3) and thus to occasions such as Amalek's attack on Israel at Rephidim (Exod. 17:8–13), at the beginning, though it never actually identifies the people who so attacked over the years. Israel's story is one long tale of assault by unnamed foes, among whom the Israel that uses the psalm can thus locate its own attackers. In the second colon, the Israel that is invited to speak may thus be the worshipping congregation that is essentially identical with the Zion of v. 5 that is under attack now; that would parallel the usage in Ps. 124. The colon might even be literally inviting the actual present congregation to join in the psalm, though that seems a rather prosaic understanding. The colon more likely has rhetorical than rubrical significance. Indeed, the difference in the context in this psalm suggests that it is more likely inviting the congregation to imagine the historical Israel reflecting on its experience.[10]

Verse 2a simply repeats v. 1a and thus continues the heightening of suspense begun by v. 1b, so that rhetorically v. 2b arrives with some force. Yet v. 2b is in itself a rather mild statement. It therefore again drives us forward.

[3]Over my back plowers [MT] faithless people [LXX, 11QPs[a]] plowed,
they made their long furrow(s).
[4]Yhwh—he is faithful;
he cut the rope of the faithless.

The second pair of lines might be read as describing a specific, more recent experience than the recurrent one described in vv. 1–2; v. 4 would then be a statement of faith about what Yhwh is now committed to doing.[11] But the parallel in the sequence describing what people did to

9. Cf. Crüsemann, *Studien zur Formgeschichte*, 168–73. Seybold (*Psalmen*, 129) takes it as an individual's recollection, with which Israel is invited to identify. Cf. also Spurgeon's comments, *Treasury of David*, 6:108.

10. Gunkel (*Psalmen*, 558–59) notes that v. 1b makes clear that the psalm indeed refers to the community and not an individual.

11. DG 60c nuances this in taking the qatal in v. 4b as precative.

"me" and then how their destructive purpose was frustrated, in vv. 1–2 and then in vv. 3–4, suggests rather that vv. 3–4 go over the same ground as vv. 1–2. In this second sequence, both the attacks and the deliverance are described much more vividly, though there are two ways of reading the description. It might be that the image changes, and Israel is not now an individual human being but an ox hauling the plow. The plowers, then, are not only plowing the ground but plowing the animal, whipping it so that deep furrows appear down its back. Verse 4 will then refer to the freeing of the animal from the ropes that tie it to the plow.[12]

But less inference is required if we read vv. 3–4 as in metaphorical continuity with vv. 1–2. The personified Israel is now lying on the ground. Figuratively what happened to that person is that they were like the ground itself when it was being plowed before sowing. The plowers (as MT calls them) who were clearly *faithless people (so LXX, 11QPs[a]) did their job well. They plowed long furrows: down the victim's back. Perhaps there is a reference to war crimes (cf. Amos 1), but if so the practice has become a metaphor applied to the personified Israel, so that its significance is not so different from that of Mic. 3:12, which threatens that Zion will be plowed up. But it may be that the description of the fate of the personified Israel itself involves a metaphor, and what the enemy did to this individual was beat him or whip him or tie him up (see v. 4b) so as to leave long weals down his back.

Whatever the precise significance of the action, it is a frightening description. It is then doubly confronted by v. 4. Suddenly the first word in the line introduces a whole new factor. Where has Yhwh been before? Yhwh has been rhetorically and practically missing, but now bursts onto the scene. There is not even a "but" to announce that another factor is about to intervene. Further, the word order puts "Yhwh" first; usually such sentences put the adjective first (e.g., 92:15 [16]; 100:5; 103:8; 111:4; 113:4; 135:5; 138:6; 145:8, 9, 17, 18). Further, the psalm leaps beyond Yhwh's actual action, or perhaps stands back and looks behind it, in declaring that Yhwh is *faithful.

Again that heightens suspense, making us ask what was the evidence of this and what it was that dealt with the issues raised by v. 3a. The second colon at last tells us. The plowmen were *faithless people who had tied up "Israel" with rope in taking him captive, like Samson (Judg. 15:13–14; 16:11–12). Yhwh burst in and cut the rope. Israel bound free, from Egypt, from Amalek, from Moab, from Philistia, from Assyria, from Babylon. . . .

129:5–8. The prayer or declaration of confidence. A recollection such as that in v. 4 can be both an expression of pain and an invitation to

12. Cf. Keel, *Symbolism*, 98.

hope. Here the latter predominates. As we note in the introduction to the psalm, the verbs that express that hope may be understood as statements of confidence or as prayers.

> [5]May they/They shall be shamed and turn away back,
> all who are against Zion.

Israel had all those attackers or assailants (*ṣārar*, v. 1). Now Zion has people *against it (*śānēʾ*); it has enemies. On the basis of what Yhwh did in the past, the psalm pleads that the enemies may turn back in disgrace, or it declares that they will; either way, the expression is a hendiadys. There is no metaphor here; they are besiegers or battlers, and the psalm wants to see this army flee. Again, they are not identified. Presumably they are groups such as appear in Ezra-Nehemiah, but their not being identified makes the psalm accessible in different contexts.

> [6]May they/They shall become like the grass on roofs,
> which before it has been plucked, has withered,
> [7]With which a reaper has not filled his hand,
> a gatherer his arm,
> [8]And passersby have not said,
> "Yhwh's blessing to you;
> we bless you in Yhwh's name."

The psalm moves back to simile, which it develops in a rhetorical tour de force for its extent and its irony. It also incorporates a neat paronomasia, as shame (*yēbōšû*, v. 5) and withering (*yābēš*) are closely related; the two words form a bracket round vv. 5 and 6. The image of withering is a familiar one; people witnessed nature withering every year during the summer, and experienced it especially sharply from time to time through drought or locust epidemic (see Joel 1). The image thus recurs in laments, usually as a self-description: I or we are withered like grass (Pss. 22:15 [16]; 90:6; 102:4, 11 [5, 12]; Isa. 40:6–8; Ezek. 37:11). It also makes a powerful image for the downfall and ruin of another (Job 15:30; 18:16; Isa. 19:5, 7; 40:24). In Isa. 37:27 Assyria is Yhwh's means of making cities like shriveled grass on roofs, and the psalm's picture is of Yhwh doing that again.

Roofs in Israel were made of soil. Grass seeds would blow there and begin to take root, but they would not be able to put down the roots that would make proper growth possible. Grass could thus start to grow, but it would not flourish. The development of the simile in vv. 6b–8 combines this reference to grass on roofs, now spoken of as if it were grown for harvesting and used as animal feed, with reference to grass and vegetation in general, which are purposefully grown (*ḥāṣîr* can have both the narrow and the broader meaning). So we are invited to imagine the grass on a roof having that potential value, but the value is never realized because before it is ready for plucking, it withers. That is how things will be for the people who attack Zion.

To underline the irony, v. 7 goes on to speak further of that imaginary harvest with its reapers and gatherers. Reaping is the general term, but it applies especially to the actual cutting of the vegetation, which involves taking a handful of grass and cutting it. Gathering then refers more specifically to the collecting of what has been cut and its binding into sheaves. The reapers and gatherers thus respectively fill a hand and an arm (literally, the fold in the front of a garment) with what they are harvesting. But the grass on the roof will not produce enough for that. That is how things will be for the people who attack Zion.

The closing line pushes the irony further as it pictures passersby greeting the harvesters with the blessing that accompanies the anticipation of a good harvest, as in Ruth 2:4. No doubt at one level the greeting would be traditional and the meaning of the words could not be pressed; they parallel greetings such as *shalom* or "goodbye" (God be with ye). Yet the words would be an encouragement to the harvesters and to the people shouting the greeting as they anticipated the results of this crucial work. The doubling of the blessing in v. 8b–c underlines the point and brings the psalm to an end with a tricolon. In Ruth 2:4, too, there are two phrases of greeting, and there the second is a response to the first. Tg assumes this is also so here; v. 8b is the greeting of the passersby, v. 8c the response of the harvesters. Either way, the words further underline the significance of the moment, with a double irony. One level of irony is embodied in the "not" in v. 8a. This affective greeting is one that no one will offer, because on a roof there is no harvest to be reaped, gathered, and blessed. Yet the other level of irony is that this is actually good news, because the whole long sentence is part of a prayer that this will be the fate of Zion's attackers. "The abundant blessing of Psalm 128 contrasts with the absence of blessing in Psalm 129."[13]

Theological Implications

Western Christians very often see being Christian as an essentially individual matter. Their membership in the body of Christ is quite a secondary aspect of Christian faith. Even more markedly, individual Christians and churches often see themselves as an essentially contemporary phenomenon. It is as if we were the first-ever Christian generation. The

13. Schaefer, *Psalms*, 309.

psalm invites a congregation to see itself as one in life with the people of God over the centuries, with Israel and with the church over two millennia. Its particular reason for doing so is that it sets our generation's experience of decline and weakness, marginality and harassment, in the context of a story running through millennia, which has moved through cycles of defeat and deliverance. The fact that God has not let this people disappear, even though it has often experienced reversal and defeat, is reason for encouragement when we ourselves experience decline and defeat.

Psalm 130

From the Depths of Trouble and Waywardness

Translation

Song of the Ascents.

1From the depths I have called you, Yhwh:
2my Lord, listen to my voice.
May your ears become attentive
to the sound of my plea for grace.

3If you keep acts of waywardness, Yah,
my Lord,[1] who can stand?
4Because pardon is with you,[2]
so that you may be revered.[3]

5I have looked to Yhwh, my spirit has looked;
I have waited for his word,

1. Codex C has *yhwh* here and in v. 6, as do some later MSS in vv. 2, 3, and 6.

2. Not "with you there is pardon," since the article on *hassĕlîḥâ* suggests that it is the subject (Franz Sedlmeier, "'Bei dir, da ist die Vergebung, damit du gefürchtet werdest,'" *Bib* 73 [1992]: 473–95 [see 484]; cf. Allen, *Psalms 101–150*, 252). Cf. v. 7.

3. Vrs vary here, perhaps reflecting the unfamiliarity of *yārē'* niphal.

[6]My spirit [has waited][4] for my Lord, more than guards[5] for the morning,
guards for the morning.

[7]Wait[6] for Yhwh, Israel,
because with Yhwh the commitment,
and the redemption with him, is great.[7]
[8]He is the one who will redeem Israel
from all its acts of waywardness.

Interpretation

Like Ps. 102, this became one of the seven traditional Penitential Psalms; unlike that psalm, Ps. 130 does reflect an awareness of needing to seek forgiveness. Admittedly, it would be possible to understand the psalm as a testimony to the answering of such a prayer (vv. 2–4 are then the recollection of it), but it is then surprising that there is no account of how the prayer was answered. More likely the calling, looking, and waiting are continuing, and this is a prayer psalm. Its opening word and its closing two lines indicate that like other prayer psalms, it presupposes a context in which the suppliant has been overwhelmed by trouble of some kind. But it presupposes that this experience resulted from the suppliant's wrongdoing, and it focuses on the consequent need of forgiveness. It thereby distinguishes itself from the majority of prayer psalms that presuppose that the suppliant is a person of commitment and that there is no such rationale for the experience of suffering. In its stance it thus compares with the prayers in Ezra 9, Neh. 9, and Dan. 9 (the noun "pardon" in v. 4 comes otherwise only in Neh. 9:17 and Dan. 9:9). It also compares with the characteristic OT attitude toward the exile (in contrast to its attitude toward some other reversals in Israel's experience) as resulting from Israel's waywardness.

4. 11QPs[a] provides *hwḥlty*, and Vrs have different versions of vv. 5–6. Perhaps there were other forms of the Hebrew text, or perhaps copyists and translators are modifying or handling loosely a text with ellipses and repetitions. See, e.g., Štephan Porúbčan, "Psalm cxxx 5–6," *VT* 9 (1959): 322–23; N. Tromp, "The Text of Psalm cxxx 5–6," *VT* 39 (1989): 100–103.

5. Vrs. take *šōměrîm* to mean "watches" (and the *min* to mean "from"), but the participial form indicates a reference to "watchers" in MT.

6. Vrs take *yaḥēl* as jussive, "may Israel look"; this makes good sense, but one would expect *yĕyaḥēl* (as in Mic. 5:6).

7. The inf. abs. *harbēh* can be used as an adverb, adj., or noun meaning "much"; here the context points to an adj. The word order *wĕharbēh ʿimmô pĕdût* suggests it is not attributive ("with him is great redemption") but predicative (cf. BDB). I then assume that the predicate also applies to the previous colon.

Those links also suggest that although it is an "I" psalm that would be quite open to being used in connection with an individual's waywardness and the trouble this had brought, it contains no explicit indication that either the suffering or the sin is particularly the suppliant's own. The "I" only calls, looks, and waits. Thus the psalm could also be used by the community in connection with the waywardness that has characterized its corporate life, and the trouble this has led to. The "I" could then be a priest speaking for the community[8] or an individual such as Nehemiah (see Neh. 1) who identifies with his community.

The psalm divides neatly into four two-line sections. The first two sections address Yhwh, with a plea for attentiveness (vv. 1–2) and a statement of confidence in Yhwh's pardon (vv. 3–4). The latter two refer to Yhwh in the third person. One describes the suppliant's waiting in a way that re-expresses this confidence but also occupies the place of both lament and plea in other psalms (vv. 5–6).[9] The psalm never actually asks Yhwh for anything but attentiveness, which may be a paradoxical indication of that confidence in implying the conviction underlying other prayer psalms that if one can get Yhwh's attention, action will follow.[10] The psalm closes with a challenge to Israel to look to Yhwh for forgiveness and redemption (vv. 7–8). Given that this last section is explicitly an exhortation, it makes sense to infer that this is also so in vv. 5–6. Thus the first half of the psalm addresses God, and the second half addresses the congregation. In content and theme, however, one can also read the four sections as an *aba′b′* sequence.[11] If the psalm does envisage an individual suppliant, the implication of the unexpected closing exhortation to Israel is that the psalm points to a parallel understanding of the relationship of individual and community to that presupposed by Ps. 129. The individual's experience with Yhwh again provides a model for understanding Yhwh's relationship with the community.

The psalm manifests some neat patterns of parallelism, repetition, and ellipse. Each pair of lines contains two references to God, Yhwh or Yah being paired with "my Lord" in the first three sections; the repetition of "my Lord" is unusual. In each of the first two, the expressions for God are juxtaposed, while in vv. 5–6 they come at the same point in the line. Verse 2b–c parallels and expands on v. 2a; the word for voice/sound (*qôl*) recurs in v. 2a and 2c. "Acts of waywardness" recurs from v. 3 in v. 8. The movement from v. 3 to v. 4 ("because") involves

8. Cf. Mowinckel, *Psalms*, 1:222.

9. It is "a hidden complaint" (Mandolfo, *God in the Dock*, 89–90).

10. Robert C. Dentan thus calls it a psalm of trust ("An Exposition of an Old Testament Passage," *Journal of Bible and Religion* 15 [1947]: 158–61 [see 159]).

11. So Beat Weber, "'Wenn du Vergehen aufbewahrtest . . . ,'" *BN* 107–8 (2001): 146–60 (see 147).

an ellipse. The qatal verb in v. 1 referring to an activity in the past that continues into the present is taken up in v. 5 by qatal verbs that have similar significance. The word in v. 3 for Yhwh's keeping or guarding acts of waywardness (*šāmar*) recurs with reference to the guards in v. 6. The description of pardon as "with" Yhwh in v. 4 is taken up in the description of commitment and redemption as "with" Yhwh in v. 7. "Looking" recurs within v. 5a with the object "Yhwh" stated only the first time and with "my spirit" changing the subject the second time. Then in v. 5b the parallel "waiting" appears, with the object modified to "his word," and the verb recurs in v. 7. "My spirit" recurs in v. 6 from v. 5, with the ellipse that makes "has waited" also apply there, with a reversion to the original object, "Yhwh." "Guards for the morning" recurs within v. 6. In v. 7, "is great" in the third colon also applies in the second. "Redemption" in v. 7 is picked up in "redeem" in v. 8. The effect of these patterns is to bind the psalm together in dense and intricate fashion.

Song of the Ascents.

Heading. See glossary.
130:1–2. A plea for Yhwh's attention.

1From the depths I have called you, Yhwh:
2my Lord, listen to my voice.
May your ears become attentive
to the sound of my plea for grace.

The "depths" of the sea come with literal reference in Isa. 51:10 and Ezek. 27:34 and with metaphorical reference (as here) to overwhelming personal devastation in Ps. 69:2, 14 [3, 15], where it denotes the effect of the assault of human attackers, and that makes sense here. Ernesto Cardenal thus paraphrases:

From the depths, I cry to you, O Lord!
I cry in the night from the prison cell
and from the concentration camp
From the torture chamber
in the hour of darkness
hear my voice
my S.O.S.[12]

12. "I Cry in the Night from the Torture Chamber: Psalm 129," in *Mission Trends No. 3: Third World Theologies*, ed. Gerald H. Anderson and Thomas F. Stransky (New York: Paulist Press, 1976), 39–40.

The suppliant's experience is therefore not very different from that implied in Ps. 129. "Depths" does not suggest a subjective awareness of being in the depths of despair; nor is this language used elsewhere of being overwhelmed by the depths of sin.[13] It indicates the objective fact of being engulfed in a "sea of troubles," which might include illness as well as the attacks of enemies.[14] The more general image of deep waters indicates the waters of death or of Sheol (see on 124:4–5; and Jon. 2), which overwhelm us because the world under the earth, where we go when we die, is also a realm characterized by water.[15] Thus the psalmist is praying as from the dead. This made it possible for Catholic devotion to make this a psalm prayed on behalf of the dead, in connection with the celebration of All Saints and All Souls Days.[16]

While the qatal verb *qārāʾtî* might then be performative,[17] it makes as much sense to see the qatal as indicating that the suppliant has been calling Yhwh for some while (the verb is again used in its rather peremptory way, with a direct object). This also makes it possible to take this qatal as parallel in significance to the ones in v. 5. The second colon then parallels the first (if that first verb is performative, v. 2a constitutes the content of the call, or is the beginning of this). Yhwh becomes "my *Lord"; each term both suggests God's mighty power and God's personal relationship with the suppliant. They mean this God has the power and the obligation to respond. "Listen to my voice" also complements the qatal verb in v. 1 by virtue of being an imperative. Yet this verb, in turn, is less peremptory than it might have been, as the suppliant uses the long form of the imperative (*šimʿâ* rather than *šĕmaʿ*).

In substance, though not in words, v. 2 then builds in "terrace" fashion. Verse 2b–c restates v. 2a, takes it further, and underscores it: v. 2b restates "listen," v. 2c restates "to my voice." "Your ears" nicely complements "my voice," while in v. 2c the restatement is closer in Hebrew, as "sound" is literally "voice," repeating that word from v. 2a. The jussive form again perhaps makes for a less peremptory impression than an imperative, as may the reference to a plea for *grace, which underlines the suppliant's need and lack of any basis for appealing to Yhwh.[18] The

13. Against, e.g., Lindström, *Suffering and Sin*, 369–75.

14. Allen, *Psalms 101–150*, 255.

15. On the image and the stimulus of its allusiveness, see Harry P. Nasuti, "Plumbing the Depths," in *The Idea of Biblical Interpretation*, ed. Hindy Najman and Judith H. Newman (James L. Kugel Festschrift; Leiden: Brill, 2004), 95–124.

16. See the comments in, e.g., Spurgeon, *Treasury of David*, 6:121; Richard J. Pettey, "Psalm 130," in *The Psalms and Other Studies on the Old Testament*, ed. Jack C. Knight and Lawrence A. Sinclair (Joseph I. Hunt Festschrift; Nashotah, WI: Nashotah House Seminary, 1990), 45–53 (see 51–52).

17. So DG 57b.

18. Cf. McCann, "Psalms," 1205.

significance of that will emerge in the next verse. On the other hand, the verbal expression "become attentive" (or even "be attentive," if that is an overtranslation) raises the question whether Yhwh is being inattentive at the moment.

130:3–4. A statement of confidence. The plea for attention could have featured in any prayer psalm. It is this second section that makes clear the distinctive concern of Ps. 130, its recognition that the suppliant comes before Yhwh as a wrongdoer, and its implication that the suppliant's wrongdoing lies behind its speaking "from the depths." After the plea for attention, one might have expected a plea for Yhwh to *do* something: in this context, to forgive the suppliant and bring about a restoration from the overwhelming consequences of wrongdoing at which the psalm's first word hinted. Yet oddly, the suppliant does not ask Yhwh for forgiveness but instead reflects on how things would be if Yhwh did not forgive, and expresses confidence that God does.

> 3If you keep acts of waywardness, Yah,
> my Lord, who can stand?

In speaking of keeping *waywardness, the psalm utilizes the common verb *šāmar*, used to refer to guarding a city (127:1) or guarding people from danger (121:3–8); compare v. 6. EVV translate by using metaphors such as "keep account," but it is hard to parallel this stretching of the verb's meaning. Rather the psalm envisages the possibility that Yhwh might keep careful watch over our waywardness and make sure none of it escapes. Job 14:16–17 provides the nearest parallel to this use of the verb, though it speaks in terms of "watching over" rather than simply "watching." Watching or keeping would be the opposite stance to the instinct to throw our acts of waywardness into the sea (Mic. 7:19). It would mean preserving them.[19] A Baylor University survey of American attitudes toward God revealed that nearly half of the Christians surveyed characterized God as centrally judgmental and critical, involved in punishing people either now or later. If this were so, the psalm comments, none of us would survive.[20] The psalm again uses a common word, "stand," and leaves the context to determine its nuance. If it meant "stand before Yhwh," one might expect the psalm to say so (cf. 76:7 [8]), though the next line might hint in this direction. Used absolutely, as here, it can mean "abide" (cf. 102:26 [27]), and that makes sense.

In the two cola, it is this time the archaic *Yah that is complemented by "my *Lord," but with similar implications to the combination in vv.

19. Cf. Anne Marie Sweet, "Pilgrimage and Reconciliation," *Bible Today* 38 (2000): 150–55 (see 153).

20. Cf. Mays, *Psalms*, 406.

1–2a. At the same time, the implicit admission of waywardness in v. 3a makes the appeal to "my Lord" somewhat paradoxical.[21] That description presupposes a master-servant relationship in the context of which the servant can appeal for the master's support and provision.[22] But can a disobedient servant do that? Logically, no; hence the appeal for grace in v. 2. The servant can make such an appeal only on the basis of a conviction that the master does not behave on a merely contractual basis. Verse 4 will spell that out.

> [4]Because pardon is with you,
> so that you may be revered.

The transition here involves an ellipse; it presupposes the fact that Yhwh does not keep acts of waywardness and that therefore we do stand, because with Yhwh there is pardon.[23] For the verb, see on 103:3. As there, it comes in association with "waywardness," which suggests the psalm is recalling the character of Yhwh as self-revealed in Exod. 34:9 and is implicitly appealing to that. Thus "the very fact that thou art God is to me a sure guarantee that thou wilt be merciful."[24] The psalmist stands (or lies prostrate) before Yhwh like a guilty person standing (or lying prostrate) before the king and throwing himself or herself on the king's mercy. Pardon is "with" Yhwh: it is Yhwh's possession, or something in Yhwh's mind, or something that sits next to Yhwh ready to be sent out on its work (like Yhwh's commitment or truthfulness or might; see on 96:6).[25]

Verse 4b also involves a surprising segue. "Since it is God that he is primarily concerned with, the forgiveness of sins does not have the effect of soothing and lulling his religious perceptions, but on the contrary of revealing the humanly incomprehensible greatness of God."[26] Indeed, this is not merely the effect of that forgiveness but (part of?) its aim. JM 169g does reckon that *lĕmaʿan* here means "with the result that" rather than its usual "so that," as it probably does in 51:4 [6], but it seems a shame to water the statement down to this.[27] Indeed, "with you there is pardon, so that you are revered" might simply not be true; forgiveness need not lead to revering. Rather the colon makes the bolder paradoxical

21. Cf. Allen, *Psalms 101–150*, 256.

22. Cf. Kraus, *Psalms 60–150*, 467.

23. Cf. GKC 163a–b.

24. Calvin, *Psalms*, 5:131. See further John Owen's monumental exposition of the psalm, focusing especially on this verse: "A Practical Exposition upon Psalm cxxx," in *The Works of John Owen* (repr., Edinburgh: T&T Clark, 1862), 6:325–648.

25. See BDB on *ʿim*.

26. Weiser, *Psalms*, 774.

27. So also at 30:12 [13]; EVV rightly follow JM only at 51:4 [6].

statement that the object of Yhwh's pardoning is that we *may* *revere Yhwh. If forgiveness is near Yhwh's heart, so that in a sense it can be taken for granted, there is a risk that this would indeed lead to taking it for granted, and to taking Yhwh for granted, in a bad sense. We can sin so that grace may abound (Rom. 6:1). Not surprisingly, Yhwh works the logic in a more profound way, a logic that Paul then assumes in Rom. 6:1–14. In pardoning us, Yhwh aims to arouse a gratitude that will lead us to commit ourselves to obedience. To put it another way, God's kindness is meant to lead us to repentance (Rom. 2:4). Of course, as usual Yhwh risks disappointment.

Franz Sedlmeier sees this as the key line in the poem, pointing to reverence for God as central to the notion of living a transformed life in relationship with God.[28]

130:5–6. The statement of dependence. The psalm now speaks *about* Yhwh rather than *to* Yhwh, perhaps addressing the self, but perhaps beginning the address to the community that is explicit in vv. 7–8.

> [5]I have looked to Yhwh, my spirit has looked;
> I have waited for his word,

The suppliant prays because of being overwhelmed. By its nature that experience usually implies something that is more than momentary. As in v. 1, I take the qatal verbs as pointing to an activity that has been going on for a while, rather than as active verbs used with stative meaning[29] that one might translate by simple present verbs (cf. EVV). Either way, they might then have two significances. They could suggest commitment to Yhwh and acceptance of dependence on Yhwh, thus overlapping with the statement of confidence that can appear in a prayer psalm. Or they could underline the suppliant's need and thus overlap with the lament or protest that often appears in a prayer psalm. The ambiguity of the line's significance symbolizes the tension expressed by the notion of looking or waiting, the tension between hoping and possessing,[30] which is inherent in a "theology of hope."[31] The overwhelming and the turning to Yhwh that this has necessitated have been a reality for a while. But the further transition into vv. 7–8 implies that confidence is stronger than protest. The verb *qāwâ* (piel) suggests an attitude of expectancy

28. Sedlmeier, "'Bei dir, da ist die Vergebung, damit du gefürchtet werdest.'"

29. So JM 112a; DG 57, remark 1.

30. Cf. Weiser, *Psalms*, 775.

31. Gerstenberger, *Psalms*, 2:356, referring to Jürgen Moltmann, *Theology of Hope* (New York: Harper; London: SCM, 1967). Edmund Steimle focuses his exposition of the psalm on the motif of waiting ("Wait," *Union Seminary Quarterly Review* 22 [1967]: 139–45).

or waiting, looking for something to happen, looking for Yhwh to act. It implies a recognition that individually and corporately we may have little control over our lives; we cannot control whether we get better from an illness, nor can we control our political destiny. Indeed, when Israel attempts to do either, it is subject to critique. Its vocation is to live life in the expectation that Yhwh is going to act and to live straining its eyes to see that act.

The line is full of repetition with development that underlines their point. First, "I have looked" is underscored by "my spirit has looked"; for "my spirit" (*person) TNIV has "my whole being." "I have *waited for his *word" repeats the point once more, using a synonymous verb and at last providing the verbs with an object. The word for which the psalm waits is the declaration that Yhwh has heard the prayer and is committed to answering it, so that the issuing of the word initiates the process whereby the answer becomes a reality (cf. 56:4, 10 [5, 11]; 107:20). In this context, it would at least begin as a word of pardon, Yhwh's declaring through a person such as a priest, "your sins are forgiven," though it might go on to a promise of deliverance.

> 6My spirit [has waited] for my Lord, more than guards for the morning,
> guards for the morning.

The repetition continues with the resumptive "my spirit" (*person), though the line then lets the superfluity of verbs in v. 5 continue their effect into v. 6, where there is no verb. The presupposed verb does have a new object, "my *Lord," again complementing "Yhwh" in the previous line; the person of "my Lord" thus also complements "his word." The suppliant wants to see the personal action that follows from the issuing of the word. The larger novelty in the line is the simile. The guards reappear from 127:1. We noted how they battle against sleep in order to stay alert in the small hours. They long for morning to come, so that they can give in to sleep. Or perhaps they are looking to the dawn with another kind of anticipation: Tg assumes that these are ministers waiting for the time to offer the morning sacrifice, which comes with the dawn. Or perhaps dawn is the time when the particular dangers of night are over (see on 121:3); the guard is relieved when morning comes because these are now past. The suppliant then longs for the Lord's words and the Lord's action because these mean the end of the relentless pressure that currently prevails.

The repetition in the second colon slows the line down and makes us wait for what will come next, matching the content of the words. It further underlines the commitment of the waiting, and thus the urgency of the need.

130:7–8. The testimony. If one took the psalm as a liturgy, then vv. 7–8 might be a priestly response to vv. 1–6, which would then imply that vv. 1–6 are indeed by nature the community's prayer rather than an individual's, another instance of the community praying in the manner of an individual. But it is more straightforward to take vv. 7–8 as the equivalent to a suppliant's exhortation to other people to take the same stance as the suppliant, such as often appears in a psalm.[32] Usually a psalm does that on the basis of a testimony to Yhwh's having acted; here it presupposes that the suppliant knows that Yhwh has heard the prayer (though it does not tell us how) and it issues its invitation simply on the basis of the truth of its statements about Yhwh, which it here reformulates.

7Wait for Yhwh, Israel,
because with Yhwh the commitment,
and the redemption with him, is great.

So the suppliant urges on the people as a whole the same attitude of looking or *waiting to which vv. 5–6 have testified, and reformulates the basis for this in terms of Yhwh's *commitment and Yhwh's *redemption, which, like pardon (see on v. 4a), are "with" Yhwh. "Three fundamental characteristics . . . are set forth almost as intimate friends and companions of God. Wherever the Lord goes, they are there accompanying and going with God."[33] Furthermore, they are great; the last line will spell out the implications of that.

8He is the one who will redeem Israel
from all its acts of waywardness.

What is it that makes the commitment and the *redemption so great? A Christian would be inclined to read the reference to redemption in v. 7 as denoting forgiveness and spiritual renewal, and v. 8 might seem to confirm that. The OT perspective would be capable of including all this (it knows that God forgives and renews), but it would not be confined to it. Redeeming Israel from its *waywardness (cf. v. 3) would first mean delivering Israel from the mess it had got itself into through its waywardness, delivering it from the depths that had overwhelmed it. "How will He redeem me when I am full of iniquity? He will first 'redeem Israel from all their iniquities'; i.e., He will forgive them their sins and inspire

32. They have been taken as a later addition (e.g., Seybold, *Psalmen*, 492), though the repetitions that characterize the psalm continue here: cf. Rick R. Marrs, "A Cry from the Depths," *ZAW* 100 (1988): 81–90 (see 87–90).

33. Miller, *Interpreting the Psalms*, 142.

them to repent wholeheartedly. Then He will return His captivity."[34] The greatness of Yhwh's commitment and redemption lies in the fact that Yhwh brings about such deliverance, and does so in respect to *all* Israel's acts of waywardness that had taken it to the destruction of state, monarchy, and temple, and left it (if the psalm comes from the Persian period) still living with the aftermath of those events. The greatness of Yhwh's commitment and redemption means that these experiences will not have the last word. Yhwh is the one who punishes, but does not leave Israel in its misery but delivers it from the consequences of its waywardness.

Theological Implications

Gosbert T. M. Byamungu suggests that Zacchaeus the outcast (Luke 19:1–10) is one who embodies the cry, the repentance, and the waiting of which the psalm speaks, and he finds Jesus embodying vv. 7–8.[35] Claus Westermann notes how the psalm is controlled by a movement that takes it from "from the depths" to "the redemption with him is great"; in the middle stands "my spirit [has waited] for my Lord, more than guards for the morning."[36] But within the internal life of the psalm itself, there is no movement; the depths are as deep at the end as they are at the beginning. Something similar was true of the German church in the 1930s. Earlier, Westermann began his dissertation on the Psalms with a reference to that church struggle, noting how "in the present transitions and disasters the church has been confronted anew with the question of the praise of God."[37] In the 1930s the church praised God as well as prayed "out of the depths." People discovered that there they learned not only how to be steadfast but how to praise. Ironically, the psalm is also inscribed on a chapel wall at Dachau,[38] where the depths indeed stand for the depths of death and for a waiting that sees no response.

Although Luther was fond of Ps. 130, as of the other penitential psalms, because of their Pauline resonances, his actual exposition of it is for the most part rather routine ("We shall omit profound exegesis here").[39] But his fondness on this basis does fit with the fact that John Wesley,

34. Qimchi, as translated by Rosenberg, *Psalms*, 3:496.

35. "Grace as Subversive Surprise," *Ecumenical Review* 56 (2004): 334–41.

36. Westermann, *Living Psalms*, 121–22.

37. *The Praise of God in the Psalms*, 5.

38. See James Limburg, "De Profundis," *CurTM* 26 (1999): 117–22 (see 119).

39. *Selected Psalms*, 3:191; he is referring to the allegorical exposition he often provides elsewhere. He did also produce a hymn version of the psalm. See further Jörg Jeremias, "Psalm 130 und Luthers Nachdichtung," *Theologische Beiträge* 20 (1989): 284–97.

on the day of his listening to a reading of Luther's preface to Romans at Aldersgate Street, had earlier listened to the choir at Saint Paul's Cathedral sing this psalm.[40] Luther does close with the striking declaration, "Whoever wants to be merciful to himself, to him God will be unmerciful; and whoever is unmerciful to himself, to him God will be merciful."[41] Alongside that, one might put Werner H. Schmidt's observation that in this psalm one finds the radical concept of grace that Rudolf Bultmann missed in the OT (one finds it elsewhere, too, of course).[42]

40. *The Journal of the Rev. John Wesley* (repr., London: Dent; New York: Dutton, 1906), 1:101–2.

41. *Selected Psalms*, 3:194.

42. "Gott und Mensch in Ps. 130," *TZ* 22 (1966): 241–53 (see 253).

Psalm 131

How I Gave Up Trying to Fix Things, and So Should You

Translation

Song of the Ascents. David's.[1]

1Yhwh, my heart has not been lofty,
my eyes have not looked high.
I have not gone about among great things,
among wonders beyond me.
2No, rather[2] I have conformed,
and stilled, my spirit:
Like one nursed with its mother,
so is my spirit nursed with me.

3Wait for Yhwh, Israel,
from now and forevermore.

1. "David's" is missing from Tg and some LXX MSS.
2. Lit. "If I have not . . . [then may I be cursed (or the like)]." On *'im-lōʾ*, see BDB 50.

Interpretation

Psalm 131 pairs with Ps. 130 rather like Ps. 112 with Ps. 111.[3] The psalm again starts from the position of an "I," who speaks through vv. 1–2, and then closes with an exhortation to Israel in v. 3, whose first colon corresponds to 130:7a and its second to 121:8b and 125:2c. In its overall content, however, the psalm otherwise contrasts with Ps. 130, which stood out from prayer psalms because of its stress on the suppliant's waywardness. Psalm 131 resembles other prayer psalms in its affirmation of the stance the suppliant has taken to life, though compared with other psalms, it is a torso. One could bring the two psalms together by seeing Ps. 131 as a working out of the nature of the waiting that Ps. 130 describes. To put it another way, the bulk of Ps. 131 corresponds to vv. 5–6 in Ps. 130, though in Ps. 131 the declaration addresses Yhwh. Thus Ps. 131 might function as a declaration of trust or confidence or commitment, of the kind that enables the worshipper to approach Yhwh with confidence, or as a thanksgiving that one has been able to take that stance and it has worked. Either way, the fact that the psalm begins with a denial suggests that the opposite might be suspected,[4] and v. 2 rather confirms that there was an issue to be faced here.[5]

If vv. 1–2 are a thanksgiving, this especially fits the line that follows in v. 3. Once again, one might take the psalm as a liturgy in which vv. 1–2 are the words of the congregation to Yhwh and v. 3 the response of a priest, but there are no particular pointers in that direction. The psalm reads naturally as the declaration of an individual, who might indeed be a priest or leader speaking on the people's behalf, who then commends to the congregation the stance described.[6] The comparison with a baby and a mother is no particular reason to reckon that the psalmist *is* a mother,[7] and v. 1 more likely implies a man in a position of leadership, but clearly the psalmist has at least watched what goes on between a child and a mother and drawn inferences for theology and spirituality from it.

3. James Limburg, "De Profundis," *CurTM* 26 (1999): 117–22 (see 120).

4. Schaefer, *Psalms*, 312.

5. Cf. Grossberg, *Centripetal and Centrifugal Structures*, 46.

6. So, e.g., Bernard P. Robinson, "Form and Meaning in Psalm 131," *Bib* 79 (1998): 180–97 (see 192–93).

7. Against, e.g., G. Quell, "Struktur und Sinn des Psalms 131," in *Das ferne und nahe Wort*, ed. Fritz Maass, BZAW 105 (L. Rost Festschrift; Berlin: Töpelmann, 1967), 173–85; Seybold, *Psalmen*, 495. See also Ulrike Bail, "Die Psalmen," in *Kompendium Feministische Bibelauslegung*, ed. Luise Schottroff and Marie-Theres Wacker (Gütersloh: Kaiser, 1998), 180–91 (see 188–89); Eberhard Jüngel, "Psalm 131," in *Einfach von Gott reden*, ed. Jürgen Roloff and Hans G. Ulrich (Friedrich Mildenberger Festschrift; Stuttgart: Kohlhammer, 1994), 240–42; Melody D. Knowles, "A Woman at Prayer," *JBL* 125 (2006): 385–91.

Song of the Ascents. David's.

Heading. See glossary. There would be food for thought in the notion that as "David's" this might be a psalm for the king to take note of and live by (it would be a separate question whether it dates from the time when there were kings; there are no indications of a date). There were kings who provided positive and negative embodiments of v. 1 (see the comment); and v. 2 sets up a demanding countercultural challenge for a king or any leader.

131:1–2. The declaration to Yhwh.

1Yhwh, my heart has not been lofty,
  my eyes have not looked high.
I have not gone about among great things,
  among wonders beyond me.

As usual, one might translate the qatal verbs as quasi-stative ("is not lofty . . .") rather than active, but the consistent use of the qatal more likely indicates that the psalm refers to a practice from the past that continues into the present. And as usual, we narrow down the poignancy of the verbs for "be lofty" and "look high" (*gābah*, *rûm*) if we take them as unequivocally denoting pride or ambition. In themselves they simply denote "be lofty, be high," so that pride or ambition is but a further connotation. The heart can be lofty in a positive sense (2 Chron. 17:6, though the precise sense is not clear there), and raising the eyes can have a positive sense (e.g., Ps. 123:1, though there the verb is *nāśā'*). But being lofty or high is dangerous because objectively, in itself, it suggests a challenge to the one who is lofty and high, and because subjectively it is almost impossible to be lofty and high without becoming people who see themselves as impressive and important, as godlets. The difference between God and us is that God never thinks he is us. So the wise person flees becoming important, knowing it is almost certain to mean peril and downfall.

The theme is expounded most systematically in Isa. 2:5–22. Uzziah provides an example: when he became strong his heart became lofty, and that led to his trespassing against Yhwh by undertaking priestly acts (2 Chron. 26:16; cf. 32:25). Being lofty in heart suggests having a high opinion of oneself. The high opinion may be justified; the problem is what it leads to. High eyes are a little different. They are the first thing Yhwh is against in Prov. 6:16–19 (cf. 30:13; also Ps. 18:27 [28]).[8] The context there implies a

8. Walter Beyerlin (*Wider die Hybris des Geistes: Studien zum 131. Psalm,* Stuttgarter Bibelstudien 108 [Stuttgart: Katholisches Bibelwerk, 1982], 71–80) emphasizes the psalm's Wisdom connections, with Job as well as Proverbs.

self-assertiveness over against other people, not over against God. It suggests something more like ambition than pride. But both a lofty heart and high eyes lead to action that treats me as the only person that counts.

"Great things" are most often great acts of God (e.g., 71:19, where Yhwh is the one "on high"; also 106:21), and thus "wonders" follows on naturally in the parallelism. The verb is *hālak* in the piel, which here has its intensive significance, suggesting "walk with determination" or "go about." The line is concerned with more than seeking to understand things that are too great for human comprehension. Rather the suppliant has avoided trying to go about doing great wonders, like God, rather than walking in faithfulness (Prov. 8:20). The psalm testifies to having escaped "vain ambition."[9] It opposes the *hybris* of the spirit.[10]

> 2No, rather I have conformed,
> and stilled, my spirit:
> Like one nursed with its mother,
> so is my spirit nursed with me.

The opening "No" brings to an impressive climax the sequence of "no's" that has run through v. 1.[11] The verse comprises two lines in which the first raises questions that the second clarifies, as often happens with parallelism. In doing so, it utilizes a severalfold paronomasia.[12] Its general function is to describe a stance that contrasts with v. 1. Prosaically put, "Rather I have made my spirit like a nursing child with its mother by stilling it."

The first verb (*šāwâ* piel) usually denotes making something like or the same as something else.[13] Only in the second colon do we discover what is being so conformed ("my spirit"),[14] and only in the parallel line

9. H. Stephen Shoemaker, "Psalm 131," *RevExp* 85 (1988): 89–94 (see 93).

10. Cf. Beyerlin, *Wider die Hybris des Geistes*.

11. Ibid., 35.

12. For what follows, cf. in part Crow, *Songs of Ascents*, 96.

13. It is a confusing verb. The piel of *šāwâ* I means "level off" in Isa. 28:25, and from this has been inferred a meaning "settle/soothe" in the psalm (*HALOT*); this meaning has also been inferred for the enigmatic Isa. 38:13, but that involves interpreting the obscure by the obscure. A related meaning has been inferred by connecting the verb with *šāwâ* II (so Aq, Jerome, Tg; the roots are differently analyzed in BDB and *HALOT*) and reckoning that it means "cause to lie down." But the verb's more usual root meaning "be like" fits if we allow for its significance being explained by the second colon. Indeed, Sym assumes that the subsequent verb *dômamtî* comes not from *dāmam* ("to be still") but from *dāmâ* (or a homonym), which also means "be like." So v. 2a already involves one or perhaps two paronomasia.

14. There is thus no need to hypothesize the loss of a noun in v. 2a (against Oswald Loretz, "Zur Parallelität zwischen KTU 1.6 II 28–30 und Ps 131,2b," *UF* 17 [1986]: 183–87 [see 184–85]).

do we further discover what it is being conformed to. Meanwhile, what broke the construction in the first line was a second verb that indicates that this conforming involved stilling, but only in the second line do we discover what its stillness looks like.

EVV take the comparison as with a weaned child, but the image of a weaned child with its mother is odd. It has been conjectured that the expression takes up the likelihood that in a traditional culture a child will never be satisfied with what it can get at the breast, so that a child that has been weaned and is getting its satisfaction from regular food but can still lie at its mother's breast for comfort will therefore be more likely to be content and stilled.[15] But this is simply an imaginative and complex conjecture. It involves less imagination to reckon that *gāmul* here refers not to the actual weaning of a child but to its having come off the breast at the end of a feeding (cf. Rashi).

That would link with the more basic meaning of the expression *gāmal ʿal* (the preposition is in any case odd in connection with nursing or weaning), which denotes to do something for someone or to give something to someone.[16] Like those opening expressions for being lofty or high (v. 1), it can have a positive or a negative sense, and the context determines which applies. In 103:2 the psalm utilizes its neutrality but then picks up the negative sense in 103:10 (cf. 94:2). For the positive sense, see 119:17, and especially 116:7, where the context particularly parallels the idea here. So the expression plays with the two possible positive meanings of the expression of *gāmal ʿal*, as LXX and Sym imply in translating in accordance with the narrower meaning in v. 2b and the broader meaning in v. 2c. The suppliant is like a child that has been provided for by its mother through being nursed, and therefore lies with her content.

The third and fourth cola are parallel *k* expressions, and EVV translate *k* "like" each time. This seems to correspond with MT's understanding, since MT locates the midpoint of the verse after v. 2b and thus dissociates the two *k* expressions. But Jerome and Sym perceive that such double *k* expressions idiomatically "signify the completeness of the correspondency between two objects."[17] The simile both explains the way the suppliant's spirit has been made like something else and indicates what "stilling" looked like.

The fourth colon in typical fashion for this group of psalms repeats what has preceded, but does so with variation. "My spirit" is now the

15. See, e.g., Anderson, *Psalms*, 2:878.

16. Cf. P. A. H. De Boer, "Psalm cxxxi 2," *VT* 16 (1966): 287–92 (see 291–92); also Willem A. VanGemeren, "Psalm 131:2—*kegamul*," *Hebrew Studies* 23 (1982): 51–57.

17. BDB 454. Admittedly the m. ptc. should strictly be f., but such disagreement is common when the m. expression precedes the f. expression.

subject of the statement, "like one nursed" is now pointed "like the one nursed," and "with" now has a suffix and changes its nuance. "With me" (*'ālay*) thus has the kind of meaning it has in 42:4, 5, 6, 11 [5, 6, 7, 12]; 142:3 [4]; 143:4, "to give pathos to the expression of an emotion, by emphasizing the person who is its subject, and who, as it were, feels it acting upon him."[18]

131:3. The exhortation. The suppliant commends to the people the stance that has been described in v. 2.

> [3]Wait for Yhwh, Israel,
> from now and forevermore.

In taking up the exhortation from 130:7 (see note and comment), the psalm moves in a direction we would not have anticipated. It has not previously been explicit that the suppliant needed to wait, and the context gives the exhortation a different meaning here. Verses 1–2 imply that the suppliant could have reached out aggressively and assertively to gain or achieve something, but resolved not to do so and instead took a quietist stance. The situation is therefore rather different from one in which people are overwhelmed and cry out from the depths. But in its different circumstances it is the same stance the psalm now commends to Israel.

The final colon makes for a more shocking move. It is rare for a psalm to think in anything like eschatological terms; commentators who use the word "eschatological" use it in a rather uneschatological sense, to refer in rather more general terms to the hope for a new act of God.[19] Here the psalm commends a quietism that lasts forever. Israel needs to be prepared to settle down for the long haul with circumstances such as those of the Persian period described in Ezra and Nehemiah and forgo any attempt to bring in the kingdom of God, which is the venture of a lofty heart and eyes that look high. It needs to be prepared to wait forever.

Theological Implications

Individual believers are fond of the idea that they should seek to make a difference, and the church is fond of the idea that it should seek to bring in or further or extend the kingdom of God. The psalm suggests that the task of the people of God is rather to wait for the kingdom of

18. BDB 753.
19. E.g., McCann, "Psalms," 1205, though not in connection with Ps. 131!

God, and Jesus also takes this view. Instead of being lofty and looking high and going about thinking that we can do wonders that are actually too great for us, the suppliant invites us to relax like a child in its mother's arms. This is a statement that will infuriate readers, which as usual shows how important it is.

Psalm 132
The Reciprocity of Prayer

Translation

Song of the Ascents.

1Yhwh, be mindful for David
  of all his being troubled,[1]
2In that he swore to Yhwh,
  vowed to Jacob's Strong One:
3"If I go into my tent, my house,
  if I climb into my bed, my couch,[2]
4If I give sleep to my eyes,
  slumber to my eyelids,
5Before I find the place that belongs to Yhwh,
  the dwelling that belongs to Jacob's Strong One. . . ."

6Now: we heard of it at Ephrata,
  we found it in the lands of Jaar.
7Let us go into his dwelling,
  let us bow down at his footstool.
8"Rise, Yhwh, to your settlement,
  you and your mighty chest,

1. For the pual inf. *ʿunnôtô* LXX implies a noun form such as *ʿanwātô*; the meaning would be the same (though LXX takes it to mean "his humility").

2. Lit. "the tent of my house," "the bed of my couch"; genitive of definition (GKC 128m).

9As your priests clothe themselves in faithfulness
  and the people committed to you resound."[3]

10For the sake of David your servant,
  do not turn away the face of your anointed.

11Yhwh swore to David in truthfulness;[4]
  he will not turn from it:
The fruit[5] of your body
  I will place on the throne that belongs to you.
12If your descendants keep my covenant,
  my declarations,[6] which[7] I will teach them,
Their descendants, too, forever,
  will sit on the throne that belongs to you.

13Because Yhwh chose Zion;
  he wanted it as a seat that belongs to him.
14This is my settlement forever,
  where I will sit, because I wanted it.
15Its supplies I will greatly bless,
  its needy I will fill with bread.
16Its priests I will clothe in deliverance,
  its committed people will greatly resound.

17There I will make the horn that belongs to David flourish;
  I have set up the flame that belongs to my anointed.
18His enemies I will clothe in shame,
  but upon him his crown will sparkle.

Interpretation

Like many other psalms collected as Songs of the Ascents, Ps. 132 does not correspond very closely to any of the regular ways of speaking to Yhwh that appear through the Psalter, but like the other members of

3. The word order suggests that these are circumstantial clauses (see *TTH* 156–69; DG 135–37).

4. MT accents and LXX takes *ʾĕmet* as direct object, "a truthfulness" (cf. *HALOT*), but this concrete usage is hard to parallel. Tg rather takes the word as adverbial acc. (cf. BDB; JM 102d). There is no need for the "it" of v. 11b to have an actual noun as antecedent.

5. Lit. "from the fruit."

6. The anomalous pl. *ʿēdōtî* might be a composite of *ʿēdōtay* (my declarations) and *ʿēdutî* (my declaration) (cf. Johnson, *Sacral Kingship*, 20) or might be a northern form (Rendsburg, *Linguistic Evidence*, 89) or an Aramaism (GKC 91n).

7. The relative need not be expressed in poetry and gives some emphasis to the relative clause.

this group, it can be seen as a variation on one of those types. In this case it is a prayer psalm that incorporates a response from Yhwh: a prayer to Yhwh relating to David (vv. 1–10) and a promise by Yhwh relating to David (vv. 11–18). Each half comprises ten lines, each half beginning and ending with references to David (vv. 1–2 and 10, vv. 11–12 and 17–18).[8] Both prayer and promise also incorporate within this frame an undertaking related to Yhwh's dwelling or settlement, one undertaking made by David and one made by Yhwh (vv. 3–9 and 13–16). The psalm's dual theme recalls the dual theme of Yhwh's choice of Jerusalem and of David, announced in 1 Kings 8:16; 2 Chron. 6:6. The speaker might be the current anointed himself, who can pray for himself in the third person; or the speaker might be a priest, or the people, the "we" of v. 6.

There is thus a linear or logical relationship between the two halves of the psalm and also a series of parallels between them. Both involve oaths, by David and then by Yhwh. David's oath concerns a place/dwelling that belongs to Yhwh; Yhwh's oath concerns a throne that belongs to David and a horn and lamp that belong to David. Both concern themselves with Yhwh's settlement in Jerusalem. Both have the priests clothed in faithfulness/deliverance and the people committed to Yhwh resounding (with David's enemies clothed differently). Both pray on the basis of the relationship between Yhwh and David. As well as being a prayer and the recollection of a promise, the psalm is a neatly formed piece of poetry characterized by features that also appear elsewhere in the Songs of the Ascents, such as elegant structuring, suggestive imagery, paronomasia, and repetition and variation.

The prayer related to David thus bases its appeal on David's commitment regarding Yhwh's dwelling or settlement, with the follow-up references to Yhwh's place or footstool or chest. On the other hand, although the prayer relates to David, it is not actually a prayer for David but for his successors (see v. 10); David's commitment is the basis for a plea that Yhwh should stay committed to these successors. Likewise, the account of Yhwh's promise begins from the fact that Yhwh made an oath to David himself (v. 11) but then immediately goes on to the fact that its beneficiaries are David's successors (v. 12), and the promise that there will be a lamp for David in Zion is fulfilled as much in them as in him (v. 17). Both the prayer and the recalling of the promise, then, belong not in David's day but sometime afterward. Indeed, in 2 Chron. 6:41–42, Solomon appeals to vv. 8–10 in his prayer at the dedication of the temple, and Solomon was clearly the first person open to being the beneficiary of

8. Terence E. Fretheim ("Psalm 132," *JBL* 86 [1967]: 289–300 [see 291–92]) argues that v. 10, in paralleling v. 1, begins the second half of the psalm (cf. Fokkelman, *Major Poems*, 3:293). But this makes for a jerky transition to v. 11 and spoils aspects of the parallelism between vv. 1–10 and 11–18.

the promises. This part of Solomon's prayer does not come in the earlier version in 1 Kings 8; it is part of the rewriting of Kings in Chronicles that brings its significance up to date for people after the exile. The fact that the text could be so meaningful in the Persian period shows that there need be no presupposition that this psalm that focuses on David and his successors must come from the time of the monarchy. David's commitment and Yhwh's responsive commitment to him remained of key importance when the monarchy was gone.

For Chronicles, that Yhwh indeed fulfilled this commitment to David by going to dwell in the sanctuary in Jerusalem in Solomon's day (and has now returned there after the exile) is of key importance for Chronicles' little community focused on Jerusalem, which has nothing like the significance and independence that it had in David's and Solomon's day. For Chronicles the focus of David's commitment, and of Yhwh's responsive commitment, lies on the references to Yhwh's dwelling and settlement; Yhwh has answered the prayer and fulfilled the promise. Conversely, Chronicles gives no indication in general that it focused on the monarchy's reestablishment: in other words that it had a messianic perspective. It may well have presupposed that Yhwh might in due course grant such a reestablishment, but its overt emphasis lies on the faithfulness of Yhwh actually embodied in the dwelling of Yhwh in Zion in the present.

The wording of Chronicles' version of vv. 8–10 also reflects the language of Isa. 55:3–5, which declares that Yhwh's commitment to David is fulfilled in Yhwh's commitment to the community as a whole and does not think in terms of a future individual Davidic king. (The fact that Chronicles was responsible for this most substantial difference in the wording of the two passages may suggest that it also lies behind the other detailed differences between the two versions of the text.) But Isa. 55 is explicit that it is offering a reworking of Yhwh's promise to David. The psalm begins from the original version, which pointed to a sequence of Davidic kings as well as emphasized the temple.[9] Other voices than that of Chronicles in the postexilic Jerusalem community did overtly speak of a future realization of the promise about the monarchy. Whereas in Ps. 89 the anointed king may still be reigning but has been humiliated, starting at least with Zerubbabel the postexilic community was familiar with the experience of having a person in its midst who should be king but is not, and v. 10 could refer (or could be made to refer) to such a person. The prayer's implication would then be that the anointed should

9. Thus Randy G. Haney concludes his study of the psalm by commenting that it is all about royal power, about the renewal of the dynasty (*Text and Concept Analysis in Royal Psalms* [New York: Lang, 2002], 151). This seems more plausible than the view of Jean-Marie Auwers ("Le Psaume 132 parmi les graduels," *RB* 103 [1996]: 546–60), who attributes to the psalm the view I associate with Chronicles.

actually be able to reign. But the psalm might equally be a prayer for the Davidic king and a recollection of Yhwh's commitment to him that comes from some time between Solomon and Zedekiah.

In principle, Gunkel's great achievement in inventing form criticism was to free the study of the Psalms from the futile attempt to focus the understanding of each psalm as a one-of-a-kind response to a unique historical context. Unfortunately, scholarly study nevertheless resisted the invitation to give up the fruitless (or overfruitful) attempt to discern when psalms were written, so that an interchange over the date of Ps. 132 at the end of the twentieth century showed that the world of scholarship has made no progress over the question whether the psalm belongs to the early monarchy or the postexilic period than was the case when Kirkpatrick laid out those possibilities at the beginning of the century.[10]

Perhaps worse, in attempting to move the focus of the question from once-for-all historical contexts to recurrent social contexts, Gunkel and his successors set scholarly study on another wild goose chase that has been just as fruitless (or overfruitful) and no more constructive than the one it replaced. It became the convention to interpret the psalm against its possible social context and in light of redactional processes it might have gone through, which has involved positing a liturgical background for and use of the psalm in an attempt to resolve unclarity by speculative hypotheses concerning matters external to the psalm. Not surprisingly, instead of resolving the questions, this has tended to multiply them.[11] Presumably the context in which people pray this prayer for the anointed is the worship of the temple in Jerusalem, and perhaps there was a regular occasion when the people used it thus. But we do not know when this might be. One can imagine that the psalm might be a liturgy in which the people or the choir says vv. 1–10 and a priest says vv. 11–18. It might also be that the references to movement (e.g., v. 7) reflect the use of the psalm itself in a procession, as the accompaniment to a ritual. But again, this is simply speculation.

Song of the Ascents.

10. See Antti Laato, "Psalm 132 and the Development of the Jerusalemite/Israelite Royal Ideology," *CBQ* 54 (1992): 49–66; and idem, "Psalm 132," *CBQ* 61 (1999): 24–33; Corrine L. Patton, "Psalm 132," *CBQ* 57 (1995): 643–54. See further Stephen Breck Reid, "Power and Practice," in *Psalms and Practice*, ed. Reid, 40–51; in light of the impasse, he goes on to consider the psalm as performative speech.

11. For redactional theories about the psalm, see Cornelius B. Houk, "Psalm 132," *JSOT* 6 (1978): 41–48 and 54–57; R. E. Bee, "The Textual Analysis of Psalm 132," *JSOT* 6 (1978): 49–53; and idem, "The Use of Syllable Counts in Textual Analysis," *JSOT* 10 (1978): 68–70; Saur, *Königspsalmen*, 225–48.

Heading. See glossary. It may have been the fact that the psalm does refer to movement to Jerusalem that encouraged its incorporation into the Songs of the Ascents; the pilgrims were involved in making the statement in v. 7 and came to Jerusalem to celebrate the fact that Yhwh had indeed answered the prayer and kept the promise.

132:1–2. The prayer for David.

1Yhwh, be mindful for David
of all his being troubled,

Such a plea for *mindfulness could be made on David's own behalf (cf. 25:6–7; 74:2; 136:23) or could mean that he is the basis of an appeal on someone else's behalf (Exod. 32:13; Deut. 9:27). It is only as the psalm unfolds that it will become clear that this prayer works in the latter way. It is a prayer for the later community, based on who David was and what he did. It is identified with him, so Yhwh "owes" them in "owing" him.

Specifically, the basis of the prayer is his being troubled or made *weak. There is only one place in the OT where a word from *ʿānâ* II unequivocally applies to David, *ʿŏnyî* in 1 Chron. 22:14, where the reference matches the present context very well. There David refers to the vast expenditure he has undertaken in providing for the temple that Solomon will build. The pual verb that comes here does come in a different connection in Lev. 23:29, and the usage is illuminating because (oddly for a pual) it refers to self-weakening, self-affliction. And the psalm's point is that David indeed imposed expenditure or weakening or trouble or affliction on himself in making it possible for Yhwh to settle in Jerusalem. The lexica also list *ʿānâ* III (Eccles. 1:13; 3:10), "be occupied/busy with," and these resonances sit well next to those of the occurrence of *ʿānâ* here and of *ʿŏnyî* in 1 Chron. 22:14.[12] With any of these implications, the word introduces the theme that will be expounded in vv. 2–9.

The fact that 1 Chron. 22:14 likely comes from later than the psalm and may be dependent on it (like 2 Chron. 6:41–42) means that Chronicles may again be interpreting the psalm. If we do not take Chronicles as the clue to understanding the psalm, this opens up another possibility. David was never weakened or troubled or afflicted, but Yhwh warned Solomon that this would happen to David's sons (1 Kings 11:39; *ʿānâ* piel). And indeed it did. Now the OT can use the name David not just to denote David ben Jesse but also to refer to whoever is the "David" of the day (see Hos. 3:5), the person who now embodies David. Verse 1 might then be directly a prayer for the current Davidic king (as it is anyway

12. Cf. Seybold, *Psalmen*, 497.

indirectly), as one who has been weakened through all those invasions and attacks that characterize the story of Judah.

[2]In that he swore to Yhwh,
vowed to Jacob's Strong One:

There is no doubt that v. 2 refers to David ben Jesse, though there is no account in the OT narrative of his swearing an oath in connection with what now follows, as there is no account of Yhwh's swearing an oath in the manner of vv. 11–18. In both cases the psalm expresses the implications of David's and Yhwh's actions.

"He [David] swore to [*lĕ*] Yhwh" corresponds to "Yhwh, be mindful for [*lĕ*] David." David's swearing is the basis for the appeal. In the parallelism of the line, "swore" (*šāba'* niphal) refers to the solemnity of the oath, "vowed" (*nādar*) to its content, as in English. The former is the more general word and the latter the more specific: vowing refers to what you will do, swearing to the fact that you cannot get out of it. Likewise "Yhwh" is the familiar term for Israel's God, while "Jacob's Strong One" is the rarer term. Outside this psalm, it comes only in Gen 49:24 (where Jacob himself speaks) and Isa. 49:26; 60:16 (also "Israel's Strong One" in Isa. 1:24). But *'ābîr* (the presumed absolute form) resembles *'abbîr*, another word for "strong one," referring to human beings, heavenly beings, or animals (22:12 [13]; 50:13; 68:30 [31]; 76:5 [6]; 78:25), and this spelling difference may have been introduced only to preserve a difference from the term with that other reference. Either way, the title denotes the might of God who is involved with Jacob and before whom no human or other heavenly strength can be a threat. Neither form of the word is ever brought into collocation with *'ānâ* or related words, but it is suggestive that the "Strong One" is here set over against the one who let himself be weakened.

132:3–5. David's commitment. As the declaration about David's oath reflects an imaginative reworking of the OT story, so the content of it expresses symbolically the nature of the king's commitment in a way that corresponds to other Middle Eastern literature.[13]

[3]"If I go into my tent, my house,
if I climb into my bed, my couch,
[4]If I give sleep to my eyes,
slumber to my eyelids,

13. Gerstenberger compares another Sumerian prayer (cf. the introductory comment on Ps. 127), of Gudea, the third-millennium king of Lagash in southern Mesopotamia (*Psalms*, 2:365, quoting from *Sumerische und akkadische Hymnen und Gebete*, ed. A. Falkenstein and W. von Soden [Zürich: Artemis, 1953], 154). See further Keel, *Symbolism*, 269–80.

[5]Before I find the place that belongs to Yhwh,
the dwelling that belongs to Jacob's Strong One. . . ."

The oath takes the common form of an unfinished self-curse (cf. 131:2); we are to imagine what might be the possible consequences of default. In vv. 3–4 David envisages several everyday acts, working out the possible prospects logically and sequentially through the two lines and thus building suspense. He could go inside, he could go upstairs, he could go to sleep. . . .[14] This process is enhanced by the unnecessary doubling of words for home and for sleeping place in v. 3 to produce rather quaint construct phrases, and by the unnecessary repetition of the description of going to sleep itself in the parallelism of v. 4, all of which underlines David's determination. "Tent" is an anachronism for a dwelling, though a common one (e.g., 84:10 [11]; Isa. 16:5). Etymologically the word for "bed" (*ʿereś*) suggests a bed frame, while the word for "couch" (*yāṣûaʿ*) suggests something spread out (cf. 139:8). If there is a substantial difference between v. 4a and 4b, then the second colon would suggest letting oneself get drowsy and letting one's eyelids droop, while the first would denote being fast asleep with one's eyes shut, which is the reverse of chronology. Perhaps we are to understand "or even" in connection with v. 4b; or perhaps the parallelism works by using the more common words first and the rarer ones second.[15]

David will do none of that until . . . (v. 5). The ancient versions take v. 5 to denote a place *for* Yhwh; it refers to David's intent to provide Yhwh with a dwelling in Jerusalem. Although he moves from speaking of a tent or a house (words he could have used with reference to Yhwh) to speaking of a place and a dwelling, the substance of the line would then make clear that the oath is not random. He has a house; Yhwh does not. The substance, though not the words, corresponds to his words in 2 Sam. 7:1. David has a cedar-paneled house. The covenant chest lives in a tent, a more literal one, a tent dwelling (2 Sam. 7:6; the words are doubled, like the ones in v. 3 of the psalm), though Yhwh of course is quite happy about that. David wants to provide Jacob's Strong One with the appropriate great or multiroomed dwelling (*miškān* as in 2 Sam. 7:6, but in the intensive plural).[16] In the first colon he speaks in terms of a "place," which sounds vaguer and could therefore be nuanced by the parallel word; but "place" is often a term for a sanctuary. It recurs

14. Tg refers the first clause to having sex with his wife, which might be implicit somewhere in the three lines; Gunkel (*Psalms*, 566) compares 2 Sam. 11:9–13.

15. Verse 3 works neatly *abcda′b′c′d′*; v. 4 works *abcdd′c*, with the *ab* elements repeating the pattern of v. 3 and the end of the four-colon clause sequence advertised by the reversal of direct and indirect object at the close.

16. Cf. Pss. 43:3; 46:4 [5]; 84:1 [2] (GKC 124b, e–f).

in Deut. 12 and in 2 Chron. 6:20–26. Its derivation from *qûm* suggests it points not merely to a location but to something that has been set up. David is committed to finding a structure, a dwelling.

But the following verses will suggest that v. 5 rather denotes the place and dwelling that Yhwh already has.[17] David's concern for the place/dwelling that belongs to Yhwh (*lĕ*, repeated) will be balanced by Yhwh's concern for the throne that belongs to David (*lĕ*, repeated) in vv. 11–12. It is this already-existing place/dwelling that David needs to "find" (cf. v. 6). According to 1 Sam. 6, after its Philistine adventures the covenant chest came to be located at Kiriat-Jearim, ten miles west of Jerusalem. But apparently Kiriat-Jearim did not become a sanctuary, certainly not *the* sanctuary. Immediately after the story of the chest's arriving at Kiriat-Jearim, we hear of Samuel gathering the people before Yhwh at *Mizpah*, as he does again for Saul's proclamation (1 Sam. 7:5; 10:17), while he confirms Saul's kingship before Yhwh at *Gilgal* and Saul makes his own notorious offerings there (1 Sam. 11:14–15; 13:8–15). Kiriat-Jearim was not in undisputed Israelite territory or undisputed Yhwh territory (in 2 Sam. 6:2 it is referred to as Baale-Judah, and David's collecting the chest involves his taking 30,000 troops). This shrine where the chest was located plays no part in Israel's life through the period of the leadership of Samuel or Saul, in fact within the lifetime of virtually anyone in David's day. David himself is subsequently twice anointed at Hebron and later moves his center to Jerusalem without reference to it (2 Sam. 2–5). In 1 Chron. 13:3 he observes that Israel had not had recourse to it through Saul's reign.[18] Against the background of that story, it is quite an intelligible idea that David should commit himself to locating the place or dwelling that belonged to Yhwh, in the sense that the chest was there. Conversely, David does not need to *find* the place where Yhwh is henceforth to reside; he knows where that is. He has a plan. What he has to do is find the place where the chest now is.

132:6–9. The people's determination. There is some jerkiness about the transition from vv. 1–5 to vv. 6–9. Who are the "we," and how do their words relate to what has preceded? In a sense they continue the words of the "I" in vv. 3–5 and thus continue David's words even though they move to "we." The people who joined with David now associate themselves with the action that issues from David's resolve (cf. 1 Chron. 13 more emphatically than 2 Sam. 6). Although vv. 2–5 spoke of David making an oath at the beginning of the sanctuary-finding process, vv. 6–7 jump forward to speak of the process whereby the people began to implement

17. Cf. Briggs, *Psalms*, 2:467. For the use of *lĕ* in this way, cf. Job 28:1, where "the place for gold" means "the place where people find gold."

18. According to 1 Sam. 14:18 MT, Saul had access to the chest, though LXX has "ephod" instead.

the oath. Another jump forward is then involved in vv. 8–9 as they recall the words the people then uttered. The jerkiness of this transition is both augmented and ameliorated if we associate the "we" with the people who spoke in v. 1, the people who asked Yhwh to be mindful of David. They are then identifying themselves with that process just described. It is as if they were themselves involved when their ancestors undertook this action with David. And this identification might also indicate that they are people involved in a liturgical reenactment of those events, as happens in a Jewish celebration of Passover or a church dramatization of the Easter story, though we have no evidence of that.

6Now: we heard of it at Ephrata,
we found it in the lands of Jaar.

Ephrata is the name of the place where Rachel died, though there is some confusion over its location; it is also a name for the area of Bethlehem (e.g., Ruth 4:11; Mic. 5:2 [1]), so that David was an Ephratite (1 Sam. 17:12).[19] That would obviously be an apposite place to hear David's actual oath, or for the "we" to imagine hearing it, when David was ruling at Hebron, further south of Jerusalem, and thinking of moving the covenant chest to Jerusalem and building a sanctuary there (2 Sam. 5–7). The chest itself was actually located at Kiriat-Jearim, "the town of Jearim," whose area is here referred to in the parallel colon.[20] It has been hypothesized that Ephrata was also a name for Kiriat-Jearim (see BDB), but that is hardly necessary or advisable. It would be a big coincidence if Ephrata were (a) well known as the place David came from, (b) otherwise unmentioned as a term for the Jaar area, but (c) nevertheless the place this passage refers to. Rather, there is movement between the two cola, from the place where one could have heard the oath to the place David then went to.

That would imply that there is also movement in the reference of the "it." "We found it" has been reckoned to refer anticipatorily to the chest, and in substance that is right, but the psalm has not actually referred to the chest, and "it" is feminine both times.[21] More likely, then, the second "it" is the place or dwelling of v. 5; "place" was masculine singular, "dwelling" feminine plural, so feminine singular (the regular

19. "Ephratite" is also the word for someone from Ephraim (Judg. 12:4–6; cf. 1 Sam. 1:1), but this hardly means that Ephrata could mean Ephraim; and anyway, Jaar was on the border of Judah and Benjamin, not in Ephraim.

20. *Ya'ar* is the regular word for a wood, and LXX, Jerome take it in this sense. A. Robinson ("Do Ephrathah and Jaar Really Appear in Psalm 132,6," *ZAW* 86 [1974]: 220–22) also emends out of existence the first name.

21. Jerome has m. suffixes (though in his exposition in *Homilies*, 1:331, he applies LXX's f. to Mary); cf. Gunkel, *Psalmen*, 569; and Otto Eissfeldt's comments, "Psalm 132," in Eissfeldt, *Kleine Schriften* (Tübingen: Mohr, 1966), 3:481–85 (see 483).

way of referring to an indeterminate "it"), makes a good compromise. Retrospectively, that suggests that v. 6a denotes "we heard *of* it" (cf. the use of the verb in 44:1 [2]; 48:8 [9]), that is, "heard of the place and dwelling" (cf. NRSV). Back in Ephrata, the location of David's home and broad clan base, people first heard of where the shrine was and set off to find it, as David had determined (v. 5).

> 7Let us go into his dwelling,
> let us bow down at his footstool.

Out of the context, these clauses could represent the commitment of Israel to go to Jerusalem to the dwelling and footstool that came to be there, but in the development of the drama in the psalm it is too soon for that, and the repeat of the word "dwelling" pending the move to "settlement" confirms that this determination refers to the journey to Jaar. Perhaps "found" in v. 6 still meant "located," if v. 7 represents the people's consequent determination actually to go to Kiriat-Jearim. After taking up the expression "dwelling" from v. 5, the people gloss that as Yhwh's footstool. In Lam. 2:1, this expression may refer to the Jerusalem sanctuary (cf. "place for his feet" in Isa. 60:13); the picture is then of Yhwh enthroned in the heavens, with the sanctuary as footstool. But in 1 Chron. 28:2 the term may naturally refer specifically to the chest, the resting place for Yhwh, who is enthroned *in* the temple. Psalm 99:5 may have the same understanding, the cherubim on which Yhwh is enthroned being the temple cherubim that represent the heavenly cherubim. Here, the sequence of verbs points in that direction. First the people go into the shrine, then they bow at the footstool.

> 8"Rise, Yhwh, to your settlement,
> you and your mighty chest,

The imaginative recollection or reliving of the event continues. David and the people are not satisfied that Yhwh should have a dwelling at Kiriat-Jearim; they have a plan for a permanent settlement in Jerusalem. Like "tent," "dwelling" suggests some ambiguity over its permanency. Although "dwell" and the associated nouns often refer to permanent dwellings, the vast majority of occurrences of the word "dwelling" denote the moveable sanctuary whose construction is described in Exodus. The word is also used to refer to Yhwh's "tent-dwelling" (2 Sam. 7:6), which Yhwh rather preferred because of its mobility but which was a cause of embarrassment to David. David wanted to build for Yhwh, and specifically for the covenant chest and Yhwh's footstool, a settlement (*mĕnûḥâ*), a place that would signify permanency (1 Chron. 28:2; cf.

1 Chron. 6:31 [16]). In some way the chest (mentioned here alone in the Psalms) suggests the presence of Yhwh, a dynamic presence and one that could mediate Yhwh's powerful presence in war; so it is "the chest of Yhwh's might."[22] On their journey to the promised land, the place of settlement, Moses would say as the chest set out each day, "Arise, Yhwh, may your enemies be scattered, may those who are against you flee from before you" (Num. 10:35). Those words have not been uttered for a century; now they are uttered one more time, but with the intention of getting Yhwh and the chest to move, not from a long-time halt back to ongoing action, but from a long-time halt to a properly settled place. After the exile, there would be no covenant chest for people to call on and thus this recollection would have some poignancy, though the loss of the chest would be no obstacle to mentioning it in connection with these earlier events.

> [9]As your priests clothe themselves in faithfulness
> and the people committed to you resound."

Presumably the priests and people are those who accompany the move of the chest, as they accompanied it on that earlier journey in Num. 10. The expression "the people *committed to you" does not appear there; it is almost exclusively a Psalms term. That lifts the veil from the fact that this whole account is both a recollection of events that the people heard about in their story and one with which they themselves identified. Likewise the description of the priests as clothed in *faithfulness no doubt has in mind the priests of the day in which the psalm was used. There is no reference to priests in 2 Sam. 6, though there is in 1 Chron. 13, and much more in 1 Chron. 15 after things went wrong at the first attempt to get the chest to Jerusalem. Perhaps the reference to priests clothed in faithfulness draws attention to the importance of the priests doing their work properly, otherwise disaster can follow. Tg takes the committed people to be the Levites, which further underlines the point. *Resounding, too, is a word that belongs much more in the Psalms than elsewhere to describe Israel's ongoing worship, though no doubt it would be a good summary of the noise described in 2 Sam. 6; 1 Chron. 13; 15.

132:10. The plea resumed.

> [10]For the sake of David your servant,
> do not turn away the face of your anointed.

22. LXX has "your holy chest."

The point about all that recollection in vv. 2–9 with its links with a possible reenactment of the events is to back up the plea with which the psalm opened, and the first half of the psalm comes to a climax and closes with a reformulating of that plea. David showed himself indeed to be Yhwh's servant, willing to be troubled in the sense of having his resources spent to undertake the work on Yhwh's sanctuary. It was in connection with his desire not only to move the chest to Jerusalem but to provide Yhwh with a settled home there that Yhwh, notwithstanding having some unease, made the extraordinary commitment to David described in 2 Sam. 7. That related not only to him but to his descendants.

And the real focus of the prayer is the current descendant of David, the current *anointed (Tg takes the anointed to be Solomon). Indeed, we have noted that it is possible to speak of this person as the current David, and one could so understand the parallelism here. But parallelism does not exclude movement between cola, and following on v. 1 (and vv. 1–9 as a whole), the first colon more likely refers to David ben Jesse. This will be confirmed by vv. 11–12, which surely refer to that David. "Anointed" describes a person who has had olive oil poured or smeared over him by Yhwh's representative as a sign of his designation to serve Yhwh as a priest or a king, his initiation into that service, and his consequent special status. Outside the OT it comes to be used in reference to a figure to appear in the future, but within the OT it refers to an existing king or priest (e.g., 2:2; 18:50 [51]; 89:51 [52]; more loosely in 105:15). The psalm's assumption is that any anointed king will come before Yhwh like a suppliant who comes to show his face before the king himself and plead for some favor. It asks that Yhwh will no more turn away his face than the king would turn away a suppliant's face. This term for rejecting someone, making the person turn around and go away, comes elsewhere only in 1 Kings 2:16–20 of Adonijah making a bold request of Bathsheba and Bathsheba of Solomon (and when the psalm is quoted in 2 Chron. 6:42). The form of expression points away from the idea that the psalm is messianic in the sense that Israel currently has no anointed king. Rather it does have an anointed (whether he is actually king or not), and the psalm asks for Yhwh to be responsive to him.

132:11–12. "Yhwh, be mindful for David," the first half of the psalm began (v. 1). "Yhwh swore to David," the second half begins, as a response reminding whoever spoke at the beginning about the antecedent event that means their plea will be answered; "swore" itself then picks up from v. 2.

Yhwh's actual oath then mirrors David's in v. 2. David made his oath and fulfilled it; Yhwh now makes his oath. The order of events corresponds to that in 2 Sam. 6–7 and 1 Chron. 13–17, even though they mention no actual oaths. In substance v. 11 also relates to v. 10 in providing the basis for reckoning that the prayer would be answered. The original oath might be delivered by a prophet such as Nathan; in worship it might be delivered by such a prophet, or by a priest.[23]

> 11Yhwh swore to David in truthfulness;
> he will not turn from it:
> The fruit of your body
> I will place on the throne that belongs to you.

Although the OT narrative does not have Yhwh swearing an oath to David, Ps. 89:3, 35, 49 [4, 36, 50] has Yhwh doing so in connection with the promise of sons to succeed him (cf. also 110:4); in this connection it, too, also refers to David as Yhwh's servant and Yhwh's anointed and to Yhwh's covenant, and has Yhwh swearing by his "*truthfulness" (*ʾĕmûnâ*; cf. *ʾĕmet*). Both psalms thus relate Yhwh's oath to the community's prayer for the king as David's successor; it is because Yhwh swore an oath that it can lean on Yhwh. Yhwh cannot get out of keeping this commitment. The *truthfulness with which Yhwh swore is Yhwh's own truthfulness, the inherent need to be true to who Yhwh is. "Your words will become truthfulness" (2 Sam. 7:28; *ʾĕmet*, as here).

Thus v. 11b draws out an inevitable implication of v. 11a. The affirmation about turning has different reference from the one it had in v. 10, but rhetorically the recurrence of the actual verb gives the affirmation the air of a positive response to v. 10.

The content of the oath, then, is that David's own offspring will succeed him. In substance this content is thus the same as that in 2 Sam. 7:12, though in its wording it is quite different. While this might reflect the existence of different traditions, it is just as likely that either or both issue from the creativity of their authors. In 2 Sam. 7:12–15 the promise refers to David's immediate successor, even if the subsequent reference to David's throne being established forever may imply a look far beyond David's day (though it could just imply "to the end of your life"). In the psalm, the form of expression in v. 11 does not make clear whether Yhwh refers to David's single immediate successor or to a line of descendants; v. 12 will imply the latter. The expression for "your body" (lit. "your insides") usually refers to the womb, but it can also be used of the insides of a man (Judg. 3:21–22). Likewise, the phrase "the fruit of your body" might usually refer to a woman (Ps. 127:3) but could also be used in addressing a man (e.g., Mic. 6:7), whose insides make their own

23. Hilber (*Cultic Prophecy*, 101–15) compares with Assyrian cultic prophecy, the comparison suggesting that vv. 11–18 reflect actual oracles rather than being merely a psalmist's construction.

contribution to procreation.[24] Either way, the image of fruitfulness is a suggestive one. God has given the body a natural capacity to produce seed and make it grow into something complete and mature with the capacity for self-reproduction, essentially like that from which it came.

Yhwh's promise is not merely that David will have offspring (actually he already has many) but that they will occupy his throne. Yhwh's taking care for the throne that belongs to him matches David's taking care for the place/dwelling that belongs to Yhwh (v. 5).

> **12** If your descendants keep my covenant,
> my declarations, which I will teach them,
> Their descendants, too, forever,
> will sit on the throne that belongs to you.

Yhwh continues in a way that might seem to compromise the apparently unequivocal nature of the oath in v. 11, though again the verse overlaps with the substance if not the words of 2 Sam. 7:14–15. When Saul did wrong, he and his line were rejected. In 2 Sam. 7:14–15, Yhwh promised not to take that action again. When Solomon does wrong, Yhwh will "correct him" or "chasten him" in the manner of a teacher or parent (rather than punish him in the manner of a court of law) but will not withdraw commitment from him. The passage does not explicitly refer to Yhwh's making a covenant in this connection, though 2 Sam. 23:5 does so. But in any case, in the psalm the argument goes in a different direction. The *covenant to which Yhwh here refers is not the covenant commitment that Yhwh made (as in Pss. 89:3, 28, 34, 39 [4, 29, 35, 40]) but the covenant commitment that Yhwh expects of David's descendants. Such expectations of covenantal commitment are expressed in 25:10; 44:17 [18]; 103:18, though there they relate to the covenant with Israel rather than with David, and perhaps that is presupposed here.[25]

Either way, "covenant" here has similar meaning to *declarations; both terms refer to expectations that Yhwh lays down. Indeed, Yhwh will be involved in an ongoing teaching relationship with David's descendants, of the kind that Ps. 119 keeps describing for people in general. To judge from that parallel, the basic covenant requirements and thus the declarations are fixed, and the teaching will not necessarily involve new content. But Yhwh will be active in bringing home its significance and

24. Unless one treats the construct "the-fruit-of-your-womb" as meaning "your fruit that comes from the womb" (of its mother) (JM 140b); cf. expressions such as "the-house-of-my-prayer," which means "my house of prayer."

25. See the discussion in Philip Nel, "Psalm 132 and Covenant Theology," in *Text and Context*, ed. W. Claassen, JSOTSup 48 (F. C. Fensham Festschrift; Sheffield: Sheffield Academic Press, 1988), 183–91.

demand. As in Ps. 119, this does not mean Yhwh inscribes these declarations into people's brains so that they become part of their instinct, like the instinct to eat or sleep. Pupils can resist their teachers. There is no learning without teaching, but teaching requires a response.

If they do respond and keep Yhwh's covenant declarations, then their descendants in turn will sit on the throne that belongs to David (that phrase again), and this arrangement will hold forever. What happens if they do not do so? The implication should be that David's throne will fall. (And of course it did; Yhwh kept the covenant commitment for four hundred years, but has then abandoned it for 2,500 years, or turned it into something else.) Psalm 89 is more explicit. There, the principle applied to Solomon is extended to his descendants; Yhwh will take action against rebellious kings, but will not abandon them, because of that commitment to David and Solomon. Psalm 132 does not say this. But perhaps its presupposition is that the question does not arise because at least the present king or the present anointed is keeping the covenant and the declarations.

132:13–16. Yhwh's commitment to Zion. The "because" that follows points to an answer to the question just raised, though in the manner of this psalm it skips a stage or two of the argument. There are two reasons for Yhwh to keep David's descendants on the throne: their responsiveness to Yhwh, if they manifest this, and Yhwh's responsiveness to David. Verses 13–16 abandon the former and begin from the latter.

> 13Because Yhwh chose Zion;
> he wanted it as a seat that belongs to him.
> 14This is my settlement forever,
> where I will sit, because I wanted it.

Once again the psalm offers an extra perspective on the story in 2 Sam. 6–7. There, the only person who did any choosing of Zion was David (though the verb does not occur). Only in Solomon's time does Zion become the city Yhwh chose (e.g., 1 Kings 8:44, 48; 11:13, 32, 36; 2 Chron. 6:5–6, 34, 38). It became it again after the exile (Zech. 1:17; 2:12 [16]; 3:2). Wanting is a stronger, affective, and rarer verb to accompany choosing; it, too, was David's business (2 Sam. 3:21), then Jeroboam's (1 Kings 11:37), and only here becomes Yhwh's. Zion becomes the seat (*môšāb*) that belongs to him (*lĕ* again), the place where Yhwh sits. The term applies to Yhwh's dwelling only here (it refers to a human dwelling in 107:4, 7, 36), but it makes a link retrospectively with the sitting of v. 12 and that of v. 14, again suggesting the interwovenness of Yhwh's activity and the king's activity. David chose, Yhwh chose; David wanted, Yhwh wanted; David sat and will sit, Yhwh sat and will sit.[26]

Verse 14 thus restates the point, adding only that the seat is also a "settlement," the people's word in v. 8. Once again, then, Yhwh takes up the human action and affirms it. The significance of this is underlined by the other major difference between vv. 13 and 14. In v. 13, Yhwh is referred to in the third person; in v. 14 Yhwh explicitly speaks. Admittedly, the resumption in v. 14 may indicate that Yhwh continues to speak in v. 13, self-referring in the third person; Yhwh then speaks through vv. 11c–18. But the form of expression in v. 13 distances Yhwh from the statement and reminds us that it is the psalmist who makes the declaration directly; there is then a move back in v. 14 to Yhwh's speaking in person to affirm it.

15Its supplies I will greatly bless,
its needy I will fill with bread.
16Its priests I will clothe in deliverance,
its committed people will greatly resound.

Yhwh's own words continue in a series of further declarations of intent. Zion is the source of blessing as Yhwh's life flows out from there, but here it is also the recipient of blessing through Yhwh's presence settling there. As happens with urbanization, one of the results of development of the state with its capital in Jerusalem and the building of its temple there was the development of the gap between the well-off and the *needy. Yhwh makes a point of noting that the needy are the special beneficiaries of the blessing of Zion. But in a postexilic context, "the needy" comes to be not a characterization of a segment within the community but of the community as a whole (e.g., Hag. 1:1–11), and the parallelism could imply that here. "Greatly bless" (the construction involves emphasis by preceding the verb with its infinitive) pairs with "fill"; "bread" pairs with "supplies."

Verse 16 continues to expound how Yhwh's presence in this settlement will mean abundance, not merely survival; it repeats v. 9 with variation, beginning again with the fact that Yhwh is the one who clothes the priests. Perhaps it follows from this that they are now clothed in *deliverance. They stand and minister as witnesses to the fact that Yhwh is Israel's great deliverer. Thus blessing and deliverance (Yhwh's regular activity in providing for people and Yhwh's occasional acts in rescuing them)

26. Elizabeth F. Huweiler ("Patterns and Problems in Psalm 132," in *The Listening Heart*, ed. K. G. Hoglund and others, JSOTSup 58 [R. E. Murphy Festschrift; Sheffield: Sheffield Academic Press, 1987], 199–215 [see 209]) compares the twofold use of "sit" with the twofold use of *bayit* in 2 Sam. 7.

come together in the two lines, in a suggestive way. The lines thus bear comparison with Isa. 61:9–11, where the same two themes recur along with other motifs paralleled in the psalm, again in the context of the pressures of the postexilic community.

In response to all that, Zion's *committed people indeed greatly *resound (the verbal idiom from v. 15 recurs).

132:17–18. The psalm once again returns to Yhwh's commitment to David.

> [17]There I will make the horn that belongs to David flourish;
> I have set up the flame that belongs to my anointed.

The last section begins by bringing together Zion ("there") and David for the last time. David has been vital to Zion; Zion will be vital to David. It is indeed the case that Zion becomes a resource for blessing and deliverance as well as a recipient of it. Verse 17 once again uses the *l* expression that came in vv. 5, 11, and 12. As there, in poetry the absence of the article does not mean it refers to *a* horn or lamp (one that does not yet exist); it denotes *the* horn and lamp that David already has. Indeed, one might have thought that David's metaphorical horn (the embodiment of an animal's strength) had already grown quite big, but it will continue to flourish or will grow even more. NRSV has "sprout," which rather suggests the beginning of new growth or the initial blossoming of growth,[27] but *ṣāmaḥ* naturally suggests proliferation and thriving (104:14; 147:8). It is somewhat ironic that while the noun "*anointed" (to recur in the parallel colon) does not become a messianic term until after OT times, the less familiar noun from this verb, *ṣemaḥ*, used in the literal sense of flourishing growth in 65:10 [11], becomes such a term within the OT (see especially Jer. 23:5). The psalm's point is that the full growth of David's horn is not something that will have to wait until the end; it will be a continuing reality in Israel's experience.

The guarantee of that future flourishing is the action that Yhwh has taken already in setting up the lamplight that belongs to the anointed. As in v. 10, whereas the first colon refers directly to David ben Jesse, the expression "my anointed" is not confined to David personally but covers whoever sits on David's throne in succession to him. Indeed, the whole promise might be a quite separate one from that in vv. 11–12, a promise given in the later context of the psalm rather than restating Yhwh's original promise to David.[28] "Setting up a flame" refers elsewhere to Aaron's putting in place the lights and other things in the meeting

27. Thus Goulder (*Psalms of the Return*, 94) sees v. 17 as evidence that there was no Davidic king at the time.

28. So Allen, *Psalms 101–150*, 266.

tent (Lev. 24:3–4). These lights are not freestanding lampstands but the various flames that burn on the candelabra. Here David is the candelabra and his successors are the individual lights that burn from him. The OT narrative seems to refer back to this promise as the guarantee that Yhwh will continue to keep David's light shining when it might have been allowed to die out, as, for instance, in 2 Kings 8:19 and 2 Chron. 21:7, though there it spells the word *nîr*, not *nēr*. In Aramaic *nîr* can mean a yoke and the servitude a yoke can symbolize, while Akkadian also has the word *nîru*, which denotes a yoke, and figuratively a king's dominion; awareness of this may lie behind that alternative spelling.[29] If so, *nîr* offers an interpretation of *nēr*. The flame that belongs to the anointed is David's yoke, David's rule.

> **18**His enemies I will clothe in shame,
> but upon him his crown will sparkle.

David's rule will not be confined to Israel. Aaron sets up the lamps in the meeting tent before Yhwh; Yhwh sets up the lamp that belongs to David before his enemies. While the promise would apply to internal enemies, it would more commonly need to apply to other peoples who think they can resist the yoke of Yhwh and Yhwh's anointed (Ps. 2), but are in for a rude awakening. The verb "I will clothe" recurs from v. 16, with contrasting but complementary implications to the ones that apply there.

The final colon contrasts with that but also makes for further links with v. 17. The reference to David's crown could support the view that *nēr* suggests dominion; for people who were not aware of that possible nuance of *nîr*, the specific reference to David's crown means that in any case the notion of David's rule over the nations is brought into association with the reference to the horn and the flame. As in 89:39 [40], the word for crown is not the everyday, more secular word *ʿăṭārâ* but *nēzer*, a word with more religious associations. Its mother verb means to consecrate, so that this crown is a symbol of the king's dedication to Yhwh.[30] Its resonances thus match those of the description of the king as Yhwh's anointed. It also resembles *nēṣer*, another word for flourishing growth that becomes a messianic term within the OT (for instance, Isa. 11:1), and these resonances may also hang around the word. That possibility is heightened by the verb *yāṣîṣ* in the last colon. It adds to this richness of allusion, since it can refer both to the flourishing blossom of a flower and to the shining of gold or precious stone. Both overtones

29. See *TDOT* 10:18; *DCH*.

30. Cf. LXX *hagiasma*, Sym *hagiasmos*, Jerome *sanctificatio*; also Aq *aphorisma*; contrast Tg *kĕlîlêh*.

take aspects of the imagery in vv. 17–18 further. The colon thus closes the psalm and Yhwh's promise with a subtle and rich picture of a crown sparkling and growth abounding.

Theological Implications

The nature of the psalms is that they commonly express one voice, such as that of the congregation addressing God, or God addressing the congregation. Psalm 132 involves a conversation and reminds us that this is an aspect of the nature of worship. Indeed, one might argue that Ps. 132 thereby reminds us of a central aspect of worship that other psalms no doubt presuppose but do not make explicit.

The worship conversation concerns the past and the future. In this particular case, the congregation appeals to its own past. Theologically, one might have expected this to be the past of Yhwh's deeds, the story of Yhwh's great acts of deliverance, but in this case the congregation appeals to its own acts, and in particular to the acts of its great hero, who was fortunately also someone of great commitment to Yhwh. It identifies with that hero in more than one sense. It can move easily from quoting his words and actions ("I") to speaking in terms of a "we" representing the people associated with him in those words and actions, but also representing its own identification with those words and actions. In Christian worship, when we ask "Were you there when they crucified my Lord?" we invite people so to identify. It is the fact that the psalm can do this that gives point to its recollection in vv. 1–10; otherwise it would have no point. David's actions carry credit with Yhwh, not just for himself and not just for the people of his day, but also for his successors and for their successors. As Presbyterians we can appeal to what John Calvin did, Lutherans to what Martin Luther did, Episcopalians to what Thomas Cranmer did, Pentecostals to what Aimee Semple McPherson did, Charismatics to what John Wimber did. . . . Of course this presupposes that we do identify with the "trouble" they took or experienced. . . .

Yhwh also appeals to the past; that is the way Yhwh offers the congregation the reassurance it seeks. This past was not merely an act of David but a reactive response of Yhwh. In David's story as a whole, Israel's narrative put Yhwh's initiative first (1 Sam. 16; 1 Chron. 11:1–3), but in the segment of the narrative to which the psalm refers (2 Sam. 5–7; 1 Chron. 13–17), Yhwh's promise to David is a reaction to David's initiative. Yet this again does not let a later generation off the hook. The OT as a whole presupposes a complex interplay between the commitment of God and human beings that can no more be reduced to a formula than can the commitment of human beings to one another. That is, we mislead ourselves if we declare that the relationship between God and human beings is or is not conditional or unconditional or contractual. We do better to refer to it as covenantal, as long as we do not let that declaration get confused by assimilating what we mean by a covenant to what Israel means by a *bĕrît*. Here, I use the word "covenant" with more the meaning it has when Jonathan and David enter into a covenant, or when people covenant themselves to one another in marriage. Those relationships presuppose a mutual commitment, but they are not exactly conditional or unconditional or contractual. They are more personal than such categories imply. The psalm sets alongside each other the oath Yhwh swore to David regarding his successors, and the necessity that these successors keep Yhwh's *bĕrît*, but wisely declines to make more explicit the relationship between these two; that would be to turn a mutual commitment into a contract. David's commitment to Yhwh wins Yhwh's commitment to David and to his successors. Yhwh's commitment to David must win the commitment of David's successors to Yhwh. Only then will the whole deal work. The consequence in v. 12 is a logical one, not a contractual one.

The psalm points to another, even more remarkable, feature of the relationship between divine and human initiative. It is said that "if you build it, they will come." But this psalm says, "If you build it, he will come." Israel's narrative did not attribute the taking of Jerusalem or the building of the temple to Yhwh's initiative, but to David's. Yet here, "Yhwh chose Zion" (v. 13). Rhetorically, Yhwh did that in Solomon's day; that is, it is Solomon's temple dedication prayer that first speaks of Yhwh choosing Zion, while Jeroboam is the first person who hears Yhwh confirm that this happened. These two narratives point to two contexts when Yhwh's choice of Zion becomes significant. The one is when the people are away from the land, and especially when they are in exile; the other is when other people such as Ephraim declare that Zion is not chosen.

All this is the more remarkable because of the extraordinary contrast between vv. 13–14 and the narrative in 2 Sam. 7:1–11 (1 Chron. 17:1–10 broadly follows). There, David is uneasy because he is living (*yāšab*) in a house and Yhwh has settled him in his position in safety (*nûaḥ* hiphil), but Yhwh is living (*yāšab*) in a tent. That makes him want Yhwh to have a house to live in (*yāšab*). Yhwh's reaction is to declare entire satisfaction with having lived in a tent or dwelling (*yāšab, ʾōhel, miškān*) and then to declare the intention to establish a place (*māqôm*) for Israel where they may dwell (*šākan*). In this psalm, in vv. 1–8 David does not wish to enter his tent/house until he finds the place/dwelling that belongs to Yhwh. Then the people hasten to go to that dwelling, and subsequently they urge Yhwh to go to "your settlement" (*mĕnûḥâ*). The content of vv.

1–8 thus broadly matches David's attitudes in 2 Sam. 7:1–11. But Yhwh's response in the narrative and here in vv. 13–14 is quite different. There, Yhwh confronts David over his desire to build a house and puts the stress back on the primacy of Yhwh's action in relation to him; it is Yhwh who will establish a place for Israel and enable them to dwell there, not David who will find Yhwh's place/dwelling, though Yhwh will eventually let David's successor build a house for Yhwh. Here, Yhwh not only chooses Zion but *wants* it as a seat, a place to live (*môšāb*), a settlement (*mĕnûḥâ*). The contrasting attitudes Yhwh expresses to the temple compare with the contrasting attitudes Yhwh takes to the monarchy itself, especially in 1 Sam. 8–12. In some superficial sense they represent contradiction, but they do so necessarily, because radical theological ambiguity attaches to both monarchy and temple. The desire for a monarch involves a rejection of Yhwh's kingship and leads Israel into great waywardness, but it is also the means of Yhwh's taking Israel's story to its greatest heights and of providing it with the key category whereby the Scriptures will conceptualize the redemption of the world. The proposal for a temple involves skewing the relationship between divine and human initiative and between a commitment to Yhwh in worship and in the rest of life, and also threatens to tie Yhwh down to one place. But it makes Yhwh wondrously and surely accessible to people and constitutes a sacrament of that presence for people when Yhwh is not active in their public life.

In the conversation represented by this psalm, both congregation and Yhwh speak about the future as well as about the past, but they do so on the basis of the observations about the past. It is because of what David did in the past that the people can ask that their future be secured, through Yhwh's being mindful of David and not turning away his successors. It is typical of such prayers in the Psalms thus to be rather unspecific and to go for the basic attitude on Yhwh's part that can then issue in whatever Yhwh decrees.

In response, Yhwh makes promises about the future that build on what Yhwh said in the past. Yhwh is interestingly more specific. (We should be concrete about what we intend to do but let other people decide on the specifics of what they are going to do?) David's descendants will sit on his throne. Yhwh will stay in Jerusalem forever. Yhwh will provide for its people, and specifically for its needy. Yhwh will make sure that David's successors exercise authority in the world and that his enemies are disgraced. Of course the trouble with being specific is that you can be checked up on, and Yhwh has often not done those things. And that reflects (among other things) the fact that declining to call the relationship conditional does not mean that failing to keep Yhwh's *bĕrît* has no consequences, any more than is the case when friends betray each other or a husband or wife is unfaithful.

The reciprocity in this relationship, in regard to the past and the future, links with an implicit reciprocity in the psalm's rhetoric. The psalm addresses Yhwh in vv. 1–10 and reports Yhwh's words in vv. 11–18. It does not make explicit who speaks in v. 1, and thus in vv. 1–10 as a whole, or who is addressed in v. 11, or actually who speaks in v. 11. The actual oath that follows is Yhwh's and it addresses David, but who is uttering it in Yhwh's name, and who is being told about it? If there were a vocative at the beginning of v. 11 like the vocative at the beginning of v. 1, to whom would it refer? Since vv. 11–18 respond to vv. 1–10, the voice in v. 1 and the ears in v. 11 will be the same. They are those of the congregation, perhaps represented by a leader such as a priest, or even by the current "anointed" in person, though the "we" in vv. 6–7 suggests that this is not simply a private conversation between the anointed and Yhwh. Likewise, the priests and committed people of vv. 9 and 16 are surely assumed to be present when the psalm is used; they are not merely present in it rhetorically.

Yet further, throughout the psalm both Yhwh and the people are actually addressed, implicitly where this is not so explicitly. In vv. 1–10 the congregation speaks to Yhwh (perhaps via the person of its leader) but also speaks to itself and begins to encourage itself. In vv. 11–18 Yhwh speaks to the people (perhaps via the person of a priest or prophet) and encourages them, but the words come from a human mouth that Yhwh overhears in the worship of the congregation and in the context of a psalm that as such is actually addressed to Yhwh. Thus even the second half of the psalm is "motivating and urging God to answer the petitions of the first half."[31] Once again, both implied audiences, God and congregation, are necessary to an understanding of worship.

31. Jacobson, *"Many Are Saying,"* 100 (he italicizes the first three words), referring to Tryggve N. D. Mettinger, *King and Messiah* (Lund: Gleerup, 1976), 100.

Psalm 133

How Wondrous Is Living as One

Translation

Song of the Ascents. David's.[1]

[1]Now: How good and how lovely
is kinfolk living[2] as one.
[2]Like good oil upon the head,
going down upon the beard,
Aaron's beard, which goes down
upon the collar of his clothing.[3]
[3]Like the dew of Hermon,[4] which goes down
upon the mountains of[5] Zion.
Because there Yhwh commanded the blessing,
life for evermore.[6]

1. Omitted by Tg, some LXX MSS, though not by 11QPs[a].
2. Lit. "the living of kinfolk."
3. "His clothing" is here the f. *middôtāyw*. The OT elsewhere uses m. *mad* rather than f. *middâ*, but the f. appears in Qumran Hebrew (see *DCH*), though 11QPs[a–b] have *mdyw*. In the OT, *middôtāyw* would thus otherwise mean "his measurements," and *ʿal-pî middôtāyw* would then mean "according to his measurements." But this requires some stretch to make it mean "over his body" (Allen, *Psalms 101–150*, 276; cf. Crow, *Songs of Ascents*, 107–8).
4. Rashi takes v. 3 to mean "so" (compare the *k . . . k* in 131:2), but it is hard to see wherein lies the comparison between the oil and the dew.
5. For the form *harĕrê*, cf. 87:1; 11QPs[a] has the more familiar *hr*.
6. 11QPs[a–b] add "Well-being on Israel," as in 125:5; 128:6.

Interpretation

The psalm is both centrally simple and clear, and also complex and puzzling. In a sense it says everything it has to say in its first line; the rest is exposition of that point in a sequence of similes and explanations. Syntactically, indeed, I have construed the entire psalm as one sentence, vv. 2–3 comprising a massive enjambment, though it is also possible to take vv. 2 and 3 as independent sentences ("It is like . . . ," "It is like . . ."). "Psalm 133 . . . starts but never really ends. Its point . . . is made in the first verse, and then it chases a chain of similes into a verbal whirlpool and stops, never really clarifying itself."[7]

Why is it making its affirmation? In itself, its central observation would be at home in Proverbs, and in that context could be designed to encourage harmony in the community. Yet its form is not characteristic of OT Wisdom. In Proverbs, many sayings comment on things being *ṭôb*, but nearly always in the context of saying that something is "more good," "better," than something else. Commentators say that it is characteristic of Egyptian wisdom, but only one example, in Ptah-Hotep, ever seems to be quoted.[8] Similes of the kind that the psalm uses appear in Wisdom, but also in the Psalms and the Song of Songs, and the psalm's lyrical opening recalls other Psalms (e.g., 84:1 [2]; 135:3) and Song of Songs (e.g., 1:16; 7:6 [7]) more than Proverbs.[9] This lyricism might simply express wonder that people actually are living as one or sometimes do so (for instance, at one of the festivals). Its references to Aaron, Hermon, and Zion (none of which would be expected in Proverbs) cohere with its appearing in the Psalter, not in a Wisdom work. If the psalm links with wisdom thinking, it does so by applying wisdom thinking to some aspect of worship life and utilizing worship life to illumine an aspect of wisdom thinking; it is hardly a wisdom poem.[10]

Its lyricism could be capable of motivating people who are not living as one. In the context of the Songs of the Ascents, it suggests a feature for which families would hope when they gathered for pilgrimage, but enunciating the point reflects wittingly or unwittingly a realistic awareness

7. Ziony Zevit, "Psalms at the Poetic Precipice," *HAR* 10 (1986): 351–66 (see 356).

8. See Hermann Gunkel, *Introduction to Psalms*, completed by Joachim Begrich (Macon, GA: Mercer University Press, 1998), 301; the text referred to appears in *ANET*, 414a. Gunkel also refers to Sir. 25:4–5.

9. On its use of metaphor, see Brian Doyle, "Metaphora interrupta," *ETL* 77 (2001): 5–22.

10. Against Gunkel (e.g., *Psalmen*, 570). Even removing the references to Aaron and Zion (cf., e.g., Seybold, *Psalmen*, 500; also O. Loretz, "Die Ugaritistik in der Psalmeninterpretation," *UF* 4 [1972]: 167–69) does not greatly facilitate this designation, since it still lacks distinct wisdom features.

that such gatherings would generate all manner of conflict. Simmering family tensions would have plenty of opportunity to receive expression, and competition for scarce resources such as places to stay and supplies of water would encourage tensions between different groups. Rivalries between clans would also have opportunity to find expression. Outside of the pilgrimage context, politically the psalm could encourage harmony and reconciliation between the northern and southern clans during the monarchic period,[11] while in the Persian period it could likewise confront the tensions between the Judean and Samarian communities. In a local context, it could encourage the members of a household to stay together or live in harmony, maybe especially after the death of the head of the household.

Like other Songs of the Ascents, the psalm utilizes "terrace" parallelism: "how good" (*mah-ṭôb*) and "[the] good" (*haṭṭôb*); "like good oil" and "like Hermon dew"; "upon the head" and "upon the beard"; "going down upon," "which goes down upon," and "which goes down upon" (the actual verb form is the same each time); "the beard" and "Aaron's beard."[12]

Song of the Ascents. David's.

Heading. See glossary.
133:1–3. A lyrical affirmation of life together.

1Now: How good and how lovely
is kinfolk living as one.

Kinfolk are literally siblings (*ʾaḥîm*), but the term applies to members of extended families and thus village communities; "living as one" would be a desirable feature of a village's life. The OT's first reference to whether kinfolk can live as one is Gen. 13:5–8, where scarce resources cause conflict; the issue recurs in Gen. 36:6–7. In the context of the settled life of Israelites, the issue would arise when the head of the household dies (the background of Gen. 36). Then the question is whether his offspring are to continue to live as one household tending the family land (as presupposed by Deut. 25:5–10) or to divide it among them. One can imagine that conflicts could continue to arise even after they have divided the land. Who has the best land? Who has nearest access

11. Cf. Stig Norin, "Ps. 133," *ASTI* 11 (1977–78): 90–95; Adele Berlin, "On the Interpretation of Psalm 133," in *Directions in Biblical Hebrew Poetry*, ed. Elaine R. Follis, JSOTSup 40 (Sheffield: Sheffield Academic Press, 1987), 141–47.

12. See further David T. Tsumura, "Sorites in Psalm 133,2–3a," *Bib* 61 (1980): 416–17 ("sorites" is a more precise term for the phenomenon as it appears here).

to water? Thus living as one suggests both physical proximity and harmony. While *šebet* can denote simply "sitting," so that "sitting as one" could denote sitting together to eat (e.g., at a festival),[13] the way those other passages speak of "living as one" makes it more likely that this is the point of the exclamation.

"Good" hints that something is not only right and proper but also delightful or good-looking; this is part of the point of the repeated reflections in Gen. 1. "Lovely" then does not so much add a different quality to "good" as nuance it; one is to expect that the good will be lovely.

> [2]Like good oil upon the head,
> going down upon the beard,
> Aaron's beard, which goes down
> upon the collar of his clothing.

Two sorts of significance attach to the pouring of oil on the head. It is a sensuous pleasure.[14] Oil makes the face shine and thus adorns the person on a festive occasion, so that such makeup suggests rejoicing (cf. Pss. 23:5; 141:5; Eccles. 9:7–8); LXX has "perfume" for "good oil." Then in a religious context a priest or king had oil poured on his head as a sign of his appointment by Yhwh and his dedication to his work. Here the splendor of the pouring is emphasized in two ways. This is not ordinary oil but good oil, which might imply it was perfumed, and there is a vast quantity of it. The point about the reference to the beard is not that the beard as such is especially significant but that its reaching down to the beard suggests abundance.

The second line makes explicit which of the daubings of oil is referred to (see Exod. 29:7; Lev. 8:12); it is Aaron's beard that we are talking about.[15] One is not to think of a beard growing down from the center, from a man's chin, but of the beard that a priest lets grow in sidelocks (Lev. 21:5), which thus fall down onto his robes. "Aaron" might stand not just for the man himself (with people imagining the story in Exodus and Leviticus) but for each high priest who succeeds him. The parallel colon then further underlines the abundance of the pouring. Grammatically, the subject might be Aaron's beard or the oil, but there might be little point in merely observing that his beard so extended, and the psalm may presuppose that if the beard extends, so will the oil; that is how the oil gets right down. Tg takes the *peh* of Aaron's clothes as their hem, which would further underline the point and make for a really spectacular

13. Cf. Thijs Booij, "Psalm 133," *Bib* 83 (2002): 258–67.

14. Cf. Doyle, "Metaphora interrupta," 22.

15. This seems more likely than that v. 2c–d expounds a separate simile (so Wilfred G. E. Watson, "The Hidden Simile in Psalm 133," *Bib* 60 [1979]: 108–9).

anointing, but the word usually means "mouth," and in this context more likely it denotes the opening at the top of his clothing through which his head would go (cf. LXX, Jerome). One might have thought this would all get rather messy and unpleasant; that is not the psalm's perspective. The abundance of oil suggests abundance of sacred festivity and thus a powerful image for the wonder of a community living as one, not least the community that looks to Aaron as a key figure in its life.

3Like the dew of Hermon, which goes down
upon the mountains of Zion.
Because there Yhwh commanded the blessing,
life for evermore.

The second simile is constructed with broad similarity to the first, yet with marked differences that keep readers on their toes. Thus the first colon is constructed differently after the "like"; the second is more like v. 2b, though the participle is prefixed by the relative like that in v. 2d; and then the second line goes its own way.

Dew might seem a feeble image compared with that abounding oil, but dew plays a key role in the maturing of crops in the summer, when there is no rain. Thus Isaac's blessing of Jacob begins with reference to dew from the heavens (Gen. 27:28; cf. Deut. 33:13, 28); the context reflects how crucial dew is to the harvest (cf. Zech. 8:12). The absence of dew is thus in its way as devastating as the absence of rain (2 Sam. 1:21; 1 Kings 17:1; Hag. 1:10). So a king's favor is like dew on the grass (Prov. 19:12). Dew brings new life (Isa. 26:19). Yhwh will be like the dew to Israel, and as a result it will blossom and flourish (Hos. 14:5 [6]).

Commentators routinely observe that presumably the implication of the phrase "dew of Hermon" is that the dew of Mount Hermon was proverbially heavy. Apparently Hermon-like dew would then be an image for plentiful dew refreshing the mountains of Zion. This expression refers to Zion as set in the midst of other mountains, that is, the hills on which Jerusalem itself is set and then the wider circle of mountains such as the Mount of Olives. The spatial image takes up that of v. 2: metaphorically speaking, Hermon's dew falls on the lower mountains of Zion as Aaron's oil runs down his face to his collar. One implication is that Hermon submits itself to Zion, one very impressive sacred mountain submitting to another apparently less-impressive one (cf. 68:15–16 [16–17]).

In connection with the assumption that the dew of Mount Hermon was proverbially heavy, commentators often quote comments from George Adam Smith to this effect.[16] But he is not actually commenting on

16. *The Historical Geography of the Holy Land* (London: Hodder, 1894), 65–66.

Hermon but on the land of the Bible in general. And the idea that this mountain such a long way from the sea became well known for its heavy dew may be inherently implausible.[17]

Further, there is a layering about the imagery here that makes the psalm's lyricism more complex. An aspect of its subtlety is that oil and dew form a pair (Gen. 27:28), with oil being a figure for rain. So the reference to dew makes us reconsider v. 2 and to infer that it points to the importance of rain coming down. Conversely, however abundant its dew, Hermon's more obvious feature and asset in this connection is the snow that caps it all year, like oil poured on its head and covering the top part of its "clothing." It is this snow that maintains the flow of such rivers in Israel as do flow through the summer. So oil points to rain, and dew may be an image for snow. That reality of physical geography becomes an image for the community centered on Zion. Unity among Israel's kinfolk has an effect on the community around Zion, the Judean community, like the effect Hermon-like dew has on the olives and grapes on those mountains.

The closing enjambment reinforces the point in a subtle way. The blessing to which it refers is not directly the benefit that the community receives from the unity of its kinfolk; the word "blessing" is hardly used in that way. The blessing is the creative effect of the dew on those grapes and olives. Yhwh commanded that blessing there (for the expression, cf. Lev. 25:21; Deut. 28:8). Yhwh ordered that Zion would be a place where harvests flourished because (among other things) plentiful dew would fall there at the time it was needed. In a broader sense, Yhwh thereby commanded that there would be life there, the kind of life that makes it possible for people to sit under their vine and fig tree and enjoy a life that lasts, undisturbed by danger or loss or disappointment (Mic. 4:4; cf. Zech. 3:10). That is blessing. But by speaking of Zion in these terms, the psalm more directly suggests that Zion would be the source of such blessing, no doubt not just for its immediate environs but for the land as a whole. "All goodly rewards and comforts come out of Zion."[18] It is the community's gathering for the festivals there that opens it to the blessings that Yhwh commands from there. By implication, the oneness of kinfolk as they gather in Zion is part of opening up the blessing. Being in Zion is the key to the togetherness or unity that the psalm speaks of.[19]

17. Cf. J. P. M. van der Ploeg, "Psalm cxxxiii and Its Main Problems," in *Loven en geloven* (N. H. Ridderbos Festschrift; Amsterdam: Ton Bolland, 1975), 191–200 (see 198–99).

18. *Midrash on Psalms*, 2:338.

19. Cf. Patrick W. Skehan, *Studies in Israelite Poetry and Wisdom*, CBQMS 1 (Washington, DC: Catholic Biblical Quarterly, 1971), 63.

A feedback mechanism then operates. The psalm takes the fulfillment of this precious promise as also a figure of something. Kinfolk living together in harmony is a means of the blessing being released. But the blessing is also an image for the wonder of kinfolk living together in harmony. This is as wonderful as that blessing, that life, that enjoyment of sitting under your vine and fig tree as the sun begins to cool and the afternoon breeze arrives. Actually there is a tighter link between the two, because there is no satisfactory sitting under the vine or fig tree if there is conflict among the kinfolk. But the psalm's direct point is to invite people to reflect on the joy of the blessing that comes from the dew and then take that as an image for the blessing of harmony in the community. It is not something to be taken for granted or imperiled but something to be cherished and safeguarded.

Theological Implications

This principle applies to all aspects of community life, but the presence of the psalm in the Psalter, and the particular terms in which it speaks, reminds the community how significant for the worshipping community is living as one. According to Augustine, this little psalm begat the monasteries, whose members are not merely *monos* in being isolated but *monos* in the sense of "one."[20] Indeed, Jerome comments, "This psalm is truly the psalm of convents and monasteries. It may even be applied to the churches, although, because of the great diversity in personal interests on the part of the members, there does not in the Christian assembly appear to be the same degree of harmony."[21] Cassiodorus notes that nevertheless the church should not evade its vision.[22]

But the most spectacularly unanswered prayer in world history is Jesus's prayer in John 17:20–23. Christian kinfolk live in breathtaking disharmony. This devastates their witness as it removes the goodness and the loveliness from them; it removes their joy and surrenders their blessing. The psalm invites us to consider the loveliness of kinfolk living as one and to meditate on the images for this that it offers, to see if this inspires us to live as one.[23] Calvin's caveats[24] show how scandalous is the psalm's conviction and how unanswerable the prayer.[25]

20. *Psalms*, 622–23.
21. *Homilies*, 1:333.
22. *Psalms*, 3:332.
23. Cf. Spurgeon, *Treasury of David*, 6:167–69.
24. *Psalms*, 5:164–65.
25. See further Mays, *Preaching and Teaching the Psalms*, 140.

Psalm 134

The Reciprocity of Praise and Blessing

Translation

Song of the Ascents.

[1]Now: worship Yhwh,
all you servants of Yhwh,
who stand in Yhwh's house[1] through the night.[2]
[2]Raise your hands to the sanctuary,[3]
worship Yhwh.

[3]Yhwh bless you yourself[4] from Zion,
the maker of the heavens and the earth.

Interpretation

Like Ps. 133, Ps. 134 addresses not Yhwh but other people, and the way it, too, opens with "Now" and closes with reference to Yhwh's blessing

1. LXX adds "in the courts of our God" (cf. 135:2); it then links "through the night" to the next line (as does Jerome).

2. Lit. "in the nights"; JM 136b suggests that the pl. denotes "in the night hours."

3. There is no prep. expressed, and TNIV has "in," perhaps reckoning that the *b* in v. 1c carries over. But elsewhere one raises one's hands "to" something or someone (e.g., 28:2; cf. LXX, Jerome).

4. I add "yourself" to make clear that the "you" is now sg.

encourages us to take the two psalms as a pair. The first two lines are a summons to worship of the kind that commonly forms the opening to a hymn, but usually that leads into the content or reasons for the worship (cf. Ps. 135). In contrast, Ps. 134 issues only the summons to praise ("if psalm 133 could be characterized as never really ending, this psalm may be described as never really starting").[5] In this respect it significantly parallels Ps. 150. Psalm 134 closes off the Songs of the Ascents with a bare summons; Ps. 150 will close off the entire Psalter in a similar way. The implication might be that after all that has been said in Pss. 120–33, a final summons to praise is all that is needed to close off the sequence; the previous fourteen psalms provide the reasons and the content for the praise it urges.

The psalm's closing line then corresponds in an inverted sense to the close of several of the Songs of the Ascents, which move from the way Yhwh deals with an individual to the implications of this for Yhwh's dealings with the community (e.g., Ps. 130). In Ps. 134 the movement is reversed. Verses 1–2 issue their challenge to the "servants of Yhwh"; v. 3 then declares Yhwh's blessing for the individual. A comparison with an example such as Ps. 121 suggests that the psalm also presupposes a liturgical movement. The voice that speaks in vv. 1–2 is the voice that is responsively addressed in v. 3. This makes for another link with Ps. 133, as the reciprocity of the psalm embodies the "living at one" that Ps. 133 celebrates.

One can imagine the psalm being used in worship, but we do not know how, nor do we know its date.

Song of the Ascents.

Heading. See glossary. If the fifteen "Songs of the Ascents" were used in some way as a sequence, Ps. 134 might have been used at the end of the sequence as people were coming to the end of their pilgrimage.

134:1–2. The summons to praise.

[1]Now: worship Yhwh,
all you servants of Yhwh,
who stand in Yhwh's house through the night.

The people bidden to *worship are Yhwh's servants; the term usually denotes Israelites in general, who "stand" before Yhwh in the temple (e.g., 2 Chron. 7:6, the same participle as here). But the psalm could also be used as a bidding to ministers in particular (so Tg). In the

5. Ziony Zevit, "Psalms at the Poetic Precipice," *HAR* 10 (1986): 351–66 (see 358).

context of a pilgrimage, pilgrims about to leave Jerusalem might thus commission the ministers who usually look after the temple worship on their behalf. Nehemiah 12:44–46 speaks of Judah thus rejoicing at the work of the priests and Levites who "stand" (again the same participle) in the temple.[6] Or laypeople in general might use the psalm as the day comes to an end thus to commission the ministers to do the work that they undertake on the community's behalf during the night. Given that the word for "worship" etymologically suggests "bow the knee," the description of the servants as people who "stand" in Yhwh's house draws attention to the fact that they are involved both in symbolic submission to Yhwh and in symbolic waiting on their master. Standing is the posture of people who are present, alert, and ready to do whatever their master wants done.

There are no regular acts of worship to be offered during the night, though there are tasks to be undertaken in connection with keeping watch and preparing for the next morning. Perhaps the people who stand there by night are the guards waiting for the morning (so Tg; cf. 130:6), or other worshippers who show up at the temple before dawn even breaks (cf. 119:148). First Chronicles 9:27, 33 refer to the Levites having work to do day and night. But perhaps the reference to the night simply gives specificity to the colon; v. 1a–b implicitly refers to what happens during each day and v. 1c makes it more concrete with regard to the night.

> 2Raise your hands to the sanctuary,
> worship Yhwh.

This further physical activity involves the body in yet another way. Raising the hands is a gesture of appeal (e.g., 28:2), and there are no unequivocal examples of its signifying simply exultation (like the sports enthusiast punching the air); even 63:4 [5] can refer to prayer rather than praise. So it is likely that raising the hands is a gesture of dependence on Yhwh that complements direct worship of Yhwh, and in a way constitutes worship because it connotes that dependence. Raising the hand(s) is also a posture of blessing (Lev. 9:22), which would lead well into v. 3,[7] though it is odd that the further exhortation to worship then intervenes. But the latter does complete a frame around vv. 1–2. These worshippers are in the earthly sanctuary, so that the sanctuary to which they raise their hands is the heavenly one where Yhwh "really" lives (cf. 150:1), the sanctuary of which the earthly one is a symbol and outpost.

6. Cf. Kirkpatrick, *Psalms*, 772.
7. Crow, *Songs of Ascents*, 126.

Through the line there is another striking complementarity over the posture for worship, as the exhortation to raise the hands is paralleled by the further exhortation to *worship, which points to bowing the knee. Here perhaps we are to imagine people standing up with their hands raised and then bowing down, before a heavenly or an earthly lord; both are postures of submission and obeisance.

134:3. The declaration of blessing.

> [3]Yhwh bless you yourself from Zion,
> the maker of the heavens and the earth.

The opening colon corresponds to 128:5, where the singular "you" refers to the individual rather than to the congregation addressed as one unit. The first words also correspond to those of the priestly blessing in Num. 6:24, where again the singular "you" refers to the individual Israelite. While it might thus be that the speaker of vv. 1–2 (himself a priest?) turns from speaking to the whole congregation or the body of ministers to address the individual, perhaps the individual pilgrim,[8] the dynamic of the psalm parallels that of psalms such as Ps. 121 and makes more sense if we reckon that the servants who have been addressed in vv. 1–2 now respond with a declaration of blessing for the one who addressed them there. Like the lines in Num. 6:24–26, the psalm thus assumes that Yhwh's blessing applies not only to the community in general but specifically to an individual such as this worship leader. (Of course we now assume that it applies to the individual and need reminding that it applies to communities.) His fellow ministers and/or fellow worshippers pray and promise that Yhwh will grant him fullness of life in response to the way he commits himself to his ministry. The reciprocal nature of vv. 1–2 and v. 3 is underlined by the repetition of the verb *bārak*, now meaning bless rather than worship.

Over against Num. 6:24, the psalm adds that it is "from Zion" that Yhwh will bless, from the place where these servants stand worshipping, the place that Yhwh has made the source of blessing, precisely because it is the earthly symbol and equivalent to the real sanctuary in the heavens. The movement into the second colon corresponds to the movement in vv. 1–2 between the earthly sanctuary and the heavenly one. Blessing comes from Zion because Zion is the earthly embodiment of that heavenly sanctuary from which Yhwh rules as the maker of the heavens and the earth, lord of all their power and resources; the

8. Cf. Pierre Auffret, "Note on the Literary Structure of Psalm 134," *JSOT* 45 (1989): 87–89 (see 87).

recognition of Yhwh as maker of the heavens and the earth is especially at home there in Zion (see 121:2).[9]

Theological Implications

The relationship of worship and blessing is reciprocal. "The members of the congregation join in this continuous unbroken circle of divine blessing by calling upon the priests to 'bless' Yahweh and are now . . . able to receive for their part the blessing of God which the priests, acting as God's mediators, impart to them."[10] But because the pronoun is singular, "let none of you say, It cometh not to me. Knowest thou of whom he speaks, 'the Lord bless thee out of Zion.' He blessed one."[11]

9. W. F. Albright contrasts "From Zaphon Baal will bless thee" in an Aramaic text ("Notes on Psalms 68 and 134," in *Interpretationes ad Vetus Testamentum pertinentes* [Sigmund Mowinckel Festschrift; Oslo: Land og Kirke, 1955], 1–12 [see 6–8]).

10. Weiser, *Psalms*, 786–87.

11. Augustine, *Psalms*, 624.

Psalm 135

How to Use Scripture in Praise

Translation

1Praise Yah,
praise Yhwh's name,
praise, you servants of Yhwh,[1]
2You who stand in Yhwh's house,
in the courts of our God's house.

3Praise Yah, because Yhwh is good;[2]
make music to his name because it is lovely.[3]
4Because it was Jacob Yah chose for himself,
Israel as his treasure.
5Because I myself acknowledge
that Yhwh is greater,[4]
that our Lord is greater, than all gods.

1. 11QPs[a] has the cola in the order 1c, 1b, 1a.

2. 11QPs[a] has "praise Yhwh because he is good," an easier reading; MT's reading reflects the link between v. 3 and 147:1.

3. "He is lovely" (cf. NRSV) is grammatically possible, but the immediate antecedent is "his name." But because the name stands for the person, in substance it makes little difference. "It is lovely" corresponds more closely to 147:1, which v. 3 is following, though there it is making music that is lovely, and here the parallelism suggests "it" is the name rather than the making music.

4. In isolation one would translate simply "great," but the complementary nature of the cola suggests that as *gādôl* carries over into v. 5c, so the comparison begins in v. 5b and "than all gods" also applies here. This is more explicit in Exod. 18:11, which the psalm turns into a two-part poetic line. Cf. Dahood, *Psalms*, 3:260.

6All that Yhwh wants, he has done,
in the heavens and on the earth, in the seas and all the depths,
7One who makes clouds rise from the end of the earth,
who made flashes of lightning for the rain,
who brings out[5] wind from his storehouse,
8The one who[6] hit the firstborn of Egypt,
human beings and cattle,
9Sent signs and portents in the midst of[7] Egypt
against Pharaoh and against all his servants,
10The one who hit many nations
and slew strong kings,[8]
11Yes, Sihon king of the Amorites,
yes, Og king of Bashan,
yes, all the kingdoms of Canaan,[9]
12And gave their land as a possession,[10]
a possession for Israel, his people.

13Yhwh, your name endures forever;
Yhwh, your fame endures through all generations.
14Because Yhwh governs his people,
gets himself relief over his servants.

15The images of the nations are silver and gold,
the work of human hands.
16They have a mouth but they do not speak,
they have eyes but they do not see.
17They have ears but they do not pay attention;
no, there is no breath[11] in their mouth.
18The people who make them will become like them,[12]
everyone who relies on them.

5. The odd form *môṣēʾ* for *môṣîʾ* reflects the form *wayyôṣēʾ* in Jer. 10:13, whence this line comes.

6. The relative prefix *šĕ* is not required and thus adds some emphasis; so also in v. 10.

7. On the form of *bĕtôkēkî*, see on 116:19.

8. The *w*-qatal verb could be explained as coordinating two verbs referring to the same event or as reflecting later usage when *w*-consecutive is going out of use; but most likely it reflects the fact that vv. 8–12 continue the participial construction begun in v. 7 (GKC 116x; JM 121j).

9. In Aramaic usage, the *lĕ* before each of the nouns in v. 11 could be the sign of the object, but v. 10 corresponds to regular Hebrew usage, so more likely the *lĕ* is something like an emphatic particle (*HALOT* 510–11; Dahood, *Psalms*, 3:262). DG 94, remark 8, sees it as introducing a noun in apposition. 4QPs[k] corrects the first *l* to *ʾt*, but leaves the second and third; 4QPs[n] corresponds to MT.

10. On the *w*-qatal verb, see the note on v. 10.

11. The *yeš* ("being of," "there is") is pleonastic.

12. LXX, Jerome have jussive.

19Household of Israel, worship Yhwh;
household of Aaron, worship Yhwh.
20Household of Levi, worship Yhwh;
you who revere Yhwh, worship Yhwh.
21Yhwh be worshipped from Zion,
the one who dwells in Jerusalem;
praise Yah.[13]

Interpretation

Whereas the last of the Songs of the Ascents (Ps. 134) comprised a call to worship that provided no reasons or content, the first of the two praise psalms that now follow resumes the call in terms that overlap with that (vv. 1–2) but then goes on to provide this worship with multiple reasons or content. The opening lines of reasoning (vv. 3–5) summarize the point in terms of Yhwh's relationship with Israel and then of Yhwh's superiority over other gods. The main section develops these aspects of praiseworthiness in reverse order, in terms of Yhwh's actions in relation to Israel (vv. 6–14) and of the inadequacy of gods who can be imaged (vv. 15–18). A further call to worship, closing with the exhortation "praise Yah" in the same way as the psalm began, acts as an inclusion round the whole (vv. 19–21). The name Yah or Yhwh occurs in a striking pattern: nine times in vv. 1–6, not at all in vv. 7–12, three times in vv. 13–14, not at all in vv. 15–18, and six times in vv. 19–21.[14] The names are associated with God's relationship with Israel, expressed in God's activity as it directly affects Israel and in Israel's worship, but they are missing when the psalm speaks of God's acts of power in relation to other peoples and of the uselessness of images.

The psalm has many links with other Scriptures; for the most part it seems likely that it has utilized them rather than vice versa. Indeed, "if ever the term 'mosaic' applied to a psalm, then it is to Ps. 135," which marks the end of the line of such developments in the OT.[15] Verses 1–2 combine material from 113:1; 134:1–2; 116:19; v. 3 reflects 147:1, though the combination of good and lovely also recalls 133:1; the talk of choosing Israel as a treasure in v. 4 corresponds to Deut. 7:6 and 14:2; the confession in v. 5 corresponds to Exod. 18:11; v. 6a compares closely with Ps. 115:3; v. 7 is a variant on Jer. 10:13; v. 8 summarizes Exod. 12:29; v. 9 corresponds to Deut. 6:22; 34:11; vv. 10–12 are a variant on 136:17–22; v. 13 is a reworking of Exod. 3:15, though v. 13b also corresponds to Ps.

13. LXX links with Ps. 136.
14. Fokkelman, *Major Poems*, 2:298.
15. Mathys, *Dichter und Beter*, 260–61.

102:12 [13]; v. 14 is identical to Deut. 32:36; vv. 15–18 are a variant on Ps. 115:4–8; vv. 19–20 then overlap with Ps. 115:9–11; v. 21 reflects the language of a number of lines in the Psalms, but the "from Zion" is an especially striking parallel with Ps. 134:3, noteworthy because it involves a quite novel reworking of the significance of the words as they are used in a new context (as also happens in v. 3).

Presumably the psalm's relationship with these other Scriptures from the Torah, the Prophets, and the Psalms indicates that it comes from a late period in OT times (which also fits with the use of the relative prefix *šĕ*), but we have no basis for being more precise than that. Nor can we know how this relationship worked. In principle it seems likely that many of the links came about through the psalmist's familiarity with Israel's story as this was celebrated in worship and with the tradition of psalmody as this was used in worship; indeed, the psalmist might well have been the sort of person who led this worship. In this sense one should not imagine the psalmist poring over scrolls and lifting phrases from written documents. Indeed, the relationship of this psalm to other psalms might not be one of direct dependence but of parallel dependence on a shared tradition. On the other hand, in the psalmist's period it is likely that scrolls of the Torah and perhaps of the Prophets in something like the form we know them were present in the temple, and it might be that some material did have its origin in reflection on such scrolls.

Presumably the psalm was used in worship, but we have no basis for saying how.

135:1–5. The encouragement to worship, and its fundamental content or rationale. Two opening lines are all encouragement, two closing lines are all reasons or content, and the intervening line combines the two.

1Praise Yah,
praise Yhwh's name,
praise, you servants of Yhwh,
2You who stand in Yhwh's house,
in the courts of our God's house.

The psalm begins with words from 113:1, though the second and third cola are transposed under the influence of 134:1–2, which v. 2a goes on to follow. The people who are to *praise *Yah and praise Yhwh's *name are again Yhwh's servants who stand in Yhwh's house, which as in Ps. 134 could be applied either to the congregation as a whole or specifically to the ministers and choirs.

The final colon compares with 116:19a, except that "our God" replaces "Yhwh." "Our God" compares with the reference to "our Lord" in v. 5; see the comment. The expression "our God's house" recurs especially in

Ezra 8:17–33; Neh. 10:32–39 [33–40].[16] The parallelism of v. 2 also adds the reference to the courtyard, the family meeting place in a house; in the case of this quasi-palace, it is naturally a multiple courtyard. The court is the heart of the design of a house, and therefore of a temple. "Whoever stands in the court stands in the midst of the God's house."[17]

> 3Praise Yah, because Yhwh is good;
> make music to his name because it is lovely.

Only here does "Praise *Yah" come anywhere other than as the opening or closing phrase of a psalm; the unique usage reflects the fact that the psalm is here reworking 147:1. The line thus constitutes a resumed beginning of the psalm. The encouragement to *praise is repeated and then paralleled with reference to making *music: praise suggests an inarticulate but excited voice, while music suggests the also inarticulate but perhaps more orderly sound of musical instruments. The parallelism also adds the first reasons for enthusiasm about Yhwh. Yhwh is *good; to put it another way, Yhwh's *name (which again means Yhwh in person, Yhwh as known in the presence of the people) is lovely (which nuances "good" here, as in 133:1).

> 4Because it was Jacob Yah chose for himself,
> Israel as his treasure.

The basis or substance of the worship is the event that embodied Yhwh's goodness and loveliness in relation to Israel. The reality of Yhwh's choice is given a vivid alternative formulation in the parallelism by speaking of Israel as a possession that is especially valuable to Yhwh (a *sĕgullâ*; for the down-to-earth sense, see 1 Chron. 29:3; Eccles. 2:8). The word comes only here in the Psalms. It goes back to Exod. 19:5, but it appears in connection with reference to Yhwh's choosing Israel in Deut. 7:6 and 14:2. Its links with the exodus will be spelled out in vv. 9–14.

> 5Because I myself acknowledge
> that Yhwh is greater,
> that our Lord is greater, than all gods.

The second "because" takes further the account of how or why people are to worship, but takes it in a new direction by speaking not of Yhwh's relationship with Israel but of Yhwh's greatness. In substance there is

16. Cf. Gerstenberger, *Psalms*, 2:379.

17. Keel, *Symbolism*, 128. Keel goes on to discuss how there were several courts in the temple at different periods.

thus an ellipse between vv. 4 and 5. Two declarations are juxtaposed; they are rhetorically left independent, but in substance they are related. The psalm will go on to speak of Yhwh's acts in relation to Israel and other peoples, which give expression to both these truths about Yhwh. Following on that, it will ridicule the images that these other peoples rely on, and v. 5c is the truth that underlies that ridicule. As usual the OT does not dispute the existence of other *ʾĕlōhîm* but affirms that there is such a difference in stature between them and our *Lord that one really needs a different word to describe them, or at least to be able to call one God and the others merely gods.

Verse 5 appears in a variant form on the lips of Jethro in Exod. 18:11. There, Jethro's qatal declaration "I acknowledge" is performative, "I hereby acknowledge," and this understanding also makes sense here. The fact that these are originally the words of a man who is acknowledging the significance of what Yhwh has done in delivering Israel from the Egyptians heralds the focus on the events associated with this in vv. 5–14. It also hints at a deconstruction of the Israel focus of the psalm, heralded by vv. 3–4. Is Yhwh good for other peoples if Yhwh chose Israel and apparently not other peoples? Jethro assumed this might be so.[18]

Here, the "I" is presumably that of the minister who leads the people's worship, the person who has been uttering the exhortations in vv. 1–4 and will continue to speak through the rest of the psalm. Here he makes explicit his personal commitment to the truths of which he speaks. In this respect the declaration also recalls Joshua's in Josh. 24. By that declaration in a superficial sense Joshua distinguished himself from the people with some emphasis, but in a deeper sense this was designed to draw them into making the same individual, personal commitment that he was making. The same will apply here. The minister speaks of his own commitment in order to draw others into joining him. The point is expressed in the major difference from Jethro's words, the addition of "our Lord," which also follows up the allusion to "our God" in v. 2. The expression "our Lord" comes in the Psalms only in 8:1, 9 [2, 10]; 147:5. It makes for a striking complement to the first-person singular style of the line. The leader implies that Yhwh is indeed his Lord, but Yhwh is also our Lord, and he wants people to affirm that. Recognition of Yhwh needs to be individual, but it is a recognition of the God of the whole community.

135:6–14. The psalm now celebrates some of those events that brought Israel into being. Verses 6–7 spell out Yhwh's greatness in terms of power, in language that may suggest reference to the Red Sea deliverance and/

18. Cf. Ruth Scoralick's discussion of Pss. 135 and 136, "Hallelujah für einen gewalttätigen Gott?" *BZ* 46 (2002): 253–72 (see 269).

or to Sinai. Verses 8–12 are then divided into two by the relative expressions that open vv. 8 and 10; vv. 8–9 refer to the exodus and vv. 10–12 to the conquest of the land. Finally vv. 13–14 restate the implications of those events, completing a bracket opened by vv. 6–7. Grammatically, the whole section seems to be one sentence, with vv. 7–14 hanging on v. 6 as a huge enjambment and spelling out its implications.

> [6]All that Yhwh wants, he has done,
> in the heavens and on the earth, in the seas and all the depths,

The first colon corresponds to 115:3, with the addition of reference to "Yhwh." While the stative verb can naturally be reckoned to refer to all that Yhwh "wants" (cf. Tg; though LXX and Jerome have past verbs), the qatal verb *ʿāśâ* suggests the whole line refers to actual deeds of Yhwh, and this fits with the account of Yhwh's deeds that will follow. Likewise the reference to acts in the heavens and on the earth, in the seas and all the depths, could suggest reference to the acts of creation. But talk of sea and depths also occurs in connection with the Red Sea deliverance in Exod. 14–15.

> [7]One who makes clouds rise from the end of the earth,
> who made flashes of lightning for the rain,
> who brings out wind from his storehouse,

The verse is a variant on Jer. 10:13; the main difference is that the participles at the beginning of the first and last cola are qatal verbs in Jeremiah. The line describes Yhwh's capacity to bring about a storm: summoning the clouds full of rain from the far horizon, making lightning flash as it often does ahead of rain as if creating a path for it,[19] and releasing wind. The psalm utilizes three different models for the divine causality involved in the event. The first colon suggests Yhwh working through natural processes. The second has Yhwh specially bringing into being each natural phenomenon, without there being any link between them; the different aspects of a storm are all discrete phenomena. The third uses a metaphor, Yhwh as the householder who keeps a multiplicity of resources in storage already in being, and available for use whenever they are needed. Once again the language is such that it could refer simply to Yhwh's activity as lord of creation, but in 77:16–18 [17–19] this kind of language is used metaphorically in connection with the Red Sea event (cf. also 18:14–15 [15–16]). Yhwh's powerful and terrifying acts are like those of one who brings about a violent storm. Of course the Red

19. Keel, *Symbolism*, 212.

Sea deliverance literally involved wind (e.g., Exod. 15:8, 10), and Sinai involved flashes of lightning (Exod. 19:16).

> 8The one who hit the firstborn of Egypt,
> human beings and cattle,
> 9Sent signs and portents in the midst of Egypt
> against Pharaoh and against all his servants,

If v. 7 does refer to the Red Sea and/or Sinai, v. 8 then goes behind it to the event that finally brought about the exodus; and certainly v. 9 then goes behind that to the earlier warning signs that Yhwh gave the pharaoh. Verse 8 summarizes Exod. 12:29. Verse 9 corresponds more closely to the language of Deuteronomy, especially 6:22; 34:11, while the unusual expression for "in the midst of" parallels 116:19, where it is applied to Jerusalem.

> 10The one who hit many nations
> and slew strong kings,
> 11Yes, Sihon king of the Amorites,
> yes, Og king of Bashan,
> yes, all the kingdoms of Canaan,
> 12And gave their land as a possession,
> a possession for Israel, his people.

The account of these further acts has a much less direct relationship with the account in the Torah, which does not talk of Yhwh hitting or slaying Sihon, Og, and the other kingdoms; indeed, it does not make Yhwh the subject of verbs in relation to them at all. It is Israel that defeats, slays, and devotes (as commissioned by Yhwh, of course). The psalm takes up the language Exodus used of Yhwh's action against the pharaoh and applies it to the nations in Canaan and then takes up the language used of Israel's action against the kings and applies it to Yhwh's action. But the phraseology of the psalm anticipates that of 136:17–22, and it is perhaps Ps. 136 that has introduced this innovation, though if so Ps. 135 reworks it so that vv. 10a and 11c refer to the nations/kingdoms and vv. 10b–11b to their rulers.

If there is a particular segment of the Torah that the psalms reflect in their account of Sihon and Og, it is the summary account in Deut. 3–4 with its reference to Yhwh doing battle with "all the kingdoms" as well as those two, and specifically to Yhwh's intention "to drive out from before you greater and stronger nations than you, to take you in, to give you their land as a possession" (Deut. 4:38). In the psalms, the repetition of "a possession" before the continuance of v. 12b emphasizes the significance of this notion: *those peoples'* land became a *possession* for Israel!

[13]Yhwh, your name endures forever;
Yhwh, your fame endures through all generations.
[14]Because Yhwh governs his people,
gets himself relief over his servants.

The acclamation is the kind that recurs in the Psalms; that in the second colon corresponds to 102:12 [13]. Yhwh's fame (*zēker*) is Yhwh's *name as proclaimed when people tell the story of what Yhwh has done for Israel, Yhwh's title. But behind passages such as 102:12 [13] is Yhwh's own declaration concerning the name in connection with its revelation and interpretation in Exod. 3:15. Yhwh says, "This is my name forever, this is my title through all generations." "Yes," the psalmist responds, "Yhwh is your name forever; Yhwh is your title through all generations." The context in Exodus perhaps explains the repetition of the name itself at the beginning of each colon here in the psalm. There is an awareness of wonder about the very declaring of the name, given that context.

Then v. 14 corresponds exactly to Deut. 32:36. The broader setting there has some ambiguity and irony about it; it is not always easy to see where the words refer to action against Israel and where they refer to action against the nations. There and here, LXX and Jerome translate the verb for govern (*dîn*, a synonym of *šāpaṭ*) "judge." But in the context of the psalm there is no doubt that Yhwh's governing operates in Israel's favor.

This does not in itself establish the nuance of the parallel verb *nāḥam* (hitpael). The verb is a feelings word; the niphal suggests feeling grief or regret or finding relief or comfort, and the rarer hitpael has a similar range of meanings. So the idea will be that Yhwh is moved by the needs of Israel as "his people," "his servants," and gets relief in connection with those feelings by acting on Israel's behalf in relation to its foes.

In the parallelism, then, "governs" is an action word and "gets himself relief" is a feelings word; the action implements the feelings, and the feelings impel the action. Then "his servants" gives specificity to "his people" and explains why Yhwh must take action: a master is bound to his servants. In turn, these two cola about Yhwh's action and feelings explain why Yhwh's name and fame endure forever and through all generations; as they have. The two cola work *abb'a'* (Yhwh governs his people, over his servants gets himself relief), which advertises that we here come to the end of a section.

135:15–18. The contrast: the nations' images. Implicitly, this description of the divine images that other peoples manufacture contrasts with the description of Yhwh in vv. 8–14 and especially vv. 13–14. The lines are virtually the same as 115:4–6, 8 and thus continue from the link in v. 6 with 115:3. Given that the psalm comes from the time when victory has been won by a commitment to worship Yhwh alone (worship of other deities is not the problem in the later postexilic period that it was in earlier centuries),[20] the polemic is actually odd; or rather, this is not polemic but a victory song.

15The images of the nations are silver and gold,
the work of human hands.
16They have a mouth but they do not speak,
they have eyes but they do not see.
17They have ears but they do not pay attention;
no, there is no breath in their mouth.
18The people who make them will become like them,
everyone who relies on them.

At first the opening description might seem rather complimentary. Silver and gold are metals of great value, and the work of human hands is not to be despised. Yet the first word in the sentence is "their images": fancy putting that word next to the dynamic description of Yhwh that has occupied vv. 6–14! Come on, says the psalm, we are talking about something that is made by human beings. How can they represent God? (Christians who accept that point about images also have to apply it to the words we devise to describe God. They are just our words. They cannot encapsulate the living God.)

But the result of this valuable and skilled work is something that does not work. The things the hands make have the attributes of personhood, but they are useless. The images are only pretend. They have mouths, eyes, and ears, but they cannot speak, see, or pay attention (here Ps. 135 uses a different verb from the more common "listen" in Ps. 115). The implication is that Yhwh has a real mouth, eyes, and ears, even if these are invisible. Yhwh really can speak, see, and pay attention. The image-worshippers of course believed that their gods could do that; they would say that the artificial or static nature of their bodily parts should not be taken as an indication of incapacity on the part of the deities themselves. But Israel knew that the images were giving unwitting testimony to the real nature of the actual deities. Deities other than Yhwh cannot speak, see, or pay attention to their devotees, and the fact that their mouth, eyes, and ears are only pretend gives neat expression to that fact. And this means they cannot act on behalf of the people who make the images and rely on them, who thus end up as incapable as they are of speaking, seeing, or paying attention; that is, they too

20. Mowinckel, *Psalms*, 1:98.

end up dead. That point is more explicit in v. 17b, the colon that most differs from Ps. 115.[21]

135:19–21. The closing exhortation to worship forms an inclusion with vv. 1–3.

[19]Household of Israel, worship Yhwh;
household of Aaron, worship Yhwh.
[20]Household of Levi, worship Yhwh;
you who revere Yhwh, worship Yhwh.
[21]Yhwh be worshipped from Zion,
the one who dwells in Jerusalem;
praise Yah.

Verses 19–20 again bear comparison with 115:9–11, where also the psalmist issues a bidding to Israel, the household of Aaron, and people who revere Yhwh, though the bidding each time is to rely on Yhwh, following up the comment in 115:8 (cf. v. 18 above). The addition of reference to the household of Levi makes it clearer that the people who revere Yhwh are the people as a whole; the addressees in vv. 19–20 come in *abb′a′* order (Israel, Aaron, Levi, people who revere).

When Ps. 115 draws to an end, it does in due course get to a declaration about worshipping Yhwh, and it closes with "praise *Yah" (115:18). Here *worship has the focus: the word comes five times. "Yhwh be worshipped" is a common enough exclamation (e.g., 106:48; 124:6), but "from Zion" is a unique addition,[22] though comparison with Ps. 134 may help to elucidate it. Psalm 134 presupposed the more familiar notion that Yhwh's *bĕrākâ* comes to people from Zion, but it also has people in Yhwh's house lifting their hands to the sanctuary (in the heavens). Here the psalm implies that the worship that is offered in Zion to the one who dwells in Jerusalem goes up from there to Yhwh's heavenly dwelling. Therefore, it says, *praise *Yah.

Theological Implications

Two aspects of the psalm's relationship with earlier "Scriptures" are significant. I put "Scriptures" in quotes because there may be a sense in which the term is anachronistic; we do not know in what sense these

21. Rather neatly, there *ʾap* refers to the nose; here it is the particle "No" (though Tg assumes it refers to a nose). Ps. 115 refers to smelling *(yĕrîḥûn)*, Ps. 135 to breath (*rûaḥ*). Ps. 115:7 probably does go on to refer to breath, though it does so in a different way.

22. Even a "peculiar" one according to Kraus (*Psalms 60–150*, 491), who therefore wonders about emending it.

writings would be Scriptures or whether the community would use that word to describe them or what it would mean by the word if they did, though we have noted that it seems likely that the Torah and perhaps the Prophets would be in existence in something like the form we know. And if there were such things as master copies of them, they would be copies the temple had. It is noteworthy that the psalm incorporates material that also appears in all three sections of the Scriptures, the Torah, the Prophets, and the Writings.

On one hand, it is those earlier Scriptures that provide the psalmist with the raw material with which to worship. They shape the psalm's understanding of Israel as Yhwh's chosen and Yhwh's treasure and of Yhwh as the greatest of all heavenly beings. Yhwh is the lord of nature, and that lordship is expressed in the way Yhwh has acted on a once-for-all basis in Israel's history. Israel is Yhwh's people, and its land is its secure possession. In response to Yhwh's saying, "This is my name forever," the psalm says, "Yes, this is your name forever." Yhwh governs and Yhwh gets relief from supporting Israel, and Yhwh's passion and activity contrast with the incapacity of images to do anything.

On the other hand, the psalmist works creatively with these raw materials. The psalmist does so in two senses. First, they become part of a new whole that is greater than the parts. And second, individual words within that new whole stimulate the psalmist into saying something new that does not emerge from their original meaning. Not only is worship good and lovely, and not only is living as one good and lovely; Yhwh in person is good and Yhwh's name is lovely. Not only did Israel slay kings who attacked it, Yhwh did so (the psalm's hardheaded boldness about saying this contrasts with modernity's queasiness). Not only does blessing for Israel come out of Zion, worship of Yhwh comes out of Zion.

The Scriptures are the community's resource for the shaping of its praise. They operate that way in both a left-brained fashion and a right-brained fashion, or both in a way that observes the norms of exegetical method and in a way that lets the Holy Spirit and the human spirit come to new insights with the stimulus of these words.

Psalm 136
Yhwh's Commitment

Translation

[1]Confess Yhwh, because he is good
(because his commitment is forever).
[2]Confess the God of gods
(because his commitment is forever).
[3]Confess the Lord[1] of lords
(because his commitment is forever),

[4]The sole worker of great wonders[2]
(because his commitment is forever),
[5]The maker of the heavens with discernment
(because his commitment is forever),
[6]The beater out of the earth over the waters
(because his commitment is forever),
[7]The maker of the great lights
(because his commitment is forever),
[8]The sun to rule over the day
(because his commitment is forever),

1. Honorific pl. (cf. *IBHS* 7.4.3b).
2. 11QPs[a] and some LXX MSS omit "great."

9The moon and the stars to rule over the night [3]
(because his commitment is forever),

10The hitter of Egypt in their firstborn
(because his commitment is forever),
11And bringer out of Israel from their midst
(because his commitment is forever),
12With a strong hand and an outstretched arm
(because his commitment is forever),
13The divider of the Reed Sea apart[4]
(because his commitment is forever),
14Who let Israel pass through the midst of it
(because his commitment is forever),
15Who shook Pharaoh and his army into the Reed Sea
(because his commitment is forever),
16The taker of his people through the wilderness
(because his commitment is forever),
17The hitter of great kings
(because his commitment is forever),
18Who slew majestic kings
(because his commitment is forever),
19Yes, Sihon, king of the Amorites
(because his commitment is forever),
20Yes, Og, the king of Bashan
(because his commitment is forever),
21Who gave their land as a possession[5]
(because his commitment is forever),
22A possession for Israel his servant
(because his commitment is forever),

23Who was mindful of us in our humiliation
(because his commitment is forever),
24Who tore us away from our foes
(because his commitment is forever),
25The giver of food to all flesh
(because his commitment is forever).

26Confess the God of the heavens
(because his commitment is forever).[6]

3. Lit. "the sun for rule . . . the moon and the stars for rules," where the word is pl., presumably because both moon and stars are involved.

4. Lit. "into divisions." Nicely, v. 13 also divides the psalm into two (Fokkelman, *Major Poems*, 3:309).

5. On the *w*-qatal verb, see the notes on 135:10, 12.

6. LXX, Jerome repeat v. 3 as a final line.

Interpretation

This further praise psalm again begins and ends with an exhortation to praise (vv. 1–3, 26). The reasons for or contents of the praise in terms of Yhwh's acts then occupy the whole of the space in between, comprising twenty-two lines, the number of letters in the alphabet.[7] This account begins and ends in participles (vv. 4–10, 25); in between it interweaves participles (vv. 13, 16–17), *w*-consecutives (vv. 11–12, 18–20, 24), *w*-qatals (vv. 14, 15, 21) and a relative clause (v. 23). Participles are a common way to go about describing God, whether in praise or in theological affirmation or in polemic, and the continuing of participles with finite verbs is a common idiom.[8] This long sequence of participles and participle substitutes all depends on the references to Yhwh in vv. 1–3; "Psalm 136 holds the record as regards the use of enjambment," which is "the crucial factor in the profile of the song."[9]

The verbs concern the acts of Yhwh in creation (vv. 4–9), in bringing Israel from Egypt to Canaan (vv. 10–22), and in caring for Israel subsequently and for all flesh (vv. 23–25). The mismatch between the analysis by topic and by grammatical form (the movement between participles and finite verbs) suggests that the former should not be allowed too much authority. In particular, the psalm itself (like the OT narrative) does not make a division between Yhwh's acts in creation and in Israel's origins. By means of the relative clause with which vv. 23–25 begin, it makes more of a distinction between Yhwh's acts in Israel's origins and Yhwh's acts in the worshippers' experience, but still not a sharp distinction.

Distinctive to this psalm is the refrain affirming Yhwh's *commitment, which occupies the second colon of each line. Possibly this is a congregational or choral response to the voice that declaims each first colon (cf. Ezra 3:11); and possibly the *kî* with which it opens is simply the marker of direct speech and should not be translated. According to Rabbi Judah, Ps. 136 *is* the Great Hallel, but others saw the Great Hallel as beginning with Ps. 120 or with Ps. 135.[10] That associates the psalm with Passover, though we do not know whether it was used at Passover, or at some other festival, in OT times.

136:1–3. Exhortation to praise.

7. Cf. Gerstenberger, *Psalms*, 2:385.

8. See GKC 116x; JM 121j.

9. Fokkelman, *Major Poems*, 3:311. On its rhetorical features, see Pierre Auffret, "Rendez grâce au Seigneur," *BN* 86 (1997): 7–13.

10. *Midrash on Psalms*, 2:324. Christoph Levin ("Psalm 136 als zeitweilige Schlussdoxologie des Psalters," *SJOT* 14 [2000]: 17–27) sees Ps. 136 as the closing psalm of the Psalter at one stage; it would fittingly fulfill that role.

[1]Confess Yhwh, because he is good
(because his commitment is forever).
[2]Confess the God of gods
(because his commitment is forever).
[3]Confess the Lord of lords
(because his commitment is forever),

The exhortation parallels that in Pss. 134 and 135, but the verb is now *confess rather than praise or worship. This verb, most at home in thanksgivings or testimonies, prepares us for the declaration of Yhwh's acts that will dominate the psalm. "Confession" or "testimony" is a more appropriate term than "thanksgiving," since the psalm does not focus simply on giving thanks to Yhwh for things done on the people's behalf but on giving broader testimony to what Yhwh has done from creation onward, and thereby on drawing attention to who Yhwh is.[11]

Within the opening colon the reason or basis for confession is again that Yhwh is *good. Elsewhere that confession seems to be the beginning of the refrain that continues with the declaration that Yhwh's *commitment is forever (see 2 Chron. 5:13; 7:3; Ezra 3:11; cf. Pss. 106:1; 107:1; 118:1, 29; also 100:5).

Verses 2–3 then complement the confession that God is good with a declaration about Yhwh's relationship with other gods and lords. The declaration goes back to Deut. 10:17, where NJPS translates "God supreme and Lord supreme." The construct expression can indeed be a way of expressing the superlative (compare "holy of holies" meaning "most holy"). But 135:5 does assert Yhwh's superiority over other gods and lords, suggesting that the construct expression in Deut. 10:17 and here is not merely a superlative. The peoples around Judah worshipped many gods, but Yhwh is the God over all gods and the Lord over all lords. Like other psalms, Ps. 135 thus assumes the existence of many other heavenly beings but affirms Yhwh's superiority to and authority over them. Yhwh is God over against (mere) gods, Lord over against (mere) lords. Only Yhwh really deserves the title God or Lord (the conviction is not the same as merely being monotheistic).[12]

136:4–9. Yhwh's acts as creator. This section of praise begins and ends with a four-word first colon, contrasting with the three-word first cola in vv. 5–8.

[4]The sole worker of great wonders
(because his commitment is forever),

11. Cf. Mays, *Psalms*, 419.
12. See the comment on 118:27.

The praise begins by acknowledging Yhwh as one who does wonders, *niplāʾôt*. This term most often refers to events such as the Red Sea deliverance, but in 89:5 [6] the related noun *peleʾ* refers to the wonders of creation, and so must *niplāʾôt* here, as it is spelled out in vv. 5–9.[13] Describing them as great wonders might seem redundant: are there any small wonders? (Actually, yes: see 139:14.) But the adjective underlines their significance. The declaration that Yhwh is the only one to do such wonders (cf. 72:18) takes further the description in vv. 2–3, further asserting the unique deity of Yhwh as creator over against the alleged power and activity of the alleged creator gods of other peoples.

5The maker of the heavens with discernment
(because his commitment is forever),
6The beater out of the earth over the waters
(because his commitment is forever),

The heavens and the earth form an obvious pair for first mention; one can imagine that many of the first cola such as these in vv. 5a and 6a would form a natural pair if the psalm did not incorporate the refrain. Maker and beater out also form a pair, both verbs applying to both objects (Yhwh beats out the sky in Job 37:18); the former is the general word, the latter gives more precision to what Yhwh has to do in getting the heavens and the earth into the form we know. Beating out the earth (like a sheet of metal) is the image in Isa. 42:5; 44:24. No doubt "with discernment" applies to the making and beating out of both heavens and earth; the entire task would require insight and skill. Even "over the waters" might be reckoned to apply to the heavens as well as the earth (see Gen. 1), though it applies particularly to the earth as laid over the waters that surround it and burst through it as springs. Gen. 1 implies that Yhwh indeed applied discernment in undertaking the complex, careful, and orderly task of making the world, but Prov. 3:19–20 makes that point explicit, while Jer. 10:12 makes explicit that it is Yhwh's own discernment. The psalm's omitting the pronominal suffix proclaims that creation embodied actual discernment (the world is a cleverly designed and executed project), not merely that this was Yhwh's discernment.

7The maker of the great lights
(because his commitment is forever),

13. See Pierre Auffret, "Note sur la structure littéraire du psaume cxxxvi," *VT* 27 (1977): 1–12 (see 1–2); more broadly on the structure, see also Jacob Bazak, "The Geometric-Figurative Structure of Psalm cxxxvi," *VT* 35 (1985): 129–38; Claus Schedl, "Die alphabetisch-arithmetische Struktur von Psalm cxxxvi," *VT* 36 (1986): 489–94.

[8]The sun to rule over the day
(because his commitment is forever),
[9]The moon and the stars to rule over the night
(because his commitment is forever),

The description of the creation of the sun, moon, and stars compares with that in Gen. 1:16–18, where God makes the two great lights (there *mĕʾōrōt*, here the more common *ʾôrîm*) to rule the day and the night (though the psalm says "rule over"). Genesis 1 keeps sun and moon in their place (Babylonian religion turned them into deities) by not naming them; they are simply the greater and the lesser light. The psalm (not needing to safeguard against that error?) calls them by their familiar names. Genesis 1 likewise simply mentions the creation of the stars as an afterthought, keeping them, too, in their place (Babylonian astrological study emphasized them). The psalm associates them with the process of ruling. Sun, moon, and stars rule over day and night by deciding when they begin and end (the crucial role of the sun in making things grow is ignored). Through their creation "not only space but time is God's gift."[14]

136:10–22. Yhwh's acts in delivering Israel and giving it the land. Like the Torah story, the psalm goes on to Yhwh's activity toward Israel, and gives that much more space. Unlike the Torah story, it leaps straight from creation to the exodus, omitting the stories of the ancestors. Also omitting Sinai, it then focuses on the Red Sea deliverance, the wilderness journey with its victories, and the gift of the land.

[10]The hitter of Egypt in their firstborn
(because his commitment is forever),
[11]And bringer out of Israel from their midst
(because his commitment is forever),
[12]With a strong hand and an outstretched arm
(because his commitment is forever),

"Hitting" Egypt (*nākâ* hiphil) is a verb the Torah applies to the disasters Yhwh brought on Egypt, specifically to the killing of the firstborn (Exod. 12:12, 13, 29). This was the act whereby Yhwh asserted ownership over the firstborn, demonstrated power over Egypt and its gods, punished it for its resistance to Yhwh's purpose, and drove it to release Israel. Yhwh thus hit Egypt "in [the person of] their firstborn."

"Bring out" (*yāṣāʾ* hiphil) is the standard expression to describe that release (e.g., Exod. 12:17, 51); the colon as a whole most closely corresponds to Yhwh's declaration of intent in Exod. 7:5.

14. Allen, *Psalms 101–150*, 297.

In turn, the emphasis on the power that Yhwh thus showed is expressed in a phrase that recurs in Deuteronomy (4:34; 5:15; 7:19; 9:29; 11:2; 26:8), usually in combination with the verb "bring out." It emphasizes the effort Yhwh put into delivering Israel and thus the extraordinary nature of the event itself (again the absence of pronominal suffixes on hand and arm helps to emphasize this, though suffixes are often omitted in references to parts of the body). Much critical study of the OT doubts whether there ever was an exodus, or at most sees it as a small-scale escape by a few state serfs. Israel consistently remembered it as something much more extraordinary, perhaps an evidence that it could hardly have been such a nonevent.

13The divider of the Reed Sea apart
(because his commitment is forever),
14Who let Israel pass through the midst of it
(because his commitment is forever),
15Who shook Pharaoh and his army into the Reed Sea
(because his commitment is forever),

Three lines on the Red Sea event succeed three lines on the creation of the planets and three lines on the exodus. Although occupying less space in the Torah than the events leading up to the exodus, in Israel's thinking the Red Sea event was the crucial act of deliverance. Before it, Israel had escaped but was not safe; despite the death of the firstborn, the pharaoh had not finally acknowledged Yhwh's authority. After it, Israel was safe, because Yhwh had asserted authority in a definitive way over the pharaoh.

It was "dividing the Reed Sea into divisions" that made it possible for Israel to pass through its midst.[15] "Divide" (*gāzar*) is distinctive to the psalm; elsewhere the verb is *bāqaʿ*. Further, in Exodus Yhwh is not the subject of the verb (see Exod. 14:16, 21–22; contrast Neh. 9:11; Ps. 78:13; Isa. 63:12).[16] Isaiah 51:9 speaks of Yhwh cleaving Rahab (*ḥāṣab*), utilizing motifs from Middle Eastern myth, and the psalm also points to those notions; the Ugaritic equivalent of *gāzar* occurs in what may be a similar context.[17]

On the other hand, the vivid "shook" corresponds to Exod. 14:27: Yhwh shook off Pharaoh and his army as easily as one shakes off an insect (cf. 109:23). No very strong hand or outstretched arm was needed.

15. On Reed Sea/Red Sea, see on 106:7.

16. Cf. the comment on 135:10–11.

17. So René Dussaud, *Les Découvertes de Ras Shamra (Ugarit) et l'Ancien Testament* (Paris: Geuthner, 1941), 84 (cf. Kraus, *Psalms 60–150*, 499); but Dahood (*Psalms*, 3:266) with uncharacteristic restraint warns that the meaning of the Ugaritic word is uncertain.

16The taker of his people through the wilderness
(because his commitment is forever),

Taking the people (literally, causing them to go) through the wilderness with its dangers is a theme that recurs in Deuteronomy (8:2, 15; 29:5 [4]). This aspect of the story is curiously understated, as even those passages indicate; LXX adds an extra line, extending the recollection of Deut. 8:15, "the bringer out of water from the basalt rock. . . ." But this does draw attention to the fact that Yhwh is "taking" them (*môlîk*), an activity that involves putting a great and majestic king (*melek*) such as Sihon or Og in his place.[18]

17The hitter of great kings
(because his commitment is forever),
18Who slew majestic kings
(because his commitment is forever),
19Yes, Sihon, king of the Amorites
(because his commitment is forever),
20Yes, Og, the king of Bashan
(because his commitment is forever),

The celebration speeds on to the successes heralding Israel's capture of the land of Canaan, though again it curiously focuses on some preliminary victories. The Torah does not use "hitting" or "slaying" language for these victories, as it does in relation to the Egyptians (though see Num. 32:4). The psalm adapts that language for Yhwh's action toward Egypt and Israel's action toward the kings they subsequently defeated (Num. 31:8; Deut. 1:4; 2:33; 3:3; 4:46) and applies it to Yhwh's own action in relation to the kings. "Great kings" and "majestic kings" is the psalm's distinctive formulation, though it again implies a reminiscence of the exodus–Red Sea story, where greatness and majesty are key themes (Exod. 14:31; 15:6, 10, 11, 16). Moses's recollection in Deut. 2–3 reflects how significant were the victories over Sihon and Og as the firstfruits of victory over the peoples of the land and the great victories whose tale the Torah itself tells.

21Who gave their land as a possession
(because his commitment is forever),
22A possession for Israel his servant
(because his commitment is forever),

18. Fokkelman, *Major Poems*, 3:309, noting that "the hitter," *lĕmakkēh* (v. 17), extends the paronomasia.

The land of Sihon and Og went to the clans that settled east of the Jordan, but vv. 21–22 will have in mind the gift of all the lands belonging to the various Canaanite peoples. Deuteronomy 4:21, 38 speak of Yhwh giving these lands to Israel as a *possession, though the precise formulation here (*lĕnaḥălâ*) corresponds most closely to Josh. 11:23. Compared with that, once again Yhwh here becomes the subject of the giving of which Joshua is the subject there. As was the case in 135:12, the repetition of "a possession" before the continuance of v. 22 emphasizes the significance of this notion: *those people's* land became a *possession* for Israel! The repetition also slows the verse down and lulls the reader into a false sense of security (all we are getting here is repetition) before the continuation says something rather new in describing Israel not merely in conventional terms as "his people" (as in 135:12) but as "his servant." That designation of Israel is otherwise confined to Isa. 41–49; Jer. 30:10; 46:27–28. The land is a gift from the Lord of lords to this Lord's closest servant.

136:23–25. Yhwh's acts in rescuing and providing. The relative prefix *še* marks a new beginning, and the language of these last three lines is much more distinctive.

> 23Who was mindful of us in our humiliation
> (because his commitment is forever),
> 24Who tore us away from our foes
> (because his commitment is forever),
> 25The giver of food to all flesh
> (because his commitment is forever).

One can imagine readers relating this confession to four experiences. First, it summarizes Yhwh's involvement with Israel described through vv. 10–22, which began with Yhwh being *mindful of Israel in its affliction (Exod. 2:24; 6:5). This affliction is then reconfigured as humiliation or being brought low (*šēpel*) at the foes' hand, while Yhwh's deliverance is reconfigured as tearing the people away from these foes. The third colon then summarizes the way Yhwh provided for the people in the wilderness (cf. 105:40).

Second, it summarizes Yhwh's involvement with Israel after giving them the land. In the "judges" period Israel was again brought low by its foes, and again knew Yhwh being mindful of it and tearing it away from these foes.

Third, the confession summarizes Israel's experience in the exile, a further and cataclysmic experience of being brought low at its foes' hand (see Lam. 1:5, 7). That was what Yhwh had long threatened (see especially Isa. 2), but Yhwh also promised to revive the people who have been brought low (Isa. 57:15).[19] For the context of exile Yhwh promised to be mindful of the covenant (Lev. 26:42, 45), and was so mindful (Isa. 63:11), and from their foes there Yhwh tore them away (responding to the plaint in Lam. 5:8, where the verb recurs).

Fourth, it summarizes Judah's experience after the exile. There again in their lowly state foes assailed them (Ezra 4:1; Neh. 4:11 [5]), and there again Yhwh was mindful of them, as Nehemiah had asked (Neh. 1:11). In vv. 23–24 for the only time the psalm speaks in terms of "us," suggesting that the postexilic community's experience is at least a level of experience that is presupposed here.

If we do not link v. 25 with Yhwh's provision of food in the wilderness, it forms an inclusion with vv. 4–9 in taking us back to Yhwh's provision for the world as creator (cf. 104:27–28; 145:15). But in following vv. 10–24, it "makes the recitation of the Lord's mighty works a preface to every blessing said over the food we eat. It became apparent here why our Lord taught us to pray for the coming of the reign of God and the gift of daily bread in one short prayer. All of history and each day of living are contained in the story of the Lord's steadfast love."[20]

136:26. The closing exhortation to praise.

> **26**Confess the God of the heavens
> (because his commitment is forever).

All that has intervened since vv. 1–3 gives ample reason for *confessing the God of the heavens. The title follows well on v. 25: Yhwh is not merely the God of Israel but the God of the heavens who is the God of all flesh. The title recurs in the Persian period, a context in which it affirmed that Yhwh is not merely a little local Judean deity but the one God of all the world (e.g., Ezra 1:2; Neh. 1:4; Dan. 2:18).

Theological Implications

Psalms such as Ps. 136 are often called "historical psalms," but their purpose is not merely to recount Israel's history, as the refrain in Ps. 136 repeatedly makes explicit. "By way of the refrain, the psalmist affirms that every aspect and moment of Israel's story . . . is pervaded by and dependent upon God's steadfast love."[21] That applies not only to Israel's story; the

19. EVV have "lowly," which gives a misleading impression; the idea of the word is not that people are subjectively lowly but that they are objectively so.

20. Mays, *Psalms*, 421.

21. McCann, "Psalms," 1224. Cf. Dirk J. Human, "Psalm 136," in *Psalms and Liturgy*, ed. Dirk J. Human and Cas J. A. Vos, JSOTSup 410 (London and New York: T&T Clark, 2004), 73–88 (see 74).

psalm presupposes a comprehensive relationship between praise and the whole world and the realm of human affairs.[22] "Creation represents the beginning of the history of God's covenant relationship with humankind. It is *only* the beginning of that history, and not the totality; it establishes the foundation or stage upon which the rest of history can unfold. And it is *truly* the beginning of that history, and not an independent topic that can be considered in isolation from its narrative context."[23]

In general, Yhwh's commitment is expressed in the way Yhwh goes about being both good and being God of gods and Lord of lords. It would be no use if Yhwh were inherently good but not committed to us; it would be frightening if Yhwh were supreme God and supreme Lord but not committed to us. But Yhwh's being good *and* supreme God, supreme Lord, is something to confess.

Yhwh's commitment is expressed in the wonders of the heavens and the earth, in the way the cosmos is, and the way it works together with the sun, moon, and stars ruling over and thus serving the world (cf. 33:6–7; Gen. 8:22–9:17).

Yhwh's commitment is expressed in being prepared to take violent action against imperial powers that seek to constrain other peoples, so as to show who is Lord and to give these peoples their freedom. This is bad news for the major powers of Europe, North America, and Asia, but good news for the little peoples whom the big powers dominate.

Yhwh's commitment is expressed in taking Israel through the wilderness. As the church in Europe wanders through the wilderness and the church in the United States enters that wilderness, it does so with Yhwh's commitment to taking it through and on toward its destiny.

Yhwh's commitment is expressed in being prepared to hit and kill powers that attack Israel. The kings the psalm mentions, Sihon and Og, were not ones Israel was commissioned to attack and kill. They made the mistake of attacking Israel instead of letting Israel pass on its way. Yhwh is prepared to take violent action against such peoples, as against Egypt, and to use such people's stupidity as a means of fulfilling the intention of taking Israel to its destiny. It is possible to scorn the notion of God's love because it seems to mean that God has nice feelings for us but does not actually do anything. The psalm assumes that love issues in action. God's love can be terrifying.[24]

22. See M. E. Andrew, "Praise in Asia," *East Asia Journal of Theology* 3.1 (1985): 107–11 (see 109). There is thus some appositeness in Mary F. Copeland's "An African-American Heritage Version of Psalm 136," *Journal of Religious Thought* 45.2 (1989): 93–85.

23. Francis Watson, *Text and Truth* (Edinburgh: T&T Clark; Grand Rapids: Eerdmans, 1997), 267.

24. Cf. Ruth Scoralick's discussion of Pss. 135 and 136, "Hallelujah für einen gewalttätigen Gott?" *BZ* 46 (2002): 253–72 (see 253–54).

Yhwh's commitment is not something that operates merely in the distant past on behalf of our ancestors. It operates now in connection with situations in which we are brought low, to ensure that we, too, are torn away from our foes.

Finally, Yhwh's commitment is not one that operates only toward Israel or the church. It operates as Yhwh provides food to all flesh, in the human and the animal world. There is enough food in the world for all to eat, and that is an expression of the commitment to the world that the God of the heavens makes.

"*Commitment" represents the word *ḥesed,* which is notoriously untranslatable. But "that which in *ḥesed* 'defies all translation' . . . is in fact translated in a most spectacular way in this whole psalm."[25]

25. Jean-Claude Margot, "And His Love Is Eternal," *BT* 25 (1974): 212–17 (see 217).

Psalm 137
Being Mindful of Jerusalem

Translation

[1]By the rivers of Babylon,[1]
there we sat, yes, and wept,
when we were mindful of Zion.
[2]On the poplars in its midst
we hung our lyres.
[3]Because there our captors
asked for the words of a song,
Our mockers[2] for joyfulness:
"Sing us one of the Zion songs."

1. LXX precedes the opening line with the heading "David's." Some LXX MSS rather or additionally refer to Jeremiah. See the discussion in James L. Kugel, "Psalm 137," in *In Potiphar's House* (San Francisco: HarperSanFrancisco, 1990), 173–213 (see 174–80).

2. The hapax legomenon *tôlālênû* is puzzling. Sym offers good sense in translating "mockers" and thus implying that the word comes from *tālal* II, though this verb is elsewhere hiphil; the by-form *hātal* or *hālal* could generate the same meaning. On any theory, the pointing is odd, but it generates paronomasia between *tôlālênû* and *tālînû* ("we hung up") in v. 2: we hung up our lyres, and they mocked us for doing so. LXX has another word for captors, presumably a guess from the parallelism. Tg "plunderers" translates as if the verb were *šālal*, though this does not necessarily imply it had that word. Jerome has "people who afflict us," perhaps suggesting a form of *yālal*, people who make us howl; but *yālal* hiphil means "howl," not "make us howl." See further the discussion in Barthélemy, *Psaumes*, 822–25; also G. A. Rendsburg and S. L. Rendsburg, "Physiological and Philological Notes to Psalm 137," *JQR* 83 (1992–93): 385–99 (see 396–99).

[4]How are we to sing Yhwh's song
on foreign soil?

[5]If I put you out of mind, Jerusalem,
may my right hand put out of mind. . . .
[6]May my tongue stick to my palate
if I am not mindful of you,[3]
If I do not lift up Jerusalem
above the pinnacle[4] of my joyfulness.

[7]Yhwh, be mindful for the Edomites
concerning Jerusalem's day,
The people who were saying, "Expose it, expose it,
to the foundations of it."[5]

[8]Madamoiselle Babylon, to be destroyed,[6]
the good fortune of the person who recompenses you
for the dealings you had with us.
[9]The good fortune of the person who seizes your babies
and dashes them on the crag.

Interpretation

Psalm 137 is the great exception to the rule that the psalms do not reveal their historical context, except that even it is not an exception. In the end it proves the rule in the sense that it tests it but vindicates it. It has a background in the destruction of Jerusalem in 587 BCE and the exile of many Judeans to Babylon. But was it written in Babylon during the exile or in Jerusalem (or Babylon) after the exile? Its opening and closing lines give the impression that the psalmist's own community experienced the exile and the Babylonians' mocking and that Babylon's fall to the Persians has not yet happened. Yet its talk of having sat "there" suggests that the psalmist is back in Jerusalem, and Jerusalem in the Persian period is where Edom's encroaching on Judah is an increasing problem and where the fact that the psalm's sole plea relates to Edom becomes more intelligible. Admittedly, in Pss. 48:6 [7] and 76:3 [4] "there" applies to Jerusalem and does not imply that the psalmist was somewhere else (the implication is "in this place at that time"), and the generation who experienced the fall of Jerusalem could also be especially incensed

3. The suffix *-kî* is the long, Aramaic-like form; as in 103:3–5, it makes for paronomasia, indeed for rhyme, here with *lĕḥikkî* at the end of the previous colon.

4. Lit. "head."

5. Lit. "in it."

6. For the passive *haššĕdûdâ*, Sym, Tg, Syr imply active *haššôdĕdâ*.

about Edom. Conversely the pain of Judah's treatment by Babylon need not be confined to the generation that was actually exiled, while the imperial authority that controls and oppresses Judah after the exile could be thought of as Babylon (Ezra 5:13; Neh. 13:6), and Babylon itself was not destroyed in 539. Thus vv. 8–9 would still make sense after the exile. Indeed, both Edom and Babylon became symbols of oppressive powers; perhaps neither term refers to the historical Edom or Babylon. It is thus impossible to be clear whether the psalm belongs in the exile or afterward, but it is easy to imagine it being used in either context. Indeed, such a psalm would help to "rekindle and sustain hope" over the long haul.[7]

Like many of the Songs of the Ascents (Pss. 120–34), Ps. 137 represents a unique take on the nature of one of the standard psalm forms; it is a distinctive kind of community prayer psalm. (It also compares with the Songs of the Ascents in its focus on Zion; in Book V, Zion is otherwise mentioned only five times.) Verses 1–4 are a variant on the protest that is part of a prayer psalm, but they include no invocation of Yhwh. Verses 5–6 are a variant on the vow of commitment that is part of a prayer psalm, though it is an affirmation of commitment to Jerusalem rather than to Yhwh. Only with v. 7 does the psalm address Yhwh, with its one explicit plea, though its focus on Edom means it is strangely unrelated to the rest of the psalm with its focus on Babylon. Verses 8–9 might be seen as a variant on the declaration of confidence in the fulfillment of Yhwh's promises that can close a prayer psalm.[8] As a community prayer psalm (see the repeated "we"/"us"), it presumably would have been used in the kind of services of prayer and lament to which Lamentations belongs and of which Zech. 7–8 still speaks after 539. Subsequently it came to be used at services on the Ninth of Ab in July–August, marking the various destructions of Jerusalem.

Verse 3 refers to "Zion songs," and one might see Ps. 137 as an ironically inverted version of a Zion song such as Pss. 46; 48; 76; and 84.[9]

7. See Ada María Isasi-Díaz's reflection on the psalm's significance for her as a Cuban exile, "By the Rivers of Babylon," in *Reading from This Place*, ed. Fernando Segovia and Mary Ann Tolbert (Minneapolis: Fortress, 1995), 1:149–63 (see 158).

8. Further on the psalm's structure, colometry, and rhetorical features, see Pierre Auffret, "Essai sur la structure littéraire du psaume 137," *ZAW* 92 (1980): 346–77; idem, "Souviens-toi YHWH," *BZ* 41 (1997): 250–52; F. Renfroe, "Persiflage in Psalm 137," in *Ascribe to the Lord*, ed. Lyle Eslinger and Glen Taylor, JSOTSup 67 (P. C. Craigie Memorial; Sheffield: Sheffield Academic Press, 1988), 509–27; David Noel Freedman, "The Structure of Psalm 137," in *Near Eastern Studies in Honor of William Foxwell Albright*, ed. Hans Goedicke (Baltimore: Johns Hopkins Press, 1971), 187–205; Morris Halle and John J. McCarthy, "The Metrical Structure of Psalm 137," *JBL* 100 (1981): 161–67.

9. Cf. Willy Schottroff, *"Gedenken" im Alten Orient und im Alten Testament*, WMANT 15 (Neukirchen: Neukirchener Verlag, 1964), 145; Ulrich Kellermann, "Psalm 137," *ZAW* 90 (1978): 43–58 (see 50–55).

It makes an absolute commitment to staying mindful of Zion in the manner of a Zion song (vv. 5–6) and it expresses the mindfulness of Zion intrinsic to a Zion song, but it does that with tears rather than joy (v. 1). It knows that joyful praise characterizes a Zion song, but the people of whom it speaks have hung up their lyres (v. 2). It knows that this praise in Zion is due to reach the ends of the earth, but the imperial power of which it speaks asks to hear Zion songs only as an expression of mockery (v. 3). It knows that Judah's vocation is to sing such songs, but how can it do so on foreign soil? (v. 4). It knows that a Zion song often expresses wonder at the city's defenses and its deliverances, and at the nations' astonishment at these, but it must itself draw attention to the city's fall and destruction and ask for action against a nation that encouraged it (v. 7). It knows that a Zion song can declare the "good fortune" of people associated with Zion, but it has to redirect that declaration (vv. 8–9). "Psalm 137 transforms the Zion-song into the Jerusalem lament."[10]

The psalm has virtually no parallelism between the cola within lines, but substantial parallelism between lines, in vv. 1 and 2, 3a–b and 3c–d, 5 and 6a–b, 6b and 6c–d, 8 and 9.

137:1–4. The protest. The opening and closing cola form the painful frame around vv. 1–4, with their reference to the rivers of Babylon and to foreign soil. In the third colon and the third colon from the end, the references to Zion set up the painful contrast over against these. The second colon and the second from the end likewise set up a contrast between weeping and singing. The intervening cola in vv. 2–3 underline the pain of those contrasts by describing the attitude of the overlords who had forced people to experience this pain and now add to it. The ninefold occurrence of the ending *-nû* (we, our, us) underlines the pathos of the lines.[11]

The whole is a protest, but whom does it address? There is no positive indication that it addresses Yhwh, and the reference to Yhwh in v. 4 works against our simply assuming that (after all, many psalms speak to the people or to the king rather than to Yhwh). Rather the psalmist (who will speak in the first person in vv. 5–6) here gives voice to the way the community reflects to itself on its experience.

1By the rivers of Babylon,
there we sat, yes, and wept,
when we were mindful of Zion.
2On the poplars in its midst
we hung our lyres.

10. Adele Berlin, "Psalms and the Literature of Exile," in *Book of Psalms*, ed. Flint and Miller, 65–86 (see 71).

11. Allen, *Psalms 101–150*, 307.

The "rivers" of Babylon may be a plural that signifies "the great river,"[12] the Euphrates itself, or may refer to humanly constructed tributaries, dug to provide irrigation. Either way Jerusalem has no watercourses like Babylon's, and one could imagine that people might rejoice at the opportunity to gather by them under the shade of the trees that v. 2 refers to, with the chance to sit, talk, play, and sing, and perhaps vv. 5–6 will recognize that it could be tempting to do that. But people's actual and proper attitude toward Babylon and Zion is weeping. Exiles usually grieve as they miss their homeland, though they may adjust; and if they do not adjust, the next generation will. The Judean exiles did so settle down, and the next generation had no more desire to go live in the backwaters of Jerusalem than present-day Jewish residents of New York or Los Angeles. In contrast, this psalm recalls being "*mindful of Zion." The object of their mindfulness is thus not actually Jerusalem, the capital city with its location on the map, but Zion, the place that Yhwh chose and made a commitment to, where Yhwh came to dwell (see Ps. 132).

"Be mindful" implies not just an accidental remembering but a deliberate focusing of attention and thought, a focused mindfulness on the part of a community gathered for recollection. Ezekiel refers to the community living (*yāšab*) by the Chebar River (Ezek. 3:15),[13] and Ezra gathered his caravan by the Ahava River for fasting, self-affliction, and prayer (Ezra 8:21). Perhaps v. 1 presupposes that people are consciously sitting before God and consciously weeping before God for their affliction and their waywardness, praying toward Jerusalem as envisaged by 1 Kings 8:46–48.[14] But the psalm does not say they were praying, and we have noted that vv. 1–4 do not address God. The words more recall the way Isa. 40:27 has people talking about God rather than talking to God (cf. Exod. 2:23). Thus they may be more an expression of religious depression.[15]

The word *ʿărābâ* can refer either to the willow or to the Euphrates poplar, which is somewhat like a willow; the latter is likely to be strictly correct in a Babylonian context.[16] Apparently the Judeans hung up their *lyres on these trees rather than play them. While it would not be

12. So GKC 124e.

13. Shimon Bar-Efrat ("Love of Zion," in *Tehillah le-Moshe*, ed. Mordechai Cogan et al. [Moshe Greenberg Festschrift; Winona Lake, IN: Eisenbrauns, 1997], 3–11 [see 5]) suggests that *yāšab* means "dwell" here.

14. Cf. Kraus, *Psalms 60–150*, 502.

15. Spieckermann, *Heilsgegenwart*, 116.

16. So J. V. Kinnear Wilson, "Hebrew and Akkadian Philological Notes," *JSS* 7 (1962): 173–83 (see 175); Michael Zohary, *Plants of the Bible* (Cambridge: Cambridge University Press, 1982), 130–31.

surprising if the lamenting implied by v. 1 involved musical accompaniment, the vast majority of references to lyres connect them with praise (e.g., Pss. 92:3 [4]; 98:5; 108:2 [3]; 147:7; 149:3; 150:3). Hanging up one's lyre signifies publicly (and before God?) that one has given up praise.

> [3]Because there our captors
> asked for the words of a song,
> Our mockers for joyfulness:
> "Sing us one of the Zion songs."

Verse 3 expresses a more specific reason why people had hung up their lyres and given up praise. What the captors request is not merely a song (so EVV) but "the words of a song." It is the words that give them something to scorn and give the captives something to lament. The reference to "captors" is also significant because of where the psalm will go in vv. 7–9. While the word comes in Ps. 106:46 and in Solomon's prayer in 1 Kings 8 and 2 Chron. 6 as it looks forward to exile, it also comes in promises of Yhwh's putting down Babylon in Jer. 50:33, and most significantly Isa. 14:2, where it follows up the specific promise about that reversal that v. 9 will claim.

"Asked for" carries over into the next, parallel line, where as subject "our mockers" parallels "our captors," and as object "joyfulness" parallels "the words of a song." The joyfulness might be that of the exiles ("Come on, sing a joyful song")[17] or might be the audience's ("Come on, entertain us"). Either way, the request is a cruel one underlining the captives' lack of anything to rejoice at.

Specifically, the captors ask for a song about Zion. One look at such songs (e.g., Pss. 46; 48; 76; 84) reveals the pain they would now cause the captives. Yhwh has not stopped Jerusalem from falling or asserted authority over the nations. Zion is not the most beautiful height, the joy of all the earth. Yhwh has not broken the weapons of the peoples who war against Zion. When Lam. 2:15–16 pictures people wandering past Jerusalem scorning the theology of the Zion psalms, one suspects they are at least in part the externalization of the Judeans' own feelings; compare the "where is your/their God?" of passages such as Pss. 42:3, 10 [4, 11]; 79:10; 115:2. This is at least part of what is going on in Ps. 137. The problem lies not merely in what the captors are saying, but in what the captives' own hearts are saying. To sing such songs might be an act of faith, but in the context it would feel more like an act of folly.

17. Harris Lenowitz takes *śimḥâ* to have the concrete meaning "joyful song" (see "The Mock-*śimḥâ* of Psalm 137," in *Directions in Biblical Hebrew Poetry*, ed. Elaine R. Follis, JSOTSup 40 [Sheffield: Sheffield Academic Press, 1987], 149–59). Cf. LXX.

[4]How are we to sing Yhwh's song
on foreign soil?

In a sense the answer is, "very easily." Theologically, the exiles know that Yhwh is not located in Judah in such a way as not to be present elsewhere; at least, the Psalms are very often declaring that Yhwh is Lord of the entire world, and the Prophets are quite often asserting that Yhwh is active in places such as Assyria and Babylon. Yhwh had spoken to Abraham in Babylonia, and Ezekiel saw Yhwh there. But the kind of song the psalm refers to can hardly be sung there. The people are on foreign soil because Yhwh has abandoned them, whereas those psalms talk about Yhwh gaining the victory over their foreign oppressors. In the exile Yhwh is not reigning, except in a rather Pickwickian sense; it will be when Yhwh puts Babylon down that Yhwh will be reigning again (cf. Isa. 52:7–10). Meanwhile, it is no more possible to sing Yhwh's song on foreign soil than to do so in Sheol; this is not a realm in which Yhwh chooses to be active and can therefore be confessed. There is no act of Yhwh to sing of here.

Yet the following lines raise the question whether the psalm goes on to treat the question as more than rhetorical, by indicating how people are to sing Yhwh's song on foreign soil.[18]

137:5–6. The promise of commitment. The temptation that would go along with the impossibility of singing a Zion song, a Yhwh song, would be the temptation deliberately to forget about Jerusalem and about Yhwh. To judge from Nehemiah, that was an issue for people in Jerusalem itself (Neh. 7:4; 11:1–2).[19] The psalm continues not to address Yhwh, but it does now address Jerusalem and promises not to forget it. It has already referred to a mindfulness that found it impossible to sing, but in the end that kind of mindfulness will not do. The psalmist knows that people have to make a commitment to singing Zion songs even if it hurts. They cannot put Zion out of mind. Otherwise they will not be able to speak or sing at all. Ultimately there is a theological reason for this. The Zion songs spoke in light of the fact that Yhwh had chosen Zion as a place to dwell. Even though this seems not to have been part of Yhwh's original plan, Yhwh had gone along with David's ideas, and it was now there that Yhwh was prepared to take on the world's opposition to Israel, which was also opposition to Yhwh's own purpose. It will be there in due course that this clash will come to a

18. So George Savran, "'How Can We Sing a Song of the Lord?'" *ZAW* 112 (2000): 43–58.

19. Gregory Vall, "Praying in the Messianic Spirit," *Bible Today* 38 (2000): 156–61 (see 159).

head when the world's powers crucify Jesus. Psalm 137 presupposes "the nonnegotiable, scandalous particularity of Jerusalem."[20] It is a city that cannot be spiritualized.

The psalmist now speaks as an "I." As in 135:5, the "I" draws attention to the psalmist's personal commitment in order to make a distinction over against the community and also to draw other people to identify with it. As involuntary exile becomes voluntary dispersion, each individual needs to take on a commitment to Zion. Ezra and Nehemiah instance this; they evidently had a burden for Jerusalem not shared by all their contemporaries, and it led them to take personal action on its behalf (in Ezra's case, seeking to involve other people so that the "I" indeed becomes a "we").

> **5**If I put you out of mind, Jerusalem,
> may my right hand put out of mind. . . .

Putting out of mind (*ignore) is the opposite of being mindful. But further, whereas the invitation in v. 3 suggests reference to the psalms that speak of Zion, the spiritual center of Israel's faith, instead the psalmist now speaks of keeping in mind Jerusalem, the nation's political as well as spiritual capital. It is as if the psalmist says, "I will not sing you a merely religious song, but I will sing you a song of defiance, a promise that I will never forget my homeland, and that there will one day be a reckoning for what you have done."[21] Initially people can hardly forget Jerusalem, but time is passing, and it will become easier. Perhaps the psalm is looking back on the taunting and hanging up of lyres; that is not present reality.

The self-curse that the psalmist imposes in the second colon involves repeating the verb from the first, but without an object, so that it parallels other self-curses that leave the curse's sanction unstated (e.g., 132:3–5). The KJV assumes that the verb implies as object "its cunning," its skill in playing the lyre, and this fits v. 6a–b.[22]

> **6**May my tongue stick to my palate
> if I am not mindful of you,

20. Brueggemann, *Message of the Psalms*, 74.

21. See Jonathan Magonet, "Some Concentric Structures in Psalms," *Heythrop Journal* 23 (1982): 365–76 (see 375–76); cf. idem, *Bible Lives* (London: SCM, 1992), 20–22.

22. LXX, Jerome might imply repointing the qal *tiškaḥ* to niphal *tiššākaḥ* ("may my right hand be put out of mind"), but that is little improvement. EVV "wither" gives excellent sense, but the foundation for it lies in a speculative extension of the meaning of an obscure Ugaritic verb (see *HALOT*). The same result may be gained by emending to *tikšaḥ* from an otherwise unknown verb that can be related to an Arabic root (Israel Eitan, "An Identification of Tiškaḥ Yĕmīnī," *JBL* 47 [1928]: 193–95).

If I do not lift up Jerusalem
above the pinnacle of my joyfulness.

Verse 6a–b parallels v. 5 in *abb'a'* order. The tongue sticking to the palate would make it impossible to speak or sing at all. The self-curse thus draws attention to the fact that mindfulness is not merely something that goes on inside the head. It is expressed in the way we talk and sing. And these lines are not merely an affirmation of love for Jerusalem but a curse on one's own hand and tongue, the greatest curse that a musician could utter.[23]

The second line spells out yet further what this mindfulness means. The mindfulness that exalts Jerusalem lifts it up, exalts it over anything else in which we might find joy. Once again the self-curse takes up the opening verses of the psalm. How can our mockers ask joyfulness of us? There can be no joyfulness over Zion at that moment. In what, then, can there be joyfulness? There had better not be anything else that makes us joyful.

137:7. The plea. For the first time the psalm explicitly addresses Yhwh, the only person who can be addressed if the psalm is to ask for anything.

[7]Yhwh, be mindful for the Edomites
concerning Jerusalem's day,
The people who were saying, "Expose it, expose it,
to the foundations of it."

Once again the topic is *mindfulness, not now people's actual mindfulness (v. 1) or their promised mindfulness (vv. 5–6), but the mindfulness they seek from Yhwh. The plea concerns their foes, but surprisingly it is Edom, not Babylon. In the context of postexilic Judah, this could reflect Edom's encroachment on Judean territory, but the verse itself more directly points to the immediate aftermath of the fall of Judah. The OT narrative makes no reference to the Edomites' involvement in Jerusalem's fall, but the psalm refers to it as a well-known fact, and Obad. 10–14 speaks of it at some length (cf. Lam. 4:21–22). Gloating and joyfulness (cf. v. 3) were among the attitudes Obadiah there attributes to the Edomites. In this connection Obad. 10–14 refers ten times to the "day" of Jerusalem's calamity, the day when Yhwh's wrath was expressed against Jerusalem: compare the many references to Yhwh's day of wrath in Lamentations (e.g., 1:12; 2:1, 21, 22). Lamentations also speaks of Judah's enemies having longed to see this day (2:16). Ezekiel has Edom welcoming the Babylonian troops,

23. Magonet, *Bible Lives*, 21–22.

encouraging them to make a thorough job of the city's destruction, and joining in bringing punishment on Jerusalem (Ezek. 25:12; 35:5). "Expose" (*ʿārâ* piel) initially suggests the motif of the city as a woman who is stripped and shamed (cf. Isa. 3:17; Lam. 4:21),[24] but the second colon then speaks more realistically about the city itself, whose very foundations are exposed when its buildings and walls are burned or torn down.

Ezekiel 25:12–14 declares that Yhwh would bring recompense on Edom for its action against Judah and would do so through Israel itself (cf. Obad. 17–21; Jer. 49:7–22 lacks the reference to Israel's own action). The psalmist asks Yhwh to act in accordance with that commitment but apparently does not look forward to taking action in person.

Typically the plea is quite unspecific in the action it looks for; it is concerned to get Yhwh to act but content to leave it to Yhwh to determine what the action should be.

137:8–9. The declaration of confidence. It is a plausible suggestion that the meetings for lamentation and prayer would also include the seeking of a word from God,[25] and it is a plausible view that God's response would be to remind people of words spoken previously that related to the present situation (cf. Pss. 60; 108).[26] The declaration of confidence takes up Yhwh's promises and declares an assurance that they will find fulfillment. This will then deal with the issue raised in vv. 1–4. Commentators refer to vv. 8–9 (and v. 7) as a curse,[27] but the only curse in the psalm is the self-curse in vv. 5–6.

> 8Madamoiselle Babylon, to be destroyed,
> the good fortune of the person who recompenses you
> for the dealings you had with us.

Whereas there is a plea about Edom, there is no plea about Babylon, only an expression of confidence concerning its fate. The reason is that Yhwh has made promises concerning this matter; all the psalm needs to do is declare the conviction that Yhwh will act as promised. The term

24. William John Lyons takes shame as one of the keys to understanding the vehemence of the psalm and its desire for the children to be killed ("A Man of Honour, A Man of Strength, A Man of Will?" *Didaskalia* 16.2 [2005]: 41–68).

25. Kraus, *Psalms 60–150*, 502.

26. Graham S. Ogden ("Prophetic Oracles against Foreign Nations and Psalms of Communal Lament," *JSOT* 24 [1982]: 89–97) argues that Jer. 49 and Obadiah are responses to Ps. 137; he does not take account of the psalm's key links with Isa. 13. It is hard to date all these oracles after the exile, and the parallel with Pss. 60 and 108 supports the idea that Ps. 137 is referring back to an existent oracle. Kellermann ("Psalm 137," 55–58) sees the psalm as responding to prophecies about Edom given in worship.

27. E.g., Gerstenberger, *Psalms*, 2:392, though he notes that the Psalms never say "may x be cursed," as in, e.g., 2 Sam. 16:5–10 (but see Ps. 119:21).

"Mademoiselle Babylon" already heralds this: the expression comes elsewhere in declarations of Babylon's fall (Isa. 47:1; Jer. 50:42). The term's own resonances are thus sinister. The expression is more literally "daughter Babylon"; it is a construct, but it does not mean "daughter of Babylon" (compare expressions such as "City of Pasadena"). It does not imply that Babylon has a father but rather that it is like a refined young woman. The passive participle that follows (*šĕdûdâ*) immediately makes the line's sinister nature explicit. To judge from the rest of vv. 8–9, Babylon has not yet been destroyed; the participle refers to what is going to happen (so Th); compare the promises in passages such as Jer. 51:48, 53, 55, 56.[28] Destruction (*šōd*) is to come upon Babylon from the Almighty Destroyer (*šadday*; Isa. 13:6). This need not mean that the psalm dates from before Babylon's fall in 539, both because this did not involve the city's destruction and because the OT sees the Babylonian empire living on in the Persian administration.

Who is to be responsible for this destruction? Ultimately it is Yhwh; the human agent is unnamed. The psalm does again imply that it is not the suppliants who expect to undertake it. They believe that the destroyers are privileged, people of *good fortune, but Babylon's destruction is not the suppliants' own task. Their task is simply to trust Yhwh to fulfill the promises they have been given. They know from the prophets that God is one who recompenses, and who is committed to "recompensing" Babylon in accordance with its "dealings" (e.g., Jer. 51:6, 24, 56; cf. Obad. 15).

> 9The good fortune of the person who seizes your babies
> and dashes them on the crag.

The final line gives terrifying concrete form to the declaration of *good fortune in v. 8. The words are chilling, but hardly surprising. They are a recurrent OT image for what happens in war (e.g., 2 Kings 8:12; Hos. 10:14; 13:16 [14:1]; Nah. 3:10). As I write, it is happening in Iraq every day. Indeed, a nation may make a point of killing its enemies' children, because they are its future. When the Babylonians captured Jerusalem, they made a point of killing the two sons of the Judean king Zedekiah to make sure they would not become the focus of attempts to restore Davidic rule in Jerusalem (2 Kings 25:7).

Yet we should not press the psalm's metaphorical language. None of the passages that refer to smashing children are simple reports of someone's action; all come in the words of prophets, apart from this psalm that appeals to the words of prophets. Zedekiah's sons were not actually smashed on a crag and neither are the children of Iraq, and it is unlikely

28. Cf. *IBHS* 37.4d; DG 110 says "possibly" the meaning is thus gerundive.

that this is what the psalm literally envisages. Middle Eastern writings like to express things concretely rather than abstractly, in terms

> which frequently signify a reality far larger than their concrete meaning. . . . We need to consider . . . whether these "little ones" ought not to be understood just as symbolically as "Mother Babylon." The inhabitants of the oppressor-city or the children of the ruling dynasty concretize the continuation of the unrighteous empire. . . . One might translate: "Happy is he who puts an end to your self-renewing domination!" Stated thus, the sentence would presumably offend no one, though it too implies brutal consequences. Its brutality, however, is cloaked in the broad mantle of abstract formulation. Such an (often dangerous) dissociation of concrete reality from idea is as foreign to the ancient Near Eastern mode of perception as the dissociation of body and spirit. Ancient Near Eastern perception usually preserves the continuity between the *concretum* and its related abstract.[29]

The psalm's words are also not surprising because all they are doing is expressing confidence that Yhwh will fulfill the promises made by the prophets. It is not devising from scratch the most vicious image it can think of to express the warped nature of its mind but taking up Yhwh's own image. There is some appropriateness to it: Yhwh had declared the intention to do this to Judah's children and had used Babylon as the means of doing so; again, it is an image (Jer. 13:14; 51:20–23). Further, Yhwh had declared that Yhwh's enemies (soon in the passage to be identified with Babylon) would be seized by excruciating pains like those of childbirth and that Babylon's children would be smashed before their eyes (Isa. 13:6, 16). The Babylonians would be thrown down from the crags (Jer. 51:25).

Thus the psalm develops no new ideas for the way Babylon might be punished. Every word in this chilling declaration takes up Yhwh's promises (as the closing declaration in a prayer psalm sometimes does) and envisages them being fulfilled.[30] Then justice will have been done.

Theological Implications

James S. Lowry represents a standard view of Ps. 137 in describing it as starting noble but becoming mean.[31] If there is movement within

29. Keel, *Symbolism*, 9.

30. Cf. Calvin, *Psalms*, 5:196–98. Tg has a striking expansive translation whose effect overlaps with this concern in seeing vv. 5–6 as Yhwh's own words and vv. 7–9 as the words of Michael and Gabriel (see Moshe J. Bernstein, "Translation Technique in the Targum to Psalms," in *Society of Biblical Literature 1994 Seminar Papers* [Atlanta: Scholars, 1994], 326–45 [see 342–43]).

31. "By the Waters of Babylon," *Journal for Preachers* 15.3 (1992): 26–33 (see 28). Cf. Weiser's imaginative account of the psalmist's psychological movement through the psalm (*Psalms*, 794–97).

the psalm, it rather starts with denial and a breakdown in relationship, and moves to recognition and communication. The beginning is aware of grief and abuse, but the community talks only to itself about it. In the last part it at last addresses God, but in doing so it also comes to express the longing in its heart concerning Jerusalem and concerning itself. Paradoxically, the captors and the mockers apparently facilitated that. If they had not urged the exiles to sing about Zion, it might have been easier to put Jerusalem out of mind. Instead the exiles are driven to express their commitment to keeping Jerusalem in mind and thus to turning to Yhwh rather than continuing to turn in on themselves, in order to urge Yhwh to keep in mind the way Edom had treated Jerusalem. And perhaps expressing themselves about the city is the halfway house to expressing themselves about the way the Babylonians had treated them. So now denial and a failure to talk to Yhwh has given way to communication with Yhwh and an owning of their pain and longing.

There is certainly a lesson here for the bourgeois average reader of the psalm and of this commentary, for we prefer denial and a reluctance to express our hearts to God over recognition and communication. And of course we are not people who have gone through the experiences the psalm speaks of or can imagine doing so. From a Nigerian perspective, David Tuesday Adamo comments on the fact that the prominence of prayer for God's punishment of one's enemies in such a psalm troubles Western Christians but does not so trouble African indigenous churches. Rather than psalms of violence and hate, these are psalms of protection and defense. People are aware that enemies will use spiritual means such as curses to cause harm to them, and traditional religion gives people charms and recitations to counteract these. When people came to believe in Christ, these means of protection became forbidden, but they discovered the imprecatory psalms and came to use them in this way.[32]

Athalya Brenner sets alongside the psalm an account of the Christian slaughter of the Jewish community in the Polish town of Jedwabne in 1941, which included putting children on pitchforks and throwing them onto the smoldering coals of the barn where their parents had been burned to death.[33] And Primo Levi wrote a modern version of the psalm

32. See, e.g., "The Use of Psalms in African Indigenous Churches in Nigeria," in *The Bible in Africa*, ed. Gerald O. West et al. (Leiden: Brill, 2001), 336–49.

33. "'On the Rivers of Babylon' (Psalm 137), or Between Victim and Perpetrator," in *Sanctified Aggression*, ed. Jonneke Bekkenkamp and Yvonne Sherwood, JSOTSup 400 (London and New York: T&T Clark, 2003), 76–91. She refers to Jan T. Gross, *Neighbors: The Destruction of the Jewish Community in Jedwabne, Poland* (Princeton: Princeton University Press, 2001).

in light of Auschwitz.[34] "P. D. James in her mystery *Original Sin*[35] has a character say to her Jewish colleague: 'If I had a God, I'd like him to be intelligent, cheerful and amusing.' He said, 'I doubt whether you'd find him much of a comfort when they herded you into the gas chambers. You might prefer a God of vengeance.'"[36]

Erich Zenger concludes that

> Psalm 137 is not the song of people who have the power to effect a violent change in their situation of suffering, nor is it the battle cry of terrorists. Instead, it is an attempt to cling to one's historical identity even when everything is against it. Still more, it is an attempt, in the face of the most profound humiliation and helplessness, to suppress the primitive human lust for violence in one's own heart, by surrendering *everything* to God—a God whose word of judgment is presumed to be so universally just that even those who pray the psalm submit themselves to it.[37]

I am not sure we can know that this is the motivation or intent of those who composed the psalm or who first prayed it, but this understanding does emerge from the nature of the psalm. It likewise implies that "it is an act of profound faith to entrust one's most precious hatreds to God, knowing they will be taken seriously."[38] Perhaps it is when we do this that we can sing Yhwh's song on foreign soil.

The psalm is thus not merely an exercise in the movement between orientation, disorientation, and renewed orientation. Or rather, its capacity to undertake that movement is not merely a process within the community's spirit, a coping mechanism that might have little to do with theological and ethical truth. It is of fundamental importance to our proper understanding of its movement that in its entirety this movement takes place within what we might call a scriptural perspective (though of course that way of expressing the point is anachronistic). The perspective on Zion/Jerusalem in vv. 1–6 is not merely that of any people who miss their homeland but the perspective of people who know that Zion/Jerusalem is of key importance for God's purpose in the world. And the plea and declaration in vv. 7–9 are not merely the understandable vitriol of such a people but an appeal for action in accordance with declarations that Yhwh has given Judah. We have noted that through several prophets Yhwh has made declarations about Edom and about Babylon in words that are reflected in the closing verses of the psalm; the psalm

34. Loretz, *Psalmstudien*, 331–50 (see 331), referring to *If This Is a Man* (New York: Orion, 1959).

35. (New York: Knopf, 1995), 232.

36. Allen, *Psalms 101–150*, 310.

37. Zenger, *A God of Vengeance*, 48.

38. Brueggemann, *Message of the Psalms*, 77.

is simply asking for the implementation of those declarations of intent. (If the prophets' words are actually responses to the psalm, this does not affect the point; perhaps it makes it stronger.)

In the case of the psalm's actual prayer, concerning Edom, the words are extraordinarily mild compared with the promises of the prophets about Edom. All the psalm asks for is that Yhwh should be mindful of what Edom did. There are paradoxical features to Yhwh's response to this plea. In the exile Edom lost its monarchy and its independence, like Judah itself, though on some theories this would have already happened by the time the psalm was written. In the Second Temple period, under pressure from the Nabateans the Edomites continued to expand into Judean territory, and Hebron became their capital. Then after the Maccabean revolt, Judah came to control Edom/Idumea, and eventually the people accepted the Jewish religion. The Herodian dynasty that came to rule Judah was of Idumean origin, and many Idumeans joined with Judeans in following Jesus (Mark 3:8). It thus rather looks as if Yhwh no more implemented warnings about casting off Edom than warnings about casting off Judah. In the context of Jesus's coming, Edom remained as theologically ambiguous as Judah itself.

All this is illuminated by comments of Dietrich Bonhoeffer on psalms such as this. He takes up the fact that the psalms entrust to God the taking of vengeance on wrongdoing rather than taking it into our own hands. We have noted that in this particular case, Yhwh had declared the intention to use Judah to that end, but the psalm does not ask for that aspect of Yhwh's promise to be implemented, and although Judah does come to take control of Idumea, this leads to the Idumeans coming to worship Yhwh and in due course to be drawn to Jesus.

But, Bonhoeffer comments, only people who have not sinned against their enemies can leave vengeance in God's hands. The prayer for divine vengeance is the prayer that God's justice will be carried out in the judgment of sin. But "as a sinner I too am under this judgement." And God's judgment has been fulfilled, in a mysterious way. "God's vengeance fell not on the sinners, but on the only sinless One, the Son of God, who took the sinners' place." It was because he was doing this that he could pray "Father forgive them." "No one but he who himself suffered the wrath of God could utter such a prayer. That was the end of all illusions about a love of God who does not take sin so very seriously. God hates and condemns his enemies in the only just One," and he is the one who can therefore pray for their forgiveness. So when as a Christian I pray for God's vengeance, I know how God has already answered that prayer in the affirmative. "Even today it is only through the Cross of Christ, through the satisfaction of God's vengeance, that I can believe in God's love and forgive enemies." On the other hand, Bonhoeffer notes that

God's vengeance must fall on all who oppose Christ. Because they have declined to let Christ be the one who bears it for them, they must bear God's curse for themselves.[39]

Not surprisingly, the NT simply spells out the implications of the character of Yhwh. When Yhwh offers a self-description in terms of being characterized by compassion, grace, commitment, and a willingness to carry people's waywardness, but also by a willingness to attend to people's waywardness (Exod. 34:6–7), Exodus does not say that this applies to Israel but not to the rest of the world (how could Yhwh thus be morally incoherent?). Edom, too, experiences Yhwh that way. As Ps. 137 can pray for Yhwh to be mindful of Edom's wrongdoing, so the NT can pray that people who preach another gospel or do not love Jesus may be cursed (see Gal. 1:8–9; 1 Cor. 16:22) or can ask when the blood of martyrs will be avenged (Rev. 6:10), and Jesus can declare it impossible that his people's religious leaders should escape being sentenced to hell (Matt. 23:33). Here "the stark claims of the holy God override all our conventional humaneness."[40] In light of the way the NT speaks, it is therefore not so surprising that Ps. 137 seems not to have troubled Christians in ancient contexts. Cassiodorus comments, "Our devoted love is not required in the case of those to be condemned by the Lord's judgment."[41]

Whatever the desires in the hearts of people who say the psalm, their words leave it to God to decide which side of that character God gives expression to.

39. Dietrich Bonhoeffer, *The Psalms* (Oxford: SLG, 1982), 21–22.

40. Brueggemann, *Message of the Psalms*, 76.

41. *Psalms*, 3:363.

Psalm 138

Before Gods, Kings, Enemies

Translation

David's.

[1]I will confess you[1] with all my heart;[2]
before the gods I will make music for you.
[2]I will bow down to[3] your holy palace,
and I will confess your name for your commitment and for your truthfulness,
Because you have made great above all[4]
your name, your word.
[3]On the day when I called, you answered me;
you make me defiant in spirit with strength.

[4]All the kings of the earth are to confess you, Yhwh,
because they have heard the words of your mouth.
[5]They are to sing of Yhwh's ways,

1. 11QPs[a] has "Yhwh" here (cf. LXX, Syr, Tg), the appellative one would expect, conforming to 9:1 [2].

2. LXX has an extra colon, "because you listened to the words of my mouth."

3. Not "in" (Jerome).

4. MT links "above-all-your-name," which is hard to make sense of. I have reckoned that we should delete the second *maqqēp*. 11QPs[a] has *kwl*, and according to JM 14c, other MSS apart from Codexes L and C have *kōl* for *kol* (and cf. Barthélemy, *Psaumes*, 832–33).

because Yhwh's honor is great.
6Because Yhwh is on high, but he sees the lowly;
lofty, he acknowledges from afar.

7Though I walk in the midst of trouble you will give me life;
on account of the anger of my enemies you will extend your hand.[5]
You will deliver me with your right hand;[6]
8Yhwh—he will bring it to an end on my behalf.
Yhwh, your commitment lasts forever;
do not let go the works of your hands.

Interpretation

The psalm is a thanksgiving or testimony, though like other psalms in this last part of the Psalter it varies the usual pattern. Verses 1–2b express the expected commitment to confession and vv. 2c–3 recount the answer to prayer that the psalm celebrates, though rather briefly and generally. It thus contrasts with the extensive declaration in vv. 4–6 about the kings' recognition of Yhwh for who Yhwh is. Finally vv. 7–8 end the psalm with an extensive affirmation of confidence in Yhwh and an unexpected closing plea, all implicitly based on the experience of Yhwh's deliverance.

The reference to the effect that Yhwh's words and actions have on the kings of the earth (vv. 4–6) suggests the psalm is the thanksgiving of a king or governor. In Pss. 2, 72, 89, and 110, the kings of the earth or all the kings are set over against the king of Israel or Judah, and in Pss. 48, 68, 76, and 148, they are set over against Israel or Judah as a whole (speaking as "we" rather than "I"), though in Pss. 102 and 119 they may be set over against an ordinary individual. But the psalm could doubtless also be used by the whole congregation or by an ordinary individual.[7] Its location among other postexilic psalms is the only pointer to a date.

5. I follow the understanding of v. 7a–b suggested by MT accents, which gives good parallelism. EVV redivide the cola and do make the prosody easier by linking "you will give me life" with "on account of the anger of my enemies," but the resultant clause is difficult and the parallelism is lost. For *ʿal ʾap*, cf. 2 Kings 24:20; Jer. 32:31; 52:3, each time with reference to the fall of Jerusalem; the construction there is unclear, but the meaning of the phrase itself is clear enough.

6. There is no prep., and LXX and Jerome take "your right hand" as the subject; but the fact that Yhwh is the subject in v. 7b would suggest that Yhwh is again the subject in v. 7c (cf. 108:6 [7]).

7. Cf. Mowinckel's comments (*Psalms*, 2:36) on the fluid boundary line between private and public/royal thanksgivings (and prayer psalms).

The psalm reuses many familiar phrases: see v. 1a (9:1 [2]), v. 2a (5:7 [8]), vv. 4–5 (102:15 [16]), v. 6 (113:3–6), v. 8a (57:2 [3]), v. 8b (136 throughout). It is said to be dependent on Isa. 40–66,[8] but it is hard to identify specific verbal links, and its themes belong as much to other psalms.

David's.

Heading. See glossary. Some LXX MSS add "Zechariah's," which invites us to read the psalm as a celebration of the community's reestablishment in Jerusalem after the exile.

138:1–3. The pledge to testimony, and the content of the testimony.

[1]I will confess you with all my heart;
before the gods I will make music for you.
[2a–b]I will bow down to your holy palace,
and I will confess your name for your commitment and for your truthfulness,

The key word "*confess" frames the pledge, the first time yiqtol, the second time cohortative, so that the parallelism involves some heightening and a higher degree of commitment in that last colon. Confession is a matter of words; the intervening cola speak of the *music that goes with the words, and the bodily bowing down that accompanies words and music. Accompanying the four parallel verbs are a variety of complements. The psalm speaks of the depth of the whole person's participation in this confession; it involves the whole inner being, the voice, and the body. It speaks of the one who is to hear the testimony. Implicitly, no doubt, it is the person's community, who are to be built up by it, but explicitly it is Yhwh, who is being thanked and glorified. It also speaks of a further audience of other deities (LXX "angels" is not so far out), whom the testimony reminds to keep acknowledging Yhwh as the only real God. Perhaps there is a confrontational edge to the "before" (cf. 23:5), which would fit the references to the gods in 135:5; 136:2–3.[9] While bowing down *in* the temple, Yhwh's earthly home, the worshipper is bowing down *to* Yhwh's "*holy palace" in the heavens, where that court sits. Finally, the psalm gives the reason for confessing Yhwh's *name, Yhwh's *commitment and *truthfulness, whose outworking will be described in the next two lines.

[2c]Because you have made great above all
your name, your word.

8. E.g., Anderson, *Psalms*, 2:901.
9. Cf. McCann, "Psalms," 1231, 1232.

Initially, however, the testimony refrains from speaking in concrete terms about Yhwh's act and focuses rather on its implications. Through what happened, Yhwh was magnified "above all," perhaps in particular above the gods v. 1 referred to. First, it was Yhwh's word (*statement) that was magnified, the word by means of which Yhwh declares an intention and fulfills it, makes a promise and keeps it. Thus it was Yhwh's *name that was magnified; Yhwh's name suggests Yhwh's character as (for instance) embodying commitment and truthfulness (v. 2b), two divine qualities that are linked in the revelation of the meaning of Yhwh's name in Exod. 34:6.

> 3On the day when I called, you answered me;
> you make me defiant in spirit with strength.

At last we get some concrete account of what Yhwh did, though it is still not very specific; but this does make the testimony easily transferable from one worshipper to another. The two cola embrace three key features of such a testimony. First, "I called." Then "you answered," on the very day, if we may press the meaning of *bĕyôm* (cf. NRSV, though the expression can simply mean "when"). It seems that here the "answering" covers both the assurance that Yhwh has heard the prayer and also the act that followed, because the parallel colon goes on to the result of that act. When one has seen Yhwh act, it changes one's stance in the world. Yhwh's acting has made an ongoing difference to the worshipper's spirit.[10] Indeed, it was action that has made a big difference: the verb *rāhab* means to act stormily or boisterously.[11]

138:4–6. The response expected of the kings of the earth. It is not enough for Yhwh to be acknowledged by the powers in the heavens; Yhwh's honor is to be acknowledged on earth as it is in heaven.

> 4All the kings of the earth are to confess you, Yhwh,
> because they have heard the words of your mouth.

The key verb "*confess" recurs, but the psalm illustrates the dynamic or ideology of a testimony psalm, which is that one person's confession comes also to be expressed by others who hear what Yhwh has done for

10. EVV translate the yiqtol verb as past, referring it to Yhwh's action in response to the prayer; yiqtol verbs in the Psalms can have that reference. But accounts of Yhwh's acts do not usually refer to the subjective difference they make to the suppliant; that belongs more to a psalm's account of the ongoing difference that Yhwh's act makes. So it makes sense to give the yiqtol verb its more regular meaning.

11. Jerome, Aq imply a form of *rāḥab*, "enlarge," as in 4:1 [2]; Vg and perhaps LXX imply a form of *rābâ*, "increase," as in 18:35 [36].

that person. Admittedly, it is usual for that response to be spoken of in terms of praise rather than confession, because by definition "confession" relates to what Yhwh has done for the worshipper(s) personally. Further, while many psalms expect the nations to come to recognize and praise Yhwh, only here do kings confess Yhwh. The psalm may imply "they will" or "they should," but it is hard to know what it means by this expectation. Perhaps it is simply a way of emphasizing the wonder of what Yhwh has done.

Initially the reason for the kings' confession is that they have heard the words of Yhwh's mouth. Presumably these *statements are the declarations of intent that Yhwh made in response to the suppliant's plea (cf. v. 2c–d). But in themselves those words would not provoke confession; it is acts that do that. So the logic of the line continues in the verses that follow, and it is vv. 4–6 as a whole that give the basis for the kings' confession.

5They are to sing of Yhwh's ways,
because Yhwh's honor is great.

Thus v. 5a complements v. 4 in two ways. First, it adds singing to confession. It indicates that the kind of praise that is signified by the kings' confession requires music for its affective significance. Mere words are not enough, as is the case for the person for whom Yhwh has directly acted (v. 1). Second, it adds Yhwh's "ways" to Yhwh's "words." Yhwh's ways include the habit of acting as well as speaking in response to the plea of people who cry out; and the kings will or should express their joyful recognition of that. That will be their way of recognizing that Yhwh's "*honor is great." This honor is expressed in the fact that Yhwh is one who hears a person's cry, speaks in response, and acts in response.

6Because Yhwh is on high, but he sees the lowly;
lofty, he acknowledges from afar.

The last line about the kings' confession spells out further wherein Yhwh's honor lies. It is again characteristic of a thanksgiving psalm that it moves from testimony regarding what Yhwh has done to recognizing what this evidences concerning what Yhwh does do and who Yhwh is. Usually the confessor makes this move; here it is the kings joining in the confession who make it. The act to which v. 3 referred evidences the point in v. 6 and makes it possible to reaffirm the truths it utters. They are not new truths but truths that can now be reaffirmed. The two cola are parallel, and each needs to be filled out from the other: from v. 6a, "because," "Yhwh," "but," and "the lowly" apply to v. 6b; from v. 6b, "from afar" applies to v. 6a. Prosaically put: "Because Yhwh is on high and lofty, but he sees and acknowledges the lowly from afar."[12] High and lofty are parallel terms in Isa. 2:12–15, where they describe the loftiness that needs to be put down; in Isa. 57:15 Yhwh becomes one who is "on high" but who also dwells with people who are "lowly in spirit." Here the kings anticipate that experience of being put down and seek to put themselves in the way of Yhwh's acknowledging the lowly, with the wisdom that Ps. 2:10 urges upon them, as they recognize that Yhwh is actually the one who is on high and lofty. If the psalm is one that a king or governor uses, then his own self-description as "lowly" refers to the experience of being put down, from which Yhwh has delivered him (cf. the description of kings as "lowly" in Ezek. 17:6, 14, 24).

Yhwh's honor thus lies not merely in being on high and lofty but in fulfilling the ideal of any kingship, that the king does not sit in his palace in comfort enjoying his position of prestige and authority far away from ordinary people in their need. Even though his position means he is far away from them in their everyday lives, he sees the lowly in their need and *acknowledges them with the kind of acknowledgment referred to in passages such as Gen. 18:19 and Amos 3:2. It means considering someone and thus making them someone you commit yourself to by acting on their behalf.

138:7–8. In vv. 4–6, we can see the suppliant's continuing testimony behind the one expected of the kings; the last three lines return to the suppliant's direct testimony. Again in the manner of a thanksgiving psalm, it expresses that point in terms of the suppliant's ongoing trust.

7Though I walk in the midst of trouble you will give me life;
 on account of the anger of my enemies you will extend your hand.
You will deliver me with your right hand;
 8aYhwh—he will bring it to an end on my behalf.

EVV translate the yiqtol verbs in v. 7 as present like those of v. 6, while LXX translates the ones in v. 7b–c as past, but Jerome more appropriately renders them all as future (like the verb in v. 8a). They are declarations of confidence for the future, which is often the way a testimony ends.

The suppliant knows that one experience of divine deliverance does not mean that life will be smooth forever. God's people are not immune from trouble (though that can sometimes be so), but neither are they overwhelmed by trouble (though that can also be so); they live by the dynamic of trouble and deliverance. That is what the psalm expects

12. Vrs take "lofty" as the object of the verb in v. 6b (cf. NRSV, TNIV), but this misses the way the parallelism works.

for the future; perhaps it applies especially to leaders, which provides another reason for hiding among the baggage when one might be in danger of being drafted.

The image of "walking" in the midst of trouble suggests that "trouble" is abstract for concrete and the psalm is referring to troublemakers; *ṣārâ* is embodied in *ṣārîm*. The parallelism in the second colon confirms that. Walking in the midst of enemies threatens death; in light of the experience of Yhwh's deliverance, the suppliant is even more convinced than before that it will actually be a context in which Yhwh will safeguard life. So "on account of the anger of my enemies" gives precision to "though I walk in the midst of trouble." And "you will extend your hand" indicates what will be involved when "you will give me life."

Verse 7c then continues the parallelism; "you will *deliver me" reexpresses "you will give me life," and "your right hand" gives precision to "your hand" (it does not imply that v. 7b refers to Yhwh's left hand). Thus the parallelism in the three cola works *aba′cb′c′*.

MT then understandably takes this as the end of the line, but thereby leaves v. 8a isolated; it does not really fit with v. 8b–c. I rather take it as extending the parallelism yet again, while also making a particular link back with v. 7a. Thus the two lines work *abb′a′*. The verb "bring to an end" is a rare one, but it comes in a similar context in 57:3 [4], where "extend" and "deliver" also occur. There it refers to bringing an end to destruction; here its implicit object is the "trouble" of v. 7a.[13] "Yhwh" comes in emphatic position before the verb.

8bYhwh, your commitment lasts forever;
do not let go the works of your hands.

The psalm almost closes with the familiar declaration about Yhwh's *commitment that formed the refrain in Ps. 136 (see also v. 2 of this psalm). But then it actually closes with a plea. In this context "the works of your hands" will be Yhwh's acts of deliverance (e.g., 92:4–5 [5–6]; 106:13; 107:22, 24; 111:2, 6, 7; 118:17; 143:5; 145:4, 9, 10, 17), and the plea urges Yhwh not to abandon such acts. As troubles will recur, so the pattern of Yhwh's acting needs to continue. Metaphorically, the psalm thus urges Yhwh not to "give up" such works (cf. Deut. 4:31; 31:6, Josh. 1:5), but the verb refers literally to dropping something or letting one's hand drop in the midst of doing something (cf. Josh. 10:6).

13. LXX, Tg have "requite," as if the verb were *gāmal* not *gāmar*, and Mitchell Dahood ("The Root GMR in the Psalms," *Theological Studies* 14 [1953]; 595–97) supports this, but it is better to keep the distinction; Aq, Sym have "bring to an end."

Theological Implications

In its three sections the psalm focuses on the gods, the kings, and the enemies. Admittedly the first section mentions the gods only once, but it is a distinctive reference that bears some comparing with Ps. 82. Precritical interpretation took *'ĕlōhîm* to refer to human judges or kings,[14] an unlikely piece of interpretation that suggests the text is actually saying something interesting. Like many psalms, this one simply assumes the existence of other divine beings, yet treats them in a way that will make it clear that they are nothing compared with Yhwh. But they cannot be ignored. They are real. They are subordinate to Yhwh, but they have to be kept in their place (cf. Ps. 82). The suppliant is playing a part in that process by reminding them that Yhwh alone is the one who delivers. Yhwh's word and name are above all.

The second section has kings called or expected to join in the suppliant's testimony—indeed *all* the kings of the earth. Psalms regularly expect the nations to do that, but the focus on their kings here is unique. The introduction of their testimony, and the content of it, further underlines the implications of the comment about the gods. In the heavens there is no one like Yhwh; on earth, in their way kings are supposed to be like Yhwh, because their vocation is to reign in the manner described in v. 6 (compare Ps. 72). The psalm has them acknowledging where their own true honor needs to lie.

The third section focuses on the enemies. It assumes that enemies are a fact of life. By implication, Yhwh has rescued the suppliant from enemies; Yhwh will need to do so again. Circumstances will find the suppliant walking in the midst of trouble in the sense of being surrounded by troublemakers, the victim of the anger of enemies. The psalm issues a reminder that the way to handle that reality of human experience is not to gird up our own anger but to remind ourselves and Yhwh of the way Yhwh delivers and of the reality of Yhwh's commitment.

14. See, e.g., Tg; Syr; Ibn Ezra.

Psalm 139

Yhwh Can Know All about Me

Translation

The leader's. David's. Composition.

1Yhwh, you have examined me and got to know me,[1]
2you yourself have got to know my sitting and my rising,
you have gained insight into my intention, from afar.
3My journeying[2] and my reclining you have measured;
with all my ways you have become familiar.
4For there is not a word on my tongue:
there, Yhwh, you have got to know all of it.
5Behind and in front you have bound me;
you have put your hand on me.
6Your knowledge[3] is too extraordinary for me;
it has gone high, I cannot prevail over it.

7Where could I go from your spirit,
where could I flee from your face?

1. The suffix on the first verb carries over onto the second. In light of vv. 23–24, Jan Holman sees v. 1 as precative ("Analysis of the Text of Ps. 139," *BZ* 14 [1970]: 37–71, 198–227 [see 39]); but this seems neither justified nor necessary.

2. The parallelism with "reclining" suggests that *ʾorḥî* is more likely inf. construct from *ʾāraḥ* than a form of the noun *ʾōraḥ*.

3. The suffix carries over from "your hand"; cf. LXX.

8If I were to climb up to the heavens, you would be there,
and if I were to make Sheol my bed, there you would be.
9Were I to take the wings of the dawn,[4]
settle on the far side of the sea,
10Even there your hand would be leading me away,
your right hand would be taking hold of me.
11Were I to say,[5] "Yes, the darkness will seize me,[6]
light will be night around me,"
12Even darkness is not dark for you;[7]
night is light like day;
darkness and light are the same.

13Because you are the one who created my heart;
you were weaving me in my mother's womb.
14I confess you, because I was set apart[8] awesomely;[9]
your acts were extraordinary
So I myself acknowledge you[10] full well;
15my frame was not concealed from you,
When I was made in secret,
embroidered in the depths of the earth.
16Your eyes saw me as an embryo.
And on your scroll were written, all of them,[11]
The days that were shaped,
when there was not one among them.[12]
17So for me, how formidable were your intentions, God,
how mighty was the sum of them.

4. LXX has "take my wings [to] the dawn [i.e., the east]," implying *kĕnāpay*, which gives better parallelism, as v. 9b refers to the west.

5. On the *w*-consecutive in a hypothetical clause, see GKC 111x, 159f.

6. I follow *HALOT* in this understanding of *šûp* here and in its other occurrences in Gen. 3:15; Job 9:17.

7. Probably not "is not too dark for you"; see GKC 133c, note 2.

8. LXX takes *niplêtî* as niphal from *pālāʾ* and translates "I was marveled at." The Hebrew verb is actually then difficult to make sense of (it should really mean "I am marvelous"), and EVV paraphrase. But in any case, it looks like a form from *pālâ* rather than *pālāʾ* (cf. Barthélemy, *Psaumes*, 842; C. John Collins, "Psalm 139:14," *Presbyterion* 25.2 [1999]: 115–20); contrast *niplāʾîm* in the next colon, which makes for a paronomasia. Some LXX MSS imply *niplêtā*, "you are wonderful." So perhaps 11QPs[a], though the reading is unclear; but cf. the next note.

9. GKC 118p, *IBHS* 10.2.2e take *nôrāʾôt* as accusative of manner; DG 88, 117, remark 2, notes that f. pl. is esp. characteristic of this usage but suggests it is better to describe it as an adverbial usage. For *nwrʾwt* 11QPs[a] has *nwrʾ ʾth*, "you are awesome."

10. The suffix on "I confess you" carries over to this parallel verb.

11. The suffix anticipates "the days" in the next colon.

12. I follow K's *wĕlōʾ* (cf. Vrs, though the Tg traditions vary). Q's *wĕlô* (cf. 11QPs[a]) would imply "and for it [my embryo] [there was] one [day] among them," one day for it to be born.

18Were I to count them, they would be more than the sand;
I have come to an end,[13] and I am still with you.

19If only you would kill the faithless, God;
murderous people, leave me,
20People who speak of you in connection with deception,
who have lifted you up[14] in connection with emptiness, as your foes.[15]
21Do I not oppose the people who oppose you, Yhwh,
and do I not repudiate the people who rise up against you?[16]
22I totally oppose them;[17]
they have become enemies for me.
23Examine me, God, and know my mind;
test me and know my concerns.
24See if there is an idolatrous way in me
and lead me in the ancient way.

Interpretation

A little like Ps. 89, the first three-quarters of Ps. 139 has great significance in its own right but its particular meaning in its context emerges only at the end.[18] The psalm begins (vv. 1–6) with a declaration that Yhwh knows all about the suppliant, who seems in general quite happy and not insecure or regretful about this. Admittedly, v. 5 is more ambiguous in that respect, and v. 6 is rather overawed by it. In vv. 7–12 the suppliant makes a similar declaration about Yhwh's presence. There is nowhere one could go to get away from Yhwh, however hard one tried. Here there is rather more solemnity about the matter, because it means there is no escaping Yhwh's punishment, though vv. 10–12 are more ambiguous in

13. LXX takes *hĕqîṣōtî* as a form from *qîṣ*, "wake up," but this makes poor sense. More likely it comes from a by-form related to *qāṣaṣ* and its derived noun *qēṣ*, "end" (cf. NJPS, NRSV).

14. In form, MT *nāśu'* is passive ptc., hard to make sense of in the context, which points to *nāśĕ'û* (cf. 11QPs[a]); see Barthélemy, *Psaumes*, 849–50. The suffix on the verb in the first colon also applies to this verb; thus the construction is not so different from that in 24:4 in Codex L, "lift up your person [*nepeš*] in connection with emptiness."

15. LXX naturally takes *'ārêkā* to mean "your cities," and Gene Rice renders "they have carried away thy cities to destruction," referring to the exile ("The Integrity of the Text of Psalm 139:20b," *CBQ* 46 [1984]: 28–30). But this is a sudden and isolated historical reference. I rather follow Jerome, Tg, Aq, Sym in understanding *'ār* to mean "foe," as in 1 Sam. 28:16.

16. The colon involves a nice paronomasia, as "repudiate" is *qûṭ*, "rise up" is *qûm*, and both words are hitpolel. One would expect *ûbĕmitqômĕmêkā*; the omission of the *m* heightens the paronomasia.

17. Lit. "with completeness of opposition I oppose them."

18. Cf. Mowinckel, *Psalms*, 2:75.

the opposite direction from that in vv. 1–6 (they can be read as solemn or encouraging). A third declaration relates to time rather than space (vv. 13–18), affirming the nature of Yhwh's involvement from the earliest beginning of life in unequivocally positive terms, speaking of "confessing" and "acknowledging." But then, as in Ps. 89, there follows a sharp transition to the last quarter of the psalm, vv. 19–24. This expresses a wish that Yhwh might kill violent people, declares opposition to people who oppose Yhwh, and urges Yhwh to examine the suppliant's mind to check whether there is secret idolatry there. This last section makes clear its link with what precedes by taking up the verbs from v. 1 in v. 23, as the suppliant willingly submits to the scrutiny of which the opening verse spoke.

Once more the psalm constitutes a distinctive take on one of the familiar forms. The past tense declarations that open Ps. 139 recall those in a thanksgiving psalm, while the psalm closes with a plea. Kraus[19] infers that vv. 19–24 constitute the plea whose answer vv. 1–18 relates. This requires considerable inference; a thanksgiving psalm regularly makes clear when it is recalling its plea (e.g., Pss. 116; 118; 138). If anything, then, vv. 1–18 record Yhwh's past activity, and vv. 19–24 build a plea upon it, as happens in other psalms. But the content of vv. 1–18 makes them rather different from a thanksgiving, and the psalm is something more like "a prayer of confidence and trust,"[20] closing with a declaration of commitment and a plea.[21] It thus compares with Pss. 4; 14; 16; 27; 115; and 125. Each of the first three sections is slightly longer than its predecessor (five lines, then six, then eight; eleven cola, then thirteen, then sixteen). They express confidence and trust in different ways, in relation to knowledge, presence or space, and time; and in their interests they thus overlap with Wisdom, and specifically Job,[22] though like Job they expound these themes in the context of a personal relationship with Yhwh rather than in terms of a discussion of omniscience, omnipresence, and omnificence. The emphasis lies on the fact that *you* know everything about *me* and that *you* are present everywhere that *I* am. It lies not on God's having predestined everything that happens to me or that I do but on the fact that *you* have set *my* destiny within your purpose.[23]

19. *Psalms 60–150*, 512.

20. Bratcher and Reyburn, *Handbook on the Psalms*, 1123.

21. Mowinckel (*Psalms*, 2:74) reverses the balance in seeing the psalm as a prayer psalm with a substantial hymnic introduction; cf. John M. Bullard, "Psalm 139," in *Society of Biblical Literature 1975 Seminar Papers* (Missoula, MT: Scholars, 1975), 1:141–50.

22. Cf. Helen Schüngel-Straumann, "Zur Gattung und Theologie des 139. Psalms," *BZ* 17 (1973): 39–51. But she notes that wisdom influence does not preclude a cultic context; cf. also L. C. Allen, "Faith on Trial," *Vox Evangelica* 10 (1977): 5–23 (see 9–10).

23. Miller, *Interpreting the Psalms*, 146–47. Cf. Siegfried Wagner, "Zur Theologie des Psalms cxxxix," in *Congress Volume: Göttingen 1977*, VTSup 29 (Leiden: Brill, 1978), 357–76.

Thus in vv. 1–6, theological issues "are not formulated as a doctrine but, as befits a psalm, confessed in adoration."[24] "You" is thus the main subject of the verbs. In vv. 7–12 "I" is the subject more often than "you."[25] But the section is more threatening (cf. Amos 9).[26] Verses 13–18 then return to the more positive with their "I confess." There is nothing threatening here; Gerstenberger calls vv. 17–18 "hymnic adoration."[27] Again, the appeal of vv. 19–24 is not that of someone philosophically perplexed by the problem of evil but of someone facing evil in their community and perturbed about what it does to the community's relationship with Yhwh. "The figure of an 'I-thou relationship'" is "the unifying thread of the whole texture of the discourse."[28]

Verses 1–6 express their confidence and trust with some ambiguity that arises from their relationship to the plea that will eventually come. It is not unreasonable that a plea for God to examine us should have some ambiguity about it, because even though we know that God can do that and we recognize that we cannot deceive God about our commitment, but believe we can survive God's examination, we know that our own hearts are deceptive, indeed consummately so (Jer. 17:9–10). So we know that we may be self-deceived about our own convictions concerning our commitment to doing right. It will not be unreasonable for such a plea also to imply some ambiguity about the fact that there is no place where God cannot reach us (vv. 7–12); if we are self-deceived, we turn out to have reason to try to find such a place (cf. Amos 9:2–4). Only as we look back at God's involvement in our lives from the beginning (vv. 13–18) can we risk unequivocal confession and praise, yet that involves again acknowledging that as someone involved with me from the earliest beginnings of my life, Yhwh knows all about me, which means that even this praise ends with some implicit ambiguity: can I make the declaration with which it closes, about still being with Yhwh?

The psalm makes effective use of parallelism, in all but one line of the first section, throughout the second, in much of the third, and throughout the fourth. But it uses the principle of parallelism in a much broader fashion as it keeps repeating its points in successive lines, using different imagery. Thus the first section really makes one point in ever varying

24. Kidner, *Psalms*, 2:464; cf. Mowinckel, *Psalms*, 1:91.

25. Cf. Fokkelman, *Major Poems*, 2:303. Karl-Heinz Bernhardt also compares Jer. 23:23–24, though he does not see Ps. 139 or Jer. 23:23–24 as threatening in the manner of Amos 9 ("Zur Gottesvorstellung von Psalm 139," in *Kirche–Theologie–Frömmigkeit* [G. Holtz Festschrift; Berlin: Evangelische Verlag, 1965], 20–31).

26. Cf. Kidner, *Psalms*, 2:464.

27. *Psalms*, 2:404.

28. J. Holman, "A Semiotic Analysis of Psalm cxxxviii (LXX)," *OtSt* 26 (1990): 84–100 (see 93).

ways through vv. 1–5 until it comes to its concluding comment in v. 6. The second section likewise keeps expressing its one point in varying ways. The third section repeats this technique until it comes to its concluding comment in vv. 17–18. The last section varies this slightly, though again the bulk of it repeats variants on its basic point, and vv. 23–24 bring it to its conclusion. The first and third sections speak mostly in qatal verbs about what Yhwh has done; the second and fourth speak mostly in yiqtol terms about what could or needs to happen. The two middle sections also make effective use of poetic imagery in the way they talk about the suppliant's possible journeying around the cosmos and about the forming of the person in a mother's womb. The first two sections also abound in merisms and opposites: sitting and rising, journeying and reclining, behind and in front, heavens and Sheol, dawn and the far side of the sea, darkness and light, night and day.[29]

The psalm's actual language raises difficulties. It contains a number of rare words, and phrases that are difficult to construe. We do not know whether this is an aspect of its poetic nature or whether it indicates that its author uses a dialectical form of Hebrew or whether the unusual expressions (for example, the words for intention [vv. 2, 17], recline [v. 3], word [v. 4], go up [v. 8], and foes [v. 20]) indicate Aramaic influence and thus suggest a postexilic date.[30] Nor do we know what would be the specific reason for someone using the psalm. "For this psalm, a classic 'Sitz im Leben' is no longer ascertainable."[31] One could imagine it being used by someone who has been accused of wrongdoing. The logic of the psalm is then that the seriousness of the acknowledgment in vv. 1–18 makes it unlikely that someone would be willing to say the psalm before God and not mean it.[32] But there is no actual declaration of innocence such as appears in other psalms, and it might simply be used as a more general act of commitment against wrongdoing.

The leader's. David's. Composition.

29. Schaefer, *Psalms*, 327; cf. Jože Krašovec, "Die polare Ausdrucksweise im Psalm 139," *BZ* 18 (1974): 224–48. On the structure and the rhetorical features in the psalm, see Pierre Auffret, *La sagesse*, 321–82; idem, "O Dieu, connais mon coeur," *VT* 47 (1997): 1–22; Jan Holman, "The Structure of Psalm cxxxix," *VT* 21 (1971): 298–310; idem, "A Semiotic Analysis of Psalm cxxxviii (LXX)."

30. On links with material from other cultures, see Hildebrecht Hommel, "Das religionsgeschichtliche Problem des 139. Psalm," *ZAW* 47 (1929): 110–24.

31. Wagner, "Zur Theologie des Psalms cxxxix," 359.

32. For theories regarding how the psalm might be used in this connection, see Ernst Würthwein, "Erwägungen zu Psalm 139," *VT* 7 (1957): 165–82; J. L. Koole, "Quelques remarques sur Psaume 139," in *Studia biblica et semitica* (T. C. Vriezen Festschrift; Wageningen: Veenman, 1956), 176–80; Allen, *Psalms 101–150*, 324–25.

Heading. See glossary.

139:1–6. The suppliant begins by declaring, "Yhwh, you have come to know all about me." DG 57 sees the sequence of qatals and wayyiqtols in vv. 1–6 (only the very last verb in v. 6 is a yiqtol) as having present reference, while translations mix present and past. Taking the whole as having past reference, though with implications running into the present, seems less arbitrary.

Why would someone speak of Yhwh's knowing everything about them? Jeremiah does so when under attack from people, in the conviction that Yhwh knows he is faithful and will therefore act against his attackers (Jer. 11:20; 12:3). Psalm 17:3 speaks in similar terms of a confidence that Yhwh will find the suppliant truly committed, which is part of the basis for an appeal for Yhwh's deliverance from attackers (cf. 26:2–3; 44:21).

1Yhwh, you have examined me and got to know me,
2you yourself have got to know my sitting and my rising,
you have gained insight into my intention, from afar.
3My journeying and my reclining you have measured;
with all my ways you have become familiar.

So the psalm opens with five parallel cola, which I take as a tricolon and a bicolon, the first three cola beginning with their verbs, the last two reversing the order of the clauses and putting the objects first. All six verbs (there are two in the first colon) refer to a process whereby Yhwh has got to know all about the psalmist. The first (*ḥāqar*) speaks of examining or searching out; the word is used for searching a city or investigating an issue or searching land to find somewhere to live. It thus refers to the process by which a person discovers something that they would not otherwise know. A concrete example would be the investigative process whereby Yhwh comes to know that Abraham really reveres Yhwh (Gen. 22:1, 12). It is the process through which God comes to gain insight into things (v. 2b), to discern things. To describe this process whereby God finds things out, vv. 1–2 thus use familiar verbs, and then in a way characteristic of parallelism between cola but here used for this extended parallelism, v. 3 uses two rarer verbs to restate the point. "Measure" (*zārâ*) comes only here, though the related word for a span (*zeret*) is more familiar.[33] The verb suggests the picture of God extending the span of a hand over something, to get the dimensions of it. "Become familiar with" (*sākan* hiphil), in turn, involves a unique use of a slightly more familiar verb; usually one becomes familiar with

33. BDB treats this as a specialized meaning of *zārâ* meaning scatter or winnow, but *HALOT* more plausibly treats it as *zārâ* II, a denominative from *zeret*.

doing something, but here Yhwh has become familiar with what the suppliant does.

The verbs then have a series of parallel objects. First it is simply "me." The second colon gives that precision in speaking of "my sitting and my rising," a merism that suggests all my movements at home. The doors of the house do not keep Yhwh out. The third colon is even more searching as it refers to my thinking or intention in the sense of my purpose or aims or striving or desires (*rēaʿ*). Yhwh can decide to look not just into my house but into my mind and sees not only what I do but what I plan to do and want to do. The expression "from afar" will then apply at least to v. 2a as well as v. 2b; being in the heavens does not stop Yhwh from gaining knowledge of what goes on a long way away.[34] In v. 3, the objects of which Yhwh gains knowledge are outside the house and not merely inside. Yhwh has got the measure of when I go out to do something and when I come home and lie down. In fact, Yhwh has become familiar with all my ways, with everything I do. While the verbs might thus suggest that the suppliant has undergone some special investigative procedure, some trial (compare the Achan story, Josh. 7), the objects indicate that the psalm refers to a much more general scrutiny by Yhwh.

> 4For there is not a word on my tongue:
> there, Yhwh, you have got to know all of it.

Formally, v. 4 relaxes the parallelism, but the whole line is broadly parallel with what precedes, as it adds the fact that Yhwh has also come to know (that verb comes for the third time) everything that I say. There need be no implication that Yhwh knows things before I say them; rather the point is that Yhwh knows everything I do say. So (for instance), if I make an undertaking, Yhwh knows; if I give evidence in court, Yhwh knows; if I plan a crime with my friends, Yhwh knows.

> 5Behind and in front you have bound me;
> you have put your hand on me.

So it is as if there has been an invisible presence in front of me and behind me, able to have access to all that I do or think or say. "Bind" (*ṣārar*) is a neatly ambiguous verb; one can bind things to protect them or to restrict them. Likewise Yhwh's hand could be like the hand of the FBI, or it could be the hand of a supporter. The person who has nothing to hide has nothing to fear of Yhwh's binding or of the touch of Yhwh's

34. Th. Booij ("Psalm cxxxix," *VT* 55 [2005]: 1–19 [see 3]) suggests that "from afar" has temporal rather than spatial meaning, "long before."

hand any more than of Yhwh's knowing. It is only the faithless person who has reason to dislike the idea of Yhwh always being present.

> 6Your knowledge is too extraordinary for me;
> it has gone high, I cannot prevail over it.

EVV reckon that this kind of knowledge on God's part is too "wonderful" for me, but it is not especially obvious what that would mean or how it fits into the context. The adjective *pil'î* comes only here and in Judg. 13:18 (where the meaning is also not very obvious), but the verb *pālā'* can refer to things that are extraordinarily difficult to do or understand (Ps. 131:1; Job 42:3; Prov. 30:18). This connotation makes sense here and leads well into the second colon.[35] There, the first verb is another qatal, like the verbs through vv. 1–4, suggesting that it refers once more to the process whereby Yhwh has come to know the suppliant; it does not make a general statement ("it is high"), though that could be inferred. Yhwh's knowledge of the suppliant has attained a great height (in English we might rather say a great depth or breadth); the word suggests the safety of inaccessibility. Thus the second verb spells out its implications. The suppliant therefore cannot prevail over it,[36] cannot evade it or defeat it.

139:7–12. The second section declares, "Yhwh, I cannot go anywhere that you cannot find me. I could try to do that, like Jonah, but I could not do so."[37]

> 7Where could I go from your spirit,
> where could I flee from your face?
> 8If I were to climb up to the heavens, you would be there,
> and if I were to make Sheol my bed, there you would be.

In the parallelism within v. 7, "go" is a neutral term, while "flee" indicates the kind of going the line refers to. It presupposes that the suppliant might have reason to flee, the kind of reason vv. 19–24 will presuppose. But it is impossible to escape from Yhwh, and specifically to escape from Yhwh's spirit or face (EVV "presence"). The former suggests Yhwh's dynamic power; the latter suggests the look that generates blessing for people who belong to Yhwh but trouble for people who do not.

To what place might we flee? Suppose we flee as far away as possible. Fleeing up to the sky, if we could do it, would get us away from human

35. Cf. Holman, "Analysis of the Text of Ps. 139," 48.

36. Not "cannot attain to it" (cf. LXX, Jerome); *yākal lĕ* elsewhere always denotes prevailing over, and this makes better sense here.

37. Wagner ("Zur Theologie des Psalms cxxxix," 361–62) compares vv. 1–18 more broadly with the relationship of a prophet to Yhwh.

beings but not, of course, away from Yhwh. Going in the opposite direction, down to Sheol, and making it into our place to sleep, would also evade human beings, and we might have thought it would also evade Yhwh, because Yhwh in general leaves Sheol to its own devices. But this does not mean that Sheol is beyond Yhwh's reach. Yhwh can have access there at will, as happens when Yhwh raises someone from death.

> [9]Were I to take the wings of the dawn,
> settle on the far side of the sea,
> [10]Even there your hand would be leading me away,
> your right hand would be taking hold of me.

Not much less ambitiously, the suppliant imagines taking refuge from Yhwh somewhere on earth itself. The expression "wings of the dawn" perhaps refers to the speedy way the dawn moves from east to west, a thousand miles an hour or so. "Though one should fly with the speed of light, he could find no recess where he would be beyond the reach of divine power."[38] If one could hitch one's wagon to the dawn, or move with the speed of the dawn, one could then soon settle down in the far west, the other side of the Mediterranean, far away from where Yhwh takes an interest.

But one would not find that this evaded Yhwh's reach. While leading is usually a positive image, this is not always so; in Job 12:23 it suggests a more restraining control (cf. Ps. 67:4 [5]), and that fits the context here. It is made more explicit in the second colon by "taking hold of me," which is regularly a negative notion (e.g., 119:53; 137:9). "Right hand" likewise gives precision to "hand." Among other Middle Eastern peoples, different deities controlled different regions or parts of the cosmos. Israel knew that Yhwh controlled them all.[39]

> [11]Were I to say, "Yes, the darkness will seize me,
> light will be night around me,"
> [12]Even darkness is not dark for you;
> night is light like day;
> darkness and light are the same.

A reverse movement to that in vv. 9–10 is one not with the light but against the light, into the darkness, to a place where light will become darkness and that will seem a good thing. To be seized by darkness might seem a bad experience, but not when one is seeking to evade Yhwh. Indeed it might seem a plausible view that darkness as opposed

38. Calvin, *Psalms*, 5:212.
39. Keel, *Symbolism*, 48, 49.

to light would make a feasible place to hide from Yhwh, like Sheol as opposed to the heavens (indeed, perhaps darkness stands for Sheol).[40] It is, after all, the realm of light that characterizes Yhwh, the one who introduced light into darkness.

But actually that means that Yhwh can enter the realm of darkness and not be overcome by it. Darkness and light are all the same to Yhwh. There is no escape there.

"In Yahweh the dualism, the opposition between light and darkness is resolved, is neutralized."[41]

139:13–18. The psalm now looks to the mystery of human birth. It twice makes a declaration about the way Yhwh had been involved in the origin of the suppliant (vv. 13, 14c–16) and responds to that with wonder (vv. 14a–b, 17–18). But the reason for speaking of this activity corresponds to the agenda of vv. 1–12: because Yhwh was involved in the shaping of the person (v. 13), Yhwh knows all about it (vv. 14c–16). Perhaps the implication is that because Yhwh knew all about what was going on then, a fortiori Yhwh can know all that is going on now. But more explicitly, the section suggests that the outline of a person's life, the days that will unfold for them, is written into their origins. If Yhwh is involved in and knows all about the origins, then, Yhwh knows about the life that will follow. All this undergirds the convictions of vv. 1–12. The reference to Yhwh's involvement relates especially to vv. 7–12; the reference to Yhwh's knowing relates especially to vv. 1–6.

13 Because you are the one who created my heart;
you were weaving me in my mother's womb.
14a–b I confess you, because I was set apart awesomely;
your acts were extraordinary

It will be some time before the logic of the "because" emerges. The idea is that Yhwh knows all about me and that I can never evade Yhwh because Yhwh was involved in my life from the very beginning. Yhwh created my heart—literally, my kidneys. LXX and Jerome assume that *qānâ* means "get" or "possess" (cf. Prov. 1:5; 4:5, 7), which would make a good link with what precedes, but the second colon points to the meaning "create" (cf. Deut. 32:6) and provides a vivid concrete image for the process of creation. It likely means that the reference to the kidneys alludes to the physical insides of the person, which one could picture as being woven, rather than to the emotions or will or conscience, which kidneys can denote.

*Confession usually applies to the concrete good things that Yhwh does for one personally, so it is a vivid verb to apply to that process of

40. So Roger Lapointe, "La nuit et ma lumière," *CBQ* 33 (1971): 397–402.
41. Wagner, "Zur Theologie des Psalms cxxxix," 366.

creation or weaving. It reminds us of how individual a process it is; each person is individually woven or plaited by God. In general and in particular, then, human beings are set apart; they are distinctive creatures. And the way Yhwh has formed them makes them great wonders. The second colon restates the point. In the context, Yhwh's "acts" will refer to that same process of activity that brought each individual into being; the plural is often used of a deed that we might think of in English as one "act" (e.g., Gen. 20:9; Exod. 5:4). The terms "create," "set apart," "awesome," "acts," and "extraordinary" are all more familiar in connection with the great deeds whereby Yhwh brought Israel to birth; they are here applied to the birth of an ordinary human being.[42] The obverse of that point is also instructive. Most Israelites did not experience the exodus or the deliverance at the Red Sea, but they did experience the wonder of human birth, and maybe this can help them appreciate the wonder of Yhwh's bringing Israel into being.

The psalm is a piece of poetry, not a part of a law code, so it is not a knockdown proof text to demonstrate that abortion is wrong. But the wonder it expresses at the growth of a fetus and at Yhwh's involvement in this process is grounds for reckoning that a decision to cause a woman to miscarry is not merely one involving a decision about what happens to her body. It involves terminating a project that Yhwh is involved in. One would need special reasons to do that.

> **14c**So I myself acknowledge you full well;
> **15**my frame was not concealed from you,
> When I was made in secret,
> embroidered in the depths of the earth.

I link v. 14c with what follows to produce more plausible bicola through vv. 14–15. The psalm resumes the confession of v. 14a in order to restate the way Yhwh was involved in the suppliant's shaping. The word for frame (*ʿōṣem* instead of the usual *ʿeṣem*) refers to a bone, and more generally to the bodily frame of the person growing inside its mother.

To describe its making, the psalm returns to a variant on the image from v. 13b: the intricacy of its making, reflected in the extraordinary, tiny, detailed form of a baby when it is born, is rather like embroidery. The reference to being made in secret suggests the mysterious way this process of growth happens inside the baby's mother, though the parallel expression "the depths of the earth" sets that mystery in a broader context. The phrase apparently involves the transferring of a metaphor.

42. Cf. William P. Brown, "*Creatio Corporis* and the Rhetoric of Defense in Job 10 and Psalm 139," in *God Who Creates*, ed. William P. Brown and S. Dean McBride (W. S. Towner Festschrift; Grand Rapids: Eerdmans, 2000), 107–24 (see 113–14).

There is a sense in which earth is our mother, so our mother can be spoken of as if she were the earth. It is from the earth that humanity is made (Gen. 2:7). A converse way of thinking has us returning to our mother's womb when we die (Job 1:21). It is in her depths that we are shaped. No human being witnesses that intricate process. It happens in secret. But it is not concealed from Yhwh.

16Your eyes saw me as an embryo.
And on your scroll were written, all of them,
The days that were shaped,
when there was not one among them.

So if Yhwh wishes, Yhwh can watch the process of a baby's growth in the womb. Indeed, the psalm declares the conviction that Yhwh did indeed watch this process, in the suppliant's case. Verse 16 goes on to a further implication. There is a sense in which the person's shaping in the womb also determines the person's life. It decides how clever they are, how strong they are, what weaknesses they have, and so on, and how long they will live. Environmental factors and personal decision making enter into the outworking of this, but they cannot evade the constraints of what goes on before birth. In this sense, what we are and how long we live ("the days that were shaped") are predetermined. And the one who could witness the shaping of the person could also therefore know how the person would turn out and how long the person would live, and know all that before one of those days had arrived. Perhaps medicine will advance to the point that we can know all this about a baby before its birth and have it all in a person's records. It is as if Yhwh has already done that and has that information on file. Perhaps its implication goes beyond divine foreknowledge to divine predetermination. We do not make the decisions about our days, about when we are born and when we die; God makes those decisions (Job 14:5).

17So for me, how formidable were your intentions, God,
how mighty was the sum of them.
18Were I to count them, they would be more than the sand;
I have come to an end, and I am still with you.

The psalm returns again to wonder, marveling at what Yhwh had decided and knows about the suppliant. Although the word for "be formidable," *yāqar*, most often means "be valuable" (so the adjective in 116:15; cf. TNIV), this hardly fits here. But the verb and related words also come to suggest things that are important or that have honor or weight (e.g., Ps. 49:12, 20 [13, 21]; Esther 1:4; Eccles. 10:1), and that works; the parallel in v. 17b fits with it. Or one could take "formidable" to have the sense of "difficult," which it can have in Aramaic (Dan. 2:11).[43] How extraordinary is the fact that way back then, Yhwh was aware of, thought about, and made decisions about the entirety of the suppliant's life. "Intentions" (*rēaʿ*)[44] is picked up from v. 2. There the psalm recognized that Yhwh knew the suppliant's intentions; retrospectively v. 16 introduces an irony into that reference with its recognition that Yhwh is also one with intentions, on a broader and more imposing scale.

So Yhwh knows all about and makes decisions about the origins, and thus about the whole life, of the suppliant. And how much there is there! If one were to attempt to count all those facts, they would be more than the grains of sand on the seashore. In the parallel colon, the reference to my end looks as if it links with the focus on my beginning earlier in the section. As Yhwh was present and involved with my beginning, so I am with Yhwh now that I have come to an end of what Yhwh has envisaged for me thus far. (It would make for even better completion of the section if one could reckon that v. 18a refers to the future end of the suppliant's life, but the qatal verb hardly allows that.) The reversal of the expression (I am with Yhwh, as opposed to Yhwh being with me) suggests my commitment to Yhwh rather than Yhwh's to me, and it prepares the way for vv. 19–24. From the beginning to the present, the suppliant has been with Yhwh.

139:19–24. The final six bicola divide into three pairs, a wish (vv. 19–20), a declaration of commitment (vv. 21–22), and a plea (vv. 23–24).

19If only you would kill the faithless, God;
murderous people, leave me,
20People who speak of you in connection with deception,
who have lifted you up in connection with emptiness, as your foes.

The sudden plea is a surprise, but it brings the psalm to its point. "The plaintiff is not meditative."[45] The suppliant wants Yhwh to kill the *faithless person and urges "murderous people" (lit. "men of bloods") to go away. The parallelism combines singular "faithless" and plural "murderous people" and initially thus defines faithlessness in this context as murder; the kind of faithless people the psalm is concerned about is people who take the lives of others. Subsequent lines will make specific that in this psalm the problem is not that these people are threatening the suppliant's own life (the fact that there is no lament or protest in

43. So *HALOT*.

44. Not merely "thoughts"; cf. Liudger Sabottka, "*Rēʿêkā* in Ps 139,17," *Bib* 63 (1982): 558–59.

45. Robert B. Coote, "Psalm 139," in *The Bible and the Politics of Exegesis*, ed. David Jobling et al. (N. K. Gottwald Festschrift; Cleveland: Pilgrim, 1991), 33–38 (see 37).

the psalm fits with the suppliant's claim that the problem is Yhwh's enemies, not the suppliant's). The desire that they should go away might imply they are trying to pressurize the psalmist into joining them. But the parallelism of a plea for God to kill them with an exhortation to them to go away might indicate that we should not take either verb too woodenly. The point of both is to indicate that the suppliant will have nothing to do with them and totally repudiates what they stand for. Indeed, if the suppliant actually were a faithless person, v. 19a would amount to a self-curse.

The enjambment in v. 20 then further defines the nature of these people's faithlessness in another direction, and carries implications for what the suppliant is claiming. The faithless and murderous are not simply flagrant and outrageous in their treachery and viciousness. They act by deception. They might then be the sort of people who live religiously upright lives and are well respected in the community, but when they speak of Yhwh or take up Yhwh's name, they do so "in connection with deception/emptiness." The two cola are thus parallel in their verbs (though one is yiqtol, one qatal) and in those *l* expressions. Typically, the second tightens the screw because it takes up the third of Yhwh's "Ten Words" at Sinai (though it omits the expression "your name"). These people do not take seriously one of the basic covenantal requirements; hence the description of them as "your foes" (not "my foes"). In the Decalogue and here, the expression "lift up in connection with emptiness" is somewhat enigmatic, though its general meaning is clear enough. It implies attaching Yhwh's name to something that has no substance. Empty speech is speech that is only words; there is no reality equivalent to it. So "false witness" in the Exodus version of the Decalogue is "empty witness" in the Deuteronomy version. It involves saying that something happened or that one saw something when this is not the case. Taking up Yhwh's name, or taking up Yhwh, in connection with emptiness makes that worse, because it associates Yhwh with the deception, presumably by swearing on oath before Yhwh. That is the way people go about faithlessness and murder.

The lines that follow suggest other possible connotations for v. 20. Taking up Yhwh's name in connection with emptiness can be a religious offense: emptiness characterizes the images that other peoples worshipped as if they were deities with substance when they were not. So v. 20 could denote people who are Yhwh's foes in the sense that they have (in effect if not in word) turned their back on Yhwh in their religious life as well as in their moral and social life.

> [21]Do I not oppose the people who oppose you, Yhwh,
> and do I not repudiate the people who rise up against you?

[22]I totally oppose them;
  they have become enemies for me.

"Do I not?" is a way of saying "I certainly do, and you know it!" The line makes more explicit how the foes are not the suppliant's but Yhwh's. The suppliant promises to treat them as personal enemies. It might be tempting to tolerate them or collude with them for the sake of harmony in the community, or even to cooperate with them and join in their deceptiveness in order to share in the profit they get from it. Instead, the suppliant promises to take the courageous stand of opposing them. The second colon goes beyond the first in the strength of its main verb. Both are words that can refer to feelings (cf. EVV "hate" and "loathe/abhor") but can also refer to attitudes or commitments; the latter will be at least as important as the former here, as the next line implies.

In v. 22, EVV's "perfect hatred" may give the wrong impression. While the psalm certainly implies that the suppliant's virulent opposition to the faithless is morally upright (and that any other attitude would be morally wrong), this opposition is perfect in the sense of being complete, total, and utter (cf. TNIV "I have nothing but hatred"). Thus the second colon restates the first.

[23]Examine me, God, and know my mind;
  test me and know my concerns.
[24]See if there is an idolatrous way in me
  and lead me in the ancient way.

The point of the plea that closes the psalm is not that the suppliant wonders whether it was all right to express those thoughts in vv. 19–22.[46] The question rather is, Does the suppliant really mean it? Is this fierce hostility to faithless people the real thing? The suppliant therefore invites God to undertake the investigation that the very first colon of the psalm spoke of as an established fact. The psalm expresses a willingness to submit to God's examination and knowledge of the suppliant's *heart or mind. God can investigate the suppliant to find out whether the profession of hostility to faithless people is genuine. The parallel colon then repeats the verb "know," like the second colon at the beginning of the psalm, though it precedes it with another verb, "test," so that the second colon with its two verbs more completely parallels the first. One would therefore expect that the rare word with which the line closes, *śarʿappîm*, paralleling "mind/heart," would mean something like "thoughts" (cf. Tg). But the dictionaries reckon it to mean something

46. Cf. Gene Rice, "Psalm 139," *Journal of Religious Thought* 37 (1980–81): 63–67.

more like "anxieties" (cf. the only other occurrence, 94:19). If that is right, then perhaps it points to the worries the suppliant has about the possible success of the faithless.

The last line first repeats the point again and then takes it further. By examining and testing, Yhwh can see if there is in the suppliant "the way of the idol [*ʿōṣeb*]." BDB takes this as *ʿōṣeb* I, meaning hurtfulness, but that does not fit very well in the context. Jerome and Tg rather reckon that the word is *ʿōṣeb* II, a word for an idol (as in Isa. 48:5), which fits motifs in vv. 19–22. The abjuration affirms that the suppliant had not been involved in worshipping other gods.[47] This then suggests that "the way of age" in v. 24b is not the way that lasts forever but the way of old, the ancient way (cf. Tg "the way of the upright of old"; and Jer. 6:16; 18:15), the proper way that goes back to Israel's beginnings before its corruption.

Theological Implications

There are several contrasts between the meaning of Ps. 139 and the common Christian understanding. First, Christian devotion uses vv. 1–18 in isolation from vv. 19–24, to encourage people with the fact that Yhwh knows all about us, will never let us go, and has been involved with us from our earliest beginnings. This edifying practice obscures the psalm's point, which lies in the relationship between these facts and the commitment made in vv. 19–24. It may therefore not be an edifying practice, because it lets Christians off the hook of the psalm's challenge, the demand that we come before God as people committed to God's ways and that we express that commitment in a resolute opposition to wrongdoers. The psalm affirms that love is not the only principle of godly life. We are indeed commanded to love our enemies but not to love God's enemies;[48] God, after all, does not seem to be doing so when (for instance) sending them to hell. Or as Jesus puts it, it is important to be prepared to hate people (see EVV for vv. 21–22), and not just God's enemies or our own enemies (Luke 14:26).

Another way to put the point about letting readers off the hook would be to underline the ambiguity about the facts concerning Yhwh's knowledge of us and our accessibility to Yhwh in vv. 1–12. In the psalm "God is at once a glorious and an oppressive presence."[49] The psalm is "a

47. So, e.g., Würthwein, "Erwägungen zu Psalm 139," 173–74.

48. Augustine, *Psalms*, 640.

49. Walter Harrelson, "On God's Knowledge of the Self," *CurTM* 2 (1975): 261–65 (see 262). Cf. Eberhard Baumann, "Der 139. Psalm," *EvT* 11 (1951): 187–90; Yair Mazor, "When Aesthetics Is Harnessed to Psychological Characterization," *ZAW* 109 (1997): 260–71.

celebration of God's invasion of our privacy."[50] In classes on the Psalms, I always ask students whether they think these verses are good news or bad news, and they always divide between people who see them as good news, people who see them as bad news, and people who perceptively discern that it depends on who you are. There is inherent in the psalm a recognition of this ambiguity, which is a recurrent feature of the Scriptures. While they often do their work on us by being crystal clear in their meaning, on other occasions they do their work by being allusive and requiring us to work out what we would mean by them. Instead of our reading them, they read us. The way we read this psalm reveals something to us about ourselves, and God and invites us to ask why we read it the way we do and to try the other reading.

In Christian theology the psalm has a part to play in the argument over God's knowledge between adherents of "classical theism" and "open theism." For the former, the psalm is a parade proof text for the idea of God's omniscience,[51] but actually it points in the opposite direction. Apart from the question whether it is universalizable (that is, Can we move from "God knows all about me" to "God knows all about everyone"?), it does not say or imply that omniscience is inherent in God. On the contrary, it repeats and repeats the fact that God has found out about the suppliant. It indicates (as many other passages do) that God can find out everything, but not that God automatically knows everything.[52] Over against open theism, however, it does not fit with the thesis that the future is inherently unknowable. It declares that God could and did know about the days of the suppliant's life from their very beginning. God can know the future.

50. William P. Brown, "Psalm 139," *Int* 50 (1996): 280–84 (see 283).

51. Cf. the cover subtitle of Edward J. Young's exposition *Psalm 139* (London: Banner of Truth, 1965), "A Study in the Omniscience of God."

52. Young comments that the psalm cannot mean that God came to know the psalmist through a process of investigation, because that would mean that God was not omniscient and was not the God of the Bible; the language must therefore be poetic (*Psalm 139*, 15–16). But he gives no evidence that God must be omniscient, nor does he discuss the biblical evidence to the contrary, or suggest on what basis we decide that the Scriptures do not mean what they say.

Psalm 140
Caught in Their Own Trap

Translation

The leader's. Composition. David's.

1Rescue me, Yhwh, from the evildoer,
will you guard me from the violent person,
2People who have thought up evil things in their heart,
who stir up[1] war every day,
3Who have sharpened their tongue like a snake;
a spider's[2] poison is under their lips. (Rise.)

4Keep me, Yhwh, from the hands of the faithless,
will you guard me from the violent person,
People who have thought up how to trip my feet,
5eminent people who have hidden a trap for me, and ropes,
Who have spread a net by the side of the track;
they have set out lures for me. (Rise.)

6I say to Yhwh, You are my God;
give ear, Yhwh, to the sound of my prayer for grace.
7Yhwh my Lord, the strength that delivers me,
you have shielded my head on the day when I took up weapons.[3]
8Yhwh, do not grant the desires of the faithless;
do not let his scheme succeed, the people who are on high.[4] (Rise)

1. *Yāgûrû* is a form from *gûr,* which overlaps in meaning with *gārâ*.

2. *ʿAkšûb* is a hapax, but *ʿakbîš* is a spider; 11QPs[a] has this (cf. Tg). LXX "asp" is likely a guess.

3. Lit. "the day of weaponry."

4. Or "[so that] they are on high" (cf. *TTH* 64). NRSV moves the verb to the next line and emends it from *yārûmû* to *yārîmû*; the fact that this involves transposing the word

9The head[5] of the people who surround me—
may the trouble from their lips cover them.[6]
10May burning coals tumble[7] on them with fire,
may it cause them to fall[8] into pits,[9] not to rise.[10]
11The person with the tongue that speaks violence—may he not stand firm in the land;
may evil hunt him into pens.

12I have come to acknowledge[11] that Yhwh will make
a judgment for the weak,
a decision for the needy.
13Yes, the faithful will confess your name;
the upright will live in your presence.

Interpretation

Psalm 140 announces with its first word that it is a prayer psalm. The first twelve lines in fact comprise four three-line prayers. There is no opening appeal for Yhwh to listen (though that eventually comes in v. 6); instead the psalm hastens directly and urgently into an appeal for rescue, with a description of the people the suppliant needs

---

with "Rise" suggests that if the verb originally belonged with v. 9, this was before the psalm reached its final form. Mitchell Dahood takes the word as a divine title, "Exalted One" ("The Composite Divine Title in Psalms 89,16–17 and 140,9," *Bib* 61 [1980]: 277–78).

5. Jerome, Sym take this as *rōʾš* II (poison), which fits the general context but does not fit so well into the sentence; the familiarity of *rōʾš* I would more likely make a reader give the word the usual meaning. Either way, there is a nice link with v. 7b, emphasized by the paronomasia and similarity in meaning of *sākak* (shield) and *kāsâ* (cover).

6. So Q. K has a pl. verb, which would imply "may they [impersonal] cover them [with] the trouble from their lips." This would lead well into the impersonal verb in v. 11a K.

7. So Q's niphal. K has hiphil, "may they [impersonal] cause burning coals to tumble." For the use of the verb *mûṭ*, cf. 55:3 [4]; Mitchell Dahood ("'A Sea of Troubles,'" *CBQ* 41 [1979]: 604–7) suggests that in both passages *yāmîṭû* rather represents a word from *nāṭâ*.

8. NJPS takes the sg. verb as impersonal, but it is less jerky to assume that in the context of the parallelism between vv. 9 and 10 the sg. word in v. 9b is the subject.

9. On *mahămōrôt*, see *HALOT*. TNIV "miry pits" implies a link with Arabic and/or Ugaritic roots (cf. BDB; Dahood, *Psalms*, 3:305).

10. The word order is "may there tumble on them coals in the fire, may they cause them to fall in pits not to rise." MT, LXX link "in the fire" with the verb that follows, but this confuses the imagery of the line; the reference to falling into pits takes up the hunting imagery, and "fire" does not belong there. Jerome takes "coals in the fire" to mean "coals of fire" (for which see, e.g., 18:12–13 [13–14]), a questionable move, but its dividing the line into two cola after that phrase makes good sense.

11. Qimchi assumes that K *ydʿt* is second person, "you know," addressed to God (cf. Gunkel, *Psalmen*, 595; Seybold, *Psalmen*, 519), but this would be harsh in the context. GKC 44i; JM 42f assume it is first person, as presupposed by Q, written defectively.

rescue from. This contains the material one would find in a lament, though it is expressed in a long enjambment attached to the plea (vv. 1–3). The second section reprises that appeal with a similar structure; MT reads it as two tricola, but it is similar in structure to the opening section (vv. 4–5). The third section begins with the delayed appeal for attention, confesses what Yhwh has been for the suppliant in the past, and then reprises the plea for deliverance (vv. 6–8). The fourth section expresses the point in a different way, comprising entirely a series of jussive pleas about what needs to happen (vv. 9–11). Finally, the suppliant expresses a certainty that Yhwh will indeed act on behalf of the weak and that the faithful will therefore have reason to confess Yhwh's name (vv. 12–13).

The word "Rise" (*selâ*) comes at the end of each of the first three sections; for complete logic one would expect another after v. 11. Dictionaries usually connect the word with the root *sālal*, "rise." Elsewhere it comes at the end of lines in psalms without any consistent patterning. While it sometimes comes at the end of sections, as here, it often comes in the middle of a section or in the middle of a sentence (Pss. 67, 68). It may be a liturgical or musical direction ("raise the voice"?), but we do not know. I understand that David Allan Hubbard advocated the theory that it was what David said when he broke a string, which is the most illuminating theory because there is no logic about when you break a string, and there is no logic about the occurrence of *selâ*.

The psalm works with close parallelism within the lines.[12] Each of the first four sections refers to the attackers in both the singular and the plural. In describing the situation out of which the prayer comes, it follows other psalms in using imagery from hunting, war making, and legal procedures (cf., for instance, Ps. 7). We can no more infer from the imagery that the suppliant was fighting a literal battle or defending a literal accusation than being literally hunted. Like Ps. 139, it contains a large number of hapaxes and also a number of unusual word forms; these are usually taken as indications of a postexilic date, but they have also been taken as indications of an early date.[13] On the latter assumption, Tg works out the implications of a link with David himself; on the former assumption, one can imagine it on the lips of a leader such as Nehemiah. If the Psalter is by definition a book of texts used in corporate worship, and specifically in the temple, then this will suggest that Ps. 140 was used by suppliants there, though there is no specific indication of that within the psalm, nor of how it was used.

12. On rhetorical features in the psalm, see Auffret, *Merveilles à nos yeux*, 202–17.

13. See Dahood, *Psalms*, 3:301. Rendsburg (*Linguistic Evidence*, 95–97) sees it as a northern psalm, others as a royal psalm (e.g., Eaton, *Kingship and the Psalms*, 63–64).

The leader's. Composition. David's.

Heading. See glossary. "In this psalm there are echoes of the Psalms of David, Psalms 52–71, in almost every verse."[14] The heading "David's" here might thus have distinctive resonances. It suggests both an analogy with the sense in which the Torah is "Moses's" and the Proverbs "Solomon's," being ultimately dependent on David because David is the person who stands behind the temple and its worship, and also an awareness of dependence on those "David" psalms and thus of being inspired by them.

140:1–3. The first appeal: rescue me.

1Rescue me, Yhwh, from the evildoer,
will you guard me from the violent person,
2People who have thought up evil things in their heart,
who stir up war every day,
3Who have sharpened their tongue like a snake;
a spider's poison is under their lips. (Rise.)

The psalm begins with a vivid verb that more literally suggests pulling someone out from a situation, in this case wresting one from the grasp of the evildoer (*bad person); the complementary verb speaks more mildly (in the yiqtol rather than the imperative) about being protected, as if the crisis is not yet so actual. On the other hand, the very general description as "bad" (which will imply "trouble," the bad experience brought to the suppliant) is given more bite by the word "violence" (*ḥāmās*), which comes three times in the psalm (and nowhere else in the second half of the Psalter). It can denote general lawlessness or outrage (e.g., Gen. 6:11, 13), but the references in the Psalms all make sense taken as denoting violence that is lawless and outrageous, often because it is exercised by means of the law (55:9 [10]; 58:2 [3]; 72:14; 73:6; 74:20). Very unusually, in vv. 1 and 4 the word is plural, perhaps suggesting "violent deeds." The line works *abb′a′*, so that the violent person comes next to the evildoer at the middle of the line. The plural verbs in v. 2 and the other plurals that will follow suggest that the singular terms in v. 1 are collectives, though they would doubtless help to give concreteness to the portrait and make it possible for people to apply them literally when (like Nehemiah) they were attacked by individuals.

Verse 2 explicitly begins as a relative clause, and I take the rest of vv. 2–3 as continuing this clause, which begins a series of descriptions of the evildoer and violence.[15] These are too varied to take them all as

14. Goulder, *Psalms of the Return*, 251.
15. Cf. Briggs, *Psalms*, 2:502, 503.

literal descriptions of actual opponents; as is often the case, the psalm brings together a variety of descriptions. Different suppliants might then apply different descriptions more or less literally to their own situation. First, the evildoers are people who have thought up "evil," or *bad things (the word recurs from v. 1), in their *heart; this is no shallow intention or casual deed but one carefully and deliberately thought through. In the parallel colon, "stir up," "war," and "every day" sharpen the morally neutral "think up," the more general "evil things," and the qualifier "in their heart."

The further description in v. 3 involves a metaphor and a simile; while the two cola are again parallel, the line as a whole also parallels v. 2. Metaphorically, people have sharpened their tongue; it is like a sword (cf. 64:3 [4]) that can kill a person through the implementing of the plans referred to in v. 2a, which comes about in the war making referred to in v. 2b. But the danger of their tongues also makes them snakelike. A snake's danger might be located in its tongue because a snake's words are crafty; they catch people out (Gen. 3). But the second colon makes explicit that here as elsewhere the idea is that the tongue is where the poison of a snake or a poisonous spider is located. Its tongue is its sword. A snake's hissing is suggested in the words as the sound "sh" comes in the words for sharpen, tongue, snake, and spider.

140:4–5. The second appeal: Keep me.

4Keep me, Yhwh, from the hands of the faithless,
will you guard me from the violent person,
People who have thought up how to trip my feet,
5eminent people who have hidden a trap for me, and ropes,
Who have spread a net by the side of the track;
they have set out lures for me. (Rise.)

The second section begins and proceeds with less urgency than the first. "Keep me" conveys less sense of crisis than "rescue me"; apparently the "hands" are not yet clutching, only reaching out to do so. Perhaps v. 1 was anticipating such a further development rather than indicating that it was yet a reality. But the adding of hands to heart, tongue, and lips indicates that the assailant's whole person is given to these attacks.[16] The bad person of v. 1 has become the *faithless person. The parallel colon, v. 4b, simply repeats v. 1b; the line as a whole works *abb′a′*, like v. 1, with the faithless and the violent thus next to each other and reinforcing each other.

Verse 4c likewise begins like v. 2 but then offers a more concrete object for the planning of the violent. The image is actually more violent than

16. Cf. Schaefer, *Psalms*, 329.

the translation "trip" implies; it suggests a forceful thrusting of the kind that will cast someone down. The parallel colon (v. 5a) begins to explain how that will work, giving precision to the metaphor in v. 4c and making clear that it comes from hunting. A trap (*paḥ*) is strictly a snare for birds, so the ropes are not to tie up the creature when captured. They might be ropes that the hunter pulls to close the trap,[17] or nooses;[18] the latter possibility heightens a feature of vv. 4c–5, that the psalm describes a variety of different ways of catching someone, with snares of one kind or another. The ropes are the first of a number of links with Ps. 18 (the next is the "lures" later in this verse; and see v. 10).[19] "Eminent" (see on 94:2; in itself it does not mean "arrogant," though no doubt these people were that) adds to the description of the attackers, as people with a position in the world who are therefore a sharper threat. As in the first section, singular words in the first line are complemented by plurals in the second and third.

The third line develops the metaphorical description of these people's planning to bring about the suppliant's downfall, or rather adds variant metaphorical descriptions of it. It was as if they were spreading a net by the side of the track along which an animal would walk (presumably the net is on the track itself, but the hunters work from the side), or putting down bait to lure a bird or an animal into a trap.

140:6–8. The third appeal: Give ear to me. The section again comprises three lines, but these are three separate sentences, with three invocations of Yhwh; v. 6 is spelled out in vv. 7–8.

6I say to Yhwh, You are my God;
give ear, Yhwh, to the sound of my prayer for grace.

I take the opening verb as a performative qatal, "I hereby say," rather than a recollection of a previous statement. The content of the statement then comprises a declaration about who Yhwh is, with a plea built onto it, though if we were to open quotation marks before "You are my God," it would be hard to know when to close them. The statement appeals to the personal relationship between the suppliant and Yhwh. The suppliant is someone committed to Yhwh and to no other god. The appeal built on that is the delayed plea for Yhwh to give ear to this prayer for *grace. It is another indication that the psalm works in reverse to an order of urgency.

17. So Rashi, 739.

18. Cf. Keel, *Symbolism*, 93.

19. "Ropes" should hardly therefore be emended (against, e.g., Gunkel, *Psalmen*, 594); cf. Goulder (*Psalms of the Return*, 252), though he does repunctuate (as do NRSV and TNIV).

[7]Yhwh my Lord, the strength that delivers me,
you have shielded my head on the day when I took up weapons.
[8]Yhwh, do not grant the desires of the faithless;
do not let his scheme succeed, the people who are on high. (Rise)

As a personal confession, v. 7 parallels v. 6a. First, "my *Lord" reprises the fact that I have been committed to Yhwh. Then it goes on to give the other side of the covenantal picture, the fact that Yhwh has been committed to me. Yhwh has been "the strength of my deliverance," the strong one who has *delivered me. The second colon spells out how that has worked, in another metaphor (or perhaps a literal reality). A warrior's head is a weak point in his person; he cannot wholly protect his head, and a blow on the head is especially dangerous. The colon suggests a further point. A warrior can have the best offensive and defensive armor in the world but discover that an enemy can find a fatal weak point in it (see 1 Kings 22:34), not least in regard to his head (see 1 Sam. 17:49). The suppliant has proved that it was at least as important to fight with Yhwh's protection as with the best weaponry in the world.[20]

In turn v. 8 parallels v. 6b in constituting the plea that builds on the confession. The argument "I have been committed to you; you must be committed to me" is complemented by the argument "You have been committed to me in the past; you must be committed to me in the present." The "desires of the *faithless" are the desires that their plans (v. 2) and their devices (vv. 4c–5) attempt to further, by means of the scheme they formulate. As "scheme" parallels "desires," the rare verb "make succeed" (*pûq* hiphil) parallels "grant." "The people who are on high" then apparently parallels "the faithless," as "the eminent" did in vv. 4–5, plural again complementing singular.

140:9–11. The fourth appeal: May the attackers drink their own medicine. The suppliant turns from seeking rescue to seeking that the faithless experience what they seek for others. Perhaps this is simply another way of making the same point: rescue and protection from them requires that they be put down. "The evil has to be fought at its roots, i.e., right where the deadly planning is going on: in the minds and lives of the wicked adversaries."[21] Three parallel jussives make this point, which is heightened by the extraposed construction in vv. 9 and 11b and the comparable locating of the subject at the beginning of the colon in

20. Reading vv. 6–7 together, one could understand the verb in v. 7b as precative; vv. 6 and 7 are then neatly parallel (cf. DG 60). But more common Hebrew usage encourages one rather to see vv. 7–8 as paralleling v. 6, with the whole of v. 7 a statement and the whole of v. 8 a plea.

21. Gerstenberger, *Psalms*, 2:411.

v. 11a. The use of jussives rather than pleas underlines the conviction that there is a process of justice built into the structure of reality. Within this framework, the psalm does not need to appeal for interventionist divine action, only for this inbuilt process to work out.

> [9]The head of the people who surround me—
> may the trouble from their lips cover them.

The jussives begin where the psalm began, with the role of words in bringing trouble to people. So the psalm asks that the trouble intended or actually caused by the lips of the people who surround the suppliant might fall on the head of these people themselves in such a way as to cover it and overwhelm them. Part of the poetic justice this will involve is the contrast in the experience of people who look to Yhwh (v. 7b).

> [10]May burning coals tumble on them with fire,
> may it cause them to fall into pits, not to rise.

The middle line puts the point more vividly. Commentators make a link with the story of Sodom and Gomorrah,[22] but the language does not correspond as closely as it does to other passages in the Psalms. To judge from 120:4, burning coals would suggest burning arrows; the context there parallels this prayer's concern with attacks and deceit. The burning coals are thus an instance of the attackers drinking their own medicine. The flaming arrows might be shot by human warriors or by warrior Yhwh (cf. 18:8, 12–14 [9, 13–15], where they denote lightning). Their effect will be to burn up the attackers who surround the suppliant.

The second colon parallels the second colon in v. 9; the "trouble from their lips" is again the subject of the verb.[23] It makes the same point as the first colon, in a less scary metaphor, though one just as definitive in its implications. It again corresponds to the attackers' own plans or acts (see vv. 4–5). Here the hunting aims at capturing a large animal in a pit; the imagery especially links with v. 4c. The idea is to get the animal into the pit and then be able to kill it. It will never climb out. So the psalm asks that this should be the hunters' fate. Then the object of the hunt is safe.

> [11]The person with the tongue that speaks violence—may he not stand
> firm in the land;
> may evil hunt him into pens.

22. E.g., Anderson, *Psalms*, 2:916; contrast Briggs, *Psalms*, 2:504–5.
23. Taking Yhwh as subject (Gerstenberger, *Psalms*, 2:411) fits the context less well.

Literally, "May the person of tongue not stand firm in the land; the person of violence, may evil hunt him into pens." In the parallelism "person of violence" thus clarifies the enigmatic "person of tongue." The person with the tongue that speaks violence will be the person with the sharpened tongue (v. 3). That person's aim is to gain further power and/or security in the land by removing the suppliant from a position of power or by taking over the suppliant's land. The psalm asks for the appropriate opposite. The parallel colon takes up the references to the violent person (vv. 1, 4) and to evil, that which is *bad (vv. 1, 2), then again takes up the idea of hunting and for the first time uses that verb in the phrase that expresses something quite the opposite to standing firm in the land. "Pens" (*lĕmadḥēpōt*) is another new word, but overlapping in form as well as meaning with "trip" in v. 4 (*lidḥôt*).[24] Evil is thus personified as something capable of getting out of hand; the attackers thought it was their tool, but the suppliant asks that they may find it is out of their control. In this fourth section, plurals in vv. 9–10 are complemented by the singular expressions in v. 11, the reverse of the order in previous sections.

140:12–13. The statement of faith. The statements in these final lines suggest that there has been a shift in the suppliant's thinking and attitudes. Verses 1–11 imply that the suppliant keenly and urgently looks for Yhwh's deliverance; vv. 12–13 imply a confidence that this deliverance will be forthcoming. Perhaps a minister brings a word of assurance after v. 11; or perhaps bringing these needs to Yhwh generates the awareness of having been heard and a certainty that Yhwh will act.

12I have come to acknowledge that Yhwh will make
a judgment for the weak,
a decision for the needy.

As usual, one could translate *yādaʿtî* "I acknowledge," or simply "I know," but this loses aspects of the likely dynamism of the statement. Through vv. 1–11 it did not look as if the suppliant acknowledged these facts with the certainty that the psalm now articulates. And the suppliant is expressing not merely a head awareness ("I know") but a moral commitment to living in light of what one knows ("I acknowledge"). The truth that the suppliant has come to own is a variant on the conviction expressed in vv. 6 and 7, but in those verses there was a certain tension between the statements of faith and the pleas, an implication that present

24. It is a hapax from a verb meaning "push." BDB and *HALOT* take it as a noun meaning "push," but both the pl. and the preposition are then difficult. NJPS gives it a more concrete meaning, following Moshe Greenberg, "*Mzmwr Qm*," in *Eretz-Israel* 14 (1978): 88–99, *125 (see 93–94); he compares the discussion of trapping birds in *m. Šabbat* 13.5.

experience was not fitting the statements of faith. The suppliant has now come out the other side of that tension. Yhwh has not yet acted, but the suppliant is newly confident in Yhwh's action. The way the psalm now speaks also contrasts with that in vv. 9–11, which envisaged evil working out its own consequences; here Yhwh acts.[25] The two expressions of that action are stated in parallel terms, of a judgment and a *decision for the *weak and the *needy. At the same time the psalm wisely hedges its bets in the way it expresses itself. It does not actually say that Yhwh will make a judgment or a decision for *me* as a weak or needy person, even though those terms are surely ones designed to apply to the suppliant. Faith knows what God *can* do, but not what God *will* do.

> **13**Yes, the faithful will confess your name;
> the upright will live in your presence.

The psalm continues to speak in faith but also to hedge its bets. The corollary of Yhwh's taking the action v. 12 spoke of is the response of the *faithful, the upright. Both words are plural, so they do not simply apply to the suppliant. The statements are more explicitly generalizations that do not pretend that every faithful and upright person is always in a position so to *confess Yhwh's *name because of what Yhwh has done for them, or that they always live "with your face" (as the closing expression literally goes), with Yhwh's face shining on them in blessing. Sometimes, Israelites will have noticed, the faithful and upright get martyred. But the suppliant knows that this fact should not make us lose sight of the fact that the faithful and upright in general do experience Yhwh answering the pleas expressed in the psalm, and they therefore have reason for confession and for continuing to live with joy before Yhwh.

Theological Implications

Psalm 140 has been described as "one of the less pleasing examples of a lamenting prayer."[26] It contains no high spiritual aspirations or admission of wrongdoing and focuses on praying for protection and for the destruction of enemies. Yet apparently Paul was happy with it (see Rom. 3:13). "The New Testament treats the Psalter as a major witness to human depravity (most of Rom. 3:10–18 comes from the Psalms), largely

25. Cf. Fokkelman, *Major Poems*, 3:317.

26. William R. Taylor, "The Book of Psalms," by Taylor et al. in *The Interpreter's Bible*, ed. G. A. Buttrick (Nashville: Abingdon, 1955), 4:1–753 (see 718); cf. Bratcher and Reyburn, *Handbook on the Psalms*, 1134. Hauge starts with this comment in his study of the psalm (*Between Sheol and Temple*, 10).

because it exposes this element in us of sheer malice."[27] And the psalm has also been described as part of "the Word of God" that expresses the voice of one "hungering and thirsting for righteousness."[28] "Few short Psalms are so rich in the jewelry of precious faith."[29]

What decides such differing assessments? Nothing in the psalm, of course; they are determined by the attitudes interpreters bring to the psalm. Paul's use of it ignores its own meaning in generalizing from a description of particular people to a description of all humanity, but it does start from the assumption that the psalm offers reliable testimony to an understanding of humanity. The critical assessment expresses the attitude of bourgeois modernity. The critics will see themselves as following Jesus's commitment to loving one's enemies; but then the New Testament has Jesus speaking rather frequently about his enemies being burned in fire (Tg assumes that v. 10 refers to Gehenna) (e.g., Mark 9:42–48), which suggests that his followers' attitude needs to be more nuanced than that and that the psalm might not be so incompatible with that of Jesus. Augustine and Spurgeon start like Paul from an attitude that would not think of questioning the Scriptures, though Augustine is inclined to read Christ into all the Psalms while Spurgeon reads a cleaned-up version of David into them.

We all read Scripture as who we are and risk seeing only our own faces at the bottom of the hermeneutical well. Is there any escape from that? Perhaps we need to read Scripture "as" someone else, as the kind of person for whom the psalm was written, people actually surrounded by others who are making plans to kill them.[30] A read of the newspaper does not make it difficult to identify such people for whom we might pray the psalm. For them, it is vital that the world is a moral place in which we may look for troublemakers to find trouble recoiling onto their own heads and a place in which Yhwh sometimes intervenes to ensure that this happens, thus giving the faithful something to confess and the prospect of living with God's face.

27. Kidner, *Psalms*, 2:468.
28. Augustine, *Psalms*, 641.
29. Spurgeon, *Treasury of David*, 6:293.
30. Cf. McCann, "Psalms," 1241.

Psalm 141
Set a Watch at My Mouth

Translation

Composition. David's.

¹Yhwh, I call you, hurry[1] to me,
  give ear to my voice when I call to you.
²May my plea stand firm before you with incense,
  the lifting of my hands with the evening offering.

³Set a watch at my mouth, Yhwh,
  keep guard[2] at the door of my lips.
⁴Do not turn my heart to something evil,
  to having dealings in faithlessness
  with people who do harm.
So I shall not eat of their delights;
  ⁵the faithful may hit me with commitment[3] and rebuke me.

1. *HALOT* takes this as *ḥûš* II, the sole instance where it means "take notice." It seems more plausible to take it as a slightly extended use of *ḥûš* I.

2. LXX takes *niṣṣĕrâ* as a noun for "watch"; Jerome, Tg more plausibly take it as a form of the qal impv. of *nāṣar* (on which see GKC 20h, 48j).

3. With Vrs, I take *ḥesed* adverbially.

Choice oil [MT]/The oil of the faithless [LXX][4] is not to adorn my
head,[5]
because my plea will continue to be[6] against their evil deeds.
6Their leaders will have fallen[7] on the sides of[8] the crag,[9]
and they will listen to my words, because they were delightful.

7Like someone cleaving and splitting the earth, [MT]
[or] Like a millstone that splits on the earth, [11QPs[a], LXX][10]
our bones[11] have been scattered at the mouth of Sheol.
8Because my eyes are toward you, Yhwh my Lord;
on you I rely, do not expose my life.
9Keep me from the sides of the snare they have laid for me,
the lures of people who do harm.
10May the faithless fall into their own nets all at once;[12]
as for me—while[13] I pass by.

Interpretation

The psalm presupposes a similar need and a similar response to that lying behind Ps. 140. Here, too, the suppliant speaks of faithless people laying snares, pleads for Yhwh's attention and help, and looks to the assailants being caught in their own traps. But this response has a different balance. Not only does it begin with the appeal for Yhwh's attentiveness

4. MT's phrase might simply mean "oil on the head," but *rōʾš* means "chief, best" in a similar context in Exod. 30:23. Either way, the colon involves a paronomasia with "my head" at the end of the colon. For *rōʾš* LXX implies *rāšaʿ*.

5. I derive *yānî* from *nāwâ* I (cf. LXX). BDB less plausibly derives it from *nāwāʾ*, with the final *ʾ* omitted (contrast *yānîʾ* in Num. 30:8 [9]); the colon will then mean "may my head not oppose choice oil."

6. *Kî-ʿôd ûtĕpillâ*: the initial *û* "is probably only an extreme instance" of the construction whereby resumptive *w* follows an expression for time (*TTH* 123β).

7. The qatal is past from the perspective of the line as a whole; in English idiom, "when they have fallen . . . , they will listen. . . ." NJPS takes both verbs as precative, but there is little that points in this direction.

8. For *yādîm* meaning "sides," see BDB 390.

9. R. Tournay ("Le Psaume cxli," *VT* 9 [1959]: 58–64 [see 60]) takes "crag" as a term for Yhwh (but there is no parallel in the Psalms for that word being a title as opposed to an epithet) and takes *šōpĕṭêhem* as honorific pl. referring to Yhwh (but there is no parallel for that, specifically not 58:11 [12] to which Tournay appeals).

10. MT has *pōlēaḥ ûbōqēaʿ* (cf. Jerome, Aq, Sym, Tg); LXX implies *pelaḥ yĕbuqqaʿ*, and 11QPs[a] can be read as suggesting these consonants (see Barthélemy, *Psaumes*, 864).

11. "My bones" (11QPs[a]) and "their bones" (LXX MSS, Syr) are readings that make the text easier.

12. MT links *yaḥad* with the second colon, but the meaning is then difficult. Jerome, Tg, Sym rather link with what precedes (cf. 40:14 [15]; 88:17 [18]; 133:1).

13. For this meaning of *ʿad*, see BDB 725.

that was long delayed in Ps. 140; here that appeal runs through two whole lines and is expressed in a distinctive way in vv. 1–2. Here the suppliant is aware of the ease with which it is possible to be drawn into behavior like that of the faithless, and after the appeal for attentiveness it focuses on that possibility (vv. 3–5); in Ps. 140 the suppliant sensed no such danger or pressure. Here that plea is followed by the psalm's one line of confidence concerning an answer to the prayer (v. 6); there is not the confident ending that closes Ps. 140. Only with the last section (vv. 7–10) does the psalm come to describe the trouble the suppliant is in, declare reliance on Yhwh, and plead for deliverance and for the faithless to fall into their own nets—the motifs that dominate the bulk of Ps. 141. The concern with sins of speech also gives the psalm a link with Wisdom concerns that parallel Ps. 140.[14] And the unexpected move to "our" in v. 7 may indicate that like Ps. 140, the psalm would naturally be used by a king or other leader.

As is the case with Ps. 140, the psalm has some distinctive expressions, such as *dal* (door) and *manʿammîm* (delights), which might point to a northern origin[15] or a late origin; but R. Tournay compares the psalm (in particular, v. 7) with Ps. 53 and suggests the time of Sennacherib's invasion.[16] There is insufficient evidence to argue for a date. It contains a number of instances of paronomasia, in vv. 3 and 7 (at my mouth, at the mouth of), 3 and 9 (set a watch, keep), 4 and 6 (delights, be delightful), 5 MT (choice, head), and 6 (leaders, fall).

Composition. David's.

Heading. See glossary.

141:1–2. The suppliant first appeals for Yhwh to be attentive to this prayer.

[1]Yhwh, I call you, hurry to me,
give ear to my voice when I call to you.

Like "I say to you" in 140:6 [7], the opening qatal verb is performative, "I hereby call you," rather than referring to the way the suppliant has been calling for a long time (contrast 130:1). The form with direct object, "I call you," practically "I summon you," is also boldly peremptory (as

14. On rhetorical patterns between Pss. 140 and 141, and within Ps. 141, see Auffret, *Merveilles à nos yeux*, 218–35.

15. So Rendsburg, *Linguistic Evidence*, 99–102.

16. "Psaume cxli," *RB* 90 (1983): 321–33. Klaus Seybold ("Psalm 141," in *Biblische Welten*, ed. Wolfgang Zwickel, OBO 123 [M. Metzger Festschrift; Göttingen: Vandenhoeck & Ruprecht, 1993], 199–214) seeks to trace its redactional history.

in 130:1). The boldness is expressed further in the imperative "hurry to me." This is not a novel boldness (cf. 22:19 [20]; 38:22 [23]; 40:13 [14]; 70:1 [2]; 71:12); evidently it is fine to urge God to hurry up. All those other passages urge Yhwh to hurry to help; here (and in 70:5 [6]) the suppliant urges simply "hurry to me," and does so in the context of a plea for attentiveness. The suppliant wants Yhwh to pay attention *now*. On the other hand, the parallel colon is more polite; the imperative "give ear" has the courteous *-â* sufformative and is followed by "I call to you" rather than "I call you."

[2]May my plea stand firm before you with incense,
the lifting of my hands with the evening offering.

The parallel line might seem to undo the stress on hurrying; if the suppliant wants the plea to stand there firm before Yhwh, this implies not expecting Yhwh to respond instantly. But this is to be prosaic with imagery. In v. 1 the suppliant was the hurting child and Yhwh was the father or mother urged to give immediate attention. In v. 2 the suppliant is the petitioner standing before the king in his capacity as supreme court, pressing for action but recognizing the king's position of authority. Lifting one's hands is a gesture of appeal that accompanies the actual plea. Incense and evening offering also stand in parallelism, though that might have varying implications. In the narrow sense, the evening "offering" (*minḥâ*) would be a grain offering, but the word can also be used in a broader sense to include animal sacrifices, so that the evening offering could refer to the animal sacrifice made each evening. "Incense" might then refer to the actual smoke from the sacrifice, which goes up to Yhwh with the pleasing aroma of a barbecue, or it might refer to the burning of fragrant spices to accompany the sacrifice itself; but if "offering" has the narrower meaning, "incense" will refer to the incense offering that accompanied a grain offering. There is no word for "with"; Vrs supply "as," but this may give a false impression. Prayers accompanied offerings, so that as usual worship of Yhwh is multifaceted; it involves words, music, gestures, and offerings. Prayers would not be substitutes for offerings unless offerings were impossible for some reason.[17]

141:3–6. The plea for help in staying faithful.

[3]Set a watch at my mouth, Yhwh,
keep guard at the door of my lips.

17. Cf. Briggs, *Psalms*, 2:507.

We often wish we had something to stop hasty or hurtful statements emerging from our mouth. This is not the need the psalm refers to. Rather it takes up the fact that our mouths are a major means of wrongdoing because of their role in deceptiveness and plotting. The suppliant asks to be held back from such forms of speech. The parallel words "watch" and "keep guard" recur from 140:4 [5], with the striking difference that there the psalm spoke of protection from other people, whereas Ps. 141 speaks of protection from oneself. To put it a different way, we need protection from other people's attacks, but also from other people's influence. Proverbs recognizes the importance of speech but with realism rather holds back from telling people to control their mouths (see Prov. 10:31–32; 13:3; 15:2, 28; 16:23; 21:23), while Ps. 39 begins by recalling that this is an impossible project.[18] In connection with the moral aspect to this, the pressure from within and without to join with other people in the way they use speech to further their scheming, Ps. 141 recognizes that we need Yhwh to do something to turn us into people who want to use speech for the furtherance of truth and faithfulness, not of our own interests.

> **4a–c**Do not turn my heart to something evil,
> to having dealings in faithlessness
> with people who do harm.

In making that explicit, this tricolon looks behind and in front of the mouth. Behind the mouth is the *heart, the inner thinking that expresses itself in words. In front are the deeds that put the words into action; "having dealings" makes the point with some emphasis (more literally, "dealing [with] dealings"). Specifically the dealings are things that involve evil (*bad) and *faithlessness, as in the parallel 140:1, 4 [2, 5], with people[19] who do *harm. (LXX, Sym, Jerome take "something evil" as "an evil word"; the word *dābār* can mean either a thing or a word, and between vv. 3 and 4b, the meaning in v. 4a could go either way.)

NJPS and TNIV take v. 4a to mean "Do not *let* my heart turn to something evil," but it is doubtful whether the hiphil can have this merely permissive sense,[20] and the parallel with the verbs in v. 3 also points to a strong understanding of the way Yhwh is involved in our moral life. The terms in vv. 3 and 4 are the converse of talk of hardening someone's heart or stiffening their resolve; they parallel talk of softening someone's

18. Contrast Gerstenberger, *Psalms*, 2:414–15.

19. Th. Booij ("Psalm 141," *Bib* 86 [2005]: 97–106 [see 98–99]) takes the unusual pl. *ʾîšîm* to mean "people of stature."

20. Cf. JM 54d, note 3; and contrast the examples in *IBHS* 27.5. But see Ernst Jenni, "Kausativ und Funktionsverbgefüge," *TZ* 48 (1992): 77–88.

heart. They do not imply that Yhwh manipulates our brains or forces us to act in a way alien to us. Rather Yhwh acts like a friend (or an enemy) who can persuade us to act in a way we would not otherwise do.

> 4dSo I shall not eat of their delights;
> 5the faithful may hit me with commitment and rebuke me.
> Choice oil [MT]/The oil of the faithless [LXX] is not to adorn my head,
> because my plea will continue to be against their evil deeds.

The chain of thought is elliptical, though less so if we treat v. 4d with v. 5, so that vv. 4d–5 become two parallel lines.[21] Like the talk of people who do harm, talk of eating their delights is a novel formulation in the psalm over against Ps. 140. There is nothing wrong with delights (*manʿammîm*); the word comes only here, but related words denote things that are properly sources of delight (e.g., Prov. 24:4, 25). The problem lies in joining with the faithless in their delights; perhaps the delights are ill-gotten, or perhaps one has got too closely involved in the lives of the faithless (cf. Ps. 1:1). So the suppliant makes a commitment to declining enjoyment with the faithless, and also, conversely, to accepting tough treatment from the *faithful, presumably in case of failure with regard to the possibilities v. 4 spoke of. Such an attack would actually be an expression of the *commitment of the faithful (cf. Prov. 27:6).

The second line (v. 5b–c) then expresses another form of the self-denial v. 4d spoke of. The parties where people partook of delicacies would be ones where people were adorned and made up with appropriate festivity, and perhaps so adorned by their hosts (cf. 23:5); the suppliant knows that it will also be necessary to have nothing to do with that. Indeed, v. 5c may suggest that the suppliant speaks of having nothing to do with any kind of festivity. The necessity to keep maintaining the plea for Yhwh to act against their evil deeds (*bad)[22] makes that inappropriate (cf. Jer. 16:1–9). There are more solemn things to do.

> 6Their leaders will have fallen on the sides of the crag,
> and they will listen to my words, because they were delightful.

The psalm expresses the suppliant's conviction about the downfall of the faithless, and does so with force by looking beyond that event to the realization it will bring them. The leaders are the *decision makers; again there is an ironic link with the preceding psalm, whose closing

21. TNIV renders v. 5a–b "Let a righteous man strike me—that is a kindness; let him rebuke me—that is oil on my head. My head will not refuse it"; that involves rather more connecting of dots.

22. Or "because of their evil deeds/troubles" (cf. Booij, "Psalm 141," 101).

statement of confidence used the related noun in speaking about Yhwh's making a "decision" on behalf of the poor and needy. The sins of speech to which this psalm refers are ones that implicate the leaders of the community who make judicial decisions. In turn, the reference to the crag recalls 137:9; these decision makers will have had the experience that is there projected for Babylon's offspring. There is a paronomasia between "fall" and "leaders," from the verbs *šāmaṭ* and *šāpaṭ*; such leadership appropriately or naturally leads to a fall.

Paradoxically, but typically in the OT, whereas v. 6a suggests that the leaders lose their lives, v. 6b apparently has them then realizing how they were wrong, and responding. Possibly the "they" of v. 6b is the faithless people in general and it was only their leaders who fell. Or possibly this "they" is impersonal. But possibly one should let the paradox stand and recognize that the language about a fatal fall should not be pressed. This would fit with the fact that v. 6 (like 137:9) likely speaks metaphorically; in order for the psalm's expectations to be fulfilled, it need not indicate literally how they need to fall. And/or possibly one should see the cola as offering the leaders two alternatives. Either they fall, or they listen. What they will then come to see is that the suppliant's words were actually delightful; the description is picked up from v. 4d. This psalm and the previous one (see 140:3, 9, 11 [4, 10, 12]) have made clear that the words of the faithless themselves are anything but delightful, hence the need to avoid coming to talk like them (v. 3). Of course they thought of their words as delightful (cf. Prov. 3:17), and they no doubt saw people such as the suppliant as hopelessly impractical in declining to be economical with the truth. But the leaders' fate, actual or contemplated, will enable them or their people to see the truth.

141:7–10. The plea for protection and the fall of the faithless. Rather jerkily, the psalm comes at last to protest at how the faithful have been treated and to plead for divine action.

[7]Like someone cleaving and splitting the earth, [MT]
[or] Like a millstone that splits on the earth, [11QPs[a], LXX]
our bones have been scattered at the mouth of Sheol.

MT's opening image apparently comes from plowing, which involves the farmer breaking up the clods mercilessly to make the soil open to the rain and seed and to new growing. That is how it has been for the people whose bones have been scattered. Syntactically, in enunciating the comparison the relationship between the two cola breaks down, but the comparison is clear enough. The alternative version is smoother: imagine a millstone dropped and shattering.

But who is having this shattering experience? Who are the "we" of v. 7b? TNIV takes v. 7 as the words of the leaders in v. 6, but there is no indication of that, and when Pss. 118, 122, and 123 move between "I" and "we," the "we" refers to the community. More likely, then, v. 7 indicates that the suppliant who has spoken as a lone individual elsewhere in the psalm is actually a member of a community under pressure. So it is the faithful in general who are like people broken into pieces, like the shattered millstone, or like those clods of earth, like the bones scattered over the plain in Ezek. 37. The closing reference to the mouth of Sheol makes for a nice link with v. 3 but also puts the point more frighteningly. It is as if the people have been swallowed up by Death, who has then spat out their bare bones and left them; the psalm uses as a metaphor language that comes from Canaanite myth, like 49:14 [15].[23] Perhaps, then, MT's syntax does not break down; perhaps v. 7a is extraposed and Sheol is the one who resembles someone breaking up and cleaving into the earth.

> 8Because my eyes are toward you, Yhwh my Lord;
> on you I rely, do not expose my life.

As is often the case (not least in Ezek. 37), in v. 7 the psalm thus talked as if people are dead, but it spoke in hyperbole. As one of the faithful, the suppliant is alive enough to be looking to Yhwh for protection. The psalm asks that the suppliant's life (*person) may not be exposed, or made vulnerable to death. The verb takes up from 137:7 (see also Isa. 53:12). To that end, the suppliant *relies on "Yhwh my *Lord."

The reference to the suppliant's eyes broadens further the references to different parts of the body in the psalm. The hands are lifted, the lips and mouth are to be guarded, the heart is not to be turned, the head is not adorned, the bones are scattered, but the eyes are focused.

> 9Keep me from the sides of the snare they have laid for me,
> the lures of people who do harm.

The last two lines recall the twofold plea for deliverance and punishment that often appear in a prayer psalm. The verb picks up from v. 3a (there the noun *šomrâ*, translated "watch"), while "sides" picks up from v. 6, referring to the two halves of the net or the two arms of the trap that come together to capture the bird (this fits with the likelihood

23. See John Barclay Burns, "An Interpretation of Psalm cxli 7b," *VT* 22 (1972): 245–46; Benedikt Hartman, "Exegetische und religionsgeschichtliche Studie zu Psalm 141:5d–7," in *Tradition and Re-interpretation in Jewish and Early Christian Literature*, ed. J. W. van Henten et al. (J. C. H. Lebram Festschrift; Leiden: Brill, 1986), 27–37.

that v. 6 speaks metaphorically, as this verse does). So the psalm here recognizes a need to be protected from people who do *harm (cf. v. 3) as well as from oneself, and it asks for an experience that is the opposite of the fate wished on the adversaries; it asks to be kept from their fate. The references to snares and lures summarize the imagery expounded at greater length in Ps. 140.

10May the faithless fall into their own nets all at once;
as for me—while I pass by.

So the converse to the plea for protection is the jussive wish for evil to bring its own consequences; the psalm again follows Ps. 140 both in the use of the jussive and in the assumption that consequences work themselves out in natural if unexpected ways. On the one hand, the *faithless (they recur from v. 4, where they also stood next to "people who harm," as here) fall into their own nets. Literally, they fall into his own net, the net each of them made individually.[24] On the other, the suppliant meanwhile passes without incident along the track where the nets are laid.

Theological Implications

The similarity to Ps. 140 in the latter part of the psalm highlights two differences in its earlier part. One is the plea for Yhwh to protect the suppliant from coming to share the sins of the faithless. Christians often look askance at the Psalms' confidence in claiming a commitment to Yhwh; here, at least, the suppliant recognizes that this claim cannot be made cheaply. It requires Yhwh to be at work in relation to one's heart, mouth, and action. The point is put negatively. The suppliant does not need Yhwh to start from scratch; the right commitment already characterizes heart, mouth, and action. But no one can be sure of maintaining today's commitment tomorrow. Yet Yhwh can exercise decisive influence over us for good or bad, in the way that our family and friends do, multiplied by a thousand. Our friends and family can dangle delights in front of us, legitimate delights that could issue from right living or forbidden delights that could issue from wrongdoing. Yhwh can do that more powerfully, and did so in relation to Pharaoh to harden him. If Yhwh does that to us, it does not mean we become helpless and hopeless, but it sure puts pressure on. We are well-advised

24. DG 26, remark 2; cf. GKC 145m.

to beseech Yhwh to influence us toward what is good by reminding us of its delights.

The other feature that distinguishes the psalm over against Ps. 140 is the appeal for attention that occupies the verses preceding those pleas in vv. 3–4. They underline how important those pleas are.

Psalm 142

How to Get Prayer to Work

Translation

Instruction. David's. When he was in the cave. Plea.

[1]With my voice I will cry out to Yhwh,
with my voice I will appeal for grace to Yhwh.
[2]I will pour out my murmuring before him,
my trouble I will proclaim before him.

[3]When my spirit faints away within me,
you yourself know my path.[1]
On the way that I walk
people have hidden a snare for me.
[4]Look [MT]/I look [11QPs[a], LXX, Jerome, Tg][2] at my right hand and see:
for me there is no one who recognizes me.

1. The *w*-consecutive serves as the apodosis to the temporal clause (cf. GKC 112oo; see also *TTH* 128; DG 106a).

2. MT *habbêṭ* is inf. abs. (for impv. one would expect *habbēṭ*); 11QPs[a], LXX, Tg have first-person verbs, which could be an interpretation of the inf. For "and see," they continue first-person verbs, whereas MT has impv. *rĕʾēh*. This could be a slip for inf. abs. *rāʾōh*, which would make possible a first-person translation of the whole line ("Looking . . . and seeing . . ."). Barthélemy (*Psaumes*, 867) sees the first-person understanding as designed to eliminate a "fine anthropomorphism," but bidding Yhwh to look and see has many paral-

Shelter has departed from me,
there is no one who inquires about my life.

5I cry out to you, Yhwh,
I say, You are my refuge,
my allocation in the land of the living.
6Attend to my resounding,
because I have been brought very low.

Rescue me from the people pursuing me,
because they are too strong for me.
7Bring me out of prison,
to confess your name.
The faithful will surround me,
because of the way you deal with me.

Interpretation

Another individual prayer psalm speaks out of awareness that people have set snares on the suppliant's path. Yet compared with Pss. 140 and 141, there is even less focus on this. The emphasis lies on the suppliant's isolation and the consequent extremity of the suppliant's dependence on Yhwh; there is nowhere else to turn. The psalm begins with a declaration of intent to cry out to Yhwh (vv. 1–2), describes the suppliant's need (vv. 3–4), issues the actual cry to Yhwh, appealing for attention (vv. 5–6b), and then pleads for the act of deliverance that will bring Yhwh glory (vv. 6c–7).[3]

A further difference from Pss. 140 and 141 is the heading making a concrete link with David's life and reflecting the language of David's story. This need not mean the psalm is intended for a king or leader (David might be a model for an ordinary believer, as he became in Christian piety), though it might be so used. It is usually reckoned that the psalm headings that make a link with an incident in David's life are later than the psalms themselves and make their link on the basis of verbal connections that are seen subsequently. In this psalm, isolated from the other psalms with concrete headings, the verbal connections look more intrinsic to the psalm and appear too numerous to be coincidental. Perhaps, then, the psalmist wrote a "David psalm" for individuals to use, based on the David story.

Another distinctive feature is the way the psalm reflects the phraseology of other psalms, in addition to 140 and 141 and David's story, though

lels, so why should this instance be eliminated? More likely the double inf. abs. is original, and the question is whether it should be read as imperatival or as first person.

3. On rhetorical patterns in the psalm, see Auffret, *Merveilles à nos yeux*, 236–48.

regularly it manifests slight variation from them. Verse 1 almost corresponds to 77:1 [2]. "Murmuring" and "trouble" in v. 2 parallel 77:2–3 [3–4]. "When my spirit faints away" (v. 3a) corresponds to 77:3b [4b], but Ps. 142 adds "within me," a distinctive expression that comes (for instance) in 131:2; this fills out the line in the place of the opening reference to murmuring, which Ps. 142 has already taken up in v. 2. In its relationship with other psalms, it parallels Ps. 135. As is the case with that psalm, the author hardly composes by scrolling through a Psalter and lifting out phrases, but rather composes as a person who lives from day to day with the phraseology of the psalms as they were used in worship and naturally falls into its phrases, or into variants on them.

Spurgeon comments that "the intense personality of the prayer is noteworthy,"[4] while Weiser enthuses lyrically over the psalm as a "deeply felt," "fervent and moving lament which arises out of the most intense physical and mental suffering. . . . In the midst of his isolation the worshipper reaches out with trembling hands and with a heart full of childlike trust for the one last support left to him." It is "an intimate prayer which appeals to us so much because of its simplicity and humility."[5] It thus illustrates the way in which personal piety and depth of dependence on Yhwh coexist with a piety that naturally expresses itself in scriptural terms, in the way that much Protestant piety echoed the phraseology of the King James Bible.

Verses 1–2 address other people rather than Yhwh, which suggests that the psalm is one that an individual prays in the company of others. Further, prayer offered "before Yhwh" likely indicates prayer prayed in the temple. But we do not know anything about its specific worship setting or its date.

Instruction. David's. When he was in the cave. Plea.

Heading. See glossary for *David's and *plea. This is the only "Instruction" in Books IV or V (there are ten earlier). If we assume that this word in headings comes from *śākal* I, then "instruction" is one possible meaning; it will suggest that this is a psalm offering a pattern for prayer or praise. But "contemplative poem" and "skillful poem" are other possibilities.[6] Klaus Koenen suggests the word rather comes from *śākal* II and means "antiphonal song."[7]

The reference to a concrete context in David's life is also the only instance in Books IV or V; perhaps this one follows Ps. 57. The most detailed

4. *Treasury of David*, 6:324.
5. *Psalms*, 815, 817.
6. See BDB.
7. "Maśkil-'Wechselgesang,'" *ZAW* 103 (1991): 109–12.

story about David and a cave is 1 Sam. 24, but there is no implication that David's spirit failed there; that would rather suggest his stay in the cave of Adullam (1 Sam. 22). The verbal links with these stories come in the appeal in vv. 6c–7.

142:1–2. A declaration of intent to cry out to Yhwh.

[1]With my voice I will cry out to Yhwh,
with my voice I will appeal for grace to Yhwh.
[2]I will pour out my murmuring before him,
my trouble I will proclaim before him.

The two-line opening comprises four parallel cola that also form two pairs, arranged *abcabc′* and *abcc′b′a′*. The suppliant announces an intention in four ways. The verbs are yiqtol, not cohortative, and could be translated as present, but I take them to refer to the prayer that the psalm will go on to utter.[8] They are all forceful words, announcing that the prayer will involve *crying out in urgent need, appealing for Yhwh's *grace, pouring out without restraint, and proclaiming (*nāgad* hiphil). One usually proclaims what Yhwh has done, but the psalm will proclaim the background to what Yhwh needs to do. The center of each colon identifies the object of the prayer: to Yhwh, to Yhwh, before him, before him. Then in the first two cola the repeated "with my voice" emphasizes the out-loud nature of the prayer. When you want to get someone's attention, you do not whisper, or just say it inside, as if the person were inside you rather than independent of you, existing really and objectively outside you.[9] And in the second pair of cola the verbs have objects, one referring to the problem, "my trouble," one to the nature of the suppliant's prayer, "my *murmuring." In none of this is the psalm yet directly addressing Yhwh (that will come later). Perhaps it is rather addressing the congregation with a statement of intent and thereby resisting the isolation it will speak of later. But perhaps it is also addressing Yhwh indirectly, to begin the process of getting Yhwh to respond.

The two lines compare with the two-line opening to Ps. 141 but also contrast with it. The doubled "with my voice" and the verb "cry out" contrast with the ordinary verb "call," and the four yiqtols contrast with the qatals. And whereas Ps. 141 calls out to Yhwh in the traditional fashion of such a prayer psalm, this psalm will not address Yhwh until vv. 3–4 and not cry out to Yhwh until v. 5.

8. Vrs have a complicated variety of tenses through vv. 1–2.

9. Though Augustine comments that prayer needs to be inward not just outward (*Psalms*, 648); it is addressed "to Yhwh," "before him," not to or before other human beings.

142:3–4. The suppliant addresses Yhwh: this is my need.

[3]When my spirit faints away within me,
you yourself know my path.
On the way that I walk
people have hidden a snare for me.
[4]Look [MT]/I look [11QPs[a], LXX, Jerome, Tg] at my right hand and see:
for me there is no one who recognizes me.
Shelter has departed from me,
there is no one who inquires about my life.

Again there is a certain parallelism between the two verses. Verses 3a–b and 4a–b allude to what Yhwh can know and what the suppliant knows. In other contexts, Yhwh's knowing can be an encouragement to the suppliant; Gerstenberger describes v. 3a–b as a statement of confidence.[10] But here the point of the line is further to press the suppliant's plight on Yhwh. Yhwh *does* know the path I have to tread with its dangers (v. 3a–b) and/or *can* know what is happening to me (v. 4a–b MT); and therefore Yhwh should do something about it. On one hand, the suppliant's spirit flags; literally "my spirit faints upon me," as if my own tiredness is becoming a burden that falls on me from outside (see on 131:2). But Yhwh knows. On the other, Yhwh can look at the suppliant's right hand, where a powerful supporter might be expected to stand (e.g., 16:8; 109:31; 121:5) and can see that there is no one there, "no one who recognizes me" or has regard for me and therefore cares what is happening to me and offers me support. Or (if we follow the other tradition), I know and see that, and I draw Yhwh's attention to it; so one way or another, Yhwh knows.

Then vv. 3c–d and 4c–d focus on the need that Yhwh can know. Some anonymous "people" have laid a "snare for me"; the words exactly correspond to words in 140:5a [6a], though there the people are more identified and ropes are added to the snare. Shelter has vanished or perished (*ʾābad*); the noun makes for an interesting contrast with the declaration attributed to David in 2 Sam. 22:3 (and in Ps. 59:16 [17] if read in light of the heading). And no one asks about me (or about my life, my *person); the verb most often refers to having recourse to Yhwh or some other such resource, but it can also refer to Yhwh searching for us, inquiring about us. In combination with the references to a shelter and to someone at my right hand and someone who recognizes me, consciously or unconsciously the suppliant is suggesting that Yhwh is not fulfilling the role one would have expected.

The parallelism between the verses is accompanied by some parallelism between the lines, so that the section is tightly bound together.

10. *Psalms*, 2:418; cf. Kraus, *Psalms 60–150*, 531.

Verse 3a–b and 3c–d both begin with *b*-expressions and have their main verb in the second colon. Then in v. 4a–b and 4c–d, each second colon begins *ʾên*, "there is no one" (the first is preceded by a *w*). And the lines have different subjects. Verse 3 refers to the suppliant's attackers. Verse 4 refers to the attitude taken by the rest of the community as a consequence of the attacks upon the suppliant. No one wants to have anything to do with a person in that position. Is another effect of vv. 1–2 to make the people who hear the psalm feel uneasy about their attitude?

142:5–6b. The suppliant appeals for Yhwh to give ear.

> 5I cry out to you, Yhwh,
> I say, You are my refuge,
> my allocation in the land of the living.

The opening verb recurs from v. 1 but is now performative qatal; the suppliant is fulfilling the intention announced in v. 1 and is actually *crying out to Yhwh. The first colon introduces the whole of vv. 5b–6.

"I say" is then another performative qatal. In the absence of any other "shelter" (v. 4), the suppliant says, "You are my refuge." This is a similar but more common term to describe Yhwh (e.g., 91:2, 9; 94:22; with the literal sense, 104:18). In parallel with that description is "allocation" (see on 119:57), which fits here in light of its common link with the experience of a family's vulnerability. The family's possession of an allocation of land in the land of Israel gives it security there. Possessing Yhwh as an allocation in the land of the living (see 27:13; 52:5 [7]; 116:9; Job 28:13; Isa. 38:11), as opposed to Sheol, the land of the dead, gives the suppliant security there. At least, that is the theory. The question is whether Yhwh is going to make this work out.

> 6a–bAttend to my resounding,
> because I have been brought very low.

The appeal for attention takes up those declarations in v. 5b–c (the words almost correspond to 17:1b); its coming so late in the psalm compares with Ps. 140. Yhwh must listen to the noise the suppliant makes, noise that issues from how low the suppliant has been brought (Sym's *lalia* gets nearest to preserving the meaning of *rinnâ*, *resounding). "My place in the land of the living is very precarious," is the implication. The verb for "be low" (*dālal*) links with the word for poor (*dal*), so the language takes further that image of insecurity; here the words almost correspond to 79:8c. But perhaps it also hints that to be brought low is to be brought to the verge of Sheol (cf. 141:7). The suppliant is fainting in spirit because external circumstances are so threatening.

142:6c–7. The suppliant appeals for Yhwh to act.

> 6c–dRescue me from the people pursuing me,
> because they are too strong for me.

At last the psalm comes to the plea for Yhwh to act. Here there is no appeal for punishment for the pursuers, the people laying the traps, only for escape from them. "Pursuing" is the participle David uses in the cave story in 1 Sam. 24:14 [15], and the explanation "because they are too strong for me" makes another link with David's testimony in 2 Sam. 22:18, where the words are identical. That makes it also significant that "rescue" (*nāṣal* hiphil) is the verb David uses to describe Yhwh's deliverance in 2 Sam. 22:49 (though v. 6c is also very similar to words in Ps. 7:1b [2b], in another psalm given a concrete link with David's life, and 31:15a [16a]).

> 7Bring me out of prison,
> to confess your name.
> The faithful will surround me,
> because of the way you deal with me.

The plea for Yhwh to act continues. While LXX and Jerome assume that "prison" has literal reference, Aq and Sym use words that could suggest a more figurative confinement,[11] and it would be wooden to assume the word must refer to a literal prison. Neither is there positive reason to connect it with exile as a prisonlike experience. Rather the metaphor of prison provides another image to describe the suppliant's situation earlier in the psalm. Over against "the land of the living" (v. 5c) it could suggest Sheol (cf. v. 6b) and imply a sense of being at Death's doors (cf. 141:7). This term and others in the verse again recall the David story. "Prison" (*masgēr*) is a rare word, but "imprison" or "shut up" (*sāgar*) recurs in the story of David and Saul (1 Sam. 23:7, 11, 12, 20; 24:18 [19]). The prison is the place where someone seems to be given over to their enemies; the suppliant asks that things may not turn out like this. The links we have noted make it significant that "bring me out"[12] (*yāṣāʾ* hiphil) is another verb David uses retrospectively in 2 Sam. 22:49. The plea for Yhwh to act soon gives way to another concern, for Yhwh to be praised, again linking with 2 Sam. 22. The object of Yhwh's bringing about a release from danger is that the suppliant will *confess Yhwh's *name, as David undertakes (2 Sam. 22:50).

11. Cf. Theodoret, *Psalms*, 2:342.

12. Literally, "bring out my *person/life"; the sequence "cry out" and *nepeš* thus appears in vv. 5–7 as it did in vv. 1–4 (Watson, *Classical Hebrew Poetry*, 290).

The link with David also gives resonances to the unusual word for "surround" (*kātar* hiphil). In isolation one might link it with the word for a crown (*keter*; so Tg, Sym, NJPS); in Aramaic it comes to mean "wait expectantly" (so LXX, Jerome). But one of the word's five other occurrences (in the piel) describes the strong ones of Bashan "surrounding" David (if we read Ps. 22 in light of the heading), in a negative sense (Ps. 22:12 [13]; there the verb is piel). Now the suppliant will be surrounded in a positive sense, by the *faithful. This will especially contrast with the isolation v. 4 spoke of. "Deal" (*gāmal*), too, recurs from 1 Sam. 24:17 [18]. Yhwh's dealings contrast with Saul's. That occurrence reflects how the verb does not mean "deal well" with someone (contrast EVV here). It is a neutral word. Saul has to add "good" and "bad" to make his point. Here it is the context that makes it clear that Yhwh's dealings are good, like David's but not like Saul's. The link with this passage also adds resonance to the reference to the faithful, because the same verse has Saul acknowledging that David in his dealings with Saul is more faithful than he is.

Theological Implications

How does prayer work? That is, how do you win Yhwh's response to your need? The psalm's four sections suggest four answers. First, talk about the way you are going to pray, maybe to other people, remembering that Yhwh can overhear what you are saying. Yhwh's overhearing is not a threat but a blessing; when we overhear something not addressed to us, it can affect us more than hearing something that was addressed to us. Second, talk directly to Yhwh about how things are, about the nature of your need, and about what Yhwh knows. Even if Yhwh knows, talking about these things brings them to Yhwh's attention, opens up the possibility of pushing them to the top of Yhwh's agenda, and means that relationships between us and Yhwh are true and open. Third, ask for Yhwh's full attention on the basis of Yhwh's being the only person who can help. Fourth, urge Yhwh to help, and point out how this will bring Yhwh glory. These convictions that the psalm assumes are not ones Christians often assume about prayer.

Psalm 143

No Living Person Is Faithful before You

Translation

Composition. David's. [LXX adds, When his son is pursuing him.]

1Yhwh, listen to my plea,
give ear to my prayer for grace in your truthfulness,[1]
answer me in your faithfulness.
2And do not contend with your servant,
because no living person is faithful before you.

3Because the enemy has pursued me,
has crushed me to the earth,
has made me live in darkness like people long dead.
4And my spirit has fainted away within me;[2]
inside me my heart is desolated.

5I have been mindful of the days of old,
I have talked of all your acts,
I would murmur about the deeds of your hands.

1. MT links "in your truthfulness" with what follows, but more likely the two cola comprising v. 1b–c are parallel and the two *b* expressions divide between them.

2. The *w*-consecutive apparently denotes consequence (see F. A. Gosling, "An Interesting Use of the Waw Consecutive," *ZAW* 110 [1998]: 403–10).

6I have stretched out my hands to you,
my whole being has been like thirsty earth in relation to you.
(Rise.)[3]

7Answer me quickly, Yhwh,
my spirit is spent.
Do not hide your face from me,
so that I shall be like the people who go down to the Pit.
8Make me hear of your commitment in the morning,
because it is on you that I have relied.

Make known to me the way that I should walk,
because it is to you that I have lifted myself.
9Rescue me from my enemies, Yhwh,
with you[4] I have covered [myself].[5]
10Enable me to learn to do what is acceptable to you,
because you are my God.
May your good spirit lead me[6]
on level ground.[7]

11For the sake of your name, Yhwh, will you give me life,
in your faithfulness will you bring me out of my trouble.
12And in your commitment will you put an end to my enemies,
destroy all the people who are attacking me,
because I am your servant.

Interpretation

Once again "the triangle enemies-God-I is explored."[8] This prayer psalm begins with an invocation of Yhwh and a plea for Yhwh to listen (vv. 1–2), an explanation in terms of the attacks of an enemy and their effect on the suppliant (vv. 3–4), and a reminder of how the suppliant has been relating to Yhwh through this experience, closing with the marker "Rise" (vv. 5–6). The remainder of the psalm comprises a long

3. See the introduction to Ps. 140.

4. Lit. "to you"; *ʾel* is used in a pregnant sense, suggesting "coming to you for covering" (cf. GKC 119g; JM 133b; BDB 40b; Allen, *Psalms 101–150*, 351).

5. *Kissitî*, piel but lacking an object, recurs in Deut. 22:12 with oneself as the implicit object; here, indeed, *napšî* in the previous line might be understood as the object. Jerome implies *kussētî*, "I was covered." Kraus (*Psalms 60–150*, 535) suggests *kĕsutî*, "[was] my covering."

6. Or, "[By] your good spirit will you lead me" (cf. 51:12 [14]; Dahood, *Psalms*, 3:325). Anarthrous "good" (contrast Neh. 9:20) is odd but explicable (GKC 126z; JM 138f). MT accents imply "Your spirit is good; lead me."

7. NRSV "on a level path" follows MSS that assimilate to 27:11.

8. Fokkelman, *Major Poems*, 3:318.

plea (vv. 7–12).[9] It is thus possible to subdivide the first part in terms of its structure and subject or function. Each subsection is marked by an opening tricolon; God is the subject in vv. 1–2, the enemy the subject in vv. 3–4, and the suppliant the subject in vv. 5–6. The second part similarly closes with a tricolon, but the formal or substantial subdivisions are not as clear. It does comprise renewed pleas for Yhwh to listen (vv. 7–8b), a double plea for Yhwh to rescue, set in the distinctive context of a double appeal for teaching and leading (vv. 8c–10), and a closing double plea for deliverance and for the putting down of the suppliant's enemies (vv. 11–12). Each subsection contains a renewed invocation of Yhwh. Verse 2 led the church to designate Ps. 143 as one of the seven Penitential Psalms, but Spurgeon notes that it is "rather martial than penitential."[10]

As in preceding psalms, the suppliant might be an ordinary individual beset by enemies within the community or a king or leader beset by external enemies; the appeal as "your servant" (vv. 2, 12) might support the latter. It again has phrases in common with preceding psalms, such as the references to an enemy "pursuing" and to "my spirit fainting within me," to "murmuring," "bringing out of trouble," and "destroying," which recall Ps. 142. But most of these phrases also appear in other psalms, and Ps. 143 has a number of other such links, which gives it a relationship to other psalms somewhat like that of Pss. 135 and 138. Distinctively, it has a number of further links with Isa. 56–66. All this suggests that it comes from after the exile and deals with issues raised by those chapters. They accuse the community of unfaithfulness to Yhwh; the psalm implicitly declares that where such accusations are true, prayer such as this would be impossible. But such accusations are not true of this suppliant in this context, and therefore it is possible to call on Yhwh in the way the psalm does.

Composition. David's. [LXX adds, When his son is pursuing him.]

Heading. See glossary.
143:1–2. The opening invocation and plea for Yhwh's attention.

1Yhwh, listen to my plea,
give ear to my prayer for grace in your truthfulness,
answer me in your faithfulness.
2And do not contend with your servant,
because no living person is faithful before you.

9. Auffret (*Merveilles à nos yeux*, 249–61) rather sees the major division in the psalm after v. 7.
10. *Treasury of David*, 6:334.

The opening invocation leads into a threefold positive appeal, for Yhwh to listen, give ear (a more forceful, less familiar expression in the parallel colon), and answer (an even more direct and specific bidding, opening the brisk and unexpected third colon) the *plea or prayer for *grace that will eventually follow in vv. 8c–12. The terms are thus familiar but vigorous and plainspoken, and they lean hard on Yhwh.

In contrast, the continuation of this plea in v. 2 is a novel one. In isolation, v. 2a might be read in light of Absalom's revolt, referred to in LXX's heading, and linked with David's sin against Bathsheba and Uriah, which issued in the disintegration of his family;[11] but v. 2b will point in a more general direction. "Contend" is more literally "enter into a *decision" (*bôʾ bĕmišpāṭ*; cf. Job 22:4). Similar phrases can refer to a more open, mutual process of decision making (e.g., Job 9:32, where the verb is plural), but this second-person expression takes the perspective of the person bringing the case, one who (the speaker also knows) can be confident of winning. Verse 2b confirms this implication. It is Yhwh who makes the authoritative decisions about whether a person counts as *faithful.

143:3–4. The declaration of need.

3Because the enemy has pursued me,
has crushed me to the earth,
has made me live in darkness like people long dead.
4And my spirit has fainted away within me;
inside me my heart is desolated.

The "because" follows on from vv. 1–2 as a whole, and specifically from v. 1, rather than from v. 2. The verbs are qatal; I take them to refer to acts in the past that continue their effect into the present.[12] The psalm returns to a more conventional agenda; the talk of an enemy "pursuing" recalls 142:6 [7], but more closely 7:5a [6a]. Likewise the second colon recalls 7:5b [6b] but also Isa. 57:15 with its reference to being crushed; and the third recalls Isa. 59:9–10 with its reference to darkness and to being like dead people, though it more closely corresponds, with one difference in word order, to Lam. 3:6.[13] The three cola develop in impact as they speak of pursuing (which likely implies death), of crushing to the earth (which also likely suggests death and burial and ending up in Sheol), and of living in the dark (which then also is likely a term for the

11. As Theodoret hints, *Psalms*, 2:343.

12. Cf. NRSV for v. 4; it then has present for v. 5. NJPS has aorist throughout, TNIV present throughout.

13. There one would have to read it as a 2-2 bicolon; if that understanding holds here, then v. 3 becomes two bicola.

realm of death), and finally explicitly refer to being in the same position as people who have been long dead.

Similarly v. 4a combines the phraseology of 77:3 [4] and 142:3 [4], but the verb in v. 4b (*šāmam* hitpolel) recalls Isa. 59:16; 63:5 (there are only two other occurrences), while Isa. 57:15 (just noted) refers to the *heart of the people who are crushed, and to their spirit. The enemy is in focus throughout vv. 3–4, but the "I" as the victim of the enemy action is just as prominent: the first two cola end with "my *person" and "my life" (as objects), the last two with my spirit and my heart (as subjects).[14]

143:5–6. The recollection. NJPS has aorist verbs, NRSV and TNIV present verbs; I have reckoned that the qatal verbs in vv. 5a–b and 6 again refer to past acts that continue into the present and that in this context the yiqtol in v. 5c likely also refers to the past but makes explicit that this act was an ongoing one.

5I have been mindful of the days of old,
I have talked of all your acts,
I would murmur about the deeds of your hands.
6I have stretched out my hands to you,
my whole being has been like thirsty earth in relation to you. (Rise.)

Recollecting how things once were is a common feature of a prayer psalm, adding to the force of the lament by contrasting past and present, and counteracting it by implying possibilities concerning Yhwh's action in the present. It would not be surprising if the locus of the mindfulness, talking, and murmuring was the worship of the temple, which celebrated the deeds of Yhwh's hands, Yhwh's acts, and the days of old. All three verbs come together in Ps. 77:3 and 11–12 [4, 12–13]. In v. 5a the phrase "days of old" corresponds to 77:5 [6], v. 5b as a whole exactly corresponds to 77:12a [13a], and the reference to *murmuring uses the language of Ps. 142:2 and of Ps. 119. Verse 5b–c works *abb′a′*, with the qatal and yiqtol verbs complementing each other and the two *b*-expressions at the center.

The psalm thus takes up familiar language from prayer psalms. But the recollection also has defensive implications. "You have not been mindful of me," Isa. 57:11 declared (Isa. 63:11 adds, "he was mindful of the ancient days," but it is not clear who is the subject of the verb). The suppliant says, "I have been mindful." "Your tongue talks wickedness," Isa. 59:3 declared; "I have talked of all your acts," the suppliant says, suggesting the frequent use of the verb "talk" (*hāgâ*) to suggest talking meditatively in connection with one's relationship with Yhwh.

14. Cf. Fokkelman, *Major Poems*, 3:319.

This link continues in v. 6. “I have stretched out my hands” to this people, says Yhwh (Isa. 65:2), and implies that they have not responded. “I have stretched out my hands to you,” says the suppliant. This time the second colon recalls the language of Ps. 63:1 [2], though the actual phrase “thirsty earth” corresponds to Isa. 32:2.[15] “I am definitely not guilty of failing here,” the suppliant is asserting.

143:7–8b. The renewed plea for Yhwh to respond.

> [7]Answer me quickly, Yhwh,
> my spirit is spent.
> Do not hide your face from me,
> so that I shall be like the people who go down to the Pit.
> [8a–b]Make me hear of your commitment in the morning,
> because it is on you that I have relied.

The three lines are parallel. Each begins with a verbal expression, first “Answer me, and that quickly,” second “Don’t hide your face,” because that issues in the opposite, in extended inaction, and third, “Make me to hear of your *commitment,” speak to me a message that tells me you are going to act in commitment to me. Then in each second colon the plea is backed up by some reasoning, lying in how tough things already are, in the fearful prospect of their getting worse, and in the stance the suppliant has been taking to Yhwh.

Psalm 102 begins, “Yhwh, listen to my plea” (cf. v. 1a above), then urges “Do not hide your face from me,” and subsequently pleads, “Hurry, answer me,” and declares, “My days are spent.” Psalm 28:1 urges Yhwh to listen to the suppliant “or I shall be like the people who go down to the Pit” (and in the next line asks Yhwh to listen to “my prayer for grace”: cf. v. 1b here). Other psalms speak of proclaiming Yhwh’s commitment in the morning (59:16 [17]; 92:2 [3]); this suppliant wants Yhwh to speak of this *commitment at that moment, the archetypal time of deliverance but also a time of worship. Thus the psalm continues to pray in the patterns that earlier psalms offer. But while (for instance) declarations of reliance on Yhwh are common in the Psalms, here a significant intertext is Isa. 59:4, where Yhwh comments on the people’s reliance on wrongdoing. In keeping with previous lines, v. 8b declares that the place where the suppliant has been placing reliance does not give Yhwh reason not to respond to this prayer.

143:8c–10. The plea for guidance and rescue follows on the plea for Yhwh to hear and respond. Again each line includes a plea in the first

15. Stefan Paas (“A Textual Note on Psalm 143,6,” *ZAW* 113 [2001]: 415–18) takes *ʿăyēpâ* as coming from *ʿwp* II and meaning dark, but this also involves reading *b* for *k* (“in” for “like”).

colon and backs it up with some reasoning in the second, except in v. 10c–d, where the second colon simply completes the plea. The distinctive feature of this plea is its recognition that in the present context questions about the suppliant's commitment and about Yhwh's commitment have to interweave. For all the professions of faithfulness and looking to Yhwh, the suppliant is aware of the point that Isa. 56–66 presses, that there have been circumstances in which Yhwh's declining to have mercy and deliver has related to the people's declining to walk Yhwh's way. And for all the professions of faithfulness and looking to Yhwh, the suppliant also shares the awareness expressed in Ps. 141 and Ps. 119 that we need Yhwh to act within us if we are to fulfill a commitment to walking in Yhwh's way. We need Yhwh's teaching, and we need it to reach us in effective ways. But we also need Yhwh's deliverance. These two needs are expressed respectively in the first and third lines and in the second and fourth lines of the section; that is, vv. 8c–d and 10a–b balance, as do vv. 9 and 10c–d. These are not separate needs. The suppliant knows that only as people walk in Yhwh's way can they expect Yhwh to rescue them, and thus asks Yhwh to take action with regard to these very different needs of ours.

8cMake known to me the way that I should walk,
because it is to you that I have lifted myself.
9Rescue me from my enemies, Yhwh,
with you I have covered [myself].

The desire that Yhwh should make known the way we should walk is a dominant motif in Ps. 119, but questions about the way in which the people walked surface in the polemic in Isa. 56–66 with which previous lines of the psalm have links (see 57:17; 65:2). Verse 8c asks to be kept from the failure that the prophecy speaks of. In the parallel colon, as in v. 8b, the crucial factor is the person who is the indirect object of the verb (there it was "on you," here "to you"); "lifted myself," or "lifted up my soul," compares with Pss. 25:1; 86:4. In other contexts it suggests in particular the expression of longing or desire, and here NJPS's paraphrase "set my hope" likely gives the right impression.[16]

On the basis of that openness to Yhwh, the psalm then pleads for rescue from enemies. The words correspond to 59:1 [2]; hence the enemies are now plural, as they are there. The expression in the parallel colon is oddly formulated, but a consideration of it in the context of Isa. 56–66 again

16. Michael L. Barré ("Mesopotamian Light on the Idiom *nāśāʾ nepeš*," *CBQ* 52 [1990]: 46–54) suggests "I took myself to you" in the sense of "I took refuge with you," but this degree of precision involves more inference. Keel suggests "I lift up my life" in the sense of committing my life (*Symbolism*, 321).

helps, because Isa. 59:6 has Yhwh declaring (in another obscure passage) that people will not be able to "cover themselves" (*kāsâ* hitpael) by means of the resources they manufacture. The suppliant has not sought to find other sources of cover, only the protection that lies in Yhwh; again the word order puts the emphasis on the verb's indirect object.

> [10]Enable me to learn to do what is acceptable to you,
> because you are my God.
> May your good spirit lead me
> on level ground.

Verse 10a, too, fits the general concern of Ps. 119, where the plea "enable me to learn" comes eight times (also twice in Ps. 25). But while *rāṣôn*, "what is acceptable," does come in the Psalms (e.g., 40:8 [9]), it is a key term in Isa. 56–66 (see 56:7; 58:5; 60:7, 10; 61:2), so again the slant that the psalm puts on the concern running through Ps. 119 is that it expresses a commitment to avoiding the wrong that Isa. 56–66 attacks. It is necessary to be committed to a life and a form of worship acceptable to Yhwh. The backing for that (v. 10b) restates this commitment. The beginning of the psalm made "I am your servant" an implicit basis for prayer, and v. 12 will pick up that phrase, but it always needs to be complemented by this correlative expression. The fact that I am Yhwh's servant means Yhwh has accepted an obligation to me; the fact that Yhwh is my God means I have accepted an obligation to Yhwh.

Talk of Yhwh's leading and of Yhwh's "good spirit" parallels Neh. 9:19–20 (the latter phrase comes only in these two places in the OT), there to describe the way Yhwh led the people and instructed them on their wilderness journey. The psalm asks that this may also be the suppliant's experience. But again the talk of Yhwh's spirit leading the people fits with Isa. 56–66 (see 57:18; 58:11; 63:10–14). At the moment, the suppliant walks treacherous, uneven ground, and is in danger of falling. The plea for rescue asks for the journey to involve level ground instead of this (cf. Pss. 26:12; 27:11).

143:11–12. The two closing lines of yiqtol statements might be declarations of confidence[17] but are more likely the double wish that often appears in prayer psalms.

> [11]For the sake of your name, Yhwh, will you give me life,
> in your faithfulness will you bring me out of my trouble.

On one hand, the suppliant appeals for life, another recurrent plea in Ps. 119 (the imperative comes nine times); and with "for the sake of

17. So Calvin, *Psalms*, 5:254.

your *name," compare 25:11; 31:3 [4]; 109:21. Once more the concern for Yhwh's name also appears in Isa. 63:12, 14. The appeal to Yhwh's *faithfulness opens up an inclusion with v. 1, as well as making a link with Isa. 59:9, 14, 16, 17, while reference to bringing out of trouble links both with Ps. 142:2, 7 [3, 8] and with Isa. 63:9. Once more the psalm aligns itself with the Psalms' tradition of prayer and also seeks to demonstrate that it passes any test set by Isa. 56–66.

> 12And in your commitment will you put an end to my enemies,
> destroy all the people who are attacking me,
> because I am your servant.

On the other hand, if there is to be an end to trouble, that requires doing something about those enemies (see v. 9). The first verb, *ṣāmat*, is one that mainly appears in the Psalms (e.g., 94:23). Equivalents in other languages can mean "silence"; the Hebrew verb generally means "do away with," but it may sometimes have that other meaning.[18] If so, the ambiguity is resolved by the verb "destroy" (*'ābad* piel). That verb makes for a striking link with 142:4 [5] but also constitutes a plea that Yhwh will fulfill the promise in Isa. 60:12. The appeal to Yhwh's *commitment balances that to Yhwh's faithfulness in v. 11; these attitudes require that Yhwh put down as well as bring life.

Verse 12c offers closing grounds for Yhwh's so acting, pairing with v. 10 and with the opening prepositional expressions in vv. 11a, 11b, and 12a, and thus making up for the lack of such a phrase in v. 12b while also formally providing the psalm with an inclusion (see v. 2) and a tricolon ending. These links make it likely that it implies "destroy them because I am your servant" rather than "they are attacking me because I am your servant," though both will be true.

Theological Implications

"Psalms 7 and 26 are there in the Psalter along with Psalms 143 and 130, the prayers to be judged along with the prayers not to be judged, the profession of righteousness and the confession of sinfulness."[19] But there is some ambiguity about the declaration that "no living person is faithful before you." One implication is that no one is faithful by the standard of Yhwh's faithfulness, which is the ultimate in faithfulness. Yhwh's faithfulness never fails; human faithfulness, toward Yhwh and

18. See *HALOT*; and cf. TNIV here.
19. Mays, *Psalms*, 433.

toward other people, always does, at some point or other. Like Job, the suppliant is thus aware of falling short of Yhwh's expectations of us as human beings, and knows that if Yhwh cares to apply absolute standards when people approach Yhwh's throne, then there is no hope of a favorable hearing (cf. Job 4:17; 7:20–21; 15:14; 25:4). But "no living person is faithful before you" can simply recognize realistically a fact about power and authority (cf. Job 9:2). Whether or not the human being is faithful, the point is that Yhwh is the one who makes the decisions about that. So all suppliants can do is cast themselves on the mercy of the one who has that power.

There is no implication here that in the suppliant's day Israel has become aware of human sinfulness in a way it was not before, as if there were any period in Israel's life when people were not aware that v. 2b was true, in either of its possible senses. At least, recognition of the shortcoming of our human faithfulness is implicit in Israel's narrative from the beginning; great heroes such as Abraham, Moses, and David would have to agree with v. 2. It is also implicit in the Prophets, where Isaiah and Jeremiah would also have to agree with it. Conversely, Job remains convinced of his personal integrity, in the way that the psalms usually are, and his story affirms his integrity, even while he and other participants grant the point made in v. 2. But the suppliant is not paralyzed by this point in the way that Job (not unreasonably) is. The appeal to being Yhwh's servant reflects that; it is the first indication of a way of thought paralleling Ps. 119, where it is a common appeal.[20]

Like the rest of the OT, the psalm thus assumes that generally speaking our sins do not separate us from Yhwh because Yhwh is one who carries our sins, as the Psalms sometimes recall (Pss. 25:18; 32:1, 5; 85:2 [3]; 99:8). The psalm thus helps Paul with his argument in Rom. 3.[21] The basis for understanding Yhwh's relationship with Israel and with the world is that it is the working out of Yhwh's truthfulness and faithfulness rather than being based on nonexistent human faithfulness.

Of course our sins can sometimes separate us from Yhwh; the exception that proves the rule is Isa. 59:2, where the context makes clear that in this instance they have done so. Yhwh can decide that enough is enough, that there will be no mercy on this occasion, and that prayers will not be answered. But generally (as James 2:13 puts it), mercy triumphs over judgment. In Ps. 143, the suppliant wants to make sure that this is one of those occasions and that Yhwh will act in accordance with usual habit. Why should it seem important to make sure of that? The psalm

20. Cf. Gerstenberger, *Psalms*, 2:422.
21. See Richard B. Hays, "Psalm 143 and the Logic of Romans 3," *JBL* 99 (1980): 107–19.

does not imply that the suppliant's suffering results from sin.[22] But the suppliant's stance does contrast with the one that predominates in the Psalms, in which suppliants protest their commitment rather than acknowledging the way they come short of Yhwh's standards. In other similar prayers, the plea is "Decide for me, Yhwh, in accordance with my faithfulness" (7:8 [9]).[23] Here the suppliant wants to make sure of not being caught by Isa. 59:2.

It is not surprising that the awareness expressed by v. 2 leads into the plea for divine guidance in one's religious and moral life expressed in vv. 7–10. When Christians think and pray about divine guidance, we are inclined to relate it to life decisions: Shall I marry this person, shall I apply for this job? When the New Testament speaks of being led by the Spirit, it has in mind moral leading, being led in God's ways, and in this respect it follows the pattern of psalms such as Pss. 119 and 143. As Christians, we are inclined to assume that we generally know what we should do in our moral and religious lives, even though we grant that we may need God's help in enabling us to do it. These psalms make more allowance for our capacity to deceive ourselves about that. They know we need God to break through our self-deception and enable us to see how we should walk and what is acceptable to God.

Surprisingly, again, we might think, the psalm then sees no tension between its openness to God as the one who must decide about our faithfulness and lead us in the right way and the desire for putting down our attackers expressed at the end of the psalm.

22. Lindström, *Suffering and Sin*, 117–28; this conclusion holds whether or not one accepts his account of the psalm's redactional history.

23. Cf. Mays, *Psalms*, 432.

Psalm 144

The Interplay between Past Praise and Present Context

Translation

David's. [LXX adds, concerning Goliath.]

1Yhwh be worshipped, my crag,
the one who trains my hands for encounter,
my fingers for war,
2My committed one[1] and my fastness,
my haven and for me[2] the one who enables me to escape,
My shield and the one in whom I have sheltered,
the one who subdues my people [MT, LXX]/peoples [11QPs[a], Tg,
Syr, Aq, Jerome] under me.[3]

3Yhwh, what is a human being that you should acknowledge him,
a mortal that you should think of him,

1. Lit. "my commitment," abstract for concrete; cf. Jon. 2:8 [9], and the use of "my deliverance" (Pss. 38:22 [23]; 62:2, 6 [3, 7]).

2. *Lî* comes at the end of the colon; MT accents link it with the next colon, but 2 Sam. 22:2 (it does not come in the Ps. 18 version) links it thus with what precedes, where it fits more naturally.

3. Perhaps the abbreviated pl. *'my* was misunderstood; or perhaps *'ammî* was assimilated to Ps. 18:47 [48].

[4]A human being who resembled a breath,
his days like a passing shadow?[4]

[5]Yhwh, spread your heavens and come down,
touch the mountains so that they smoke.
[6]Flash lightning and scatter them,
send your arrows and rout them.
[7]Send your hands[5] from on high,
snatch me away, rescue me,
From the great waters,
from the hand of foreigners,
[8]People whose mouth has spoken emptiness,
and their right hand is a deceitful right hand.

[9]God, a new song I will sing for you,
on a ten-stringed harp I will make music for you,
[10]The one who gives deliverance to kings,
who snatches away his servant David.

From the deadly sword[6] [11]snatch me away,
rescue me, from the hand of foreigners,[7]
People whose mouth has spoken emptiness,
and their right hand is a deceitful right hand.

[12]In that[8] our sons are like saplings,
nourished in their youth,
Our daughters like a corner pillar,
carved[9] according to the pattern of a palace,
[13]Our storehouses full
of provisions of every kind,
Our sheep in thousands,
in myriads in our fields,
[14]our cattle laden,

4. The word order suggests that v. 4 is not simply two regular independent clauses (so EVV): they might be circumstantial ("When a human being resembled . . .").

5. Vrs assimilate to the usual sg. "hand."

6. Lit. "from the bad sword."

7. Making "from the deadly sword" the beginning of a new line generates more plausible lines through vv. 10–11. Perhaps we should also link "rescue me" with the previous colon, to match v. 7.

8. Commentators make heavy weather of the *ʾăšer*, but its varied (though less usual) uses (see BDB, *HALOT*) make it quite possible here. Jerome, Aq, Sym, have "so that." NRSV's turning it into a wish is harder to justify.

9. BDB and *HALOT* derive *mĕḥuṭṭābôt* from *ḥāṭab* I, but that seems to mean "chop." It might come from *ḥāṭab* II, "colored," but Briggs plausibly sees the verb as a by-form of *ḥāṣab*, "hew [stone]" (*Psalms*, 2:524).

There is no breach and there is no going out,[10]
and there is no cry in our squares:
15The good fortune of the people for whom it is like this;
the good fortune of the people whose God is Yhwh.

Interpretation

Psalm 144 contains a rich combination of building blocks, but the prominence of vv. 5–8 and 10c–11 suggests it is a prayer psalm enhanced by a variety of other elements that all contribute to its functioning as a prayer. A long and complex declaration of Yhwh's praiseworthiness and a correlative acknowledgment of humanity's transience (vv. 1–4) lead into the first plea (vv. 5–8). As happens in other psalms, the sequence then repeats; a further declaration of Yhwh's praiseworthiness (vv. 9–10b) leads into a further plea (vv. 10c–11). The second sequence is much shorter than the first, though each time the declaration and the plea are of similar length; the second plea is largely a repetition of the first. The distinctive closing declaration of good fortune (vv. 12–15) may be seen as a variant on a declaration of confidence in Yhwh. The psalm's content suggests it was meant to be prayed by a leader, who is not David but can claim Yhwh's way of relating to David as a way Yhwh might reasonably be expected to relate to him. This might be another king, or a postexilic governor; Aramaisms (the words for "snatch away" and "kind," and the relative in v. 15b) point in the latter direction.[11]

The psalm has a very close relationship with existent psalmody, reworking a number of verses from Ps. 18 and elsewhere. Thus vv. 1–2 take up 18:2, 34, 46–47 [3, 35, 47–48]; v. 3 takes up 18:4 [5]; vv. 5–11 take up 18:9, 14, 16, 17, 44–45, 50 [10, 15, 17, 18, 45–46, 51], and 33:2–3. There are also phrases that parallel Pss. 39, 102 and 104. Verses 12–15 have no similar parallels elsewhere.[12]

David's. [LXX adds, concerning Goliath.]

Heading. See glossary. Tg likewise refers to the sword of v. 10 as Goliath's.

10. The f. ptc. functions as an abstract noun (cf. GKC 122s).

11. Saur (*Königspsalmen*, 249–68) sees the psalm as having a more theological or theoretical role in this context, teaching what the place of the king should be (e.g., subordinate to Yhwh). But Eaton, for instance, links the whole psalm with the monarchic period, seeing Ps. 18 as actually the "answer" to Ps. 144 (*Kingship and the Psalms*, 127–28).

12. On rhetorical patterns in the psalm, see Auffret, *Merveilles à nos yeux*, 262–76.

144:1–2. A declaration about Yhwh's praiseworthiness. In light of where the psalm will go, there is some formal similarity with the opening to Ps. 89, but the praise's function is rather different. There it begins a long quasi-confession of Yhwh as creator and covenanter, a quasi-confession because it eventually leads to a confrontation. "Here its function is to support the subsequent prayer of lament as a persuasive acknowledgment of Yahweh's power."[13]

¹Yhwh be worshipped, my crag,
the one who trains my hands for encounter,
my fingers for war,
²My committed one and my fastness,
my haven and for me the one who enables me to escape,
My shield and the one in whom I have sheltered,
the one who subdues my people [MT, LXX]/peoples [11QPs[a], Tg, Syr, Aq, Jerome] under me.

The declaration about Yhwh as the one to be *worshipped begins by taking up words from the close of Ps. 18 rejoicing in what Yhwh has done for the king; here that will introduce a plea concerning what Yhwh needs to do for the current suppliant. Verse 1 suggests two aspects to what Yhwh has been for the king; v. 2 parallels v. 1, spelling out these two aspects at greater length. There is some tension between them.

First, Yhwh is protector. In v. 1 Yhwh is a *crag where the king can take refuge from danger, like a bird fleeing there, or a human being or an animal taking refuge from a flood. In v. 2, Yhwh is the one who is *committed to the king. Yhwh is a fastness, the place where a man on the run can take refuge from people pursuing him. Or Yhwh is a haven, a high tower (see on 94:22), which might again be a natural stronghold or a structure within the city that can provide another refuge if a besieging army breaks through the city's defenses. Or Yhwh is one who enables the leader to escape, like David coming to the rescue of his family when they had been captured by Amalekites (1 Sam. 30); the "for me" underlines the point. Or Yhwh is a shield, one who deflects the flaming arrows of the enemy and makes sure they do not hit the king. Or Yhwh is the one in whom he has sheltered, like a bird sheltering under its mother's wings (Ps. 91:4) or like a small nation relying on the power of a bigger one (Isa. 30:2).

All that would imply that the suppliant does nothing and leaves Yhwh to take action. But (second), Yhwh is also one who "trains my hands for encounter." There is some irony in the verb, which was just used in the appeal to be taught ways that are acceptable to Yhwh (143:10; cf. Ps. 119).

13. Allen, *Psalms 101–150*, 361.

Here the point is underlined by the parallel colon. It gives precision to "hands" by referring to "fingers." Then, whereas etymologically "encounter" (*qĕrāb*) simply denotes people coming near each other, "war" makes inescapable their reason for doing so. The psalm thus gives two cola to the point about Yhwh's teaching the psalmist how to make war that gets just one colon in 18:34a [35a]. Verse 2 then goes on to describe Yhwh as the one who subdued people "under me."[14] 11QPs[a], Jerome, Syr, and Aq (and an MT "sebir," an alternative reading either rejected or suggested by the Masoretes) have Yhwh subduing "peoples," the word one would expect; it comes in Ps. 18:47 [48]. MT and LXX have a much more interesting declaration about Yhwh subduing "my people," the word used in the version of the psalm in 2 Sam. 22:44. The striking comment fits David's achievement on the way to becoming king over the whole land, and also LXX's heading to Ps. 143 (though not LXX's heading to this psalm). There were many subsequent occasions when a king or governor needed Yhwh to subdue the people under him, though the reading would also provide ideological support for rulers whose people's rebellion was quite justified.

144:3–4. The acknowledgment. Like vv. 1–2, these lines have a formal parallel in Ps. 89 (see vv. 47–48 [48–49])[15] but fulfill a different function. There they seek to arouse divine compassion; here they express self-humbling before God as a follow-up to vv. 1–2. They still thus play a part in preparing the way for the prayer that follows.

> [3]Yhwh, what is a human being that you should acknowledge him,
> a mortal that you should think of him,
> [4]A human being who resembled a breath,
> his days like a passing shadow?

Whereas Ps. 8 expresses astonishment at Yhwh's mindfulness of and attention to human beings in general, Ps. 144 is expressing the leader's astonishment at Yhwh's *acknowledgment of and thinking about him as a human being in the way vv. 1–2 have implied. Why should Yhwh be training his fingers when Yhwh's own fingers have undertaken a much bigger project than this leader could ever dream of (cf. 8:3 [4])? There is little difference in meaning between the two terms for humanity; both suggest humanity in its weakness.

Further, in Ps. 8 the implicit rationale for its rhetorical question lies in the contrast between the immensity of creation over against the

14. *Rādad* more resembles the verb for "subdue" (from *yārad* hiphil) in 2 Sam. 22:48 than the one in Ps. 18 itself (from *dābar* piel).

15. Cf. Werner H. Schmidt, "Kritik am Königtum," in *Probleme biblischer Theologie*, ed. Hans Walter Wolff (G. von Rad Festschrift; Munich: Kaiser, 1971), 440–61 (see 460–61); cf. Allen, *Psalms 101–150*, 361.

lowliness of humanity. Here v. 4 implies a different rationale. Yhwh's being goes back as far as one could imagine and will go on as far as one could imagine. This human being, like all others, is as short-lived as a breath and lives for only a day. The comparison with a breath or a passing shadow parallels passages such as 39:5 [6] and 102:11 [12]. Why should Yhwh bother, as vv. 1–2 have presupposed that Yhwh does? Yet Yhwh does bother.

144:5–8. The plea. There has been no hint so far that the leader stood in need of Yhwh's acting; it would not have been a surprise if the psalm had continued to be an act of praise. Yet without any indication of the nature of this need, the psalm is suddenly pleading vividly for the kind of intervention described in Ps. 18 (the inspiration for vv. 1–2).

5Yhwh, spread your heavens and come down,
touch the mountains so that they smoke.
6Flash lightning and scatter them,
send your arrows and rout them.

Thus v. 5a turns 18:9a [10a] from confession to plea in asking for Yhwh to split apart the sky (cf. Isa. 64:1 [63:19b]; Mark 1:10; not to bend it, as LXX, Jerome have, which makes little sense), to break through it and come down to earth to act.[16] Verse 5b then utilizes language that recalls Yhwh's appearance at Sinai, when the mountain smoked as a result of Yhwh's coming down on it (Exod. 19:18), but more closely corresponds to Ps. 104:32. The psalm urges Yhwh, as well as doing that thing that Ps. 18 testified to, also to do that thing that Yhwh did at Sinai and that Ps. 104 says Yhwh habitually does. The smoking will be the indication that Yhwh really is here and active. The language in vv. 5–6, which also appears in Canaanite portrayals of Baal, goes back to the dramatic and overwhelming experience of a storm with its associated thunder, lightning, rain, and steam rising from the ground. These speak of something that embodies breathtaking power and suggest someone who embodies, controls, harnesses, and utilizes that.

The exhortation in v. 6 reworks 18:14 [15]. Here the "them" lacks an antecedent, at least in the immediately preceding lines, but it is not difficult to determine that it is enemies that the suppliant wants to see scattered and routed. It is Yhwh who will bring that about. As "rout" re-expresses "scatter," so "send your arrows" re-expresses "flash lightning." The flash of lightning in a storm, part of what makes a mountain smoke (v. 5b), provides an image for the weapons Yhwh lets loose in routing

16. Norman C. Habel ("'He Who Stretches Out the Heavens,'" *CBQ* 34 [1972]: 417–30) associates this usage with the employment of the phrase to describe Yhwh's creative activity in terms of pitching a tent, but this hardly works in the present context.

the leader's enemies. The implication will be that all the leader has to do is collect the spoil.

> 7Send your hands from on high,
> snatch me away, rescue me,
> From the great waters,
> from the hand of foreigners,
> 8People whose mouth has spoken emptiness,
> and their right hand is a deceitful right hand.

One might have reckoned that the leader will therefore hardly need the protection or war-making ability that vv. 1–2 spoke of, but the action against the enemies will actually involve saving and rescuing, if not enabling. Verse 7 re-expresses material from 18:16–17 [17–18]; the foreigners come from 18:44–45 [45–46]. The imagery pictures Yhwh in a different way from vv. 5–6, not as coming down from the heavens in the phenomena of a storm but as reaching down from the heavens. The plural "hands" is unusual (the word does not come in Ps. 18); usually Yhwh uses both hands to create but stretches out only one hand to help (cf. 138:7–8).

The plural "hands" also contrasts with the singular "hand" of the enemy. The peril is that of someone caught by a flash flood, to which some of the imagery in vv. 1–2 could relate. Such tumultuous waters become a figure for political powers asserting themselves against Israel, and thus by implication against Yhwh (cf., e.g., 95:4; 124:1–5).

In Ps. 18 the enemies were simply strong. Here they are deceptive. What they say turns out to be empty; their actions belie it. They seal their words by raising their hand in taking an oath (Deut. 32:40) and/or perhaps by shaking hands (Prov. 6:1), but their actions also belie the gesture. The language of deception might especially fit the diplomatic relations of the postexilic period such as are pictured in Nehemiah, though there were also deceptive relations of this kind in the monarchic period. But the selective way Ps. 144 uses Ps. 18 gives a quite different tone to the way it speaks of the enemies, and it makes the language of divine action more metaphorical.[17]

144:9–10b. A further declaration about Yhwh's praiseworthiness is not so surprising; such an undertaking has a place in a prayer psalm as it looks forward to God's having answered the prayer. But the suddenness and unmarked nature of the transition is surprising, and the content of the praise relates more obviously to what Yhwh has already done. The apparent promise of praise is actually more a second declaration

17. See Jannie H. Hunter, "Interpretationstheorie in der postmodernen Zeit," in *Neue Wege*, ed. Seybold and Zenger, 45–62 (see 58–60); cf. Mathys, *Dichter und Beter*, 262–66.

of Yhwh's praiseworthiness that prepares the way for a second plea. It thus parallels the opening of Ps. 89.

> 9God, a new song I will sing for you,
>   on a ten-stringed harp I will make music for you,
> 10a–bThe one who gives deliverance to kings,
>   who snatches away his servant David.

Verse 9 adapts phrases from 33:2–3, turning these into a neatly parallel bicolon. The address to "God" rather than Yhwh contrasts with Ps. 33; it is characteristic of Pss. 42–83, the "Elohistic Psalter." The new song might imply a newly composed *musical composition, accompanied by the *harp, though this may be prosaic; all that might be required to fulfill this commitment to a new song would be a familiar song sung with new enthusiasm in light of Yhwh's new act.

The description of Yhwh as "one who gives *deliverance to kings," which would justify the praise in v. 9, generalizes from 18:50 [51] and 33:16–17. This will be an encouragement to the suppliant, who needs to be clear that Yhwh's action in relation to David was not unique to him. Verse 10b makes the specific point about David, in Ps. 144's own way; the verb *pāṣâ* with this meaning comes only in this psalm (vv. 7, 10, 11). In a preexilic context there would be an ambiguity about whether "David" refers specifically to David ben Jesse or to the current "David" (cf. Hos. 3:5), an appropriate ambiguity because the presupposition of the psalm would be that Yhwh's relating to David (confessed in Ps. 18) should be the pattern for Yhwh's relating to subsequent "Davids."

144:10c–11. A further plea.

> 10cFrom the deadly sword 11snatch me away,
>   rescue me, from the hand of foreigners,
> People whose mouth has spoken emptiness,
>   and their right hand is a deceitful right hand.

So it transpires that vv. 9–10b were not a promise of praise for when the prayer has been answered but the lead-in to a further plea building on the declaration in vv. 9–10b, as vv. 5–8 built on vv. 1–4. Indeed, the plea simply repeats material from vv. 7–8, except that "from the deadly sword" replaces "from the great waters." The expression involves a metonymy, but otherwise replaces a metaphorical expression with a literal one.

144:12–15. The statement of confidence. The last section jumps beyond the relief of an immediate crisis to an experience of the fullness of life when God grants full blessing on top of deliverance. In broad terms it corresponds to the promises of Deut. 28:3–8; it also fits with the expectations that follow from having Yhwh's man leading the people (cf. Ps. 72). And it jumps out of the individual concerns of the leader to those of the nation for whom he fights. I take vv. 12–14 as an extensive extraposed clause anticipating the "like this" of v. 15.[18]

> **12**In that our sons are like saplings,
> nourished in their youth,
> Our daughters like a corner pillar,
> carved according to the pattern of a palace,

This vision of the future looks first to the coming generation, as people often do. The young men will be like plants; the term most often refers to young trees such as olives and vines. These will not be like the plant in Isa. 53:2 but like plants that have been properly fed and watered at the time they needed it, when they were growing.

So the men will be strong, and the young women will be good-looking, shapely like the carved or striped decorative pillars in a palace, specifically at the corners of walls, where their shape is most visible. Tg nicely has the young men nourished on the Torah and the young women fit to be the wives of priests.

> **13**Our storehouses full
> of provisions of every kind,
> Our sheep in thousands,
> in myriads in our fields,
> **14a**our cattle laden,

Two cola then describe the provisions of the people, and two more the sheep that are a source for milk and wool. Verse 14a is less clear. The word for cattle, *ʾallûp*, usually refers to the captain of a unit of the people (cf. TNIV mg). But another root *ʾālap* means "learn, get to know," and linked with it is another word, *ʾallûp*, meaning a friend (someone you know) and another meaning cattle, in the sense of oxen who are trained to help with plowing and other tasks. Although MT's verse division suggests it took it another way, LXX, Jerome give it the last meaning, which fits the context best. Applied to these beasts, the pual participle from *sābal* ("bear a load") will denote the fact that they are laden with the results of a good harvest.[19]

18. LXX takes it as a description of the prosperity of the enemies, which requires it to change the suffixes from first to third person.

19. Cf. Tg. GKC 122e takes the phrase to denote cows that are pregnant, even though the word is m. LXX and Jerome take the word to mean fat.

[14b–c]There is no breach and there is no going out,
and there is no cry in our squares:

Qimchi understands "breach" (*pereṣ*) to refer to a miscarriage, which would fit with MT's verse division. The word does refer to a baby bursting out of the womb in Gen. 38:29, but that links with the baby's name being Perez (explanations issue from names rather than vice versa). *HALOT* likewise understands "going out" to refer to miscarriage. The parent verb *yāṣāʾ* can certainly refer to birth, but it is doubtful if there is any other basis for understanding it to denote miscarriage.[20] Much more commonly "breach" refers to an event such as breaking through a wall or breaking it down (cf. Neh. 1:3; 2:13; 4:3, 7 [3:35; 4:1]; 6:1), and "going out" refers to leaving a place; the two words come together in this connection in Amos 4:2–3. All this suggests that v. 14b–c takes us back to the circumstances presupposed by the psalm, with the king, and therefore the people, under pressure from foes. The vision concerns a time when there will be no more breaching of the city walls and thus no one having to leave the city to go off into exile when the city has been captured, or perhaps no one having to go out from the city to engage a hostile army. And therefore there will be no cry of grief and anguish in the city's streets as people experience death and destruction (for this word for "cry," cf. Jer. 46:12).[21]

[15]The good fortune of the people for whom it is like this;
the good fortune of the people whose God is Yhwh.

Indeed, the *good fortune of that people for whom it is like this, the people whom this leader governs, the people referred to in v. 2. This is a people that has proved what it is like to have Yhwh as its God (not merely to have a king on its throne!). Verse 15b reworks 33:12 (cf. also Deut. 33:29).

Theological Implications

If Ps. 144 comes from the monarchic period, it presupposes that Yhwh's involvement with David is not just for David ben Jesse but for

20. *HALOT* refers to Exod. 21:22, but that is a problem in itself (contrast NRSV with TNIV there).

21. On the terms in v. 14, see further Joseph Ziegler, "Ps 144,14," in *Wort und Geschichte*, ed. Hartmut Gese and Hans Peter Rüger (K. Elliger Festschrift; Neukirchen: Neukirchener Verlag, 1973), 191–97; R. Tournay, "Le psaume cxliv," *RB* 91 (1984): 520–30.

each David who reigns on the throne of Judah. It invites such Davids to go back to Yhwh's dealings with that David and declare that Yhwh is also their protection and education, even as they recognize their human limitations. It invites them to urge Yhwh to intervene in spectacular ways to deliver them and to expect Yhwh to fulfill the vision of a good life for the whole community based on the fact that Yhwh is not merely the monarch's God but the people's God.

If Ps. 144 comes from the Second Temple period, it presupposes that the fact that there is no current David does not mean the Davidic promise is dead. It invites the leader of the community (perhaps a descendant of David, but perhaps not) to worship Yhwh in the way that David did and also to reckon that the possibility of divine intervention can always be urged on Yhwh. The Davidic promise is not irrelevant for today's crises. It does not have to wait for the End to find fulfillment.

That is the implicit assumption in the story of Judah as Chronicles tells it for the Second Temple community. Chronicles also implies another assumption. Perhaps a new Davidic leader will arrive at the End, though this is not of great relevance to the Judean community as it lives its ongoing life. But Yhwh makes with the community the commitment once made to David (Isa. 55:3–5). The Davidic promise can be fulfilled now for this community. It can lay hold on Yhwh in the way the psalm does.

In whichever framework the psalm is used, it takes up the declarations in Ps. 18 and elsewhere but refracts them through the lens of present situation and need. It knows people need Yhwh to teach them how to fight and puts more emphasis on this than Ps. 18 did. It knows their feebleness, something that applies to the leader or the community[22] that uses the psalm in a distinctive way (contrast the general point about humanity in Ps. 8), and it inserts that into its reworking of Ps. 18, as a paradoxical reason why Yhwh should intervene in the community's life, not a reason why Yhwh should not. It is realistic about its experience of Yhwh's intervention and less supranatural in its expectations about this than Ps. 18 was. Yet it does expect a new act of Yhwh to which it will therefore respond with a new song; its God is not one who merely sits in the gallery watching what happened on earth but not acting there.

Its experience of other peoples is more of their deceptiveness than of their brute strength, and it needs deliverance from that. It yearns for a quiet life in which young people grow up strong and handsome, flocks flourish and crops thrive, and war becomes a thing of the past. While it is possible that vv. 12–15 are based on a psalm that is otherwise lost,

22. Oswald Loretz (*Die Königspsalmen* [Münster: Ugarit, 1988], 177–208) sees vv. 12–15 as indicating that the originally royal psalm is democratized for use by the community.

there is no evidence for that, and it is food for thought that perhaps vv. 12–15 are the psalmist's own composition expressing what the community distinctively wanted to say to Yhwh, the vision that they did not find in the praise and prayer material they inherited in anything quite like the form they wanted to articulate, and that they therefore needed to articulate in a unique way. If so, it is the sharpest example of a feature of the psalm as a whole, that it lives with a conversation between what it found in the praise and prayer of the past and what it needed to say in its context. Merely to keep saying what was said in the past does not do; merely saying what we think we need to say does not do. The interplay between these is vital to a real and true community relationship with God and a life of prayer.

Psalm 145

Thine Is the Kingdom, the Power, and the Glory, Forever and Ever

Translation

Praise. David's.

[ʾ] 1I will exalt you,[1] my God, the king,[2]
 and worship your name forever and ever.
[*b*] 2Every day I will worship you
 and praise your name forever and ever.

[*g*] 3Yhwh is great and much to be praised;[3]
 of his greatness there is no fathoming.
[*d*] 4One generation shall laud your deeds to another,
 declare your mighty acts.[4]

1. The yiqtol might denote "I will exalt" or "I do exalt"; the cohortative in v. 1b resolves the ambiguity. Verse 2 follows the same sequence.

2. The noun with the article is in the vocative (cf. GKC 126e; JM 137g; DG 30, remark 1; *IBHS* 13.5.2).

3. As at 96:4; 113:3, the context suggests that the ptc. is gerundive (contrast NJPS).

4. LXX, Tg have sg. "your might." A jussive understanding of the yiqtols here and in following verses fits better with the cohortatives and gerundive in vv. 1–3, though Fokkelman (*Major Poems*, 2:312) comments that "there is hardly any distinction between the

[*h*] **5**Of your majestic and glorious splendor
and of your wondrous acts I will murmur. [MT]
[or] Of your majestic and glorious splendor they shall speak;
of your wonders I will murmur. [11QPs[a], LXX][5]
[*w*] **6**And people shall talk of the might of your awesome acts,
and your greatness [Q, LXX, Tg]/great acts [K, Jerome]—I will proclaim it.[6]

[*z*] **7**They shall pour forth the celebration of your great goodness,[7]
resound at your faithfulness.[8]
[*ḥ*] **8**Yhwh is gracious and compassionate,
long-tempered and great in commitment.
[*ṭ*] **9**Yhwh is good to all,
his compassion is over all he has made.

[*y*] **10**All that you made shall confess you, Yhwh,
and the people committed to you shall worship you.

[*k*] **11**They shall talk of the glory of your reign,
speak of your might.[9]
[*l*] **12**To make his mighty acts[10] known to human beings,
the glorious splendor of his reign.[11]
[*m*] **13**Your reign is a reign over all ages,
your rule over all generations.

[*n*] Yhwh is trustworthy in his words,
committed in all his deeds. [11QPs[a], LXX][12]
[*s*] **14**Yhwh upholds all who are falling,
lifts up all who are bowed down.
[ʿ] **15**The eyes of all look to you
and you give them their food at its time.
[*p*] **16**You open your hand
and fill all living things with favor.[13]

---

poet's use of the indicative and of the gerund." TNIV has present-tense verbs, but these are harder to fit with the context.

5. LXX has a third-person pl. verb in v. 5b.

6. LXX, Tg have a third-person pl. verb.

7. Following DG 42, remark 1, in reckoning that the adj. precedes the noun. BDB 913a; GKC 132b suggest rather that *rab* is treated as a noun, "the greatness of your goodness."

8. Sym, Jerome have "faithful deeds."

9. Jerome has "mighty deeds."

10. LXX has "your might."

11. LXX has "your reign."

12. 11QPs[a] has "God" for "Yhwh."

13. Tg assumes that the colon refers to the *rāṣôn* of the living things, that is, "their favor," or "their desire," in keeping with the use of the word in PBH (*DTT* 1492), but this

[*ṣ*] **17**Yhwh is faithful in all his ways,
committed in all his deeds.
[*q*] **18**Yhwh is near to all who call him,
to all who call him in truth.
[*r*] **19**He implements his favor for the people who revere him,[14]
and listens to their cry for help and delivers them.
[*š*] **20**Yhwh watches all who are dedicated to him[15]
and all the faithless he destroys.

[*t*] **21**My mouth shall speak Yhwh's praise,
and all flesh shall worship his holy name
forever and ever.

Interpretation

This praise psalm is an incomplete alphabetical psalm in MT, lacking a *nûn* line. Since many alphabetical psalms are incomplete, there is no presumption that it was originally complete. 11QPs[a] and LXX provide a *nûn* line; we do not know whether this tradition remedies a lack in the original or preserves a lost line.[16] The stimulus and constraint of the alphabetical form enable the psalm to expound the variegated nature of the act of praise and its content. Its alphabetic structure constitutes an appropriate poetic form in that connection. The psalm offers praise from A to Z to God described from A to Z. "The entire alphabet, the source of all words, is marshalled in praise of God."[17]

The psalm thus incorporates the two classic elements in a praise psalm, the nature of praise and the reasons for praise, the latter in terms of Yhwh's acts and personal qualities. There is no exhortation to other people to praise Yhwh, such as usually appears in a praise psalm and will appear through Pss. 146–50, yet Calvin is doubtless right that "David

meaning does not otherwise occur in the OT; LXX and Jerome more plausibly refer it to Yhwh's *rāṣôn* (cf. *HALOT*).

14. Not only Tg but other Vrs (and *HALOT*) take *rāṣôn* here to refer to the "favor," or desire of the people who revere Yhwh, but the fact that the word never means this elsewhere in the OT is again an obstacle (see on v. 16); rather the genitive is objective, as in 106:4, not subjective.

15. 11QPs[a] has "who revere him."

16. Barnabas Lindars ("The Structure of Psalm cxlv," *VT* 39 [1989]: 23–20) argues strongly that the *n* line is original, Reuven Kimelman ("Psalm 145," *JBL* 113 [1994]: 37–58 [see 49–51]) that it is secondary. Babylonian Talmud *Berakot* 4b sees in its omission a desire not to recall the declaration that Israel "fell" (*nāpal*).

17. Adele Berlin, "The Rhetoric of Psalm 145," in *Biblical and Related Studies Presented to Samuel Iwry*, ed. Ann Kort and Scott Morschauser (Winona Lake, IN: Eisenbrauns, 1985), 17–22 (see 18).

does not so much tell us what he would do himself, as stir up and urge all others to this religious service of offering to God the praises due to his name."[18]

While working with the alphabet, the psalm also has a second structure or movement of thought:

A commitment to worship by the psalmist (vv. 1–2)
  Reasons for worship: Yhwh's greatness (vv. 3–6)
    Reasons for worship: Yhwh's goodness (vv. 7–9)
A commitment to worship by creation and by the community (v. 10)
  Reasons for worship: Yhwh's greatness (vv. 11–13b)
    Reasons for worship: Yhwh's goodness (vv. 13c–20)
A commitment to worship by the psalmist and by all creation (v. 21)

This movement of thought is not formally marked. There is no "because" to bridge the commitment to worship and the reasons for worship, and references to commitment to worship spill over into the sections on the reasons for worship in vv. 3–7 and 11–12. Conversely, the reason for worship in terms of Yhwh's greatness is anticipated in v. 1 with the acclamation of Yhwh as king. In this sense the outline of the psalm just suggested simplifies it, and other ways of describing its structure could bring out other aspects of its nature. But the movement from speaking of Yhwh's greatness to speaking of Yhwh's goodness is without marker or spillover; vv. 3–6 and 11–13b are all about Yhwh's greatness, vv. 7–9 and 13c–20 are all about Yhwh's goodness, with the last of these sections subdividing into four lines relating to the whole creation and four relating to Yhwh's people. Yet the movement between these parts of the psalm is seamless, which encourages the making of a link between greatness and goodness and the inference that Yhwh's greatness expresses itself in goodness.

Within this structure, the psalm underlines its points in two ways. One is the repetition of individual words or similar expressions. The word "all/every" comes in vv. 2a, 9a, 9b, 10a, 13a, 13b, 13d, 14a, 14b, 15a, 16b, 17a, 17b, 18a, 18b, 20a, 20b, 21b. It thus links with worship, with Yhwh's greatness, and with Yhwh's goodness, though especially with the last. The word points to the all-embracing nature of the worship of Yhwh (it covers all time, all people, and all creation) and to the fact that Yhwh's greatness extends to all ages, but it especially emphasizes

18. *Psalms*, 5:270.

the all-embracing reach of Yhwh's goodness. The universality suggested by the use of the word "all" is also expressed by the use of the varied temporal expressions for "forever" (vv. 1–2, 21) and by references to generations (vv. 4, 13a–b).

The other way the psalm underlines its point is by the accumulation of words of similar meaning. It refers to exalting, worshipping, praising, lauding, murmuring, talking, proclaiming, pouring forth, resounding, confessing, and speaking (but not fathoming). It refers to Yhwh's greatness, mighty acts, majesty, glory, splendor, wondrous acts, might, awesome acts, reign, and rule. It refers to Yhwh's goodness, faithfulness, grace, compassion, long-temperedness, commitment, and trustworthiness. It describes Yhwh upholding, lifting up, giving, opening the hand, filling, being near, listening, delivering, watching, and destroying. The addition of those concrete accounts of the way Yhwh's goodness expresses itself also has the effect of doubling the length of the second section on Yhwh's goodness, vv. 13c–20. The result is to accumulate a many-sided though overlapping account of the nature of worship, of Yhwh's greatness, of Yhwh's goodness, and of Yhwh's concrete positive involvement with humanity.[19]

Aspects of the psalm's language (e.g., the verb "lift up," mostly known from Aramaic; the word "reign"; and the use of *l* to mark the direct object in vv. 14a, 14b, and 16) suggest it comes from the Second Temple period. Westermann argues that it illustrates the way fellowship with God has become a matter of private devotion in this period,[20] but the argument is thin and sits oddly with the later prominence of the psalm in synagogue worship; *b. Berakot* 4b declares that "whoever repeats it three times a day may be sure that he is a child of the world to come." One can easily imagine that it was already used in worship in the Second Temple period; this might explain some of the variants between MT and the LXX and other traditions listed in the textual notes. The 11QPs[a] version seems to be adapted, especially by the addition of a refrain like that in Ps. 136, so as to function as a worship text. Although "I" features in vv. 1–6 and 21, there is no particular indication that its praise would be particular to an individual or to a leader; the "I" is that of each worshipper or of a worship leader speaking for the community.

19. On rhetorical features of the psalm, see Leon J. Liebreich, "Psalms 34 and 145 in the Light of Their Key Word," *HUCA* 27 (1956): 181–92 (see 187–90); Pierre Auffret, "Essai sur la structure littéraire du Psaume 145," in *Mélanges bibliques et orientaux en l'honneur du M. Henri Cazelles*, ed. A. Caquot and M. Delcor, AOAT 212 (Neukirchen: Neukirchener Verlag, 1981), 15–31; Berlin, "Psalm 145"; Kimelman, "Psalm 145"; Lindars, "Structure of Psalm cxlv."

20. *Living Psalms*, 224.

Praise. David's.

Heading. See glossary. Psalm 145 is the last David psalm, bringing Pss. 138–45 to a conclusion, as well as the first of a sequence of praise psalms with which the Psalter closes. "Praise" comes in a heading only here; in the psalm it recurs in v. 21, so that the word forms an inclusion.

145:1–2. The psalmist's commitment to worship.

[ʾ] 1I will exalt you, my God, the king,
and worship your name forever and ever.
[*b*] 2Every day I will worship you
and praise your name forever and ever.

The opening first-person yiqtol verb provides the psalm with a word beginning with *ʾālep* (*ʾărômimkā*), whose objects affirm that Yhwh is both "my God," the one committed to me and to whom I am committed, and "king," announcing a theme the psalm will develop. Human communities physically exalt people as a way of signifying that they are to be honored, and this provides a metaphor for our honoring of God; it is like putting a human king on a high throne. The second colon goes beyond the first in speaking of a *worship of Yhwh's *name that will go on "forever and ever," a "devotional hyperbole."[21] Literally, it will go on for my lifetime, but that is forever as far as I am concerned. This is a king whose exaltation far exceeds that of a human king, in the attitude we take to it and in how long it lasts.

The psalm then reaffirms the lifelong nature of this *worship and complements that with a reference to its frequency (*bĕkol-yôm*). The time references form a frame around the *abb′a′* line. Within the frame, likewise the physical prostration implied by "worship" is complemented by its verbal (or nonverbal, but at least vocal) enthusiasm as *praise of Yhwh's *name.

145:3–6. Yhwh's greatness. In the manner of a praise psalm, after vv. 1–2 the psalm comes to focus more on the content of or reasons for this praise; indeed, we might see this as the content of the praise that vv. 1–2 undertook to offer. The theme of Yhwh's greatness is announced in the opening colon; the term recurs as an inclusion in the closing colon.

[*g*] 3Yhwh is great and much to be praised;
of his greatness there is no fathoming.
[*d*] 4One generation shall laud your deeds to another,
declare your mighty acts.

21. Goulder, *Psalms of the Return*, 280.

The *praise begins with a statement spelling out the implications of the opening description of Yhwh as king. Yhwh is, simply, great (*gādôl*). We say someone is great when we are astonished at the dimensions and magnitude of their achievements. The second colon goes beyond the first in emphasizing that Yhwh's achievements are not merely monumental but so immense that we could not get our minds around them.

It follows that Yhwh should be praised not only by me in the whole of my lifetime (vv. 1–2) but beyond my lifetime, from one generation (*dôr*) to another. This praise is now described as lauding (*šābaḥ*), which suggests commendation (the affirmation "Yhwh is great" would count), and declaring (*nāgad* hiphil), which suggests speaking of things that have happened, of things someone has done. The line works *abcc′b′* with the verbs framing the objects that people will laud and declare: Yhwh's deeds and, to be more specific, Yhwh's mighty acts. The word *gĕbûrâ* is not common in this plural, concrete sense. It can refer to the events at the beginning of Israel's story (Deut. 3:24) but more often to the mighty acts that subsequent generations experience in their own lives (Pss. 20:6 [7]; 71:16; 106:2).

[*h*] 5Of your majestic and glorious splendor
and of your wondrous acts I will murmur. [MT]
[or] Of your majestic and glorious splendor they shall speak;
of your wonders I will murmur. [11QPsa, LXX]
[*w*] 6And people shall talk of the might of your awesome acts,
and your greatness [Q, LXX, Tg]/great acts [K, Jerome]—I will proclaim it.

The first colon is a rare three-word construct chain of synonyms, "the splendor [*hādār*] of the majesty of your glory"; but (alphabetic considerations aside) one could put the words in any order as they pile up to highlight and emphasize, simply, Yhwh's honor, magnificence, and grandeur. "Wondrous acts" then parallels these qualities; it is in these acts that the qualities are expressed and evidenced. They are again the events in the time of Moses but also the wonders Israel continues to experience in its history (105:2, 5; 106:7, 22; 107:8, 15, 21, 31). Speaking is sharpened as *murmuring; in 11QPsa and LXX, third- and first-person verbs complement each other in the parallelism.

That parallelism recurs in v. 6, with "and" first providing the needed *w* for the line. "Awesome deeds" once again characterizes events such as the Red Sea deliverance and events in Israel's later experience (65:5 [6]; 66:3, 5; 106:22). These are not just powerful (v. 4) and amazing (v. 5) but deeds that draw forth reverence and submission to Yhwh. In v. 6b "proclaiming" is more forceful than "talking of," and in Q abstract "greatness" builds on the reference to the concrete acts, the reverse order to that in v. 5.

145:7–9. Yhwh's goodness. Again, the theme is announced in the opening line and repeated in the closing line as an inclusion.

> [*z*] 7They shall pour forth the celebration of your great goodness,
> resound at your faithfulness.
> [*ḥ*] 8Yhwh is gracious and compassionate,
> long-tempered and great in commitment.

People will thus bubble up with such talk of Yhwh, gushing it forth like a spring or fountain gushing water. The talk is now characterized as the commemorative celebration (*zēker*) of Yhwh's "great *goodness," which would especially happen in worship. To restate the point, they will *resound at Yhwh's *faithfulness. Those mighty, wondrous, awesome deeds were not merely deeds of power, designed to arouse astonishment, but deeds that expressed goodness and faithfulness. Or rather, part of their might, wonder, and awesomeness lay in the way they served goodness and faithfulness.

The need for a *ḥêt* word leads to describing Yhwh as gracious (*ḥannûn*), one of the first terms in the classic description of Yhwh in Exod. 34:6–7, which brings with it other terms from that description: compassionate, long-tempered, and big in *commitment. The order with graciousness first is common in later writings (e.g., Neh. 9:31).[22] These were also qualities of Yhwh's mighty, wondrous, and awesome deeds, as the original self-revelation in Exod. 34:6–7 implied.

> [*ṭ*] 9Yhwh is good to all,
> his compassion is over all he has made.

But the psalm likes the word *good (*ṭôb*; cf. v 7), which does not appear in Exod. 34:6–7 but sums up much of its revelation concerning what Yhwh is; here it is spelled out in compassion, the first word that characterizes Yhwh in that revelation.

So far the psalm has implicitly concerned itself with Yhwh's relationship with Israel and Yhwh's deeds in Israel's history. Other praise psalms invite the whole world to join in praising Yhwh for these acts (cf. v. 21). Psalm 145 goes beyond that in speaking of Yhwh's generosity and compassion extending to everyone or everything, to all creation. It never defines "everyone" or "everything," and initially we might assume it refers to everyone within Israel. But its terms sound as if they refer to all humanity and all creation, and the more the psalm repeats such

22. Briggs, *Psalms*, 2:529.

terms, the more implausible it becomes to limit their reference. Yes, Yhwh is committed to all creation. One could see this as an outworking of Yhwh's being not only "my king" or "our king" but "the king" (v. 1). A focus on Israel does not stop the psalm from keeping the whole world in mind.

145:10. The whole world's commitment to worship. The declaration follows on that in vv. 1–2, but now the worship is not confined to the psalmist, appropriately in light of vv. 3–9.

> [*y*] 10All that you made shall confess you, Yhwh,
> and the people committed to you shall worship you.

The *yôd* line thus has that whole creation *confessing Yhwh (*yôdûkā*), in light of v. 9, and parallels that with all the *committed people offering their *worship, in light of the earlier comments on Yhwh's marvelous acts on behalf of Israel. The two cola work *abb′a′*.

145:11–13b. Yhwh's greatness. The theme is picked up from vv. 3–6, but it is now expounded in terms of Yhwh's reign or kingship, the motif introduced in the very first colon of the psalm. The word "reign" comes in the first and last lines as an inclusion. It might be significant that this theme features in the *klm* lines of the poem, which correspond to the root letters of *melek* (king) in reverse order.[23]

> [*k*] 11They shall talk of the glory of your reign,
> speak of your might.
> [*l*] 12To make his mighty acts known to human beings,
> the glorious splendor of his reign.
> [*m*] 13a–bYour reign is a reign over all ages,
> your rule over all generations.

Glory (*kābôd*), talk, and might recur; "speak" parallels "talk" without adding much color, while "reign" sits happily alongside terms such as "greatness" and "majesty" and picks up the opening acknowledgment of Yhwh as king.

To generate a *lāmed* word for v. 12 the psalm uses an infinitive (*lĕhôdîaʿ*), thus for the only time making one line directly dependent on another rather than self-standing. The rest of the line reuses words we have become familiar with in the psalm.

The psalm then runs with the word "reign," which provides it with a *mêm* word (*malkût*), and in this connection it returns to talk of "forever" and of the generations. In vv. 1–2 that talk related to human acknowledgment; in v. 13a–b it relates to the reign that this acknowledgment

23. So Wilfred G. E. Watson, "Reversed Rootplay in Ps 145," *Bib* 62 (1981): 101–2.

recognizes. The line is a variant on Dan. 4:3, 34 [3:33; 4:31]; perhaps the formula comes from the context of worship and Nebuchadnezzar is portrayed as giving Yhwh the recognition that belongs in that worship.

145:13c–20. Yhwh's goodness, expressed in commitment. 11QPs[a] and LXX divide vv. 13c–20 into two four-line subsections. Each begins with a double noun clause affirming Yhwh's goodness, followed by identical second cola affirming Yhwh's commitment. Each opening line is then followed by three verses spelling out the implications of that description more concretely; vv. 13c–16 do that for creation in general, vv. 17–20 for Yhwh's people.[24]

> [*n*] **13c–d**Yhwh is trustworthy in his words,
> committed in all his deeds. [11QPs[a], LXX]
> [*s*] **14**Yhwh upholds all who are falling,
> lifts up all who are bowed down.

Glory, reign, might, majesty, splendor, and rule are worryingly power-focused words. It is therefore reassuring that v. 13c–d in the version in 11QPs[a], LXX reverts to the moral qualities of this powerful being, who is trustworthy (*neʾĕmān*; *true) and *committed, in word and deed, and in all these words and deeds.

The psalm's new direction might seem surprising because kings and other people in power can be tempted to ignore the weak. But it might seem predictable because that is exactly not what they are supposed to do. As wealth is granted in order to be shared, so power is granted in order to be exercised on behalf of the needy. Yhwh's commitment as king is thus expressed in v. 14 in a concern for such people. The verbs and the participles complement each other, the second colon going beyond the first. Where people are falling, Yhwh puts out a hand to take hold of them and prop them up (*sômēk*) in order to stop them from actually falling over. Where they are bowed down, Yhwh lifts them up again. If Yhwh stops people from falling, how can there be people who need lifting up? The first participle is active, the second passive, so perhaps v. 14b refers to people who have been knocked over by someone. Or perhaps the psalm makes the two affirmations because that is how things are. Yhwh does stop people from falling. If that does not work out, then Yhwh lifts them up. Or perhaps it is affirming that there is no one but Yhwh who upholds and lifts up; there is no other God active in our lives to whom people may look.

> [ʿ] **15**The eyes of all look to you
> and you give them their food at its time.

24. Cf. Allen, *Psalms 101–150*, 369.

[*p*] **16**You open your hand
and fill all living things with favor.

Yhwh's upholding and lifting in itself would make everyone's eyes (*ʿênê*) look to Yhwh; the verb *śābar* (piel) suggests a looking with expectancy. But v. 15b indicates that the psalm has gone in another direction. It has in mind the resource to which the whole creation looks for food, and it affirms that the one who unfailingly provides support also unfailingly provides sustenance. Or (in parallel with the possibility raised in connection with v. 14) given that sustenance sometimes fails, perhaps the psalm's point is that Yhwh is the only one who ever provides sustenance; there is no other God to look to. Yhwh does so "at its time." "There is a certain time appointed for harvest, vintage, and hay crop. . . . We have no small reason to admire the seasonableness with which the different kinds of fruit and aliment are yearly produced."[25]

Are we then worryingly subservient to nature's time frame or schedule (which might not match human need)? First, Yhwh gives with an open hand (*pôtēaḥ*), like a person feeding animals who allows them to take as much as they like. Yhwh does not dispense in small, measured amounts. The parallel colon re-expresses the point by speaking of Yhwh filling all living things; the word "all" once again recurs. All living things get enough to make them quite satisfied, and all this is an expression of Yhwh's favor or good pleasure (cf. 106:4), of Yhwh's love.

These two lines are variants of 104:27–28.

[*ṣ*] **17**Yhwh is faithful in all his ways,
committed in all his deeds.
[*q*] **18**Yhwh is near to all who call him,
to all who call him in truth.

The noun clause parallels that comprising v. 13c–d and opens the second subsection within vv. 13c–20. The need of a *ṣādê* word leads to a reaffirmation that Yhwh is *faithful (*ṣaddîq*), which draws in its train the declaration that Yhwh is *committed. Once again the psalm declares that this applies to all Yhwh's ways and all Yhwh's deeds.

Declaring that Yhwh is near (*qārôb*) to all who call ("all" again recurs twice in v. 18) follows on from preceding verses, but it also returns the psalm to its focus on Yhwh's own people, who in a more explicit sense call Yhwh. They can cry out in danger or hunger, and Yhwh is near; they just need to call "in truth." The English expression may suggest that people's inner feelings correspond to their outward profession or

25. Calvin, *Psalms*, 5:279. See also the comment on Ps. 104:27.

act, but the biblical expression is more inclined to suggest that people's profession and act at one point must be consistent with their profession and act at another: for instance, it would not count as true calling if they were hedging their bets and also calling Baal. "The contrast to *bʾmt* . . . would be *lšwʾ* (Exod. 20:7)."[26]

> [*r*] **19**He implements his favor for the people who revere him,
> and listens to their cry for help and delivers them.
> [*š*] **20**Yhwh watches all who are dedicated to him
> and all the faithless he destroys.

Verse 19 implicitly links with v. 18b: people who call in truth are people who *revere Yhwh. For them Yhwh does act with favor (*rāṣôn*). That is then spelled out in a new way as listening and *delivering, though listening and delivering was implicit in all the earlier talk about wonders and awesome deeds done for Israel, for these are Yhwh's way of delivering. "Calling in truth" is spelled out yet again by the reference to a "*cry for help"; who we cry out to when we need help indicates whom we revere.

The last line of description of Yhwh coheres with vv. 18–19's move from Yhwh's regular care for people to Yhwh's response to them in crises. Watching (*šômēr*) the people who are *dedicated to Yhwh and destroying the *faithless to stop them from acting oppressively is how Yhwh exercises that care. The *abb'a'* order of the cola expresses their complementary and contrasting nature.

145:21. The psalmist's and the whole world's closing commitment to worship.

> [*t*] **21**My mouth shall speak Yhwh's praise,
> and all flesh shall worship his holy name
> forever and ever.

The closing tricolon moves back to the giving of *praise rather than the content of praise; the word (*tĕhillâ*) both provides the *t* word and forms an inclusion with the heading to the psalm. *Worship also recurs in vv. 1 and 21 and near the center, in v. 10. Verse 21a, like vv. 1–2, again expresses the worshipper's personal commitment to praise. Verse 21b–c, like the main part of the psalm, once more moves on to the inclusive nature and permanence of this worship. "*Holy *name" is a new expression, but holiness sums up the metaphysically unique person of Yhwh that the psalm has explored in many of its epithets for Yhwh. The opening two cola work *abb'a'*.

26. Kraus, *Psalms 60–150*, 548.

Theological Implications

The prayer encouraged by this psalm is the kind embodied in the Lord's Prayer,[27] which works out the psalm's implications.

The psalm begins by describing Yhwh as "my God" and emphasizes the great acts of Yhwh's love toward Israel, but it goes on to address Yhwh as "*the* king" and to emphasize Yhwh's being God of the whole world, of the whole of reality. To use a phrase that became popular in the Second Temple period, Yhwh is the God of heaven. The Lord's Prayer sums this up in addressing God as our Father who is in heaven. The psalm urges that Yhwh be exalted, worshipped, and praised; the Lord's Prayer urges that God's name be hallowed. The psalm announces that its concern is Yhwh as *the* king, and Kraus describes *malkût* as "the principal term in Psalm 145."[28] It thus helps to explicate what God's kingdom or reign is. It speaks by faith of the world acknowledging the glory of Yhwh's reign; the Lord's Prayer says, "May your reign become a reality." The psalm knows that kingship means being able to exercise your power on behalf of the needy, and it thus has Yhwh filling all things with divine favor, divine desire, divine will; the Lord's Prayer says, "May your will be done." The psalm rejoices in Yhwh's goodness, has people looking to Yhwh for their needs, and has Yhwh giving generously to them; the Lord's Prayer asks for bread for each day. The psalm knows that Yhwh is gracious, compassionate, and long-tempered; the Lord's Prayer can therefore pray for the forgiveness of our sins. The psalm knows it is possible not to call on Yhwh in truth; the Lord's Prayer asks for us not to be led into temptation, pulled into falsehood and false ways and the acknowledgment of false gods. The psalm has Yhwh upholding the falling, lifting up the bowed down, watching over us, and destroying the faithless who oppress us; the Lord's Prayer asks that we may be delivered from evil. "Thine is the kingdom, the power, and the glory, forever and ever" is the thought that the psalm expands.[29] "Forever and ever, Amen" is a conclusion it emphasizes.

27. Cf. Erich Zenger, "'Dass alles Fleisch den Namen seiner Heiligung segne,'" *BZ* 41 (1997): 1–27; cf. Reinhold G. Kratz, "Die Gnade des täglichen Brots," *ZTK* 89 (1992): 1–40 (see 25–28).

28. *Psalms 60–150*, 549.

29. Kirkpatrick, *Psalms*, 813.

Psalm 146
On Leaders

Translation

[1]Praise Yah.

Praise Yhwh, my soul;
[2]I will praise Yhwh through my life,
I will make music for my God as long as I live.

[3]Do not rely on leaders, on a human being,
with whom there is no deliverance.
[4]His breath goes, he returns to his ground:
on that day his deliberations have perished.
[5]The good fortune of the people who have the God of Jacob as their help,[1]
whose expectation is in Yhwh their God,
[6]Maker of the heavens and the earth,
the sea and all that is in them.

He is one who keeps faith forever,
[7]exercises authority for the oppressed,
gives food to the hungry.
Yhwh frees prisoners,

1. On the *b* of identity, see GKC 119i; JM 133c; *IBHS* 11.2.5e.

[8]Yhwh opens the eyes of the blind,
Yhwh lifts up the bowed down.
Yhwh is dedicated to the faithful,
[9]Yhwh watches over strangers.
The orphan and widow he relieves,[2]
and the way of the faithless he subverts.
[10]Yhwh will reign forever,
your God, Zion, for all generations.

Praise Yah.[3]

Interpretation

The opening and closing bidding to "Praise Yah" (vv. 1a, 10c) forms an inclusion around Ps. 146 MT; it recurs in each of the last four psalms that follow in MT, and there are other points of connection between them.[4] The bidding marks the psalm as a praise psalm, which is confirmed by the tricolon opening the main body of the psalm (vv. 1b–2) that declares a personal intention to praise Yhwh. In terms of a praise psalm, the subsequent challenge to rely on Yhwh (vv. 3–6b) is surprising, though it does follow logically on a praise affirmation concerning Yhwh. The main body of the psalm (vv. 6c–10) develops the description of who Yhwh is, backing up the exhortation to reliance and providing the basis and the content for the exhortation to praise.

Verses 1–2, 10c and vv. 3–6b thus give contrary indications regarding the psalm's essential nature. One suggests an act of praise of the kind one expects in the Psalter, the other an exhortation to reliance on Yhwh with a didactic concern; near the end of the psalm, vv. 9c–10b with its "your God" is also implicit exhortation and recalls the way the Psalter itself opens.[5] The psalm thus holds praise and exhortation in balance. Since the "I" of vv. 1–2 goes on to address the community in general in vv. 3–4, this "I" is likely a leader; and the content suggests a minister rather than a king or governor.

The psalm takes up phrases from Ps. 145 in vv. 2, 5, 7, 8, and 10 and contains variants on many other psalms and other passages from the

2. *ʿÛd* polel, from a verb from the same root as *ʿôd*.
3. LXX, Jerome lack this phrase.
4. Emphasized by John S. Kselman, "Psalm 146 in Its Context," *CBQ* 50 (1988): 587–99; Patrick D. Miller, "The End of the Psalter," *JSOT* 80 (1998): 103–10; Erich Zenger, "'Dass alles Fleisch den Namen seiner Heiligung segne,'" *BZ* 41 (1997): 1–27; idem, "The Composition and Theology of the Fifth Book of Psalms," *JSOT* 80 (1998): 77–102.
5. Mays, *Psalms*, 440.

Scriptures, as did Pss. 142 and 143. So it is another example of the praise of the present identifying with and building on the praise of the past.

> [1a]Praise Yah.

146:1a. Introduction. "Once again . . . *Alleluia* knocks at the doors of our hearts";[6] it is sad that this word is used so casually, taking Yhwh's name in vain.[7] LXX adds "Haggai and Zechariah's," which coheres with the link between vv. 7c–9a and Isa. 42:7 and with Qimchi's comment that the opening exhortation to *praise *Yah is a response to a sense from the holy spirit that the Jews in exile are to be gathered and brought home. Jerome also links it with the reference to Zion in v. 10, which he takes to point to Zion's imminent restoration.[8] Its location raises the further question whether "Praise Yah" in this psalm and in some subsequent psalms is a heading rather than a part of the psalm that would be used in reciting it.[9]

146:1b–2. A (further) exhortation and commitment to praise.

> [1b]Praise Yhwh, my soul;
> [2]I will praise Yhwh through my life,
> I will make music for my God as long as I live.

As well as being an opening exhortation to people in general (v. 1a), *praise is now an exhortation to the self (*person; v. 1b) and a personal declaration of intent (v. 2). In the parallel cola of v. 2, the enthusiastic and ecstatic nature of praise is accompanied by the making of *music, and the commitment involved in this is underlined by the two striking temporal phrases. The Midrash points out that as we cannot praise God when we are dead (e.g., 115:17) and as we do not know when our time will come (Eccles. 9:12), we would be as well to get on with praising God now.[10] The three cola recall Ps. 104:1, 33, 35.

146:3–6b. An exhortation to reliance on Yhwh.

> [3]Do not rely on leaders, on a human being,
> with whom there is no deliverance.
> [4]His breath goes, he returns to his ground:
> on that day his deliberations have perished.

6. Cassiodorus, *Psalms*, 3:432.
7. Spurgeon, *Treasury of David*, 6:400.
8. *Homilies*, 1:393.
9. Cf. Theodoret, *Psalms*, 2:357.
10. *Midrash on Psalms*, 2:363.

This different exhortation is then a surprise, though psalms often urge people to *rely on Yhwh (4:5 [6]; 37:3, 5; 62:8 [9]; 115:9–11), and these lines take up the converse declaration in 118:8–9: it is a bad idea to rely on human beings, on leaders (*nědîbîm*; see the comment on 118:8–9). "In the book of Psalms and in the Bible as a whole, wickedness is essentially a matter of trust."[11] In substance v. 4 also recalls 144:4.[12] The psalm does not specify what sort of leaders it refers to, and Israel's experience would provide evidence for interpreting it in the broadest of senses. It is unwise to rely on imperial authorities, the leaders of other local peoples, or leaders within Israel or Judah. The two ways of describing the unwise objects of reliance, as leaders and as human beings, come in the opposite order to Ps. 118, but the implication will be similar: "Do not rely on leaders: they are only human beings." (Whereas MT divides the line 2-4 after "leaders," its point becomes clearer if we divide it 3-3 after "a human being.") Verse 3b then explains what is wrong with a human being. Its rationale again corresponds to Ps. 118, the testimony of a leader testifying that Yhwh "became deliverance for me" (vv. 14, 21).

Why does being human beings stop leaders from bringing deliverance? Verse 4 explains. "Rich power brokers, perhaps also heathen despots, radiate a deceptive power," but these leaders "have the mark of death on them."[13] They may not belong to the faithless or come short in social or moral values.[14] But however upright they are, leaders lose their breath: the use of the word *rûaḥ* hints at the contrast between divine *rûaḥ* and human *rûaḥ*. The colon also recalls the observations concerning *rûaḥ* in 76:12 [13]; Eccles. 12:7, and that concerning a return to the ground in Gen. 3:19. Here, for the human leader, it is "his" ground; *ben-ʾādam* returns to *ʾădāmâ*. Verse 4b further spells out the implications, in a more unfamiliar way ("deliberations" is an Aramaism, like the relative *še* in v. 3b). In this asyndetic line as a whole, the first colon is implicitly subordinate to the second.[15] When human beings die, their deliberations die with them. The plans to effect deliverance get nowhere. Thus, while the two cola in v. 4 are internally parallel, together they also parallel v. 3; the first comments on being a human being, and the second restates the point in v. 3b.

In 1 Maccabees 2:63, Mattathias on his deathbed urges his sons in words like those in v. 4 to remember that this truth applies to Antiochus Epiphanes.

11. McCann, "Psalms," 1263.

12. Fokkelman, *Major Poems*, 2:316.

13. Kraus, *Psalms 60–150*, 552.

14. Contrast Anderson, *Psalms*, 2:941.

15. See DG 123, remark 1. *TTH* 153.3 and JM 167a underscore this point by seeing the verbs in v. 4a as jussive and thus hypothetical, though the forms are not distinctively jussive.

[5]The good fortune of the people who have the God of Jacob as their help,
whose expectation is in Yhwh their God,
[6a–b]Maker of the heavens and the earth,
the sea and all that is in them.

After the "negative foil" with regard to the praise of Yhwh, "enhancing the ground for praise that follows" in vv. 5–6,[16] these two further cola make the positive contrast with vv. 3–4 in declaring the *good fortune of people who have Jacob's God as their *help; that formula again corresponds to 115:9–11. "God of Jacob" is a "term of endearment"[17] celebrating Yhwh's relationship with the people descended from Jacob; it perhaps draws more attention to Jacob as an individual than does his new name Israel, which became the more usual name for the people. In the parallel colon, speaking of people having their expectation in Yhwh picks up a root from 145:15 (the verb *śābar*, translated "look to").

The TNIV takes v. 6a–b as a sentence, the beginning of the sequence in vv. 6c–10.[18] A bare participle can thus constitute the predicate of a sentence whose subject is left implicit ("[He is] maker of the heavens and the earth"),[19] but it is an unusual construction, and the content of v. 6a is familiar as an enjambment following on a declaration like that in v. 5 (see 115:15; 121:2; 124:8; 134:3).[20] Verse 6a–b would likely be read as such an enjambment. Hope's basis lies in Yhwh's being creator. This might seem a surprising argument,[21] but it reappears in those other psalms. The formula's expansion in v. 6b is distinctive but comparable to expressions that come elsewhere (69:34 [35]; 96:11; also 8:5–8 [6–9]; and Neh. 9:6).[22] It contrasts with the attitude toward the sea that is often expressed in other psalms, where it is an embodiment of dynamic power asserted against Yhwh.[23] As a whole, then, vv. 5a and 6a are conventional cola that could have comprised a bicolon, but the psalmist has given each another colon to expand them into two lines.

146:6c–10b. The reminder of who Yhwh is. The bulk of the psalm comprises a description of Yhwh's key activities. Building on the

16. Allen, *Psalms 101–150*, 375; cf. Weiser, *Psalms*, 831.
17. Briggs, *Psalms*, 2:228.
18. Cf. Seybold, *Psalmen*, 535–37.
19. See *TTH* 135.6; GKC 116s; JM 154c; none gives this as an example.
20. Though unusually, here the ptc. is absolute *ʿōśeh*, conforming it to the participles in subsequent lines.
21. Cf. Calvin, *Psalms*, 5:288.
22. Keel, *Symbolism*, 35, 56–57.
23. Cf. Gerstenberger, *Psalms*, 2:438.

declaration concerning Yhwh's act of creation (v. 6a–b)[24] and coming to a conclusion with Yhwh's reigning forever (v. 10a–b), the lines between describe the deeds that characterize Yhwh's activity in the time between (vv. 6c–9).[25] Within vv. 6–10b, different cola describe Yhwh by using an anarthrous participle (vv. 6a–b, 7a–b), a participle with the article (v. 6c), an anarthrous participle with Yhwh explicitly mentioned as subject (vv. 7c–9a), or a yiqtol clause (vv. 9b–10b). While the content of the verses is straightforward enough, the formal way the clauses relate to one another is hard to see. MT has a series of tricola through vv. 6–9, which would be unusual, and ignores the way vv. 6c, 7c, and 9b look like a new start in terms of their form of expression. BHS more plausibly arranges vv. 6–10b as a neat series of bicola, but this puts the transition to a Yhwh-statement in v. 7c into the middle of a bicolon. Now v. 6a–b links easily with what precedes (see the comment) and the article on the participle in v. 6c could signal a new start, the move to a series of clauses, rather than continuing the enjambment.[26] I thus take vv. 6c–7b as one tricolon statement, vv. 7c–8b as another, and vv. 8c–10 as a series of bicola.[27]

6cHe is one who keeps faith forever,
7a–bexercises authority for the oppressed,
gives food to the hungry.

If there seems to be a big distance from Yhwh's being maker of the heavens and the earth to people's everyday lives, then vv. 6c–7b begin to bridge that distance, spelling out the implications of Yhwh's being "maker." That participle hints that creating was not something Yhwh simply undertook once. It is characteristic of Yhwh's ongoing activity. Reworking this point, v. 6c says that Yhwh did not create and then leave the world to look after itself. Yhwh is one who keeps faith, and that forever.

This is then expanded in two more participles. The first reworks 103:6, abbreviating the line so that it becomes a colon instead of expanding a colon so that it becomes a line. The second picks up an expression from 145:15, though it changes the phrase's slant by making the recipients of Yhwh's giving "the hungry" rather than "all." This pairs well with the previous colon.

24. Watson (*Classical Hebrew Poetry*, 322, 353) sees v. 6a–b as a merism spelled out by vv. 6c–9.

25. Cf. William J. Carl, "Psalm 146," *Int* 48 (1994): 166–69 (see 168).

26. Against NRSV, but with Gunkel (*Psalmen*, 612), even though he removes the article from "the one who keeps faith."

27. Cf. Allen, *Psalms 101–150*, 375.

7cYhwh frees prisoners,
  8Yhwh opens the eyes of the blind,
  Yhwh lifts up the bowed down.
Yhwh is dedicated to the faithful,
  9aYhwh watches over strangers.

The five statements in vv. 7c–9a follow naturally on those in vv. 6c–7b; they are again participial clauses, distinct by virtue of having "Yhwh" as their explicit subject. The first two rework Isa. 42:7. The prisoners will be people in confinement for political reasons, the usual reason for imprisonment in the ancient world. Opening the eyes of the blind restates that point; in the context it does not refer to healing people whose sight has gone but to freeing people in the darkness of prison to see the light again. The third colon belongs with those two and adds another formulation that follows 145:14, while also recalling in substance if not in words passages such as Isa. 51:14. Qimchi relates the descriptions through vv. 7–9 to the exile; he will have in mind the Jewish people's ongoing exile. Both the sixth-century exile and exile as a continuing reality provide contexts against which to imagine the fulfillment of these declarations and their promise to people using the psalm.

The fourth and fifth cola make statements distinctive to this psalm. Only here is Yhwh *dedicated to the *faithful, and only here does Yhwh watch over strangers.[28] But Deut. 10:18 urges people to dedicate themselves to strangers and to give them food (cf. v. 7b here). If vv. 7c–8b then invite people to see Yhwh as one who deals with people's ongoing Babylon-like exile, vv. 8c–9a invites them to see Yhwh as one who deals with their ongoing Egypt-like oppression.

9b–cThe orphan and widow he relieves,
  and the way of the faithless he subverts.

Once more the saying's form changes, though the content coheres with the description of Yhwh that has preceded. Each colon emphazes the object by putting it first, and each now uses a yiqtol verb (polel, then piel). The reference to orphan and widow continues a link with Deut. 10:18, though these categories of needy people often feature together. But the verbs are again distinctive to the psalm, the one suggesting a positive reversal, the other a negative one. The declaration affirms a pair of reversals like that in vv. 7c–8b, and like that in Ps. 1 with its reference

28. See Francisco O. García-Treto, "'El Señor guarda a los emigrantes,'" *Apuntes* 1.4 (1981): 3–9.

to the "way of the faithless" perishing. But in light of the Red Sea link in v. 10, it could also be natural to read v. 9b–c as continuing the exodus theme suggested by vv. 8c–9a; Yhwh continues to be one who relieves the oppressed and puts down the oppressor.

> 10a–bYhwh will reign forever,
> your God, Zion, for all generations.

Verse 10a reformulates Exod. 15:18, while v. 10b compares more with Ps. 145:13. Yhwh's reigning forever as king contrasts with the short-term lives of human leaders (v. 4). It adds to the encouragement to rely on Yhwh as King, and not put one's hopes on a human king (such as the king you hope to have again some day).[29] The address to Zion more likely sees the city as personifying its people than taking "Zion" as a term for the people. Either way, this last full line combines the exodus and exile motifs that have underlain vv. 6c–9. Zion's restoration will be effected by the God who began to reign at the Red Sea and reasserted that reign as Babylon fell (Isa. 52:7–10). As well as being "my God" (v. 1) and "their God" (v. 5), Yhwh is "your God" (v. 10).

146:10c. The closing exhortation.

> 10cPraise Yah.

The closing exhortation to *praise forms an inclusion with v. 1a.

Theological Implications

The psalm's comment about rulers gives it an ambiguous relationship with Ps. 2.[30] Edmund Hill comments that the psalm's first point is to praise God continually; its second is "'Never trust the politicians' . . . for any sort of political, social, national or individual salvation. Not because they are more treacherous or fickle than other men, but simply because they are just like other men—they will die, and their plans and policies and panacaeas with them." In contrast to the politicians, Yhwh keeps faith forever, exercises authority for the oppressed, gives food to the hungry, frees prisoners, opens the eyes of the blind, lifts up the bowed down, is dedicated to the faithful, watches over strangers, restores orphan and widow, and subverts the way of the faithless. Politicians do none of those things, either because they cannot, or

29. Cf. Bruce V. Malchow, "God or King in Psalm 146," *The Bible Today* 89 (1977): 1166–70.

30. McCann sees it as having the same view as Ps. 2 ("Psalms," 1263).

because they do not make it their priority. But how does God do these things? Paradoxically, it is usually through people who are willing to be involved in politics, or leadership, but who do it as God's servants and agents.[31]

31. Hill, *Prayer, Praise and Politics*, 70–73.

Psalm 147

God of Cosmos, Congregation, and City

Translation

> [1]Praise Yah,
> because[1] it is good making music for our God,
> because it is fine glorifying our praise.[2]

1. EVV begin a new sentence, "How good," and A. Anderson argues that *kî* here cannot mean "because," on the grounds that "Praise Yah" at the beginning "is outside the metrical arrangement, and it may not be an integral part of the Psalm" (*Psalms*, 2:944). But it is doubtful whether *kî* can mean "how" or that a praise psalm can begin with *kî* (Gunkel, *Psalmen*, 615). The argument thus needs to be reversed: the natural way to read the double *kî* is to take it to mean "because" (cf. LXX, Jerome), which shows that "Praise Yah" is an integral part of the psalm and is inside the metrical arrangement.

2. Vrs and EVV interpret *nā'wâ tĕhillâ* in light of 33:1 (where the phrase means "praise is fine"), but it is then difficult to construe the colon, and they vary in the way they do so; indeed, it is often difficult to see how they construe it. In fact, the parallelism with the piel inf. *zammĕrâ* suggests that Ps. 147 is using the phrase in a different way from Ps. 33. Here *nā'wâ* is not an adjective but another piel infinitive, from *nā'â*: so J. Derenbourg "Aus Briefen J. Derenbourgs an den Herausgeber," *ZAW* 5 (1985): 163–64 (see 164); cf. Josua Blau, "*Nāwā Ṯhillā* (Ps. cxlvii 1): Lobpreisen," *VT* 4 (1954): 410–11. They then take the phrase to mean "to make praise beautiful," understanding that to mean "to sing glorious praise" (NJPS). More plausibly, Kraus offers the alternative rendering "to adorn with praise" (*Psalms 60–150*, 555). Dahood (*Psalms*, 3:344) takes it as referring to Yhwh as

[2]Yhwh is the builder of Jerusalem;[3]
he gathers the exiles of Israel.
[3]He is the one who heals the broken in spirit,[4]
binds up their hurts.
[4]He calculates the reckoning of the stars,
calls all of them by their names.
[5]Our Lord is great and mighty in power;
there is no reckoning of his understanding.
[6]Yhwh restores the weak,
putting down the faithless right to the ground.

[7]Sing to Yhwh with confession,
make music to our God with the lyre.
[8]He is the one who covers the heavens with clouds,
who provides rain for the earth,
who makes the mountains grow grass.[5]
[9]He gives to cattle their food,
to the offspring of the raven when they call.
[10]He does not revel in the strength of the horse,
he does not delight in the thighs of a human being.
[11]Yhwh delights in the people who revere him,
the people who put their hope in his commitment.

[12]Glorify Yhwh, Jerusalem;
praise your God, Zion.
[13]Because he has strengthened the bars of your gates,
blessed your children within you.
[14]He is the one who makes your border peaceful,[6]
fills you with the finest of wheat.
[15]He is the one who sends his utterance to the earth;
his word runs quickly.
[16]He is the one who gives snow like wool;
he scatters frost like ash.
[17]He throws his hail like crumbs;
before his ice who can stand?
[18]He sends his word to melt them;
he blows his breath, waters flow.

---

the object of praise (with "our" carrying over from the first colon), which completes the parallelism between the cola.

3. Not "Yhwh builds Jerusalem," which would require absolute *bôneh* rather than MT's construct *bônēh*.

4. Lit. "broken of heart," though "brokenhearted" has different connotations in English.

5. Some LXX MSS add "and food for the service of people," which turns the odd tricolon into a double bicolon; but the words do not come in all LXX MSS and look like a later addition from 104:14 (Allen, *Psalms 101–150*, 382).

6. Lit. "peace."

19He declares his word[s][7] to Jacob,
his laws and his decisions to Israel.
20He has not acted thus to any nation;
the decisions—they do not know them.[8]
Praise Yah.

Interpretation

Psalm 147 fits the regular nature of a praise psalm in combining exhortations to praise with the reasons for or contents of praise. It goes through this sequence three times: vv. 1, 7, and 12 are the exhortations; vv. 2–6, 8–11, and 13–20 give the reasons or the content. In LXX, vv. 12–20 form a separate psalm, and it might be of separate origin, but it fits well enough in MT, and the inclusion "Praise Yah" (common to each of the last five psalms in MT) makes especially clear that MT does see this as one psalm. Kirkpatrick describes it as a psalm of praise for the restoration of Jerusalem;[9] this cannot be quite right, as only in v. 13 (where it uses qatal verbs to speak of Yhwh's deeds) could it be reckoned to speak of actual acts of restoration. It is a psalm of praise that celebrates Yhwh's ongoing acts rather than a commemoration of particular events. But the Jerusalem focus in the content of the praise in vv. 2, 13–14 and in the exhortation in v. 12 is unusual; it reflects the position of the postexilic community as centered on Jerusalem. This focus then combines with a stress on Yhwh's being at work in creation. The first section goes from Jerusalem to creation to restoring the weak. The second goes from creation to people who revere Yhwh. The third goes from Jerusalem to creation to Yhwh's revelation to Israel.[10]

The rhetoric of address in the psalm is complex and subtle. In the first two sections the speaker addresses the community in second-person plural verbs while also identifying with it by using the first-person plural (vv. 1, 7). The first section then goes on to speak in the third person of the beneficiaries of Yhwh's action, as well as of other entities (vv. 2–6), even though the speaker and the addressees are presumably among these beneficiaries. The rhetoric thus invites them to look at themselves from the outside, to see themselves being built up, healed, and restored even as they see the faithless being put down. That approach continues in the

7. K has sg., Q pl.

8. For MT *yĕdāʿûm* (cf. 4QPs[d]), 11QPs[a] has *hwdyʿm*, "he did [not] make them known" (cf. LXX, Tg).

9. *Psalms*, 820.

10. For further analysis, see Pierre Auffret, *Hymnes d'Égypte et d'Israël*, OBO 34 (Göttingen: Vandenhoeck & Ruprecht, 1981), 121–31.

second section, which closes by speaking in the third person of people who revere and hope. Now the addressees are invited to look at this third-person body and ask whether they fit the description. The third section operates in yet another way by addressing the city, which is again both identical with the actual people who are being addressed and distinct from them. It is distinct rhetorically and also literally distinct in that a city is more than the sum total of its current inhabitants. Yet indirectly it is these current inhabitants who are urged to offer the praise that is due from the city, precisely because they *are* its current inhabitants. And in the description of the city's experience, they see themselves. They *are* its children (v. 13). They are also the current embodiment of the Jacob-Israel of vv. 19–20.

The psalm's description of Yhwh combines noun clauses (vv. 2a, 5), verbal clauses (vv. 2b, 10, 13, 18, 20), participles with the article (vv. 3, 8, 14–16), anarthrous participles (vv. 4, 6, 9, 17, 19), and participial clauses with Yhwh as subject (v. 11). (Many of the participial expressions are continued by finite verbs; I have treated these as part of the participial construction.) This combination recalls 146:6–10, where there seemed to be some rationale in the alternation. Here, there seems no such rationale and no consistent pattern that argues for reckoning that some participial expressions depend on preceding main verbs by enjambment, or conversely that all the lines with finite verbs continue the participial construction. I thus reckon that this variation is stylistic and follow EVV in taking all the lines as independent clauses, though marking the participles with the article by the phrase "he is the one who."

Every line in the psalm involves parallelism,[11] and in most lines, at least in the first two sections, the parallelism involves marked intensifying; the second colon is more concrete or dramatic or vivid.[12] In the third section the more evident characteristic is a number of instances of assonance: notably, in v. 13, bars, blessed, within you (*bĕrîḥê, bērak, bĕqirbēk*); in v. 16, frost, like ash (*kĕpôr, kāʾēper*); and in v. 17, his hail, his ice (*qarḥô, qārātô*). The psalm as a whole continues the pattern of employing phraseology parallel to that in the immediately preceding psalms (vv. 6, 12), in other psalms (vv. 3, 10–11), and in other parts of Israel's traditions, especially Isaiah and Job (vv. 2, 4–5, 8–9). Sometimes these phrases retain the meaning they had elsewhere, but sometimes they gain new meaning (see the parallels with Ps. 33 in vv. 1c and 18b).

Presumably the psalm was used in worship, but there is no basis for guessing a specific worship setting. And although it focuses on Jerusalem

11. The inclusion "Praise Yah" and the fact that v. 8 is a tricolon hardly compromises that.

12. Cf. Bratcher and Reyburn, *Handbook on the Psalms*, 1173; they contrast Ps. 145, where the parallelism more commonly involves simpler restatement.

and was presumably used there, one could not exclude its being used in the dispersion among people for whom Jerusalem remained the pinnacle of their joyfulness (137:6).

147:1–6. The first exhortation and the first set of reasons.

> 1Praise Yah,
> because it is good making music for our God,
> because it is fine glorifying our praise.

As in Ps. 146 the opening "*Praise *Yah" will turn out to be the beginning of a bracket that v. 20c will close. But in its context in v. 1, the significance of this opening phrase is spelled out by the noun clauses in v. 1b–c. While vv. 2–6 will explain the reasons or the content of the praise, these two parallel cola in v. 1b–c[13] offer an interim rationale that raises suspense. They declare that making *music for and glorifying our God, who is our praise, are *good and fine: in each pair of expressions a standard term leads into a less familiar one. "Glorifying" or "beautifying" (cf. 93:5; Isa. 52:7) nuances "making music," making the music's point explicit. As in Ps. 146, LXX adds "Haggai and Zechariah's" (and follows it with another "Praise the Lord" to smooth the transition to the "because" clauses), which once more fits the psalm's implicit links with Jerusalem after the exile.

> 2Yhwh is the builder of Jerusalem;
> he gathers the exiles of Israel.
> 3He is the one who heals the broken in spirit,
> binds up their hurts.

The first concrete reason why praise is good and fine lies in Yhwh's relationship with the city and community the psalmist presumably belongs to. In isolation one might take Yhwh's building up of Jerusalem to refer to its physical rebuilding, and it may include that, but v. 2b likely gives precision to the matter (the expression compares with Isa. 11:12; 56:8).[14] In the sixth and fifth centuries the city had a key need that its population should be built up by exiles exercising their freedom to move "back" to the city. It would be prosaic to link v. 2a with Nehemiah's building of the walls of the city, though v. 13 may refer to that.

Verse 3 might be seen as a quite separate statement, but the collocation of brokenness of spirit and the building up of Jerusalem also appears in Ps. 51:17–18 [19–20], and the collocation of vv. 2 and 3 suggests some

13. Each line begins *kî* and follows that by an adjective, an infinitive functioning as a gerund, and an object.

14. The line works *abcb′a′*, with "Yhwh" at the center applying to both cola.

mutual nuancing. People both in Jerusalem and in exile had been broken in spirit and hurt, first by Jerusalem's fall and the exile itself, then by the ongoing broken-down state of city and community and by the ongoing pressures of life in exile. Yhwh will treat the hurt of people of Jerusalem and Judah by building up the city through drawing people back to it. Conversely, drawing people from their settled (even if still demoralized) state in exile/dispersion will involve healing their wounds so as to inspire them to make that move. The combination of brokenness of spirit and binding up also parallels Isa. 61:1; there and here, the way one treats bodily hurts (a broken limb or wound) becomes an image for the way Yhwh treats hurts in people's morale and hearts. "Broken" usually refers to the physical and "hurt" to the emotional; the verb "hurt" applies to Zion in Isa. 54:6 (see also 14:3).

> 4He calculates the reckoning of the stars,
> calls all of them by their names.
> 5Our Lord is great and mighty in power;
> there is no reckoning of his understanding.

It is natural enough that Yhwh's power as creator should be further reason for praise in a psalm, but the move from vv. 2–3 to vv. 4–5 is sudden. Perhaps the power of Yhwh evidenced in lordship in creation implicitly means Yhwh will have no trouble with the undertakings in vv. 2–3 (cf. the link with creation in 146:6–10 and other passages noted there). The two verses reflect the language of Isa. 40:26, 28, which presuppose the same link between restoration from exile and the restoring of Jerusalem on one hand and Yhwh's power as creator on the other, though the specific theological context there is different. In the background of Isa. 40:12–31 is the attractiveness of Babylonian religion with its stress on the planets and stars. The psalm hardly implies only that Yhwh can count the existent stars and address them by names, but that Yhwh counts out how many stars there should be and gives them their names (the second colon goes beyond the first).[15] It further implies that Yhwh cannot be subjected to the same calculation as they can be; the repetition of the word "reckoning" helps to make the point. It shares the perspective of other postexilic writings that in effect see the exile as continuing; but it also shares the exilic prophet's perspective, that the power and insight of our *Lord as creator means things need not stay as they are. Yhwh has the ability and the understanding to change them. Reference to Yhwh's understanding or insight thus has practical significance (Dahood translates "skill").[16]

15. Schaefer, *Psalms*, 341. The line works neatly *abcc′b′a′*.
16. *Psalms*, 3:345.

[6]Yhwh restores the weak,
putting down the faithless right to the ground.

The closing line of the first section summarizes the point, along with its implicit corollary. Restoring the *weak summarizes vv. 2–3, using the verb from 146:9. Putting down the *faithless (Babylon or Persia or the local powers that pressurize Judah) is involved in restoring the weak. The psalm's links with Isaiah likely make it no coincidence that *šāpal* is a favorite verb in Isaiah in this connection (e.g., Isa. 13:11), but it is nice that Israel is now the beneficiary of Yhwh's "putting down" the faithless rather than its victim (as in Isa. 2). The connotation of "underworld" or Sheol may attach to "ground" here.[17]

147:7–11. The second exhortation and the second account of the reasons.

[7]Sing to Yhwh with confession,
make music to our God with the lyre.

"Make *music" with the *lyre parallels "sing," the tune and the lyric combining, rather than the tune and the object ("glorifying") as happened in v. 1. "*Confession" here is used in the loose sense of appreciation for Yhwh's ongoing, regular acts rather than for acts undertaken for this individual or this community.

[8]He is the one who covers the heavens with clouds,
who provides rain for the earth,
who makes the mountains grow grass.
[9]He gives to cattle their food,
to the offspring of the raven when they call.

An unexpected tricolon begins the subsection giving the reasons for thanksgiving. Its content is also unexpected as the whole of vv. 8–9 relates to the gift of rain and its crucial role for the animal world. The three cola in v. 8 are parallel but also form a sequence. First, Yhwh brings the cloud cover that promises rain. Then, Yhwh brings forth the rain from it. Thereby Yhwh makes the grass grow. This leads directly into v. 9a, since the grass is the animals' feed; v. 9b parallels v. 9a, though Yhwh will need to do something different for the offspring of the raven, which do not eat grass.[18] Thus when feeding the ravens in Job 38:41, Yhwh supplies

17. So Dahood, *Psalms*, 3:345.

18. In the line, the verb and object in v. 9a carry over to v. 9b, so the whole of v. 9b parallels "to cattle" in v. 9a.

"provision." In general and in particular, the Scriptures that the lines parallel come in Job 38 (though also see Ps. 104:14), which also talks about cloud and rain and covering. And the burden of much of Job 38–39 is Yhwh's care for the created world, which does not focus on humanity.

> 10He does not revel in the strength of the horse,
> he does not delight in the thighs of a human being.
> 11Yhwh delights in the people who revere him,
> the people who put their hope in his commitment.

Once more the declarations move in an unexpected direction, though one that makes it possible to infer a link with the context. The lines overlap with Ps. 33:17–18 (see also 20:7 [8]), while Isa. 31:1–3 adds human beings to horses as unwise objects of trust. In the ancient world "the admiration accorded to the horse was based primarily on its military capabilities," and Israelites, as much as anyone, could become "infatuated" with them. The psalm confronts that.[19] The Judeans might reckon that their military and human resources were key to Jerusalem's upbuilding and security. Verse 10 undermines that assumption. Yhwh is not infatuated with military hardware and human strength.

The key to restoration and blessing lies in being people who *revere Yhwh and put their hope in Yhwh's *commitment. Revering and hoping are complementary attitudes.[20]

147:12–20. Once again the psalm resumes exhortation and backs it with further reasoning.

> 12Glorify Yhwh, Jerusalem;
> praise your God, Zion.

The distinctive word is "glorify" (*šābaḥ,* as in 145:4), but the direct address to Jerusalem/Zion is also distinctive. The city has been the explicit or implicit topic throughout, but only here is it bidden to do the worshipping. The notion fits the personification of Jerusalem/Zion in passages such as Isa. 49–54.

> 13Because he has strengthened the bars of your gates,
> blessed your children within you.
> 14He is the one who makes your border peaceful,
> fills you with the finest of wheat.

19. Keel, *Symbolism*, 239.

20. As in v. 9, two of the three words in the first colon ("Yhwh delights") carry over to the second, so that the whole of v. 11b parallels "those who revere him" in v. 11a.

For the first time in the psalm the praise's rationale is expressed in a regular *kî* clause; the psalm continues to address the city, but thus indirectly addresses its inhabitants and the people who actually sing the psalm or listen to it being sung. The rationale's perspective differs from what has preceded but complements it; the two lines are parallel. Further, whereas v. 7 spoke of thanksgiving, which one might have expected to lead into a statement of what Yhwh had done, only here does such a statement come. And no doubt the qatal verbs refer to something that Yhwh has been doing and carries on doing, as is suggested by the participles that continue the statement.

On one hand, Yhwh looks after the city's defense. In Isa. 45:1–2 Yhwh is opening Babylon's gates and breaking down its bars; now Yhwh is strengthening Jerusalem's. In Neh. 3, Nehemiah and his forces are "strengthening" the city's "gates" and "bars"; here Yhwh is doing so. Presumably the implication is that the psalm comes from later than Nehemiah. In the parallelism of the lines, the border in v. 14a will be the city limits, in effect the wall in which those gates and bars feature. The word comes in this connection in parallelism with "gates" in Isa. 54:11–12, which also speaks of the "peace" of the city's "children." And in this context, the city's shalom will be more its peace than its general well-being.

On the other hand, the two second cola indicate that the psalm does presuppose *shalom* in the broader sense, for blessing and shalom are closely related ideas. In turn, blessing will imply fruitfulness (again, cf. Isa. 54), and the fruitfulness of the ground accompanies that; for "the finest of wheat," compare 81:16 [17].

Luther comments that "the word 'bars' . . . we must understand not only as the iron bar which a smith can make, but, by synecdoche, everything else that helps to protect us, such as good government, good city ordinances, good order, stern punishments, and pious, faithful, and wise rulers." These, too, are God's gifts, as is the city itself being full of people, and its enjoyment of peace and of daily bread. For all, we should be grateful and not merely self-congratulatory.[21]

15 He is the one who sends his utterance to the earth;
his word runs quickly.
16 He is the one who gives snow like wool;
he scatters frost like ash.
17 He throws his hail like crumbs;
before his ice who can stand?
18 He sends his word to melt them;
he blows his breath, waters flow.

21. *Selected Psalms*, 3:113, and further 113–23. Luther further interprets "peace" of the internal harmony of the city rather than its security from outside attackers.

The significance of v. 15 becomes clear when we reach the end of vv. 15–18. Within v. 18 there is a link between Yhwh's word and what happens in nature, and this is also presupposed on a broader canvas in vv. 15–17. Yhwh "sends his utterance to the earth" in a quite down-to-earth sense; the "earth" is the earth that is affected by snow, frost, hail, and ice. The utterance or word is the one that operates in Ps. 33:4–9 as well as in Gen. 1, when God speaks and things come into being in nature. Both the utterance and the word are personified as something sent like an aide and hastening to fulfill its commission like an aide, as in Ps. 107:20.[22]

The emphasis on God's acting by speaking reappears in Job 37:2–6, 12, and the series of natural phenomena again parallel Job 37–38: snow (37:6; 38:22); frost (38:29); hail (38:29); ice (37:9). The end of the little sequence in vv. 16–17 is marked by the different form of expression in v. 17b. Over against v. 15, in vv. 16–17 Yhwh becomes the direct agent of what happens in nature. Yhwh makes the snow cover the ground in the way a woolen fleece covers a sheep. Yhwh scatters frost like a man throwing the ashes out of the fireplace. Yhwh throws hail like someone scattering bread crumbs. Snow, frost, hail, and ice are known in parts of Israel, though they are infrequent occurrences, and like the descriptions of animals in Job, the description of these phenomena may not issue from personal experience but from traditional poetic resources that reflect the experience of other peoples and/or other places.

Verse 18 varies the forms of expression again in noting the reversal of the acts in vv. 16–17. Once more Yhwh "sends his word," and it melts snow, frost, hail, and ice. To put it another way, Yhwh breathes (that is, the wind [*rûaḥ*] blows), and the frozen waters flow again. Here again the language overlaps with 33:6, but the implication is different. There the breath breathes out words that do the work; here the breath stands for the wind. Throughout the four verses, as in vv. 8–9, there is little concern with humanity (for instance, with the trouble or relief that these acts bring to humanity), except insofar as humanity is included in v. 17b. Once more the psalm compares with Job in its focus on Yhwh and nature in a way that largely ignores humanity. Its emphasis on Yhwh's power in nature is nevertheless an encouragement.

> **19**He declares his word[s] to Jacob,
> his laws and his decisions to Israel.

22. Although the language of sending a word is distinctive to the psalms, a Sumerian hymn personifies the deity's word in a way that is otherwise similar: see Kraus, *Psalms 60–150*, 558, quoting from A. Falkenstein and W. von Soden, eds., *Sumerische und akkadische Hymnen und Gebete* (Zürich: Artemis, 1953), 224.

[20]He has not acted thus to any nation;
the decisions—they do not know them.
Praise Yah.

Yhwh's word is the means whereby Yhwh acts in nature. It is also the means whereby Yhwh acts in history. Yhwh "declares his words" via the prophets and thereby reveals to Israel what is about to happen, so that when these events take place, people may know and be reassured that it is indeed Yhwh who has acted. The language is especially characteristic of Isa. 40–48 (e.g., Isa. 41:26; 42:9; 43:12; 44:8); these chapters are ones that commonly refer in parallelism to "Jacob-Israel" as the beneficiaries of these acts, which may explain the sudden move from talk of Jerusalem to talk of Jacob-Israel here. Acts such as the ones vv. 13–14 spoke of are ones Yhwh thus announced the intention of performing. It is an aspect of Yhwh's ongoing relationship with Jerusalem.

In other contexts, one would take the subsequent reference to Yhwh's *laws and *decisions (*ḥôq*, *mišpāṭ*) as denoting the obligations that Yhwh places on Israel, but in this context that would be an implausibly sharp change of direction. The context and the parallelism has prepared us to take these two words as continuing the reference to Yhwh's own acts rather than acts Yhwh expects of the people. The laws are decrees about what should happen to Israel (cf. 2:7; Mic. 7:11; Zeph. 2:2). The decisions are ones Yhwh has made concerning Israel's destiny: the word recurs in the singular with this meaning in Isa. 40:14, 27; 42:1, 3, 4.

Whereas other nations can perceive God's action in nature, Yhwh does not declare to them the decrees and the decisions. They do not have this kind of knowledge (Isa. 45:20). It is this that establishes that Yhwh is the only real God (cf. Isa. 41:26–28; 43:11–13; 44:6–8; 45:20–22). Only Jacob-Israel possesses this revelation. It is not Yhwh's intention that the nations remain ignorant of it (cf. Isa. 45:20–25), but this is not a psalm that draws attention to that in the way that Pss. 96–98 (and 148) do. Its concern is to hearten Jacob-Israel with the wonder of Yhwh's grace that has given it unique insight into what Yhwh is doing with it, even when it is scattered, broken, hurt, and weak.

The final "*Praise *Yah," completing an inclusion around the psalm, forms an appropriate response to this.

Theological Implications

One of Rudolf Bultmann's distinctive emphases, in the last decades of modernity, was a stress on "demythologizing." According to Bultmann, references in the NT (or the OT) to angels or demons, or to the ultimate

End or the ultimate Beginning, are not objective statements about what actually is or will be or once was; that is to misunderstand their mythical form of expression. They are really statements about the attitudes we need to take. Statements about creation, for instance, are not statements about something God once did back at the Beginning but about our utter dependence on God for our lives now.

> Faith in creation . . . is not a theory about the past. It does not have its meaning by relating what took place at some earlier time and no longer concerns man in the present, but rather speaks precisely about man's present situation. It tells him how he is to understand himself now; and the reference to the past is only for the purpose of teaching him to understand his situation in the present.[23]

Bultmann was wrong in what he denied but right in what he affirmed. It is implausible to suggest that all those lengthy and complex accounts of the Beginning are merely disposable husk; the Bible is making statements about something Yhwh once did, even if it uses poetic form in doing so. But Bultmann was right that the point about those statements is their significance for now. The point is reflected in the way Isa. 40–55 uses the verb "create" to refer to things God is doing in the time of the prophet and the prophet's hearers and not just to acts of creation back at the Beginning.

The psalm presupposes and works with that point. It moves effortlessly between talk about God's relationship with creation and God's activity in restoring the community in the present. Its instinct is to reckon that when we see the people of God scattered, broken, hurt, and weak, what it needs to know is that Yhwh is the loving, powerful, insightful creator of the world. That is reason for hope and for not placing our trust in resources located within creation. And when as the people of God we experience God strengthening the bars of our gates and providing for us richly, we experience the creator's provision. Conversely, when we think about creation, we need to see that the love, power, and insight of God as the creator are significant for the destiny of the people of God. It is as the creator that Yhwh is the one who builds up Jerusalem. And it is the one who acts by speaking within nature who acts by speaking now and implements decisions for our destiny and for the world's. "His salvific activity is creative. His creative activity is salvific."[24] The creation of the world and the history of Israel belong together.[25] Yhwh is God of cosmos, creation, and city.[26]

23. Rudolf Bultmann, *Existence and Faith* (repr., London: Collins Fontana, 1964), 207–8.

24. Kraus, *Psalms 60–150*, 559.

25. Cf. the trenchant comments of Francis Watson in *Text and Truth* (Edinburgh: T&T Clark; Grand Rapids: Eerdmans, 1997), 265–67.

26. Mays, *Psalms*, 441.

Psalm 148

Creation's Ring of Praise

Translation

1Praise Yah.

Praise Yhwh from the heavens,
praise him on high.
2Praise him all his aides,
praise him all his army [K]/armies [Q].
3Praise him sun and moon,
praise him all bright stars.
4Praise him highest heavens
and waters that are above the heavens.
5They are to praise Yhwh's name,
because he is the one who commanded and they were created.[1]
6He established them forever and ever;
he made a decree, and it will not pass.[2]

7Praise Yhwh from the earth,
sea monsters and all depths,

1. "He is the one who commanded" corresponds to the opening of 33:9b; LXX precedes it with a colon equivalent to 33:9a.

2. Not "a decree that cannot be transgressed," or "a limit that cannot be passed"; either requires us to take the third-person verb as impersonal and thus passive (cf. NRSV), which is not a natural understanding where "a decree" is inviting us to take it as subject.

[8]Fire and hail, snow and fog,
storm wind doing his word,
[9]Mountains and all hills,
fruit trees and all cedars,
[10]Animals and all cattle,
creeping things and winged birds,
[11]Kings of the earth and all nations,[3]
leaders and all rulers of the earth,
[12]Youths and girls, too,
old people with young people.
[13]They are to praise Yhwh's name,
because his name alone is on high.
His majesty is over the earth and the heavens,
[14]but he has lifted up a horn for his people, [MT]
but he will lift up a horn for his people, [LXX][4]
Praise for all those committed to him,
the Israelites, the people who come near him.[5]

Praise Yah.

Interpretation

This further praise psalm again comprises exhortations to praise and *kî* clauses detailing the reasons for praise or the content of praise. It does so in two sequences relating to the world above and the earth itself (vv. 1–6 and 7–14), the whole being bound by the inclusion "Praise Yah." Whereas the OT often presupposes a threefold distinction of the cosmos into the world above, this world, and the world below, here the psalm works with a twofold distinction between the heavens and the earth. They are summed up in the reverse order resumptively in v. 13c as the survey comes to a close and the last two lines of the psalm turn in an unexpected though familiar new direction. The omission of reference to the world below

3. On the suggestion that *lĕʾummîm* means "rulers," see *CP*, 254–55. Barr there argues that reference to the nations is entirely in place here, but it is odd, and more likely that the construct "kings of" governs both nouns (on this usage see JM 129b).

4. For MT *wayyārem*, LXX implies *wĕyārēm*.

5. Gunkel takes v. 14b–c as a subscript (*Psalmen*, 617, 618); other peoples do have subscripts for hymns, and cf. Hab. 3, but there are no other examples in the Psalter. R. A. F. MacKenzie ("Ps 148,14bc," *Bib* 51 [1970]: 221–24) suggests that originally v. 14b–c was the heading for Ps. 149. The fact that many of its words reappear in Ps. 149 argues against that; there is not usually much verbal overlap between a psalm's heading and its contents, whereas in Pss. 145–50 there are several examples of the words of one psalm being taken up in the next. Further, the purported heading is again unlike any other in the Psalter. But in any case, the presence of the inclusion "Praise Yah" at v. 14d and again at 149:1a makes clear that v. 14b–c is now part of Ps. 148.

coheres with the awareness that there is no praise to emerge from there because Yhwh is not active there (e.g., 30:9 [10]). The merism "heaven and earth" itself implies everything, but the psalm underlines the point in describing the agents of praise by using the word "all" nine times; the whole creation joins in. The "all" is spelled out selectively in the mention of various elements within creation. This is particularly evident in the second section. It does not mention every meteorological phenomenon or every tree or every category of people (there is no mention of priests, prophets, scribes, singers, chiefs, mothers, slaves, sojourners, and other groups)[6] but it gives concrete expression to the totality by mentioning some instances of different categories.

As happens with other types of psalms, Ps. 148 gives great emphasis to one element in the form and lets the rest almost fall away. Here the emphasis is on the exhortation to praise. It thus contrasts with Ps. 147 and other praise psalms in which the reasons for or contents of the praise have the emphasis (e.g., the creation psalms 8; 19; also 93).[7] So in each section the predominant motif is the bidding to praise, or rather the entities urged to join in the praise (vv. 1–4, 7–12). After a resumptive jussive demanding praise of Yhwh's name (vv. 5a, 13a), only in vv. 5b–6 and 13b–14c are the exhortations backed up by the reasons for or the content of this praise.[8] Further, the psalm again gives predominant attention to the creation, as the agent of praise, not as the reason for praise (as in Ps. 147). Through vv. 1–10 what we see as the inanimate creation is urged to give praise. Only in vv. 11–13 does the psalm speak of human praise, and here the psalm offers another contrast over against Ps. 147, because it is the peoples of the whole earth who are bidden to praise. Only in the final verse does Israel come into purview, not as agent of the praise but as the reason for it. In Ps. 147 the nations did not know Yhwh's decrees and decisions; now they know them and give praise for them.

The account of the elements of creation has parallels in Egyptian wisdom, and such material may have been adapted here and turned into worship.[9] But much of the resemblance to these sources is shared with a resemblance to Mesopotamian and Egyptian hymnody,[10] while

6. Gerstenberger, *Psalms*, 2:450.

7. Cf. Westermann, *Living Psalms*, 256.

8. Further on the psalm's rhetorical features, see Auffret, *La sagesse*, 383–404.

9. So Gerhard von Rad, "Job XXXVIII and Ancient Egyptian Wisdom," in von Rad, *The Problem of the Hexateuch and Other Essays* (Edinburgh: Oliver and Boyd; New York: McGraw-Hill, 1966), 281–91; also Keel, *Symbolism*, 56–60.

10. See Delbert R. Hillers, "A Study of Psalm 148," *CBQ* 40 (1978): 323–34; cf. Lothar Ruppert, "Aufforderung an die Schöpfung zum Lob Gottes," in *Freude an der Weisung des Herrn*, ed. Haag and Hossfeld, 275–96 (see 286–94).

the psalm also relates to Gen. 1 and Ps. 33, or to creation itself, at least as much as to such sources.[11] A notable stage in the psalm's own afterlife is its incorporation in expanded form in the Benedicite, the praise song of Shadrach, Meshach, and Abednego, in LXX.

148:1–6. The exhortation to the world above.

1Praise Yah.

Praise Yhwh from the heavens,
praise him on high.
2Praise him all his aides,
praise him all his army [K]/armies [Q].
3Praise him sun and moon,
praise him all bright stars.
4Praise him highest heavens
and waters that are above the heavens.

After the opening exhortation (LXX again adds "Haggai and Zechariah's"), the main bidding starts not with the agents of *praise but with the location of praise: it is to come "from the heavens" and thus from "on high" (v. 1).

Its actual agents, the entities addressed in v. 1 and located in the heavens and on high, are first Yhwh's aides and armies, the supernatural agents through whom Yhwh acts in the heavens and on the earth. The *aides (*mal'ākîm*) are the beings through whom Yhwh's will is implemented in the heavens and on the earth; they are really the same beings spoken of as gods in passages such as Ps. 82, though the bidding also compares with that in Ps. 29. The armies are perhaps the same entities spoken of in a different way. The term emphasizes their number (especially in Q) and their strength and power. They are the supernatural forces through whom Yhwh's will is imposed in the heavens and on the earth.

Sun, moon, and stars itemize part of this army's membership. Other peoples thought of these as deities who determined what happened on earth; the OT stresses their subordination to Yhwh (cf. 147:4 and its background in Isa. 40:26). If they are involved in deciding what happens on earth, this is strictly as Yhwh's agents. Perhaps they do so only in the demythologized sense assumed by Gen. 1:16–18.

But perhaps sun and moon and stars appear just as the impressive objects in the sky that they are. That seems to be true of the highest heavens and the waters above the heavens. The former may suggest an awareness of some depth of field about the heavens; there are parts farther away than others, an idea that eventually solidified as the view

11. See Spieckermann, *Heilsgegenwart*, 50–59.

that the heavens have three or seven levels. The latter term refers to the reservoirs of water that Yhwh keeps above the sky, from which the earth is watered (cf. Gen. 1:6–8). The different formulation in v. 4b, without the repetition of the verb, hints that the bidding is coming to an end.

> 5They are to praise Yhwh's name,
> because he is the one who commanded and they were created.
> 6He established them forever and ever;
> he made a decree, and it will not pass.

All those entities in vv. 2–4 are to "*praise Yhwh's *name," v. 5a declares, resumptively. The jussive declaration might raise more sharply the question, "Why should they praise Yhwh's name?" Verses 5b–6 give the answer. Only now does a *kî* clause say something of the reasons for the praise the psalm calls for. These entities in the heavens owe Yhwh this praise because it is only through Yhwh's action that they exist. The language of v. 5b again recalls that of Gen. 1 as well as that of Ps. 33. It speaks of Yhwh "commanding" in connection with creation as Ps. 33:9 does, but of the heavens and the earth being "created" (for the niphal of *bārā'*, see Gen. 2:4). The connotation of "creating" is to act with utter sovereignty (rather than to be "creative" in our sense), and the verb thus re-expresses Yhwh's sovereignty over the heavenly entities that vv. 2–4 have implied.

Verse 6 re-expresses that point, spelling out how creation is an act of sovereignty. Elsewhere the Psalms grant the possibility that the heavens and the earth might pass away (102:26 [27]), but that is a possibility acknowledged to make a contrast between their inherent finitude and Yhwh's infinitude. By virtue of Yhwh's action, the heavens and the earth will not actually pass away, because Yhwh established them as a permanency. The heavens share in the permanence of the earth itself (Gen. 9:11). No doubt Yhwh could decide to bring them to an end (though that statement in Gen. 9:11 has given Yhwh little room to maneuver). But unless Yhwh so decides, they are established. No one else can bring them to an end without Yhwh's connivance. Yhwh made a decree (cf. 147:19), and Yhwh's decrees do not become obsolete—again, unless Yhwh decides they shall.

148:7–14. The exhortation to the world below.

> 7Praise Yhwh from the earth,
> sea monsters and all depths,
> 8Fire and hail, snow and fog,
> storm wind doing his word,
> 9Mountains and all hills,
> fruit trees and all cedars,

[10]Animals and all cattle,
creeping things and winged birds,
[11]Kings of the earth and all nations,
leaders and all rulers of the earth,
[12]Youths and girls, too,
old people with young people.

Again the bidding begins from the location of the praise (with v. 7a compare v. 1b–c), but it goes on more quickly to the agents of the praise. "Earth" evidently has a broad sense, referring to the earth as opposed to the heavens, because the first entities summoned to praise from the earth are entities that live in the sea. The sea monsters and the depths recall Gen. 1:2, 21 (though there "deep" is singular). They bellow, and thus praise Yhwh. Both sea monsters and depths can suggest dynamic powers asserted against the forces of order, so it is noteworthy that the second section of praise begins with such rather worrisome entities.[12] The implicit emphasis of the colon is that there is nothing to be anxious about here. The monsters and the depths have also been demythologized and deprived of any power but the power to praise.

Verse 8 continues to speak of entities from the earth in the broad sense. Fire (in the context, lightning), hail, snow, fog (the word is usually translated smoke, but in the context fog makes more sense, or the steam that can rise from the ground in a storm),[13] and storm wind might all be reckoned to come from the heavens. But it is on the earth that they do their work, fulfilling Yhwh's word of command. As well as making explicit that these entities within creation are subordinate to Yhwh, "doing his word" perhaps hints at where the psalm will eventually conclude, as these "natural" phenomena often accompany or make possible the action of Yhwh whereby Israel is delivered and its enemies are put down (cf. Ps. 18). They contribute to Yhwh's praise in this way, too.

The psalm now looks around the regular world and sees the features of life in a land such as Israel: mountains and hills that dominate its landscape and from which wheat waves in praise, trees that bear fruit, and trees that contribute to the building of the temple or simply wave their branches and thus join in praise.

Finally, within the world of nature, the psalm returns to the perspective of Gen. 1 with its summons to animals, cattle, creeping things, and winged birds (Gen. 1:21, 24–25).

So far, humanity has no overt place in this summons to praise. The view of creation is even less centered on humanity than is that of Gen.

12. Cf. Westermann, *Living Psalms*, 258.

13. LXX, Jerome have "ice," which makes less sense and has less etymological justification.

1. Its perspective thus has the potential to counter the way humanity is set to destroy creation.[14] But as Gen. 1 eventually comes to the human beings created in God's image, so in v. 11 the psalm eventually comes to humanity, thus portraying "a symbiosis of human and nonhuman in praise."[15] Worryingly at first, it focuses on kings, leaders, and rulers. Genesis 1 contrasts with the Middle Eastern view that it is the king who is made in God's image; it democratizes that idea and declares that all men and women are. Does Ps. 148 go back on that?

Verse 12 reassures us. Not only does this bidding to praise address men and women; it also addresses young men and young women, and both old and young. It thus parallels the promise of the outpouring of Yhwh's spirit in Joel 2:28 [3:1]. Further, this bidding goes not just to Israel's young and old, but to the young and old of the world. Its different form of expression ("too," "with") hints that the list is coming to an end.

13They are to praise Yhwh's name,
  because his name alone is on high.
His majesty is over the earth and the heavens,
  14but he has lifted up a horn for his people, [MT]
  but he will lift up a horn for his people, [LXX]
Praise for all those committed to him,
  the Israelites, the people who come near him.

Praise Yah.

All these inanimate and animate objects and people, everything and everyone in this created world, are to "*praise Yhwh's *name." The jussive declaration parallels the one in v. 5a and might again raise more sharply the question, "Why should they praise Yhwh's name?" Verses 13b–14 give the answer. As happened in the first section, at last we get a *kî* clause giving some rationale for the praise. For all the impressiveness of many of the entities named so far, there is nothing as impressive as Yhwh: "His name alone is on high."

As MT sees it, that statement is in turn spelled out in an unexpected third colon that turns v. 13 into a tricolon; another then follows in v. 14a–c. The statement in v. 13b is then based in the fact that the earth and the heavens are what they are; the return to a reference to the heavens makes a link with the first section and advertises that the psalm is drawing

14. See Margot Kässmann, "Covenant, Praise and Justice in Creation," in *Ecotheology*, ed. David G. Hallman (Geneva: World Council of Churches; Maryknoll, NY: Orbis, 1994), 28–51 (see 32–36).

15. Terence E. Fretheim, "Nature's Praise of God in the Psalms," *Ex auditu* 3 (1987): 16–30 (see 28).

near to its end and summing up the whole. The very nature of creation testifies to the majesty of the creator whose name stands over it. Praise, therefore, is appropriate.

But two tricola here are an unlikely development, and I rather take v. 13c as beginning a new line that summarizes where we have been so far before moving in another, unexpected direction in v. 14a. The statement of fact (MT) or of hope (LXX) in this second colon is brief, but following on vv. 1–13 it conveys great power. The psalm has not invited us to think about Israel at all. It has concerned itself entirely with "the heavens and the earth" as a whole, undifferentiated. It has enthused over Yhwh's relationship with the entire heavens and earth, including the whole of humanity. Suddenly, just before the end, comes a big "but" (though LXX and Jerome take it as an "and"). Its content is very different from a "but" like that in 89:38 [39] or 44:9 [10], but its unexpected nature and thus its effect are analogous. As in other psalms, it turns out that these entities are to give praise not only for Yhwh's activity in creation but also for Yhwh's acts toward Israel. The God of the heavens and the earth has lifted up (MT) or will lift up (LXX) a horn for a particular people, with whom God identifies. The horn is a symbol of strength, because an animal's horn is a key focus of its strength in fighting. Perhaps the colon implies that it is Yhwh's horn that is lifted in asserting strength in relation to other peoples, or perhaps it implies that Yhwh gives strength to the people itself so that it can stand up to its attackers; either way the description re-expresses a theme from Ps. 147.

The last regular line of the psalm might then give a reason why this people is to be an object of praise or admiration on the part of the entities that have occupied us through the bulk of the psalm (cf. Deut. 26:19). But the psalm's drama is increased if we rather assume that *praise has its regular meaning. The lifting up of that horn gives a new reason for *praise on the part of this people whose nature is to be a people *committed to Yhwh. We know who that people is, yet the final colon of the main body of the psalm still brings it to a climax by actually naming this people and then by defining them in yet another and more novel way as "the people who come near him." That is what Israel is privileged to do in its worship. Or perhaps this last phrase describes Israel as "the people to whom he comes near" (cf. 145:18).[16] Coming near is what Yhwh does in lifting up a horn for Israel, whichever way we understand that phrase. Either way, the congregation overhearing this summons to praise is openmouthed on hearing the last line.

16. That is, this is then not the adj. with a third-person suffix but the inf. abs. with a third-person suffix, and the suffix is subjective not objective.

Theological Implications

What does it mean to speak of the heavens and earth praising Yhwh, and why should they do so? *Praise is an inarticulate noise, a la-la-la-la sound, so being unable to articulate sentences is no barrier to giving praise. Much of the heavens and the earth is noisy, and its noise has the ring of praise about it. Its noise draws attention to the one who made it the way it is. As the Psalms see it, silence cannot be praise (except when silence is a mark of trust or submission in particular circumstances). Praise requires noise, and much of creation expresses itself in noise. And the reason why creation should so express itself is that it is secure in the way Yhwh established it. We might say that the noise creation makes is built into its nature by the way God created it. The music of the stars and the swish of the waters, the bellowing of the sea creatures and the howl of the wind, the laughter of young people and the gossiping of old people, all reflect the way Yhwh created them. Every shout, every roar, and every tweet draws attention to the one who made them that way.

So creation, just for being what it is, has plenty of reason for praise. Yet the last three lines of the psalm suddenly give it extra reason for praise. Creation itself looks at what Yhwh does with Israel and finds itself drawn with Israel into even more of that inarticulate worship. For reasons this psalm does not explore, what Yhwh does with Israel is so important that the whole creation joins in praise for it. Perhaps inarticulate worship is the only kind appropriate to the wonder of what Yhwh does in the world and with Israel.

Yet it would be too much to claim that all creation worships Yhwh by making a noise. Much of creation is literally silent. The summons to praise has some other rhetorical significance. Perhaps it chiefly works by personalizing creation, by speaking metaphorically. If creation were capable of making a noise in Yhwh's honor, then it would be appropriate for it to do so. And perhaps we need to reflect on the aim of its rhetoric and consider how this rhetoric works. Presumably the psalm is sung in the temple, and while the entities addressed in vv. 1–6 are listening, those addressed in vv. 7–14 are not. The people who actually hear the psalm, the people who overhear it though they are not directly addressed by it, are Israelites gathered for worship. The psalm's effect is to arouse their wonder, commitment, reverence, and hope in relation to Yhwh as the one who deserves all these entities' praise. It is to draw them into the praise to which all these other entities are directly invited. The closing verse makes that explicit when it comes to its actual reference to what Yhwh has done for Israel.

Psalm 149
Preparing to Leave the Sanctuary

Translation

1Praise Yah.

Sing for Yhwh a new song,
his praise in the congregation of the committed.
2Israel is to rejoice in its maker;[1]
the children of Zion—they are to joy in their king.
3They are to praise his name with dancing,
with tambourine and lyre they are to make music for him.
4Because Yhwh delights in his people,
he will adorn the weak with deliverance.

5The committed are to exult in their honor,[2]
they are to resound on their beds,
6Acclamations of God in their mouth[3]
and[4] a two-edged sword in their hand,

1. JM 136e; *IBHS* 7.4.3d; DG 20c take the form as honorific pl., but GKC 124k sees it as actually sg. Goulder (*Psalms of the Return*, 298) suggests that it might be numerical pl., referring to Yhwh's aides as involved in creation, but it is hard to find clear parallels for this idea, and the parallelism of the line works against it.

2. The suffix on "their beds" also applies to "honor."

3. Lit. "their throat."

4. Tg renders *w* "like," and Raymond J. Tournay ("Le psaume 149 et la 'vengeance' des pauvres de YHWH," *RB* 92 [1985]: 349–58) understands similarly; but see Gottfried Vanoni,

7To execute redress among the nations,
rebukes among the countries,[5]
8To bind their kings with shackles,
their nobles with iron chains,
9To execute among them the decision put into writing:
this will be glory for all his committed people.

Praise Yah.

Interpretation

Yet again a psalm takes a familiar form and does something distinctive with it. After the opening "Praise Yah," the first section (vv. 1b–4) follows the form of a praise psalm, with three lines of bidding to praise and a line of reasons for or content of praise. The second section (vv. 5–9b) begins as if it is a third-person variant on another bidding, which one would expect to be followed by further reasons or content. Instead, it takes off in a different direction and never returns. In theme it resembles the anticipatory praise or prophetic praise of Isa. 42:10–17, which begins exactly like v. 1. In that passage, vv. 10–12 constitute a bidding to praise, and vv. 13–17 provide its grounds or content: Yhwh is about to march out as a warrior, triumph over enemies, and lead the blind home.[6] Thematically, the sequence here is similar, though the statements about warlike action come in infinitives rather than yiqtols. (The bidding in v. 1b also parallels the one that opens Pss. 96 and 98; there the biddings lead into "proper" *kî* clauses, with noun clauses, qatal verbs, and yiqtol verbs.) More significantly, that reflects how the warlike action is to be undertaken not by Yhwh but by the people bidden to give praise. Thus the description of this action does not constitute part of the grounds for praise, either in form or in substance. In form it is an extension of the description of the people who offer the praise, and in substance it draws attention away from their worship to the action they are due to undertake, not after their worship but interwoven with it.

"Zur Bedeutung der althebräischen Konjunktion *w=*: Am Beispiel von Psalm 149,6," in *Text, Methode und Grammatik*, ed. Walter Gross et al. (W. Richter Festschrift; St. Ottilien: EOS, 1991), 561–76; then Jochen Sautermeister, "Psalm 149,6 und die Diskussion um das sogenannte *waw adaequationis*," *BN* 101 (2000): 64–80.

5. As usual, Codex L misdivides *balĕʾummîm* as *bal-ʾummîm*.

6. See John Goldingay and David Payne, *A Critical and Exegetical Commentary on Isaiah 40–55* (London and New York: T&T Clark, 2006), 233, which notes that the term "eschatological praise" is less appropriate. On the connections between Ps. 149 and Isa. 40–66, see Bernard Gosse, "Le psaume cxlix et la réinterprétation post-exilique de la tradition prophétique," *VT* 44 (1994): 259–63.

The psalm closes with another "Praise Yah" to form an inclusion (vv. 1a, 9c). Inside this inclusion come double references to the committed (vv. 1 and 9, with another in v. 5 that might qualify this to be called the psalm's key word)[7] and inside them, references to Yhwh as king and to the nations' kings (vv. 2 and 8).[8]

The opening reference to the congregation of the committed indicates more specifically than most that the psalm presupposes a setting in this congregation's worship, though it is no more specific than others in identifying that worship occasion. Indeed, the phrase need not imply that the congregation is assembled in the temple at all. The parallels with 2 Chron. 20 and Judith 15, noted below (as well as with Exod. 15)[9] warn us against assuming that a celebration such as the one the psalm urges must belong in the temple rather than in the world outside, and most dancing to which the OT refers (see v. 3) takes place in the world outside, not in temple worship.

The psalm takes up prophetic material in Isaiah and Jeremiah, suggesting it belongs in the postexilic period, as does the description of the people as only the children of Zion,[10] and in different ways its stance fits that expressed in Chronicles and Nehemiah.

149:1–4. Biddings to praise, and their reasons.

1Praise Yah.

Sing for Yhwh a new song,
his praise in the congregation of the committed.
2Israel is to rejoice in its maker;
the children of Zion—they are to joy in their king.
3They are to praise his name with dancing,
with tambourine and lyre they are to make music for him.

After the opening "*Praise *Yah," v. 1b corresponds to 96:1a; 98:1a, though there the bidding addresses the whole world. It also corresponds to Isa. 42:10a and then continues to do so with the first word of the parallel colon; but Isa. 42:10 also goes on, "[his praise] from the end of

7. Cf. Norbert Lohfink, *Lobgesänge der Armen* (Stuttgart: Katholisches Bibelwerk, 1990), 121.

8. Cf. Fokkelman, *Major Poems*, 2:321–22; and further on the psalm's rhetorical features, Auffret, *Merveilles à nos yeux*, 277–84; Willem S. Prinsloo, "Psalm 149," *ZAW* 109 (1997): 395–407.

9. Anthony R. Ceresko ("Psalm 149," *Bib* 67 [1986]: 179–94) sees the psalm as a whole as focusing on the exodus (vv. 1–4) and the conquest (vv. 5–9): it thus looks to rejoice in the new exodus and to make a commitment to a new conquest.

10. Cf. Goulder, *Psalms of the Return*, 298.

the earth."[11] The contrast in v. 1c is thus the sharper as it makes clear that the psalm's bidding addresses Israel, like the not-quite-identical Ps. 33:3a. It is actually rare for the worshipping people to be identified as the congregation of the *committed (cf. 22:22, 25 [23, 26]; 35:18; 40:9–10 [10–11]; 107:32), and the *qāhāl* can assemble outside of the temple. So v. 1 could imply worship in the temple or in the world, such as later verses point to.

The move to jussive verbs with v. 2 again parallels Ps. 98 and Isa. 42:10–17, though there it might reflect the fact that psalm and prophet are commanding the praise of peoples and creatures who are not present in the congregation's worship. Where the worshippers are present, the effect of the jussive is to distance them from the bidding and make them look at themselves in the third person. In light of the link with Isa. 42:10–17, it is noteworthy that Isa. 40–55 likes to describe Yhwh as Israel's or Zion's maker (44:2; 51:13; 54:5) and also speaks of Yhwh as Israel's king (43:15, after "creator of Israel"; 44:6). It was in the events from the exodus to Sinai that Yhwh brought Israel into being and became its king. Passages such as 54:1, 13 also think of the community as Zion's children, though that phrase comes only in Joel 2:23 and Lam. 4:2. Those passages make clear that "children of Zion" is a term of endearment that recognizes the way these children have been devastated and desolate; it declares that they are now going to be able to rejoice.

The expression of *praise for Yhwh's *name, with tambourine (or hand drum)[12] and *lyre to make *music, recalls the tone of Yhwh's promises in Jer. 30–31, specifically 31:4, 13. Along with the links with Isa. 40–55, the verse thus suggests a rejoicing in what Yhwh has done or will do in fulfilling the prophets' promises and restoring the people, and in particular the city. In Jer. 31:4, at least, there is no suggestion that the dancing takes place in temple worship.

4Because Yhwh delights in his people,
he will adorn the weak with deliverance.

Why this singing, praising, rejoicing, joying, dancing, and making music? In coming to the explicit basis or content of the psalm's praise,

11. Robert C. Culley (*Oral Formulaic Language in the Biblical Psalms* [Toronto: University of Toronto, 1967], 58) sees the recurrence of this phrase as reflecting the use of stock formulae. But the many direct links between these last psalms in the Psalter and other biblical writings, not least the links between this psalm and Isa. 40–66, and the recurrence of "his praise," suggest that a direct link here is more likely.

12. So H. Seidel, "Ps. 150 und die Gottesdienstmusik in Altisrael," *NedTT* 35 (1981): 89–100 (see 95); I. H. Jones, "Musical Instruments in the Bible, Part I," *BT* 37 (1986): 101–16 (see 112–13).

v. 4 spells out the answer in terms again recalling Isa. 40–55. Israel is Yhwh's servant, and Yhwh's servant is one in whom Yhwh delights (cf. Isa. 42:1). Israel is *weak (cf. Isa. 49:13; 51:21; 54:11) but is one Yhwh is committed to adorning (cf. Isa. 55:5; 60:9; 61:3) with *deliverance (cf. Isa. 49:8; 51:6, 8). The Isaiah passages use the qatal in speaking of Yhwh adorning Israel, but it is the instantaneous qatal that refers to an act that is certain enough to be described as already having happened. The psalm's yiqtol recognizes that this adorning is still future. This highlights the fact that although v. 4 functions as giving the reasons or contents for the praise commissioned in vv. 1–3, its reasoning is somewhat paradoxical, like that in Isa. 42:10–17. The basis for praise lies not in something Yhwh has yet done but in an attitude of Yhwh (v. 4a) that will issue in action in the future (v. 4b). (The point would require only slight restating if we follow EVV in translating the verb "he adorns.")

149:5–9. A further bidding to praise.

5The committed are to exult in their honor,
they are to resound on their beds,

The bidding to the *committed resumes the exhortation to praise in third-person form, urging that people exult and *resound at the honor that is coming to them. While Isa. 40–55 speaks only of the honor coming to Yhwh through delivering Israel, Isa. 61:6 speaks of the community itself enjoying the nations' honor. The rare verb "exult" (*ʿālaz*) described the attitude of Israel's attackers in Ps. 94:3 (subsequent lines will take further links with Ps. 94). It is now the people committed to Yhwh who will do the exulting. While the word can refer to exulting in Yhwh, like its English equivalent it is not one that especially refers to temple worship.

Commentators have hypothesized that these "beds" are places in the temple where people slept when staying there overnight, but the OT does not refer to such customs and only makes negative reference to beds in connection with religious practices (e.g., Isa. 57:7–8). It seems wiser to understand the reference to beds in light of the way the OT does refer to them; again, it is not a word that makes us think of temple worship. Not surprisingly, people lie in bed chiefly in connection with sleep, sex, and sickness, though the OT also mentions the bedroom as a place of privacy[13] and thus of plotting (e.g., Ps. 36:4 [5]). It is familiar with the notion of lying awake in bed, tossing and turning (Job 7:4) or depressed (1 Kings 21:4) or weeping (Ps. 6:6 [7]), and with lying down

13. Cf. Ceresko, "Psalm 149," 186. Augustine (*Psalms*, 679) takes v. 5 to refer to sincerity.

and fasting as an act of repentance (1 Kings 21:27).[14] The last seems most significant.[15] The exilic and postexilic community was demoralized and lamented, and it fasted in connection with the devastation of Jerusalem. The connection of "beds" with repentance makes sense in the context if the psalm is urging people to start exulting and resounding at the honor that contrasts with their current weakness, and (in effect) to repent over the city's ashes, or at least if it is promising that they are going to have cause to do so.

> 6Acclamations of God in their mouth
> and a two-edged sword in their hand,
> 7To execute redress among the nations,
> rebukes among the countries,

The asyndetic enjambment re-expresses the point and takes it further. Exulting means that words exalting Yhwh will be in their mouth; they will be lifting Yhwh up in light of the deliverance that is coming. Verse 6a could thus be a continuation of the summons to praise, in a novel form. But the parallel colon again directs us away from temple worship. Instead of lying demoralized on their beds, people are to get up and wield their swords (lit. "a sword of mouths," a devouring sword).[16] The exile meant that Yhwh turned back the edge of the king's sword (89:43 [44]), but after the exile the community learned how to use its swords again (Neh. 4:13, 18 [7, 12]). It does not achieve things by using its sword independently of Yhwh's action (cf. Ps. 44:3, 6 [4, 7]), but neither does Yhwh usually take action independently of the people using their swords.

If the reference to the sword stood in isolation, one might interpret it less literally. Rashi understood "a two-edged sword in their hand" as another way of saying "acclamations of God in their mouth"; in Cassiodorus, the two-edged sword is the Scriptures comprising OT and NT.[17] It has been suggested that the colon refers to a ritual sword dance,[18] but we know of no such custom in Israel. Although in later times there was indeed a fire dance at Sukkot, vividly described in *m. Sukkah* 5.3–4,[19] it involved no swords. But in any case, the psalm goes on to describe actions

14. Compare also Hos. 7:14 (cf. Michael L. Barré, "Hearts, Beds, and Repentance in Psalm 4,5 and Hosea 7,14," *Bib* 76 [1995]: 53–62), though the context there is elusive. Notger Füglister ("Ein garstig Lied," in *Freude an der Weisung des Herrn*, ed. Haag and Hossfeld, 81–105 [see 101–5]) sees this bed as the place where people lie in death, so that the colon refers to their resurrection; this requires considerable reading into the text.

15. Cf. Jerome, *Homilies*, 2:426.

16. Kirkpatrick, *Psalms*, 831.

17. *Psalms*, 3:460.

18. E.g., Mowinckel, *Psalms*, 1:181.

19. Cf. Goulder, *Psalms of the Return*, 299.

that look very literal, and its perspective corresponds to that of the OT elsewhere. We have noted the swords in Neh. 4. Second Chronicles 20 also vividly describes a gathering for worship in the temple when Judah is under attack from the Moabites and others, worship that continues as the people go out for the victorious battle (which is admittedly one in which the Judeans did not actually have to fight). Following Judith's decapitation of Holofernes and the army's slaughter of his army, Judith 15:12–13 has the women dancing in procession in something like the fashion of this psalm, with the men following in their armor with songs in their mouths.[20] Indeed, v. 6b makes one reread v. 6a and wonder whether that refers to the kind of acclamation of Yhwh that an army would give in battle.[21]

The OT speaks much of the sword in connection with the devastation of Judah and Jerusalem, but the psalm promises that it will not be like that when the nations come to attack Jerusalem the next time. It was necessary for Judah to be put down for its wrongdoing, but it is also necessary for other nations to be put down for their wrongdoing. So there will be *redress and rebukes. In 94:1 Yhwh is God of redress (cf. 18:47 [48]; 79:10); the day when the community is restored is the day when Yhwh takes redress (e.g., Isa. 47:3; 59:17; 61:2; 63:4). Here it seems that Israel is involved in the taking of redress, though to translate *nĕqāmâ* as vengeance gives a misleading impression (see on 94:1). Indeed, the function of the redress is to rebuke them (cf. the word order in 141:5). It is to put them in their place, to chastise them for their attitudes and get them to see the truth about their position in the world and before Yhwh. Again, however, whereas in 94:10 it is Yhwh who rebukes the nations, here Israel is the means of issuing that rebuke.

8To bind their kings with shackles,
  their nobles with iron chains,
9To execute among them the decision put into writing:
  this will be glory for all his committed people.

Praise Yah.

The further account of the way this redress and rebuke will be administered continues to follow the promises of Isa. 40–55. Those chapters speak of kings being put in their place, of people coming to Israel in shackles (Isa. 45:14). Noteworthy is the reversal this involves over against Israel's own earlier experience. The word for "chains" comes otherwise

20. Cf. Gunkel, *Psalmen*, 620.

21. Prinsloo ("Psalm 149") sees v. 6 with its combining of praise and the sword as summing up the psalm as a whole.

only at 105:18; the verse also refers to iron (cf. 107:10, 16). And bound has been the position of the community itself (Isa. 61:1).

But Yhwh has made a *decision (cf. 146:7; 147:19–20) concerning these nations and their leaders; it is the negative side to the decision spoken of in Isa. 42:1–4. The decision is written. It is written in the Torah, Tg explains; Qimchi refers to Deut. 32:41. And/or it is written in the prophets, the Midrash comments, citing Mal. 4:1 [3:19] and Isa. 66:20, 24.[22] It is even written in the Psalms; the Midrash cites 104:35.[23] Yes, this will be glory for Yhwh's *committed ones, to replace the glory that they lost (Lam. 1:6). The reference to the committed joins the bidding "*Praise *Yah" (and the reference to kings in v. 8) in forming an inclusion for the psalm.

Theological Implications

In the context of modernity, as usual a psalm that speaks of inflicting violence meets with the disapproval of European and American commentators, both Christian and Jewish[24] (it does not meet with the disapproval of Christian and Jewish commentators in earlier times or outside Euro-America). First Maccabees 2:42 speaks of "the congregation of the committed" and implies that the psalm came true in the victory over Antiochus; Theodoret is explicit in seeing this to have been so.[25] Commentators routinely speak, with implicit disapproval, of its use by Caspar Schopp (the name is variously spelled) to encourage Roman Catholic princes to fight the Thirty Years' War and by Thomas Müntzer to stir up the Peasants' War.[26] Walter Brueggemann remarks that "this psalm is extremely problematic because . . . it combines 'praise the Lord' with 'pass the ammunition.'" But he goes on, "If this psalm becomes too dangerous to sing in our more bourgeois liturgies, then we may want to consider how such liturgy becomes innocuous and cuts God off from God's deeply rooted social intention."[27]

22. *Midrash on Psalms*, 2:385.

23. Ibid.

24. E.g., Buttenwieser, *Psalms*, 690, who calls it "spiritually valueless."

25. *Psalms*, 2:371.

26. They seem to follow Rowland E. Prothero, *The Psalms in Human Life* (London and New York: Nelson, 1903), 143; he gives no references, and I have been able to find none. But apparently Anabaptist Bernhard Rothmann did make use of the psalm in his tract "On Vengeance" (1534; *Die Schriften Bernhard Rothmanns*, ed. Robert Stupperich [Münster: Aschendorf, 1970], 285–97; see Erik Betten, "Bernhard Rothmann's 'Bericht von der Wrake' and the Dutch Anabaptists," http://docserver.bis.uni-oldenburg.de/publikationen/bisverlag/2001/boeing01/pdf/transfer.pdf).

27. Brueggemann, *Psalms and the Life of Faith*, 124, 125.

Interpreters likewise render it innocuous when they reassure us that it does not mean what it says or that it does not apply to us. It is as if they think that by doing so they reduce the chance of people picking up the sword, as if it is the Scriptures that make them do so. More likely the opposite is the case; people make up their minds to take up the sword and then use the Scriptures to justify their doing so. But by simply declaring that the Scriptures are not relevant (for instance, by seeing the psalm as outdated by the NT), we leave people to make war without taking any notice of the Scriptures. Instead of questioning the premise that the Scriptures have something to say, we are driven by the psalm to accept it and press people to be bound by its principles.[28]

> There is a clear marker that distinguishes the violence that takes hold of God's kingdom from that which wreaks destruction in our world—a difference between the saints' violence, always conjoined with God's high praise, and the unholy violence that rings as shrill mockery in God's ears. . . . Every kind of godless violence is directed at getting something or holding on to it—power, oil, satisfaction, vengeance, personal or national security. But the battle of the saint is always fundamentally directed toward giving praise to God.[29]

Of course, we who feel uneasy about it are members of the great war-making nations, and what we have to be wary of is the fact that this is a psalm for the weak, not the powerful.[30] Augustine knows that in his day the kings and nobles have become Christians, so v. 8 is a puzzle.[31] And it is this fact that makes modern Euro-American interpreters uneasy. We are designed to be the psalm's victims, so we had better make it innocuous. Fortunately, Pss. 148 and 149 offer the nations alternative destinies. We can choose Ps. 148, but we need to be frightened by Ps. 149 first.

How ironic that the Psalter should draw toward its end with a psalm that looks outside the worship of the temple to what happens in life outside, yet how appropriate as we prepare to leave that sanctuary constituted by the Psalter itself. Indeed, the Psalter is in the midst of closing as it opened; this psalm links with the psalms with which the Psalter began.[32] The penultimate psalm compares with the second psalm,

28. Cf. Calvin's comments, *Psalms*, 5:316–17.

29. Ellen F. Davis, "Self-Inflicted Violence," in *The Art of Reading Scripture*, ed. Davis and Richard B. Hays (Grand Rapids: Eerdmans, 2003), 294–99 (see 296); though as her title implies, she applies the psalm to the "violence" we inflict on ourselves, in repentance.

30. Gerstenberger, *Psalms*, 2:457.

31. *Psalms*, 680.

32. Cf. Oswald Loretz, "Psalm 149 und H. Gunkels Historismus," *UF* 25 (1993): 289–310; revised version in Loretz, *Psalmstudien*, 351–80.

which also talks of nations and countries and their kings and leaders, though it democratizes its commission and its promise.[33] And there is no indication that the psalm should be understood eschatologically, any more than is the case with Pss. 1–2. Its promise and its warning apply now.

33. Cf. Schaefer, *Psalms*, 344–45; Keel, *Symbolism*, 303; Lohfink, *Lobgesänge der Armen*, 124–25.

Psalm 150

The End of Prayer Is Praise

Translation

[1]Praise Yah.
Praise God in his sanctuary,
  praise him in his strong firmament.[1]
[2]Praise him for his mighty acts,
  praise him in accordance with his immense greatness.
[3]Praise him with the blast of the horn,
  praise him with harp and lyre.
[4]Praise him with tambourine and dancing,
  praise him with strings and pipe.
[5]Praise him with loud cymbals,
  praise him with noisy cymbals.
[6]Every breath is to praise Yhwh;
  praise Yah.

Interpretation

The closing psalm, like so many in the last part of the Psalter, again starts from one of the regular psalm types but then transforms it. This praise psalm comprises nothing but an exhortation to praise. Reasons for praise

1. In the construct expression "the firmament of his strength," the absolute noun presumably functions adjectivally (for analogous expressions, see 61:3 [4]; 62:7 [8]; 68:33 [34]; 89:10 [11]; 110:2; 132:8, also "immense greatness" in v. 2). It is thus odd that NJPS has "the sky, his stronghold."

do come in two prepositional expressions in v. 2, but there are no actual clauses to give content to the praise. Admittedly it would be wooden to treat this fact about the psalm's form as if it said the final word about its significance. The very fact that this is the last psalm in the Psalter makes it unlikely that worshippers saw it as comprising only a bidding to praise. In Christian usage, when people say "Praise the Lord," the words are formally merely a bidding, but in function are themselves an expression of praise. "Praise is implicit throughout the very exhortation itself."[2] But its focus on the act of praise makes it a proper close for the Psalter; it is perhaps an equivalent to the codas that close its first four books. Once we have seen what it is, we can see that this is the only way the Psalter could close. To attempt to say something final about Yhwh would inevitably be anticlimactic. Everything that the previous 149 psalms have affirmed about Yhwh offers the reasons and the content for this praise.

In itself it details the where, why, how, and who of praise.[3] After the opening "Praise Yah," the first line notes the location of this praise (v. 1b–c), the second line its basis (v. 2), three lines its accompaniment (vv. 3–5), and one line who is to offer it (v. 6). As with Ps. 149, it is initially natural to assume that its praise is offered in the Jerusalem temple, though the opening line points in another direction, as does the instrumentation detailed in vv. 3–5, and the prescription in v. 6.

The reference to the ram's horn rather than the metal trumpet to which Chronicles refers and the use of the word for cymbals that otherwise comes only in 2 Sam. 6:5 may suggest that the psalm is a preexilic one, held back in the Psalter to use at the end of the final groups of psalms, which are mostly postexilic.

1Praise Yah.
Praise God in his sanctuary,
  praise him in his strong firmament.
2Praise him for his mighty acts,
  praise him in accordance with his immense greatness.

150:1–2. The psalm begins as it means to go on, with a bidding to *praise. In different contexts *qōdeš* could refer to the temple on earth or the temple in the heavens (or to Yhwh's own holiness); here the parallel colon dispels any ambiguity. While *rāqîaʿ* refers to the sky, that translation would give a misleading impression, since the psalm is thinking of the solid dome in the heavens, above which Yhwh's throne sits, securely established by Yhwh. If the "in" expressions tell us where God is, it would be natural to reckon that the entities called on to praise are worshippers

2. Mowinckel, *Psalms*, 1:83.
3. Kidner, *Psalms*, 2:490–92.

in the earthly temple. But Ps. 148 called for praise from the heavens, on the part of Yhwh's aides, and it would be just as plausible here to reckon that the bidding refers to praise offered in the heavenly sanctuary. The temple choir likely commissions this praise, but the entities expected to offer it may not be the congregation in the earthly temple but the beings in the heavenly sanctuary and the other beings implied by v. 6.[4]

In the only indication of a reason for this *praise, "mighty acts" recurs from 145:4, 12, and 106:2, where it denotes the acts whereby Yhwh brought Israel into being and delivers Israel, though we should perhaps not reduce the expression to too much precision; it could also include Yhwh's acts of creation. Verse 2b issues an even more demanding bidding in urging that the praise should correspond to Yhwh's immense greatness.

3Praise him with the blast of the horn,
praise him with harp and lyre.
4Praise him with tambourine and dancing,
praise him with strings and pipe.
5Praise him with loud cymbals,
praise him with noisy cymbals.

150:3–5. Six cola itemize the sound that conveys this *praise. They include instruments that belong more in temple worship and those that belong more outside it; every means is summoned to magnify Yhwh. They include instruments that would be played by priests (the horn), by Levites (harp, lyre, cymbals), and by laypeople (tambourine, strings, pipe). "The Psalmist, therefore, in exhorting believers to pour forth all their joy in the praises of God, enumerates, one upon another, all the musical instruments which were then in use, and reminds them that they ought all to be consecrated to the worship of God."[5] There is no reference here to words or to feelings of adoration; all the emphasis lies on noise.

The horn is the instrument by which one issues a blast, rather than plays a tune. It may come first because the sounding of a horn announces or initiates things, such as the beginning of worship, rather than being an actual part of them.[6] *Harp and *lyre are then the regular stringed imstruments to which the psalms refer.

4. See H. P. Mathys, "Psalm cl," *VT* 50 (2000): 329–44 (see esp. 339–43).

5. Calvin, *Psalms*, 5:320 (though he then comments that this only applied to believers when they were under the law). On the instruments, see Joachim Braun, *Music in Ancient Israel/Palestine* (Grand Rapids: Eerdmans, 2002), 16–32; J. H. Eaton, "Music's Place in Worship," *OtSt* 23 (1984): 85–107; Keel, *Symbolism*, 335–52; H. Seidel, "Ps. 150 und die Gottesdienstmusik in Altisrael," *NedTT* 35 (1981): 89–100; Edo Škuij, "Musical Instruments in Psalm 150," in *The Interpretation of the Bible*, ed. Jože Krašovec (JSOT Sup 289; Sheffield: Sheffield Academic Press, 1998), 1117–30.

6. Cf. Allen, *Psalms 101–150*, 404.

Tambourine (or hand drum) and dance recur from 149:3; they go together, because women play this instrument as they dance (cf. Exod. 15:20). Strings (which comes only here) is another stringed instrument or might stand for stringed instruments generally. It is Tg that suggests that *ʿûgāb* is a pipe; it might in turn suggest wind instruments in general. None of the instruments in v. 4 are associated with temple worship, though they can be associated with the praise of Yhwh in other contexts.

The third line notes the characteristic double nature of cymbals, that they are (literally) cymbals of hearing and cymbals of shout; they make themselves heard. The two expressions might denote two different kinds of cymbals (e.g., something more like castanets and something more like actual cymbals)[7] or two different functions fulfilled by the same instruments at different times (e.g., encouraging people to listen to what is about to happen and telling them it is time to shout in acclamation).[8] One might compare the use of bells in Latin worship, which give signals to the congregation regarding what is going on. But the only other occurrence of this word is 2 Sam. 6:5 (Chronicles has a different word for the cymbals used on this occasion and on other occasions in the temple).

6Every breath is to praise Yhwh;
praise Yah.

150:6. As happens in Ps. 148, a sequence of imperatives gives way to a jussive at the end (cf. also Ps. 149, though there the balance of imperatives and jussives is reversed). Every breath may denote every human being or every living creature (cf. Gen. 7:22) or every breath applied to a musical instrument.

I take the closing "*praise *Yah" as constituting the second colon of the final line as well as forming an inclusion with v. 1a, much as the opening "Praise Yah" was part of the opening line in Ps. 147 and even more as it was part of the closing line in Ps. 104.[9]

Theological Implications

The Psalter has been dominated by prayer. But it did not start there, and it does not end there; "the end of prayer is praise."[10] Further, the enthusiasm about noise in worship that dominates this psalm issues

7. Cf. *HALOT*.

8. So I. H. Jones, "Musical Instruments in the Bible, Part I," *BT* 37 (1986): 101–16 (see 110–11).

9. Cf. Fokkelman, *Major Poems*, 2:323.

10. Peterson, *Answering God*, 121.

the Psalter's closing piece of advice to intellectual and socially activist readers of the Psalms. It ignores the possible anti-intellectual or escapist implications of its enthusiasm in order to fulfill this function.[11] It is prepared to take that risk in order to remind us that sharp thinking and social function are not the only important things in the world. Indeed, it makes no reference to intelligent content, sincerity of heart, integrity of life, feelings of joy, or commitment of love. It closes with simple enthusiasm. It expresses "lyrical self-abandonment, an utter yielding of self, without vested interest, calculation, desire, or hidden agenda."[12]

The Psalter thus takes big risks with both its closing psalms, though their riskiness offers mutual safeguard. The closing juxtaposition of Pss. 149 and 150, like the opening juxtaposition of Pss. 1 and 2, does hold together "complete devotion to God" with "intense political resolve."[13] Further, while Ps. 1 concerns the individual, Ps. 150 concerns the community, not just Israelite and not just human and not just earthly. And while Ps. 1 "asserts in a decisive way that life under torah is the precondition of all these psalms," Ps. 150 "states the outcome of such a life under torah," in "*unencumbered praise*." Thus "the expectation of the Old Testament is not finally *obedience,* but *adoration*."[14]

> I urge those reading this book, if it seems to be a fit and proper work of commentary, to reap benefit from them. If, on the other hand, we have not in some cases arrived at the Spirit's hidden mysteries, do not be too hard on us: what we succeeded in finding we proposed to everyone without stint, and what we learned from the Fathers we were anxious to offer to posterity. The labor undergone was ours; for others free of labor is the benefit we offer. I ask them to repay the labor with prayers, so that relying on them we may add actions to words, and reap the beatitude that arises from both.[15]

> Who would even dare to assert that anyone has completely understood one single psalm?[16]

11. So Allen, *Psalms 101–150*, 405; Brueggemann, *Israel's Praise*, 148.
12. Walter Brueggemann, "Bounded by Obedience and Praise," *JSOT* 50 (1991): 63–92 (see 67).
13. Brueggemann, *Psalms and the Life of Faith*, 125.
14. Brueggemann, *Message of the Psalms*, 167.
15. Theodoret, *Psalms*, 2:374.
16. Luther, *Selected Psalms*, 3:284.

Glossary

The following comments relate to words marked * in the commentary. Entries mostly refer to passages from Pss. 90–150 but are generally not exhaustive.

Acknowledge (*yāda'*). The verb covers the range of the English word "know," in that it can refer to knowing facts and knowing people, to head knowledge and experiential knowledge. But it also covers the range of English words such as "acknowledge" and "recognize." It thus suggests a knowing that issues in a response of the will. EVV occasionally reflect this in their translations, but it is worth asking more broadly whether in a given context *yāda'* refers to something more than head or heart knowledge (92:6 [7]; 94:10).

Against, be (*śānē'*). EVV usually translate "hate," but it regularly refers to action rather than emotion. The participle is a standard word for "foes" and thus refers to their hostile actions rather than to their negative feelings. To be against wrong is to repudiate it (97:10).

Aide (*mal'āk*). The LXX translates the word by *angelos*, "messenger," which is then represented in English as "angel." But *mal'āk* comes from a root denoting "work." Although a *mal'āk* can function as a messenger, this is just part of a broader role fulfilled by someone who functions as servant of a king and sees that the king's decisions get implemented; see 91:11.

Anointed (*māšîaḥ*). A *māšîaḥ* is someone who has had oil poured or smeared on him, in accordance with Middle Eastern custom, as a sacramental sign of his designation and authorization to fulfill tasks. It is not a participle, like the English word, but a noun and thus designates an ongoing status rather than drawing attention to an event. We could invent the word "anointee" to translate it. In Israel priests and kings could be so designated (see 132:10, 17). Literally, they were anointed by other human beings, but these were acting on Yhwh's behalf so that by this rite people became "Yhwh's anointed." In Qumran documents it comes to refer to a future king or future priest, but in

OT times it refers to an actual one, not a Messiah in the sense of a leader to come in the future.

Ascents (*maʿălôt*). The Songs of the Ascents comprise Pss. 120–34. They have some distinctive linguistic features such as the use of the relative prefix *še* more often than *ʾăšer* and some recurrent phrases such as "maker of the heavens and the earth" and "from now and forevermore," which might be reckoned to constitute a stair- or terrace-like pattern. There have been imaginative attempts to see them as a sequence, but "there is no universally accepted understanding of the designation nor of the nature of the group"[1] (of course the pessimist could add that there are few universally accepted understandings of anything in the Psalms). In 2 Kings 20:9–11, *maʿălôt* mean "steps," though in a metaphorical sense (contrast Jerome with LXX), and according to Rashi's comment on Ps. 120, the Levites sang the fifteen psalms on the fifteen steps by which one would make the ascent from the court of Israel to the court of the women. But *m. Sukkah* 5.1 and *m. Middot* 2.5 note only that the number of psalms and the number of steps correspond, not that the psalms were sung there. Qimchi on Ps. 120 offers the interpretation that is now usual, that the psalms were used by pilgrims climbing up to Jerusalem. It has been argued that they were written or redacted to form a coherent collection,[2] but the diversity among them in form, subject matter, and apparent dating supports the view that they are of separate origin but came to form a resource book for pilgrims.[3] Each psalm then works individually. Given that most psalm titles (especially ones that refer to occasions when the psalms were used) are later than the psalms themselves and tell us not about the original context in which they were used but about ways they were subsequently reused, it makes sense if this is also true of the Songs of the Ascents. It would both explain how this group of psalms is collected together and account for the fact that individually they are so diverse. GKC 127e suggests that the term originally referred to the collection as a whole, when it would mean "the Songs of Ascents." Only subsequently was it adapted for attaching to the psalms individually as the slightly anomalous expression that strictly means "the song of ascents."

Authority (*mišpāṭ*). EVV usually translate the noun and the verb *šāpaṭ* by words such as "judgment," "justice," or "judge," and they do sometimes refer to judicial action, but this is but one aspect of a broader meaning that more

1. Grossberg, *Centripetal and Centrifugal Structures*, 15. Crow surveys the history of the interpretation of the term (*Songs of Ascents*, 4–25).

2. See, e.g., Allen, *Psalms 101–150*, 193–97; Auffret, *La sagesse*, 439–531; Crow, *Songs of Ascents*; Grossberg, *Centripetal and Centrifugal Structures*, 15–54; Leon J. Liebrich, "The Songs of Ascents and the Priestly Blessing," *JBL* 74 (1955): 33–36; Klaus Seybold, "Die Redaktion der Wallfahrtspsalmen," *ZAW* 91 (1979): 247–68; Hendrick Viviers, "The Coherence of the *Maʿălôt* Psalms," *ZAW* 106 (1994): 275–89; Erich Zenger, "The Composition and Theology of the Fifth Book of Psalms," *JSOT* 80 (1998): 77–102 (see 92). These works also discuss the theories concerning the meaning of the term "Songs of Ascents."

3. Cf. Klaus Seybold, *Die Wallfahrtspsalmen* (Neukirchen: Neukirchener Verlag, 1978), 84.

commonly runs through the use of the words. They denote the exercise of authority or governance and thus the making of decisions for people. In the Psalms, this is particularly significant when they speak of God ruling or governing (not judging) the world, or making decisions for the poor (not judging them; 96:13; 98:9; 103:6; 146:7). They are fundamentally power words; it is thus possible for *mišpāṭ* to be exercised in an unjust way and it is worth asserting that Yhwh's authoritative decisions are characterized by *faithfulness (119:7; cf. 96:13; 98:9).

Bad (*ra'*). Like the English word, *ra'* covers both wrongdoing and calamity, as in the expression "bad things happen to bad people."

Bow low (*hištaḥăwâ*). There are two rival parsings of the verb; BDB takes it as hitpalel from *šāḥâ*; *HALOT* as eshtafel from *ḥāwâ*. Either way, it denotes bowing right down. EVV often render it "worship," but it refers to the physical act of prostration rather than the attitude that accompanies this act, and it can refer to a proper prostration before a human being.

Comfort (*nāḥam* piel, *neḥāmâ*). The verb and the noun can refer both to the declaring of comforting words (Isa. 40:1) and to the taking of comforting action (Isa. 52:9). The context will need to indicate whether the words refer to facts or to feelings or to both.

Commitment, committed (*ḥesed, ḥāsîd*). EVV translate *ḥesed* by expressions such as "steadfast love" and "constant love." It is sometimes described as covenant love, though in the OT it rarely appears in the company of the word "covenant." It is used in two connections: when someone makes an act of commitment for which there is no reason in terms of prior relationship, and when someone keeps their commitment when they might be expected to abandon it (e.g., because the other person has done so). It is the Hebrew equivalent to the Greek *agapē*. "Yhwh's committed ones" is a term to describe Israelites; like the NT term "saints," it is an honorific term and might not correspond to their actual stance in relation to Yhwh. In the second century *ḥăsîdîm* came to be a term for Jews who really were committed to Yhwh, but there is no indication that in the Psalter it means a group within Israel.

Composition (*mizmôr*). See *Music.

Confess, confession (*yādâ* hiphil, *tôdâ*). EVV translate with "give thanks," "thanksgiving," or similar words, which express one aspect of their significance; they denote people addressing Yhwh with their appreciation for what Yhwh has done for them. Strictly they refer to what Yhwh has done for one personally and directly (109:30), though they also come to denote acknowledging what Yhwh did long ago for one's people or for what Yhwh regularly does (111:1). The verb can also be used with regard to sins (32:5), which shows that it denotes the owning of the truth of something, whether something good or bad. Further, giving thanks for what Yhwh has done is always undertaken for other people to hear. Thanksgiving is essentially testimony.

Covenant (*bĕrît*). A covenant is a solemn undertaking that is sealed and thus properly binding. It may be a one-sided undertaking by one person to another (e.g., by Yhwh to David, 89:3, 28, 34, 39 [4, 29, 35, 40]; or by Yhwh to Israel,

105:8, 10; 106:45; 111:5, 9; or required by Yhwh of Israel, 103:18; 132:12). Or it may be an agreement between two parties, which in the Psalms comes only between human partners (83:5 [6]).

Crag (*ṣûr*). A *ṣûr* is a "rock" (so EVV), but specifically it is a high rock that is difficult to access and therefore a potentially secure place of refuge.

Cry for help (*šāwaʿ, šawʿâ*). The verb and the noun are nicely similar to the verb *yāšaʿ* (hiphil), "*deliver"; they refer to a cry for deliverance in danger.

David's (*lĕdāwid*). MT designates Pss. 101, 108–10, 122, 124, 131, 133, 138–45 *lĕdāwid* (a number of others also are "David's" in 11QPs[a] or LXX). In the OT, the name can refer to David ben Jesse, or to a later Davidic king, or to a coming David. In any of those senses, in the Psalms it might indicate that the psalm in question was written for David or about David or to David, or that it was written by David, though it is unlikely that any of these Davids personally wrote any of the Psalms.[4] It may often invite us to imagine David using the psalm.

Decision, decisiveness (*šāpaṭ, mišpāṭ*). See *Authority.

Declaration (*ʿēdût*). Yhwh's declarations (also *ʿēdâ*, but the word occurs only in the plural) are solemn statements expressing Yhwh's expectations. Their etymology links them with the verb *ʿûd* meaning "testify," which draws attention to the solemnity of Yhwh's declaring them.

Dedicated, be (*ʾāhēb*). EVV translate "love," but its connotations suggest at least as much a commitment of the will as a feeling (122:6). Thus loving Yhwh's commands suggests obeying them and not just liking them (119:47). It is the antonym of "be *against."

Delight (*šāʿaʿ, šaʿăšuʿîm*). Paradoxically (in view of what is said above under "*dedicated, be"), Yhwh's teaching is also something we delight in (*šāʿaʿ*; the noun is *šaʿăšuʿîm*). In ordinary usage the word suggests a child's uninhibited, carefree playfulness (Isa. 11:8; 66:12; cf. the noun in Prov. 8:30–31; Jer. 31:20).

Deliverance (*yāšaʿ*). EVV render *yāšaʿ* and its related nouns by words such as "save" and "salvation" (96:2), but in Christian thinking these words are inclined to suggest saving people from God's wrath and giving them eternal life. The OT does believe that people are forgiven and put into relationship with God (though they also know that death is the end; see *Sheol). But they do not use these words to refer to those realities. Deliverance involves Yhwh's saving people from other people or from calamity. EVV sometimes use words such as "victory" or "triumph" (98:1), but this obscures the meaning of the word in another direction.

Face (*pānîm*). The word *pānîm* is also the Hebrew word for "presence," since a person's presence and attitude are suggested by the look on their face. It is the face that turns and looks, that notices and acts in love, commitment, generosity, deliverance, and blessing. The shining of the face implies looking on people with a life-giving smile, with love and generosity, and acting accordingly. If someone can be prevailed on to smile at a suppliant, all else will follow. So seeking God's

4. See the introduction in the first volume of this commentary.

face means seeking for God to look at us in such a way as to act thus, and seeing God's face means seeing such prayers answered as we experience vindication and deliverance. To come "before Yhwh" is literally to come "to Yhwh's face." On the other hand, hiding the face, turning the face from people's oppression and need, means ignoring that need, a terrifying act because it means there will be no deliverance or blessing (102:2 [3]). But it is a comforting act when Yhwh's face is averted from our sin (51:9 [11]) and when Yhwh's face is against wrongdoers (34:16 [17]).

Fail (*ḥāṭāʾ, ḥaṭṭāʾ*). The words are regularly translated "sin." In ordinary usage the verb meant to aim at something and fail to reach it or fall short of it. Applied to the moral and religious realm, the words do not suggest that we try our best but fail; we fall short because we do not aim right or because we aim in the wrong direction.

Faithful, faithfulness (*ṣaddîq, ṣedeq, ṣĕdāqâ*). EVV render with words such as "just" and "righteous," which conveys part of their significance. They do connote doing the right thing, but they refer to doing the right thing in light of our relationships and commitments rather than merely in light of an objective standard of justice and righteousness or being righteous in our individual personal morality. So God is *ṣaddîq* to us when forgiving our sins and when protecting or delivering us (143:11). "Faithful" or "faithfulness" thus corresponds to the words' significance. Further, *ṣĕdāqâ* often accompanies *mišpāṭ* (*authority) to connote the decisive exercise of authority on behalf of people with whom one is in relationship (EVV have expressions such as "justice and righteousness"; 99:4).

Faithless (*rāšaʿ, rešaʿ*). EVV translate "wicked, wickedness." They are the antonyms of *ṣaddîq, ṣedeq*, and *ṣĕdāqâ*, and thus denote a failure to do the right thing in light of our relationship with and our commitments to someone.

Falsehood (*šeqer*). The word can refer to deceptive relationships with Yhwh; that is, it can refer to people who are secretly having recourse to other gods as well as Yhwh. It can also denote deceptive relationships with others; that is, when people are making accusations of wrongdoing of which the accused are innocent. This alleged wrongdoing might itself involve either recourse to other gods or wrong done to other people. Falsehood is what does not correspond to reality. It is testimony that does not correspond to what happened, or an image that corresponds to no reality and thus cannot save, or a promise that does not come true.

Forever (*lĕʿôlām*). The expression literally means "to an age." The context must guide us in determining how long the "forever" is. In passages such as 119:89, it does refer to Yhwh's being everlasting. In passages such as 110:4, it suggests "throughout your lifetime."

Good (*ṭûb, ṭôb*). The words are wide-ranging antonyms of *raʿ* (*bad), so they can refer to doing what is good as opposed to what is wicked but also to experiencing what is good as opposed to what is bad—that is, blessing. While *ṭôb* thus means "good" in as general a sense as the English word, "to speak of God as good is to affirm that the Lord is the source of all that makes life possible and worthwhile, the deliverer of those in trouble and distress, the one who, in making this whole universe, marked it forever as 'very good.'"[5] As LXX puts it, God is *chrēstos*: kind, bountiful, and generous. Goodness involves more than doing what is merely objectively right.

Good fortune (*'ašrê*). The formula in EVV "blessed are those" or "happy are those" represents the plural construct noun *'ašrê*, "the blessings of," which is a different expression from the regular word for "bless," *bārak*. Whereas *bārak* suggests making fruitful, *'ašrê* is a broader word that actually corresponds more closely to the English word "blessings." The Hebrew is a noun exclamation, without a verb. This construct plural is the only form in which the word occurs (a similar noun *'ōšer* comes once, in Gen. 30:13). It is not numerical plural but intensive plural.[6] Further, it does not mean "blessing" in a merely "spiritual" sense, though it would include that—the expression would hardly be applied to godless people merely because they did well in life. But it is a less religious-sounding or liturgical word than the English word "blessed." It suggests that people's whole lives work out well. The contexts of the declaration suggest that it has two aspects. Positively, Yhwh gives all good things (84:11–12 [12–13]; cf. 112:1–3; 128; 144:15). Negatively, Yhwh sees people are delivered from trouble and preserved in crises (65:4 [5]; 94:12). It "is not a wish and not a promise. . . . It is a joyful cry and a passionate statement."[7]

Grace (*ḥēn*, *ḥānan*). Like Greek *charis*, Hebrew *ḥēn* and the verb *ḥānan* (more frequent in the Psalms) suggest favor shown to people when they have no basis for demanding it. Grace is the positive, generous attitude a person shows to someone else when there is no existent relationship or desert that the latter could appeal to. In human relationships, it corresponds to the way we may ask someone else to "do us a favor." It is a generosity or mercy shown because the person showing it wishes to do so; its basis emerges from the giver rather than because of the recipients' worthiness. Thus etymologically *taḥănûnîm* (116:1) are prayers for Yhwh to show grace in responding to a plea, appeals to Yhwh's nature as one who acts with favor and grace toward people irrespective of their deservingness but because that is indeed Yhwh's nature.

Harm (*'āwen*). It has been argued that "people who do harm" (*pō'ălê-'āwen*; 92:7, 9 [8, 10]) are people who use words to cause harm by the manipulation of demonic power, but the Psalms' language is too general to infer this or any other specific and precise connotation for the phrase.[8] It simply denotes causing harm to someone. But the language's generality means that psalms in which it appears are open to being used by people under various forms of verbal attack that threaten their well-being and life.

5. Patrick D. Miller, "Psalm 136:1–9, 23–26," *Int* 48 (1995): 390–93 (see 391).

6. Cf. BDB.

7. Martin Buber, *Good and Evil* (New York: Scribner's, 1952), 53. Waldemar Janzen ("'Ašrê in the Old Testament," *HTR* 58 [1965]: 215–26) renders it "enviable."

8. See, e.g., *TDOT* or *NIDOTTE* on *'āwen*.

Harp (*nēbel*). The *nēbel* is perhaps a variant on the *kinnôr*, *lyre. It sometimes explicitly had ten strings, whereas the lyre had less, and the harp may have been a louder and/or deeper instrument.[9]

Heart (*lēb*, *lēbāb*). The *lēb* or *lēbāb* is the center of the person and thus the place where the person thinks things through and comes to decisions; the English word "mind" covers much of its meaning. It is much rarer in the OT than it is in English for the heart to suggest the emotions. So a person without heart is a senseless person (95:10 NJPS).

Help (*ʿāzar*, *ʿēzer*, *ʿezrâ*). The context in which the words are used shows how helping does not denote assisting people who are doing their part but rescuing people when they are helpless, people such as the wretched or the orphan, who have no protection and no resources. "Help" is thus a rather feeble equivalent for *ʿēzer*, which suggests a powerful person taking decisive action on behalf of a weak person who is in dire need. In English, without "help" we might manage OK but a little less comfortably; in Hebrew, without *ʿēzer* we would often be dead (94:17; 107:12; 118:13; 124:8 in their context).

Holy, holiness (*qōdeš*). Holiness points to the distinctiveness and separateness of God over against humanity. God's holiness denotes God in person; God *is* the holy one (99:3, 5, 9). Thus God speaks "by his holiness," that is, "by himself" (108:7 [8]). Holiness then points to the distinctiveness and separateness of places that belong to God (99:9; 150:1) and of people who belong to God (106:16). It is not directly a moral category—it is more like "divine" over against "human" than "righteous" over against "wicked"—though because Yhwh *is* a moral character, it comes to have moral implications (see 15:1 and 24:3 in their contexts).

Honor (*kābôd*). The word *kābôd* (EVV "glory") suggests the visible splendor of a monarch or some other important person, glorious in their impressive array, and thus it is used of the splendor of Yhwh as King (102:15–16 [16–17]). The visible honor is then assumed to be an appropriate outward expression of the intrinsic worth (cf. the verb *kābēd* piel in 91:15)—though this may not always be so (49:16–17 [17–18]). The adjective *kābēd* means "heavy," and a person of honor is a person of weight.

Ignore (*šākaḥ*). The verb can suggest forgetting something accidentally, but more often it denotes deliberately putting something out of mind (119:16, 61, 83, 93, 109, 139, 141, 153, 176). It is thus the opposite of being *mindful.

Integrity (*tāmîm*, *tām*). EVV often have words such as "blameless" or "perfect" (101:2, 6). Over against the first, *tāmîm* is a positive word; it does not suggest the absence of something, and specifically not the absence of blame. Over against the second, to be *tāmîm* does not imply being sinless (Job was *tām*, but he knew he was not sinless). Etymologically, the words suggest "whole," but they do not have psychological connotations. They suggest a fundamental orientation of one's life toward what is right.

9. See Joachim Braun, *Music in Ancient Israel/Palestine* (Grand Rapids: Eerdmans, 2002), 22–24; Keel, *Symbolism*, 346–49.

Law (*ḥōq*, *ḥuqqâ*). A *ḥōq* or *ḥuqqâ* is a statute or decree, etymologically something that has been prescribed or inscribed (*ḥāqaq*).

Lord (*ʾădōnāy*). This word looks as if it would mean "my lords," but it usually refers to Yhwh. There are two ways of understanding the ending.[10] The plural may be honorific, a plural of majesty, so that the expression means "my Lord." This fits (e.g.) 130:2, 3, 6. But Ugaritic had a sufformative similar to this *-āy* with an emphatic or intensifying sense, so this sufformative might function simply to reinforce the meaning of the word; an English equivalent might be "*the* Lord." The ancient versions render simply "the Lord."

Lyre (*kinnôr*). To judge from the OT and from archeological discoveries, the *kinnôr* was the most common Israelite musical instrument, an equivalent of a guitar or banjo, but freestanding or handheld. It could be plucked or strummed.[11]

Mindful, be (*zākar*). As the antonym of *ignore, *zākar* usually suggests not an accidental remembering but a deliberate holding in mind or applying of the mind, which then issues in action (106:4, 7, 45; 137:1, 6, 7); it can refer to the present and future as well as the past.

Most High (*ʿelyôn*). In ordinary usage *ʿelyôn* denotes something high (Neh. 3:25), and thus it designates Yhwh as the exalted one (97:9). It could suggest Yhwh's exaltation over the world and over other deities, and might point especially to Yhwh's power. Apparently it was a title of God as worshipped by the pre-Israelite people of Jerusalem and came to be an honorific title for Yhwh (cf. Gen. 14:18–22; also Num. 24:16).

Murmur (*śîaḥ*, *śîḥâ*). The words are traditionally translated by words such as "meditate" (Ps. 119) or "lament" (cf. BDB). But what would be the relationship between these meanings? The first translation points us to the fact that the words suggest something broader than lament; they imply strong inner feelings, which may be of a lament or protest kind but need not be.[12] The second translation points us to the fact that they suggest something more vocal than meditation; they imply strong feelings that are outwardly expressed.[13]

Music (*zāmar* piel). EVV often take the verb to denote praise (98:4–5), but it is the regular Hebrew word for making music in a general sense. It thus draws attention to the musical aspect to both praise and prayer. The term "composition" (*mizmôr*) recurs in psalm headings. LXX translates this term *psalmos*, a song sung to the harp, but in English "psalm" came to be a specifically religious song, whereas *mizmôr* simply denotes a musical composition.

Name (*šēm*). As in English, in the OT someone's "name" is sometimes simply a label they go by, though even then (as in English) the name summons up the person; when we think of someone's name, we think of the person. Thus

10. See, e.g., *IBHS* 7.4.3e–f, which reckons that the second understanding is always correct.

11. See Braun, *Music in Ancient Israel/Palestine*, 16–19; Keel, *Symbolism*, 346–49.

12. Cf. Sigmund Mowinckel, "The Verb Śiªḥ and the Nouns Śiªḥ, Śiḥā," *ST* 15 (1961): 1–10.

13. Cf. Hans-Peter Müller, "Die hebräische Wurzel שיח," *VT* 19 (1969): 361–71.

the name Yhwh (the pronunciation was probably originally Yahweh) draws attention to the person. But sometimes names have a meaning that can suggest the nature of the person or their parents' hopes for the person or their position or their job (e.g., Grace, Faith, Duke, Smith). Thus the name Yhwh could remind people that Yhwh is the God who will always be there, being what people need God to be in different situations. To praise that name (or any name), trust in the name, or take the name lightly is then to praise the person, trust in the person, or take the person lightly. Conversely, to eliminate the name is to eliminate the person. For Yhwh's name to act is for Yhwh to act, and the fact that the name sums up the person's character means that a key act under pressure is to call on Yhwh's name and thus summon Yhwh in person. The actual uttering of the name makes the presence of the person a reality, just because the name expresses who the person is. Acting for the sake of the name implies acting in accordance with who the person truly is, and demonstrating that.

Needy (*'ebyôn*). Along with "poor" and "*weak," *'ebyôn* is one of the OT's words for people without resources. While these words can be used more or less synonymously, *'ebyôn* draws attention in particular to the vulnerability that poverty brings to someone.

Orders (*piqqudîm*). *Piqqudîm* are things Yhwh appointed (*pāqad*).

Person (*nepeš*). *Nepeš* is a word of wide-ranging meaning. It can denote the person as a whole, or the person's inner being, outer being, or life. EVV often translate "soul," which can be appropriate, but it is misleading to think of *nepeš* as denoting the soul as the real person within a disposable shell called the body (see 121:7).

Plea (*tĕpillâ*). The background of *tĕpillâ* lies in the deliberations of a court. The verb *pālal* often refers to a court's proceedings (a *pālîl* is a judge), so that in a *tĕpillâ* people cast themselves in their need on the mercy of Yhwh's court.

Possession (*naḥălâ*). Etymologically *naḥălâ* suggests something we possess by inheriting it; hence EVV's "inheritance." But even Yhwh can have a *naḥălâ* (94:5, 14); the word denotes a secure possession, without focusing on how it comes to be that.

Praise (*hālal*). The verb denotes making a la-la-la-la sound or ululating. It thus suggests the enthusiasm expressed in wordless vocal noise. The word *tĕhillâ* (hitpael) presumably then suggests such wordless praise, though its appearance in the heading to Ps. 145 may indicate that it was used in a broader sense to denote enthusiastic praise. The expression "praise Yah" (*hallĕlû-yāh*) usually opens psalms, and it has been suggested that when it appears at the end of a psalm (Pss. 104; 106; 113; 115; 116; 135; 146; 147; 148; 149; 150) it has been displaced from the beginning of the next psalm. But this sometimes produces duplication because the next psalm already begins thus (and it cannot apply to Ps. 150). So it seems that the expression can come at the beginning or the end or both.

Rebellion (*peša'*). *Peša'* is traditionally translated "transgression," but it denotes an offense against a person, not a law, and in nonreligious contexts the word suggests rebelling against a human authority such as a parent or an emperor.

Recourse, have (*dāraš*; *bāqaš*). Hebrew uses *dāraš* and *bāqaš* (piel, "seek help from") more or less as synonyms (105:3–4). Both relate to treating someone as a resource for guidance and help. Translations such as "seek Yhwh" are misleading if they suggest seeking a religious experience; the verbs denote looking to Yhwh as one who can and must be our resource.

Redeem, redemption (*pādâ*, *pĕdût*). The words literally refer to the paying of a price to set free someone who has been enslaved, but the religious use of the words seems to ignore the price-paying element and focuses on the wondrous freedom that a redeemer's action brings to a slave.

Redress (*nĕqāmâ*). The words is conventionally rendered "vengeance," but it does not have the connotations of personal feeling and revenge that "vengeance" suggests. Rather it indicates punishment exacted by a competent authority in a way appropriate to the wrong done that thus puts things back in order.

Rely on (*ḥāsâ b*). This is what a person does in relation to something that provides protection, such as a shield (144:2). In relation to God, it is commonly what the Davidic king does (18:2, 30 [3, 31]), but it also characterizes the relationship between Israel and God.[14] Mediating between the natural image of taking refuge and the metaphor of reliance is the fact that the wings of the cherubim dominate the temple's inner sanctuary, while carvings of cherubim appear elsewhere in the temple. While the cherubim function mainly to provide Yhwh with transport, it would not be surprising if they also suggested protection. This verb could then denote taking refuge in the temple, though we should not press the image. None of the occurrences of the verb mention the temple, and all apply the verb directly to Yhwh. If the temple was a place of asylum, then this likely has become a metaphor for finding refuge with Yhwh in a more general sense. Relying on Yhwh is thus similar to trusting in Yhwh; contrast *ḥāsâ b* with *ḥāsâ taḥat* "take refuge under" (91:4).

Resound (*rānan*, *rinnâ*). The verb and the noun suggest making a na-na-na-na sound; they thus compare with *hālal* and *tĕhillâ*. Like these words, they refer to the sound people make rather than the significance of the sound. To resound can be a mark of praise or protest (cf. 106:44).[15]

Restore (*gā'al*). In ordinary life, a restorer (*gō'ēl*) is a person who accepts a moral obligation to use his resources or energy for the benefit of someone in need from his extended family, for instance by buying them out of slavery or pursuing a murderer. The image is then applied to Yhwh, who is the one who restores Israel from slavery or from the control of the Pit (103:4; 107:2).

Revere (*yārē'*). The verb covers both negative fear and positive reverence that issues in obedience (103:17–18). One has to discern from the context which meaning applies to the verb and associated nouns.

Seek help (*dāraš*; *bāqaš*). See *Recourse.

14. See *TDOT*.

15. N. E. Wagner, "*Rinnâ* in the Psalter," *VT* 10 (1960): 435–41.

Sheol (*šĕʾôl*). Sheol (116:3; 139:8; 141:7) is the name of the place where dead people are, a nonmaterial equivalent to the grave as the location of their bodies. It is not a place of punishment (except insofar as people go there before their time); people exist there in a state of inactivity. Yhwh does not generally choose to intervene there, so there is nothing to give thanks to Yhwh for there (although the word could be connected with the verb *šāʾal* meaning "ask," the OT never makes that link). It can also be referred to as the Pit (103:4), which reflects the fact that people's bodies could be buried in a grave pit.

Statement (*ʾimrâ, ʾēmer, ʾōmer*). The words can refer to both promises and commands and they are sometimes translated thus, but they actually denote simply something a person "said" (*ʾāmar*).

Teaching (*tôrâ*). The word is often translated "law," but this is misleading,[16] since it covers "teaching" in a broader sense. While it appears twenty-five times in Ps. 119, *word, *decision, *declaration, command, *order, *law, and *statement all come 19 to 24 times, which shows that *tôrâ* is not the dominant word that it became later. It does not yet refer to Scripture or to Genesis to Deuteronomy or part of it. Psalms does not refer to Yhwh's "teaching" as that of Moses (as Ezra and Nehemiah do) or as a book (as Deuteronomy does).[17] While *tôrâ* would cover the contents of these, it would also cover a priest's instruction of individuals, a wisdom teacher's instruction, and a prophet's teaching.

True, truthfulness (*ʾĕmet, ʾĕmûnâ*). The words refer to the truthfulness of a person or a statement, in the sense of their reliability. A truthful person is one who is steadfast in keeping commitments (91:4; 100:5). A truthful statement is one that can be relied on, in the manner of a promise.

Wait (*yāḥal*). To wait is to take the attitude of hopefulness that looks with expectation for the implementation of a promise (119:43, 49, 74, 81, 114, 147; 130:5, 7).

Waywardness (*ʿāwōn*). This word for sin (103:3, 10) comes from a verb (*ʿāwâ*) meaning to leave the path (106:6). In fact, there are two roots *ʿāwâ*, one meaning "twist," and one meaning "go astray," not in the sense of accidentally losing one's way but of deliberately choosing the wrong road. A passage such as Jer. 3:21 suggests that people could be aware of the latter connotation of *ʿāwōn*. Sin involves skewing one's way.[18] But *ʿāwōn* might also suggest the first idea, the idea of perversity—people are twisted or crooked in their ways.

Weak (*ʿānî, ʿānāw*). A weak person is someone who is vulnerable and powerless, often through circumstances such as having no surviving family (109:16, 22; 147:6). Such people are open to being victimized and hounded by the contrivances of others in the community who feel no obligation to its weaker members but rather use their weakness to their own advantage. EVV translate by words such as "afflicted," "poor," "oppressed," and "meek," but these words do not denote an inner humility, nor do they point to a group or party

16. See, e.g., A. Robert, "Le sens du mot Loi dans le Ps. cxix," *RB* 46 (1937): 162–206.

17. Cf. Jon D. Levenson, "The Sources of Torah," in *Ancient Israelite Religion*, ed. Patrick D. Miller et al. (F. M. Cross Festschrift; Philadelphia: Fortress, 1987), 559–74.

18. See *TLOT* 862–66.

within the community as a whole.[19] Further, here as elsewhere, "weak" is a way Israel characterizes itself over against other peoples when it wants to call on or glorify Yhwh's help (149:4). The broader idea of the weakness and vulnerability of the individual and of Yhwh's commitment to punishing anyone who sheds the blood of such a person has become a figure that characterizes the attitude of strong, oppressive nations toward a weak, vulnerable one, and Yhwh's involvement in this situation.

Well-being (*šālôm*). The word has wide-ranging meaning. It can denote peace from war or peace between people in the community (120:6–7) or the widest prosperity, good fortune, and blessing (119:165). One has to discern from the context which nuance applies.

Willful (*zēd*). The willful (119:21, 51, 69, 78, 85, 122) are arrogant people who decide for themselves how to run their lives, people who make up their own mind about behavior (cf. Prov. 21:24).

Word (*dābār*). Yhwh's word is often a command (119:17), but it also can be a promise (119:49); the two are connected, because Yhwh's word both issues instructions and promises that good consequences will follow from heeding them. The phrase "according to your word" refers to the word of promise thus attached to the word of command (119:9, 25).

Worship (*bārak* piel). With God as subject, the verb means to bless, to make someone fruitful (132:15), but this makes poor sense when God is the verb's object (134:1–2). It then derives its meaning from the noun *berek* "knee" and denotes bending the knee in prostration before Yhwh (cf. *bow low).

Yah (*yāh*). This short version of the name Yhwh is much more common in Books IV and V of the Psalter than in Books I–III, especially in the expression "Praise Yah." But its first appearance in Exod. 15:2 may suggest it is an old form of the name (perhaps older than Yhwh, the version given to Moses in Exod. 3). If so, here it is an archaism, perhaps as preserved through its use in worship.

19. See Kraus, *Psalms 1–59*, 93–95.

Bibliography

For works relating to individual psalms, the footnotes contain bibliographical detail; a later reference to the same work in the treatment of the same psalm uses a short title. This bibliography comprises more general works, which are always referred to by a short title in the footnotes.

Allen, Leslie C. *Psalms 101–150*. Rev. ed. Word Biblical Commentary. Nashville: Nelson, 2002.

Alter, Robert. *The Art of Biblical Poetry*. New York: Basic Books, 1985.

Anderson, Arnold A. *Psalms*. 2 vols. New Century Bible. London: Oliphants, 1972.

Anderson, Bernhard W. *Out of the Depths*. Rev. ed. Philadelphia: Westminster, 1983.

Athanasius, Archbishop of Alexandria. *Letter to Marcellinus concerning the Psalms*. http://www.kensmen.com/catholic/psalmsathanasiusletter.html.

Auffret, Pierre. *Merveilles à nos yeux: Étude structurelle de vingt psaumes dont celui de 1Ch 16,8–36*. Beihefte zur Zeitschrift für die alttestamentliche Wissenschaft 235. Berlin: de Gruyter, 1995.

———. *La sagesse a bâti sa maison*. Orbis biblicus et orientalis 49. Göttingen: Vandenhoeck & Ruprecht, 1982.

———. *Voyez de vos yeux: Étude structurelle de vingt psaumes, dont le psaume 119*. Vetus Testamentum Supplements 48. Leiden: Brill, 1993.

Augustine of Hippo. *Expositions on the Book of Psalms*. In vol. 8 of *The Nicene and Post-Nicene Fathers*, series 1. Edited by Philip Schaff. Edinburgh: T&T Clark, 1886–89; repr., Grand Rapids: Eerdmans, 1989. Also http://www.ccel.org/fathers2/NPNF1-08/TOC.htm.

Barthélemy, Dominique, and J. T. Milik. *Qumran Cave 1*. Discoveries in the Judaean Desert I. Oxford: Clarendon, 1955.

Barthélemy, Dominique, et al., eds. *Critique textuelle de l'Ancien Testament: Tome 4. Psaumes*. Orbis biblicus et orientalis 50.4. Göttingen: Vandenhoeck & Ruprecht, 2005.

Bratcher, Robert G., and William D. Reyburn. *A Handbook on Psalms*. New York: United Bible Societies, 1991.

Brenner, Athalya, and Carole Fontaine, eds. *Wisdom and Psalms*. Feminist Companion to the Bible, second series, 2. Sheffield: Sheffield Academic Press, 1998.

Briggs, Charles A., and Emilie Grace Briggs. *A Critical and Exegetical Commentary on the Book of Psalms*. 2 vols. International Critical Commentary. Repr., Edinburgh: T&T Clark, 1986–87.

Broyles, Craig C. *The Conflict of Faith and Experience in the Psalms*. Journal for the Study of the Old Testament: Supplement Series 52. Sheffield: JSOT, 1989.

Brueggemann, Walter. *Israel's Praise*. Philadelphia: Fortress, 1988.

———. *The Message of the Psalms*. Minneapolis: Augsburg, 1984.

———. *The Psalms and the Life of Faith*. Minneapolis: Fortress, 1995.

Buttenwieser, Moses. *The Psalms*. Repr., New York: Ktav, 1969.

Calvin, John. *Commentary on the Book of Psalms*. 5 vols. Repr., Grand Rapids: Eerdmans, 1948–49.

Cassiodorus, Senator. *Explanation of the Psalms*. 3 vols. Mahwah, NJ: Paulist Press, 1990–91.

Chrysostom, John. *Commentary on the Psalms*. 2 vols. Brookline, MA: Holy Cross Orthodox Press, 1998.

Craigie, Peter C. *Psalms 1–50*. 2nd ed. With supplement by Marvin E. Tate and W. Dennis Tucker. Word Biblical Commentary. Nashville: Nelson, 2004.

Crenshaw, James L. *The Psalms*. Grand Rapids: Eerdmans, 2001.

Crow, Loren S. *The Songs of Ascents*. Society of Biblical Literature Dissertation Series 148. Atlanta: Scholars Press, 1996.

Crüsemann, Frank. *Studien zur Formgeschichte von Hymnus und Danklied in Israel*. Wissenschaftliche Monographien zum Alten und Neuen Testament 32. Neukirchen-Vluyn: Neukirchener Verlag, 1969.

Dahood, Mitchell. *Psalms*. 3 vols. Anchor Bible. Garden City, NY: Doubleday, 1966–70.

Driver, G. R. "Textual and Linguistic Problems in the Book of Psalms." *Harvard Theological Review* 29 (1936): 171–95.

Eaton, John. *Kingship and the Psalms*. London: SCM, 1976.

———. *Psalms*. Torch Bible Commentaries. London: SCM, 1967.

Flint, Peter W. *The Dead Sea Psalms Scrolls and the Book of Psalms*. Leiden: Brill, 1997.

Flint, Peter W., and Patrick D. Miller, eds. *The Book of Psalms*. Vetus Testamentum Supplements 99. Leiden: Brill, 2005.

Fokkelman, J. P. *Major Poems of the Hebrew Bible*. Vols. 2–3. Assen: Van Gorcum, 2000–2003.

García Martínez, Florentino, et al. *Qumran Cave 11*. Discoveries in the Judaean Desert XXIII. Oxford: Clarendon, 1998.

Gerstenberger, Erhard S. *Psalms*. 2 vols. The Forms of the Old Testament Literature 14–15. Grand Rapids: Eerdmans, 1988–2001.

Goulder, Michael D. *The Prayers of David*. Journal for the Study of the Old Testament: Supplement Series 102. Sheffield: JSOT, 1990.

———. *The Psalms of the Return*. Journal for the Study of the Old Testament: Supplement Series 258. Sheffield: Sheffield Academic Press, 1998.

———. *The Psalms of the Sons of Korah*. Journal for the Study of the Old Testament: Supplement Series 20. Sheffield: JSOT, 1982.

Grossberg, Daniel. *Centripetal and Centrifugal Structures in Biblical Poetry*. Society of Biblical Literature Monograph Series 39. Atlanta: Scholars Press, 1989.

Gunkel, Hermann. *Die Psalmen*. 5th ed. Göttingen: Vandenhoeck & Ruprecht, 1968.

———. *The Psalms*. Philadelphia: Fortress, 1967.

Gunkel, Hermann, and Joachim Begrich. *Introduction to Psalms*. Macon, GA: Mercer University Press, 1998.

Haag, Ernst, and Frank-Lothar Hossfeld, eds. *Freude an der Weisung des Herrn: Beiträge zur Theologie der Psalmen; Festgabe zum 70. Geburtstag von Heinrich Gross*. Stuttgart biblische Beiträge 13. Stuttgart: Katholisches Bibelwerk, 1986.

Habel, Norman C., ed. *The Earth Story in the Psalms and the Prophets*. Earth Bible 4. Sheffield: Sheffield Academic Press; Cleveland: Pilgrim, 2001.

Haglund, Erik. *Hisorical Motifs in the Psalms*. Coniectanea biblica: Old Testament Series 23. [Lund]: Gleerup, 1984.

Hauge, Martin R. *Between Sheol and Temple*. Journal for the Study of the Old Testament: Supplement Series 178. Sheffield: Sheffield Academic Press, 1995.

Hilary of Poitiers. *Homilies on the Psalms*. Pages 236–48 in vol. 9 of *The Nicene and Post-Nicene Fathers*, series 2. Edinburgh: T&T Clark. Repr., Grand Rapids: Eerdmans, 1989. Also at www.ccel.org/fathers2/NPNF2-09/Npnf2-09-20.htm.

Hilber, John W. *Cultic Prophecy in the Psalms*. Beihefte zur Zeitschrift für die alttestamentliche Wissenschaft 352. Berlin: de Gruyter, 2005.

Hill, Edmund. *Prayer, Praise and Politics*. London: Sheed & Ward, 1973.

Hossfeld, Frank-Lother, and Erich Zenger. *Psalms 2: A Commentary on Psalms 51–100*. Hermeneia. Minneapolis: Fortress, 2005.

Howard, David M. *The Structure of Psalms 93–100*. Winona Lake, IN: Eisenbrauns, 1997.

Ibn Ezra. *Tĕhillîm*. In *Miqrāʾôt Gĕdôlôt*, vol. 10. Repr., New York: Pardes, 1951. Also reprinted in A. J. Rosenberg, *Psalms*. 3 vols. New York: Judaica, 1991. Referred to without page numbers.

Jacobson, Rolf. *"Many Are Saying."* Journal for the Study of the Old Testament: Supplement Series 397. London: T&T Clark, 2004.

Jeremias, Jörg. *Das Königtum Gottes in den Psalmen*. Forschungen zur Religion und Literatur des Alten und Neuen Testaments 141. Göttingen: Vandenhoeck & Ruprecht, 1987.

Jerome [Eusebius Hieronymus]. *The Homilies of Saint Jerome.* Vol. 1, *1–59 on the Psalms*. Fathers of the Church 48. Washington, DC: Catholic University of America, 1964.

Johnson, Aubrey R. *The Cultic Prophet and Israel's Psalmody*. Cardiff: University of Wales, 1979.

———. *Sacral Kingship in Ancient Israel.* Cardiff: University of Wales, 1955.

Keel, Othmar. *The Symbolism of the Biblical World.* New York: Seabury, 1978.

Kidner, Derek. *Psalms*. 2 vols. Tyndale Old Testament Commentary. London: Inter-Varsity, 1973.

Kirkpatrick, A. F. *The Book of Psalms*. Cambridge Bible for Schools and Colleges. Repr., Cambridge: Cambridge University Press, 1910.

Koenen, Klaus. *Jahwe wird kommen, zu herrschen über die Erde: Ps 90–110 als Komposition*. Weinheim: Beltz Athenäum, 1995.

Kraus, Hans-Joachim. *Psalms 1–59*. Minneapolis: Augsburg, 1988.

———. *Psalms 60–150*. Minneapolis: Augsburg, 1989.

Lindström, Fredrik. *Suffering and Sin.* Stockholm: Almqvist, 1994.

Lipiński, E. *La royauté de Yahwé dans la poésie et le culte de l'ancient Israël.* 2nd ed. Brussels: Academie voor Wetenschappen, Letteren en Schone Kunsten van België, 1965.

Lohfink, Norbert, and Erich Zenger. *The God of Israel and the Nations: Studies in Isaiah and the Psalms*. Collegeville, MN: Liturgical Press, 2000.

Loretz, Oswald. *Psalmstudien*. Beihefte zur Zeitschrift für die alttestamentliche Wissenschaft 309. Berlin: de Gruyter, 2002.

———. *Ugarit-Texte und Thronbesteigungspsalmen*. Münster: Ugarit, 1988.

Luther, Martin. *First Lectures on the Psalms*. 2 vols. In *Luther's Works,* vols. 10–11. St. Louis: Concordia, 1974–76.

———. *Selected Psalms*. 3 vols. In *Luther's Works,* vols. 12–14. St. Louis: Concordia, 1955–58.

Mandolfo, Carleen. *God in the Dock*. Journal for the Study of the Old Testament: Supplement Series 357. London: Sheffield Academic Press, 2002.

Mathys, Hans-Peter. *Dichter und Beter*. Orbis biblicus et orientalis 132. Göttingen: Vandenhoeck & Ruprecht, 1994.

Mays, James L. *Preaching and Teaching the Psalms*. Louisville: Westminster John Knox, 2006.

———. *Psalms.* Interpretation. Louisville: Knox, 1994.

McCann, J. Clinton. "The Book of Psalms." In *The New Interpreter's Bible*, edited by Leander E. Keck. Vol. 4, pages 639–1280. Nashville: Abingdon, 1996.

Midrash on Psalms, The. 2 vols. New Haven: Yale University Press, 1959.

Miller, Patrick D. *Interpreting the Psalms.* Philadelphia: Fortress, 1986.

Mitchell, David C. *The Message of the Psalter: An Eschatological Programme in the Book of Psalms*. Journal for the Study of the Old Testament: Supplement Series 252. Sheffield: Sheffield Academic Press, 1997.

Mowinckel, Sigmund. *The Psalms in Israel's Worship*. 2 vols. Oxford: Blackwell, 1967.

Peterson, Eugene. *Answering God*. Repr., San Francisco: Harper, 1991.

———. *Where Your Treasure Is: Psalms That Summon You from Self to Community*. Grand Rapids: Eerdmans, 1993.

Qimchi, David. *Tĕhillîm*. In *Miqrāʾôt Gĕdôlôt*, vol. 10. Repr., New York: Pardes, 1951. Also reprinted in A. J. Rosenberg, *Psalms*. 3 vols. New York: Judaica, 1991. Referred to without page numbers.

Raabe, Paul R. *Psalm Structures*. Journal for the Study of the Old Testament: Supplement Series 104. Sheffield: JSOT, 1990.

Rashi. *Tĕhillîm*. In *Miqrāʾôt Gĕdôlôt*, vol. 10. Repr., New York: Pardes, 1951. Also reprinted in A. J. Rosenberg, *Psalms*. 3 vols. New York: Judaica, 1991. Referred to without page numbers.

Reid, Stephen Breck, ed. *Psalms and Practice*. Collegeville, MN: Liturgical Press, 2001.

Rendsburg, Gary A. *Linguistic Evidence for the Northern Origin of Selected Psalms*. Atlanta: Scholars Press, 1990.

Ridderbos, N. H. *Die Psalmen*. Beihefte zur Zeitschrift für die alttestamentliche Wissenschaft 117. Berlin: de Gruyter, 1972.

Rienstra, Marchienne Vroon. *Swallow's Nest: A Feminine Reading of the Psalms*. Grand Rapids: Eerdmans, 1992.

Rogerson, J. W., and J. W. McKay. *Psalms*. 3 vols. Cambridge Bible Commentary, New English Bible. Cambridge: Cambridge University Press, 1977.

Rosenberg, A. J. *Psalms* (with translation of Rashi and other commentaries). 3 vols. New York: Judaica, 1991.

Saur, Markus. *Die Königspsalmen*. Beihefte zur Zeitschrift für die alttestamentliche Wissenschaft 340. Berlin: de Gruyter, 2004.

Schaefer, Konrad. *Psalms*. Berit Olam. Collegeville, MN: Liturgical Press, 2001.

Seybold, Klaus. *Introducing the Psalms*. Edinburgh: T&T Clark, 1990.

———. *Die Psalmen*. Tübingen: Mohr, 1996.

Seybold, Klaus, and Erich Zenger, eds. *Neue Wege der Psalmenforschung: Für Walter Beyerlin*. 2nd ed. Freiburg: Herder, 1994.

Slomovic, Elieser. "Toward an Understanding of the Formation of Historical Titles in the Book of Psalms." *Zeitschrift für die alttestamentliche Wissenschaft* 91 (1979): 350–80.

Soggin, J. Alberto. *Old Testament and Oriental Studies*. Rome: Biblical Institute Press, 1975.

Spiekermann, Hermann. *Heilsgegenwart: Eine Theologie der Psalmen*. Forschungen zur Religion und Literatur des Alten und Neuen Testaments 148. Göttingen: Vandenhoeck & Ruprecht, 1989.

Spurgeon, C. H. *The Treasury of David*. 6 vols. Repr., London: Marshall; Grand Rapids: Zondervan, 1963.

Stec, David M. *Targum of Psalms*. Collegeville, MN: Liturgical Press, 2004.

Tate, Marvin E. *Psalms 51–100*. Word Biblical Commentary. Dallas: Word, 1990.

Terrien, Samuel. *The Psalms*. Grand Rapids: Eerdmans, 2002.

Theodoret of Cyrus. *Commentary on the Psalms*. 2 vols. Washington, DC: Catholic University of America, 2000–2001.

Trudiger, Peter L. *The Psalms of the Tamid Service*. Vetus Testamentum Supplements 98. Leiden: Brill, 2004.

Ulrich, Eugene, et al. *Qumran Cave 4*. Part 11, *Psalms to Chronicles*. Discoveries in the Judaean Desert 16. Oxford: Clarendon, 2000.

Watson, Wilfred G. E. *Classical Hebrew Poetry*. 2nd ed. Journal for the Study of the Old Testament: Supplement 26. Sheffield: JSOT, 1986.

Weiser, Artur. *The Psalms*. London: SCM; Philadelphia: Westminster, 1962.

Westermann, Claus. *The Living Psalms*. Grand Rapids: Eerdmans; Edinburgh: T&T Clark, 1989.

———. *The Praise of God in the Psalms*. Richmond: Knox, 1965. Enlarged ed. titled *Praise and Lament in the Psalms*. Atlanta: Knox, 1981.

Whybray, R. Norman. *Reading the Psalms as a Book*. Journal for the Study of the Old Testament: Supplement Series 222. Sheffield: Sheffield Academic Press, 1996.

Zenger, Erich. *A God of Vengeance?* Louisville: Westminster John Knox, 1996.

Subject Index

Author Index

Index of Scripture and Other Ancient Writings

Old Testament

Genesis

Exodus

Leviticus

Numbers

Deuteronomy

Proverbs

Rabbinic Writings

Babylonian Talmud

ʿAbodah Zarah

Berakot

Midrash Tehillim/Psalms

Mishnah

Middot

Pesaḥim

Šabbat

Sukkah

Taʿanit

Tamid